INDIAN AFFAIRS
ANNUAL
2008

INDIAN AFFAIRS ANNUAL 2008

(In 9 Vols.)

Vol. 8

Chronology of Events

(16-01-2008 to 29-02-2008)

Shailendra Sengar

KALPAZ PUBLICATIONS

KALPAZ PUBLICATIONS

DELHI - 110052

Indian Affairs Annual 2008

Rs. 6300 (Set)

ISBN: 81-7835-693-7 (Set)
ISBN: 81-7835-701-1 (Vol. 8)

Published in 2008 in India by
Kalpaz Publications
C-30, Satyawati Nagar,
Delhi-110052
E-mail: kalpaz@hotmail.com
Phone : 9212729499

Laser Type Setting by: Quick Media, Delhi
Printed at : Singhal Print Media, Delhi

INDIAN AFFAIRS ANNUAL 2008

Chronology of Events

(16-01-2008 to 29-02-2008)

5513. (16-1-2008) CHANDIGARH : The Vice President of India Mohd. Hamid Ansari addressed the 57th Annual Convocation of Panjab University at Chandigarh today. Following is the text of his Convocation Address: "Nature is evolutionary, but has occasional spurts of cataclysmic activity and tectonic shifts. The University of Panjab was born at Simla in 1882 and prospered at Lahore. Panjab University, however, took shape in difficult times in 1947 and has made a name for itself through the grit and excellence of students, researchers and teachers. I, therefore, deem it a privilege to be its Chancellor and to preside over this Convocation. A university, it is said, is the place from where men and women start the journey to the Eternal City, imagine and develop the ideas and ideals that give shape to it, and traverse the many paths leading to it. For this reason alone, the annual Convocation is an event of significance since it marks the formal completion of the first stage of that journey. Since the beginning of time, humankind has debated the meaning of existence. Amidst a diversity of answers, the centrality of Change has not been disputed. The idea of change, its meaning and inevitability, therefore, needs to be etched on the minds of all those who leave the sanctuary of the University today to plunge themselves into the world beyond. A century earlier, a university degree was considered a recipe for steady and dignified existence in a society characterised by settled equations and relationships.

5514. (16-1-2008) NEW DELHI : The Railways have generated Rs. 33757.87 crore of revenue earnings from freight traffic during the first nine months (*i.e.* April-December 2007) of the current financial year 2007-08 as compared to Rs. 30242.78 crore during the corresponding period last year, registering an increase of 11.62 per cent. Railways carried 571.35 million tonnes of freight traffic during April-December 2007 as compared to 527.95 million tonnes carried during the corresponding period last year, reflecting an increase of 8.22 per cent. The Net Tonne Kilo Metres (NTKM) went up from 346259 million during the months of April-December 2006 to 367601 million during April-December 2007, with an increase of 6.16 per cent. The earnings from freight traffic during the month of December 2007 was Rs. 4341.47 crore, compared to Rs. 3739.92 crore during the corresponding period last year showing an increase of 16.08 per cent. Railways carried 69.97 million tonnes of freight traffic during the month of December 2007 as compared to 63.56 million tonnes of freight traffic during the corresponding period last year, registering an increase of 10.08 per cent. The Net Tonne Kilo Metres (NTKM) went up from 41384 million during the month of December 2006 to 46140 million during December 2007, showing an increase of 11.49 per cent. Of the total earnings during the month of December 2007, Rs. 1660.43 crore came from transportation of 30.24 million tonnes of coal, followed by Rs. 674.68 crore from 11.92 million tonnes of iron ore, Rs. 329.73 crore from 3.40 million tonnes of foodgrains, Rs. 328.42 crore from 6.63 million tonnes of cement, Rs. 255.89 crore from 2.26 million tonnes of iron & finished steel, Rs. 245.21 crore from 2.99 million tonnes of petroleum oil and lubricant (POL), Rs. 230.78 crore from 3.44 million tonnes of fertilizers, Rs. 183.52 crore from 2.39 million tones of container service, Rs. 74.06 crore from 1.05 million tonnes of raw material for steel plants except iron ore and Rs. 358.75 crore from 5.65 million tonnes of other goods.

5515. (16-1-2008) NEW DELHI : Department of Commerce is facilitating a project entitled "eTrade" among all trade regulatory and facilitating agencies like Customs, Directorate General of Foreign Trade (DGFT), Sea Ports, airports, CONCOR, Banks etc., to provide 24X7 electronic delivery of efficient service to Exporters/ Importers. Currently, Exporters/ Importers have to maintain multiple bank accounts at their Head Offices/ Ports, Airports etc., to handle their export-import transactions. With a view to facilitate trade, a series of meetings were held and finally at a meeting convened by the Commerce Secretary, Shri G.K. Pillai, on 20.12.2007, it was decided that all Exporters/ Importers would need to maintain only one core-banking enabled bank account at national level for transactions with any of the stakeholders for trade. This would include Customs, DGFT, Ports, airports, Banks etc. All the concerned Government agencies have been advised to facilitate e-payment using single core-banking enabled bank account of Exporters/ Importers in the country. Exporters/ Importers would declare to all the agencies their one bank account in any core-banking enabled branch anywhere in India for all payments/ receipts, including Drawback. This would come into effect throughout India.

5516. (17-1-2008) NEW DELHI : The Cabinet Committee of Economic Affairs has approved the Central Sector Scheme of providing 1 lakh jobs per annum in the private sector to the persons with disabilities, with a proposed outlay of Rs. 1800 crores, during the 11th Plan Period. In addition, the Committee has also approved a provision of Rs.16 crore for making adequate publicity of the Scheme. The employees with disabilities, with monthly wage up to Rs.25000/- per month, working in the private sector would be covered. The scheme has been made applicable to the employees with disabilities covered under the Persons with Disabilities (Equal Opportunities, Protection of Rights and Full Participation) Act, 1995 and the National Trust for Welfare of Persons with Autism, Cerebral Palsy, Mental Retardation and Multiple Disabilities Act, 1999. The scheme will be applicable all over India on enrolment of the employees in Employees Provident Fund (EPF) and the Employees State Insurance (ESI), under the Employees Provident Fund and Miscellaneous Provisions Act, 1952 and Employees State Insurance Act, 1948. The Government will make payment of the employer's contribution to the Employees Provident Fund and Employees State Insurance for the first three years. The Scheme has been evolved in detailed consultation with the Ministry of Labour and Employment and is proposed to be implemented in a coordinated matter through existing mechanism *i.e.* Employees Provident Fund Organization (EPFO) and Employees State Insurance Corporation (ESIC). The scheme will address the most important aspect of rehabilitation of persons with disabilities is economic rehabilitation, which can be achieved by providing employment or through self-employment. Government has already been promoting the self-employment of persons with disabilities by providing vocational training and loan on concessional rates through National Handicapped Finance and Development Corporation (NHFDC). Employment of persons with disabilities in the Government is promoted through reservation. However, employment opportunities in the Government have been shrinking over years. Therefore, it had become necessary that employment opportunities for the persons with disabilities be created in the private sector by giving incentives to the employers.

5517. (17-1-2008) SHIBPUR : The Vice President of India Mohd. Hamid Ansari addressed at the Closing Ceremony of the Sesqui-Centenary Celebration of the Bengal Engineering and Science University at Shibpur in West Bengal today. Following is the text of the Vice President's address on the occasion : "It is an honour for me to be present today at the closing ceremony of the Sesqui-Centenary celebrations of the Bengal Engineering and Science University. It is a unique experience to be in an institution founded in 1856, one year prior to the first war of independence. It has also been a long journey from the Bishop's College in British India to the Bengal Engineering College in independent India, then on to a deemed University and finally to a State University. What began as a college to meet the requirements of trained engineers for the PWD Department has today blossomed into a premier academic institution that has made significant contributions to the development of engineering and technology studies in India and I am confident will continue to do in the India in the future. Engineering and technical education in the country occupies a critical role in our knowledge economy. While India produces over 400,000 engineers every year, it is nowhere close to the number of engineers required by our industry and economy. The skills deficit that we face in our country needs to be remedied at the earliest. Remedial measures have a long gestation period, yet the first step in that direction must be taken today. I would like to emphasize on four issues that must be addressed to raise the standards of technical education in the country. First, the general quality of engineering and technical college faculty in the country leaves much to be desired. Our premier engineering colleges fail to attract and retain the best of their faculty. We need to revisit the terms and conditions guiding the appointment of faculty members and have systemic flexibility to enable engineering institutions to attract and retain talented faculty. Second, industry-academia interaction is currently limited to some of the elite institutions and is not a generic feature of engineering and technical institutions. This should be remedied and the curriculum and teaching methodologies should take into account the relevance of engineering education for Indian industry and economy. The first step towards enhancing interaction of engineering colleges with industry is through the faculty of these institutions. We must facilitate their temporary movement to the industry to gain experience and knowledge of the latest and best industry practices. Third, engineering and technical institutions should serve as foci of research and development activities. Unfortunately, over the years, engineering colleges have not fostered R&D activities. Engineering research continues to be undertaken in specific government institutes. This needs to change. Fourth, the inter-linkages between the various levels of the engineering and technical education pyramid have weakened over the years. The linkages between vocational and technical institutes, polytechnics, state-level engineering and technical colleges and elite national institutions such as NITs and IITs have frayed. The regulatory mechanisms governing these various levels are also different further weakening the exchange of information and expertise across them. We need to examine how best to strengthen such linkages.

5518. (17-1-2008) NEW DELHI : The Trade Minister of Australia, Mr. Simon Crean accompanied by a delegation called on Shri Sharad Pawar, Minister of Agriculture here today. Both sides appreciated the growing economic cooperation between the two countries and reiterated the need for increase in trade between the two countries to enhance economic cooperation between India and Australia. The Indian side raised the issue of mango export to Australia. The Australian trade Minister agreed to convey the Indian concerns to Australian government and promised that Australian government would address the issue in right earnest to facilitate mango export from India to Australia. The Agriculture Minister referred to the issue of food security and informed the Australian delegation of the efforts being made by the Indian scientists to develop drought resistant seed variety to meet the challenge of the adverse impact of climate change affecting the agriculture in particular. The Australian delegation voiced its concern regarding the subsidies declared by the Government of India for sugar industry. They were of the view that these were non-compliant with the WTO regime. Officers present from the Indian side explained the background necessitating the subsidies stating that the subsidies were being extended to make payments to the sugarcane farmers and were in a way helping the international sugar prices to remain firm. It was emphasized that these measures were within the WTO mandated regime. Both the Ministers expressed hope that some solution would be found to settle the issue through discussion between the two governments.

5519. (17-8-2007) NEW DELHI : The Bharatiya Janata Party has noted the comment of the Prime Minister, Dr. Manmohan Singh in an interview to a national news magazine. The Prime Minister thanks his destiny which put him in office. He charges BJP for having organized *Havans* to cut short his life. Prime Ministers have in the past made statements which are capable of criticism. But the content of this statement can only be described as "rubbish". It has taken the Prime Minister three long years to discover the non existent *havans* organized against him. The BJP treats the Prime Minister as a political opponent and not an enemy. We wish him a very long life. May he live long and see after his tenure comes to an end how India is governed much better by others after him. The Prime Minister must acknowledge that the BJP also had a role in shaping his destiny. Had we not vehemently opposed the first choice of the Congress, Dr. Manmohan Singh as the second preference would have never made to office.

5520. (17-1-2008) NEW DELHI : Over 500 NCC cadets and officers were hosted by Gen Deepak Kapoor at his residence this evening. These included the contingents from Vietnam, Bhutan, Kazikisthan, Singapore, Maldives, Nepal, Bangladesh; Sri Lanka etc. The Indian cadets were drawn from all the states and union territories. They shared with Gen Kapoor their hopes and aspirations. Many of them desired to opt for Army as their career. Army Chief commended the cadets' motivational levels and camaraderie and congratulated them for the forthcoming 59th Republic day of India.

5521. (17-1-2008) NEW DELHI : Minister of Tourism & Culture, Smt. Ambika Soni, held a review meeting of tourism and culture projects pertaining to the State of Punjab in Hoshiarpur yesterday. Tourism Minister of Punjab, Shri, Hira Singh Gabria, senior officers of the Union and the State government were present on the occasion. The minister reviewed the projects under the 10th Five Year Plan during which time an amount of Rs 47.74 crore was sanctioned, out of which an amount of Rs 31.50 crore was released. During 2006-07 alone an amount of Rs. 24.52 crores was sanctioned, out of which an amount of Rs. 13.10 crores was released. In recognition of the potential of tourism in the State, a number of initiatives were undertaken during the tenth plan period such as integrated development of Amritsar, Attari-Wagha, Patiala, Kapurtala and Ropar as tourism destinations. Integrated development of Freedom Circuit and integrated development of destination pilgrim circuit 'Land of Gurus and Saints' were other major initiatives during the period. For the development of Hoshiarpur as a tourism destination in the year 2007-08, Rs 4 crore has been sanctioned-for environmental up-gradation of Bajawra fort, development of VV Research Institute and others. In order to promote Punjab as an international tourism destination, Ministry of Tourism has provided the consultancy through the Asian Development Bank and facilitated preparation of Tourism Master Plan of Punjab through United Nations World Tourism Organisation. The Union Ministry of Tourism is already running Institute of Hotel Management at Gurdaspur. With a view to creating employment opportunities for the youth of Punjab, Hon'ble Minister had cleared one more IHM at Boothgarh and discussed the possibility of setting of a Food Craft Institute for skilled development in the hospitality sector in an area to be identified later in consultation with State Government. The Minister also reviewed the progress of the project for development of Jallianwalabagh National Memorial which is slated to be completed by 31st March, 2008. She emphasized on the timely completion of the project along with the Sound and Light show. The Maharaja Ranjit Singh Panorama project, which had been launched in July, 2006 at the Rambagh Heritage Garden, was also appraised and the Minister expressed satisfaction on the popularity of the Panorama and its good upkeep. The development of Anandpur Sahib and Talwandi Sabo, as a part of the Ter-centenary celebrations of the Guru-ta-Gaddi, at a proposed cost of nearly Rs.180 crores, is also in the last stage of approval by the Union Cabinet. The proposal to name the route from Punjab to Huzur Sahib Nanded as Guru Govind Singh Marg, is also being taken up for approval of the Central Government and is likely to be approved shortly. The Minister will review other matters related to Culture Ministry during her next visit. The Minister underlined the importance of timely completion of Central projects like National Rural Employment Guarantee Program which are pending implementation with the State Government. As per the guidelines, the implementation of the projects is the responsibility of the State Government.

5522. (17-1-2008) NEW DELHI : On the wake of 31st Anniversary Celebration of Indian Coast Guard a painting competition was organised today at Coast Guard headquarters, to commemorate the occasion. Children across 30 schools in Delhi participated in this competition, which was held in two categories. The school children who participated in this competition with great enthusiasm exhibited their skills and expressed concern over national security by painting their views which indicated high levels of awareness about the growing threat to the nation. In the middle school category students from Raisina Bengali School sweeped the Awards as they occupied all the four positions. First Prize went to Sushmita Chatterjee and Second, Third and Fourth Prize went to Ankita Malakar, Kaushik Barua and Subhodeep Sarkar, respectively. In the High School category Mohini Bhowmik of Raisina Bengali School secured the First Prize and the Second Prize went to Pramod Kumar of NP Boys Sr Secondary School. Mrs. Sandhya Prasad Wife of Vice Admiral Y Prasad, Ex Vice Chief of Naval Staff (Retd) graced the function and distributed prizes to the winners.

5523. (17-1-2008) NEW DELHI : Prof. Saifuddin Soz, the Union Minister for Water Resources released the "National Disaster Management Authority Guidelines for Management of Floods" compiled by the National Disaster Management Authority (NDMA) at a function here today. Gen. N.C. Vij, Vice Chairman of the NDMA presided over the function, Dr. Mohan Kanda, Member, NDMA made a presentation of the guidelines and Smt. Gauri Chatterjee, Secretary, M/o Water Resources addressed on the occasion. Addressing on the occasion, Prof. Soz said that for the development of flood prone areas and upliftment of the people, it is necessary that floods are managed effectively. He said that floods in India are annual feature and the area frequented by the floods, are comparatively backward and the people living there are, economically weak and socially backward. The Minister said that floods being a state subject, the primary responsibility for their management lie with the states, however the Government has taken a number of steps towards lending a helping hand to them. The policy statement made in Parliament in 1954 and subsequent appointment of various committees, task forces, working groups etc. to look into the problem of floods and suggest measures for their management is a pointer to the importance attached by the Government to the flood management. The most notable ones were High Level Committee on floods (1957), Ministers Committee on Floods (1964), Rashtriya Barh Ayog (1980) and the Task Force on Flood Management & Erosion Control (2004). The institutional capability of the Central Water Commission (CWC) was strengthened by creating a separate flood wing in 1954. Establishment of Ganga Flood Control Commission and Brahmaputra Board to look into the problem of floods in Ganga and Brahmaputra river basins respectively were other measures, taken by the Government in the field of flood management. The Minister informed that it is proposed to take up flood management programme at a cost of Rs. 8000 crore in the 11th Plan to assist the states in execution of the flood management works. It has given immense satisfaction to announce that the scheme has already received in principle approval of the Union Cabinet. Another scheme costing Rs. 1500 crore to take up river management works in border areas of the country and critical flood management works in the Brahmaputra and Barak river basins are also in the process of approval. It is also proposed to give adequate funds to the CWC to undertake improvements and expansion of its flood forecasting and warning network.

5524. (17-1-2008) NEW DELHI : The Economic Advisory Council (EAC) to the Prime Minister released its review of the Economy 2007-08, which is an update on the Economic Outlook for 2007, at a Press Conference in New Delhi today. Addressing the Press, Chairman EAC, Dr. C. Rangarajan said that the economic growth of the country in 2007-08 is likely to be 8.90 per cent with Agriculture growing at 3.6 per cent, Industry 9.7 per cent and Services 10.3 per cent. He also projected a baseline growth of 8.5 per cent in 2008-09.

5525. (17-1-2008) NEW DELHI : The Union Cabinet today gave its approval for setting up of a Greenfield International Airport through the Public Private Partnership (PPP) at Kannur, Kerala. The decision for setting of a Greenfield

International Airport will meet requirements of increasing air traffic in that region. BACKGROUND The airport will be built over 2000 acres of land and will have a single runway. The project would be implemented through the Public Private Partnership (PPP) route. The total project cost is Rs. 929.5 crores.

5526. (17-1-2008) NEW DELHI : The Union Cabinet today gave its 'in-principle' approval for transfer of Dr. Ambedkar International Airport, Nagpur to the Joint Venture Company comprising AAI and Maharashtra Airport Development Company Ltd. For upgradation of the airport to a world class Multi Modal International Passenger and Cargo Hub (MIHAN). The Union Cabinet also gave its approval to invest an amount of Rs. 4.90 crore by AAI in the equity of the Joint Venture Company. Development of Dr. Ambedkar International Airport, Nagpur to a World Class Multi Modal International Passenger and Cargo Hub is expected to help in improving tourism and international trade in the region as well as enable optimum utilization of the airport. Development of MIHAN will also fulfil the long cherished demand of the public of the Vidarbha region.

5527. (17-1-2008) NEW DELHI : Shri Kamal Nath, Union Minister of Commerce and Industry, has announced that India and Syria have agreed to make concerted efforts to raise the level of bilateral trade to a respectable level commensurate with the potential of the two countries. This was agreed during the first session of the India-Syria Joint Commission Meeting (JCM) held here during 15-17 January, 2008 where Mr. Abdullah Dardari, Deputy Prime Minister for Economic Affairs of the Syrian Arab Republic was also present. Both sides agreed to enhance cooperation in various sectors for mutual benefits. Leaders of both the delegations pressed the need for greater interaction between the business communities of the two countries and it was decided that both the countries would exchange visits of delegation and participate in fairs, exhibitions and buyer-seller meets. The session was also attended by Dr. Ghias Barakat, Minister of Higher Education; Dr. Ahmed Khaled Al-Ali, Minister of Electricity; and Dr. Tayseer Suleiman Ridawi, Head of State Planning Commission of the Syrian Arab Republic. Observing that both the countries were maintaining very cordial political and economic relations, Shri Kamal Nath informed that the two countries also shared common views on most of the multilateral issues. Both the countries also expressed their keenness to cooperate on all matters of mutual interest and of interest to the international community.

5528. (17-1-2008) NEW DELHI : The Government today has given 'in principle' approval to the Government of Kerala (GoK) for setting up of a Greenfield International Airport through the PPP route at Kannur in relaxation of the Policy on Airport Infrastructure relating to Greenfield Airports. The proposed Kannur airport is located in Kannur district and falls outside the municipal limits of Kannur. The site is at about 80 km aerial distance from Calicut airport, about 229 km from Cochin airport and 125 km from the Mangalore airport. GoK has strongly recommended the project since this would promote tourism and trade in Northern Kerala. The proposed airport will also act as a cargo hub for perishable cargo like cut flowers, vegetables, fruits, sea food etc. Ministry of Tourism, GoI has also supported the setting up of the airport since it has potential to open up tourism for North Kerala, which has not seen sufficient tourism development. As per a study conducted by AAI, major impact of the proposed Kannur airport will be felt at Calicut airport. With the commissioning of Kannur airport, 55% traffic of Calicut airport is expected to get diverted. The estimated loss of revenue due to the diversion of traffic on account of the proposed Kannur airport will be to the extent of 27.6% at Calicut airport, 5.1% at Cochin airport, 3.0% at Bangalore airport, 1.5% at Trivandrum airport and 0.75% at Mumbai airport. Since airports at Calicut and Trivandrum are AAI airports, the proposed airports could impact the revenue of AAI. The remaining are private airports. Indian aviation sector has been witnessing robust growth in the recent years and this trend is expected to continue in future for quite some time belying all traffic projections. It is expected that all the above airports would record impressive financial performance in future. Certain activities at the airport like Security, Air Traffic Control, Customs, Immigration, MET etc. would be reserved for GOI entities. These would be performed by the relevant central government agencies. Provision of these services would be on cost recovery basis and the airport operator would enter into agreement with the respective agencies. it would be part of revenue expenditure and as such would not be capitalized. For performance of these services at the airport, necessary provisions would need to be made by the relevant government agencies to ensure that there is sufficient capacity to provide these services, as and when required.

5529. (17-1-2008) NEW DELHI : More than 57 MW of Wind Power capacity has been commissioned in the country during last month under Grid Connected Sector. With these achievement in the sector to 623.37 MW against a target of 1500 MW for 2007-08 and cumulative achievement in the sector reaches to 7717.27 MW. During the same period, 20.25 MW of Biomass Power capacity was also commissioned taking the achievement in the sector to 132.50 MW against a target of 275 MW for 2007-08. This takes cumulative achievement in the sector to 1273.13 MW. Under Off-Grid Systems, 9.00 MW biomass co-generation (non-bagasse) project were commissioned during the month. The cumulative achievement in the sector reaches to 40.20 MW. Besides this, 8 projects have been completed in the States of Chhatisgarh, Gujarat, Orissa & West Bengal during the month under Test Projects on Village Energy Security Programme. A total of 22 test projects have been completed so far. Indian Renewable Energy Development Agency Limited disbursed a loan amount of Rs.21.29 crore during this period taking the cumulative disbursement of Rs. 255.22 crore against a target of Rs.550 crore for 2007-08.

5530. (17-1-2008) NEW DELHI : The Wild Life Crime Control Bureau with its four regional offices at New Delhi Kolkata, Mumbai and Chennai and three sub regional offices have been made operational since last three months. The Bureau has coordinated with various agencies in seizure of 32 otter skins and arrests, near Panipat, Haryana and Gastropod shells attempted export as Mother of Pearl in costume made jewellery in Mumbai. It also facilitated seizure and arrest of schedule I & IV gastropod at Delhi and one leopard skin at Dharamtola, Kolkata More than 320 bags of Sassurea lappa, a scheduled species of Medicinal Plan in Wild Life (Protection) Act 1972 has been seized at Delhi The Bureau is examining the cases of Star Tortoise smuggling detected at Mumbai and Chennai Air ports and Red Sanders smuggling to Nepal and gathering intelligence in this field. Training of various central enforcement agencies at exit points-CISF, BSF, ITBP, SSB, DRI has been being organized at Wild Life Institute of India. It will commence from 4th of next month. Besides this, Training Workshop with National Tiger Conservation Authority and TRAFFIC is being organized for three days at Bandhavagrh from 23rd of this month. A programme to educate international tourists to decrease demand for wildlife and its products is being finalized with Ministry of Tourism. The Bureau will soon release a manual/guide for enforces on Red Sanders.

5531. (17-1-2008) NEW DELHI : Retail prices of farm commodities monitored by the Department of Consumer Affairs have generally remained steady or shown mixed trend over the week ending January 11, 2008. During the week ending January 11, 2008 Prices of wheat remained steady at all the monitoring centres. Prices increased only at Ahmedabad. Prices of sugar remained steady at all the monitoring centres. Prices increased only at Delhi, Jaipur and Thiruvananthapuram and declined at Hyderabad. Prices of gram dal have remained steady across all the monitoring centres and declined at BHUBANESHWAR and Chennai. Prices of tur dal remained steady in all locations, and declined at Jaipur, Bhubaneshwar, and Hyderabad. Out of 1.29 MT pulses contracted for import, 0.91 MT have arrived in the country.

5532. (17-1-2008) NEW DELHI : The Cabinet Committee on Economic Affairs today gave its approval for gauge conversion of Ratlam-Mhow-Khandwa-Akola (472.64 km). The cost of the Ratlam-Mhow-Khandwa-Akola gauge conversion would be about Rs.1421.25 crore. There existed a meter gauge North South Link between Jaipur and Secunderabad covering 1469 kms. The line connected major townships like Jaipur, Ajmer and Chhitaurgarh in Rajasthan, Ratlam, Indore, Mhow and Khandwa in Madhya Pradesh, Akola, Purna and Mudkhed in Maharashtra and Manoharbad and Secunderabad in Andhra Pradesh. Out of 1469 kms on this route, 805 kms from Jaipur to Ratlam and Secunderabad to Purna have already been converted to BG. The work on Akola Purna section covering 210 kms is targeted for completion by March 2008. Thus section from Ratlam to Akola covering about 454 kms is approved for gauge conversion. Ratlam-Akola conversion will restore shorter alternative North South route link connecting Secunderabad, Chennai with Jaipur, Ajmer, Ratlam, Indore, Khandwa, Akola and other towns in

North West Rajasthan. The route will provide broad gauge connectivity for carrying food grains / oil cakes, cement from Nimach / Chittaurgarh area & various products from Pithampur Special Economic Zones near Mhow to Southern States. It will also facilitate movement of military personnel & equipments to/from Mhow containment.

5533. (17-1-2008) NEW DELHI : The Cabinet Committee on Economic Affairs today gave its approval for revision in the criteria under the Kasturba Gandhi Balika Vidyalaya (KGBV) Scheme as per the following: (i) For Rural areas-blocks where the female literacy rate is below 30% would qualify as educationally backward blocks for the purpose of this scheme. (ii) For Urban areas-Out of the 338 town/cities identified by the Ministry of Minority Affairs having concentration of minority population, 94 towns/cities having female literacy rate below the national average of 53.76% (as per 2001 Census) would qualify for the purpose of the scheme. The revision would ensure access to education to the most deprived section if girls through provision of additional residential schools for girls at upper primary level in blocks having very low female literacy rate (below 30%) and urban areas with female literacy below national average (53.67%) as per 2001 Census.

5534. (17-1-2008) NEW DELHI : The Cabinet Committee on Economic Affairs today gave its approval for the Central Sector Scheme of providing 1 lakh jobs per annum to the persons with disabilities, with a proposed outlay of Rs.1800 crore during the 11th Plan Period. In addition, CCEA also approved a provision of Rs.16 crore for four years for making adequate publicity of the Scheme. The implementation of the scheme will lead to considerable social profit and goodwill as the persons with disabilities, who are otherwise in a disadvantageous position, will get regular employment in the organized sector.

5535. (17-1-2008) NEW DELHI : The Union Cabinet today gave its approval to fill up 246 technical posts through the direct recruitment method in partial relaxation of the guidelines of the ADRP Scheme in 6 Organizations *viz.* Tea Board, Coffee Board, Rubber Board, Spices Board, Marine Products Export Development Authority (MPEDA), Export Inspection Council of India (EIC) under the administrative control of the Department of Commerce and also gave its approval for exemption of all technical posts from the application of Annual Direct Recruitment Plan (ADRP) as recommended by the Committee of Secretaries. By exempting these posts from ADRP, Strategic functions services rendered by the Commodity Boards etc. which include (a) R&D, development and extension services and market development and (b) research, increasing production, replantation and rejuvenation activities etc. can be sustained on regular basis.

5536. (17-1-2008) NEW DELHI : The Union Cabinet today gave its approval for signing of a MoU between India and Southern African Customs Union (SACU) for exchange of tariff concessions on a select list of products. The MoU will facilitate the expansion of trade between the Parties by providing the mechanisms and conditions to negotiate a Preferential Trade Agreement (PTA) between the Parties, in conformity with the rules and principles of the World Trade Organisation (WTO).

5537. (17-1-2008) NEW DELHI : The Union Cabinet today gave its approval for implementation of the revised guidelines for converting individual dry latrines into pour-flush latrines of the Centrally Sponsored Scheme of Integrated Low Cost Sanitation Scheme (ILCS) at a total financial implication of Rs. 715.48 crores with a Central subsidy component of Rs. 545.16 crores. The Scheme will convert 6 lakh dry latrines into water borne flush toilets in the country from the year 2007-08 to 2009-10. The States/UTs will be requested to take appropriate action to implement the scheme on priority basis.

5538. (17-1-2008) NEW DELHI : The Union Cabinet today gave its approval for introduction of a Bill, namely the Constitution (Scheduled Tribes) Order (Amendment) Bill, 2008 in Parliament by amending the Constitution (Scheduled Tribes) Order, 1950 for giving effect to the modifications in the list of Scheduled Tribes relating to the State of Arunachal Pradesh. The modified list of Scheduled Tribes in the State of Arunachal Pradesh will satisfy the aspirations of the 'Nyishi' community regarding removal of the term "Dafla" and insertion of 'Nyishi" in the list of Scheduled Tribes in Arunachal Pradesh. Pradesh.

5539. (17-1-2008) NEW DELHI : The Union Cabinet today gave its approval for an additional release of Rs. 530.06 crore towards waiver of overdue interest in the 31 districts in the four State of Maharashtra, A.P., Karnataka and Kerala. This is the additional share of Govt. of India as 50% of the overall financial implication of Rs. 3778.37 crore in this relief package *i.e.* the difference between the expected final share of Rs. 1889.19 crore minus the original estimated amount of Rs. 1359.13 crore. This decision will give benefit to the borrowers whose loans were overdue as on 01.07.2006 in the 31 debt stressed districts of Maharashtra, A.P., Karnatka and Kerala.

5540. (17-1-2008) NEW DELHI : The Union Cabinet today gave its approval for signing of Treaty between India and Australia on Mutual Legal Assistance in Criminal Matters and also to ratify the Treaty. The Treaty will improve the effectiveness of both countries in the investigation and prosecution of crime, including crime related to terrorism and tracing restraint and forfeiture of the proceeds and instruments of crime, through cooperation and mutual legal assistance in criminal matters. India has already signed similar Treaties / Agreements on Mutual Legal Assistance in Criminal Matters with Switzerland, Turkey, United Kingdom, Canada, Russian Federation, France, Kyrgyzstan, Kazakhstan, United Arab Emirates, Uzbekistan, Mongolia, Tajikistan, Ukraine, United State of America, South Africa, Bahrain, Thailand, Kuwait, South Korea, Singapor, Belarus, Mauritius, Spain, Mexico, Bulgaria and Vietnam.

5541. (17-1-2008) NEW DELHI : The Union Cabinet today gave its approval for signing of the Agreement between India and Egypt on the abolition of visa requirement for diplomatic and official / service passport holders. This Agreement will facilitate visa-free travel between India and Egypt for diplomatic and official/ service passport holders while entering, transiting through and exiting from the territory of the other country. It will also facilitate in issuing of residence visa valid for duration of the assignment to the members of diplomatic/consular Missions. This Agreement will allow a citizen of one country to stay in other country's territory for a maximum period of 90 days without a visa. India has already entered into similar Agreements with 35 other countries.

5542. (17-1-2008) NEW DELHI : The Minister of State for Information Technology and Communications, Shri Shakeel Ahmed, has emphasized the great dependency on IT especially among the youth of the country. He was inaugurating the Electronics and Information Technology Exhibition-2008 (ELITEX-2008) here today. The Minister said that ELITEX offers a platform where technology solutions can be viewed, shared and used for the betterment of the people. Responding to the suggestions made by Chairman, Parliamentary Standing Committee on Information Technology, Shri Nikhil Kumar, on the recommendations of the Committee for amendments to the IT law, the Minister said that the IT law will be strengthened to deal with data crime, transmission of pictures and other kinds of cyber crime and the department will accommodate most of the recommendations made by the Standing Committee. Referring to the e-governance project of his Department, he said 25,000 crore has been earmarked for over five years. He assured Shri Nikhil Kumar that the Community Service Centres in Bihar would come up in every block by the end of March, 2009. Delivering the key note address, the Standing Committee Chairman on IT, Shri Nikhil Kumar, emphasized the need for creating a safer information society and preventing cyber crimes. He said the Standing Committee had spent a lot of time in examining issues relating to security of cyber space and had taken evidence from across the country in order to propose amendment to the IT law. A compendium of 562 technologies and products developed under the Department of IT during the past years was distributed at the event. The Minister released 9 of these technologies. As of now, Department has filed IPR for 301 Patent/Copy Right/Trademark and Design related applications were filed. Out of these 157 (132 Copy Rights, 12 Patents, 13 Trade Marks and Designs) have been granted.

5543. (17-1-2008) NEW DELHI : As per latest information received, a total mortality of 61,075 poultry birds has been reported from Birbhum, Dakshin Dinajpur and Murshidabad districts of West Bengal. Fresh cases of mortality have also been reported from the Khargram and Burwan blocks of Murshidabad district, which are adjoining the affected areas of the Birbhum district. Similalry, a fresh mortality of 347 poultry birds has also happened in the Gangarampur block in the Dakshin Dinajpur district. As per telephonic message received from the Govt.

of West Bengal today, there are reports of unusual mortality in Terhatta block of Nadia district, Kalna block of Bardhaman district and Baruipur village of South-24 Pargana district. Except for a mortality of 40 poultry birds reports from the Baruipur village, figures in respect of the other two blocks are not yet available. These deaths are being investigated by the State. Action is also being taken to collect samples and take them to the High Security Animal Disease Laboratory, Bhopal. Active surveillance is being undertaken in the affected areas of West Bengal. A total of 58 Rapid Response Teams (RRTs) are carrying out culling operations in the Birbhum district and 26 RRTs in the Dakshin Dinajpur district. In these operations, a total of 11225 poultry birds were culled and 5877 number of eggs and 1218 kg. of poultry feed destroyed. Samples collected from the Murshidabad district and further samples collected from various affected blocks of the Birbhum district have been sent to the HSADL, Bhopal. The State Government has been requested to ensure effective functioning of the culling teams and payment of compensation on-the-spot. Animal Husbandry Commissioner, who is the Chief Veterinary Officer of the Government of India is also being sent to the affected areas to assess the situation. The situation is monitored at the top levels in Government of India on a daily basis. Centre has assured all assistance to the State in terms of expertise, equipment and funds.

5544. (17-1-2008) NEW DELHI : Stage is set for people in the rural areas to look forward to getting services like birth and death certificates, use of tax payments, e-mail etc. in their gram panchayat offices itself through e-governance. The Gram Panchayat President or Sarpanch will soon be able to monitor panchayat centric schemes, do financial accounting and reporting, keep records of gram sabha and panchayat meetings' on her computer in the panchayat office through the induction of information and communication technologies (ICTs). The Expert Committee on Information Technology for Panchayati Raj submitted its recommendations to the Minister of Panchayati Raj, Shri Mani Shankar Aiyar today. The report recommends use of information and communication technologies to be an integral part of multi-mode training and capacity building. The Committee has given extensive recommendation on hardware and system software, application software, open standards, connectivity, domain specific Data and Meta Data Standards, capacity building, adoption of national panchayati portals (NPP), and facility management. With E-governance the grass root organizations will benefit in many way which would lead to decentralized planning, effective monitoring of centrally sponsored schemes (CSSs), transparency of accountability, enhance their ability to generate, manage and collect local revenue, ability to automate their own functioning, e.g; records of the minutes of meetings of the gram sabha etc.- the information made available could reflect governance structure and decisions taken, profiles of elected representatives and the role played by them; details of NGOs present in the village, to provide external visibility for all the above mentioned areas for enhanced public participation such that there is transparency and ability to facilitate social audits strengthening the Panchyati Raj based delivery systems, they can offer the citizen services that have been devolved to them with a provision of additing more services as they get devolved, provide external linkages for speedy and transparent transfer of funds; markets; communication with state and central government departments etc.; as a mechanism for capacity building. Introduction of ICTat Panchayat level will not only allow experimentation with the technology but will also give immense opportunity to the people to handle technology, be it relating to software, hardware, networking, power supply or any other issue due to which such technology has been traditionally denied to them. Such an initiative will create large-scale job opportunities at the grassroots level, as it has done in urban areas, in the form of operational services, maintenance and many other ancillary areas. The initiative would permeate a culture of ICT usage in rural areas to such a magnitude which probably no other initiative would match. The initiative will also throw up totally new challenges to ICT technology developers as they gear up to meet the requirements of technology diffusion in the villages. Finally, it is likely to create an improved cyber space covering the entire government spectrum of the country, where information could flow seamlessly.

5545. (17-1-2008) NEW DELHI : The Government today approved the transfer of Dr. Ambedkar International Airport, Nagpur to a Joint Venture Company (JVC) comprising of Airports Authority of India (AAI) and Maharashtra Airport Development Company (MADC) Ltd., for upgradation of the Airport to a world class Multi Modal International Passenger and Cargo Hub in accordance with the MoU signed on 18th December 2006. AAI has been permitted to invest an amount of Rs. 4.90 crores in the equity of the JVC. Government of Maharashtra (GoM) had proposed to develop a world class Multi Modal International Passenger and Cargo Hub airport at Nagpur (MIHAN) integrated with the existing Nagpur airport. A high level Steering Committee was constituted for this project wherein the Ministry of Civil Aviation (MoCA) and Airports Authority of India (AAI) were also represented. The Maharashtra State Road Development Corporation (MSRDC), the nodal agency for the project, got a Techno-Economic Feasibility Study (TEFS) conducted for this project through a consortium of Consultants led by M/s. L&T Ramboll Consulting Engineers Ltd., Chennai under the guidance of the Steering Committee. Consultants were of the opinion that Nagpur has very good potential for becoming an international hub airport. Detailed study of traffic data and statistics carried out for air traffic and road and railway etc. suggest that Nagpur could be developed to handle passenger traffic of 18.9 m.p.a in 2035 as against 0.2 m.p.a in 2000. Similarly, air cargo traffic forecasts suggest that as against 910 MTs cargo traffic in 2000, the total cargo traffic in 2035 could be of the order of 11,690,700 MTs. Based on these projections, the TEFS suggests a Master Plan for development of MIHAN at a total capital cost of Rs. 2,581 crores till year 2035. As against the same corresponding revenue is estimated to be Rs. 5,280 crores. Based on these inputs, the project IRR for 30 years of operations has been determined to be 14%. The project envisages expansion of the existing airport and development of new facilities in and around the same for the multi-modal transfer of passengers and cargo. Consultants have suggested formation of a special purpose vehicle with the participation of State Government and other agencies for implementation of this project.

5546. (17-1-2008) NEW DELHI : The President of India said here that "Let me first of all wish you a very happy New Year and best wishes for all your endeavours. I am particularly delighted to be here at this meeting of the 6th South Asia Regional Meeting commemorating the World Conference on Women held in Beijing in 1995, in which I had the privilege to participate as a member of the Indian delegation. India is honoured to host this Regional Meeting for the second time. I warmly welcome all delegates and wish them a pleasant stay in India. It is now over a decade since the Beijing Platform for Action was adopted. It is the time to evaluate our performance in attaining gender equality-a task that still remains incomplete in the world, in our region and in our respective countries. Amongst countries in our region, India has had a dynamic woman Prime Minister-Smt. Indira Gandhi, similarly Sri Lanka, Pakistan and Bangladesh have also had such leadership in their countries. However, it is also equally true that a significant proportion of women in our region live below the poverty line and they have not benefited from the process of globalization, resulting in a further "feminization of poverty". The performance of our region on gender related issues clearly has been mixed. This Conference provides an opportunity to share our views and our experiences in implementing decisions taken at the Beijing Conference and a unique opportunity for building fruitful partnerships within the region for gender equality, gender justice and empowerment. I am glad that SAARC is addressing gender issues. I understand that under the SAARC Development Fund, there are two pioneering projects targeting women-Women and Child Care including Immunization and Women Empowerment for home based workers. Such projects should be encouraged in our region. In India, women took part in our freedom struggle and they fought shoulder to shoulder with men. Recognising their stellar role in the freedom struggle, Pandit Nehru, our first Prime Minister, said, "most of us men folk were in prison. And then a remarkable thing happened. Our women came to the front and took charge of the struggle. Women had always been there of course, but now there was an avalanche of them, which took not only the British Government but their own men folk by surprise". Such is the strength of our women and all that is needed is to give them the opportunities and options for realizing their potential. The principles of gender equality and protecting the rights and privileges of women and children are enshrined in the Constitution of India, which not only guarantees equality to women at par with men, but it also advocates positive discrimination in favour of women, wherever necessary. These are reinforced through the passage of new legislations and amendments to existing laws so as to remove any gender bias. In the political field, by amending the Constitutional provisions, one-third of the seats have been reserved for women leaders in local bodies, both in the rural and urban areas. As a result, more than a million of our women are now politically empowered at the grassroots level.

5547. (18-1-2008) NEW DELHI : The Vice President of India Mohd. Hamid Ansari addressed at the valedictory function and the first Convocation of St. Xavier's College at Kolkata today. Following is the text of his address on the occasion: " Homecoming is a feeling that is difficult to articulate. A sense of happiness is evident. So is a flood of memories. I return to St. Xavier's to express my gratitude to the college that initiated me in disciplines which became a lifelong passion. I come also to salute an institution whose dedication to its mission is exemplary and foremost amongst them is a passion for excellence. More objectively speaking, it is always a privilege for any alumnus to return to his alma mater after half a century, to interact with a new generation of students, to share perceptions, to catch up with their vision of a new world, and their hopes and aspirations in it. History records that the rise and fall of civilisations is closely related to knowledge creation and its utilization for human advancement through techniques of production and distribution. Human history, said H.G. Wells, 'becomes more and more a race between education and catastrophe'. Hence education is critical to the wellbeing of a society. It is a public good, a basic human right, a fundamental right, and an important instrumentality for social and economic empowerment. How then do we approach the question of education, in relation to itself and in relation to society? Some in this audience may know of Lord Acton, the nineteenth century historian of liberty. He was dismissive of utilitarian education and was critical of universities 'where nothing is studied for its own sake, but only as it will be useful in making a practical man'. Notwithstanding an element of truth in it, bland advocacy of such an approach today would be socially irresponsible. A few years back a Task Force of the World Bank on 'Higher Education and Society' concluded that in the world of the 21st century, global wealth will be reckoned in terms of knowledge, skills, and resourcefulness of people. In a word, the way we work and the way we live both necessitate a change in the way we educate ourselves. The advancing tide of globalisation means that the quality of knowledge generated within higher education institutions, and its availability to the wider economy, is becoming increasingly critical to national competitiveness.Education, therefore, has to respond to the imperative of a qualitatively new situation. The challenge is to be met at all levels: primary and secondary and higher education. It is also to be addressed in institutions of vocational training. Logical sequence and pragmatic necessity both suggest a bottom-up approach. Good higher education must of necessity be premised on quality, universal, school education. Where do we stand today? Some hard facts confront us. About 2 crore children are born every year. Around 7 percent of the children do not attend school between the age group 6 to 14. Of the ones that do go through the primary and secondary schooling, about 75 lakhs appear in Class X and 38 lakhs in Class XII examinations. At both levels the pass percentage is 50-55 percent. Only 6 percent enter the university system and only 4-5 percent opts for vocational education. While the global picture about new schools and enrolment is impressive, does it tell us enough about the inroads made in the weaker and the deprived segments of society? Available data indicates that the percentage of children who do not attend school between the age group 6 to 14 from minority, SC and ST communities is higher than that of the general population. There are other questions about the content and quality of primary and secondary education. Who teaches in these schools? What is the teacher-pupil ratio? What is taught? How is it taught? Are the teachers adequately trained? Are we training them in sufficient numbers? Tenth Plan data shows that 'secondary education suffers from lack of access, low participation, and from equity and quality issues'. The all India average of the number of secondary and higher secondary schools per 100 Sq. kilometre area is only 4, and much below this in several of the larger and most populous states. Once upon a time, teachers commanded social status and elicited respect. Do we still subscribe to these values in adequate measure, and translate that respect into action? These questions about school education are relevant because schools constitute the base of the educational pyramid and determine the quality of the input into college and university education.

5548. (18-1-2008) NEW DELHI : Government of India have announced the issue of '7.95 per cent Oil Marketing Companies' Government of India Special Bonds, 2025' for Rs.11,256.92 crore (nominal). The Special Bonds are being issued to three Oil Marketing Companies as compensation towards estimated under-recoveries on account of sale of sensitive petroleum products during the current financial year. The Special Bonds are being issued at par to Indian Oil Corporation Ltd. (IOC) for Rs. 6362.25 crore, Bharat Petroleum Corporation Ltd. (BPCL) for Rs.2539.13 crore and Hindustan Petroleum Corporation Ltd. (HPCL) for Rs. 2355.54 crore on January 18, 2008 (Friday). The investment in the Special Bonds by the banks and Insurance Companies will not be reckoned as an eligible investment in Government securities for their statutory requirements. However, such investment by the insurance companies will be eligible to be reckoned as investment under "other Approved Securities" category as defined under Insurance Regulatory and Development Authority (Investment) Regulations, 2000. Further, the investment by the Provident Funds, Gratuity Funds, Superannuation Funds, etc. in the Special Bonds will be treated as an eligible investment under the administrative order of the Ministry of Finance. The Special Bonds will be transferable and eligible for market ready forward transactions (Repo). The bonds, however, will not be an eligible underlying security for ready forward transactions (Repo/Reverse Repo) with the Reserve Bank of India. Department of Economic Affairs, Ministry of Finance New Delhi.

5549. (18-1-2008) NEW DELHI : 120 films will be screened during the international and Indian section of Mumbai International Film Festival (MIFF)-2008 being held from February 3 to 9, 2008. In the International Section 44, films will be in the Competition Section and nine for the special screening whereas 54 films of the Indian category will vie in the Competition Section and 13 would be screened in the Special Category. This was stated by Shri Kuldeep Sinha,

Director, MIFF, while addressing media today. Shri Sinha said, a total of 228 films were received from 37 countries for the international Competition and 543 entered the Indian Competition Section. Final selection by the jury for the International Section comprises films from 16 countries. Maharashtra Governor Shri. S. M. Krishna would inaugurate the Festival and Minister of Information & Broadcasting and Parliamentary Affairs, Shri P. R. Dasmunsi will preside over.

5550. (18-1-2008) NEW DELHI : The Prime Minister Dr. Manmohan Singh will give away the National Bravery Awards for the year 2007 to twenty two children-4 girls and 18 boys-on January 24, 2008. Four will get the award posthumously. The coveted Bharat Award has been conferred on 17 year old Km. Babita and 15 ½ year old Master Amarjeet of Haryana who saved several school mates from drowning when their school bus fell into the Western Yamuna canal near Ganaur, Sonepat. The Sanjay Chopra Award has been given to six year old Master Yuktarth Shrivastava of Chhattisgarh who saved his sister from stray dogs. On the evening of 30 December, 2006 Yuktarth was playing with his 11 month old sister Surmayee outside their house at Panchsheel colony, Rajnandgaon. When Surmayee went a little ahead of the house some stray dogs once encircled her. Scared, Surmayee started crying. Seeing his baby sister surrounded by the dogs, Yuktarth called out to his parents for help. When no one heard his cry, Yuktarth jumped in the midst of the dogs. Picking up his sister on the laps, Yuktarth tried to shoo away the dogs. More than half a dozen dogs pounded on Yuktarth and bit him on his feet and thighs severely. Unmindful of his injuries, Yuktarth kept holding his sister and ran into the house. Yuktarth displayed exemplary courage in saving his infant sister. The prestigious Geeta Chopra Award has been conferred posthumously on 14 ½ year old Km. Lalrempuii of Hmar Veng in the Mamit district of Mizoram, who valiantly resisted a rape attempt to her last breath and lost her life. Master Raipalli Vamsi (12 years) of Andhra Pradesh has been awarded the Bapu Gaidhani Award along with Master Boney Singh (16 ½ years) of Manipur and Late Master Amol Aghi (15 years) of Haryana. On 26 October 2006, several residents of Basangi village of Andhra Pradesh had gone to the Nagavali river to take a holy dip on the occasion of 'Karthika Masam'. While bathing, eight girls (aged between 10-13 years) started drowning as the river was in spate. Hearing their cries, as well as those of their family members and friends, Raipalli Vamsi, who had also gone to the river to bathe, at once dived into the water. An expert swimmer, he managed to catch hold of two girls and brought them safely to the bank. Jumping into the water a second time, he rescued another two girls. In his third attempt, however, he could save only one more girl. The other three girls died in the incident. While Master Raipalli Vamsi saved five girls, Master Boney Singh saved two boys from drowning in a water tank near Sagolband Meino Leirak,Imphal West-I. Master Amol Aghi lost his life in chasing robbers in Geeta colony, Panipat. The other recipients of the National Bravery Awards are: Master Raveendra Halder, Master Ravi Kumar Jhariya, Master Awadhesh Kumar Jhariya, Master Manas Nishad (all from Chhattisgarh), Master Vishnu C.S., Master Bijin Babu (both from Kerala),

Master Kavvampalli Rajkumar, Master Pinjari Chinigi Sab (both from Andhra Pradesh), Km. Meher Legha (Noida, UP), Master Ankit Rai, Late Master Abhishake and Late Master Suraj (all from Haryana), Master Subhash Kumar (U.P.), Km. Congress Kanwar (Rajasthan) and Master Sunil Kumar P.N. (Karnataka).

5551. (18-1-2008) NEW DELHI : India is keen to export agricultural products and dairy & poultry products to Australia and has asked Australia to facilitate these exports through appropriate market access initiatives and removing non-tariff barriers. This was conveyed by Shri Kamal Nath, Union Minister of Commerce and Industry, during his bilateral talks with the Trade Minister Mr. Simon Crean, here today. India is also looking forward to exporting mangoes from April 2008, the Minister added. The meeting was attended by the Commerce Secretary Shri G.K. Pillai; Secretary (DIPP) Shri Ajay Shankar; Director General of Foreign Trade Shri R.S. Gujral and senior officials from various Ministries from both the countries. Shri Kamal Nath stated that "India is growing and a stable investment climate presents huge opportunities for Australian companies, particularly in energy and infrastructure sectors. Some of the major Australian companies, which have invested in India are BHP Petroleum Pty. Ltd., Telstra Corporation Ltd., Telstra Holding Pty. Ltd., Australian India Resources N.L.., BHP Steel, BHP Billiton, Rio Tinto, MIM Holdings, Snowy Mountains Engineering Corporation etc. Australia's investments in India have been US $ 1.92 billion since 1991. Indian investments in Australia are now well over US $ 1 billion and most of these are in the IT sector". The bilateral trade between India and Australia has seen a growth of 37.50% between 2005-06 and 2006-07, and the total bilateral trade during 2006-07 is US $ 7932.79 million. Bilateral trade from April to September 2007 is US $ 4967.27 million recording a growth of 29.41% for the same period in 2006. The compounded Annual Growth Rate during 2001-02 and 2006-07 is 14.14% for exports and 32.31% for imports. For total trade during the same period, the CAGR is 28.96%. India's exports to Australia in 2006-07 were US $ 924.78 million, an increase of 12.61% from 2005-06. India's imports in 2006-07 was US $ 7008.01 million, an increase of 41.64% over 2005-06. Australia's trade in services with India during 2006-07 was US $ 1895 million. Of this, the import of services was US $ 360 million and the export was US $ 1536 million. The major items of India's exports are gems & jewellery, metals, machinery & instruments, cotton yarn, fabrics, drugs & pharmaceuticals. The major imports consists of gold, coal, coke and briquettes, metal ore, metal scraps and non-ferrous metals.

5552. (18-1-2008) COIMBATORE: The Communist Party of India Coimbatore city unit has asked the State Government and Tamil Nadu State Transport Corporation to increase the number of town buses on the most congested routes for the benefit of commuters. The ninth conference of the party resolved to ask the Government to operate more town buses in West Coimbatore, especially on routes such Ondipudur to Vadavalli and Velandipalayam to Railway Station. More town buses are required from Velandipalayam, Vadavalli, Perur, Periyanaickenpalayam, Ganapathy, Peelamedu and Podanur to the city, the resolution pointed out.

5553. (18-8-2007) NEW DELHI : BJP National President Shri Rajnath Singh today said that the time had finally come when the Left Front parties with complete honesty would need to walk the talk and match words with actions. Shri Rajnath Singh said that it was indeed ironical that while on the one hand the nuclear deal with the United States had been concluded by the government, the Left Front parties despite making their opposition known in strong words, had not supported the opposition parties demand for a discussion in Parliament under Rule 184 which entailed voting. Shri Rajnath Singh criticized the hypocritical stand of the Left Front parties for indulging in another round of pretentious shadow boxing with the government. Over the last three years the Left Front parties have clearly shown that they are only willing to engage in high decibel verbal duels with the government without displaying the resolve to strike. It was high time that the Left Front parties stopped performing the role of an opposition party and simultaneously enjoy the benefits of power, he added. Shri Rajnath Singh said that the people of the country expected Shri Prakash Karat to answer the question that *"if the nuclear deal is against the nation, then will the Left Front parties now allow this government to continue functioning?"* The Left Front Parties should decide between the trappings of power and the interest of the nation, he said. The BJP President said that the entire mood in the country was against the deal. All opposition parties and the Left Front had also clearly indicated that there was no national consensus or broad political acceptability on the Indo-US nuclear deal in its present form which would not only bind but also compromise the long term strategic interests and independence of the country. Shri Rajnath Singh pointed out that ideological differences cannot be larger than the nation. If the Left Front parties honestly and genuinely believed that the Indo-US Nuclear Deal was not in the interest of the nation, then a time had come for all parties to go beyond ideological differences and display solidarity against the government on issues of national importance by taking the matter to its logical end.

5554. (18-1-2008) NEW DELHI : The Congress Party welcomes the Cabinet decision to waive agricultural credit overdues of over Rs. 550 crores. The Congress Party strongly and whole-heartedly welcomes the proposal to implement a scheme targeted at those states, those sub-regions where infant girl mortality is very high, whereby Rs. one lakh will be paid, subject to certain conditions, upon the girl child attaining an age over 18 years. The Congress Party believes that these are but two examples, out of a large array of similar examples, whereby we have successfully through legislation, through new initiatives and schemes, brought about a social and economic revolution. You will recollect that the Congress Party's approach, the manifesto, the CMP, the entire campaign, the philosophy which the Congress Party represents, is a humane, socially and economically progressive approach. Whether it is the Bharat Nirman another example of a huge ameliorative renewal scheme, whether it is the National Rural Employment Guarantee Scheme, whether it is the Protection of the Parents and the Aged or the Domestic Violence Act or the allocations for the micro-credit and the agricultural sector in the last Budget they all have singular common features. First, these features have never been inaugurated in the Republic of India earlier. Second, they seek, in some cases socially and in some cases economically to touch the poorest of the poor, those at the bottom layer of the pyramid. Third, they attack a psychological mindset, they seek to change a mindset in the social sphere. Fourth, they are fulfilment of our promises. We promise and we deliver, we promise and we perform, we promise and we actualize. And an ultimate analysis of such schemes depends on the implementation trajectory and we firmly believe that the implementation trajectory has to be micro-monitored, audited, corrected and modified. But it is the conceptualization of these schemes, it is the creation of these schemes which is novel, unprecedented and it is a first for any government and we the Congress Party are proud of it. To a question that the BJP has made strong allegations against the UPA for 33 per cent reservation for women that nothing has been done and that on the Ramsethu issue whether it is man-made or natural it should not be destroyed what do you have to say, Shri Singhvi said, both your questions are excellent examples and illustrations of the utter hypocrisy of the BJP. The BJP was in power for 5 years, what did they do for 33 per cent reservation? Did they make the same demand at that time of their government, obviously no, because they know that the Congress Party is committed to it but it is other parties' consensus and consent which is holding this back. As far as Ramsethu is concerned from 2004 and going back to 1998, document after document, meeting after meeting, quotation after quotation, minister after minister calls for the immediate implementation of the Adam's Bridge project. Fund are allocated, committees are appointed budgetary allocations are made, press conferences are held and former prime minister Shri Vajpayee calls it a grand project. The BJP manifesto says that it is our main project. And today they want to make a misleading, hypocritical, opportunistic claim for political reasons. It is a volte face, it is not so easy. To a question now that the expert committee has made it clear that Ramsethu is not a man-made structure does the Congress Party believe that like the earlier government which allowed it to go, what do you believe is in the best interest of the state and of a billion people, Shri Singhvi said, it is not the expert committee which is the final result. The expert committee is to be followed by affidavits to be followed by detailed arguments and further to be followed by order of the court.

5555. (18-1-2008) NEW DELHI : The Government has no immediate plans to go for conscription or compulsory military service, the Minister of State for Defence Shri MM Pallam Raju said here today. Talking to reporters on the sidelines of his visit to the NCC Republic Day Camp, Shri Pallam Raju denied that the Government was seized of the issue at the moment in view of acute shortage of students opting for military officers' training through the NDA and CDS exams. Lack of funds was even proving to be a hurdle to raise the strength of NCC from 13 to 15 lakhs, Shri Pallam Raju added. He said the states will have to raise their contribution to the NCC while there are plans to seek the services of Ex-Servicemen for imparting training to implement the scheme. Earlier, addressing the cadets, Shri Pallam Raju said the NCC played a critical role in moulding and motivating the youth into responsible citizens and involving them in community campaigns. He said the NCC offered a vast reservoir of trained and disciplined youth to fall back on in a crisis. Speaking on the occasion, Lt Gen Prakash S Chaudhary, Director General, National Cadet Corps, pointed out that the NCC Cadets achieved a distinction by bagging the second place in the recent National Shooting Championships, second only to the Army. The NCC cadets presented a Guard of Honour to the Minister on the occasion. Shri Pallam Raju also inspected an impressive turnout of the NCC Parade. A colourful and lively cultural programme was presented by the cadets on the occasion.

5556. (18-1-2008) PANAJI: The central emissaries of the ruling Congress and the Nationalist Congress Party, who rushed here on Thursday, held parleys with the defiant NCP legislators and other coalition members till late in the evening to salvage the seven-month-old Digambar Kamat government. The talks between the Congress and the NCP were "inconclusive" and would continue in New Delhi on Friday, said NCP leader and Civil Avian Minister Praful Patel. The Congress-led government was reduced to a minority in the 40-member Assembly on Wednesday night, after the two NCP members and an Independent MLA resigned from the Ministry and withdrew support. Earlier in the day, the Assembly session was abruptly adjourned to avert a possible defeat for the government on the floor of the House. Setting the tone for the salvage operation, NCP president Sharad Pawar issued a stern warning of "extreme action" against the rebel MLAs. Mr. Patel, who arrived here along with NCP observer for Goa D.P. Tripathy, held discussions with the MLAs amid speculation that the State unit, in a tie-up with all non-BJP groups including Independents, proposed the formation of an alternative government with Congress support. If this effort failed, they would seek BJP support. In the Congress camp, B. K. Hari Prasad, Siddarth Patel and Ms. Mabel Rebello, who rushed to Goa, held talks with partymen. Sources in the NCP said that while the disgruntled MLAs had not demanded a change in the leadership of the coalition government, they wanted the Chief Minister to function more effectively. There were also demands for divesting Dayanand Narvekar, whose style of functioning reportedly antagonised many members, of the Finance portfolio, and for berths for at least two from the supporting groups. By evening, there were signs of an end to the impasse with the NCP legislature party leader Jose Philip D'Souza; Micky Pacheco, also of the NCP; and Independent MLA Vishwajit Rane, son of Speaker Pratapsingh Rane, toning down their stand after deliberations with Mr. Patel. The three, who had resigned as Ministers, said they were confident that their grievances over the functioning of the government could be redressed through talks. Earlier as the crisis unfolded, Congress MLAs Shyam Satardekar and Mr. Gurudas Gawas made common cause with the rebel group, whose number swelled to nine. One of the Congress MLAs threatened to resign in a bid to reduce the party's strength. However, the Congress claimed the situation was under control. After talking to the MLAs of the NCP and non-Congress groups, followed by a round of deliberations with the Chief Minister in a city hotel, Mr. Praful Patel said he was hopeful that the crisis would be resolved. He said that the NCP and other party MLAs had several grievances over the functioning of the government. There was a feeling that due importance was not being given to non-Congress MLAs. Some protested that their constituencies were neglected. "I understand the issues and dialogue is on, but a solution cannot be found right now," said Mr. Patel. "We have been talking to the Congress." The NCP leader is understood to have told the Chief Minister to take all MLAs along with him. Earlier in the day, as part of the damage control exercise, the Assembly was abruptly prorogued on Thursday without passing the Appropriation bill, inviting strong protests from the BJP. Leader of the Opposition Manohar Parrikar accused Governor S. C. Jamir of committing "constitutional impropriety to salvage the tottering government" and demanded his immediate recall. The Assembly was prorogued by the Governor following the Cabinet's recommendation. The move came hours before the Assembly was to meet to take up the Appropriation Bill. Before the withdrawal of support by some members on Wednesday, the ruling coalition had 23 members-Congress (16), NCP (3), Save Goa Front (2) and Independents (1) and the United Goans Democratic Party's unattached legislator Atanasio Monserrate. The Opposition comprised 14 of the BJP, two of the MGP and one Independent.

5557. (18-1-2008) NEW DELHI : The Ministry of Railways has decided to increase the Advance Reservation period from 60 to 90 days (excluding the date of journey). The Advance Reservation Period of 90 days will be applicable w.e.f. 1st February, 2008. There will be no change in the case of certain day time Express trains like Taj Express, Gomti Express etc. where lower time limits for advance reservations are at present in force. There will also be no change in the case of the limit of 360 days for foreign tourists.

5558. (18-1-2008) NEW DELHI : The Minister of Mines, Shri Sis Ram Ola met Australian delegation to discuss enhancing bilateral cooperation in mining sector, here today. The five member delegation was led by Mr. Simon Crean, Minister for Trade, Australia. Speaking on the occasion the Minister said that Mining industries of both countries are working together to promote mineral trade and investment between India and Australia. India and Australia established a Joint Working Group (JWG) on Energy and Minerals in the year 2000 for enhancing bilateral cooperation in the energy and mineral sectors. Five meetings have so far been held. The Ministry of Mines is the nodal Ministry for the Joint Working Group on Energy and Minerals. The Ministries of Coal, Petroleum and Natural Gas, Power, Non-Conventional Energy Sources, Commerce and MEA are also represented in the Indian side. The 5th meeting of JWG was held in Canberra on 2-3 July, 2007. Australia's mining industry has always been reckoned as one of the best in the world, in terms of mineral production, the technology used and the use of environmental protection measures in the mining sector. India looks forward to Australia both in terms of Foreign Direct Investment and the superior mining technology. The potential areas for investment in mining are iron ore, bauxite, chromites, barites, china clay, potash and granite. India has evinced interest in Australia's administration of their mining regime, procedures and mining practices; Mechanised large-scale mining operations and handling arrangements; State-of-the-art technology adopted for open cast mining; Expertise in the areas of exploration, mining and environment protection and Environmental management and practices adopted in Australia's mining sector.

5559. (18-1-2008) NEW DELHI : As compared to the month of November, 2007, the All-India Consumer Price Index Numbers for Agricultural Labourers and Rural Labourers (Base: 1986-87=100) for December, 2007 decreased by 1 point each to stand at 413 (Four hundred and thirteen) points for both the series. The rise/ fall in index varied from State to State. In the case of Agricultural Labourers, 6 States reflected an increase in index ranging between 1 and 5 points; in 11 States the declining trend in index ranged between 2 and 9 points while in 3 States the index remained constant. Haryana with 441 points topped the index table whereas Manipur was at the bottom with the index level of 362 points. In the case of Rural Labourers, in 6 States, index reflected an increase ranging between 1 and 6 points; in 11 States the declining trend in index ranged between 2 and 7 points whereas in 3 Stats the index remained constant. Haryana was at the top of the index table with 439 points whereas Manipur was at the bottom with 363 points. The Consumer Price Index Numbers of Kerala for Agricultural Labourers and Rural Labourers registered the highest increase of 5 and 6 points respectively mainly due to increase in the prices of rice, coconut oil, milk, onion, tea readymade, saltish refreshment, pan leaf and hair oil. The indices in respect of Himachal Pradesh registered a fall of 9 and 7 points for Agricultural Labourers and Rural Labourers respectively mainly due to decrease in the prices of rice, wheat atta, milk, onion, vegetables & fruits, sugar and gur. Point to point rate of inflation based on the CPI-AL and CPI-RL decreased from 6.15% and 5.88% during November, 2007 to 5.90% and 5.63% respectively during December, 2007. Respective rates of inflation during December, 2006 were 8.94% and 8.31%.

5560. (18-1-2008) NEW DELHI : India and Singapore to sign Memorandum of Understanding in culture sector soon to increase bilateral cultural cooperation. The Minister for Community Development, Youth & Sports and Arts of Singapore Dr. Vivian Balakrishnan today called on Tourism and Culture Minister Smt. Ambika Soni. During their half an hour meeting here both the leaders discussed ways to strengthen bilateral cooperation in tourism and culture sectors. Smt. Ambika Soni welcoming the visiting leader said India is currently witnessing boom in tourism sector and 5 million tourists arrived in the country in 2007. She said there are some challenges such as room shortage and better connectivity and infrastructure in India and the Government is working to create more infrastructure facilities to sustain the boom. Smt. Soni said Singapore airlines has one of the largest network and this can be utilized to promote tourist circuits in India. She informed the visiting dignitary that she is going to participate in the ASEAN tourism minister's conference which is scheduled to take place in Bangkok from 21st January, 2008. Dr. Vivian Balakrishnan suggested a joint marketing strategy to promote tourism with India and Australia on trilateral basis. He showed keen interest in the steps taken by the Indian Government to sustain the tourism growth and related issues. He thanked Smt. Ambika Soni to allow exhibition of Lord Buddha Relics in Singapore and said this is a special gesture by the Government of India.

5561. (18-1-2008) NEW DELHI : Shri Murli Deora, Minister for Petroleum & Natural Gas, today inaugurated the Oil & Gas Conservation Fortnight, 2008 in New Delhi that is being observed throughout the nation with an objective of promoting fuel efficiency in the country. Petroleum Conservation Research Association (PCRA) is organizing the fortnight in association with all oil PSUs, under the aegis of Ministry of Petroleum & Natural Gas, Govt. of India. The inaugural function was also attended by Shri Dinsha Patel, MoS(P&NG), Petroleum Secretary Shri M.S. Srinivasan and senior officers of the Ministry of Petroleum & Natural Gas and Oil Sector Companies. The fortnight is observed to sensitize public on fuel efficiency and oil & gas conservation in various uses in their day-to-day lives. The inaugural function was held at Siri Fort Auditorium, New Delhi in presence of a large number of school children. "For a country like India, where 73% of its oil demand is imported and when international crude oil price has touched $100, fuel efficiency is of utmost significance", said Shri Murli Deora, Minister for Petroleum & Natural Gas, inaugurating the event. Shri Deora, while awarding the winners of essay contest on "Save Oil, Save Gas, Save our Future" that carried a first prize of Rs. 1 lac each for Hindi & English, announced that PCRA will organize national level debating competition in order to aggressively promote the concept of oil & gas conservation amongst the youths of the country. Shri Dinsha Patel, Minister of State for Petroleum & Natural Gas, addressing the gathering of oil industry and school children, called for an attitudinal change in the mindset of public and appealed to the school children to imbibe upon the habit of fuel conservation. Shri M.S.Srinivasan, Secretary, Ministry of Petroleum & Natural Gas, delivering the Chairman's address, reiterated that India is growing fast and so is her energy demand. Children therefore, from their early stage of life, should practice conservation of Petrol & Diesel. Shri Srinivasan applauded PCRA for its leading role in promoting fuel efficiency in the country. "Extended road network and effective public transport are two key factors that would considerably reduce fuel consumption of transport sector in the country", said Shri A.Sundareshan, Addl. Secretary, MOP&NG, while delivering his address. Shri

Ravi Capoor, Joint Secretary and Executive Director, PCRA welcomed the gathering and said that the city of Delhi alone wastes Rs. 994 crores per year due to idling of vehicles at traffic red lights as per a study carried out by CRRI and PCRA. For the country, the figure may well be imagined. This wastage may be saved simply by switching off vehicle engine beyond 15 seconds at traffic red lights.

5562. (18-1-2008) NEW DELHI : In exercise of the powers conferred by clause (1) of Article 217 of the Constitution of India, the President is pleased to appoint Shri Justice Jagdish Bhalla, Judge of the Chhattisgarh High Court, to be the Chief Justice of the Himachal Pradesh High Court with effect from the date he assumes charge of his office.

5563. (18-1-2008) NEW DELHI : In exercise of the powers conferred by clause (1) of Article 222 of the Constitution of India, the President, after consultation with the Chief Justice of India, is pleased to transfer Shri Justice Rajeev Gupta, Chief Justice, Uttarakhand High Court as Chief Justice, Chhattisgarh High Court. The President, after consultation with the Chief Justice of India, is pleased to transfer Shri Justice Vinod Kumar Gupta, Chief Justice, Himachal Pradesh High Court as Chief Justice, Uttarakhand High Court. They have been directed to assume charge of their respective office on or before 2nd February, 2008.

5564. (18-1-2008) JHANSI: With the critical situation in Bundelkhand region of Uttar Pradesh becoming a major political issue between the Congress and the ruling Bahujan Samaj Party, the All India Congress Committee general secretary, Rahul Gandhi, presented a virtual chargesheet against the Chief Minister, Mayawati, on the plight of the people of the backward region of State. He said he would present his report card on Bundelkhand to the Prime Minister, Manmohan Singh, and United Progressive Alliance chairman Sonia Gandhi, and assured all possible help to the people of the drought-hit region of the State. Mr. Gandhi stated that the challenge of drought could only be overcome with the joint efforts of the people of Bundelkhand, the Central and State governments.

5565. (18-1-2008) NEW DELHI : Deputy of the cultural Heritage and tourism, Iran Mr. Hossein Jafari today called on tourism and Cultural Minister, Smt Ambika Soni. During an hour long meeting here both the Leaders discussed matters related to Tourism and Culture Sectors. Both the Leaders recalled centuries old historical and cultural ties between India and Iran and agreed to strengthen bilateral cooperation further in all sectors. Smt. Ambika Soni welcoming the Iranian leader said that Iran is one country where we want to concentrate in Incredible India brand campaign. She said India is looking on closer connectivity between Indian and Iranian cities to increase people to people contact. She said that despite close proximity and historical ties both countries are needed to increase tourists substantially to further strengthen bilateral relations. She said there is a need to exchange more information on tourism sector between the two countries and familarization trips of travel writers and journalists can contribute in this direction.

Smt Soni offered to train people from Iran in the hospitality sector and food crafts institutes. She said exchange of music, dance, crafts, exhibition of artefacts in each other's country will strengthen the relationship between the two countries further. Smt Soni thanked Iran for its support to India during UNWTO session at Colombia and said Indian delegation supported Iran to become Vice President of the UNWTO executive council. The visiting Iranian leader said President of Iran is eager to increase cooperation between the two countries and activities in Culture and Tourism sectors will be accelerated to work out a model of cooperation. He said, in April, 2008 Iran will organize a cultural week in India to show case and seek attention of the people of India towards Rich Iranian culture. He recalled Iran's participation in 17th Session of UNWTO at Colombia and said Iran whole heartedly supported India's candidature for Chairmanship of UNWTO Executive Council. Iranian Leader invited Smt Soni to visit his country at the earliest possible opportunity. Smt Soni said it is my dream to go to Iran. India Tourism Dubai looks after promotion and marketing of Indian tourism in Iran. It participated in the 'Holiday Show Travel Exhibition' held in Tehran, Iran from 13th to 15th of June, 2007. The exhibition was held after a gap of 17 years. India Tourism, Dubai set up an Indian pavilion which was decorated with traditional Indian designs. India and Iran are both members of UNWTO (United Nations World Tourism Organization) and were elected to the Executive Council to represent South Asian region. The term of both countries in the Executive Council will expire in 2009.

5566. (18-1-2008) NEW DELHI : On the directions of the Union Minister for Shipping, Road Transport & Highways, Thiru T. R. Baalu, the Secretary, Road Transport & Highways held a review of the progress on access controlled Delhi-Gurgaon stretch of National Highway-8 here today. The Chairman, NHAI, senior officers of Ministry and NHAI, Concessionaire and Independent Consultant from M/s RITES were present in the review. During the review, it was reported that the major works of the facility were completed on 31st December, 2007, but some safety related components such as provision of crash barriers, completion of left in-left out configuration at Kapashera, removal of scaffoldings at some locations, backup power supply particularly for street lighting and toll operations, system for tolling and that for operations and maintenance (O&M) of the corridor, etc. were remaining so that statutory tests could be undertaken by the Independent Consultant. The Concessionaire reported that the work is continuing round the clock to complete all these remaining jobs. The Concessionaire assured to complete these works and activities by today evening so that Independent Engineer could undertake the mandatory safety, reliability and integrity tests. Based on discussions and the commitment given by the Concessionaire during the meeting, that all the above requirements would be satisfied by 23rd January, 2008, it was decided that Delhi-Gurgaon access control facility on NH-8 in its entirety would be opened on 23rd January, 2008 at 4.00 p.m. by the Union Minister for Shipping, Road Transport & Highways, Thiru T. R. Baalu in the presence of Chief Ministers of Haryana and NCT of Delhi.

5567. (18-1-2008) NEW DELHI : CPI(M) Krishna District 20th meetings would be organised from January 20 to 22 at Kandukuri Kalyana Mandapam. The CPI (M) would take out a rally from Municipal Corporation office to Gymkahana grounds on January 20. The rally would culminate in public meeting.

5568. (18-1-2008) NEW DELHI : India and Congo have agreed to explore the possibility of cooperating in industrial diamonds in view of abundance of availability of these in Congo and Indian expertise in cutting and polishing of diamonds. Congo is world's second largest producer of diamonds and Indian companies like MMTC etc. are in a position to join hands for exploitation of rich potential which exists in this sector. Shri Kamal Nath, Union Minister of Commerce & Industry, during his bilateral meeting with Mr. Endra-Philippe Futa, Minister of National Economy and Commerce of Democratic Republic of Congo, also stated that India could cooperate with DR Congo in a meaningful exploitation of minerals like copper-and cobalt which exist in huge quantity in Congo. The Indian Commerce Minister also mentioned about the abundant hydro-electric power resources in DR Congo and stated that NHPC or other Indian companies in this field could provide technical expertise in exploitation of this energy resource in cooperation with Societe Nationale D'electricite (SNEL) of DR Congo. Shri Kamal Nath also reiterated the willingness of the Indian government to offer technical expertise to Congo in modernising and managing small and medium enterprises through National Small Industries Corporation. Recalling the visit of Mr. Simon Mboso Kianputu, DR Congo Minister for Industries to India in September 2007 during which many areas of cooperation were identified particularly between the SMEs of the two countries, Shri Kamal Nath observed that import from DR Congo are increasing while exports from India have come down since 2003-04. He expressed the need for increasing trade with DR Congo in view of stabilisation of economic activity in DR Congo. He also offered Indian assistance in modernising of mining sector in Congo. The Congo delegation is on a visit to India to participate in the Partnership Summit and also visited the Auto Expo which concluded here last evening.

5569. (18-1-2008) NEW DELHI : The centenary celebrations of the Trained Nurses' Association of India (TNAI) will be held on January 22, 2008. It is indeed a proud moment for the entire nursing fraternity in the country. The TNAI had its beginning in the Association of Nursing Superintendents which was founded in 1905 in Lucknow, U.P. Then it was composed of nine European Nurses mostly employed as administrators in the hospitals. This small band of visionary women with pioneering spirit saw the need to develop nursing as a profession and also provide a forum where professional nurses could meet and plan to achieve these goals. The movement gathered momentum and in 1908, the Trained Nurses Association was established with the objective to uphold in every way the dignity and honour of the nursing profession promoting espirit de cops among all nurses and to advance professionals, educational and general welfare of nurses. TNAI believes that good health is a fundamental right of every person and that it is the responsibility of the health professionals, including nurses to provide the kind of health care, which will give each individual in society every opportunity to achieve optimum health. As a professional person each nurse is ethically and morally responsible for giving the required care. Each nurse is a member of the society and is entitled to the same individual rights, privileges and the goals of physical, mental, economic and social development as are available to other members of the society. Nursing Services in India have expanded considerably since Independence. Along with this expansion a diversification in nursing services in the medical care field has also taken place. Great imbalances in the manpower situation can be noticed as far as nursing is concerned. As compared to the developed countries, the nurse's population ratio in India is not adequate. In India there is one nurse to 2250 people while in the developed countries the number of people served by one-nurse ranges from 150 to 200. Even developing countries like Indonesia, Kenya, Srilanka and Thailand have a better nurse population ratio. The nurse patient ratio, however, varies form 1:5 to 1:60 or 1:1000 in different Institutions. Nursing profession and its practitioners complement the Health Care Services by successfully implementing the interventions that promote or restore health. Being the subsystem of health services, nursing share some common attributes like caring, assessing and monitoring health needs, advocacy and education, developing appropriate response to care gaps, coordinating and delivering health care services across the health care spectrum. Acknowledging the contributions made by the nurses to the society, our late Prime Minister Mrs. Indira Gandhiji during a programme at the All India Institute of Medical Science, New Delhi observed that "A Nurse is not merely an aid and assistant to a doctor, she has an independent part to play in many areas where doctor need not necessarily be present. In the Western world, Nurse anesthetist is properly trained, take on important duties in minor surgical procedures as also care of newborn etc. The Nurse is in her own right a key member of the medical team. Many intensive care units, dialysis units and blood banks today fall with in the realm of nursing specialties. Auxiliary Nurse Midwives (ANMs) who do such valuable field work along with health visitors should be given due recognition on the basis of equality and not be regarded as a lesser members of the profession".

5570. (18-1-2008) NEW DELHI : The National Conference on Civil Aviation was held in New Delhi today. Chief Ministers, Ministers and Chief Secretaries and other senior officials from States attended the meeting. Welcoming the gathering, the Secretary Civil Aviation at the beginning of the Conference announced that this was a Conference for the specific purpose of interaction with the State Governments, which aimed at partnership between the Central and States for the growth of the Civil Aviation sector. In his speech the Deputy Chairman of the Planning Commission Shri Montek Singh Ahluwalia said that Civil Aviation was a growing sector and a success story. He said that the tremendous expansion had taken place because of the policies of the Government to invite private money to participate in the growth. This has been beneficial to both the public and private sector and now the airport infrastructure has been witnessing significant transformation across the country. Focusing on North East, Shri Ahluwalia hoped that at the end of the 7th Plan at least one airport should be operational in each of the North East State. The Minister for Tourism and Culture Smt. Ambika Soni called for synergising Ministries of Civil Aviation and Tourism and Culture because tourism primarily depend upon connectivity facilities and perception. She called for more connectivity especially to the places, which could promote health, religious and other facets of tourism. In his speech the Minister for Civil Aviation, Shri Praful Patel said that the Civil Aviation sector has a very high growth rate in this country, which was amongst the highest in the world. The aspirations of the people and of the States have led to more connectivity within the country whereas there was only 50 airports across the country in 2004, the number is expected to double to about 100 in 2008. In this sphere he called upon the States to come forward and join the process in the next level of growth of civil aviation because the Centre alone will no more be able to cope with the tremendous growth. The States should use their infrastructure including operationalisation of the un-used airports and airstrips to bring them into the mainstream, as there is immense potential for growth. The aviation sector, he said would in the next ten years bring in investments to the tune of $115-120 billion. It would become one of the top sectors for investment and also for employment generation. Even from the tourism point of view there was immense potential especially from the domestic tourism market for which he called upon the States to promote. He called for the development of more infrastructures in the hinterland of the big States because there was demand and there were opportunities waiting to be availed. This was followed by the panel discussion with the States giving in their inputs of their problems and expectations from the Central Government.

5571. (18-1-2008) NEW DELHI : India and Hungary today held discussions to further enhance of cooperation in agriculture sector. The Indian delegation was led by Shri Sharad Pawar, Union Agriculture Minister, and the Hungarian team was led by Minister of Agriculture and Rural Development of Hungary, Mr. Jozsef Graf. Highlighting the progress made by India in the fields of agricultural research, dairy equipment and packaging poultry and livestock, Shri Pawar sought increased cooperation between India and Hungary in these areas. India also proposed to have cooperation in agricultural infrastructure, post harvest management and horticulture. It was also decided to further strengthen linkages between the G.B. Pant Agriculture University and Universities and Centres in Kaposvear, Godollo and Eger. An agreement in the field of agriculture and allied sectors is to be signed by the two Ministers this evening in the presence of the Prime Ministers of the two countries. The Agreement is overarching and provides for cooperation in agricultural research and technology, agricultural production, food processing and economic cooperation between the two countries through joint activities. Joint activities will be carried out in the field of agricultural research, agricultural production including horticulture, post harvest management, agro processing, agricultural marketing, animal husbandry, dairying and aquaculture and phytosanitary issues relating to trade in plant and animal genetic resources. The Agreement also provides for setting up a Joint Working Group to develop biennial work plan and to coordinate and monitor activities to be carried out under this Agreement. The Agreement will enter into force on the date of its signing and shall remain valid for a period of five years and will be automatically renewed for a subsequent period of five years.

5572. (18-1-2008) NEW DELHI: The Communist Party of India (Marxist) on Thursday described Prime Minister Manmohan Singh's recent three-day visit to China as "highly successful" that has positively contributed towards carrying forward the improvement of relations between the two Asian giants. In addition to a number of bilateral agreements signed in various sectors, there was a determined expression to intensify high level political exchanges between the two countries in the future, an editorial in the latest issue of party organ People's Democracy said. Hailing the main document "A shared vision for the 21st Century", the editorial noted that the document stated that both sides will work for "a fair, reasonable and mutually acceptable solution" to the border dispute. "What is important to understand is that while continuing the dialogue on the border dispute both the countries appear to have converged on the understanding that cooperation in other fields must proceed and be strengthened. It needs to be recollected that it took China more than seven decades to resolve its border dispute with the former USSR and today's Russia," it said. On the new target of $60 billion by 2010 for bilateral trade, the editorial said the fact that trade between the two countries has grown so rapidly despite many restrictions, given security considerations, in itself shows the tremendous potential of economic cooperation between India and China. "There is now bound to be a serious rethink in India on the question of visa restrictions and the blacklisting of certain Chinese companies even after they have qualified global tenders as it happened in the offshore seaport in Kerala. In this contest, it is instructive to note the economic relations between China and Taiwan. People's Republic of China having succeeded in reintegrating Hong Kong and Macau with the mainland is seeking to do so similarly with Taiwan, which it considers as an integral part of China. In spite of this position and its consequent irritants in political, diplomatic and military spheres, Taiwan remains an important economic partner, both in terms of trade and investment, with China," it said. The editorial said that perhaps the most important aspect of Prime Minister's visit has been the enlargement of the canvas on which improvement of relations is being sought. "There has been a new found sharing of concerns at the development in Pakistan and the readiness to work together to meet the consequent threats of terror. The most important, however, appears to be the recognition that stronger economic relationship between India and China could well move the centre of economic gravity of the world towards Asia. This recognition in itself will go a long way in the movement towards multi-polarity," the editorial said.

5573. (18-1-2008) NEW DELHI : Direct tax collections continued to record a growth of over 40 percent for the period April to January 15 in the current fiscal. Net tax collections stood at Rs.2,17,149 crore, up from Rs.1,52,993 crore during the same period last fiscal, registering a growth of 41.93 percent and achieving over 81 percent of budgeted direct tax target of Rs.2,67,490 crore. Corporate Tax registered a growth of 37.22 percent at Rs.1,32,948 crore, up from Rs.96,883 crore during the previous fiscal, while Personal Income Tax (including FBT, STT and BCTT) grew by 50.15 percent at Rs.83,897 crore, up from Rs.55,874 crore. Growth in Securities Transaction Tax (STT) was 78.19 percent (Rs.6,793 crore against Rs.3,812 crore) and Fringe Benefit Tax (FBT) was 64.79 percent (Rs.5,121 crore against Rs.3,108 crore). Banking Cash Transaction Tax (BCTT) grew by 15.26 percent (Rs.423 crore against Rs.367 crore). Tax deduction / collection at source increased by over 51 percent while self-assessment tax (unpaid taxes paid voluntarily before submission of tax return) increased by over 59 percent, indicating continued improvement in tax administration and tax compliance levels.

5574. (18-1-2008) NEW DELHI : In a major move aimed at cooperation between the two giant railway systems of the world, namely Indian Railways and Chinese Railways, a Memorandum of Understanding (MOU) was signed between them in the Chinese capital, Beijing, this week during the Prime Minister's recent visit to China. The MOU, valid for three years, envisages development of rail related programmes of mutual interest, consultations, training and visits to each others' facilities. The Prime Minister Dr. Manmohan Singh and the Chinese Premier Mr. Wen Jiabao were present when the MOU was signed between Shri K.C. Jena, Chairman, Indian Railway Board and Mr. Liu Zhijun, the Chinese Minister for Railways Indian Railways has, of late, made tremendous progress in different sectors of its railway operation leading to great turnaround in its functioning and is fully gearing up towards modernization, technological upgradation, capacity enhancement and development of world class services. The MOU signed with China will further facilitate progress in that direction. The areas in which cooperation with Chinese Railways will be sought are in raising of speed on existing routes, development of world-class stations, heavy haul operations, development of multimodal logistics parks and in Research and Development. The Chinese Railways' experience in the areas of Signalling & telecommunication, Traction supply, High Axle Load Operations, Design & Maintenance practices, Track Machines, Development & Operations, Multimodal Transport in Railway sector would be of benefit to Indian Railways. During this visit, detailed discussions on all aspects of railway sector were held between Chairman, Indian Railway Board, with the Chinese Minister of Railways. The Chinese side was very enthusiastic on cooperation with Indian Railways and assured all possible assistance and follow up. In near future, the concerned officials from the Chinese Railways will visit India to firm up the details and modalities of mutual cooperation. Chinese Railways carry the highest level of freight traffic in the world and also a very high level of passenger traffic. It has undertaken considerable network expansion, speed raising, modernization and technology upgradation during the last 10 years and have a very ambitious programme for the next decade too. (Photo available on pib.nic.in)

5575. (18-1-2008) NEW DELHI : Production of finished carbon steel went up by 6.6 per cent during April-December 2007 compared to the corresponding period of last year. Finished carbon steel production touched 38.05 million tonnes during the first nine months of 07-08 compared to 35.704 million tonnes during the same period in 06-07. Imports of finished carbon steel during April-December 07 went up by 66.9 per cent from 2.936 million tonnes last year to 4.9 million tonnes this year. During the same period exports recorded a rise of 9.1 per cent to 3.850 million tonnes from 3.529 million tonnes in the previous year.

5576. (18-1-2008) KURNOOL: The two-day district meet of CPI(M) got off to a start with focus on development of the district. The party planned to take up the agenda of irrigation for upland area and industrialisation of backward areas. Outlining the future programme of the party, M.A. Gafoor, MLA, said the unprecedented flood in Tungabhadra caused havoc in Kurnool city this year. The loss could not be prevented as no dam existed on the river after Hospet, 200 km upstream of the city. According to an estimate, nearly 200 tmcft water was wasted into the sea every year. If half of it was tapped and supplied to the upland areas in Aluru, Pathikonda, Kodumur and Yemmiganur constituencies, nearly 10 lakh acres could be irrigated. Either the Congress or the TDP leaders never paid their attention to using Tungabhadra water for irrigating the perennially drought hit areas of the district. He said instead of starting new industries, the existing ones were also closed leading to unemployment. As the employment dwindled, the poor resorted to migrations, he said. The government has set two backward districts-Kurnool and Anantapur, against each other by diverting water from Kurnool to Anantapur. He said GO No. 3 was issued to divert KC canal water without compensating the farmers.

5577. (18-1-2008) NEW DELHI : The Union Public Service Commission will be conducting the Combined Defence Services Examination (I)-2008 at 41 Centres in the country on 17/2/2008 (Sunday). Admission Certificates to all the eligible candidates for the Examination have been dispatched. Rejection Letters citing the grounds for rejection have also been dispatched.

5578. (18-1-2008) NEW DELHI : India has asked Indonesia to consider removing Non-Tariff Barriers (NTBs) on the import of Indian pharma products into Indonesia. During the bilateral meeting between Shri Kamal Nath, Union Minister of Commerce and Industry, and the Indonesian Trade Minister Ms. Mari Elka Pangestu, here last evening, he observed that such a step would be beneficial for Indonesia to take benefit of India's cost effective drugs and source pharmaceutical products from India. He further stated that the Indian pharmaceutical products are exported to many countries including highly regulated markets of US, Europe, Japan and

Australia. Both sides discussed the issues regarding non-tariff barriers on carbon black, wheat flour, uncoated writing and printing paper and milk products and ascertained the concerns of each other to remove barriers to free flow of trade in these goods. The meeting was attended by the Commerce Secretary Shri G.K. Pillai; Secretary (DIPP) Shri Ajay Shankar; Director General of Foreign Trade Shri R.S. Gujral and senior officials from various Ministries from both the countries, apart from the representatives of the apex chambers. Shri Kamal Nath underlined the potential of small and medium enterprises (SMEs) in both the countries and stressed the need to explore the opportunities in the markets of the other. "The Indian SMEs sector is quite strong and would welcome engagement with the Indonesian counterparts and some of the Indonesian products such as wood furniture, handicrafts, traditional textile (Batik), food processing etc. that can find good market opportunities in India", he added. The Commerce Minister stated that there is lot of scope for widening the trade basket particularly in the services sector and highlighted the strengths of financial and banking sector. He also apprised the Indonesian Minister that Indian banks are interested in having stakes in Indonesia and a few Indian banks like State Bank of India and Bank of India have already started their operations in Indonesia. He added that Indonesia should also think about investing in banking sector in India, which would enhance the confidence of Indonesian businessmen and investors to do business with India. As regards the Joint Study Group (JSG), Shri Kamal Nath informed that the first meeting of India-Indonesia JSG was held in October 2007 in Jakarta and the Group agreed to complete the Report by June 2008. The next meeting of the Group is proposed to be held in New Delhi in February 2008.

5579. (18-1-2008) NEW DELHI : The Rural Employment Generation Programme (REGP), is implemented through the Khadi and Village Industries Commission (KVIC), under the Ministry of Micro, Small & Medium Enterprises to help eligible entrepreneurs to set up village industry units and thus create employment opportunities in villages including small towns with a population upto 20,000. Under this programme, entrepreneurs can establish village industries by availing of margin money assistance from KVIC and loans from public sector scheduled commercial banks, selected regional rural banks, cooperative banks, etc., for projects with a maximum cost of Rs. 25 lakh. Under REGP, banks appraise the projects as per the scheme and take credit decision.

5580. (18-1-2008) NEW DELHI : The total approximate earnings of Indian Railways on originating basis during the period 1st January-10th January 2008 were Rs. 2005.46 crore compared to Rs. 1725.25 crore during the same period last year, registering an increase of 16.24 per cent. The total goods earnings have gone up from Rs. 1207.71 crore during 1st January-10th January 2007 to Rs. 1406.99 crore during 1st January-10th January 2008, showing an increase of 16.50 per cent. The total passenger revenue earnings during the period 1st to 10th January 2008 were Rs. 529.63 crore compared to Rs. 460.69 crore during the same period last year, reflecting an increase of 14.96 per cent. The revenue earnings from other coaching amounted to Rs. 50.89 crore during this period compared to Rs. 39.38 crore during the same period last year, showing an increase of 29.23 per cent. The total approximate number of passengers booked during the period 1st to 10th January 2008 were 194.85 million compared to 183.55 million during the same period last year, showing an increase of 6.16 per cent. In the suburban and non-suburban sectors, the number of passengers booked during 1-10 January 2008 were 116.19 million and 78.66 million compared to 109.37 million and 74.18 million during the same period last year, registering an increase of 6.24 per cent and 6.04 per cent respectively.

5581. (18-1-2008) NEW DELHI : All the States have been asked to record significant higher achievements in implementation of all the centrally sponsored schemes for rural development under operation and particularly in case of NREGS, the flagship programme for freeing villages from the scourge of endemic and chronic unemployment and which also has the potential for unleashing the capacity of rural India to create durable community assets and catch up with the nation's march towards progress. Disclosing this to media persons here today the Union Minister for Rural Development, Dr. Raghuvansh Prasad Singh said states have been told that the new opportunities and the impetus created in the areas of rural development should not be frittered away and the tempo needs to be maintained. Dr. Singh said his ministry has a number of schemes for the welfare of rural poor and development of rural areas all over the country. For the success of these, it is important that a well-oiled and proper system for monitoring is in place and periodic evaluation of the implementation status is undertaken. Besides helping in course correction and augmenting performance levels, it also helps in bringing in transparency in the process of implementation. As a part of this exercise, a comprehensive multi-level and multi-tool system of monitoring and evaluation of the implementation of its programmes has been evolved through periodic Performance Review Committee (PRC) meetings. These are held on a quarterly basis, wherein wholesale review of centrally sponsored schemes/ programmes of the Ministry of Rural Development in different States are undertaken. During the last calendar year, the four such meetings were held. As a part of this exercise, a two day Regional PRC was held here on 17th and 18th January, 2008 in which States, Union Territories, CAPART, NIRD and Planning Commission have participated. Dr. Raghuvansh Prasad Singh said that the need for proper monitoring and evaluation for success of any programme needs no elaboration. He said these are critical not only for ensuring proper implementation of schemes but also are of cardinal importance for ensuring transparency. The Minister said that since we are in last league of the current financial year, the States have been told to ensure that there is no lagging behind in terms of financial and physical performance. The Minister also said that during the 10th plan period and during the last financial year the Ministry has done remarkably well both in terms of financial and physical achievements. During the 10th Plan as against a total allocation of Rs 76000 crores, Rs 1,14,000 crores was spent. There has been a progressive increase in the budget allocation for the Ministry over the last three years. The minister said, though the review touched upon all major programmes of the Ministry, the focus of the two-day deliberations and review was on National Rural Employment Guarantee Act (NREGA). Referring to draft CAG Report on NREGA, Dr. Singh said it was his ministry that asked the CAG to have a thorough scanning of the RD schemes implemented currently and accordingly has now given instructions to the States for taking necessary action on all the issues raised in report. 17 States have communicated their views and other States were asked to ensure compliance by 31st January, 2008. It has been categorically told to all States that, apart from taking corrective measures in districts under performance audit, similar action should also be ensured in other districts. States were advised to ensure effective measures in all phase III districts so as to have totally transparent and fully accountable system in position.

5582. (19-1-2008) NEW DELHI : The Central Government has amended provisions vide Notifications No.1/2008-Central Excise (C.E.), No.3/2008-C.E.[N.T.] and 4/2008-C.E.[N.T.] all dated 18.1.2008 to exclude the benefit of area based exemption in the State of Himachal Pradesh and Uttarakhand to those units which undertake only peripheral activities. Notification Nos.49/2003-C.E. and 50/2003-C.E., both dated 10.06.2003, provide full exemption from excise duty to the units located in specified areas of Uttarakhand and Himachal Pradesh. These exemptions are intended to encourage industrial development by creation of basic infrastructural facilities and to generate employment opportunities for the local people of these states. In order to ensure genuine industrial activities in these regions, it has been decided that benefits of duty exemption should not be admissible to goods in respect of which only peripheral activities like preservation during storage, cleaning operations, packing, re-packing, labelling or re-labelling, sorting, alteration of retail sale price etc. take place. This will ensure that the intended purpose of promoting substantial industrial/manufacturing activities through grant of fiscal incentives is fully met. Even in respect of special category states in the Northeast (States of Assam, Tripura, Meghalaya, Mizoram, Manipur, Nagaland, Arunachal Pradesh and Sikkim), the benefit of excise duty exemption has been disallowed to units carrying out only such peripheral activities. Accordingly Notification Nos. 49/2003-CE and 50/2003-CE have been amended vide notification No. 1/2008-CE dated the 18th January, 2008 so as to exclude certain peripheral activities from the operation of these notifications. The benefit of the said notifications will not, therefore, be available to goods which have been subjected to only one or more of the following processes such as packing or re-packing of such goods in a unit container or labelling or re-labelling of containers, declaration or alteration of retail sale price, etc. In other words, units carrying out only such processes would not be eligible for exemption benefit and would be required to pay duty as per normal procedure. It has also been decided to prescribed a simple quarterly return for assesses availing exemptions under the said notifications in order to create a database about the actual impact of exemptions on the industrial activities in these regions. Accordingly, rule 12 of Central Excise Rules, 2002 has been amended vide notification No.3/2008-CE[N.T.] dated the 18th January, 2008 to prescribe for a Quarterly Return [notified as Form-A vide notification No.4/2008-CE[N.T.] dated the 18th January, 2008], to be filed by the assesses with the jurisdictional Central Excise Commissionerate by the 20th of the subsequent month of the quarter to which the return relates. However, for the quarter ending 31st day of December, 2007, the units have been allowed to file the return by the 20th February, 2008. The assesses may send the said return electronically or by post. Necessary arrangements have been made in the concerned Commissionerates to receive the quarterly returns. The above provisions come into effect immediately from the date of publication of the notification No.1/2008-CE *i.e.* the 18th January, 2008 and are applicable to all the existing units availing the benefits of these notifications as also to new industrial units that may be set up in future.

5583. (19-1-2008) NEW DELHI : Union Agriculture Minister, Shri Sharad Pawar today asked agricultural universities to bring out concrete proposals to transform agricultural research and education. They must focus on vital and priority areas so that the required transformation takes place and agriculture sector grows fast in the XI Plan and beyond, he said. Shri Pawar was addressing the Conference of Vice Chancellors of Agricultural Universities. Besides the VCs and other scientists, senior officers of other departments of the Ministry of Agriculture and ICAR are also participating in the two-day Conference. Shri Pawar informed that the Government has decided to support schemes for expansion of teaching facilities and enhancing research capabilities of the agricultural universities under the recently launched Rashtriya Krishi Vikas Yojana (RKVY) also. Shri Pawar focused on reorienting research and education to meet the needs of agriculture as well as the new emerging areas such as IPR, phyto-sanitary and other quality standards and food processing. He complemented ICAR for supporting the establishment of 183 experiential learning units in 143 universities for providing hands-on training to students. ICAR is also supporting a massive project for developing e-courses for B.Sc. (Agri.) and B.VSc degree programmes, creating a digital library of PhD thesis and setting up consortium for e-courses in agriculture. Shri Pawar said that the use of information and communication technology needs to be further enhanced for improving the standards of teaching. Emphasising that agriculture universities must modernized their laboratories and farms, the Minister said that not only would this help in improving the quality of research and education but by doing so the varsities would also be able to generate resources for themselves. Shri Pawar also drew attention of scientists to the likely impact of climate change on Indian agriculture. He showed his happiness that ICAR has already taken initiatives to quantify implications of climate change and mitigating the emission of greenhouse gases. He exhorted ICAR to further accelerate such studies and prepare Indian agriculture to withstand the negative effect of rise in atmospheric temperature and other changes in the climate.

5584. (19-1-2008) NEW DELHI : Following is the text of the address delivered by the Defence Minister Shri AK Antony at the NCC Investiture Ceremony held at Republic Day NCC Camp, Delhi, today:-"I am very glad to be amongst NCC cadets at Republic Day Camp-2008. I hope that this year will bring peace, happiness and prosperity to you and your families. I extend a warm welcome to all our guest cadets who have come from different countries and hope that they will enjoy their stay here. National Cadet ~ Corps (NCC) is a unique organisation of the youth, which has contributed greatly for the overall development of the youth of the nation over the years. The youth is one of the strongest pillars of our society and nation and the NCC is rendering invaluable service by grooming them. NCC has been inculcating virtues like discipline, leadership, camaraderie, team-spirit, adventure, national integration and even strengthening the bond of fraternity on a global scale. NCC cadets are making contributions not only to the Armed Forces, but also to the civil society, in general. This camp is an opportunity for all of you to know and understand more about each other's culture, customs, and language and have a first-hand experience of the unique 'unity in diversity' of our nation. NCC undertakes development work and social service schemes from time to time-tree plantation, blood donation camps, adult education, anti-dowry pledge, campaign against drugs, anticorruption and awareness programmes on AIDS and cancer. The relief work done by NCC in the wake of disasters has helped In spreading awareness among all sections of the society. I am confident that the MoU signed between NCC and UNICEF to spread literacy among the youth, especially the girl child in rural and backward areas, will go a long way in using the international experiences in educating and spreading awareness to the remotest corners of our country. Recently, the NCC has taken steps to educate the cadets through career counselling and hone their communication skills to widen their horizons and enhance the employment opportunities. From time to time, the NCC has been channelising the energy of the youth into constructive activities such as sports and adventure. Two cadets-Lajja Goswami and Akash Kumar Ravidas have won medals at international shooting competitions. I congratulate both these cadets for doing the NCC and the nation proud. NCC should endeavour to expand its utmost to reach out to the remotest village in semi-urban and rural areas of every district of our country.

5585. (19-1-2008) NEW DELHI : The project designed by students of Apeejay School, Noida won top honours in the 2007-2008 Future Cities India 2020 competition. The programme, which was launched in 2006 by the Ministry of Science and Technology and Bentley Systems, is a partnership among government, universities, and the business community. It encourages students to use their design skills, along with Bentley's software for the world's infrastructure, to help prepare India's cities for the year 2020 as it is estimated that more than 50 percent of

India's citizens will live in the country's largest cities. All submissions provided a plan for the future redevelopment of the Commonwealth Games 2010 international zone, which will consist of temporary structures-everything from media centres, entertainment facilities, and practice grounds to a commercial centre and transportation system-that will be dismantled at the conclusion of the Games. Second place honours went to DAV Public School, Gurgaon. Shri. Kapil Sibal, the Union Minister for Science & Technology & Earth Sciences, gave away the awards in a ceremony in New Delhi today. Addressing the gathering, Shri Sibal said that it is for the second straight year that students have been made aware of the enormous infrastructure challenges facing this country. Lauding the efforts of both the organizers as well as the participants, he said that the programme also planted the engineering seed in the minds of the youth with the hope that they will one day determine the infrastructure future of this great nation. Terming the Chandni Chowk as one of the most unique living heritage sites, the Minister expressed concern over the fact that it is rapidly losing its unique character. He urged upon Bentley Systems and the DST to organize a competition to develop the historic stretch from Fatehpur to Lal Quila with inputs from modern science and technology into a truly world-class heritage site that the nation could feel proud of in the years to come. Later on interacting with the media the Minister shared his vision to make this a national event open to high schools and colleges across the country so as to sensitize a much larger section of the student community to issues of development in the country where they can make a meaningful contribution too. Shri. Bhupinder Singh, senior vice president, Bentley Software, said his company shared the ministry's enthusiasm for the programme and appreciated the incredible maturity, talent, and vision the students displayed in this year's competition. Commenting on Apeejay School, Noida's win, and their experience during the 5 month long competition, Team Leader Ajaypat Jain said, "Future Cities India 2020 gave us an opportunity to serve our country in a special way-and it was an opportunity we did not take lightly. We are truly fortunate to be part of this initiative as it has given us practical experience for our future endeavours. The Future Cities India 2020 competition consisted of 14 teams representing 10 high schools. Teachers and industry mentors guided each team in designing a redevelopment plan for the post Commonwealth Games international zone. Using Bentley software, students designed an innovative functional use for the site, while keeping in mind the concerns of the neighbouring residential community and all environmental issues. Distinguished experts from the infrastructure community judged the project presentations based on five criteria: project design solution report, computer model, expenditure summary report, physical model and team presentation.

5586. (19-1-2008) NEW DELHI : Shri Sam Pitroda, Chairman, National Knowledge Commission (NKC) released here today its 2nd annual 'Report to the Nation' which was presented to the Prime Minister, Dr. Manmohan Singh, yesterday. The release took place at a Press Conference which was also attended by NKC

Members including Dr. Ashok Ganguly, Dr. Jayati Ghosh, Dr. Deepak Nayyar, Mr. Nandan Nilekani and Ms. Sujatha Ramdorai. The Report assumes importance in the context of UPA government's commitment to the knowledge initiatives in the XIth Plan endorsed recently by the National Development Council. The Plan places high priority on education as a central instrument for achieving rapid and inclusive growth with specific emphasis on expansion, excellence and equity. This is reflected in the proposed allocation of Rs. 3,00,000 crore, a five fold increase over the Xth Plan. The share of education in the total plan will accordingly increase, from 7.7 percent to 20 percent, representing a credible progress towards the target of 6 percent of GDP. The vision of the Prime Minister and support of our leadership from across the political spectrum is indeed laudable. This is a landmark initiative in the history of government planning. NKC believes the education agenda outlined in the XIth Plan is a critical step towards realizing the objective of an equitable society. It is also fundamental to our continuing growth, employment generation, infrastructure development and other developmental priorities. The second Report to the Nation includes recommendations on Portals, Health Information Network, Legal Education, Medical Education, Management Education, Open & Distance Education, Open Educational Resources, Innovation, Intellectual Property Rights, Legal Framework for Public Funded Research and Traditional Health Systems. Together, in the last two reports, the Commission has covered 20 subjects and outlined about 160 concrete action items. Most of NKC recommendations on Education, Vocational Training, Libraries, Translation, National Knowledge Network, Innovation, IPRs, Traditional Health Systems etc. are integrated in the XI Plan and adequately funded. NKC recommendations, also accessible through the web, have been widely distributed, discussed, debated and are being considered at various levels in the government for implementation. The Commission has received excellent input and advice from academicians, scientists, teachers and various other stakeholders from both public and private domains, Central and State governments and the Planning Commission. While releasing the first NKC Report to the Nation on January 12th 2007, the PM emphasized that the Commission "must be involved in ensuring the implementation of their innovative ideas". The focus of NKC work has therefore been on ensuring that while the Central government designs appropriate strategies supported by financial allocations to implement their recommendations, the Commission engages simultaneously with diverse stakeholders to build up a groundswell of favourable opinion and assist preparation of implementing strategies at the grassroots. Continuing dialogue with a wide and diverse set of stakeholders has been a critical part of its process both in formulating recommendations and in their subsequent dissemination. NKC has tried to provide a platform for sharing and debating ideas, a critical requisite for accepting and steering change.

5587. (20-1-2008) NEW DELHI : As per latest information received, a total mortality of 98,254 poultry birds has been reported from Birbhum, Dakshin Dinajpur, Murshidabad, Nadia, South 24 parganas, Burdwan and Bankura districts of West Bengal. As per the report of HSADL, Bhopal, the sample from district Bankura has also tested positive. Further, more samples from Nadia, Birbhum and Murshidabad districts have also tested positive. On 19.01.2008, a total of 60 Rapid Response Teams (RRTs) carried out operations (58 teams for culling and 2 for surveillance) in Birbhum district. 33 teams in Dakshin Dinajpur district and 16 RRTs in Murshidabad were deployed for culling operations.

5588. (20-8-2007) NEW DELHI : The entire nation is appalled by brazenness of the UPA Government in actively colluding with the accused in the Bofors bribery case. The governments headed by Congress have repeatedly subverted the CBI as a premier investigative agency to compel it to actively cooperate and collude with the accused. The entire effort of the Congress party is that the truth in the Bofors case must be given a judicial burial even if this arose out of Collusive proceedings between the accused and the CBI. After collusively obtaining a judicial burial the fraudulent argument advanced by the Congressmen is "The truth has not come out and therefore there was no truth in the allegations". Let us remind the country of the allegation against Ottavio Quatrocchi. The facts in this regard are – (a) There were five trials by the Indian army which favoured the French gun Sofma. On 31.10.1985, AE Services, a company controlled and run by Otavio Quatrocchi entered into an agreement with the manufacturers of the Bofors gun, Noble Industries. The contract stated that AE Services shall obtain the order for their guns on before 31.3.1986 If they do so, they would be entitled to a three percent commission. (b) AE Services succeeded in pursuing the Indian army to conduct the sixth trial. This sixth trial favoured Bofors. (c) To obtain the order on or before 31.3.1986 the file was pushed from table to table (including 17 tables on one day) and on 24.3.1986 the contract was allotted. AE Services earned its commission. (d) In 1993 the Swiss authorities informed the CBI that AE Services was the beneficiary of the Bofors payment and its account opening form in part B indicated Ottavio Quatrocchi as beneficiary of the account. (e) Ottavio Quatrocchi swung the deal because he was close to the powers that be. He was a close friend of the Gandhi family. (f) When the Swiss informed the Indian government of Quatrocchi involvement, he escaped from India within 72 hours. Since then he is a Fugitive.

5589. (21-1-2008) NEW DELHI : Most of Asia opened the year 2008 on a weak note with heavy selling pressure seen in most markets. Comparing the major Asian market indices as on 2nd January, 2008 with their closing today, it is seen that the Straits Times has fallen by 14.75%, Hang Sang by 13.58% and the Nikkei is down by 9.29%. The corresponding figure for BSE Sensex is 13.97%. Today the BSE Sensex has fallen by 1408.35 points or 7.41% and the NSE Nifty has closed down 496.5 points or 8.7%. As regards domestic economic conditions, the just released Review of the Economy 2007-08 by the Economic Advisory Council of the Prime Minister has estimated the rate of growth of the GDP in 2007-08 at 8.9%. Corporate profits as reflected in the third quarter 2007-08 results continue to be buoyant. Direct tax revenues have shown an increase of 42.8% this financial year (April to December, 2007). Banks have reported that investments in the pipeline are robust and credit demand is high. Thus, the fundamentals in the domestic economy are quite strong. Today's market fall reflects the continuing uncertainties in the global economy and not any change in the fundamentals of the Indian economy. Investors should take informed and responsible decisions in the situation and not be led by market rumours or any unwarranted apprehensions.

5590. (21-1-2008) NEW DELHI : The President of India, Smt. Pratibha Devisingh Patil has condoled the loss of lives in a road accident near Nashik in Maharashtra. In a condolence message to the Chief Minister of Maharashtra, Shri Vilasrao Deshmukh, the President has requested him to convey her condolences to bereaved families and her prayers for the early recovery of the injured. Smt. Patil has also said that she is sure that the Government of Maharashtra is providing all help to the bereaved families as well as providing medical facilities to the injured.

5591. (21-1-2008) NEW DELHI : The Annual Plan for Manipur for the year 2008-09 was finalized today at a meeting between Planning Commission Deputy Chairman, Shri Montek Singh Ahluwalia and Chief Minister of Manipur, Shri Okram Ibobi Singh. The Plan size was agreed at Rs.1660 crores. This includes a special plan assistance of Rs.550 crores for projects of special interest to the State. Deputy Chairman, Planning Commission, complemented the State Government for accelerating pace of development and assured that fund constraint would not be allowed to hamper progress in development. He said the Commission will ensure that there is no delay in the release of funds to the State. The State was asked to improve in the power sector reforms and performance in execution of Pradhan Mantry Gram Sarak Yojana. It was pointed out that in recognition of the need for infrastructure development, Planning Commission has agreed to give focused attention to road, power, education and health services. Funds were also been provided to improve employment opportunities. Attention was drawn to the fall in allocation to social services and high incidence of HIV cases. The Chief Minister in his remarks said that efforts were on to increase food-grain production to reduce food-grain deficit, expand horticulture area and improve processing facilities, increase per capita income to all India level and electrification of all villages by 2010-11. He said to improve infrastructure a sum of Rs.800 crores was proposed in next year's budget. He sought Planning Commission's support in early completion of Jiribam-Tupul-Imphal Railway Line, up-gradation of NH-39 and creation of additional capacity for food storage and petroleum product storage in the State.

5592. (21-1-2008) NEW DELHI : The children who have been conferred the 'National Bravery Award 2007' met with the Vice President of India Mohd. Hamid Ansari at a function here today. Twenty two children-eighteen boys and four girls have been selected for the Awards and four of them have been given posthumously. Congratulating these brave children for their courageous acts the Vice President said that this is their big achievements as they have saved the life of the people and they deserve more. He blessed them big success in their life and assured them of all sorts of assistance for their bright future. The covered 'Bharat Award' has been conferred on 17 year old Kum. Babita and 15 year old Master Amarjeet of Haryana who saved several of their school mates from drowning when their school bus fell into the Yamuna canal. The 'Sanjay Chopra Award' has been conferred to six year old Master Yuktarth Shrivastava of Chattisgarh who saved his sister from stray dogs. The prestigious 'Geeta Chopra Award' has been conferred posthumously on 14 year old Kum. Lalrempuii of Mizoram who fought vehemently against her assailant to resist a rape attempt and lost her life in the process. The selection was made by a high powered committee comprising representatives of various Ministries/Department, non-governmental organizations as well as senior members of Indian Council for Children Welfare (ICCW). The children will receive the Awards from the Prime Minister of India on 24th January 2008 and will participate in the Republic Day parade riding caparisoned elephants. These Awards were initiated in 1957 and since then a total of 732 children-530 boys and 202 girls have been given the Awards. Deserving awardees will be granted financial assistance until they complete their schooling under Sponsorship Programme of the Council. Some State Governments also provide financial assistance to them. In addition, ICCW provides financial assistance under its Indira Gandhi Scholarship Scheme to those undertaking professional courses such as engineering and medicine. For the others, this assistance is provided till they complete their graduation. The Government of India has reserved some seats for the awardees in medical and engineering colleges and polytechnics.

5593. (21-1-2008) NEW DELHI : India Post is under universal service obligation to provide basic postal facilities at affordable price throughout the length and breadth of the country. The task, of course, is daunting and challenging as well, more so in view of the fact that the present day communication business is determined by market forces. Managing the operations of 1,55,516 Post Offices in the country of which more than 1.3 lakh are in rural areas with more than 5.5 lakh employees calls for high level of managerial skills and professional commitment. While the pressure of managing the vast network spread all across the country is huge, at the same time expansion of the network to cover the hitherto un-served or under served areas is equally important. Technology induction at a large scale is, therefore, the only viable solution both for sustenance and growth as far as India Post is concerned. Adoption and assimilation of technology in India Post has gone beyond the urban locales to rural habitats across the country. Having created a base of 8,263 computerized Post Offices in the country and a pool of trained human resources, India Post is now poised to offer state of the art Internet based services throughout the country.

5594. (21-1-2008) NEW DELHI : The BJP strongly condemns the draft political document released by the CPM at its 19th party congress yesterday. The entire document smacks of political arrogance at its worst despite the fact that the Left Front parties have been conclusively pushed to the margins of the country, and their political relevance is confined only to West Bengal, Kerala and Tripura. It was indeed astonishing that the CPM has the audacity to call the BJP as its enemy number one, failing to realise that the BJP is today one of the two principal political fronts of the world's largest and truly functioning democracy, and is in power in six states on its own and in another three states in coalition. The BJP totally refutes this entire concept of terming political opponents as enemies and would like to remind Mr. Karat and his bandwagon of "leftovers" that this mindset is patently anti-democratic, irrelevant and undesirable in the interests of healthy democratic traditions. It is indeed worth pointing out that since independence, even the political forefathers of Mr. Karat have indulged in this sort of verbal assault against the nationalist and democratic forces of the country. At various points of time, the Left Front leadership has used similar autocratic and stalinist expressions against the Congress party and also described Loknayak Jai Prakash Narain in the 1970s as a rank fascist. Infact, for 45 years, the Left Front leadership did not even spare the legendary Subhash Chandra Bose from their verbal assaults. But the inbuilt democratic genes of India's masses always conclusively rejected such despicable and anti-democratic abuses during elections. Yet the Left Front leadership has remained rooted in the past and failed to evolve in sync with the will of the people. This explains the reality of their total marginalization in Indian politics where the Left Front cannot ever emerge beyond the confines of three states and where their total vote share at the national scene is nowhere close to double digits. Over the last six decades since independence, Indian politics has increasingly become bi-polar, a reality the CPM and Left Front parties have failed to either note or appreciate. The BJP and the Congress are today the two divergent poles of Indian politics. The chimera of the so called Third Front is solely to frustrate the growth of the BJP and prevent it from coming to power. This ill-conceived political gameplan is destined to fail. The people of India deserve better than an attempt to subvert the will of the masses through the formation of a Third Front. A hoisted political enterprise conceived in haste to subvert the true will of the people will never succeed. History has numerous lessons to teach. Neither the Gujral nor Deve Gowda Third Front experiments at the centre could ever last or provide a viable political alternative to the country. The only difference between then and now, is at that point the grand old man of antiquated political thought, Mr. Harkishan Singh Surjeet, was the force behind these disastrous political experiments, and today it is Mr. Prakash Karat and his team of outdated intellectuals.

5595. (21-1-2008) NEW DELHI : A 14-women hockey players were awarded today for their performance in Asian Cup (2005), Commonwealth Games (2006) and Asian Games (2006). The Secretary (Sports), Mr. S. K. Arora gave away the cheques ranging from Rs. 1.5 lakhs to Rs. 4 lakhs to these players. Speaking on the occasion, Mr. Arora said that the Ministry of Sports will give all possible support to the women's hockey team to motivate them further. The women's hockey team won the Asian Cup 2005, silver medal in the Commonwealth Games 2006 and bronze medal in Doha Asian Games in 2006.

5596. (21-1-2008) NEW DELHI : The Board of Approval of the Special Economic Zones (SEZs) met here today to consider proposals for setting up of Special Economic Zones and also approve other miscellaneous requests pertaining to SEZs. Addressing the Board of Approval members, the Chairman informed that so far formal approvals have been granted for setting up of 428 SEZs out of which 194 have been notified as on date. He informed that over Rs.52193 crores have been invested in these notified SEZs. Direct employment to over 94832 persons have been provided by the new generation Special Economic Zones. This is in addition to the employment provided by the 7 Central Government established SEZs which is over 1.81 lakh persons. In this meeting, 19 proposals for setting up SEZs, including 2 proposals for conversion of in-principle approvals to formal approvals were considered. The Board recommended grant of 11 Formal approvals (including 2 requests for conversion of In-Principle Approvals to Formal Approvals) and 1 In-principle approval. The proposals are:

5597. (21-1-2008) NEW DELHI : India is seeking investments from UK in the areas like highway projects, bridges, expressways, ports, power generation, water plants, water management techniques. This was conveyed by Shri Kamal Nath, Union Minister of Commerce and Industry, during the India-UK CEOs Round Table, here today, and added that so far investments from UK was mainly from the sectors such as telecom, chemicals, fuels, service sector etc. The Round Table was attended by Lord Digby Jones, UK Minister of State for Trade and Investment and Dr. Ashwani Kumar, Minister of State for Industry, besides senior officials from both the countries. Drawing the attention of CEOs, Shri Kamal Nath said: "We consider UK as one of the most important source of FDI for India not only amongst the EU countries but also vis-a-vis other countries in the world. With a share of 37% in EU's total outflow of FDI in non-EU countries, I think UK is a very natural and important partner for a country like India that requires massive investment for its infrastructural needs". India is now the 3rd largest foreign investor in the UK in terms of projects, second only to the US and Japan. In the first half of 2006, according to Ernst & Young's European Investment Monitor 2006 Report, Indian investment into the UK overtook Japan, making India the 2nd largest investor in the UK. UK is the 3rd largest investor in India with a cumulative inflow of US $ 4.06 billion, (6.48%) since 1991. FDI inflows from UK in 2005, 2006 and 2007 (up to October) have been US $ 219.3 million, US $ 1749.8 million and US $ 398.5 million, respectively. On the trade front, UK is the 4th largest trading partner of India with bilateral trade of US $ 9.8 billion in 2006-07, which is about 3% of India's total trade. Percentages of bilateral trade compared to total trading basket of UK (US $ 1 trillion in 2006) are negligible. This again indicates an immense potential existing between the two countries.

5598. (21-1-2008) NEW DELHI : The Government has decided to reconstitute Hindi Salahkar Samiti for the Ministry of Micro, Small & Medium Enterprises with the Minister Shri Mahabir Prasad as its Chairman. The tenure of the Samiti will be three years from the date of formation. The Samiti has 26 other members. The functions of the Samiti will be to advise the Ministry regarding progressive use of Hindi in official work.

5599. (21-1-2008) NEW DELHI : Shri V.S.Sampath today took over as the Secretary Department of Chemicals and Petrochemicals. Shri Sampath is a 1973 batch officer of the Indian Administrative Service of the Andhra Pradesh Cadre. He was the Director General National Institute of Rural Development, Hyderabad, before taking up the new assignment.

5600. (21-1-2008) BHUBANESHWAR: Expressing grave concern over the spurt in naxalite violence in various parts of the country, BSP leader and Uttar Pradesh Chief Minister Mayawati on Sunday blamed politicians who were at the helm of affairs for a long time for it. Kicking off her party's campaign here for the next Lok Sabha elections due next year, Ms. Mayawati said naxalite violence continued to be a major problem for the last 15-20 years. This was because more and more people were joining the naxalite cadre thus strengthening their outfits, she said. "People, mainly youths are joining the naxal cadre out of frustration and other compulsions," she claimed adding no one was joining the cadre on his own to become a naxalite or a terrorist. "Politicians and parties in states and at the Centre are responsible for the growth of naxal menace." Since the state governments ignore the people living in forests and remote areas, the people support naxalites to get their benefits. "The state governments which have deprived the poor people of their genuine rights are witnessing naxalite activities," she said. The Chief Minister also blamed the Centre for rise in terrorism in some border states. "Since the Centre is unable to protect international borders, terrorists from neighbouring countries sneak in," she said. Ms. Mayawati said since successive governments at the Centre adopted economic policies to benefit capitalists and not the poor, naxalisim and terrorism had been growing. "If BSP comes to power, it will ensure that the root cause of violence is addressed properly in order to check the twin problems."

5601. (21-1-2008) NEW DELHI : The Ministry of Railways has decided to increase the Advance Reservation period from 60 to 90 days (excluding the date of journey). The Advance Reservation Period of 90 days will be applicable w.e.f. 1st February, 2008. There will be no change in the case of certain day time Express trains like Taj Express, Gomti Express etc. where lower time limits for advance reservations are at present in force. There will also be no change in the case of the limit of 360 days for foreign tourists.

5602. (21-1-2008) BHUBANESHWAR: Uttar Pradesh Chief Minister and Bahujan Samaj Party president Mayawati on Sunday launched her party's election campaign in Orissa by announcing sops for both weaker sections and the economically poor among the upper caste. If voted to power in the State, the BSP Government will give patta for three acres of cultivable government land to each poor and needy family, Ms. Mayawati said at a State level Sarbajan Bhatrubhav Mahasamavesh here. As Assembly polls were to be held in Orissa simultaneously with the general elections in early 2009 there was not much time in hand to prepare for the polls, she told the thousands of her supporters who had gathered at the rally coming from different corners of the State. In an attempt to attract the upper caste people towards her party, Ms. Mayawati clarified that nobody should have the notion that BSP was devoted to the cause of the weaker sections and Dalits. "Unless those belonging to the upper caste people join the party we cannot form government to work for the benefit of all sections of the society," she said, while urging the party workers to induct upper caste people into the party.

5603. (21-1-2008) NEW DELHI : Following is the text of the address delivered by the Defence Minister Shri AK Antony at the National Seminar on Defence Standardisation held here today:-This seminar has come not a moment too soon when numerous initiatives are being taken by Government towards liberalization and modernization. This seminar is an ideal platform for all the concerned players-the research and development agencies, production agencies, quality assurance agencies and the user agencies-to come together on a common platform to debate on and evolve better methods for the scientific management of our defence inventory. The Directorate of Standardization, established in 1965, has been working on standardization and codification of defence stores towards effective logistics management by our Armed Forces. Given the size of our defence infrastructure, not only in terms of the number of personnel in uniform but also in terms of the sheer number of the variety of equipment being used, standardization provides the only answer to rationalize and effect reductions in the number of items being procured, stocked, maintained, transported and used, without degrading the operational effectiveness of our Armed Forces. Towards this end, the Directorate of Standardization has done commendable work by setting up a database on defence inventories. Over the years, it has also produced a number of standardized documents, codified a vast quantity of materials and generated several Joint Staff Qualitative Requirements. The latter is a very important area-we are now witnessing a movement towards Joint-Services efforts and commonality which implies the production, use and management of defence stores which will meet the common requirements of all the Services to the extent possible. As we increasingly globalize and cooperate across international borders on the development, production and procurement of defence stores and items with many countries, as the number of entities involved in defence material production and management grows rapidly, as the number of players, particularly from the private sector, increase with the introduction of the offset policy, it becomes all the more important to intensify our standardization and codification efforts if we are to avoid getting trapped in a logistics nightmare. Standardization is the instrument through which we can promote better understanding of requirements between the research and development agencies, the producers and manufacturers and the end users. But as I mentioned above, we in the defence sector are not an island unto ourselves. We need to not only link our efforts with our National standards organization-The Bureau of Indian Standards-but also with international organizations. I am happy to learn that this Directorate is working towards cooperation with international organizations like the Allied Committee-135 and expects to become a member of that group soon. I am sure that the Directorate of Standardization, in cooperation with all, will continue its yeoman work towards improved inventory management, better quality assurance and in promoting greater clarity and transparency in procurement of defence stores. I hope that this seminar deliberates and evolves more effective mechanisms to ensure better synergy between our technologists, suppliers and users-be they be public or private.

5604. (21-1-2008) NEW DELHI : The Defence Minister Shri AK Antony inaugurated a two-day seminar on "Synergising Defence, Industry and Technology through Standardisation-Perspective concerns and Spin offs" here today. The seminar is organized by the Directorate of Standardisation under Department of Defence Production, Ministry of Defence. Brigadier Jatender Singhla, Director, Directorate of Standardisation, delivered the opening remarks. In the 11th Plan Government has projected the need for a "National Quality and Standardisation Authority" by synergising the efforts of all the major national standardization bodies like BIS, Directorate of Standandisation, GS 1 etc. under the aegis of "Quality Council of India". The seminar is the first step in this direction. Recently the Directorate has embarked upon measures to upgrade the country's defence standardisation and codification procedures at par with international standards. It is also preparing standards for various defence equipment, weapons and other stores thus leading to better battle preparedness for the fighting forces. The Directorate has taken initiative for India to become Tier 1 level member of AC/135, an apex International body of codification. Inclusion of a mandatory clause for provision of technical parameters for codification in future procurements will ensure codification of defence equipment at the time of introduction into service. A codification software is under development in the Centre for Advance Computing and System Application, Directorate of Standardisation. The Seminar is aimed at leveraging the concepts of standardisation to a national level in order to optimize the operational efficiency of our Armed Forces. Senior functionaries of the Ministry of Defence, representatives of three Services, DRDO, PSUs and representatives of major private sector industries besides delegates from USA, Russia, South Africa and France are participating in this event.

5605. (21-1-2008) NEW DELHI : The twenty-first century is witnessing a gradual decline in fertility, and with increase in life expectancy, the society will need to grapple with issues of longevity. The cause of morbidity and mortality world over is shifting from communicable diseases a few decades ago to non-communicable diseases. The leading causes of mortality among aged people comprise respiratory problems, heart diseases, cancer and stroke. Significant causes of morbidity among this group is chronic inflammatory and degenerative conditions such as Arthritis, Diabetes Osteoporosis, Alzheimer's disease, depression, psychiatric disorders, Parkinson's disease and age related urinary problems. The biggest challenge with geriatric problem is that in most of the cases the condition cannot be attributed to a single cause or in certain conditions of neuro-psychiatric disorders like, Senile dementia, Alzheimer's depression, the structural cause is unknown. In such cases the conventional medical therapy fails to come out with effective management plan and hence is severely compromised. Another challenge with conventional medical therapy is that it does not have health-promoting agents. Ayurveda on the other hand has interventions like chayavanaprasha, triphala that enhance physiological processes that influence metabolic and immunological status. Such interventions are significant in the context of geriatric care. Rasayana therapy of Ayurveda is a dedicated stream of medication for immune promotive, antidegenerative and rejuvenative health care and is known for preventing the effects of ageing and improving the quality of life of healthy as well as diseased individuals. Scientific studies have proven the efficacious role of Rasayana remedies in the management of chronic life style related diseases and degenerative changes. Rasayana is normally advised during the degenerative phase, which starts from around 45 yrs in both male and female. A holistic system like Ayurveda approaches this condition through two-fold methods. One is a radical approach in which it recharges the whole metabolic process of the body by eliminating the toxins from the system by a three to four months rigorous and organized process known as Kutipraveeshika Rasayana. However, this process is seldom practised due to the extreme intricacy of the physiological process involved and the need for utmost care to be taken by the physician and subject including the environment where the treatment is done. Hence this Kutipraveeshika remains as a textual marvel of Ayurveda than a practical process of contemporary relevance.

5606. (21-1-2008) NEW DELHI : The Union Public Service Commission will hold the Engineering Services Examination, 2008 commencing from 7th June, 2008. The Examination will be held at various centres across the country. For details regarding the Scheme & syllabi, Centres of examination, Guidelines for filling up application form etc. aspirants must consult the Detailed Notice of the examination published in the Employment News/Rozgar Samachar dated 12th January, 2008. In case of any guidance/information/clarification regarding their applications, candidature etc. candidates can contact UPSC's Facilitation Counter near 'C' gate of its campus in persons or over Telephone No. 011-23385271/011-23381125/011-23098543 on working days between 10.00 a.m. to 5.00 p.m. The Commission also has a Website at address: http:/www.upsc.gov.in from which the candidates can obtain details of the examination as well as information about registration of their applications, venue of the examination and results etc.

5607. (21-1-2008) NEW DELHI : The Union Minister of Shipping, Road Transport and Highways, Thiru T.R. Baalu has approved a sum of Rs. 161.09 lakh for construction of High Level Bridge at 116/8 km of NH-210 across Anjukottai supply channel in Sivagangai district in the state of Tamil Nadu. NH-210 is an important National Highway passing through Trichy, Pudukottai, Sivaganga and Ramand districts in Tamil Nadu. The Highway connects many towns in Tamil Nadu and also serves as a main link to the Pilgrim centre of Rameswaram from the northern parts of the State. During rainy season, causeway is subjected to submergence causing frequent interruption of traffic. It is, therefore, necessary to construct a High Level Bridge at this location.

5608. (21-1-2008) NEW DELHI : The Home Minister has called upon the South Asian nations to use their strength in science and technology to build a robust system of prevention, mitigation and preparedness to reduce the risks of natural and man-made disasters. Inaugurating the SAARC Workshop on Application of Science and Technology for Disaster Risk Reduction and Management in South Asia here today, Shri Shivraj Patil pointed out that South Asia has the largest scientific and technical manpower in the world. Many of its scientists and technologists are supporting the most advanced scientific, research and technical institutions around the world. Some of its scientific and technical institutions are also at par with the best in the world. Drawing the attention of the workshop to the fact that various regions of the sub-continent are prone to earthquakes, Shri Patil stressed the need for sustained scientific research on earthquake, particularly in the Himalayan region, so as to be able to identify the fault zones and the return period more accurately. He said that earthquake resistant designs and technology would have greater acceptance if it makes use of local ethos and locally available building materials. Describing cyclone risk mitigation as another priority area for scientists, Shri Patil said that prediction of the precise location of the landfall was essential so that the people who would not be affected by the storm surge do not have to be evacuated. He also highlighted the need to deal with the challenges like sea level rise and climate change. The Home Minister said that India would extend all possible assistance and cooperation to all its neighbouring countries for better management of disasters in the region. Scientists and policy-makers concerned with application of science and technology for disaster risk reduction and management in the member countries of the SAARC are attending the two-day workshop. The workshop would develop a road map for regional cooperation in the field of science and technology for disaster risk reduction and management.

5609. (21-1-2008) NEW DELHI : Shri Kamal Nath, Union Minister of Commerce and Industry, is scheduled to address the annual meeting of the World Economic Forum (WEF) in Davos. The WEF meeting during 22-26 January, 2008 will be attended by a high-powered delegation that includes government representatives from both the central and state governments and key business leaders from different sectors. Shri P. Chidambaram, Finance Minister; Shri Praful Patel, Minister for Civil Aviation and Shri Vilasrao Deshmukh, Chief Minister of Maharashtra, will also participate in the WEF meeting. Shri Kamal Nath will be addressing in several important sessions at the WEF, including the sessions entitled "The Asian Century-Fact or Fiction?" on 22nd January; "India's International Agenda" on 23rd January; "New Global Challenges" on the 24th of January; and "Threats to the Global Trading System" and "WTO Informal Ministerial Gathering" on 26th January. The meetings will also be attended by the Prime Minister of Hungary, Mr. Ferenc Gyurcsany; Mr. Akira Amari, Minister of Economy, Trade & Industry of Japan; Mr. Celso Amorim, Minister of Foreign Relations of Brazil; Mr. Pascal Lamy, Director General of World Trade Organisation; Mr. Doris Leuthard, Federal Counsellor of Economic Affairs of the Swiss Confederation; Mr. Peter Mandelson, Trade Commissioner, European Commission, Brussels; Ms. Mari Pangestu, Minister of Trade of Indonesia; and Ms. Susan Schwab, US Trade Representative.

5610. (22-1-2008) NEW DELHI : Prof. Saifuddin Soz, the Union Minister of Water Resources has assured full cooperation and assistance to the Punjab Government in implementation of various ongoing schemes. This assurance was given when Punjab Chief Minister Shri Prakash Singh Badal called on him here today. In the course of the meeting, implementation of various schemes was reviewed and it was decided to expedite the works. The Punjab Chief Minister brought the notice of the Union Minister that the study conducted by the Central Ground Water Board for water logging problem in Mukatasar district of the State should be implemented early. He also said the scheme under Command Area Development should be approved for speedy implementation. The Minister appreciate the plea of the Punjab Chief Minister that Punjab deserved attention as it is supposed to be granary of the country. In the course of the meeting, Prof. Soz impressed upon the need for augmentation of ground water level in Punjab where depletion of ground water is already a matter of concern. Prof. Soz stressed that the Model Bill forwarded by his Ministry should be accepted and a law enunciated early to recharge the ground water besides organizing a movement for rain water harvesting in the entire State.

5611. (22-1-2008) NEW DELHI : As per latest information received, a total mortality of 1,13,796 poultry birds has been reported from Birbhum, Dakshin Dinajpur, Murshidabad, Nadia, South 24 Parganas, North 24 Parganas, Burdwan & Bankura districts of West Bengal. The HSADL, Bhopal has confirmed a positive result for Avian Influenza (H5) in respect of samples from Krishnanagar-I and Haringhata blocks of Nadia district, Ktugram, Jamuria and Galsi blocks of Burdwan district and Nalhati-I and Bolpur-Sriniketan blocks of Birbhum district of West Bengal on the basis of rapid tests. A number of samples from Howrah, South 24 Parganas, North 24 Parganas, Hooghly, Kolkata, West Midnapur tested at the HSADL, Bhopal turned a negative result. On 21.01.2008, a total of 258 Rapid Response Teams (RRTs) were deployed for culling, mopping up and surveillance operations. The maximum number of teams are working in Birbhum (79), followed by Burdwan (60), Murshidabad (51), Dakshin Dinajpur and Nadia (34 each). The RRTs have, up to 21st January 2008, culled a total of 2.42 lakh poultry, destroyed 88,252 eggs and about 3000 kgs of feed material. The joint teams of the Department of Animal Husbandry, Dairying & Fisheries and the Ministry of Health & Family Welfare visiting Jharkhand, Bihar, Orissa, Assam and Meghalaya are continuing their work in these states. A team has also moved to Tripura and Mizoram today.

5612. (22-1-2008) NEW DELHI : The Chief Minister of Manipur, Shri O. Ibobi Singh called on the Union Minister of Shipping, Road Transport and Highways, Thiru T.R. Baalu here this evening to discuss the road sector projects in the State. Thiru Baalu assured the Chief Minister that sanctions for the 4-laning of a stretch from Imphal to Imphal University and strengthening of km 366 to km 400 km between Pallel and Moreh of NH-39 will be given by the Ministry shortly. The issue relating to the repair of Hanlon-Tipaimukh section of NH-150 was also discussed. In this connection, the Minister directed the Secretary, Road Transport & Highways to organize a joint meeting of the State Officials and Border Road Organisation (BRO) to sort out the issue. The Minister also impressed upon the Chief Minister to issue necessary instructions to the concerned State officials to complete the pending works of repair and improvement of Senapati-Imphal section of NH-39 and utilize the budgetary allocation of Rs 25 crore under National Highways (Original works). It was also agreed upon that estimates for repair of flood damages suffered due to the rains during 2007 will also be approved by the Ministry shortly.

5613. (22-1-2008) NEW DELHI : India, with growing industrialization, has reached a crucial juncture as the country is poised to touch double-digit growth rate. The 11th Five Year Plan seeks to achieve a faster and more inclusive growth. This is possible only with effective contribution of all stakeholders. To cope with the serious manpower crunch the industrial sector is facing, and in order to increase the employability of the labour force through development of skills suitable for the ongoing industrialisation process, the Government decided to set up a corpus fund of Rs 550 crore for training one million persons above the age of 14 over the next five years under the "Skill Development Initiative Scheme". This is a centrally sponsored scheme under which an amount of about Rs 5,000 would be spent per person for providing training and certification. The Scheme will provide an opportunity to the large unskilled workforce of the country from the socially and economically disadvantaged sections, for securing jobs in both manufacturing and service sectors. The crafts which have been included cover a large spectrum from beautician and carpet weaving to engineering and information technology sectors. Well over 200 modules for employable skills as per industry and labour market demands have already been identified and course curriculum has been developed. It is hoped that this will address the requirement of industry for skilled workers. These industries include automobile, construction, refrigeration, painting, welding, carpet weaving, gem and jewellery, food industry, toy-making etc. The workers who have already acquired certain skills through many years of hands on work but with no formal certification would also be able to get tested and certified under this scheme. Testing of skills of trainees would be carried out by independent assessing bodies, which would not be involved in training delivery, to ensure that it is done impartially. The essence of the scheme is in the certification that will be nationally and internationally recognized. Training would be provided through optimal utilisation of available infrastructure in various Government and private institutions and industry. Institutions providing training under this scheme would include various Vocational Training Providers under Central and State Governments, public and private sector and industrial establishments. The objectives of the scheme include providing vocational training to school dropouts, existing workers, ITI graduates, etc. to improve their employability by optimally utilizing the infrastructure available in Government., private institutions and the Industry and to build capacity in the area of development of competency standards, course curricula, learning material and assessment standards in the country.

5614. (22-1-2008) NEW DELHI : This year Twenty Six Tableaux will participate in the forthcoming Republic day Parade-2008, where India will showcase its military might and economic strength. This year's tableaux component comprises 16 States, 09 Ministries & one department. Each tableau depicts its own story to portray themes varying from Industrial Progress to National Heritage and from Traditional Art and Culture to Legendary Personalities.

5615. (22-1-2008) NEW DELHI : Today's meeting has indeed been a significant milestone in the current political developments in the country. For the first time after the May 2004 Lok Sabha elections, all the leaders of the constituent parties of the NDA and all the chief ministers of NDA-ruled states have come together to deliberate on a common strategy for the next parliamentary elections. I sincerely convey my gratitude to all my colleagues in the alliance for reposing their trust in me by entrusting the responsibility of leading the NDA in the next Lok Sabha elections. I assure you that I shall do my utmost to discharge this responsibility successfully, and seek your continued support and cooperation in the challenging tasks ahead. At the outset, I would like to heartily thank our leader, my senior colleague for over five decades, and the chairman of the NDA, Shri Atal Bihari Vajpayee, on this occasion. I shall continue to seek, as I have done for the past five decades, his wise and inspirational guidance in the discharge of my responsibilities. I would also like to specially thank Shri George Fernandes, convenor of the NDA, and Shri Rajnath Singh, president of the BJP. The birth and evolution of the NDA is not an ordinary phenomenon. With the Bharatiya Janata Party as its strong and central pillar, the NDA represents one of the most outstanding developments in the political history of post-independence India. It indicates the maturing of Indian democracy in the direction of Good Governance, Development and Comprehensive Security.

5616. (22-1-2008) NEW DELHI : Over the years Radio as a medium of communication has played an important role in the nation's socio-cultural, political and economic development. It has the unique advantage of being receivable through low cost, battery operated, and mobile receiving sets, affordable for almost everyone, even in the rural areas. With appropriate strategies, radio can expand its reach to sparsely populated areas and remote corners of the country. In the recent years, Ministry of Information & Broadcasting has initiated a number of steps for the expansion of radio all over the country. Recognizing the potential use of the medium of radio for the betterment of the community, the Government announced a policy for the grant of licenses for setting up Community Radio Stations by the educational institutions in December 2002. Today, there are 28 such stations working in various parts of the country. The community radio aims at enhancing participation of the people in the development process and capacity building in rural areas, through education. It provides opportunities to the people to upgrade their skills and enhance their creative talents, besides preserving and promoting the traditional wisdom, knowledge and skills. Thereby Community Radio Stations (CRS) help to promote and project the local language, arts, craft, culture and traditions. CRS brings within easy reach of the rural population, topical information in areas of agriculture, social welfare, education, health and environment and help in creating rural networks for the rural cottage and village industry.

5617. (22-1-2008) NEW DELHI : The Ministry of Defence will soon be approaching the Union Government for approval of Second Phase of Married Accommodation Project to meet the shortfall in accommodation to a large number of soldiers who are leaving away from their families. Speaking to the reporters on the sidelines on a function to felicitate the National Bravery Awards 2007 winning children, here today, he said that the Government will work on a war footing to execute the project. Replying to a question on the shortfall of officers in the Armed Forces, Shri Antony said in today's scenario the children have many options and the pay packet is much better in other fields than what the Armed Forces are offering. However, he said that for the first time the Armed Forces have put their best foot forward by presenting a unified proposal to the Sixth Pay Commission. He expressed optimism that the Armed Forces would get a better deal this time. Talking to the children, the Defence Minister said that their achievements are great and are comparable to the Armed Forces, guarding the borders in inhospitable terrains and weather conditions. He wished the children best in their life. Shri Antony spent about half an hour with the children and their parents.

5618. (22-1-2008) NEW DELHI : The Wildlife Crime Control Bureau need to combine visibility as well as invisibility into its performance. Inaugurating the office premises of Wildlife Crime Control Bureau Headquarters today Ms. Meena Gupta, Secretary, Environment & Forests further elaborated that visibility is required to create awareness among people on two accounts one have to access the Bureau in time to need and second to educate them about damage to our wildlife and our heritage. Ms. Gupta expressed the hope that this will be a good beginning for very effective measures, if not to stop, to minimize wildlife crimes and to reduce smuggling of illegal trade of wildlife. She said dangers to wildlife come from borders so the Bureau has to be more vigilant at these areas. Ms. Gupta said today we realize that Government cannot do everything but Government can become very effective if we tie up with other organizations and sharing information with others. She suggested to have good network with private sectors State Governments and other Government bodies to reduce crimes in wildlife. The Secretary suggested to install a hotline so that people can access the Bureau in time of need. A manual for enforcers on Red Sanders, a tree species that is endemic to southern India, listed on Convention on Trade in Endangered Species (CITES) was released by Shri P. R. Mohanty, Director General of Forests and Special Secretary to Government of India on the occasion. The field forensic facility at Bureau Headquarter displayed the scientific identification of Shatoosh fibre, a banned wildlife fibre of "Chiru"-a tibetan antelope, other goat fibres which are commonly used, banned gastropod shells and some of their products traded; tiger, leopard fur, hair, claw identification and their fakes; some of the endangered medicinal plants like Kuth roots, Sarpgandha; ivory and bone articles; some of the endangered marine species; and the identification manuals on Mollusca (shells), Fishes, Reptiles and Amphibians. The bureau, a multidisciplinary agency consisting of officials from forests, police and revenue (customs ¢ral excise) would aim for inreased awareness amongst the international tourists to reduce demand for the wildlife and its products. As part of the strategy for a coordinated universal action in combating organized crime, strengthening of the enforcement at the international trade exit points would get emphasis as the major demand for the wildlife and its products lies in overseas markets. It is also mandated to advise policy changes, if any, based on the information/data on crime and criminality.

5619. (22-1-2008) NEW DELHI : India and Israel today held discussions to strengthen cooperation in areas ranging from research to investment in infrastructure, and cooperation at state and industry levels. The Indian delegation was led by Shri Sharad Pawar, Union Agriculture Minister, and the Israel team was led by Mr. Shalom Simhon, Agriculture Minister of Israel. Welcoming the visiting delegation, Shri Pawar called for time-bound implementation of the Work Plan agreed by the two countries in 2006. Extending India's offer for cooperation in mutually beneficial areas, Shri Pawar said that the "Indian agriculture is changing and offers tremendous opportunities for private sector to play a constructive role in all stages of agricultural chain-infrastructure, R&D extension, diversification to high agriculture, value addition and agro processing and marketing. It requires significant investment in capital and technology. The technology, however, needs to be customized to the needs of the end users. Majority of Indian farmers are small holders with limited resources. They are, however, very keen to adopt new technology which they can afford with their limited resources. I would, therefore, urge captains of Israeli industries and representatives of association of Indian Industries present here to come and work together in India which offers a huge market. I am confident that the economies of scale which will be realized while catering to such a huge market will make it possible to keep the prices of end products and services to be offered affordable and within the reach of small holder farmer." Earlier the Israel delegation visited Maharashtra, Rajasthan and Haryana. The delegation visited mandies in Haryana, and the National Dairy Research Institute, Karnal and held discussions with Rajasthan government on a project being implemented in olive cultivation.

5620. (22-1-2008) NEW DELHI : Inaugurating the centenary celebrations of Trained Nurses Association of India (TNAI), the Union Minister for Health & Family Welfare, Dr. Anbumani Ramadoss said that the Association is playing a vital role in upholding the dignity and honour of nursing profession and promoting high standards of healthcare and nursing practice in the country. Congratulating all the members of the Association on this momentous occasion, he said that nursing profession occupies a strategic position in the primary healthcare network. He added that they are the mainstay of our healthcare delivery system. Besides, Shri Arvind B. Kulkarni, President, TNAI, Sr. Gilbert, First Vice-President, TNAI, senior officials from the ministry of Health & Family Welfare and representatives from TNAI were also present at the function.

5621. (22-1-2008) NEW DELHI : The National Resource Centre for Cluster Development (NRCD) of National Institute for Micro, Small & Medium Enterprises (formerly known as NISIET) under the Ministry of Micro, Small & Medium Enterprises is organising a two-day national workshop on MSME Cluster Development on 28-29 January 2008 in New Delhi. The objective of the workshop is to bring together various organisations/institutions concerned with cluster development so as to synergise the efforts and add further momentum to cluster development in the country. For this purpose, policy makers, planners, implementers and field experts are being invited to share their experiences and to evolve new strategies for development of MSMEs through cluster development. The themes selected for discussion are a) Policy Implications for Cluster Development b) Clusters: Employment Generation and Poverty Reduction c) Business Development Services d) Investment Promotion and Technology Transfer e) Cluster Financing and Development f) Infrastructure Development and Common Facilities g) Cluster Development Implementation Strategy and h) Future Directions.

5622. (22-8-2007) NEW DELHI : During my stay of about two months in America I have had talks with a large number of friends who have contributed a lot for the OFBJP (USA) since its inception. In the backdrop of each one of them expressing a keen desire to work united for the cause of the BJP and the recent resolution adopted by the derecognized OFBJP (USA), regretting the circumstances that led to its de-recognition by the parent body and also assuring the central organization to always abide by their directions and guidance, I had ascertained the views of the Elders Council. Thereafter, the matter was discussed at the highest level in Delhi. The BJP has now decided to rescind the earlier decision to disassociate itself from the OFBJP (USA). Elections of the new president and the office bearers of his team are to be held shortly. It has been decided to postpone these elections for a few months till the present constitution of the OFBJP (USA) is reviewed and got duly approved by the parent body in Delhi. To ensure that the elections are held at the earliest, taking along all sections of the OFBJP (USA), it has been decided as an interim arrangement to appoint the following office bearers of the OFBJP (USA). They will hold charge till the new elections are held which, in any case, must not be later than March 31st, 2008. They must immediately seek fresh suggestions from all members, old and new, regarding amendments to the present constitution and send these recommendations for the formal approval to New Delhi. Shree Chandrakant Patel has ensured that this decision will be implemented immediately.

5623. (22-1-2008) NEW DELHI : Shri Arjun Singh, Minister for Human Resource Development has released today Flash Statistics: Elementary Education in India: Progress towards Universal Elementary Education (UEE) 2006-07 in the meeting of Executive Committee of the National Mission for SSA in the presence of Secretary, School Education & Literacy. This document is the second publication on the same subject and has been brought out by the National University of Educational Planning and Administration (NUEPA). One of the significant indicators that has been presented in the document is the addition of Muslim enrolment both at the primary and upper primary levels of education which has been attempted for the first time in the country. This document will further help to track progress of the States towards Universal Elementary Education (UEE) for Primary and Upper Primary levels as well as for a composite look at Elementary level of Education. The EDI as an annual exercise that will encourage the States to improve their performance. It is expected that this exercise will help more effective targeting of Sarva Shiksha Abhiyan (SSA) to the most needy districts. The Government is already focusing on districts with substantial population of Scheduled Castes, Scheduled Tribes and Minorities, educationally backward districts where there are large numbers of out of school children, high gender gap and large infrastructure gaps. The EDI is developed keeping in mind four broad parameters of access, infrastructure, teacher and outcomes related indicators. The index takes into account 23 variables for calculating EDI. These variables are for Access (Percentage of habitations not Served, Availability of Schools per 1000 Population and Ratio of Primary to Upper Primary Schools/Sections), Infrastructure (Average Student-Classroom Ratio, School with Student-Classroom Ratio greater > 60, School without Drinking Water Facilities, School with Boy's Toilet, School with Girl's Toilet), Teachers (Percentage of Female Teachers, Pupil-Teacher Ratio, School with Pupil Teacher Ratio > 60, Single-Teacher Schools (in schools with more than

15 students), Percentage of Schools with 3 or less Teachers, Teachers without Professional Qualification), Outcomes (Gross Enrolment Ratio-Overall, Scheduled Castes : Gross Enrolment Ratio, Scheduled Tribes: Gross Enrolment Ratio, Gender Parity Index in Enrolment, Repetition Rate, Dropout Rate, Ratio of Exit class over Class 1 Enrolment (Primary stage only), Percentage of Passed Children to Total Enrolment, Percentage of Appeared Children passing with 60 per cent and above Marks).

5624. (22-1-2008) NEW DELHI : Following is the text of the speech of the Minister of Tourism & Culture Smt. Ambika Soni at the India-ASEAN Tourism Ministers' Meeting In Bangkok today:-"It gives me great pleasure to lead the first Indian Ministerial level delegation to this extremely important India-ASEAN Ministerial Meeting. I wish to say how much I value my participation here. Let me take this opportunity to thank the Government of Thailand for the excellent hospitality extended to all of us. I am glad that as part of India's Look East policy since the early 1990s, we have consciously moved forward to re-establishing our historical ties with the ASEAN countries. This has been duly reciprocated by the ASEAN countries, which recognize the mutually advantageous multifaceted partnership with India. Today, India-ASEAN Cooperation has broadened to cover wide ranging areas. Tourism is an important activity between our two regions as it helps, above all, to connect our people together. The out bound tourism from India crossed 8 million in 2007; the ASEAN region is one of the prime beneficiaries of this outbound traffic from India. At the last India-ASEAN Summit in Singapore in November, 2007, Prime Minister, Dr. Manmohan Singh announced a target of one million tourist arrivals from ASEAN to India by 2010. With increased air and road connectivity between our two regions, and the vast tourism infrastructure that we are creating in our country will, I believe, make this target achievable. Common history binds our regions and people together. Our peoples have interacted with each other in various capacities since time immemorial, and in the process contributed to building a rich tapestry of cultural and religious affinities. The ASEAN Tourism Forum offers an opportunity to the region to take forward these historical linkages. With a view to sustaining these ties we are developing world class tourism infrastructure around 15 of our most important heritage sites such Taj Mahal, Hampi, Ajanta and Ellora, Bodh Gaya etc. You will be pleased to know that all these sites are now connected by air and we will encourage airlines from this region to directly operate flights without having to go via major cities. This would help to make India a short haul destination. With the support of the private sector we should be able to work out attractive tour packages that cater to the needs of the ASEAN tourists. With this objective in mind our India Tourist Office in Singapore will organize in April this year the first ASEAN-India Travel Trade Exchange "Beyond Boundaries" in which the Travel Agents and Tour Operators from all the member countries could discuss and finalize joint packages on different products. We also need to work towards greater simplification of visa procedures. Last year, India has introduced long duration visas for passengers on a pilot basis. We hope to expand this facility to ASEAN countries. Our next goal will be to introduce 'visa on arrival'. With the modernization of our airports, we are confident of putting such a facility in place. Some of the ASEAN countries have successfully introduced this facility, reaping huge benefits in terms of increased tourist traffic. India and ASEAN region are now looked upon as the economic powerhouse of the world. Therefore, investments in tourism sector could be of immense interest to our region. India has already declared Hotel and Tourism industry as high priority with provision for 100% foreign direct investment. I would like to urge the ASEAN investors to take advantage of the high returns this sector provides on investment. Another area of cooperation that I wish to highlight is the development of human resource for the hospitality sector in the region. Greater exchange of students from the hospitality training centres could be encouraged. We would gladly host such exchange programmes with any ASEAN member country.

5625. (23-1-2008) NEW DELHI : The Thirteenth Finance Commission held its first meeting with economic experts and administrators of the country under the chairmanship of Dr. Vijay Kelkar here today. The Members of the Commission, Dr. Indira Rajaraman, Prof. Atul Sarma and Shri B.K. Chaturvedi had detailed discussions with eminent economists such as Dr. Amaresh Bagchi, Dr. M. Govinda Rao, Dr. Tapas Sen, Dr. Pratab Bhanu Mehta, Dr. Haseeb Drabu as well as Professors and economists from University and reputed institutes such as The Energy and Research Institute (TERI), Public Health Foundation of India (PHFI), Indian Institute of Public Administration (IIPA), etc. The day long discussions focused on the terms of reference of the commission, its mandate, scope as well as suggestions for improving the fiances of Centre and States. The Commission held wide ranging discussions on the review of the finances of the Centre and the States and measures for maintaining a stable and sustainable fiscal environment consistent with achieving equitable growth. The operations of the States' Debt Consolidation and Relief Facility introduced on the basis of the recommendations of the Twelfth Finance Commission also came in for discussion in addition to the present arrangements regarding financing of disaster management through the National Calamity Contingency Fund. The commission will hold a series of meetings at the regional level in various parts of the country in the coming months. As part of its efforts to elicit views and suggestions, the Commission has launched a website http://fincomindia.nic.in. It would be an interactive website where general public and stake holders can submit their suggestions to the Commission online. The thirteenth Finance Commission was constituted to give specific recommendations on the sharing of tax receipts between the Centre and States and also for outlining the principles for providing grants-in-aid to the States out of the Consolidated Fund of India. The Commission will also suggest measures to augment the Consolidated Funds of the States to supplement the resources of the Panchayats and Municipalities. The Finance Commission is expected to submit its final report by October 2009.

5626. (23-1-2008) NEW DELHI : The leaders of our freedom movement realized the importance of girls' education and had put it as a prime agenda for national development. However, when India attained independence some 60 years ago, it was a formidable challenge that the new government had to face. The national female literacy rate was an alarmingly low 8.9 per cent, Gross Enrolment Ratio (GER) for girls was 24.8 per cent at primary level and 4.6 per cent at the upper primary level (in the 11-14 years age group). Social and cultural barriers to education of women and lack of access to organized schooling, had to be addressed immediately.

5627. (23-1-2008) BHOPAL : As per latest information received, a cumulative mortality of 1,16,203 poultry birds has been reported from West Bengal, of which 2407 birds died on 22.01.2008 in Murshidabad, Nadia and Bankura districts. This number stood at 1,13,796 till yesterday. The HSADL, Bhopal has confirmed a positive result for Avian Influenza (H5) in respect of samples from Dinhata-I block of Coochbehar district, Balagarh block of Hooghly district and Raniganj block of Burdwan district of West Bengal on the basis of rapid tests.

5628. (23-1-2008) NEW DELHI : Three Army personnel will be awarded the coveted Ashok Chakra, all posthumously, by the President of India on the Republic Day. These are Col Vasanth V, Captain Harshan R, and Naib Subedar Chuni. These awards were announced last year and will be received by their next of kin. Col Vasanth V of 9 Maratha Light Infantry laid down his life in a fire fight when he was personally leading an operation to flush out militants near Uri town in Jammu and Kashmir. He succumbed to his injuries before he reached the hospital. He is survived by his wife Subhashini, two daughters Rukmini and Yeshodha and parents Mr. and Mrs. Venugopal. Col Vasanth went to school at many places in Karnataka as his father was working with the LIC. His schooling took him to Mangalore, Ooty, Udupi, Shimoga, Bangalore etc. He graduated from MES College, Bangalore. He was an ardent NCC Cadet and had also participated in a Republic Day parade at Delhi. He also visited Canada on exchange programme through the NCC. Even as a youngster, he had expressed a desire to be in the army. Being a bright student, he had got selected to do an MBA in the prestigious IIM, but he chose to go to IMA, Dehradun as a Gentleman Cadet. Col Vasanth-a true idealist and a man of peace-was proud to be an officer of the Indian Army till the very end. He was no armchair idealist. He read widely about military histories and strategy and would take great care to analyse the inscrutable choices that armies have made in history. He attended many seminars and talks, and listened with care to the many different voices of our nation. He was genuinely motivated by sacrifice. He was excited about commanding the 9 Maratha LI and thrilled that he would be joining them on the frontline. For Vasanth, his lifetime commitment was simple-his word and his honour. His personal life always came second. In 1997, during a discussion with his wife, Subhashini, a Bharatnatyam dancer,

Vasanth expressed that there are a lot of people speaking about the soldiers but not many who try to depict the life of the women in their lives. He felt that she should use her talent and her experiences to tell the story of the army wife. This gave the birth to The Silent Front, an organization dedicated to the widows of martyrs. Mrs. Suhasini will receive the award bestowed on the gallant officer from the President.

5629. (23-1-2008) NEW DELHI : The Union Minister of Shipping, Road Transport and Highways, Thiru T. R. Baalu, the Chief Minister of Haryana Sh. Bhupinder Singh Hooda and the Chief Minister of Delhi Smt. Sheila Dikshit inaugurated here today the last flyovers at Rao Tula Ram Marg-Palam Mahipalpur of NH-8. With the opening of RTR-Palam flyover, the 27.70 km. Delhi-Gurgaon Access-Controlled highway project has been completed at a total cost of Rs. 710 crore. This is one of the busiest corridors carrying traffic more than 1,50,000 Vehicles per day and is the only link to the Indira Gandhi International and domestic Airport of the capital city. This project has been implemented on Build, Operate and Transfer (BOT) basis with a negative grant. The project facility will be maintained by Concessionaire for 20 years period including construction period. The user fee will be collected at three toll plaza locations with discounted rates for Local personal traffic and Local Commercial traffic. With the opening of RTR-Palam flyover, the stretch between Km 14.300 to Km 42 of NH-8 with nine flyovers would provide smooth ride to the commuters. It will now take approximately 20 to 25 minutes only to cover this stretch. The opening of entire project for public use will provide immense relief to commuters travelling between Delhi and Gurgaon. The service roads will cater to the local traffic without interfering with the long distance main traffic. This would further provide comfort to the commuters, both passenger and commercial vehicles, on this important route to Jaipur and Mumbai. For the safety of pedestrians, the project comprises of four pedestrian subways, one completed Steel Foot over Bridge, one under Construction Steel Foot Over Bridge and six proposed Steel Foot Over Bridges. These Foot Over Bridges would be located at km 11 near DSOI Gate, Dhaula Kuan in Delhi and rest in Haryana at various places like the one between Udyog Vihar and IFFCO Chowk and another at Hero Honda Chowk while two others at Khandsa Village and Narsinghpur Village respectively. The project was initially scheduled for completion in July 2005. The completion of the project has however got delayed due to complexity involved in the implementation of this project. Additional works amounting to about Rs.155 crores had to be ordered during the implementation of the projects to cater to the needs of increased traffic on this stretch. Multiplicity of agencies involved was another factor contributing for the delay. Also the increased traffic had to be managed within the space available during construction which reduced the speed of construction to some extent. The Minister of State for Defence Production, Shri Rao Inderjit Singh and Shri Sajjan Kumar, Member of Parliament were also present on the occasion.

5630. (23-1-2008) NEW DELHI : H.E. Piyabutr Cholvijarn, Deputy Minister of Industry of Thailand, led a Thai delegation comprising both the Thai public and private sectors to visit three North Eastern States of India (Sikkim, Arunachal Pradesh and Assam) from January 9-12, 2008 to follow up the earlier visit to Tripura, Assam and Meghalaya of H.E. Krirk-Krai Jirapaet, Thai Minister of Commerce, and the North-East India Trade & Investment Opportunities Week held in Bangkok in October, 2007 with a view to further promoting and strengthening Thai investment in the North East and exploring its trade potentials. H.E Piyabutr Cholvijaran's visit was in response to the invitation from Shri Mani Shankar Aiyar, Minister for the Development of the North-Eastern Region of India. The Thai delegation consisted of representatives from the Thailand Board of Investment, the Royal Thai Embassy in New Delhi, the Thai Office of Commercial Affairs in New Delhi and Thai companies in the food, construction, banking and steel industry. The Indian delegation was headed by Ms. V.S.Rao, Secretary, Ministry for the Development of the North Eastern Region. The delegation included officials of the Ministry of DoNER and Secretary (Industry) of the States of Arunachal pradesh, Assam and Sikkim. Meetings at Guwahati (Assam) and Gangtok (Sikkim) were chaired by the respective Chief Ministers of the States, Shri Tarun Gogoi and Shri Pawan K. Chamling. The meeting at Itanagar was chaired by Shri Lombo Tayeng, Minister for Public Health Engineering & Water Supply, Government of Arunachal Pradesh. The business seminars conducted in Guwahati, Itanagar and Gangtok were very successful with more than 100 people participating in each seminar and many sub-group discussions on industries of common interest to the two parties. Both sides recognized that food processing, agriculture, tourism and infrastructure improvement in roads, hydro-electricity, dams, water control in rivers, etc. are areas with the greater potential to be further pursued. The meetings concluded that there will be further cooperation through exchange of information and further visits of organized trade, investment and tourism delegations to advise and assist each other to further promote Thailand-India trade and investment. As of now, 42 proposals for Thai-North East Trade Cooperation in investment and trade are being actively pursued under the overall aegis and coordination of the Indian Chamber of Commerce, Kolkata.

5631. (23-1-2008) NEW DELHI : The total import of sensitive items for the period April-November 07 has been Rs.18702 crore as compared to Rs.16726 crore during the corresponding period of last year thereby showing an increase of 11.8%. The gross import of all commodities during same period of current year was Rs.612357 crore as compared to Rs.544674 crore during the same period of last year. Thus import of sensitive items constitute 3.07% and 3.05% of the gross imports during last year and current year respectively. Imports of spices, marble & Granite and milk & milk products have shown a decline at broad group level during the period. Imports of items *viz.* edible oil, fruits & vegetables (including nuts), cotton & silk, food grains, automobiles, products of SSI, rubber, Alcoholic beverages and Tea & Coffee have shown increase during the period under reference.

In the edible oil segment, the import has increased from Rs.7304 crore last year to Rs.8024 crore for the corresponding period of this year. The import of both crude oil as well as refined oil have gone up by 9.1% and 15.8% respectively. The increase in edible oil import is mainly due to significant growth in import of Crude palm oil and its fractions, which have gone up by 16%. Imports of sensitive items from Indonesia, Canada, China P RP, United States of America, Brazil, Sri Lanka DSR, Germany, Thailand, Japan, Guinea Bissau etc. have gone up while those from Argentina, Myanmar, Russia, Malaysia, Cote D' Ivoire, Australia, Benin etc. have shown a decrease.

5632. (23-1-2008) NEW DELHI : The Ministry of Culture in association with the seven Zonal Cultural Centres (ZCCs) is organizing 'National Folk Dance Festival' from 24th to 29th January, 2008 as part of the ensuing Republic Day celebrations. The festival carries the name 'Loktarang' and its logo is 'Peacock'. This festival is a regular event which is being organized by the Ministry of Culture every year. The objective of organizing this festival is to showcase the rich cultural heritage of our country represented through folk dances. This event will provide a unique opportunity for the people to witness colourful, vibrant and authentic folk dances drawn from various parts of the country and will go a long way in preserving, promoting and disseminating Indian folk dances as a part of Indian art and culture. Addressing media persons the Joint Secretary, Ministry of Culture Sh. N.C. Goel said here today, the six day National Folk Dance Festival will commence on 24th January, 2008. The President of India, Smt. Pratibha Devisingh Patil, will inaugurate the Festival. Tourism and Culture Minister Smt. Ambika Soni will preside over the function. The inaugural show will begin with the lighting of a lamp to invoke the Agni (Fire), the most essential of the five basic elements of life known as 'Panch Mahabhoots'. Forty two Folk dances selected from twenty eight States and two Union Territories with about seven hundred folk artists will participate in this event. Sh. N.C. Goel said entry to the event will be free of cost for general public at Hamsadhwani Open Air Theatre in Pragati Maidan on all days of the show except the inaugural function day on 24th January, 2008 when entry will be strictly on special invitation basis.

5633. (23-1-2008) NEW DELHI : The statutory inquiry by Commissioner of Railway Safety, Northern Circle, New Delhi (Ministry of Civil Aviation, Government of India) into collision of 4629 Up Ludhiana-Firozpur Sutlej Express with a mini bus No. PB 29 E 9482 while it was on the run between Jagraon and Ajitwal railway stations on Ludhiana-Firozpur single line non electrified section of Firozpur Division of Northern Railway at 08.20 hours on 14.12.2007 has revealed that the accident had occurred due to "Failure of Railway staff".

5634. (23-1-2008) NEW DELHI : The Indian Army will be represented in the Republic Day Parade on Saturday by the mounted column of 61 CAVALRY, ten mechanized columns, eight marching contingents and a fly past by the Dhruv advanced light helicopters of Army Aviation. Total of 13 serving, retired and civilian Param Vir Chakra & Ashok Chakra awardees have confirmed their participation. The Army will showcase T-90 Tanks, BLT T-72 (the Bridge Laying Tanks), 155 mm SOLTOM Guns, Smerch Racket System, Brahmos Missile (Army Variant), Tanguska Air Defence Gun System, Sarvatra Bridge, Mobile Network Connect Centre, Infantry Combat Vehicle-BMP II K and Carrier Mortar tracked Vehicle. The highlights of the DRDO Columns will include Brahmos, Experimental Tanks, NBC Recce Vehicle, Anti Submarine Warfare Tableaus, Dhanush Missile and AGNI-III Missile. The marching contingents are composed of The Punjab Regiment, The GRENADIERS, The Rajputana Rifles, The Sikh Light Infantry Regiment, The Assam Regiment, The Mahar Regiment, The 58 GTC, and the Territorial Army. There will be ex-Servicemen contingent also and that will be accompnied by Bihar Regiment Centre and AMC Centre & School Band. A total of four band contingents comprising of participation by eight regiments will provide the music for the march. The bands have been drawn from The Punjab Regiment Centre & Artillery Centre Band, The AD Arty & Guard Regimental Centre Band, The Assam Regimental Centre & Mahar Regimental Centre Band & Para Regimental Centre & Rajput Regimental Centre Band. Major General KJS Oberoi, General Officer Commanding, Delhi Area will be the Parade Commander and Second-in-command of the parade will be Brigadier HPS Dhillon.

5635. (23-1-2008) NEW DELHI : Union Agriculture Minister, Shri Sharad Pawar has asked the ICAR to reorient research and development in agriculture and bridge critical gaps wherever present. Addressing the 79th Annual General Meeting of the Council here today Shri Pawar said that the pace of innovations in agriculture universities and research institutions in India is not satisfactory and therefore, remedial steps must be taken by the ICAR. It must put in place highly skilled and competent human resources. Similarly, there is need to revise the course curriculum of agricultural education to make it more relevant, the Minister said. Shri Pawar drew the attention of the ICAR Governing Body towards the resources and facilities available under the recently launched Rastriya Krishi Vikas Yojana (RKVY) and National Food Security Mission (NFSM). The flexibility provided to States in proposing schemes under RKVY can cover seed production and multiplication, development of watersheds, creation of farmer schools and many other areas. Under the NFSM, ICAR institutes, agricultural universities and Krishi Vigynan Kendras have a role in providing technological inputs at district levels, he said. The AGM was attended by Minister of State for Planning Shri M.V. Rajashekharan, Members of Parliament, State Ministers and other members of the ICAR Society. In his presentation, DG, ICAR, Dr. Mangala Rai focused on the need for genetic improvement of crops and livestock. Other areas he highlighted for urgent attention included soil amelioration, use of organic manure, water harvesting and conservation, technologies for value addition, aquaculture and preparing for impact of global warming on agriculture.

5636. (23-1-2008) NEW DELHI : Every field of activity coins and uses terms as per expression requirements of that field. The journey of iron from ore to finished products also requires certain such terms for apt description. Knowledge of these terms commonly used in steel sector will help understand and appreciate the sector better. Sponge Iron (SI): Sponge Iron is solid metallic iron product obtained upon Direct Reduction of high-grade iron ore in solid state itself without being converted into liquid form like that in Blast Furnace. Sponge Iron named so due to its spongy microstructure is also known as Direct Reduced Iron (DRI) because of the process involved to obtain it.

5637. (23-1-2008) NEW DELHI : Among the first events of the world Economic Forum (WEF) meet at Davos, was inaugurated by Shri Kamal Nath, Minister of Commerce and Industry, opened a discussion on the Asian Renaissance, which is drawing the attention of the think tanks all over the world. As the Asian region grows in economic importance its future leadership (and growing soft power) is taken as given the world is increasingly looking at east for greater economic engagement. Shri Kamal Nath who recently released his book called India's century was the chief panelist. Shri Shashi Tharoor, former UN diplomat and Shri Kishore Mahbhubani, Dean of Lee Kuan Yew School of Public Policy, Singapore. Shri Raju Narisetti, Managing Editor, Mint, HT Media, was the moderator. The event was attended by members of the young global leaders which operate under the aegis of WEF. Commenting on the recent global market sell off, Shri Kamal Nath felt that India should be out of it soon as the changing global economic architecture means that the ingredients of fundamentals contributing to such changes are shifting with increasing importance for Indian economy. Answering questions from the young global leaders on how should we understand Asia's re-emergence and growing leadership on the world stage and will the rise of Asian economic power be accompanied by a re-emergence of Asia's soft power, Shri Kamal Nath stated that the rules of international trade are changing and west no longer can remain the custodian for such rules. Managing growth is the biggest task ahead of us, Shri Kamal Nath further underlined.

5638. (23-1-2008) NEW DELHI : The President of India, Smt. Pratibha Devisingh Patil met children who have won the National Awards for Bravery for the year 2007 at a function at Rashtrapati Bhavan today. Smt. Patil met each awardee individually after his or her act of bravery was announced. The President commended the children for showing exemplary courage in the face of overwhelming odds. The President was particularly impressed by the courage shown by one of the awardees, Kumari Congress Kunwar who resisted her family's attempts to marry her off at the tender age of 13 years. Smt. Patil said Congress Kunwar stood up against members of the family against a social evil, which destroys the lives of many young girls in the country. The President said resisting a member of the family is sometimes much more difficult than resisting outsiders in a physical act of crime. The President added that if girls can come forward in this way, many social evils, which hurt women and girls, could be eliminated. Smt. Patil also commended the other children for their bravery and said they were role models for not only for the youth but also for the nation.

5639. (24-1-2008) NEW DELHI : The President of India, Smt. Pratibha Devisingh Patil has condoled the passing away of the former First Lady, Smt. Usha Narayanan in New Delhi today. In a condolence message, she has said Smt. Narayanan was known for her active participation in the welfare and upliftment of women and children, especially from the weaker sections of society. The President also recalled, Smt. Narayanan's keen interest in gardening, which was reflected in the Mughal Gardens of Rashtrapati Bhavan when she was the First Lady.

5640. (24-1-2008) NEW DELHI : The Vice President of India, Mohd. Hamid Ansari has received, with deep sorrow, the news of the demise of Smt. Usha Narayanan, wife of former President Late Shri K.R.Narayanan. He has expressed his heartfelt condolences to her family.

5641. (24-1-2008) NEW DELHI : India has made remarkable progress since independence in various aspects of girls' education like greater access to and enrolment in schools, decline in drop out rates and in the number of out of school girls, greater transition to upper primary level and special help provided to disadvantaged sections of the society. We have also in place the constitutional and policy framework enshrining the vision of girls' education that enabled the Government to design different strategies, interventions, schemes and programmes with specific objectives that impinge on girls' education.

5642. (24-1-2008) NEW DELHI : In today's globalised world, quality and capacity of our infrastructure determines whether we end up on the winning and losing sides of the global village. There is total unanimity among the policy planners in the country that removal of infrastructural constraints is the foremost challenge to be met for our country to continue its journey on the high-growth trajectory of 9% plus GDP growth p.a. Planning Commission has estimated that removal of the infrastructure backlog would require investment of more than US$400 billion and annual investment in infrastructure has to be stepped up from the present level of 4% GDP to 8%. Such huge sums are beyond the Government's budgetary capacity. It would become even more difficult in future in view of the increasing commitments to social sector programmes like health and education and the constraints imposed by Fiscal Responsibility and Budget Management (FRBM) Act (the Act prescribes that the fiscal deficit of Central and State Governments must not exceed 9% of the GDP). Governments both at centre and states are, therefore, looking at fresh approaches to bridge the infrastructure deficit to sustain the growth momentum. It is in this context that Public Private Partnerships (PPPs) have emerged as a serious option to leverage limited public funds to attract private investment in infrastructure. Apart from easing the pressure on public finance, PPPs also allow efficiencies of private sector to be harnessed for improved project execution and service delivery. Like other infrastructure sectors, Indian Railways require massive investments to augment its carrying capacity and modernize its system. While impressive growth in traffic and revenue over the last three years on Indian Railways (freight and passenger traffic is growing at more than 9% and 7% year-after-year respectively) has brought applause from all quarters, it has also exposed the problems of congestion and saturation of the network especially on the high-density corridors connecting our four metropolitan cities. The XI Five Year Plan which is under finalization, has underscored the need to sustain the momentum and attain the projected traffic levels of 1100 million tones of freight and 8400 million passengers at the terminal year. Sizeable investment for expansion of network by way of new lines, doubling and gauge conversion, port connectivity works and augmentation of manufacturing capacity of rolling stock would need to be undertaken to attain these targets. The plan envisages a total investment of Rs. 2,51,000 crore. Of this, 95000 crore is to be raised through internal generation and Rs. 86000 crore has been sought by way of budgetary support (subject to approval by NDC). The rest Rs. 75000 crore is to be raised as extra budgetary resources. Of this, barring Rs. 40,000 crore to be raised by IRFC, most of the rest is to be raised through PPP.

5643. (24-1-2008) NEW DELHI : The President of India has been pleased to appoint General (Retd.) Joginder Jaswant Singh, PVSM, AVSM, VSM, to be the Governor of Arunachal Pradesh with effect from the date he assumes charge of his office.

5644. (24-1-2008) NEW DELHI : The Vice President of India Mohd. Hamid Ansari, has called upon the NSS Volunteers to be the role model for the society and to enlighten the next generation. He was addressing the National Service Scheme (NSS) Volunteers who have gathered in the capital from various parts of the country to participate in the Republic Day celebrations here today. The Vice President asked the volunteers to follow their motto and set their examples. He said that the volunteers will work for the eradication of social evils from the society so that the nation could achieve speedily the avowed goal of creating a society based on the equality of status and opportunity. The Vice President said that more educational institutions and universities should impart NSS activities. He said that NSS volunteers are the select few who have the capacity to build up the society and if they do it, it will be of great use not only for them but for their country too. He said that through NSS, the youth of the country can form useful, instructive and enjoyable groups and serve for the betterment of the society besides undertaking the social service activities. The Vice President said that the youth of the country work dedicatedly in developing their own personalities and thereby contributing towards the development of the nation as a whole. He congratulated the National Service Scheme volunteers for making significant contribution in social service and helping the people during national calamity. 200 NSS Volunteers of which 110 are female volunteers and 90 are male volunteers from 28 states and 2 Union

Territories are participating in this camp. The parade camp brings a Mini India to the Delhi during the month long training camp since 1988 where they not only interact among themselves but also meet and talk to national personalities and exchange their views as well as experience. The volunteers of the NSS presented a colourful cultural programme highlighting the unity and integrity of the nation. The NSS Memento was presented to the Vice President. The Secretary of the Ministry of Sports and Youth Affairs, Shri S.K. Arora and Programme Advisor of NSS Shri S.K. Rathore and a number of senior officials were present on the occasion.

5645. (24-1-2008) NEW DELHI : A day-long Conference of State Tourism Secretaries was held here today. Representatives of Ministries of Home Affairs, Defence, Delhi Police, Civil Aviation, Railways and Road Transport & Highways, also participated in the conference. Smt. Ambika Soni, Minister of Tourism & Culture in her opening statement urged the states to sensitise people about the safety and security of tourists and link it up with the economic progress of their respective states and the country as a whole. She said Tourism should be made safe and secure and states must recognize their strength in Tourism Sector and build on it. Smt Soni said that India is a safe destination and will continue to be a safe destination and, yet some unfortunate incidents of harassement of tourists which have occurred in the recent past are causing concern for all the stakeholders in the Tourism Sector. Government is committed to minimise such incidents in future. The Minister asked the state governments to have a look at the proposal of the Union Ministry of Tourism to involve Ex-Servicemen in the task of ensuring the safety and security of tourists. She said that the country has lived through incidents of terrorism and epidemics such as Bird Flu, Chikungunya, etc. and it will definitely check the menace of crime against Tourists especially women tourists. She asked the states to generate awareness among people about safety of tourists especially women tourists as India is known for its hospitality. She said the country is witnessing a tourism boom. About five million tourists arrived in the country in 2007 and the sector earned US$ 12 billion. She said that the Ministry is working towards solving the issues regarding the connectivity, shortage of hotel accommodation in the country and working closely with Ministry of Civil Aviation, Railways and Surface Transport and Highways to build up required tourism infrastructure.

5646. (24-1-2008) NEW DELHI : Shri Kamal Nath, Union Minister of Commerce and Industry, has stated that India is studying the possibilities for a long-term trade and economic cooperation agreements with China, which is emerging as a major trade partner of India. He was addressing a select group of International Business leaders at a session on "India's International Agenda" at Davos last evening, and added that this process has been boosted with the Prime Minister's recent visit to China. He further stated that India is also working on a comprehensive relationship with the Gulf Cooperation Council, and has signed framework agreements for cooperation with South African Customs Union and COMESA in Africa and with MERCOSUR and Andean Community in South America besides forming regional trade and economic alliances and signing Free Trade Agreements and Preferential Trade Agreements with other countries and trade groups, for market access and greater economic clout. India has an FTA with Thailand and a Comprehensive Economic Cooperation Agreement with Singapore. He informed that participants that India has formed a strategic trilateral group IBSA (India-Brazil-South Africa) with the two emerging powers of Africa and Latin America to promote economic, commercial and political cooperation and to advance our common interests globally. Shri P. Chidambaram, Finance Minister and Shri Praful Patel, Minister for Civil Aviation also addressed the group. Emphasising that India's international agenda is linked to its growth story and also to its increased integration with the world Shri Kamal Nath added that "this is currently only at the appetizer stage. The main course is yet to come, and I can promise you that it will be even palatable than the hors d'ouvre". As far as multilateral trade is concerned, Shri Kamal Nath stated that India has been actively protecting its trade interests and seeking to open the markets of developed countries through the WTO. "India's leadership role-as a champion of the developing world, especially under the Doha Round-has been recognized at the WTO", he added. To facilitate and complement the trade flows, the Minister added that India is focusing on integration of rail and road linkages in our extended neighbourhood. India-Myanmar-Thailand trilateral highway and Delhi-Hanoi railway are projects which will bring long-term economic benefits. He further said that India has taken its bilateral relationship with Japan with the involvement of Japanese agencies in building the Delhi Mumbai industrial corridor.

5647. (24-1-2008) NEW DELHI : Shri Kamal Nath, Union Minister of Commerce and Industry, has stated that the economic reforms in India has been largely responsible for transforming India's private sector and the growth is being driven by many companies that were set up in the nineties. New sectors such as IT and communications, and modernised old sectors such as the automobiles and pharmaceuticals are the new torchbearers, he added while addressing the Global Challengers Session at Davos today. The Minister observed that the increased openness has contributed significantly to the growing confidence of Indian firms and the scrapping of controls on expansion has allowed many Indian firms to aspire for global economies of scale for the first time. Among others, the meeting was also attended by Mr. Rahul Bajaj and leading Global CEO's. During the course of interaction with the participants, Shri Kamal Nath stressed that Indian globalisation is synonymous with Indian entrepreneurship and the domestic entrepreneurship is the engine that is driving India's growth. Indian companies are seizing the opportunities presented by new technologies and a more open economy. "Today, thanks to its innovative and entrepreneurial culture India is emerging as a hub for new software platforms, new technology development, engineering design and hi-end outsourcing", he added. The Minister further referred to the process of globalisation in India that has also resulted in important shifts in the mindsets and added that in the past, because of the restrictive economic environment, the top management in India tended to be in their comfort zones and steeped in their own cultures. "Indian leadership, both in corporate India and also in the government, is now thinking in much more ambitious terms. Corporates have the cash flows or they can generate the cash flows to think in these terms and they are willing to take the risk of global expansions. This has given us in the government the confidence that they can take on the world. Accordingly, we are creating conditions for them by creating an investment, regulatory and trade environment that is on par with the best in the world ", the Minister said. Mr. Rahul Bajaj summed it up by stating that, "A global mindset is about thinking of the whole world as your arena, being comfortable in interacting with people from multiple cultures, looking at the various markets while strategizing, leveraging talent from all cultures, making sure that all cultures are comfortable in your milieu".

5648. (24-1-2008) NEW DELHI : The Appointments Committee of the Cabinet has approved the appointment of Shri Raghav Sharan Pandey, IAS(NL:72), presently Secretary, Ministry of Steel as an Advisor to the Governor of Nagaland with the stipulation that:-(i) Shri Pandey will be reappointed as Secretary, Ministry of Steel when his term of duty in Nagaland is over; and (ii) Shri J.S. Sharma, IAS (AP:71), Secretary, Department of Fertilizers, Ministry of Chemicals and Fertilizers will hold additional charge of the post of Secretary, Ministry of Steel until Shri Pandey takes over.

5649. (24-1-2008) NEW DELHI : The officers of the Customs & Central Excise Department are considered for grant of Presidential Award of Appreciation Certificate on their achieving and maintaining excellence in the discharge of their duties. These awards are announced on the eve of Republic Day. This year 35 officers have been selected for grant of Presidential Award of Appreciation Certificate for specially distinguished record of service. These officers have exhibited exceptional commitment and devotion to duty on a sustained basis, while achieving the goals set for their organizations.

5650. (24-1-2008) NEW DELHI : Gen Deepak Kapoor, Chief of The Army Staff has taken over the mantle of Honorary Colonel of The Brigade of The Guards. Lt Gen OP Nandrajog, Colonel, Brigade of the GUARDS, formally handed over the BATON of THE HONORARY COLONEL to the Chief of the Army Staff. Brigade of The Guards is the senior most Infantry Regiment in the Indian Army with a history of over 250 years. The Gallant GUARDSMEN have been in the forefront of all Army activities and have actively participated in all operations fought by the Indian Army, including counter insurgency operations and have received commendations even from foreign dignitaries for their role in United Nation Peace Keeping Missions. The Regiment has on its roll three Victoria Crosses, five Military Crosses and two Order of British Empire prior to

Independence. After Independence the Regiment has been awarded two Param Vir Chakras, two Ashok Chakras, six Mahavir Chakras, forty one Vir Chakras, twenty six Shaurya Chakras, four Kirti Chakras and one hundred and four Sena Medals. The Regiment holds nine Battle Honours and ten Theatre Honours for operations fought subsequent to Independence. Late Field Marshal KM Carriappa OBE, the first Commander-in-Chief of Indian Army, founded brigade of THE GUARDS. Ever since, traditionally the Chief of the Army Staff is the Honorary Colonel of the Brigade of Guards. Gen Deepak Kapoor stated that he was proud to be bestowed the honour of this prestigious appointment and assured the august gathering that it would be his earnest endeavour to assist the Regiment in enhancing its glorious deeds. The investiture ceremony was attended by senior officers of the Indian Army as also by many serving and retired officers of The Brigade of The Guards.

5651. (24-1-2008) NEW DELHI : The Ministry of Labour and Employment is working on a bill to be introduced in the ensuing Budget Session of the Parliament which would make the payment of gratuity to the teachers of the private schools. Apart from this, the Unorganized Sector Workers Social Security Bill, 2007 which was introduced in Parliament in September last, is expected to be considered by the Parliament during the Budget Session along with the recommendations of the Standing Committee and the comments of the Government thereon. This information was given by the Minister for Labour and Employment Shri Oscar Fernandes at the Consultative Committee Meeting here today. Speaking on the occasion, the Minister said that the Government is committed to the welfare measures for the labour force of the country and would make every effort to protect their interests. Speaking on the issue of the 'Contract Labour', the Minister said that there is an urgent need to arrive at a consensus to find a workable solution which is acceptable to all the stakeholders *i.e.* the workers, employers and the State Governments. He reiterated that the Ministry of Labour & Employment follows spirit of Tripartite Consultations in the truest sense and would like to address the issues concerning Contract Labour in this spirit only. The Minister said that at the moment, there exists a big gap between the divergent stands taken by the Trade Unions and the employers organizations on this issue as the Trade Unions are demanding automatic absorption of contract labour while the employers are vehemently opposed to it. Shri Fernandes pointed that some of the State Governments, in tune with the changing times, have proposed measures to liberalize the Contract Labour Act to spur the growth of industry, especially the grant of exemption to Special Economic Zones and Export Oriented Units from the applicability of the Act to boost exports. Participating in the discussion, the Members lauded the efforts of the Ministry of Labour & Employment for effectively taking up the issues concerning the welfare of the labour. However, they expressed concern over the fact that the tendency to deploy Contract Labour is on the increase even in the Government sector. Responding to this, the Minister said that his Ministry is aware of the trend and was attempting to evolve the measures to protect the interest of the labour force. The Members who participated in the meeting were: S/Shri Gurudas Dasgupta from Lok Sabha; S/Shri Balihari Babu and Mohammed Amin from Rajya Sabha.

5652. (24-1-2008) NEW DELHI : The delegations of Government of India and the Government of Kingdom of Saudi Arabia met at Jeddah on 23 January, 2008 to review the bilateral air services agreement between the two countries. The last round of review had taken place in 2002. While agreeing on designation of multiple airlines, both sides also decided to enhance the existing traffic entitlement of 8500 seats per week to 20000 seats per week with immediate effect. For the Kingdom of Saudi Arabia, Calicut, Lucknow and Bangalore were included as new points of call besides Delhi, Mumbai, Chennai, Kochi and Hyderabad and Madina was included as a new point of call for the Indian carriers in addition to the existing points of Riyadh, Jeddah and Dammam. Significantly Saudi Arabia is the first country in Middle East/Gulf to get the facility of flights to Calicut. Similarly, India is the first country to be granted access to operate to Madina on schedule basis. Both sides have also decided to free up all limitations on the cargo services. There will be no restriction in terms of frequency and point of call for operating all cargo services. With the successful conclusion of this agreement, airlines of both sides will be able to add new services on the India-Saudi Arabia route, which is presently constrained due to the bilateral capacity/route limitations. This will be in the interest of the travelling people who have to presently travel through third countries and at higher tariffs due to these limitations. The Indian delegation was led by Shri R.K. Singh, Joint Secretary in the Ministry of Civil Aviation, while the Saudi Arabian delegation was led by Dr.Mohammed R. Beranji, Vice President in the General Authority of Civil Aviation of the Kingdom of Saudi Arabia.

5653. (24-1-2008) NEW DELHI : The Cabinet Committee on Economic Affairs today gave its approval for the implementation of the ongoing Plan Scheme for creation of consumer awareness during the 11th Five Year Plan Period (2007-2012) as follows: Continuing consumer awareness campaign in print/electronic/outdoor/other media covering the entire country during the 11th Five Year Plan; The awareness would help in emergence of consumers who irrespective of age, socio-economic class or gender are empowered enough to make free, fair and informed choices of products or services with the help of information, standards and safeguards that are available, accessible and responsive.

5654. (24-1-2008) NEW DELHI : The Union Cabinet today gave its approval for signing of a MoU between Ministry of Railways, Government of India and SNCF, French National Railways. The MoU will help promote cooperation in the Rail sector between French National Railways and Indian Railways. It will be signed in January 2008 during the visit of French President to India. The MoU will be valid for 3 years.

5655. (24-1-2008) NEW DELHI : The Union Cabinet today gave its approval for establishment of the All India Institute of Ayurveda in New Delhi as an autonomous organization under the Department of AYUSH and to appoint a Director with supporting staff to oversee project implementation. The decision will facilitate scientific validation, quality control & standardization and safety evaluation of Ayurveda products, standardized Ayurveda-based tertiary health delivery and to promote interdisciplinary research & education of Ayurveda at postgraduate and postdoctoral levels.

5656. (24-1-2008) NEW DELHI : The Union Cabinet today gave its ex-post-facto approval for signing of the Agreement between India and Mexico for Avoidance of Double Taxation and prevention of Fiscal Evasion with respect to Taxes on income. This Agreement will stimulate the flow of capital, technology and personnel from India to Mexico and vice-versa. It will provide tax stability and reduce any obstacles in providing mutual cooperation. India has so far signed such bilateral treaties for avoidance of double taxation with 71 other counties.

5657. (24-1-2008) NEW DELHI : The Union Cabinet today gave its approval for placing a Statement before the Parliament to convey the Government's decision for ratification of the ILO Convention No. 174 on the basis of suggestions made in ILO Convention No. 181 as guidelines for formulating and implementing national policies and programmes for prevention of major industrial accidents. The decision for Ratification of ILO Convention No. 174 will enhance the safety standards for prevention of major industrial accidents in India.

5658. (24-1-2008) NEW DELHI : The Union Cabinet today gave its approval for ratification of the Seventh Additional Protocol to the Constitution of the Universal Postal Union adopted by the XXIII Congress of the Union held at Bucharest in 2004. It would enable the Postal administration of the India to have the Instrument of Ratification signed by the President of India and have the same deposited with the Director General of the International Bureau of the Universal Postal Union through diplomatic channels along with approval of other Acts of the Union. Ratification by the Government of India of the Seventh Additional protocol to the Constitution of the Universal Postal union adopted by the XXIII Congress of 4the Union held at Bucharest in 2004 would complete a formality required by Article 25 of the Constitution of the Universal Postal Union and fulfil its commitment as required by a member country of the Union. It will also enable the department of posts to bring out administrative orders to enforce the provisions of the UPU Convention.

5659. (24-1-2008) NEW DELHI : The Minimum Support Price (MSP) of toria of Fair Average Quality (FAQ) for 2007-08 to be marketed in 2008-09 has been fixed at Rs. 1735 per quintal mainly on the basis of normal price differential between toria and rapeseed/mustard. This is Rs. 55 per quintal over the MSP of toria fixed for the previous year *i.e.* 2006-07. The National Agriculture Cooperative Marketing Federation of India (NAFED) will undertake the price support operation for toria in the marketing season 2008-09 at the fixed MSP, as was done earlier.

5660. (24-1-2008) NEW DELHI : The President of India, Smt. Pratibha Devisingh Patil, will address the Nation tomorrow on the eve of the 59th Republic Day. The address will be telecast over Doordarshan in Hindi followed by English from 7 P.M. onwards. It will also be broadcast over all Channels of All India Radio in Hindi followed by English from 7 P.M. onwards. In addition All India Radio will broadcast the regional language versions of the address over their regional channels from 9.30 P.M. onwards.

5661. (24-1-2008) NEW DELHI : Government of India launched an effective promotional campaign in London today showcasing 57 exploration blocks on offer under the seventh round of the New Exploration Licensing Policy (NELP-VII). The blocks include 19 are in deepwater, 9 in shallow water and 29 in onland. After the inaugural road show held at Mumbai on 8th January, 2008, the London road-show is the first one to be held abroad for NELP-VII. As many as 97 companies comprising 35 E&P, 27 service providers, 20 investment companies/bankers and 15 others participated in the London Road Show.

5662. (24-1-2008) NEW DELHI : The President of India has been pleased to appoint General (Retd.) Joginder Jaswant Singh, PVSM, AVSM, VSM, to be the Governor of Arunachal Pradesh with effect from the date he assumes charge of his office.

5663. (24-1-2008) NEW DELHI : Engineering Projects (India) Ltd. (EPI), a Mini Ratna Company under the Department of Heavy Industry handed over a cheque for Rs.3.54 crore on 23rd January 2008 in New Delhi to the Government towards interim dividend of 10 per cent of its paid up capital for the year 2007-08. The cheque was presented to Shri Sontosh Mohan Dev, Minister for Heavy Industries & Public Enterprises by Shri A.K. Ratwani, Chairman-cum-Managing Director, EPI. Dr. Ramesh Chandra Panda, Secretary, Heavy Industries & Public Enterprises, Dr. Surajit Mitra, Addl. Secretary, Heavy Industries & Public Enterprises and other senior officials were present on the occasion. EPI is presently executing 77 projects in India and abroad valuing over Rs.3300 crore. The projects being handled by EPI are of diverse nature comprising of Electrification Works, Process Plants, Buildings & Housing Complexes, Highways, and Project Management Services etc. EPI is consistently exceeding its targets and is most efficient public sector construction company having achieved highest turnover per employee among all construction PSUs during the year 2006-07. Its performance during the last two consecutive years has been rated as "Excellent" on MOU parameters signed with Government.

5664. (24-1-2008) NEW DELHI : Department of Animal Husbandry, Dairying and Fisheries, Govt. of India has notified Avian Influenza in poultry in a number of blocks spread over nine districts, namely Birbhum, Dakshin Dinajpur, Murshidabad, Nadia, Bankura, Malda, Cooch behar, Burdwan and Hoogly. Ministry of Health and Family Welfare (MOHFW) initiated a series of actions to assist the state in the containment operations and restrict further spread of the disease. Senior Officials from this Ministry were deputed to review the situation with State Health Authorities. The contingency plan of the Ministry of Health and Family Welfare has been implemented in affected districts. Seven Central Rapid Response Teams are assisting the State in containment operations. In all the affected areas, active human surveillance is being undertaken in the 0-3 Km zone and being further stepped up in 3-10 Km area. Persons having Upper Respiratory Infection [URI]/ Fever are being monitored. Health care facilities have been identified with isolation ward and critical care facilities for management of human cases of Avian Influenza. The animal health staff involved in the culling and sanitization operations and those involved in human health surveillance are being provided chemoprophylaxis and their health status is being monitored. No suspected human cases of Avian Influenza have been detected. Five samples tested so far have been reported negative. MOHFW has supplied 1,20,000 capsules of Oseltamivir, 5000 personal protective equipments, 5000 N-95 masks and 5 ventilators. This is in addition to 10 ventilators and 10 semi automatic analyzers supplied earlier. An additional supply of 1,00,000 capsules of Oseltamivir, 100 bottles of Oseltsamivir syrup and 5 ventilators have been sent on 23.01.2008. There is adequate stock of Oseltamivir and Personal Protection Equipments to meet further requirements. States of Jharkhand, Bihar and Assam that share a common border with West Bengal have been instructed to ban and prevent any entry of poultry or poultry related products from West Bengal into these States. Other States have also been put on alert. MOHFW has deputed Central teams to the states of Assam, Bihar, Jharkhand, Orissa and other North Eastern States to review the level of preparedness and fill critical gaps. The preparedness of the districts bordering West Bengal is also being reviewed through videoconference with state/ district authorities. MOHFW has initiated IEC campaign to sensitize the community through the visual and print media. This includes broadcast of spots on private and Government owned FM channels in West Bengal. The spots are also scheduled to be broadcast 5-6 times before and between popular programmes and the National News broadcast during morning and late evening hours in the States of Bihar, Jharkhand, Madhya Pradesh, Chhatisgarh, Uttar Pradesh, Uttaranchal, Rajasthan, Orissa, Assam, Arunachal Pradesh, Mizoram, Meghalaya, Manipur, Nagaland, Sikkim, Tripura, Jammu & Kashmir and Himachal Pradesh. Telecast of campaign on Avian Influenza through Doordarshan Kendras of Patna, Ranchi, Kolkatta and Guwahati has been initiated.

5665. (25-1-2008) NEW DELHI : The Government is going to implement Rashtriya Swasthya Bima Yozna for workers of unorganized sectors and their families from 1st April 2008. Every year 1.2 crore families of such workers, living below the poverty line, will be covered. In next five year 6 crore families of such workers consisting of around 30 crore family members will be provided the facility. Inaugurating a National Workshop on Rashtriya Swasthya Bima Yozna here today Minister for Labour and Employment, Shri Oscar Fernandes said that under the scheme 75 percent of the insurance premium will be borne by the Central

Government and remaining 25 per cent by the State Government to provide free insurance the worker. The sum insured will be 30,000 per family per annum and members of family will be covered for all hospitalization expenses, taking care of most common illness with a few common illnesses with as few exceptions as possible. The smart card provided under the scheme will not only enable cashless transactions of all covered ailments, it will be valid for use outside the states for the welfare of the migrant workers, the Minister said. Reiterating the Government commitment for the welfare of all workers, particularly those in the unorganized sector Shri Fernandes said the Government is working on schemes to provide social security cover to weavers, handloom workers, fishermen, toddy tappers, leather workers, plantation labour, beedi workers, safai karmcharis and domestic workers etc. and Rashtriya Swasthya Bima Yozna is one of such scheme, he said. The workshop was attended by the representatives of State Governments, various Central Ministries, insurance companies, World Bank, NIC and other stake holders to chalk out strategy for speedy and effective implementation of the scheme.

5666. (25-1-2008) NEW DELHI : Smt. Renuka Chowdhury, Minister for Women & Child Development, has proposed behavioral training workshops on regular basis for teachers in school to make them more sensitive about children issues. Chairing an interactive session with school principals here today, Ms. Chowdhury said that such workshops will also discuss problems of teachers and experts will provide them guidance how deal with them. The Minister said today children are in tremendous pressure and its duty of the society to bring them out of it so that holistic development of the children can be ensured. Expressing concern over recent incidents of violence and physical abuse in some schools, the minister said children can not be held responsible for such incidents, we have to identify behavioral problems such children and counsel them. Core group of teachers and parents should be formed to tackle problematic children and if necessary the groups should visit he family of such child to see if the child have any problem in family and interact with the family. Smt Renuka Chowdhury also proposed on line consultancy service for children to deal with their various problems including examination stress and sex education. She said well known experts of different field would be involved in the proposed interactive online service. The meeting convened by the Ministry of Women and Child Development to ensure safe environment for children was attended by schools principals, education experts, child psychologists, child NGOs, and representatives of UNESCO and education departments. Various issues related with children including corporal punishment, violence in school and nutritional problem were deliberated upon in the meeting.

5667. (25-1-2008) NEW DELHI : The President, Smt. Pratibha Devisingh Patil has greeted the citizens of India on the eve of 59th Republic Day. The President observed that the impressive strides of the Indian economy have resulted in the emergence of India as a powerful player in the global economy. However, she pointed out that people's participation is key to the effective implementation of programmes and projects launched by the Government. She added that there is a need to create a band of committed social workers and civil society members to spread awareness and to share the onus of implementation by joining hands with the Government. Speaking on rural economy, the President said that the slow growth in the agriculture sector is a matter of concern and there is a need to expeditiously work in the direction of bringing in a Second Green Revolution in the country. The President noted that there is a need to address social evils like child marriage, female foeticide, female infanticide and dowry, calling upon women and the youth of the country to take up the challenge to eliminate these social evils.

5668. (25-1-2008) NEW DELHI : Squadron Leader Shantanu Basu has been awarded Shaurya Chakra (Posthumous) for displaying exceptional courage and gallantry in the face of imminent death in dangerous circumstances beyond the call of duty which are in the best traditions of the IAF. Squadron Leader Shantanu Basu was on the posted strength a Cheetah Helicopter Unit at Air Force Station Leh since 22 May 06. On 11 Apr 07, Sqn Ldr Basu was detailed for an air logistics support sortie to Amar helipad located on the Siachen Glacier, as the leader in a two aircraft formation. The Siachen Glacier is the highest battlefield in the world. Flying over this vast frozen ice mass entails flying in the extremes of climatic conditions over exceedingly inhospitable terrain. The margin for error in this environment, while flying the single engine Cheetah aircraft, is practically nonexistent. Amar post has the highest helipad in the world with density altitude exceeding twenty thousand feet and is located on the Actual Ground Position Line (AGPL). The sortie was uneventful till final approach. On short finals, an overshoot had to be initiated as tail winds were encountered. The helicopter experienced a sudden loss of power and height after crossing the helipad. Sqn Ldr Basu maintained his cool in this unusual emergency and handled the situation in a competent manner displaying a high degree of professionalism. He asked his co-pilot to keep a close check on the engine parameters and initially tried to recover the aircraft by reducing the power demand smoothly. The engine jet pipe temperature (JPT) also shot up. Unfortunately, the JPT failed to respond to the emergency actions by the pilot and the aircraft continued to lose height. He therefore took the highly courageous decision of attempting to force land across the AGPL. However, due to the absence of a suitable force landing field in the harsh, snow bound and sloping terrain, the helicopter crashed, giving no chance of survival to the crew. The aircraft crashed about 300 meters ahead of Amar Helipad, in direct line of sight of the Pakistani post. Sqn Ldr Basu, a true air warrior, made the supreme sacrifice in the service of the country, displaying exceptional courage and gallantry in the face of imminent death in dangerous circumstances beyond the call of duty, which are in the best traditions of the IAF.

5669. (25-1-2008) NEW DELHI : Wing Commander Anil Kumar of Indian Air Force has been awarded Shaurya Chakra for thoroughbred soldierly attitude, display of conspicuous gallantry in the face of highly challenging task and regardless of his personal safety. Wg Cdr Anil Kumar was detailed as crew of an IAF microlight aircraft proceeding on a "Round-the-World" expedition. The expedition flew 40,529 Km, landed at 85 destinations in 19 countries and created a new world record of circumnavigating the world in 80 days, battering the previous world record of 99 days. The mission was flown in a single engine unpressurised aircraft weighing less than 300 Kg, without any redundancy features. As the expedition was undertaken without any accompanying technical, logistics or administrative support team, the officer had even maintained and rectified the aircraft at his own, a task beyond the call of duty. Wg Cdr Anil Kumar was instrumental in planning critical aspects of the mission and his decisions, especially in face of adverse weather, led to safe recovery of aircraft in several inclement situations. The officer faced adverse weather, unfamiliar operating environment and harsh terrain ranging from sub-zero Arctic to scorching deserts and tropical rainforests knowing fully well that survival in case of any eventuality would have been extremely challenging. The officer in these harsh conditions not only displayed exceptional courage but also professionalism and airmanship of an extremely high order. His fortitude and mental strength were critical for the success of the mission. Inspite of facing severe weather and life threatening technical malfunctions in the small aircraft he continued steadfast in his task despite the risk to his life, with the aim of bringing glory to the nation and to the IAF. For his thoroughbred soldierly attitude, display of conspicuous gallantry in the face of highly challenging task and regardless of his personal safety, Wg Cdr Anil Kumar has been awarded the Shaurya Chakra.

5670. (25-1-2008) NEW DELHI : Wg Cdr Rahul Monga of Indian Air Force has been awarded Shaurya Chakra for his thoroughbred soldierly attitude, display of conspicuous gallantry in the face of highly challenging task and regardless of his personal safety. Wg Cdr Monga was detailed as the Captain of the first microlight aircraft proceeding on a "Round-the-World" expedition. The expedition flew 40, 529 Kms, landed at 85 destinations in 19 countries and created a new world record of circumnavigating the world in 80 days, batteirng the previous world record of 99 days. This feat has brought glory to the country. The mission was flown in a single engine unpressurised aircraft weighing less than 300 Kg, without any redundancy features making the risk factor very high. As the expedition was undertaken without any accompanying technical, logistics or administrative support team, the officer had even maintained and rectified the aircraft on his own, a task beyond the call of duty. The officer faced adverse weather, unfamiliar operating environment and harsh terrain ranging from sub-zero Arctic to scorching deserts and topical rainforests knowing fully well that survival in case of any eventuality would have been extremely challenging. He continued undeterred, as a true soldier to achieve the assigned task. In the course of the expedition, Wg Cdr Monga became the first Indian to fly solo across the Bering Strait as well as the formidable North Atlantic. Any incident/accident would have led to a situation, where the recovery could have been nearly impossible, but unfazed by such life threatening deterrents, he flew this leg of the expedition keeping achievement of goal uppermost in his mind. The Officer not only displayed exceptional courage but also professionalism and airmanship of an extremely high order. His fortitude and mental strength were critical for the success of the mission. Inspite of facing severe weather and life threatening technical malfunctions in the small aircraft he continued steadfast in his task despite the risk to his life, with the aim of bringing glory to the Nation and to the IAF. For his thoroughbred soldierly attitude, display of conspicuous gallantry in the face of highly challenging task and regardless of his personal safety, Wg Cdr Monga has been awarded of Shaurya Chakra.

5671. (25-1-2008) NEW DELHI : Amongst various awards for Army personnel, four Kirti Chakras have also been announced. Kirti Chakra has been awarded to Major Shatrujeet Kotwal of 3 JAT and Major Suhash Chand Punia of 21 PARA (Special Forces). Kirti Chakra has been awarded posthumously to Major Kumandur Prabhakar Vinay of 53 Medium Regiment (Artillery) and Sepoy Suresh of 16 JAT. Maj KP Vinay belonged to Rajendra Nagar Colony in Hyderabad. He had his education in Vasavi Public School and College, Hyderabad. He was an alumunus of National Defence Academy. He killed two terrorists in Baramulla District of J & K on 02 Oct. 2007. He was then serving with 34 Rashtriya Rifles. He was a bachelor. He is survivied by his father Shri KR Prabhakar. Sepoy Suresh of 16 JAT was martyred in an action with militants in Kupwara Dist of J & K on 06 Oct. 2007. He killed three militants even after being injured in a fire fight with them. Maj Shatrujeet Kotwal, while serving with 34 Rashtriya Rifles also killed three terrorists in a dare devil action in Budgam Dist (J & K) on 18 Jun. 2007. An alumnus of National Defence Academy, he was commissioned in 1999. He belongs to Udhampur (J & K). Maj Subhash Chand Punia has been awarded Kirti Chakra for his gallant action in Manipur. He led the assault against militants who were entrenched in a camp on 04 May 2007. He himself killed two militants and along with his buddy killed another and injured one more.

5672. (25-1-2008) NEW DELHI : Minister of Mines and Industry, Government of Senegal, Mr. Madicke Niang called on the Minister of Chemicals and Fertilisers and Steel Shri Ram Vilas Paswan today in New Delhi. The two Ministers discussed bilateral issues related to fertilizer sector. Welcoming the Senegalese Minister Shri Paswan underlined the excellent relations between the two countries. Appreciating the recent efforts made by Government of Senegal and the IFFCO consortium for revival of ICS, Senegal Shri Paswan hoped that this would ensure stability of phosphoric production by ICS in near future. The Senegal Minister, on behalf of his government thanked Shri Paswan for strong support for the revival of ailing company ICS in Senegal through IFFCO consortium. He also sought assistance of the Indian government to the tune of US $ 20 million to strengthen and upgrade the railway line connecting the Potash mines with the port. Shri Paswan assured that the request of Senegal government will be considered in consultation with the Ministry of External Affairs. Mr. Niang also offered another Potash mine in Senegal for development by Indian entities. Thanking Mr. Niang, Shri Paswan indicated that a technical team will shortly visit Senegal to study the mines. ICS Senegal needed complete financial restructuring with substantial infusion of funds to reduce losses, replace old machinery and wipe out its debts. The two sides had agreed last month for a revival package for ICS Senegal. Under the plan, IFFCO will infuse $100 million in equity and provide another $100 million as loan over the next three years to revive the company. The restructuring of ICS Senegal will enhance the availability of phosphoric acid which will result in softening of international prices of raw material. Secretary, Department of Fertilisers, Dr. J.S. Sarma and the Ambassador of Senegal Mr. Amadou Boucoun were present during the discussions.

5673. (25-1-2008) NEW DELHI : CSIR & the French National Science Research Institute, CNRS, have entered into an agreement for the creation of Joint Research laboratory on sustainable chemistry at Interfaces. The CSIR-CNRS Memorandum was signed today in New Delhi by Prof. Samir K. Brahmachari, Director General, CSIR and Ms.Catherine Brechignac, President CNRS in the presence of Union Minister for Science & Technology and Earth Sciences Mr. Kapil Sibal and French Minister for Higher Education & Research Mrs. Valerie Pecresse. This would be a milestone of Indo-French Partnership in the field of Science & Technology, which has a long history & tradition. The Joint Research Laboratory will focus its research partnership in the areas of Green Chemistry targeting therapeutic agents for cancer and neuro disorders Protein interactions for targeting alternative drugs/ biological systems Indian Institute of Chemical Technology (IICT) at Hyderabad, one of the CSIR laboratories will be implementing the programme in partnership with CNRS laboratory for Molecular Chemistry on Molecular Photonics and University of Rennes in France.

5674. (25-1-2008) NEW DELHI : The Prime Minister, Dr. Manmohan Singh has condoled the passing away of the former first lady of India, Mrs. Usha Narayanan. The text of the PM's condolence message is a follows : "I am deeply grieved to learn of the sad demise of Smt. Usha Narayanan, former First Lady of India. A gracious and gifted personality, she was one of the outstanding First Ladies of our Republic. Her passion for reading and writing was best reflected in her numerous literary pieces which included the translation of several Burmese stories to English. A collection of her translated stories brought out in the volume "Sweet and Sour" testifies to her rich literary taste and bent of mind. A caring and compassionate person, she met the representatives of the victims of Gujarat riots of 2002 when they visited New Delhi and personally attended to them. Well known for her passion for gardening she took the novel step of introducing several European flowers such as Tulip to the Mughal Gardens of the Rashtrapati Bhavan. She was the constant source of inspiration to Late President K.R. Narayanan and played a key role in several aspects of his remarkable life and career. An indomitable fighter for the rights and empowerment of women, she will be long remembered for her profound pronouncements on gender equality. In her unfortunate passing away, the country has lost one of the cultivated, cultured and civilized persons, whose commitment to Indian values shaped her personality, universal outlook and identity. On this said occasion, I extend my heartfelt condolences to Ms. Chitra and Ms. Amrita, her worthy daughters, other members of her bereaved family, her countless friends, associates and her admirers. May the Providence rest her soul in peace and give strength and fortitude to her family members to bear this irreparable loss."

5675. (25-1-2008) NEW DELHI : On the basis of results of the written part of the Indian Forest Service Examination, 2007 held by Union Public Service Commission (UPSC) in July 2007, 129 candidates have qualified for Interview for the Personality Test. The candidature of all these candidates is Provisional subject to their being found eligible in all respects. In accordance with the condition(s) of their admission to the examination, the candidates should keep original certificates in support of their age, educational qualification, claim to belong to the Scheduled Casts/Scheduled Tribes/OBC etc. in readiness for submission at the time of their interview which would be contingent upon their producing requisite documents. All the qualified candidates will be sent Detailed Application Forms, which should be returned to the Commission within the closing date indicated in the forwarding letter thereof. In case any of these candidates does not receive a communication in this regard within two weeks of the publication of this result, he/she should immediately contact the Commission, giving his/her particulars *i.e.* roll number, full name, date of birth, address etc.

5676. (25-1-2008) NEW DELHI : The President has approved awards of 425 gallantry and other Defence decorations to Armed Forces personnel and others. This includes one Ashoka Chakra, four Kirti Chakras, 22 Shaurya Chakras, two Bar to Sena Medals (Gallantry), 107 Sena Medals (Gallantry), two Nao Sena Medals (Gallantry), three Vayu Sena Medal (Gallantry), 30 Param Vishisht Seva Medals, three Bar to Ati Vishisht Seva Medals, 52 Ati Vishisht Seva Medals, one Yudh Seva Medal, three Bar to Vishisht Seva Medals, 127 Vishisht Seva Medals, four Bar to Sena Medals (Devotion to Duty), 38 Sena Medals (Devotion to Duty), 10 Nao Sena Medals (Devotion to Duty) and 16 Vayu Sena Medals (Devotion to Duty). One Tatrakshak Medal (Gallantry), two Takrakshak Medals (Meritorious Service) and 28 Mention-In-Despatches have also been announced.

5677. (25-1-2008) NEW DELHI : The Vice President of India Mohd. Hamid Ansari has extended his warm greetings and best wishes for prosperity and happiness to the countrymen on the joyous occasion of Republic Day. The Vice President in his message said that the Republic Day celebrations encourage us to work with dedication and commitment in realizing the vision of our founding fathers. We continue our march towards the goal of achieving for all of our citizens social, economic and political justice. The need of the hour is to work together to achieve this at the earliest.

5678. (25-1-2008) NEW DELHI : A strong and resurgent India is celebrating its 59th Republic Day on 26 January 2008. This year's parade will highlight the nation's achievements in various fields, the military prowess, scintillating display of air power as also our rich and diverse cultural heritage. The Armed Forces will showcase the Bhishma T-90 tank, Bridge layer tank T-72, 155mm / 45mm Soltam Guns, Smerch Multiple Launch Rocket System, BrahMos missile, Tunguska Air Defence Weapon system, Sarvatra Bridge, Infantry Combat Vehicle BMP-II and carrier mortar tracked vehicle. The parade ceremony will commence at the Amar Jawan Jyoti at India Gate where the Prime Minister, Dr. Manmohan Singh will lead the nation in paying homage to the martyrs by laying wreath. An eternal flame burns at the Amar Jawan Jyoti to commemorate the indomitable courage of our Armed Forces personnel who have made the supreme sacrifice in the service of the motherland. The Amar Jawan, the immortal soldier, is symbolised by a reversed rifle topped by a helmet. As per tradition, after unfurling of the National Flag, the National Anthem will be played. Thereafter President Smt Pratibha Devisingh Patil will confer Ashok Chakra posthumously to Major Dinesh Raghu Raman of Jat Regiment / 34 Rashtriya Rifles, Captain Harshan of 2 Parachute Regiment, Naib Subedar Chunnilal of 8 Jammu & Kashmir Light Infantry and Col. Vasantha Venugopal of 9 Maratha Light Infantry. The parade will then commence and the President will take the salute. This year's Chief Guest in the parade will be Mr. Nicolas Sarkozy, President of France. The parade will be commanded by Major General K J S Oberoi, General Officer Commanding, Delhi Area. Brig Harvinder Pal Singh Dhillon will be the parade Second-in-Command. The marching contingents of Army will be from the Punjab Regiment, the Grenadiers Regiment, the Rajputana Rifles Regiment, Sikh Light Infantry Regiment, the Assam Regiment the Mahar Regiment, 8 Gorkha Rifles and Territorial Army (126 & 155 Infantry Battalion). The marching contingents of Navy comprising 144 men will be led by Lt. Commander Ravi Kant Pandey and the Air Force contingent comprising 148 men will be led by Sq. Ldr. Ashok Sharma.

5679. (25-1-2008) NEW DELHI : Major Dinesh Raghu Raman has been awarded posthumously with the country's highest peacetime Gallantry Award Ashok Chakra on the eve of Republic Day. The President Mrs. Pratibha Devi Singh Patil will confer the Award at the Republic Day Celebrations at Rajpath on Saturday, where three others-Captain Harshan R of 2 Parachute Regiment, Special Forces (Posthumous), Naib Subedar Chunni Lal, VrC, SM of 8 J&K Light Infantry (Posthumous) and Colonel Vasanth Venugopal of 9 Maratha Light Infantry (Posthumous), who were awarded Ashoka Chakra on the eve of Independence Day, last year, will also be honoured. Born to Shri SK Murthy and Smt Mala on Apr 06, 1978, Major Dinesh Raghu Raman (IC-59263W) did his schooling from Kendriya Vidyalaya, INA Colony, New Delhi and joined National Defence Academy in 1996. After passing out from NDA, he was commissioned into 19th Battalion of the JAT Regiment. During his short and illustrious career, Major Dinesh Raghu Raman served in various appointments and was awarded Chief of Army Staff Commendation Card in Drass during Operation Parakram. Major Dinesh Raghu Raman was posted to 34 Rashtriya Rifles Battalion (JAT) on 22 Feb 2006. In recognition of his leadership qualities and professional competence he was given command of 'C' Company at Aripanthan and had already conducted a very successful operation "OP Narawar" in June 07 culminating in elimination of 3 hard-core terrorists in his AOR. On 02 October 2007, at 0820 hrs Major Dinesh Raghu Raman deployed his company in a village in Baramulla district of Jammu & Kashmir where an encounter with terrorists had commenced. At 0855 hrs, while closing in on suspected houses, Major Raman heard shouts of a fellow officer who had been seriously injured. Displaying camaraderie and esprit-de-corps of the highest order he crawled towards him under heavy hostile fire. He extricated him and two other injured soldiers to safety. He then took on two terrorist who had caused heavy casualties to the troops and in a fierce close quarter battle shot both of them dead. The other terrorists now fired on Major Raman from another house. In the ensuing firefight, Major Raman was seriously injured. Undeterred, he continued leading and motivating his troops and pinned down the terrorists till he fell unconscious. He later succumbed to his injuries. Major Raman displayed most conspicuous bravery besides camaraderie and leadership of the highest order and made the supreme sacrifice for the nation.

5680. (26-1-2008) DAVOS : Shri Kamal Nath, Minister for Commerce and Industry has expressed hope that India and EFTA states would set the tone for a greater economic engagement between mature and developed economies for deriving benefits from greater trade and investment opportunities. Launching negotiations for a proposed broad based Trade and Investment Agreement between India and EFTA States in Davos, Switzerland here today the Minister expressed satisfaction over the present trade but stated that full potential needs to be exploited. An India-European Free Trade Association (EFTA) Joint Study Group (JSG) was established on 1 December 2006. The JSG was tasked to undertake a comprehensive view of bilateral economic linkages between India and EFTA States (Iceland, Norway, Switzerland and Liechtenstein) and to recommend measures to strengthen the economic engagement. It was also tasked to explore the feasibility of a bilateral broad based trade and investment agreement. The JSG has since met four times and has submitted its report to the Governments of India and EFTA States. Based on the study of bilateral economic linkages between India and the EFTA States, the JSG concluded that both sides should advance their economic relationship by exploiting the potential for enhancing trade and investment flows. Considering the complementary structure of the economies, the JSG concluded that both sides would significantly benefit from a bilateral broad-based trade and investment agreement. The JSG recommended that the Governments of the EFTA States and India enter into negotiations for such an agreement. The recommendations of the

JSG have been accepted by India and EFTA States. It has been agreed to constitute a Joint Task Force (JTF) comprising officials from India and EFTA States to monitor the implementation of the recommendations of the JSG and negotiate the proposed broad based Trade and Investment Agreement between India and EFTA States.

5681. (26-1-2008) NEW DELHI : The Ministry of Women and Child Development has convened a 2-day conference of State Ministers in charge of Women and Child Development on 28-29 January, 2008 to review programmes and policies related with women and children. The Government has decided to expand Integrated Child Development Services Scheme (ICDS) to ensure 14 lakh Anganwadis in operation by the end of 2008. States have been asked to identify SC and ST hamlets for opening of new Anganwadis on priority basis and to put on all the data related with ICDS on their website which should include number of beneficiaries, fund utilized and related matters. Anganwadi workers and helpers now stands cover under insurance. The conference will review implementation of these steps. Setting up of Child Right Commission at the State level for proper enforcement of children's right and effective implementation of laws and programmes relating to children and to designate a district level court as Children's Court will also be taken up in the conference. Guidelines regarding adoption of children, measures to check illegal adoptions, setting up of child welfare committees and constitute juvenile justice boards in each district by this year-end will be discussed in the meeting. Besides reviewing implementation of the protection of women from Domestic Violence Act, comment of the States will be sought about proposed Act for Protection of Women from Sexual Harassment at Workplace. Rehabilitation and reintegration of trafficked victims, appointment of Child Marriage Probationary Officer to ensure strict implementation of prohibition of child marriage, vocational training of the women in emerging sectors fashion designing, BPO, IT, airlines ticketing and travel for self employment are also on the agenda of the meeting. The Ministry is revamping scheme for working women's hostel and crèche scheme. Proposed amendments in both the schemes will be discussed during the conference.

5682. (26-1-2008) NEW DELHI : The Ministry of Rural Development has decided to celebrate the 61st year of India's independence this year by honouring Nirmal Gram Puruskar (NGP) awarded winners from across the country as State Guests on the Republic Day Parade celebrations. Addressing the media persons regarding this innovative step here to day, the Union Minister for Rural Development Dr. Raghuvansh Prasad Singh said these winner Panchayats have become role models in achieving cent percent sanitation coverage in their areas of jurisdiction and have motivated others Panchayats in building slowly but steadily open defecation free, clean and healthy villages. Moreover they showcase the progress made under Total Sanitation Campaign (TSC), the flagship programme of the Ministry. Recognizing impact of sanitation on public health, poverty reduction, economic and social development and the environment United Nation has launched 2008 as International Year of Sanitation to accelerate the progress of 2.6 billion people world wide that are without proper sanitation facilities. India is signatory to this resolution. The central objective of International year of sanitation is to put the global community on track to achieve Millennium Development Goals on sanitation. As against UN target to halve the proportion of people without access to basic Sanitation by 2015 as defined in Johannesburg Plan of Action (JoPI) India is committed to increase sanitation cover from present 50% to cent percent by 2012 AD. India is also organizing South Asia Conference on Sanitation (SACOSAN) wherein all SARC countries will participate. Dr. Singh said Rural Sanitation coverage being low in the country over the years, his Ministry has accorded one of the highest priority to promote sanitation for improving quality of life in rural area through its demand driven, community led Total Sanitation Campaign (TSC) initiated in April 1999. Currently TSC is being implemented in 578 districts spread across 30 states across entire rural India with the objective of ensuring full sanitation coverage by 2012 by providing sanitation facilities in all individual households, schools, anganwadis. The Minister for Rural Development also falicitated 43 Nirmal Gram Puruskar Awardees specially invited from different States for this years Republic Day Parade at Raj Path,New Delhi on this ocassion. These include 16 from West Bengal, three each from Bihar and Kerala and two each from Mizoram, Sikkim and Tamil Nadu and one each from the States of Chhattisgarh, Haryana, Madhya Pradesh,Gujarat, Karnataka, Orissa, Uttar Pradesh and Uttarakhand. He said the honouring of Nirmal Gram Awardees in the Republic day celebrations thus marks a watershed in bringing sanitation in the forefront of Rural Development. These role model Panchayats are silently transforming a clean and healthy rural India.

5683. (28-1-2008) NEW DELHI : The President Smt. Pratibha Devi Singh Patil has said that India needs to accelerate the pace of its development process to match up with the rapidly developing world and needs to take onboard 70% of the population living in rural areas in this march towards progress to make it a meaningful one. Smt. Patil was addressing the inaugural session of a two days National Conference of the Project Directors of District Rural Development Agencies (DRDA) organized by the Ministry of Rural Development here today. She said The National Rural Employment Guarantee scheme if implemented in letter and spirit will bring out a revolution in rural areas leading not only to immediate wage-employment generation but, also in the long run, to the rejuvenation of land, water bodies and bio-diversity. She called for sincere and prompt efforts in the implementation of employment generation schemes in the rural areas of the country and exhorted the implementing agencies to plan, implement and monitor the schemes so as to realize the objective of rural development. Smt. Patil referred to the various ongoing schemes of the Rural Development Ministry namely, the Bharat Nirman, Indira Awaas Yojana, Pradhan Mantri Gram Sadak Yojana, the swarnajayanti Gram Swarozgar Yojana (SGSY) and emphasized on the benefits for their potential of bringing about an all round development and welfare in the rural areas. She particularly underlined the importance of Bharat Nirman and its elements for ushering in a new chapter in the process of rural development in India in a time bound manner. The president said that in order to ensure that people's trust in the development mechanism is not dented it is important that the implementers at grass root level who have a face to face relation with the people play a pro-active role in understanding the needs of the people and plan and implement the schemes accordingly. She exorted the Project Directors to take initiatives and play a vital role as change agents for development so that full benefit of different schemes accrues to the poorest of the poor in the rural areas. Speaking on the occasion, the Deputy Chairman of Planning Commission Shri Montek Singh Ahloowalia said the 11th Plan emphasizes on all the key areas of of rural development so that we can achieve an inclusive growth and 70% of our population are not left out from enjoying the fruit of development and growth. He further said with the strengthening of the Panchayati Raj Institutions, there is a change of circumstances since the the DRDAs were established and the DRDAs are required to adapt to this change in circumstances so that they continue to play an important role in the implementation of the schemes. It is up to the implementing agencies *i.e.* DRDAs to draw and design the district development plan which are of cardinal importance and a constitutional requirement of our planning process. He called for better convergence at district level between various stakeholder Departments and Ministries etc. so that the funds provided for developmental schemes is utilized in a proper, systematic and transparent way and there is no overlapping of any kind.. Addressing the Project Directors as the "Local Commanders", in the battle against poverty and unemployment, the Minister for Rural Development Dr. Raghuvansh Prasad Singh said they have to play and important role not only as the agents of Government in the district but should also approach the development issue of their respective areas with a humane touch. Dr. Singh said since there is growing emphasis on rural development programmes by the Government at the centre and there is a progressing increase in the availability of funds in the last four years commensurate result and physical achievements can only come if the agencies involved in the task of development at the lowest level is geared up to the optimum. The importance of DRDA require no emphasis as over the years they have been the main stay of the development process at the district level. The minister also indicated that combined with the wage employment guarantee scheme, the SGSY has the potential to wipe out the curse of unemployment from the face of rural India. In view of this the ministry proposes to bring at least one member from each BPL family under the ambit of SHG movement by the end of 11th Plan period. This universalization of SHGs would go a long way in the overall development of the villages. He reiterated the goals under Bharat Nirman and indicated that his Ministry is committed to achieve higher goals from the ones set out under Bharat Nirman by the end of 2009.

5684. (28-1-2008) NEW DELHI : Government of India have announced the sale (re-issue) of "11.30 percent Government Stock, 2010" under Market Stabilization

Scheme for a notified amount of Rs. 3,000 crore (nominal). The Government Stock will be sold through price based auction using multiple price method. The auctions will be conducted by the Reserve Bank of India, Mumbai Office, Fort, Mumbai on January 31, 2008 (Thursday). Up to 5 per cent of the amount notified for the sale of stock is reserved for allotment to eligible individuals and Institutions on non-competitive basis as per the Scheme for Non-Competitive Bidding Facility in the Auction of Government Securities. Bids in the prescribed form obtainable from the Regional Director, Reserve Bank of India, Mumbai Office (Public Debt Office), Fort, Mumbai-400 001 and RBI website www.rbi.org.in should be submitted to that Office on January 31, 2008. The NDS members should submit competitive as well as non-competitive bids in electronic format using Primary Market Operation (PMO) module of NDS.

5685. (28-1-2008) NEW DELHI : The President of India said here that I am glad to be here at this Conference, as I strongly believe that with 70 percent of our population living in villages, the development of India will not be comprehensive or complete unless there is development in the rural areas. In the fast changing world, there is need to act with a sense of urgency to ensure that our population living in rural areas has the skills and opportunities to benefit from growth. Therefore, we will have to shed lethargy and lax attitude to achieve this objective. The 11th Five Year Plan is targeting economic growth with emphasis on inclusive growth. A major focus of our efforts must be on bringing about a visible and tangible difference in the quality of life of the rural population especially the rural poor of our country. The Ministry of Rural Development has a pivotal role in formulating programmes for sustainable income, capacity building and skill up-gradation in rural areas. On the other hand, District Rural Development Agencies, as nodal administrative units for implementation of programmes, have the challenge of actually bringing change in the lives of the people in rural areas by taking effective action for implementing programmes. The Government has put in place a framework of policies and programmes, which seek to bring about a holistic development of rural areas. They also aim to give the weaker sections of our society a security net. The Flagship programmes-Bharat Nirman and National Rural Employment Guarantee Scheme have been launched with these objectives. Bharat Nirman is shaped to address issues relating to the provision of basic infrastructure and amenities such as drinking water, roads, housing, irrigation, telephone connectivity and electrification in a time bound manner to rural areas. Construction of rural roads brings multifaceted benefits that include better prices for agricultural produce, lower prices of essential commodities for rural consumers and a better infrastructure for setting up rural and agro-industries. They also bring to the lives of the rural population, better medical care, better access to education and better availability of public services. The Pradhan Mantri Gram Sadak Yojna is a right step in this direction. Rural Housing is one of the basic requirements for human survival. Possession of a house brings about a profound social change in a person's existence. The Indira Awaas Yojana provides assistance for the construction and up-gradation of dwelling units to rural households living below the poverty line with priority being given to Scheduled Castes and Scheduled Tribes. The work of actual construction is being done directly by the beneficiary, which gives a sense of ownership and whole-hearted involvement in building the dwelling unit. The National Rural Employment Guarantee Scheme has given the right to employment to the rural poor of this country in the form of a guarantee of 100 days of unskilled work in a year. This programme if implemented in letter and spirit will bring about a revolution in rural areas leading not only to immediate wage-employment generation but, also in the long run, to the rejuvenation of land, water bodies and bio-diversity. Many a times, complaints are received that full remunerations are not being paid or payments are delayed and sometimes employment is not provided in time. Implementing agencies will have to be sincere and prompt to redress these grievances and to avoid recurrence of such incidents.

5686. (28-1-2008) NEW DELHI : The Government has set up a High Level Task Force to look into the various aspects of providing Affordable Housing for All under the chairmanship of Shri Deepak Parekh, Chairman, HDFC Ltd. The National Urban Housing & Habitat Policy (NUHHP), 2007 recognizes the need for public-private partnerships and development of various financial and operational innovations for bridging the housing shortage.

5687. (28-1-2008) NEW DELHI : In our country people belonging to various religions live in harmony, but there are occasions when the communal fabric gets disturbed, often on trivial issues. It is the responsibility of all sections of society to ensure peace and brotherhood so that all round development of the country takes places rapidly. The police have a great role to play in promotion of communal harmony and national integration. They come in contact with the general public in the process of performing their duties far more frequently then most other bodies of civil servants of the Government. In such a situation, interaction with vision, understanding, tact, compassion and humour by the police will not only raise the public esteem of the police but will also lead to a healthy police-public relationship, and secure the desired measures of public involvement and cooperation in promotion of communal harmony. Keeping this in mind, the National Foundation for Communal Harmony (NFCH) has been organizing seminars with the aim of effective sensitization of the police officers so that they become the torchbearers of communal harmony and national integration in their day to day functioning. The first such seminar was held at Haryana Police Academy, Madhuban, in August 2007 and the second one in Mumbai in October 2007. The Foundation, which is working silently for promotion of communal harmony, has also supplied reading materials on the role of police in promotion of communal harmony and national integration, constitutional and statutory provisions relating to communal harmony. These seminars have been quite successful in spreading the message of communal harmony and national integration amongst the police officers. The Foundation is an autonomous organization registered as a society under the Societies Registration

Act, 1860. It functions under the aegis of the Ministry of Home Affairs and the Union Home Minister is the Chairman of the Governing Council. The principal objectives of the Foundation is to foster communal harmony, fraternity and national integration in general, and facilitate physical and psychological rehabilitation of the child victims of caste, communal, ethnic or terrorist violence, in particular. The NFCH undertakes and assists state governments, local administration, non-governmental organizations, universities, colleges and schools, social activists, scholars, researchers and students in undertaking activities and programmes aimed at promoting harmony at local, state and national levels. Though there have been some incidents of communal violence in certain States, there has been no major communal riot in any part of the country in 2007. Pro-active role of the Central and State Governments prevented escalation of communal violence at Gorakhpur in Uttar Pradesh and Indore in Madhya Pradesh last year. All states are advised to keep a close watch on the situation with communal overtones and take early steps to prevent any flare up. Over the last five years the incidents of communal violence have gradually come down. The decline is attributed to the Centre closely monitoring the situation and keeping a strict vigil on the activities of individuals and organizations to ensure that the situation remains under control. The activities of all organizations having a bearing on maintenance of communal harmony in the country are under constant watch of the law enforcing agencies.

5688. (28-1-2008) NEW DELHI : The Urban Development Minister, Shri Jaipal Reddy today took stock of activities of the Delhi Development Authority (DDA) in a meeting of the Consultative Committee of Parliament attached to his Ministry in New Delhi. He thanked the MPs for their support to the Government on the stand taken in passing the special law last year. The Delhi Development Authority helps in house construction and also facilitates by allotting land for residential purposes through cooperative societies, auctions. It also allots residential plots. The Authority also provides land for commercial space and develops greens as per the Master Plan provisions. Among its future plans are sports complexes at Narela, Rohini, Dwarka and Karol Bagh/Rajinder Nagar/Patel Nagar. DDA has also been assigned the development of the Games village for the Commonwealth Games-2010 and development of competitive venues for Table Tennis, Badminton, Squash and Archery. The Members were given an overview of the important activities of the DDA by its Vice Chairman, Shri Dinesh Rai. Members cutting across party lines stressed the need for appropriate and timely compensation for the farmers whose land had been acquired by DDA. They felt that as per the policy they should be given alternative residential plots in the same area. DDA informed the Members that compensatory plot allotments were being done in Rohini and Narela and acquisition of suitable land for residential plots in Dwarka is under process. The Urban Development Minister urged DDA to clear all pending applications in the matter within the next three months.

5689. (28-1-2008) NEW DELHI : Minister of State for Women and Child Development, Smt. Renuka Chowdhury has urged the States to implement programmes and policies related to the children aggressively so that benefits of the schemes could be ensured to the vulnerable of the society, which accounts nearly 67% of the total population of the country. She said that in recent past the Central Government had undertaken a number of initiatives to tackle multi-dimensional problems and constraints faced by women and children which include setting up of national Child Rights Commission, amendments in Juvenile Justice Act, Child Marriage Prohibition Act and enactment of Domestic Violence Act but follow up action for effective implementation is yet to be taken by the States. Highlighting the importance of gender specific schemes for empowerment of women, the Minister said that there is need to create an enabling environment for incorporating a gender perspective and sensitiveness at all levels and stages of the developmental planning. In this process, 'we hope to achieve gender responsive budgets by reflecting the quantum of flow of funds for women in all sectors', she said. A number of States have not availed the grant under the Swayamsidha, a programme for self employment of women, she requested the States to take stock of the situation on emergency basis and ensure the receipt of the funds at an early date. She also urged them to involve the corporate sector for providing training and skill development and to increased employment opportunities for women. Expressing concern over growing incidents of violence and abuse against women and girl child, she said that States should put in place implementation mechanism such as protection officers for effective implementation of Child Marriage Prohibition Act and Prevention of Domestic Violence Act. Dissemination and awareness about the provisions of the Act in regional languages needs to be reinvigorated. The Minister said that the Government wants to set up at least one shelter home for destitute women in each District. Assessment for such shelter homes in the State particularly in areas such as religious places where a huge population of destitute widows reside is required on priority basis. Briefing about proposed Conditional Cash Transfer Scheme for girl child, Smt. Chowdhury said the Scheme would be launched very soon as a pilot project in 11 educationally backward blocks in the States of Andhra Pradesh, Uttar Pradesh, Bihar, Orissa, Jharkhand, Chattisgarh and Punjab. ICDS would be also restructured and universalized very soon. It would be implemented in mission mode status to ensure time bound and inclusive approach to reach to the most disadvantaged and vulnerable beneficiaries, particularly from the SC/ST/Minority communities she said. Urging States to entrust the work of child welfare and protection to a single Department, she said that spread over the work in different departments creates effective implementation of the programmes. She also asked the States to ensure registration of child care institutions, setting up child welfare committees, juvenile justice boards and child protection units in all districts.

5690. (28-1-2008) NEW DELHI : The Election Commission today held a briefing meeting for the Observers (both General and Expenditure) who are being deployed for the General Elections to the Legislative Assembly of Tripura. The meeting was addressed by Shri N. Gopalaswami, Chief Election Commissioner, Shri Navin B.Chawla and Dr. S.Y. Quraishi, Election Commissioners. 60 Officers are being appointed as Observers (52 General and 08 Expenditure Observers) to supervise the election process in forthcoming Legislative Assembly Elections, 2008 for Tripura. To ensure close monitoring and supervision, one General Observer per assembly constituency and one Expenditure Observer for every 7-8 constituency are being appointed in Tripura. In addition to their own duties as Expenditure Observer, each Expenditure Observer has been assigned the duties of a General Observer for one of the Assembly Constituencies under his charge. The Election Observers will reach the allotted constituencies at least one day before the last day of nomination and stay continuously in the constituencies assigned to them till the end of poll day. This would ensure immediate redressal of complaints that are received from various political parties/candidates. During the first visit, they will supervise the processes of nominations, scrutiny, withdrawal, campaign and poll. They would also be supervising preparation of Electronic Voting Machines, training of polling personnel and conduct of voter awareness programmes. All Observers have been asked to look into deployment plan of forces in the constituency. They will also be critically examining classification of hypersensitive and sensitive polling stations and monitor the process of vulnerability mapping to identify the segments vulnerable for threat and intimidation. During second visit, all Observers will monitor counting and declaration of results. Observers, who are appointed under Section 20B of the Representation of the Peoples Act, play an important role in ensuring free and fair elections. They act as crucial link between the field and the Commission. These officers remain under disciplinary control of the Commission till the end of elections. During the elections, the maximum number of vehicles that will be allowed to come within the periphery of 100 mtrs. of Returning Officers/Assistant Returning Officers office shall be three and maximum number of persons that will be allowed to enter the office of Returning Officers/ Assistant Returning Officers at the time of filing nomination shall be the candidate plus four other individuals which may include any proposer/proposers proposing the nomination of the candidate *i.e.* there can be only five people (including the candidate) who can remain present inside the Returning Officers/Assistant Returning Officers' room at the time of filing nomination. The Observers have been asked to make sure that the affidavits that are filed by the candidates at the time of nomination detailing their movable/immovable assets, qualifications, convictions, cases pending in courts, are displayed prominently and made available for public scrutiny without any loss of time. Observers have specifically been asked to tour their respective allotted Assembly Constituency extensively and build confidence among weaker and disadvantaged sections.

5691. (28-1-2008) NEW DELHI : The Prime Minister Dr. Manmohan Singh has said that the spirit of the NCC needs to be replicated in many spheres of our society to bring about constructive social changes. Addressing PM's NCC Rally in New

Delhi Dr. Singh said the involvement of youth in wide variety of national building activities will be a key determinant of our success and our excellence, he remarked. Exhorting the youth to enroll for the NCC, Prime Minister said our Government is encouraging youth movements that contribute to social and human development. He hoped that NCC Cadets will continue to enrich the legacy of NCC and contribute to the greater glory of the motherland. Earlier the NCC cadets, comprising groups from the three wings,-Army, Navy and the Air Force, presented an immaculate display of skills in warfare training. Boys and girl cadets in battle gear gave a thrilling display of Quick Reaction Teams as they were heli-dropped from an MI-17 chopper hovering 30 feet above ground, supported by mechanised infantry columns. Parasailing, flights by microlight aircraft, aeromodelling and floats displaying various adventure activities at sea were other major attractions. The Prime Minister also presented awards to the best cadets in different categories. The most coveted Prime Minister's banner and trophy went to Andhra Pradesh Directorate. Senior Under Officer HS Sandeep of Andhra Pradesh directorate received the best cadet trophy in the Army Wing Senior Division, while Cadet Tushar Mohata of Maharashtra Directorate received the Best Cadet in Senior Division Naval Wing, Senior Under Officer Shyam Sunder Bajpai of UP Directorate was adjudged the Best Cadet in Senior Division Air Wing. Best Cadet Senior Division Girls Trophy was won by Sergeant Divya A of Tamil Nadu, Pondicherry and Andaman Nicobar Directorate. In the Junior Division Girls Wing Best Cadet Trophy and Medal was won by Sergeant Narayani Anand of Punjab, Haryana, Himachal Pradesh and Chandigarh Directorate. Cadet Syed Abbar Hyder Razavi of Andhra Pradesh Directorate got the Best Cadet Trophy of Junior Division Boys Wing. In the Girls Wing Competition Maharashtra Directorate got the Best Directorate Trophy from the Prime Minister, whereas Best Directorate Trophy in Army Wing Competition went to Karnataka and Goa Directorate.

5692. (28-1-2008) NEW DELHI : The BJP is of the firm belief that the country's economic development can succeed only if agriculture is made vibrant, if the purchasing power of the farmer and the agriculture workers is substantially augmented, if more employment opportunities are created in rural India and by improving the overall living conditions of entire rural India. The NDA government, through numerous initiatives, tireless worked to improve the condition of the agricultural sector as well as rural India. Under the Congress led UPA government, many of these initiatives have unfortunately either been kept in cold storage or are being implemented at an extremely slow pace. The fundamental cause of the deterioration of the rural economy is because of the poor performance of the agriculture sector. The low growth in agriculture per capita income and increasing disparity between the per capita farm and non farm incomes has been caused by the slow growth of agricultural and rural output as compared to other sectors of the economy. The disparity would further worsen unless there is a major shift in our policies and the farmer is brought to the centre stage of all our planning exercises.

5693. (28-1-2008) NEW DELHI : A Group of Ministers has been formed to review the existing Cluster Development Programmes of different ministries of the Government. This was stated by Shri Mahabir Prasad, Minister for Micro, Small & Medium Enterprises while inaugurating the National Workshop on Micro, Small & Medium Enterprises Cluster Development here today. The Minister said that the Government extended financial assistance to the tune of Rs.61 crore for the development of 156 clusters under the Micro & Small Enterprises Cluster Development Programmes (MSECDP). Besides, diagnostic study of 172 clusters has been undertaken to understand the problems of these clusters and address them. Under MSECDP, the Government provides 90 per cent financial assistance as a soft intervention for enhancing the productivity of a cluster, whereas for establishment of Common Facility Centre, the Central Government provides a maximum of 70 per cent assistance as a hard intervention. The rest of the amount is provided by the beneficiaries of the cluster and the State Government. Under SFURTI, 124 Clusters have been approved for khadi, coir and village industry sectors. Under this scheme, for the development of each cluster an amount of Rs. 85 lakh to Rs. 1,10,000 will be spent. The National Resource Centre for Cluster Development (NRCD) of National Institute for Micro, Small & Medium Enterprises (formerly known as NISIET) under the Ministry of Micro, Small & Medium Enterprises has organised this two-day national workshop on MSME Cluster Development on 28-29 January 2008 in New Delhi. The objective of the workshop is to bring together various organisations/institutions concerned with cluster development so as to synergise the efforts and add further momentum to cluster development in the country. For this purpose, policy makers, planners, implementers and field experts are being invited to share their experiences and to evolve new strategies for development of MSMEs through cluster development. The themes selected for discussion are a) Policy Implications for Cluster Development b) Clusters: Employment Generation and Poverty Reduction c) Business Development Services d) Investment Promotion and Technology Transfer e) Cluster Financing and Development f) Infrastructure Development and Common Facilities g) Cluster Development Implementation Strategy and h) Future Directions.

5694. (28-1-2008) NEW DELHI : The body of martyr Capt Sunil Kumar Chaudhary, SM was flown in a special aircraft from Dibrugarh to Pathankot this morning and will arrive there later in the evening. Capt SK Chaudhary, SM was martyred little after noon yesterday in a counter insurgency operation in Village Barapathar (Tinsukia), Assam. In this operation the brave officer had killed two militants of 28 Bn of ULFA, even after being shot in his neck. He later succumbed to the injuries. Capt SK Chaudhary was awarded a Sena Medal for gallantry, in the awards announced day before yesterday. The award was for an operation in Nabjothi (Tinsukia) in July last year in which two militants including self styled Sgt Palash Moni, an Action Group Commander of ULFA were killed. Son of a serving Army Officer, Lt Col PL Chaudhary, his brother Ankur is a flying officer in the Air Force. The martyr belonged to New Colony, Govindsar, Kathua (J &

K). He had his early educated at Kendriya Vidyalaya, Bangalore, graduated from Pune and had done his post graduation for Garhwal University. Capt Chaudhary was commissioned from IMA, Dehradun into 7/11 Gorkha Rifles on 10 Dec 2004. He had excelled in Platoon Weapons and Machine Gun courses at Infantry School, Mhow. Before moving to counter terrorism operations, he was posted at Kolkata. The cremation of this brave officer will take place at Kathua with full military honours.

5695. (28-1-2008) NEW DELHI : The Minister of State of Commerce, Shri Jairam Ramesh will be visiting Maldives from January 29th to 31st as part of his drive to expand trade and investment ties within SAARC. He has already visited Bangladesh and is scheduled to be in Sri Lanka in two weeks time. Interactions with delegations from Pakistani and Bhutan have also taken place. In addition, Shri Ramesh has visited all the important border trade centres in the region including Petrapole, Moreh and Attari/Wagah. The visit assumes significance in light of the forthcoming SAFTA Ministerial meeting in New Delhi on March 1st-2nd, 2008. Shri Ramesh will also review the working of the Indo-Maldives Trade Agreement of 1981 in light of the changes that have taken place in the economies of both countries. India supplies essential commodities like rice, wheat flour, eggs, potatoes, stones and sand as part of this Agreement. Even though wheat exports from India are banned, as a measure of the importance it attaches to SAARC in general and Maldives in particular, India supplies wheat flour to Maldives. India accounts for around 10-11% of Maldives imports, next to Singapore and Sri Lanka and is on par with UAE. Exports from India to Maldives are presently in the region of about $ 100 million. Singapore accounts for almost 90% of the FDI into Maldives, followed by Malaysia. Shri Jairam Ramesh's visit is to explore how India can expand its trade and investment presence in Maldives, a country of great strategic significance to it. Fisheries is one important area for bilateral cooperation that is proposed to be discussed during Shri Ramesh's visit. Cooperation in tuna is one specific area that will be discussed now that India has also announced major plans to develop its tuna resources, particularly in the Andaman and Nicobar Islands. In addition, Maldives has sought India's assistance to develop it as a trans-shipment and logistics hub because of its strategic location. Maldives has also expressed in expanding the scope of training in IT.

5696. (28-1-2008) NEW DELHI : The Prime Minister, Dr. Manmohan Singh addressed the 59th Republic Day Rally of NCC cadets in New Delhi today. He asked the youth of the country to seek adventure and test their limits, not just academically but in all spheres of their personality development. Following is the text of the Prime Minister's speech on the occasion: "I am very happy to be with you today. I compliment you for your marvellous rally. What I saw today and what I saw day before yesterday, on Rajpath, make me feel very proud. The NCC inculcates among our youth the enduring values of our Republic, our civilization and our composite culture. You combine the dynamism and energy of youth with the discipline and camaraderie instilled by the NCC. This provides an inspiring example of smartness, cheerfulness and team effort. You are bound together by the commonalities of our diverse faiths and the human values which the Indian identity so majestically expresses. The bright young men and women of the NCC display the promise and hope of India to address the challenges facing our ancient civilization and modern nation. It is a matter of great pride that the NCC has come forward and discharged its duties with efficiency and effectiveness. The services rendered by you to the victims of natural and man-made disasters are truly praiseworthy. The spirit of the NCC needs to be replicated in many spheres of our society to bring about constructive social changes. The involvement of youth in a wide variety of nation building activities will be a key determinant of our success and our excellence. All of you know that India is a young nation with more than a third of our population is below the age of 20. Very few countries in the world are bestowed with such youthful human resources. I am confident that your legacy of dedicated service will inspire more and more students to join the NCC for serving the nation and enriching their lives, character and career. I take heart from the fact that the NCC cadets in our schools and colleges have been steadily growing. Pursuit of academic work in educational institutions must be accompanied by efforts for full flowering of one's personality. The youth in our educational institutions can do so by joining the NCC in large numbers. Discipline and determination are the defining attributes of any society which has made a mark in history. As we register unprecedented progress in the economic field we need to imbibe discipline and develop character more vigorously. I would like our young people to seek adventure and test their limits, not just academically but in all spheres of one's personality development. Our Government is encouraging youth movements that contribute to social and human development. The Nehru Yuvak Kendras have been activated. We are going to support youth programmes that enable our young people to get involved in spreading literacy, in rural development and other constructive avenues.

5697. (29-1-2008) NEW DELHI : The Union Minister for Rural Development Dr. Raghuvansh Prasad Singh has said that transparency and accountability are a must in the implementation process of rural development prgrammes. Addressing the inaugural session of 8th Annual Editors Conference on Social Sector Issues here today the minister said that the primary concern of Government towards improving the quality of life of the people is reflected in the launch of various schemes of his ministry. Dr. Singh said a five pronged strategy to ensure effective implementation of its programmes in transparent manner by ensuring people's participation and accountability has been adopted in this regard. The five points include Awareness Generation; Transparency; People's participation; Accountability; and Vigilance and Monitoring. The minister reiterated that in order to provide Guaranteed 100 Days Employment, the National Rural Employment Guarantee Act (NREGA), 2005 was notified on 7th September 2005 and launched on 2nd February 2006 in 200 identified districts in 27 States in its first phase of implementation and 130 additional districts in 2007-08. All the districts of the country would be covered w.e.f. 1st April 2008. On the reported shortcoming in the implementation part of Dr. Singh said it is the duty of State Governments to enact NREGA in letter and spirit and it should have to be ensured that utmost transparency be adopted during the entire process. Considering the importance of providing a dwelling unit to a shelter less rural BPL families, Indira Awaas Yojana (IAY) has been included as one of the six components of 'Bharat Nirman'. Under Bharat Nirman, 60 lakh IAY houses are envisaged to be constructed during a period of four years from 2005-06 to 2008-09. During the first two years *i.e.* 2005-07, 30.36 lakh houses have already been constructed. The Central outlay has been further increased by 39 per cent to Rs 4040 crore for the third year i.e 2007-08 to construct 21.27 lakh houses as against 15.33 lakh IAY houses during 2006-07. The likely achievement during four years *i.e.* 2005-09 is likely to be over 70 lakh as against the target 60 lakhs, The Minister added. Dr. Singh said, Rural Roads being one of the six components of the Bharat Nirman, Construction of rural roads is a part of the process of augmenting and modernizing of all weather pacca rural road infrastructure and the Ministry is implementing a Pradhan Mantri Gram Sadak Yojana (PMGSY). Under rural roads component of Bharat Nirman, it is targeted to connect 66802 habitations by constructing 1.46 lakh km. rural roads. In addition, the programme envisages upgradation of 1.94 lakh km. of existing rural roads to provide full farm to market connectivity. Up to November, 2007, 16878 habitations have been connected by constructing 49713 km. rural roads and projects for connecting 21973 habitations are in progress. In addition, 64253 km. of existing rural roads have been upgraded/renewed under the programme.

5698. (29-1-2008) NEW DELHI : The UN Assistant Secretary General for Mission Support in the Department of peacekeeping operations Ms. Jane Holl Lute accompanied by the UN Messenger of Peace Mr. George Clooney called on the Defence Secretary Shri Vijay Singh, here today. During the discussions, Ms. Lute was highly appreciative of the role played by the Indian peacekeepers in various parts of the world. She urged New Delhi to take part in the Contingent Owned Equipment (COE) Manual Review Exercise to be held at New York from 04-22 next month. Shri Singh reiterated India's commitment for UN Peacekeeping operations and assured Ms. Lute that India will send a high-level delegation to take part in the review meetings both at technical and working levels. Ms. Lute was also given an overview of the experiences of the just-returned Indian contingent of peacekeepers, especially those relating to logistic and operational aspects. The Army Headquarters gave a presentation on the various 'Commandments' given to the Indian peacekeepers such as respect for cultural ethos of the country where they are deployed and zero-tolerance for human rights violations. Ms. Lute had recently visited Congo, where she had seen the Indian peacekeepers in action. The UN Assistant Secretary General yesterday visited the 50 Para Regiment at Agra and the South-Western Army Command Headquarters at Jaipur. She evinced keen interest in the training imparted to the Indian peacekeepers to orient them to handle challenges in alien territories.

5699. (29-1-2008) HOUSTON : After successful Road Show at London on 24.01.2008 as part of Government of India's promotional campaign to show case NELP-VII exploration blocks, another Road Show abroad was held late yesterday at Houston (U.S.). Under the seventh round of the New Exploration Licensing Policy (NELP-VII) 57 blocks include 19 in deepwater, 9 in shallow water and 29 in onland. After the inaugural road show held at Mumbai on 8th January, 2008, the Houston road-show is the second one to be held abroad for NELP-VII. As many as 66 companies comprising 32 E&P, 18 service providers, 6 investment companies/bankers and 10 others participated in the Houston Road Show. A high level delegation led by Mr. Dinsha Patel, Minister of State for Petroleum & Natural Gas, which also included Mr. M.S. Srinivasan, Secretary, Ministry of Petroleum & Natural Gas, MR, V.K. Sibal, Director General, Directorate General of Hydrocarbons and Mr. Anil K. Jain, Joint Secretary, Ministry of Petroleum & Natural Gas, is currently in Houston to promote NELP-VII to prospective E&P companies and investors. Mr. Patel highlighted important features of the NELP-VII. Shri Dinsha Patel emphasised the highly attractive opportunities being offered under NELP-VII impressed upon companies to participate in the bidding process to enter into a long term beneficial relationship by becoming part of India's growing and vibrant Petroleum Sector. He mentioned that the promotional road shows for NELP-VII will also be held at Calgary, Singapore, Perth and Dubai. He invited US firms to make up for the lost opportunities in previous rounds by participating in the current offer. He pointed out that India is 5th largest consumer of energy in the world after China, Russia and Japan. Shri Patel elaborated various steps underway to bridge the gap between demand and supply of oil and gas like accelerating E&P efforts in Indian basins as well as acquiring oil assets abroad and harnessing alternative sources of energy like coal bed methane, gas hydrates, coal liquefaction, ethanol, bio-diesel, etc. Referring to excellent business relationship between India and America, Shri Patel informed that the trade between the two countries is valued at about US$ 31 billion which is about 10% of India's total trade. Some of the major stakeholders in India's upstream petroleum sector namely BG Group, Oil & Natural Gas Corporation Limited, cairn Energy and Reliance Industries Limited also made presentations during the NELP-VII roadshow about their experiences, and the plans and vision their companies had regarding India's petroleum sector, especially the upstream sector. They emphasised the strong fundamentals as well as the attractiveness of the E&P sector in India and concluded that the investment climate in India was indeed positive with very attractive fiscal terms under NELP. For the first time in NELP promotional road show, a presentation by a leading Indian offshore service providers was also included to assure the investors of the growing availability of services in India. In order to provide access to information such as salient technical data on the blocks on offer, the bid documents and highlights of NELP-VII, a special web site has been created at www.indianelpvii.com. This website can also be accessed from the Ministry's official website www.petroleum.nic.in as well as www.dghindia.org. To facilitate data viewing by Exploration and Production companies, the Government of India would also be opening data centres at Noida/Delhi, Houston, London, Calgary and Perth. The data for NELP-VII can be viewed by companies at any of these centres as well as online through website and thereafter interested companies may purchase data. Data viewing facilities at London will be available until the end of March 2008. As of today, 13 companies have already booked for NELP-VII data viewing at London data room. The major companies include ENI, Total, MOL, MITTAL, BP, StatoilHydro, Harvest Natural Resources. The bid closing date for NELP-VII is 11th April, 2008. It is expected that NELP-VII would attract a very good response from E&P companies and prospective investors and they would avail of the attractive investment opportunities being offered through NELP-VII. Government is committed to complete evaluation, award and signing of Production Sharing Contracts in a strict time frame and the whole process would be completed in a transparent manner in 3 to 4 months from bid closing date as demonstrated in past rounds of NELP.

5700. (29-8-2007) NEW DELHI : Bharatiya Janata Party national president Shri Rajnath Singh set up a committee to investigate into the recent violence against Dalits in Gohana in Haryana. The committee would be headed by Shri Satyanarayan Jatia, Member of Parliament and national president of BJP SC Morcha. Other members of the committee are Shri Kishan Lal Valmiki and Surendra Lath – both MPs. The committee is rushing to Gohana immediately and will submit its report to Shri Rajnath Singh.

5701. (29-1-2008) DINAJPUR : The Rajiv Gandhi Grameen Vidyutikaran Yojana, RGGVY, was today launched in Uttar Dinajpur District in West Bengal in the presence of Union Power Minister Shri Sushil Kumar Shinde and Union Minister for Information and Broadcasting, Shri P.R. Dasmunshi. Under RGGVY, the state of West Bengal gave 32 project proposals for 18 districts. 13 projects covering 13 districts were sanctioned during X-Plan at the estimated cost of Rs.385 crore. 3,268 villages have been electrified under RGGVY as on 18-1-2008. Funds released for West Bengal so far are to the tune of Rs.394.38 crore out of which 90% has been provided as capital subsidy by the Ministry. 6 projects &13 Supplementary projects will be taken up for implementation in the XI Plan period. Ministry of Power introduced the scheme Rajiv Gandhi Grameen Vidyutikaran Yojana (RGGVY) in April 2005, which aims at providing electricity in all villages and habitations in four years and provides access to electricity to all rural households. This programme has been brought under the ambit of Bharat Nirman. Under RGGVY, electricity distribution infrastructure is envisaged to establish Rural Electricity Distribution Backbone (REDB) with at least a 33/11 KV sub-station, Village Electrification Infrastructure (VEI) with at least a Distribution Transformer in a village or hamlet, and standalone grids with generation where grid supply is not feasible. This infrastructure would cater to the requirements of agriculture and other activities in rural areas including irrigation pumpsets, small and medium industries, khadi and village industries, cold chains, healthcare and education and IT. This would facilitate overall rural development, employment generation and poverty alleviation.

5702. (29-1-2008) NEW DELHI : Following is the text of the inaugural address delivered by the Defence Minister Shri AK Antony at National Seminar on Defence R&D and Technology Management, here today:-It gives me great pleasure to be present here today for the inauguration of the national seminar on defence R&D and technology management organized by the Society of Defence Technologists (SODET). This seminar comes at a most opportune moment when serious initiatives are being taken by Government towards strengthening our defence R&D base through the increased involvement of all players, whether private or public, Indian or foreign. Defence R&D and its integration into product improvement and development is an exceedingly complex and exacting process. This involves collaborative and network techniques so as to ensure that the output of research establishments are effectively translated into viable, state-of-the-art products. I am, therefore, pleased to note that SODET, which is a forum of defence technologists and industries, has made significant contributions towards pooling of technological resources by organizing various seminars, workshops and symposia covering themes such as corporate strategies, manufacturing technologies, intellectual property rights etc. The value of these efforts cannot be under-emphasized as the challenges before you are not small by any measure. The variables which impact our defence preparedness and threat assessments, including regional and global political dynamics, are in a state of continuous flux, forcing us to constantly reassess threats to our security. All this is compounded by the remarkable technological and scientific revolution which began in the last century and is continuing at a dizzying pace. One estimate indicates that knowledge doubles every five years. This exponential growth of technology and information makes it all the more imperative that suitable instruments are in position to ensure that defence innovations reach their intended end users, namely the Armed Forces. The ability to move with speed in response to innovations is what will determine whether a country continues to have a winning edge or not. As we increasingly globalize and cooperate across international borders for the development and production of defence products, as the number of entities involved in defence material production and management grow rapidly, and as the number of players, particularly from the private sector, increase with the introduction of the off-set policy, it becomes all the more important that all players are enabled to network effectively. In such a scenario, collaborative and networked defence R&D can go a long way in enabling the nation address technology gaps, match global standards and promote indigenization. This seminar, therefore, provides an ideal platform for the meaningful interaction of defence technologists and defence industries. I am confident that all of you will be able to deliberate and evolve more effective mechanisms for interaction amongst yourselves so as to ensure better utilization of assets and better R&D leading to improved products.

5703. (29-1-2008) NEW DELHI : "Employment and Unemployment Situation in India: 2005-06"-Report No.522 based on the data of 62nd round survey of National Sample Survey Organisation (NSSO) in the Ministry of Statistics and Programme Implementation, Government of India, has been released. The field work of the survey was carried out during July 2005-June 2006.. This report provides some broad features of employment and unemployment situation in India and some characteristics associated with them at the national and state levels. Information regarding participation in public works was collected for the first time in this round for persons of age 15 years and above in the rural areas. No separate estimate is provided for small States & UT's due to small sample size, instead, in such cases the estimates have been provided for a group of States/ UT's. The survey covered the whole of the Indian Union except (i) Leh (Ladakh) and Kargil districts of Jammu & Kashmir, (ii) interior villages of Nagaland situated beyond 5 kilometres from the bus routes and (iii) villages in Andaman and Nicobar Islands which remain inaccessible throughout the year. The survey was spread over 4,798 villages and 5,125 urban blocks covering 78,879 households (37,975 in rural areas and 40,904 in urban areas) and enumerating 3,77,377 persons (1,86,571 in rural areas and 1,90,806 in urban areas). The earlier survey on the same subject was the NSS 61st round quinquennial survey (2004-05) spread over 7999 villages and 4602 urban blocks covering 1,24,680 households (79,306 in rural areas and 45,374 in urban areas) and enumerating 6,02,833 persons. The main characteristics associated with employment, unemployment are broadly comparable at the national level. However, at State/UT level comparison of the results of this round with the quinquennial round on some of the characteristics needs to be attempted with due caution.

5704. (29-1-2008) NEW DELHI : Department of Animal Husbandry, Dairying and Fisheries has notified Avian Influenza in poultry in two more districts *viz.* South 24 Parganas and West Medinipore. With this, the number of districts affected by the Influenza has risen to 13. In the affected 13 districts, 42 blocks covering 2600 villages and four municipalities are involved. Out of these, 1027 villages are in 0-3 Km area where a population of 8,39,246 are under daily surveillance. 1998 cases fever/URI have been reported, 2 of which had contact history with poultry. There are 1573 villages in the surveillance zone of 3-10 kms where a population of 6,96,133 have been surveyed. There had been 1284 fever/ URI cases none of whom had exposure history.

5705. (29-1-2008) NEW DELHI : The Ministry of Social Justice and Empowerment has taken a major initiative of facilitating educational empowerment of the Scheduled Caste students as a part of its commitment to promote 'inclusive growth'. A new Central Sector Scheme 'Rajiv Gandhi National Fellowship (RGNF) for Scheduled

Caste students' has been introduced since the year 2005-06 for pursuing M.Phil and Ph.D. courses. This scheme was conceived to meet a long felt need in the field of higher education. It was found that the University Grants Commission (UGC), Council of Scientific and Industrial Research (CSIR) and Indian Council of Social Sciences Research (ICSSR) are offering fellowships, but they could not percolate to the Scheduled Caste students. Similar was the case in the Nationwide Eligibility Test (NET) conducted by the UGC to determine the award of fellowships for pursuing M.Phil and Ph.D Degree Courses in the universities. The Planning Commission had assessed in the year 2004 that at the all India level, only 3133 Scheduled Caste students were pursuing M.Phil and Ph.D Courses, constituting a meager 5.8 per cent of the total such registered students. Even among the registered candidates, several who could not get the general fellowships, felt constraint of financial resources. The Ministry's Scheme of Post Matric Scholarships for Scheduled Caste students could not be of much help because of inadequate provisions for maintenance allowance. The scenario, thus, virtually meant constricting opportunities of higher education to otherwise capable Scheduled Caste students. Additionally, education being a feeder to reservation in services, this also adversely affected the availability of Scheduled Caste students for appointments in academic, research and other allied institutions. The RGNF Scheme has a wide range and covers all universities and academic institutions recognized by the University Grants Commission. The eligibility conditions have been tailored to meet the needs of Scheduled Caste students. Any Scheduled Caste student admitted to M.Phil or Ph.D Degree Course in a university or academic institution recognized by the University Grants Commission is eligible for award of fellowship. There is no condition regarding clearing the NET/SLET examinations. Under the Scheme, a total of 1333 Research Fellowships (Junior Research Fellows) per year are awarded to Scheduled Caste students. In the case of non-availability of adequate number of Scheduled Caste candidates, there is a provision for carrying forward of the unavailed fellowships to the next academic session. In case the number of candidates exceeds the number of available awards, the candidates are selected on the basis of percentage of marks obtained in their post-graduate examinations.

5706. (29-1-2008) NEW DELHI : The National Council of the Bharatiya Janata Party expresses its grave concern at the ineffective governance and the complete lack of direction of the United Progressive Alliance Government at the Centre. As the UPA government nears the fourth year of its tenure, a sense of national drift prevails in the country. Never in the history has the impact of the Central government been so negligible; never has India witnessed such political ineffectiveness. The UPA Government merely occupies the seat of power; it has ceased to govern. The UPA is a motley cluster of political parties committed only to vote bank politics and unconcerned about the threats and challenges facing the nation. Ineffective governance and weak leadership are the hallmarks of the UPA government. Divisive vote bank politics is its political strategy; indecision is its recipe for survival. The victims of this political travesty are India and the Indians. National security has been compromised and the lives of ordinary people put at risk. Farmers and weaker sections have suffered from economic mismanagement. Governance in India has always given primacy to the office of the Prime Minister. The UPA's model of governance is repugnant to parliamentary democracy. The Prime Minister is a non-leader; he is at best only a chief executive officer executing the day to day governance on behalf of the extra-constitutional centres of power. As the next General elections approach, it is clear that the Prime Minister is a not a factor in the country's politics. The extra-constitutional centres of power have no parliamentary accountability. Yet they dictate and determine government decisions. Realising this skewed command structure of the Congress Party, the allies of the UPA, both within and outside the government, have pushed the government in all directions. They have sought to pander to their own narrow vote banks and hold political and economic decision-making process to ransom. The UPA has disregarded the dignity and independence of various institutions. Governors have been reduced to partisan institutions. The Election Commission has been sought to be politicized. The CBI has been functioning as a political instrument of the ruling alliance. The callousness of the UPA has led to national security being jeopardized. The UPA is unable to diagnose the problems of national security and obviously unwilling to provide appropriate and effective solutions to the problem. It views the threat to national security from the prism of vote bank politics. No wonder terrorists strike at will across the with unfailing regularity. The situation in Jammu and Kashmir continues to be a cause of concern. An unstable Pakistan in the neighbourhood has added to the worries of India. Terrorist groups both State sponsored and autonomous continue to operate from Pakistani soil. Let alone the safety of citizens of Jammu & Kashmir, even the Chief Minister of the State continues to be the most insecure person. The rehabilitation of the Kashmiri Pandits in the valley remains a distant dream. Members of the minority community even in certain areas of the Jammu Division feel insecure after being reduced to fragile targets. The only intervention of the Central government has been to organize two failed Round Table conferences and giving a clean chit to Pakistan as being a victim of terrorism and thus negating a long standing national position of terrorist organizations being allegedly operating from Pakistan. The recent initiative to compensate families of deceased terrorists in Jammu and Kashmir is an evidence of Terrorist Friendly Policies. The impact of cross-border terrorism is now been increasingly been felt even outside Jammu & Kashmir. The lowering of the guard by the UPA has resulted in a number of terrorist attacks in States governed by UPA and other pseudo-secular parties.

5707. (29-1-2008) NEW DELHI : In an overwhelming response, 24 bidders have submitted their bids for the Commercial Operation, Maintenance of Terminal Building, Development and Operation of Cargo Facilities and Cityside Development of the Udaipur Airport in Rajasthan. The Government had invited bids for Commercial Operation, Maintenance of Terminal Building, Development and

Operation of Cargo Facilities and Cityside Development of the airport. The last date for submitting bids was 24th January 2008.

5708. (29-8-2007) NEW DELHI : Bharatiya Janata Party national president Shri Rajnath Singh set up a committee to investigate into the recent violence in Agra, Uttar Pradesh. The committee would be headed by Shri Vinay Katiyar, Member of Parliament and Party National General Secretary. Other members of the committee are Shri Kishan Singh Sangwan, MP from Haryana and Subash Maharia, MP from Rajasthan and former Union Minister. The committee is rushing to Agra immediately and will submit its report to Shri Rajnath Singh.

5709. (30-1-2008) NEW DELHI : Annual Plan size for Bihar for the year 2008-09 was approved today at a meeting between the Deputy Chairman, Planning Commission, Shri Montek Singh Ahluwalia and Chief Minister of Bihar, Shri Nitish Kumar. The Plan outlay was agreed at Rs.13000 crores this includes additional Central assistance of Rs.100 crores for projects of special importance to the State. It was also agreed that on the basis of mid year performance and absorptive capacities, an additional outlay of Rs.500 crores in the special package of assistance to Bihar based on performance can be included in the Annual Plan for the year 2008-09, taking this to an effective plan size of Rs.13500 crores. Deputy Chairman, Planning Commission, Mr. Ahluwalia complemented the State Government for the major initiatives taken towards administrative reforms, decentralization and simplification of procedures, delegation of powers and also focused attention towards implementation of flagship programmes launched by the Central Government. He said this has lead to acceleration in plan expenditure. He also appreciated efforts being made for improving performance in the sectors of education, health and horticulture. Mr. Ahluwalia said that the Commission was concerned about the problem being faced by the States in executing Centrally sponsored schemes and was looking forward to suggestions aimed at improving implementation by making guidelines flexible wherever necessary. Attention was drawn to the industrial policy launched by the State Government in 2006 and it was pointed out that the policy skewed towards dependence on providing fiscal benefits in the form of subsidy and concessions for attracting investments. This was contrary to the policies being pursued by the Central Government which emphasizes for creation of enabling conditions and removal of impediments. The State Government should identify select industries/sectors which have potential endowment in Bihar in place of conventional approach of giving emphasis to sectors as a whole. Attention was also drawn to high dependence on public sector funding and it was pointed out that efforts should be made to encourage private sector funding in development programmes. The Chief Minister Shri Nitish Kumar said that special plan has been formulated to bring about improvement in sectors like power, road connectivity, irrigation, forestry and watershed development. Social sector is being given top priority. Next year 31 per cent of the development funds would be earmarked for this sector. Irrigation and flood control will also get focused attention with over 13 per cent and 10.93 per cent allocations.

5710. (30-1-2008) NEW DELHI : As per the latest report received from the High Security Animal Disease Laboratory, Bhopal, samples collected from the Suri-I block of Birbhum district, Raghunathganj-II block of Murshidabad district and Chanditala-2 block of Hooghly district have tested positive for Avian Influenza virus on the basis of the rapid tests. Sample from North 24 Parganas is under process and there is no report as yet that it has tested positive. A total of 630 Rapid Response Teams were engaged on 29.01.2008, which completed culling of 1.55 lakh birds taking the cumulative figure of culling so far to 23.23 lakh. Culling mainly remains in the areas which got affected later in the last few days. A total mortality of 1,30,170 poultry birds has been reported from Birbhum, Dakshin Dinajpur, Murshidabad, Nadia, South 24 Parganas, Burdwan, Bankura, Hooghly, Malda, Coochbehar, Purulia, Howrah and North 24 Parganas districts of West Bengal. This number stood at 1,29,777 till yesterday. It is emphasized that eating properly cooked poultry and poultry products is perfectly safe in areas not affected by virus in West Bengal and rest of the country since bird flu is restricted to certain parts of the districts affected in West Bengal.

5711. (30-1-2008) NEW DELHI : It was mid 90s. Ratnakar Shetty ran a successful Udipi restaurant in sub-urban Mumbai. He was a busy man for most part of the year. But when his children's school closed for summer vacations, Shetty yearned to visit his hometown near Mangalore and spend time with his parents. His family too looked forward for a break in the lush green surroundings of their native place. But journey wasn't any easy. He and his family had to perform an arduous road journey via Pune, Belgaum, often in cramped buses, lasting over 30 hours. Reason-there was no direct rail link between Mumbai and the port town of Mangalore. This was the plight of all South Canara people, who had made Mumbai their home. But all that changed on January 26, 1998, when the through line operations from Mumbai to Mangalore began. The Republic Day, ten years ago, was a red letter day for the Indian Railways. The day marked the dream come true of the Indian Railway's most ambitious and most difficult project after Independence. It took seven years and almost $1 billion to complete the missing rail link between Mumbai and Mangalore, winding through the tough terrain of Western Ghats and crossing the rapid flowing coastal rivers in Maharashtra, Goa and Karnataka. It also marked the successful completion of the country's first ever BOT (build, operate, transfer) project. The Konkan Railway Corporation (KR) was formed on July 19, 1990 with participation of four states viz : Maharashtra, Goa, Karnataka and Kerala with the Indian Railways. It's mandate-raise your own funds and construct with speed and economy a railway connecting Mumbai with Mangalore and pay off the loans in the promised time. It was a sweeping challenge and it met its hero in Dr. E. Sreedharan, a veteran railway man known for brisk efficiency. He was persuaded out of his retirement and made the Chairman and Managing Director of the Corporation. The largest railway project in this part of the world, threw up a whole range of difficulties-technical, financial, emotional and psychological. The rocky Sahyadris had to be bored through, 1,500 rivers had to be forded, a railway line had to be built out of nowhere. And once in a while, a poisonous snake, or a tiger, decided to take a close look at goings-on! In the face of collapsing embankments and unrelenting mountains, the engineers had to be tough. Family life took a backseat during those arduous years. Many engineers stayed away from their families during this period, not even returning home for festivals like Diwali. At the very least, working conditions were uncomfortable; in June 1994, Mahad had floods 10 to 12 feet above the road level, and when they receded, Konkan Railway jeeps had six-inch layers of silt on the seats. Dr. Sreedharan had divided the length of 760kms into 7 sectors of approximately 100kms each. Each sector had a Chief Engineer with full freedom of decision making. And with the freedom came, a definite time target. Four concrete sleeper plants were set up to manufacture the 1.3 million sleepers required for the project. Besides this, cement, steel, explosives, rails and a hundred other things had to be delivered through harsh terrain. Depots were created for these. Wherever possible design was standardized to be built with pre-stressed parts cast elsewhere. International norms were followed in evaluating and short listing contractors. Their bids were decided upon within 72 hours of opening. Independent quality assurance inspectors were appointed.

5712. (30-1-2008) NEW DELHI : Finance Minister, Shri P. Chidambaram has approved 34 Foreign Direct Investment proposals recommended by Foreign Investment Promotion Board (FIPB) in its meeting held on 18th January, 2008. The approval amounts to Rs. 2288.40 crore. The proposals are related to Ministries/ Departments, namely, Chemicals & petro-chemicals, Commerce, Health & Family Welfare, Industrial Policy & Promotion, Information & Broadcasting, Posts, Telecommunications, Urban Development and Economic Affairs. The major investment proposals pertain to the Ministries/Departments of Commerce, Information & Broadcasting, Telecommunications, Urban Development and Economic Affairs.

5713. (30-1-2008) NEW DELHI : The outstanding balance of 9.50 per cent Loan, 2008 is repayable at par on February 20, 2008 and no interest will accrue thereon from the said date. In the event of a holiday being declared on February 20, 2008 by any State Government under the Negotiable Instruments Act, 1881, the Loan will be repaid by the paying offices in that State on the previous working day. To facilitate repayment of the Loan on the due date, holders may tender the securities, duly discharged, at the Public Debt Offices, Treasuries/Sub-Treasuries and branches of State Bank of India and its Associate Banks (at which they are enfaced / registered for payment of interest) 20 days in advance of the due date for repayment.

5714. (30-1-2008) NEW DELHI : The Indian Coast Guard completes thirty one glorious years of service to the nation on Friday, Feb.1, 2008. Youngest of the four armed forces, the Coast Guard has grown from strength to strength since its formative years. The organisation that started with just two frigates and five patrol boats leased from the Indian Navy, has grown into a competent and capable force comprising 76 ships including small crafts and 45 aircraft. The force is mandated with the task of protecting the marine wealth and vast ocean resources in the enormous Exclusive Economic Zone of 2.013 million square kilometres. The dedicated efforts of the Coast Guard has resulted in saving 4,049 lives at sea to date, out of them 185 lives were saved in the year gone by-that translates to a life being saved every second day. Since inception, the Coast Guard has apprehended 9,220 foreign fishermen along with 925 fishing vessels for violating the Maritime Zones of India Act. The repatriation of these fishermen back to their countries of origin is a responsibility that also rests on the Coast Guard. 254 personnel have been repatriated to the countries of their origin in the year gone by. The Coast Guard has vigorously pursued its charter for the preservation of marine life. Every year, "Ops Olivia" is conducted to prevent the poaching of the endangered Oliver Ridley turtles along the Orissa coast. The Coast Guard has till date seized 315 boats along with 500 crew involved in poaching these protected species. The Coast Guard also coordinates the National Oil Spill Disaster Contingency Plan. Efforts are underway to make the ports and oil handling agencies self reliant in providing response to oil spills of up to 700 Tons i.e Tier 1 capability. This would leave the Coast Guard to tackle major oil spills even in the deep sea with specialised vessels. The Coast Guard is also assisting the Coastal States in setting up Marine Police Stations and training the police personnel under the Coastal Security Scheme. To date 862 police personnel have been trained and Marine Police stations set up in 41 locations. The emerging security situation in the backdrop of global terrorism calls for the Coast Guard to be at the highest state of vigil. To counter this new challenge, the Coast Guard has stepped up their aerial and surface surveillance to safeguard assets against subversive threats from the sea.

5715. (30-1-2008) NEW DELHI : Shri Kamal Nath, Union Minister of Commerce and Industry, has called for a greater economic engagement between India and Mauritius, when Mr. M.M. Dulloo, Minister of Foreign Affairs, International Trade and Cooperation, Government of Mauritius, met him here today. To strengthen the existing economic ties between the two countries, a Comprehensive Economic Cooperation and Partnership Agreement (CECPA) is under negotiation, and the Preferential Trade Agreement (PTA) is a component of the proposed CECPA, the Minister informed. During 2006-07, India's total exports to Mauritius was $ 736.53 million as against $ 199.43 million in 2005-06, with the growth rate of 269.31%. The total import stands at $ 14.51 million in 2006-07 as against $ 7.33 million in 2005-06 with a growth of 97.95%. The total trade between the two countries was $ 751.04 million in 2006-07 against $ 206.77 million in 2005-06 with a phenomenal growth of 263.23%. India has given assistance to Mauritius for its transformation into a knowledge hub in the fields of medicine, engineering, IT and has agreed to give due consideration to proposals for the setting up of centres of excellence in Mauritius in association with quality Indian educational institutions. The major export items from India to Mauritius include petroleum products, plastic & linoleum products, drugs, pharmaceuticals & fine chemicals, non-ferrous metals and transport equipments. The major import items from Mauritius to India include readymade garments, fabrics, made-ups, man-made & spurn yarn, chemical materials & products etc.

5716. (30-1-2008) NEW DELHI : Smt. Renuka Chowdhury, Minister for Women and Child Development has proposed to bring the implementation of Integrated Child Development Services Scheme (ICDS) under mission mode to ensure more focused approach. She said that it has also been decided to provide Anganwadi to the State on demand, as nutritional support to the children and women is a very high priority in the agenda of the Government. The Minister said that States have been requested to set up special monitoring cell and provide the feedback to the Central Ministry so that corrective steps could be taken immediately for the effective implementation of the ICDS while addressing the Editors' Conference on Social Sector Issues-2008 here today. Briefing about the initiatives taken by the Ministry of Women and Children for the development of children and women, the Minister said that very soon a Bill to check the sexual harassment of the women at the workplace would be brought. Steps were being taken to provide skill upgradation training to women for self-employment in partnership with industrial association like CII, ASSOCHEM. More funds are being allotted to self-help groups and micro financing for the women, she said. Besides setting up of child right commission, the Central Government has proposed an integrated child protection scheme which will be launched very soon to monitor programmes and policies related with the children at the grass root level. Under the programme, infrastructure would be created at the district level to see the implementation of the programmes and take appropriate action. Adoption laws are being simplified so that destitute and orphan children could get family care and juvenile justice act has amended to make it more children friendly. She expressed the hope very soon States would appoint Protection Officers to completely wipe out incidents of child marriage completely from the society.

5717. (30-1-2008) NEW DELHI : The President of India, Smt. Pratibha Devisingh Patil has paid her tribute to the Father of the Nation, Mahatma Gandhi in a message to Mani Bhavan Sangrahlaya, Mumbai on the occasion of his 'Asthi Visarjan' today. "The life and work of Gandhiji is a lesson about tolerance and respect for humanity. He motivated a whole nation-millions of men and women-to fight and attain freedom on the basis of satyagraha and nonviolence. Gandhiji is the Father of the Nation and a symbol of peace and harmony for the world. Gandhiji's message is universal and the observance of 2nd October as the International Day of Non-Violence by the United Nations is a global tribute to Gandhiji's vision and principles, which are even more relevant today than they were during his lifetime. Let us on this day pledge our commitment to Gandhiji's ideals and philosophy".

5718. (30-1-2008) NEW DELHI : The Union Cabinet has approved setting up of a Central Institute of Classical Tamil in Chennai. The decision has been taken for preservation and development of Classical Tamil which is an integral part of India's composite heritage. Chief Minister of Tamil Nadu has been designated as ex-officio chairperson of the institute. The institute would be set up with 100% recurring and non-recurring costs to be borne by the Central Government. The Cabinet has also gave its approval for incurring an expenditure limited to Rs. 76.32 crore over a period of 4 years for the CICT at Chennai. It also gave approval for accepting land admeasuring 17 acres, free of cost from the Government of Tamil Nadu.

5719. (30-1-2008) NEW DELHI : An agreement was signed between the National Brain Research Centre, an autonomous institute of the Department of Biotechnology represented by its director, Prof. V. Ravindranath and the Deputy Director of Inserm, in charge of the strategical affairs M. Thierry Damerval and The President of the University Paris Diderot-Paris VII Professor Guy Cousineau. The agreement signed during the recent visit of the French President to India pertained to the setting up of a joint NBRC-INSERM Associated Laboratory known as "PROTECT", an acronym for Promoting Research Oriented Towards Early CNS (central nervous system) Therapies with a view to extending and strengthening relations in the area of research on developmental brain disorders, that affects millions of children worldwide. The agreement includes a training element for building human capacity and exchange of research scientists from both countries. The mandate of the associated laboratory is to make contributions towards understanding the basic mechanisms involved in developmental brain disorders and help develop novel treatments for neonatal brain disorders. The laboratory will focus on the short term and long term consequences of maternal malnutrition on the progeny, which is an issue of great societal importance and impact. It will also focus on abnormal brain development and whether stem cells can be used in the context of developmental disorders. The associated laboratory will be headed by Dr. Shyamala Mani from NBRC and Dr. Pierre Gressens from U676, Inserm.

5720. (30-1-2008) NEW DELHI : Consequent to the recommendations of the 2nd Pay Revision Committee headed by Justice M. Jagannadha Rao for executives of Central Public Sector Enterprises (CPSEs), the Government has permitted merger of 50% of Dearness Allowance with Basic Pay to the employees of CPSEs following 1997 IDA pattern of scales of pay. The Board of Directors of respective CPSEs can decide on the merger of DA with the approval of their Administrative Ministry. The merger of 50% DA will be subject to the following conditions: (i) Portion of IDA equal to 50% of the existing basic pay in respect of employees in CPSEs following IDA pattern of pay scales at 1997 levels for employees of CPSEs may be merged w.e.f. 1.1.2007 with the basic pay of the employees and shown distinctly as Dearness Pay (DP), which would be counted for purposes like payment of allowances, transfer grant, retirement benefits, contribution to Contributory Provident Fund, Licence Fee, various advances etc. (ii) The merger of IDA equal to 50% of the existing basic pay may be allowed to employees of

CPSEs following IDA pattern of pay scales at 1997 level that are not loss making and are in a position to absorb the additional expenditure on account of merger of 50% of IDA with basic pay from their own resources without any budgetary support from the Government. The budgetary support would not be available for this purpose. (iii) Similar benefits of merger of IDA equal to 50% of the existing basic pay as at sub-para (i) above may also be extended to the employees in the IDA pattern pay scales in the Food Corporation of India. (iv) The entitlements for LTC, TA/DA while on tour and transfer would, however, continue to be governed on the basic pay alone without taking Dearness Pay into account. (v) Portion of Dearness Allowance converted into Dearness Pay would be deducted from the existing rate of Dearness Allowance while computing quantum of Dearness Allowance. (vi) The Board of Directors of each CPSE would consider the proposal for 50% merger of DA with Basic Pay for executives and workmen keeping in mind the capacity of the company to pay and submit a proposal to the Administrative Ministry which will approve the proposal with the concurrence of its Financial Advisor. There are 247 CPSEs in the country as on 31st March, 2007. In total, there are about 16.3 lakh employees in 247 CPSEs as on 31.3.2007. Approximately, 96.4% of the said workforce belong to IDA pattern scales of pay. This decision will benefit most of these employees who are on 1997 IDA scales of pay. With this, one of the major demands of employees of CPSEs has been met by the Government.

5721. (30-1-2008) NEW DELHI : The Cabinet Committee on Economic Affairs today gave its approval for the continued implementation of the ongoing Centrally Sponsored Scheme of Project Tiger during the XI Five Year Plan, at an estimated cost of Rs.600.00 crore, including the following additional components: (i) Rehabilitation/resettlement of denotified tribes/communities involved in traditional hunting; (ii) Mainstreaming livelihood and wildlife concerns in forests outside tiger reserves and fostering corridor conservation through restorative strategy to arrest fragmentation of habitats; (iii) Enhanced village relocation / rehabilitation package for people living in core or critical tiger habitats apart form settlement of rights; (iv) Safeguards / retrofitting measures in the interest of wildlife conservation; (v) Providing basic infrastructure for strengthening the National Tiger Conservation Authority and establishing a monitoring lab in the Wildlife Institute of India; (vi) Establishment and development of 8 new tiger reserves (vii) Provision of project allowance to ministerial staff working in tiger reserves (viii) Fostering ecotourism The implementation of the Scheme would benefit in: (a) protection and conservation of Endangered tiger in tiger reserves as per the recommendations of Tiger Task Force (b) curbing unlawful activities in tiger reserves by strengthening their infrastructure; (c) providing inviolate space for tiger in core or critical tiger habitats; (d) Mainstreaming tiger conservation in the landscape and (e) To provide conditions for increase in tiger population in the country.

5722. (30-1-2008) NEW DELHI : The Cabinet Committee on Economic Affairs today gave its approval for: (a) Changing the mode of upgradation of 60 km stretch of Patna-Muzaffarpur section of NH-19 & NH-77 in Bihar from BOT (Toll) to BOT (Annuity) mode. (b) Authorization to NHAI Board to take decision with regard to award of work on BOT (Annuity) mode The approval will enable the award of project and facilitate implementation of NHDP Phase-III.

5723. (30-8-2007) NEW DELHI : Mr. L.K. Advani said that my interview with the Indian Express at Hyderabad about the Indo-US Nuclear Deal is sought to be projected as the party's u-turn from its earlier position. Actually it was intended to clarify how the BJP's opposition to the agreement stems from considerations of pure national interest, and not from any kind of anti-Americanism which may be motivating the leftist parties. The position of the BJP on this vital question has been stated consistently and unambiguously in a series of statements over the last two years. Each of the statements has been fully deliberated upon and approved by the senior most leaders of the party under the guidance and in the presence of Shri Atal Bihari Vajpayee. These are the statements that my colleagues, Yashwant Sinha and Arun Shourie were asked to release to the media. These statements embody the Party's considered view on every aspect of the deal. There is no change in that position. In my interview, I sought to emphasise that the provisions of the Hyde Act militate against India's sovereignty – in particular, in regard to the conduct of our foreign policy. When enforced, they will seriously impair our nuclear weapons programme, and thereby jeopardize our strategic objectives. The 123 Agreement is the first step towards operationalizing the Hyde Act, and other US laws. Several of the requirements of those laws have been built into the 123 Agreement. Moreover, the Agreement specifically provides that, in implementing it, the party concerned – the US in this case – shall be governed by its national laws. Hence, provisions of the Hyde Act and other relevant laws shall apply with full force. These facts are indisputable – and just as unacceptable. They push the country not into a 'strategic partnership' with the USA but a 'strategic subservience' to the USA, which the BJP cannot accept. A suggestion has been made recently that, as the domestic laws of the US are the ones that are causing the problem, we should examine whether we can alter our laws, such as the Atomic Energy Act, 1962 in such a way as to insulate our strategic objectives. If that can be done, we should strengthen our laws, and, on the basis of those altered laws, renegotiate the 123 Agreement.

5724. (30-1-2008) NEW DELHI : The Cabinet Committee on Economic Affairs today gave its approval for releasing the 50% share of the Central Government for recapitalization of Regional Rural Banks (RRBs) having negative networth. The total amount of recapitalization for the 27 RRBs having negative networth has been assessed at Rs.1,795.97 crore. In view of the 50% stake of the Central Government, contribution of the share of the Central Government will be Rs.897.98 crore, towards recapitalization of RRBs. The amount shall be released to the RRBs along with the contribution by the State Government and the respective sponsor bank. Recapitalization would improve the viability of Regional Rural Banks having negative networth.

5725. (30-1-2008) NEW DELHI : The Cabinet Committee on Economic Affairs today approved the MSP of raw jute for 2008-09 season at Rs.1250/- per quintal for Tosa Desi-5 grade of jute ex-Assam as against the MSP of Rs.1055/- per quintal fixed for 2007-08 season. The increase in MSP for raw jute for 2008-09 season is Rs.195/- per quintal over the MSP fixed for the previous year. The corresponding MSP for other varieties and grades of raw jute across locations will be fixed by the Ministry of Textiles keeping in view, the aggregate scores assigned to different grades of jute, apart from their normal market price differentials. The Jute Corporation of India will continue to act as Central nodal agency to undertake price support operations and the losses incurred, if any, will be reimbursed by the Central Government. The higher MSP is expected to encourage the farmers to invest more for improving quality and yield of jute in the country.

5726. (30-1-2008) NEW DELHI : The Cabinet Committee on Economic Affairs today approved a Centrally Sponsored Scheme of pre-matric scholarship for students belonging to the minority communities through the State Governments/ Union Territory Administrations. The funds to the tune of Rs.1868.50 crore during the XI Five Year Plan (2007-2012) have been approved for the Scheme. Out of this, an amount of Rs.1408.40 crore will be borne by Centre whereas Rs.460.10 crore will be shared by the States. Union Territories would be provided 100 per cent Central assistance. The scheme will be launched during the financial year 2007-08, targeting 25 lakh scholarships for the XIth Five Year Plan (2007-2012). The scholarships will be awarded to students from the minority communities for studies in India in Government or private schools from class I to class X, including residential Government institutes, and eligible private institutes selected and notified in a transparent manner by the State Governments/UTs concerned. 30% of the scholarships will be earmarked for girl students of each minority community in a State/Union Territory and will be transferable to boy students only if eligible girl students are not available. The maximum ceiling of tuition fee entitlement would be Rs.350 per month, subject to actuals. The rates of maintenance allowance would be Rs.600 per month for hostellers from class VI onwards, subject to actuals and Rs.100 per month for day-scholars from class I onwards. Admission fee from class VI onwards would be Rs.500 per annum subject to actuals. 25 lakh scholarships will be given to the meritorious students belonging to the notified minority communities during XI Five Year Plan period for their empowerment through education which is expected to lead to mainstreaming of the minority communities.

5727. (30-1-2008) NEW DELHI : The Union Cabinet today gave its approval for allowing CPWD to proceed with the tendering process (already started) for the combined projects of construction of Afghanistan's Parliament Building and Indian Chancery Complex in Kabul.

5728. (30-1-2008) NEW DELHI : The Union Cabinet today gave its approval; (i) to provide subsidy to Government of Arunchal Pradesh for operating an exclusive MI 172 helicopter service between Guwahati and Tawang initially for a period of one year. Subsidy to State Government for operating this helicopter service beyond one year would based on review of operation of this service at the end of first year of operation; and (ii) The amount of subsidy *i.e.* actual cost of operation of helicopter service minus recovery from passengers would be met on 75:25 basis *i.e.* 75% by the Govt. of India (Ministry of Home Affairs) and 25% by the State Govt. of Arunachal Pradesh. The over all ceiling of flying hours for the proposed helicopter service in Arunachal Pradesh would be 52 hours per month. This would facilitate the movement of tourists and public between Guwahati and Tawang.

5729. (30-1-2008) NEW DELHI : The Union Cabinet today gave its approval for extension of tenure of the Commission for Economically Backward Classes not covered by the existing reservation policy for a period of six months w.e.from 1st February 2008 on the existing terms and conditions. The welfare measures recommended by the Commission would benefit economically backward sections of the society by giving them adequate representation in services.

5730. (30-1-2008) NEW DELHI : The Union Cabinet today gave its approval for extension of the term of the National Commission for Denotified Tribes and Semi Nomadic and Nomadic Tribes from 06.02.2008 to 05.08.2008. With the extensions of term granted, the Commission would be able to submit its Report to the Government.

5731. (30-1-2008) NEW DELHI : The Union Cabinet today gave its approval for extension of the term of the 2nd Administrative Reforms Commission for submission of its Reports by a period of six months, *i.e.* upto 30.09.2008. The 2nd ARC was set up to prepare a detailed blueprint for revamping the public administration system. Implementation of its Reports after due consideration is bound to improve service delivery etc.

5732. (30-1-2008) NEW DELHI : Giving a broad overview of the various ongoing activities in the health arena at the 8th Editor's Conference on Social Sector Issues organized by the Press Information Bureau, the Union Minister for Health & Family Welfare, Dr. Anbumani Ramadoss said that the National Rural Health Mission (NRHM) has set a new standards of partnerships with States where it is the States that determine what is needed to resolve the crisis of the public sector health system. The mission has delivered on every front and across social segments. The impact has been felt across States in the form of improved healthcare and greater access to healthcare.

5733. (30-1-2008) NEW DELHI : In exercise of the powers conferred by clause (1) of Article 217 of the Constitution of India, the President is pleased to appoint

(i) Shri Justice Partha Sakha Datta, and (ii) Shri Justice Prasenjit Mandal, Additional Judges of the Calcutta High Court, to be Judges of the Calcuta High Court, in that order of seniority, with effect from the dates they assume charge of their respective offices.

5734. (30-1-2008) NEW DELHI : MMTC Ltd. has declared interim dividend payout of 35% for 2007-08. During the first nine months of the current year, MMTC achieved its highest ever trading profit of Rs.250.87 crores which is 54% higher than trading profit earned by the company during corresponding period last fiscal. The Profit before tax earned by the company amounted to Rs.177.53 crores as against the Profit before tax of Rs.118.75 crores earned by the company during April 2006-December 2006. MMTC has reported its highest ever profit after tax of Rs115.53 crores which is 33% higher than the profit after tax earned by the company during corresponding period last fiscal. During the period MMTC recorded business volumes of Rs.16884 crores, which includes export business of Rs.2721 crores and import transactions totalling Rs.13350 crores. MMTC's domestic trade during the period was at Rs.813 crores. MMTC is in the process of setting up free trade and warehousing zones on lines similar to Special Economic Zones at Kandla, Haldia and Greater Noida. To accelerate growth and enhance its future sustainability, MMTC is following Public Private Partnership route and has embarked upon various strategic initiatives which include, in broad terms, setting up of a commodity exchange jointly with India-bulls, joining hands with an international producer as a joint venture partner for setting up a gold /silver medallion manufacturing unit, which would also include a gold refinery as an integral part. For effective marketing of the finished products from this unit, as well as jewellery from other sources, MMTC plans to set up in partnership with a leading Indian company, a chain of retail stores at various cities in India for medallions, jewellery and its home-grown brand of 'SANCHI' silverware.

5735. (31-1-2008) NEW DELHI : M/s VSNL, M/s Reliance and M/s Bharti Airtel Ltd., are in constant touch with Telecom Egypt to ensure the speedy repair of the SEMEWE-4 Cable (SMW-4) and FLAG Cable connecting India to Western Europe. Normally repair of such type of submarine optical fibre cable takes 15 days time for restoration, however, it is expected that the links will be completely restored by the ILD operators within 10 days by expediting the repair of cables. It may be recalled that the disorder occurred near Alexandria off the coast of Egypt yesterday. The International long distance traffic and Internet traffic to Europe and USA has got affected due to this fault. Besides India, traffic of other countries is also affected. The circuits working on these cables are being shifted by the International Long Distance operators *viz.* M/s VSNL, M/s Reliance and M/s Bharti Airtel Ltd., to other cables such as SMW-3 cable and pacific route cables etc. to restore the telecommunication links. Out of total links working on these cables, approximately 30 percent links are restored and efforts are being made on war-footing for providing alternate path to remaining links.

5736. (31-1-2008) NEW DELHI : NTPC Limited, India's largest power utility announced highest ever interim dividend of 27% amounting to Rs. 2226.28 crore for the financial year 2007-08 while announcing the unaudited results for the third quarter ended December 2007. Net sales of the company have grown by 10.8% to Rs. 26306.52 crore for the nine months as compared to Rs. 23744.83 crore in the corresponding period last year. For the third quarter ended 31st December 2007, the company has reported sales of Rs 9330.86 crore as compared to Rs. 8525.96 crore during the same quarter previous year. Profit after tax for the nine month period has registered a growth of 18.4%. The profit after tax for nine months period has crossed Rs. 6000 crore mark and is reported as Rs. 6075.34 crore as against Rs. 5130.09 crore for the corresponding period last year. Profit after tax for the third quarter is Rs. 1779.93 crore as compared to Rs 2103.38 crore in the corresponding period last year. However, if one off items are removed from the Profit after tax for the third quarter, the adjusted profit works out to Rs. 1989.88 crore as against Rs 1741.38 crore for the corresponding period last year registering a growth of 14.27%. PLF of coal based station was higher in the first nine months of the year at 93.23% as compared to 91.14% for the corresponding period last year.

5737. (31-1-2008) NEW DELHI : All India Consumer Price Index Number for Industrial Workers (CPI-IW) on base 2001=100 for the month of December, 2007 remained stationary at 134 (one hundred and thirtyfour). During December, 2007, the index recorded decrease of 6 points in Giridih centre, 5 points in Kodarma centre, 4 points each in Tripura and Labac-Silchar centres, 3 points in 3 centres, 2 points in 9 centres and 1 point in 26 centres. The index increased by 5 points in Quilon centre, 3 points in Mundakayam centre, 2 points each in Mysore and Ernakulam centres and 1 point in 12 centres while in the remaining 20 centres the index remained stationary. The decrease of 6 points in Giridih centre is mainly on account of decrease in the prices of Rice, Wheat Atta, Mustard Oil, Onion and Vegetables, while the decrease of 5 points in Kodarma centre is mainly on account of decrease in the prices of Rice, Onion and Vegetables. The increase of 5 points in Quilon centre is mainly due to increase in the prices of Rice and Fish Fresh and that of 3 points in Mundakayam centre is mainly due to increase in the prices of Rice and Fish Fresh.

5738. (31-1-2008) NEW DELHI : A total mortality of 1,31, 981 poultry birds has been reported from Birbhum, Dakshin Dinajpur, Murshidabad, Nadia, South 24 Parganas, Burdwan, Bankura, Hooghly, Malda, Coochbehar, Purulia, Howrah and North 24 Parganas districts of West Bengal. This number stood at 1,30,170 till yesterday. A total of 635 Rapid Response Teams were engaged on 30.01.2008, which completed culling of 1.94 lakh birds taking the cumulative figure of culling so far to 25.16 lakh. Reduction in the number of teams is reported to be on account of work of culling having been completed in some districts. Latest position of destruction of eggs and feed carried out till 30.1.2008 are 2,28,771 and 46,931 kg. respectively. The Agriculture Minister, Shri Sharad Pawar held a meeting with the representatives of the poultry industry on 30th January 2008 to assess the economic impact of the Avian Influenza on the poultry industry in West Bengal and in the rest of the country. Action is being taken to work out a suitable relief package.

5739. (31-1-2008) NEW DELHI : A daylong conference of Law Ministers, Law Secretaries of states and Registrars General of High Court is being held tomorrow to discuss the establishment of Gram Nyayalayas in the country. Organised by the Ministry of Law and Justice, the conference will be chaired by the Union Minister of Law & Justice, Dr. H.R.Bhardwaj. The conference would also deliberate on other related matters like time frame and financial arrangements for the setting up of Gram Nyayalayas. The Gram Nyayalayas Bill, 2007 has already been introduced in the Parliament and examined by the Department related Parliament Standing Committee. The Government has now decided to pursue the Gram Nyayalayas Bill in the Parliament for its enactment. Before enactment of the Bill, the Government has also decided that the implementation aspects in this regard should be further discussed with the Law Ministers of the States.

5740. (31-1-2008) NEW DELHI : NTPC Limited, India's largest power utility announced highest ever interim dividend of 27% amounting to Rs. 2226.28 crore for the financial year 2007-08 while announcing the unaudited results for the third quarter ended December 2007. Net sales of the company have grown by 10.8% to Rs. 26306.52 crore for the nine months as compared to Rs. 23744.83 crore in the corresponding period last year. For the third quarter ended 31st December 2007, the company has reported sales of Rs 9330.86 crore as compared to Rs. 8525.96 crore during the same quarter previous year. Profit after tax for the nine month period has registered a growth of 18.4%. The profit after tax for nine months period has crossed Rs. 6000 crore mark and is reported as Rs. 6075.34 crore as against Rs. 5130.09 crore for the corresponding period last year. Profit after tax for the third quarter is Rs. 1779.93 crore as compared to Rs 2103.38 crore in the corresponding period last year. However, if one off items are removed from the Profit after tax for the third quarter, the adjusted profit works out to Rs. 1989.88 crore as against Rs 1741.38 crore for the corresponding period last year registering a growth of 14.27%. PLF of coal based station was higher in the first nine months of the year at 93.23% as compared to 91.14% for the corresponding period last year.

5741. (31-1-2008) NEW DELHI : The National Commission for Enterprises in the Unorganised Sector (NCEUS), under the Ministry of Micro, Small and Medium Enterprises is finalising yet another report on Unorganised Sector. After holding discussions with all the stakeholders, it will be finalised and submitted to the Government by February-end 2008. This was stated by Dr. Arjun Sengupta, Chairman, NCEUS at the Editors' Conference on Social Sector Issues here today. Earlier NCEUS presented two reports to the Prime Minister, Dr. Manmohan Singh on 5th November, 2007. The two reports are on the 'Financing of Enterprises in the Unorganised Sector' and on 'Creation of a National Fund for the Unorganised Sector' (NAFUS). The recommendation on the creation of a National Fund follows from the first report. Dr. Arjun Sengupta said that the report on 'Financing of Enterprises in the Unorganised Sector' deals with financing of the enterprises in the non-farm unorganised sector. It examines in depth the status of financing of the sector and deals with deficiencies in institutional infrastructure and constraints in financing this sector. The Report, besides giving its recommendation on financing has also made a recommendation for the creation of NAFUS. The second Report submitted to the Prime Minister deals in details with the recommendation of creation of NAFUS. The Report on NAFUS gives the rationale, organizational model, functions and sources of financing of the Fund. The mandate for the creation of this Fund derives from the National Common Minimum Programme of the UPA Government. Giving the details of the proposed Fund, Dr. Sengupta said, the National Fund proposed by the Commission is envisaged as a statutory body funded by the Central Government and Financial Institutions that will primarily focus on non-farm micro enterprises with investment of less than Rs. Five lakh. The Commission's report reveals that this segment constitutes 94 per cent of all small enterprises estimated at 58 million in 2007 with a total employment of 104 million. Dr. Sengaupta further said that this Fund would be created on the pattern of NABARD and exclusively meant for meeting the financing and promotional assistance gaps in the development of the Non Farm Unorganised Sector. Being a statutory body it would leverage funds from the market and national and international institutions to meet its objectives, he added. The Commission had initially proposed a draft Bill "Unorganised Sector Workers (Conditions of Work & Livelihood Promotion) Bill, 2005" for comments and feedback. Based on the comments received from states, trade unions and others, the Commission revised the earlier proposal and has now proposed two Bills "Unorganised Non-agricultural Sector Workers (Conditions of Work and Livelihood Promotion) Bill, 2007" and the "Unorganised Agricultural Sector Workers (Conditions of Work and Livelihood Promotion) Bill, 2007" to cover unorganised agricultural workers and non-agricultural workers respectively. Part 1 of each of the Bills contains provisions relating to the regulation of conditions of work of wageworkers. Part 2 relates to the protection and promotion of livelihoods of the unorganised workers. The Draft Bills provide for basic and minimum conditions of work for all unorganised wage workers and home workers. Instead of relying on costly and time consuming legal redressal procedures, the Commission has accorded priority to conciliation and has proposed the participation of workers' representatives and elected representatives of the local bodies in the conciliation and dispute resolution committees.

5742. (31-1-2008) NEW DELHI : The Rajputana Rifles Regiment contingent has bagged the coveted award for the best marching contingent among the three services at this year's Republic Day parade. The panel of judges also selected the

Central Industrial Security Force (CISF) contingent as the best marching contingent among paramilitary and other auxiliary marching contingents. Raised in 1775, the Raj Rifle Regiment won the Indian Army's first Victoria Cross in 1856. During Kargil War the Regiment played a vital role in capturing the Tololing and Drass Sectors for which it was awarded the Battle Honour Tololing and Drass. Captain Umed Singh Mehra of this Regiment was conferred the highest peace time award, the Ashok Chakra, posthumously. The Regiment has won one Param Vir Chakra, on Ashok Chakra, ten Maha Vir Chakras and eight Kirti Chakras among the prestigious awards. It has to its credit six Arjuna Awards for excellence in sports. The Republic Day contingent of the Regiment was led by Lieutenant Anand A Shirali. On the other hand CISF is the youngest and hi-tech paramilitary force of the country. The force has been given the responsibility of providing security to airports and vital installations across the country besides heritage sites including the Taj Mahal and to VIPs. The Republic Day parade contingent was led by Assistant Commandant Onkar Singh Thakur. In the Children's pageant category, Tiranga Sakshi Hai presented by the students of Kamal Model Sr. Secondary School, Mohan Garden and Vandana International Sr. Secondary School, Sector-10, Dwarka was given the first prize. The second prize in this category went to four Government Girls Schools, Trilokpuri for their presentation Gaurav. South Central Zone Culture Centre, Nagpur was awarded third prize for its dance performance Gour Madia, the bison dance. In the tableaux category, the tableau of Kerala depicting Onam festival was awarded first prize. The second prize went to tableau from Karnataka depicting Hoysala temple. The tableau of Ministry of Human Resource Development on the theme Education of Girl child was awarded third prize.

5743. (31-1-2008) NEW DELHI : Surajkund Crafts Mela 2008 will begin from 01.02.2008. External Affairs Minister Shri Pranab Mukherjee will inaugurate the 15 day extravaganza at Surajkund, Haryana (near Delhi). Addressing media persons on the venue of the Mela, the Union Tourism Secretary Shri S. Banerjee in his capacity as Chairman of the Mela Authority said that the Mela is a part of national festival of Incredible India. He said it is one of the biggest events in the world and unique in that each participating craftsperson is an authentic and outstanding exponent of his/ her art. He said a total number of 350 craft persons/ weavers are to participate in the Mela. In addition, craft persons from SAARC countries and craft persons from the Thailand, Brazil and South Africa have also been invited. He said this year West Bengal is the theme state in the Mela and 61 craft persons from West Bengal will be participating. The major crafts which will be on display from West Bengal are Artistic Leather Craft, Brass & Bell metal, Cane & Bamboo, Ceramic, Clay dolls, Dhokra, Horn work, Jute Products, Masks & Puppets, Papier Mache, Sandalwood Carving, Artistic Weaving, Printing & Painting, Baluchari Saree and Daccai, Cotton Sarees and Jamdani, Needlwork and Embroidery. The Tourism Secretary said cultural evenings are organized at the open air theatre 'Natyashala' daily in the evening from 6.00 P.M. onwards in which renowned artistes from different fields of culture from various parts of the country are invited to perform. He said in addition, more than 200 artistes are invited to perform throughout the day in the Mela area and at Chaupal in the Mela for attraction of the tourists. Shri S. Banerjee said the Mela seeks to provide a forum to most of the states of India to showcase unique traditional cuisine for the interest of visitors/ tourists. During this Mela apart from the food stalls of West Bengal, Punjab, Rajasthan, Chattisgarh, Himachal, Maharastra, Haryana and Gujarat are being put up. He said the daily ticket for a visitor will be Rs. 35 per person. School children sponsored by their school in groups will be given entry free of cost provided they have the necessary letter and teachers accompanying them. He said free entry to school children is planned to sensitize the future generation about the crafts and culture. The children will be able to see from themselves the languishing crafts, the traditional ancient culture, the folk artistes such as Dandia, Gharba. Tarangmail, Sambhalpuri Dance, Bihu, Panthi, Rai, Dhol Nagada, Chakri, Been Sapera, Ghoomer, Puppet Show and Kachhi Ghodi & indulge in camel safari and Kite Flying etc. This kind of display of art and culture in the rural ambience has a powerful impact on inquisitive and observant minds and their thinking. This would go a long way in helping them to take these traditions further. Shri S. Banerjee said adequate arrangements have been made to maintain law and order in and around Mela area.

5744. (31-1-2008) NEW DELHI : Rarely has the discussion on the nature and extent of quality and excellence been as intense as in our times. 'Assessment for quality assurance' is widely known across the world since late 20th century. The movement may be called as the promotion of the 'Assessment Culture'. In India, it has taken a concrete shape only in the last decade of the last century, with the establishment of the National Assessment and Accreditation Council (NAAC) (in 1994) and a few other quality assessment organizations in the public domain, for the assessment of higher education institutions and programmes. The NAAC, with a vision 'to make quality the defining element of higher education in India through a combination of self and external quality evaluation, promotion and sustenance initiatives', has assessed and accredited 3,644 Higher Education Institutions (HEIs) (as on 22/12/2007) and has also undertaken a number of quality promotion activities. There is a mixed response from the HEIs and the academia, to the external quality assessment. Many institutions have voluntarily opted for NAAC assessment and proudly exhibit their accreditation status. Few others have apprehensions about the NAAC assessment process. For a deeper understanding of the complex process of external quality assessment, it may be useful to critically examine the motivational factors for readily seeking NAAC assessment on one hand and the inhibiting factors for hesitations to go for assessment on the other.

5745. (31-1-2008) NEW DELHI : The Memorandum of Understandings (MoUs) of three river water links are likely to be signed soon and there Detailed Project Reports (DPRs) would be taken up immediately thereafter. In respect of Parbati-

Kalisindh-Chambal link, the Union Minister for Water Resources wrote letters to the Chief Ministers of Rajasthan and Madhya Pradesh during January 2007 and again during August 2007. Secretary, Water Resources wrote letters to Chief Secretaries of these two States during February 2007 and again during October 2007 to expedite the matter. With the efforts, the Government of Rajasthan sent draft MoU during November 2007 to the Government of Madhya Pradesh for consideration. The Government of M.P has made further suggestion to the Government of Rajasthan and both are in active dialogue for early consensus. Regarding Par-Tapi-Narmada and Daman-Ganga link, a draft MoU for taking up their DPR was sent to both the States for concurrence during April 2007. Further, the Minister for Water Resources wrote letters to the Chief Ministers of Gujarat and Maharashtra during August 2007. Secretary, Water Resources wrote letters to Chief Secretaries of these two States during October 2007 to expedite their concurrence in this regard. Recently, during the Governing Body meeting of National Water Development Agency (NWDA) on January 9, 2008, the representatives of both the states informed that the matter is under active consideration and response would be sent soon. After persistent efforts by the Government, DPR of one of the priority links namely Ken-Betwa has been taken up by NWDA after signing of MoU between two States in August, 2005 which is likely to be completed during the year 2008. The Inter-linking of Rivers (ILR) Programme is to be pursued in fully consultative manner starting with Southern rivers. Therefore, five links in Peninsular components have been identified as priority links. The issues have also been discussed in details during the meeting of the Consultative Committee of Ministry of Water Resources chaired by the Minister for Water Resources. NWDA has completed pre-feasibility studies of all the 30 links and further feasibility studies of 14 links in Peninsular components and two links (Indian portion) in Himalayan components have also been completed. The work to prepare feasibility reports of balance links are going on.

5746. (31-1-2008) NEW DELHI : Tribal Guests invited to participate in the Republic Day Celebrations met Minister of Tribal Affairs, Shri P.R. Kyindah here today and presented colourful dances. These tribal guests included 60 tribals, one male and one female from each State, representing 37 Scheduled Tribes and 16 Primitive Tribal Groups were invited by the Ministry of Tribal Affairs. Besides witnessing Republic Day Parade tribal guests also had meeting with President, the Vice-President and the Prime Minister of India and Defence Minister. The Ministry of Tribal Affairs also took them to the various places within Delhi for sightseeing. They also enjoyed travelling in Metro Train and visit to Vrindavan, Mathura and Agra. Objective for arranging such visits is to provide opportunities to the tribals to know each other and to have glimpses of cultural heritage of other parts of the country. Felicitating the tribal guests on the occasion, Shri Kyindah said tribals represent a vibrant group of our society. Their welfare has a very high priority of the agenda of the Government. Various programmes and schemes have been initiated by the Government and focus is to provide them all possible opportunities for better education, health care and other development. He said that recently notified Scheduled Tribes and other Traditional Forest Dwellers Act would go a long way to provide land rights to the tribals. He urged for creating mass awareness about the various schemes and programmes so that target groups could take the benefit of the schemes.

5747. (31-1-2008) NEW DELHI : The Minister for Steel, Chemicals and Fertilisers has favoured higher spending by profit making companies in both private and public sector in corporate social responsibility activities. He was speaking here today after receiving the interim dividend cheque from the Manganese Ores India Limited (MOIL). He said the public sector companies under the Steel Ministry are currently spending between 2 to 5 percent of their net profit under various CSR activities and they will step up the expenditure in the coming year. Shri Paswan said, such activities have been benefiting the local population immensely in health care, improvement in educational infrastructure and civic amenities. The MOIL today presented a dividend cheque of Rs.29.69 crore to the Minister from Steel, Chemicals and Fertilisers Shri Ram Vilas Paswan. The company had announced 130 per cent interim dividend. Government of India holds 81.57 percent of the equity in the company..Presenting the cheque the Chairman and Managing Director of MOIL, Shri K.L.Mehrotra said, the company has recorded 67 per cent rise in turnover during the first nine months of this financial year. The turnover rose to Rs.491.90 crore during April-December 2008 from Rs.294.63 crore during the same period last year. Net profit during April-December 2008 recorded a rise of 156 per cent to Rs.205.50 crore from Rs.80.18 crore during the corresponding period last year. Production of Manganese ore during the same period rose 34 percent from 7,03,391 tonnes in 2007 to 9,40,185 tonnes and that of Ferro Manganese went up by 6 percent from 7,800 tonnes during the first nine months to 8,270 tonnes this year. The company has been showing excellent performance for several years. It has been getting Prime Minister's Merit Certificate for achieving excellence in fulfilling the MOU targets continuously for the past 6 years. Considering the excellent performance, the status of MOIL has been upgraded from Miniratna Category II to Category I. The company has entered into a 50:50 Joint Venture agreement with the Steel Authority of India (SAIL) for setting up a ferro alloy project at Bhilai at an estimated cost of Rs.225 crore. It has earmarked Rs.3 crore for carrying a wide variety of corporate social responsibility activities.

5748. (31-1-2008) NEW DELHI : The Union Minister of Shipping, Road Transport and Highways, Thiru T.R. Baalu has approved a sum of Rs. 13.611 crore for the procurement of Ambulances and Cranes for the year 2007-08 under the National Highways Accident Relief Service Scheme. Thiru Baalu approved a sum of Rs. 8,52,60,000 for procurement of 100 ambulances in 21 states and 4 NGOs. 96 ambulances are proposed to be given to the Police and Transport Departments of 21 States *viz.* Andhra Pradesh, Arunachal Pradesh, Assam, Bihar, Chandigarh,

Gujarat, Haryana, Himachal Pradesh, Kerala, Madhya Pradesh, Maharashtra, Meghalaya, Mizoram, Orissa, Punjab, Rajasthan, Sikkim, Tripura, Uttarakhand, Uttar Pradesh and West Bengal. In addition, four NGOs from the States of Gujarat, Maharashtra, Rajasthan and Uttaranchal would be provided one ambulances each under the scheme. The Minister has also approved a sum of Rs. 5,08,50,000/- for the procurement of 30 cranes for providing to the Police and Transport Departments of 11 States *viz.* Arunachal Pradesh, Bihar, Gujarat, Kerala, M.P, Meghalaya, Orissa, Punjab, Rajasthan, U.P and West Bengal.

5749. (31-1-2008) NEW DELHI : Chitranjan Locomotive Works (CLW) produced 134 electric locomotives against the target of 132 electric locomotives and Diesel Locomotive Works (DLW) produced 170 diesel locomotives against the target of 163 diesel locomotives during first nine months of the fiscal 2007-08 (April-December 2007). Rail Coach Factory (RCF) produced 1053 coaches against the target of 1044 coaches where as Integral Coach Factory (ICF) produced 906 coaches against the target of 912 coaches during the same period. Rail Wheel Factory (RWF) produced 101507 wheels and 33949 axles against the target of 95203 wheels and 34049 axles during April-December 2007. During the month of December 2007, CLW, DLW, ICF, RCF and RWF have produced 19 electric locomotives, 16 diesel locomotive, 118 coaches, 136 coaches, 14402 wheels and 6009 axles respectively against the target of 20 electric locomotives, 18 diesel locomotive, 100 coaches, 133 coaches, 11301 wheels and 5982 axels. The punctuality percentage of mail/express trains was 90.8 per cent in Broad Gauge and 99.1 per cent in Metre Gauge during the month of December 2007 compared to 88.8 per cent and 99.5 per cent respectively during the same period last year. Railways have realized an amount of Rs. 21 crore approximately during the month of December 2007 through ticket checking.

5750. (31-1-2008) NEW DELHI : The delegations of the Government of India and the Aeronautical Authorities of the Government of the Sultanate of Oman met in New Delhi on 29-30 January 2008 to discuss matters relating to operation of air services. While agreeing on designation of multiple airlines both sides also decided to enhance the existing traffic entitlement to 11,550 seats per week in each direction with immediate effect. For the Sultanate of Oman-Bangalore and Calicut have been included as an additional point of call besides Mumbai, New Delhi, Kochi, Thiruvananthapuram, Chennai, Hyderabad, Lucknow and Jaipur The request of the Omani side to grant Mangalore as an additional point of call in India will be considered only after Mangalore is declared an International Airport. For India the points of call in Oman are Muscat and Salalah. The designated airlines of the Sultanate of Oman can use any point an 'intermediate points' or 'beyond points' but without fifth freedom traffic rights. The designated Indian carriers can use any points in Asia including points in UAE, Qatar and Bahrain as 'intermediate points' and any point in Europe, North America and Asia including points in UAE, Qatar and Bahrain as 'beyond points'. With the overall entitlement of 11,550 seats, the designated airlines of Bahrain shall operate not more than fourteen frequencies/ 2,156 seats per week to Mumbai, seven frequencies/ 1,078 seats per week to New Delhi, seven frequencies/1,078 seats per week to Kochi, seven frequencies/1,078 seats per week to Thiruvananthapuram, seven frequencies/1,078 seats per week to Hyderabad, seven frequencies/1,078 seats per week to Lucknow, six frequencies/924 seats per week to Jaipur and six frequencies/ 924 seats per week to Bangalore. Both sides have decided to free up all limitations on the cargo services. There will be no restrictions in terms of frequency and point of call for operating cargo services.

5751. (31-1-2008) MALAPPURAM: The district conference of the Communist Party of India (CPI) will begin here on Thursday. The four-day conference will discuss in depth the recent political changes in the State as well as across the world. The party flag will be carried to Malappuram from Veliyamkode and will reach the conference venue on Thursday evening. Veteran Communist leader N.C. Moideen will hoist the party flag at Kottappadi grounds at 5 p.m. on Thursday. A mass rally, accompanied by a volunteer march, will be taken out through Malappuram town on Friday evening. The rally will begin from Munduparamba Bypass Junction at 4 p.m. CPI State secretary Veliyam Bhargavan will inaugurate the public meeting at Kottappadi grounds on Friday evening. Forest Minister Benoy Viswom, Agriculture Minister Mullakkara Ratnakaran, CPI State assistant secretary C.N. Chandran, CPI national council member M. Rahmatullah, and Deputy Speaker Jose Baby will address the public meeting. Poet Balachandran Chullikkad will inaugurate a cultural meet on Saturday evening. Minister Benoy Viswom will preside over the meet. Poets P.K. Gopi, Alankode Leelakrishnan and Manamboor Rajanbabu will address the conference. A comedy show by Jayaraj Warrier and team and musical orchestra by Tajuddeen Vadakara will follow the cultural meet. The delegates' meet will be held at Municipal bus-stand Auditorium on Saturday and Sunday. On Friday evening, drama troupe K.P.A.C. will stage its play, 'Asthamikkatha Sooryan', at Kottappadi grounds.

5752. (31-1-2008) NEW DELHI : Retail prices of farm commodities monitored by the Department of Consumer Affairs have generally remained steady or shown mixed trend over the week ending January 25, 2008. During the week ending January 25, 2008 prices of wheat remained steady at most of the monitoring centres. Prices increased only at Delhi, Jaipur and Patna. Prices of sugar remained steady at almost all the monitoring centres. Prices increased at Mumbai and Agartala. Prices of gram dal remained steady across majority of the monitoring centres. Prices increased at Jaipur, Patna, Bangalore and Thiruvananthapuram and declined at Mumbai. Prices of tur dal increased at Patna and declined at Ahmedabad, Mumbai, Chennai and Thiruvananthapuram. Out of 12.98 lakh tonne pulses contracted for import, 9.98 lakh tonne have arrived in the country by 22.1.08. In Delhi, prices of atta, gram, rice, mustard oil, tea, potato and onion held steady for one week. Prices of tur, sugar, groundnut, milk and salt held steady for one month. Prices of wheat and vanaspati, however, rose by Re 1 and Rs. 2 per kilo respectively.

5753. (31-1-2008) NEW DELHI : The delegations of the Government of India and the Government of the Kingdom of Bahrain met in New Delhi on 29-30 January 2008 to review the Bilateral Air Services Agreement between the two countries. While agreeing on designation of multiple airlines both sides also decided to enhance the existing traffic entitlement to 11,500 seats per week in each direction with immediate effect. For the Kingdom of Bahrain Hyderabad has been included as an additional point of call besides Mumbai, Delhi, Chennai, Bangalore, Kochi and Kolkata. The designated carriers of India for Bahrain can use any points in Asia including points in UAE Oman and Qatar as 'intermediate points' and any points in Europe, North America, Asia including points in UAE, Oman and Qatar as 'beyond points'. With the overall entitlement of 11,500 seats, the designated airlines of Bahrain shall operate not more than seven services per week each to/from Thiruvananthapuram, Kochi and not less than two services per week to-Kolkata. Both sides have decided to free up all limitations on the cargo services. There will be no restrictions in terms of frequency and point of call for operating cargo services. With the successful conclusion of this agreement airline of both sides will be able to add new services on the Indian-Bahrain route, which will be in the interest of the travellers. The Indian delegation was led by Shri R.K. Singh, Joint Secretary in the Ministry of Civil Aviation while the Bahrain delegation was led by Captain Abdul Raham Mohammad Al-Goaud, Under Secretary for Civil Aviation Affairs in the Kingdom of Bahrain.

5754. (31-1-2008) NEW DELHI : "Household Consumer Expenditure in India, 2005-06"-Report No. 523 based on the data of 62nd round survey of National Sample Survey Organisation (NSSO) in the Ministry of Statistics and Programme Implementation, Government of India, has been released. The field work of the survey was carried out during July 2005-June 2006. Data collected included commodity-specific information on 148 items of food, 13 items of fuel, 28 items of clothing, bedding and footwear, 18 items of educational and medical expenses, 52 items of durable goods, and about 85 other items. The present report contains the information on distribution of households and persons by 12 classes of household monthly per capita consumer expenditure (MPCE), average MPCE, composition of MPCE by item category (cereals, pulses, clothing, etc.), quantity and value of per capita consumption of different cereals, distributions of households or persons by other characteristics such as educational level, structure and area of dwelling unit, and energy sources used for cooking and lighting etc. The estimates are provided separately for rural and urban sectors at State level as well as for all-India. No separate estimate is provided for small States & UT's due to small sample size, instead, in such cases the estimates have been provided for a group of States/ UT's. The survey covered the whole of the Indian Union except (i) Leh (Ladakh) and Kargil districts of Jammu & Kashmir, (ii) interior villages of Nagaland situated beyond 5 kilometres from the bus routes and (iii) villages in Andaman and Nicobar Islands which remain inaccessible throughout the year. The survey was spread over a randomly drawn sample of 39436 households spread over 4750 villages and 5120 urban blocks, The earlier survey on the same subject was the NSS 61st round quinquennial survey (2004-05) spread over 7999 villages and 4602 urban blocks covering 1,24,644 households (79,298 in rural areas and 45,346 in urban areas) and enumerating 6,09,736 persons. The main characteristics associated with household consumer expenditure are broadly comparable at the national level. However, at State/UT level comparison of the results of this round with the quinquennial round on some of the characteristics needs to be attempted with due caution.

5755. (31-1-2008) NEW DELHI : The total approximate earnings of Indian Railways on originating basis during the period 10th January-20th January 2008 were Rs. 2037.44 crore compared to Rs. 1783.91 crore during the same period last year, registering an increase of 14.21 per cent. The total goods earnings have gone up from Rs. 1264.73 crore during 10th January-20th January 2007 to Rs. 1459.76 crore during 10th January-20th January 2008, showing an increase of 15.42 per cent. The total passenger revenue earnings during the period 10th to 20th January 2008 were Rs. 510.17 crore compared to Rs. 459.07 crore during the same period last year, reflecting an increase of 11.13 per cent. The revenue earnings from other coaching amounted to Rs. 48.17 crore during this period compared to Rs. 41.53 crore during the same period last year, showing an increase of 15.99 per cent. The total approximate number of passengers booked during the period 10th to 20th January 2008 were 177.68 million compared to 176.91 million during the same period last year, showing an increase of 0.44 per cent. In the suburban and non-suburban sectors, the number of passengers booked during 10-20 January 2008 were 100.96 million and 76.72 million compared to 102.49 million and 74.42 million during the same period last year, registering a decrease of 1.49 per cent and an increase of 3.09 per cent respectively.

5756. (31-1-2008) NEW DELHI : Wetlands are defined as lands transitional between terrestrial and aquatic eco-systems where the water table is usually at or near the surface or the land is covered by shallow water (Mitch and Gosselink, 1986). The value of the world's wetlands is increasingly receiving due attention as they contribute to a healthy environment in many ways. They retain water during dry periods, thus keeping the water table high and relatively stable. During periods of flooding, they mitigate floods and trap suspended solids and attached nutrients. Thus, streams flowing into lakes by way of wetland areas will transport fewer suspended solids and nutrients to the lakes than if they flow directly into the lakes. The removal of such wetland systems because of urbanization or other factors typically causes lake water quality to worsen. In addition, wetlands are important feeding and breeding areas for wildlife and provide a stopping place and refuge for waterfowls. As with any natural habitat, wetlands are important in supporting species diversity and have a complex of wetland values. The present review is aimed at providing, in a nutshell, the distribution of wetlands, the value of wetlands, the causes and consequences of the loss of wetlands. The review attempts to provide a glimpse of the use of modern spatial technology tools, *viz.*, Remote Sensing/GIS for obtaining an assessment, description and monitoring of inland wetlands. The review also gives a methodology for an ongoing nationwide attempt at evolving a conservation area network or a protected area network of inland wetlands.

5757. (31-1-2008) NEW DELHI : The Government has announced the National Awards for E-Governance for 2007-08. Seeking to recognize and promote excellence in implementation of E-governance initiatives, the awards will be given away by Shri A. Raja, Minister for Communication and Information Technology during the 11th National Conference on E-Governance to be held at Panchkula, Haryana on February 7-8, 2008. Grapenet, the project of Agriculture and Food Product Export Development Authority (APEDA), Ministry of Commerce & Industry, Government of India has been awarded the Gold under the newly introduced Special Sectoral Award Category, which had Agriculture as the focus sector for 2007-08. The Internet Ticketing Project of Indian Railways Catering & Tourism Corporation has been awarded the Gold in the Category-Outstanding Performance in Citizen Centric Service Delivery, while the Gold for the best government website has been awarded to the Government of Tamil Nadu.

5758. (31-1-2008) NEW DELHI : One MiG-27 aircraft of Indian Air Force Crashed near Air Force Station Hashimara on 31 Jan 08 at 1240 hrs. The aircraft had got airborne from Hashimara airbase and was on a routine training flying mission. The pilot Wg Cdr J Singh ejected safely. There was no damage to civil property and no individual was injured/killed as a result of air crash. An inquiry has been ordered to investigate the reasons for the accident.

5759. (31-1-2008) NEW DELHI : The Indian Railways set another feather to its excellent performance by dispatching Diesel Multiple Units (DMUs) coaches to Angola, the first ever export of Indian manufactured DMUs to the world market. The fifteen DMU coaches, six each for two trains and three for self propelled accident relief train, manufactured by Integral Coach Factory (ICF), production unit of Indian Railways, Chennai and exported to Angola by RITES, were flagged off for export to Angola by the Minister of State for Railways, Shri R. Velu at a ceremony at Chennai today. Speaking on the occasion, Shri Velu said that the Indian Railways has achieved another milestone as it is for the first time that such DMUs designed and manufactured by ICF are being exported. He said that this export of DMUs to Angola shall bring great laurels to Indian Railways and to our country and open new vistas for similar exports in future. ICF has always been in the forefront to accept new challenges put forth by ever increasing needs of coaching stock for Indian Railways to satisfy domestic passenger rail traffic. The present endeavour of designing and manufacture of DMUs, self-propelled accident relief train and other coaches for export to Angola is testimony of ICF's continued initiative to partner with RITES to boost exports on a sustainable basis. ICF have so far manufactured 230 varieties of different designs of coaches and is still venturing into new designs and assimilating the latest technology available to provide the best comfort to the passengers, the Minister said. The Minister further said that manufacture and dispatch of these DMUs and the self propelled accident relief train mark the successful completion of various on-going projects undertaken by RITES in Angola which include technical assistance, up-gradation of maintenance workshops and earlier export of passenger coaches manufactured in ICF and Diesel locomotives manufactured in DLW, Varanasi. The Minister appreciated RITES for achieving highest ever turnover of Rs. 265 crore in 2006-07 from export of locomotives and rolling stock as against previous best of Rs. 110 crore achieved in 2001-02. RITES has been a pioneer in executing Railway related export projects in a variety of Railway Systems of different gauges all over the world. RITES has worked in about 60 countries worldwide and has undertaken a variety of projects of versatile nature and multiple complexities. Some of the major projects have been undertaken in countries like Myanmar, Vietnam, Mozambique, Tanzania, Ghana, Zambia, Bangladesh, Sri Lanka, Sudan, Senegal, Mali and Angola.

5760. (1-2-2008) NEW DELHI : The Prime Minister, Dr. Manmohan Singh has condoled the passing away of renowned journalist Shri R.K. Karanjia. In his message the Prime Minister said, "I am deeply grieved to learn of the sad demise of Shri R.K. Karanjia, a renowned journalist of our country. Shri Karanjia was a respected and veteran journalist who received acclaim and recognition within and outside India for his rich contribution to the world of journalism. His outstanding achievements, as a media personality set many new landmarks in the field of journalism. On this sad occasion, I convey my heartfelt condolences to the members of his bereaved family and to his numerous friends, associates and admirers. I pray that the departed soul may rest in peace."

5761. (1-2-2008) NEW DELHI : The Union Minister for Rural Development, Dr. Raghuvansh Prasad Singh launched a website on National Rural Employment Guarantee Act (NREGA) here today. Addressing media persons on the eve of the completion of two years of the enforcement of the Act here today the minister said in this website www.nrega.nic.in maximum transparency will be insured through by placing all data in public domain. The web enabled MIS (www.nerga.nic.in) will be equally accessed by everyone. This includes Workers' entitlement data and documents such as registration, Job Cards, Muster Rolls; Work selection and execution data including, shelf of approved and sanctioned works, work estimates, works under execution, measurement; Employment demanded provided; and Financial indicators such as, funds available, funds used, and the disaggregated structure of fund utilization to assess the amount paid as wages, materials and administrative expenses. Since the MIS places all critical data on the web and this data is software engineered, it has significant advantages in terms of transparency as it allows cross verification of records and the generation of reports on any parameter of the Act. Dr. Singh said NREGA is being implemented with full vigour and during the year 2007-08 the Wage Employment has been provided to 2.57 crore rural households against the demand of 2.61 crore households in all phase I and II districts upto December 2007 during 2007-08. More over, 85.51 crore person days have been generated. Out of which the Share of ST & SC was 58.29% (ST-31.06%,SC-27.23%) and Women was 44%. The total funds utilization was Rs. 9105.74 crore. The wage share during the year has been 67% and expenses on material & administrative contingency have been 33% against the permissible ratio of 60:40. During the year, 1231130 works have been taken up. More than 50% of the works are on water conservation. Although the programme is not confined to BPL families, experience in almost all States is that most BPL families have been able to demand employment under NREGA. At the National level, the demand for employment is 157% of the BPL rural households. It is near 100% or more than that in most of the States. This shows that the programme has reached out to the most needy households in the States where employment demand as a percentage is more than rural BPL households. On Gender Equity: Women Work Force Participation Ratio the Minister said at the National level the Women's ratio in work force participation under NREGA is 44% which is higher than the 1/3rd earmarked for women under the Act. Dr. Singh said Field Reports yield nascent evidence of reduction in distress migration especially in Rajasthan, AP, Chattisgarh, Orissa. Positive impact on land productivity to yield additional on SC/ST farms in Chattisgarh, MP, Rajasthan. Increase noticed in workforce's awareness of minimum wages and task rates, increase in Wage earnings of workforce in wage employment programme especially in AP, TN, Maharashtra, Chattisgarh, Jharkhand, wage negotiation capacity of wage earners developing vis a vis private employment in Rajasthan, TN, Haryana, increase in Women workforce participation as compared to 26.24% in SGRY, financial inclusion in the form of savings accounts of wage earners in Banks/Post Offices started in some States like AP, Karnataka & Jharkhand, insurance of wage earners in some districts like Pakur, Gumla, Ranchi (Jharkhand), developing literacy skills among wage earners (Raichur in Karnataka), convergence with other development programmes: Jetropha (Chattisgarh, MP) Forest Nurseries (Udaipur in Rajasthan, Khandwa in MP). He said further improvements in use of MIS through computerisation of the Blocks, data consistency and GIS based planning are planned and instructions have been given that all muster rolls to be on the NREGA website, Campaign for 100% verification of muster rolls has been launched in all districts, civil society organizations have been enlisted for muster roll verification. He said Citizen Information Boards on each work site with the details of works taken up are being put in place.

5762. (1-2-2008) NEW DELHI : Government of India have announced the sale (re-issue) of "12.25 percent Government Stock, 2010" under Market Stabilization

Scheme for a notified amount of Rs. 4,000 crore (nominal). The Government Stock will be sold through price based auction using multiple price method. The auctions will be conducted by the Reserve Bank of India, Mumbai Office, Fort, Mumbai on February 7, 2008 (Thursday). Up to 5 per cent of the amount notified for the sale of stock is reserved for allotment to eligible individuals and Institutions on non-competitive basis as per the Scheme for Non-Competitive Bidding Facility in the Auction of Government Securities. Bids in the prescribed form obtainable from the Regional Director, Reserve Bank of India, Mumbai Office (Public Debt Office), Fort, Mumbai-400 001 and RBI website www.rbi.org.in should be submitted to that Office on February 7, 2008. The NDS members should submit competitive as well as non-competitive bids in electronic format using Primary Market Operation (PMO) module of NDS.

5763. (1-2-2008) NEW DELHI : Government of India have announced the sale (re-issue) of "8.20 per cent Government Stock, 2022 for a notified amount of Rs. 5,000 crore (nominal) through a priced based auction using multiple price method. Government of India have also announced the sale (re-issue) of "8.33 per cent Government Stock, 2036" for a notified amount of Rs. 4,000 crore (nominal) through a price based auction using multiple price method. The auctions will be conducted by the Reserve Bank of India, Mumbai Office, Fort, Mumbai on February 8, 2008 (Friday). Up to 5% of the notified amount of the sale of both the stocks will be allotted to eligible individuals and Institutions as per the Scheme for Non-Competitive Bidding Facility in the Auction of Government Securities. Bids in the prescribed form obtainable from the Regional Director, Reserve Bank of India, Mumbai Office (Public Debt Office), Fort, Mumbai-400 001 and RBI website www.rbi.org.in should be submitted to that Office on February 8, 2008. The NDS members should submit competitive as well as non-competitive bids in electronic format using Primary Market Operation (PMO) module of NDS.

5764. (1-2-2008) NEW DELHI : A delegation of Senior and Eminent Electronic Media Journalists and News Editors of NewsX Channel called on the Union Minister of Information and Broadcasting, Shri P.R. Dasmunsi, today and explained about the injustice and the shocking treatment being meted out to them by the security staff and other persons and later on they were sacked. Shri P.R. Dasmunsi has issued the following statement: "Keeping in view the independence and autonomy of the Media, neither the Government nor the Ministry ever interferes and shall not intervene in the internal affairs or administration of any media house or channel. But the manner in which the eminent Editors have been treated and the rights of media personnel have been reportedly infringed upon is really a matter of great concern for free and fair journalism in the country. Minister has been apprised of the serious allegations including source of channel funding which Minister is not competent to react, and accordingly, has referred the matter to the concerned desk of the Finance Ministry to ascertain the facts through their investigation wing. Minister makes an appeal to all media channels that whenever any media personnel is engaged on some contract, their contractual terms should be valued and honoured including the financial clauses. Otherwise, hire and fire mechanism shall not provide honour and confidence to the engaged media personnel in the country, wherever they may be".

5765. (1-2-2008) NEW DELHI : The Vice President of India Mohd. Hamid Ansari released the book titled "Rescuing the Future Bequeathed Misperceptions in International Relations" authored by Shri.Jagat S. Mehta, former Foreign Secretary, here today. Addressing on the occasion, the Vice President said that we are still not getting enough by way of old history and we owe to our history. Encouraging others to share their experiences. He said that the history writing should get support from all of us. Congratulating Shri Mehta for his remarkable book, the Vice President said that the book gives a complete overview of the contemporary diplomatic experiences. Earlier Shri Mehta presented a brief description of his book. The Foreign Secretary Shri Shiv Shankar Menan also addressed on the occasion. A number of dignitaries and former diplomats were present on the occasion.

5766. (1-2-2008) NEW DELHI : Dr. Shakeel Ahmed speaking in Hindi said that some of the newspapers today carried the statement of Shri L.K. Advani who has alleged that Taslima Nasreen has been kept under house arrest by the Central government. I can very well say that Taslima Nasreen is not under house arrest but due to security reasons she has been kept separately in a safe place. It has been the tradition in India that we give shelter to those who seek asylum in India but we also ask them to abide by the code of conduct and not to violate it or do anything which might hurt the sentiments of the Indian people. If Shri Advani was so concerned about Taslima then why was she not allowed to stay in Jaipur for more than 24 hours after she left Kolkata? Rajasthan is a state ruled by the BJP hence he should ask the state chief minister as to why such a thing happened. This is a sensitive issue and security is a state matter and the Centre cannot put pressure on any state. Therefore Shri Advani should think twice before making such a statement. The Congress Party had given a slogan "Congress ka haath aam aadmi ke saath" and this statement was made true when the telecom department decided to give insurance cover to all subscribers of BSNL, the biggest company in the private sector. There are around 4 crore BSNL subscribers who will be covered under this scheme which is Rs.50,000 against death or permanent disability. We do want to earn profit and also fulfil social obligations and that is what the UPA government is trying to do. To a question as to why this facility is limited to BSNL only and not to MTNL, Dr. Ahmed said that when discussions were in progress the MTNL CMD was present and was persuaded to follow this scheme and I believe MTNL will follow suit in time to come. To a question as to why Shri Murli Deora or Shri Chidambarma do not have concern about the aam aadmi? Dr. Ahmed said that they too have their concern for the aam aadmi and I can understand your point of reference to the fuel price rise. The Congress Party does not want to put burden on the aam aadmi but you all know that the price of oil has risen in the international market and therefore, our oil prices depend on the international market rate which fluctuates. The UPA government, however, is working out plans that no extra burden is thrust upon the common man but at times the price of oil depends more on circumstances beyond their control. To a question whether an increase of Rs. 2 or Rs. 1 is OK for the common man? Dr. Ahmed said that I cannot say anything. It is for the Petroleum Ministry to decide. The stand of the Congress Party is very clear and we do not want to burden the common man. To a question that Smt. Mayawati has written to the Prime Minister that Muslim and Christian Dalits too should get separate reservation. Dr. Ahmed said that this is a long-standing demand and the Muslim and Christian dalits should get all those facilities like all other dalits are getting in different communities. Suggestions have been made and the government is working on those suggestions. It is a sensitive issue therefore we would like to have a unanimous opinion on this issue by all political parties. To a question that you are talking about social obligation but the Prime Minister and Finance Minister want to divest this country of the public sector which they say is a burden on the common man? Dr. Ahmed said that he did not hear or see any statement made in this regard by the Prime Minister or the Finance Minister. To a question on the statement made by Bal Thakrey about the festival of "Chhat" performed by Biharis, Dr. Ahmed said that Shri Thakrey has made a wrong statement which hurts the faith and sentiments of all Biharis. This should be condemned by everyone and he should apologise to the nation. To a question whether the Congress Party supports the suspension of IAS officials by Mayawati in Uttar Pradesh? Dr. Ahmed said that the Congress Party does not support their suspension we are rather surprised than disappointed. The Book "Sultanpur—yesterday and today" was written by an officer of the state government and the foreword was written by a District Magistrate and the Commissioner of Faizabad and the officer had simply mentioned about the role of a public representative including Shri Rahul Gandhi, Shri Rajiv Gandhi, Smt. Sonia Gandhi and others who represented the constituency of Sultanpur and three of the Assembly segments fall under Shri Rahul Gandhi's constituency. So, it is unfortunate that a bureaucrat is appreciating the role of Shri Rahul Gandhi and if he or she is punished for this, then it is very unfortunate in our opinion.

5767. (1-2-2008) NEW DELHI : Avian influenza is an infection caused by viruses. These viruses occur naturally by birds-particularly among migratory waterfowl and ducks. Often unaffected themselves, the host birds spread the infection to domesticated chicken and ducks-that can catch the virus adapted to waterfowl and have it rapidly mutate into a form that kills in days over 90% of the entire flock and spread to other flocks. Infected birds shed influenza virus in their saliva, nasal secretions and faeces. Domesticated birds may become infected with avian influenza virus through direct contact with infected waterfowl or other infected poultry or through contact with surfaces (such as dirt cages) or materials (such as water or feed) that have been contaminated with virus. Due to significant species barrier, the virus does not easily cross over to humans. However, confirmed cases of human infection have been reported since 1997. Most cases of avian influenza infection in humans have resulted from direct contact with sick or dead infected poultry or surfaces contaminated with secretion/excretions from infected birds. During an outbreak of avian influenza among poultry, there is a possible risk to people who have contact with infected birds or surfaces that have been contaminated with secretions or excretions from infected birds. Often, flu viruses that cross from animals to humans originate in areas where people live in proximity to chickens and pigs. That is because pigs are susceptible to infection with both avian and human viruses and so are an ideal "mixing bowl" in which viruses can exchange genes. Dogs and cats are also susceptible.

5768. (1-2-2008) NEW DELHI : The total mortality of birds on 31st January 2008 was of the order of 393, all of which were reported from South 24 Parganas and Birbhum. A total mortality of 1,32, 374 poultry birds has been reported from Birbhum, Dakshin Dinajpur, Murshidabad, Nadia, South 24 Parganas, Burdwan, Bankura, Hooghly, Malda, Coochbehar, Purulia, Howrah and North 24 Parganas districts of West Bengal. A total of 421 Rapid Response Teams were engaged on 31.01.2008, which completed culling of 2.1 lakh birds taking the cumulative figure of culling so far to 27.27 lakh. The revised target of culling is 27.79 lakhs. Latest position of destruction of eggs and feed carried out till 31.1.2008 are 2,31,966 and 60,810 kg. respectively. There were reports of death of two bar-headed geese in Jammu and Kashmir. The State has reportedly sent samples to the HSADL, Bhopal, which would be tested on receipt in the said laboratory.

5769. (1-2-2008) NEW DELHI : On the occasion of the 67th Anniversary of Army Dental Corps, Mrs. Kirti Kapoor, President Army Wives Welfare Association (AWWA) launched a joint initiative by the Army Dental Corps with AWWA here today. This Mother & Child Oral Health Care Program, is the first of its kind will encompass educating the wives of the combatants about various preventive and curative measures for the better oral health of the family members. Lt Gen Paramjit Singh, Director General of Dental Services during the inauguration of the programme brought out that this endeavour will be implemented through a series of lectures during family welfare meets, free distribution of oral health pamphlets, free check ups of mothers and children and imparting training to the oral health educators and propagators. Oral health is a very good indicator of overall health practice in a community. Not only is it preventable, inexpensive and less time consuming to recognize and intervene dental problems early, but also involves primary non invasive management. Even though there are many different health issues common to both men and women, they can manifest more often and differently in women. Compared to men, genetic and hormonal factors may cause women to have more frequent and intensified responses to the oral bacteria that initiate gum problems. Oral hygiene practices, hormonal influences on women's oral health and systemic diseases, and how puberty, menstruation, pregnancy and menopause influence oral health are important and frequently overlooked women's health issues. If a child has poor oral health habits, the mother can work towards changing them provided she is aware and counselled of the status. It is much easier to modify these habits in a child than in an adult. Since a child models its behaviour after the mother, it follows that she should serve as a positive role model in oral hygiene habits. A healthy smile, good breath and strong teeth all contribute to a young person's sense of personal appearance, as well as confidence and self-esteem. In the backdrop of the armed forces scenario, the wife of the serving personnel more often than not finds herself at the helm of affairs in terms of increased responsibility of the family household and its health due to long periods of absence of the latter, attributable to unavoidable service exigencies. Therefore it is the initiative of the Army Dental Corps in association with the AWWA to launch a nationwide unique campaign to propagate and foster healthy oral health practices in the community by targeting the most effective clientele, the mother and child.

5770. (1-2-2008) NEW DELHI : The Ministry of Rural Development considers bio-diesel as a potential fuel which is capable of providing employment also at rural level and hence all possible help is being provided to promote its culivation especially in the Wasteland areas. Addressing the National Convention on Climate Change and Bio-Diesel 2008 at FICCI auditorium here today the Union Minister for Rural Development, Dr. Raghuvansh Prasad Singh asserted that apart from reducing green house gas emissions bio-feuls can be an effective options to stimulate rural development, create jobs and provide energy security. Dr. Singh said under Desert Development Programme (DDP) of his ministry an allocation of Rs. 50 crore was made to promote the cultivation of Jatropha in the rural areas last year. Dr. Singh said keeping in view the limited sources of conventional petro fuels, their escalating prices and their adverse effects on the climate globally it is high time that issues and strategies relating to bio-diesel production, conversion and utilization need to be considered and discussed with the stakeholders including the farmers. The minister said that availability of quality planting material, suitability of waste lands, rainfall, Suitable agronomic practices for cultivation of non-edible oil seed producing plants etc., are important aspects for the farmers and cultivators. The stake holders in the entire chain of bio-diesel production, conversion and utilization need to be educated and awareness need to be created through various means such as training, workshops, seminars, symposia etc. He expressed the hope that deliberations at the convention will provide valuable inputs for all those who are engaged in the promotion of Bio-fuels as substitute to petrol and diesel in the transport and other Sectors.

5771. (1-2-2008) NEW DELHI : As per data compiled by Agriculture Ministry as on today, sowing is progressing well in the present rabi season. Wheat has been sown in 275.67 lakh ha as compared to 280.63 lakh ha on the same date last year. 19.84 lakh ha area has come under winter rice as against 20.06 lakh ha last year. Coarse cereals have been sown in 67.77 lakh ha as compared to 69.4 lakh ha by this time in 2007. Barley and maize have been grown in more area than last year's {barley 7.57 lakh ha, maize 10.35 lakh ha}. Rabi oilseeds have been sown in 87.97 lakh ha as compared to 96.65 lakh ha in the last rabi. Mustard/rapeseed coverage has reached 59.04 lakh ha (last rabi, up to this time: 66.67 lakh ha). Rabi pulses cover 131.55 lakh ha (last year: 138.11 lakh ha). Gram coverage has reached 79.95 lakh ha (vs. 83.24 lakh ha by this time last year).

5772. (1-2-2008) NEW DELHI : The Appointments Committee of the Cabinet has approved the following appointments/extension:- (i) Shri U.N. Panjiar, IAS (BH: 73), presently Secretary, Border Management, Ministry of Home Affairs as Secretary, Ministry of Water Resources vice Smt. Gauri Chatterjee, IAS (WB:71) who has been approved for repatriation to her cadre; (ii) Shri Surendra Pal Gaur, IAS (UP: 74), presently Secretary, Union Public Service Commission as Chairman Inland Waterways Authority of India, Department of Shipping, Ministry of Shipping, Road Transport and Highways, in the rank and pay of Secretary, vice Shri S.B. Mathur, IAS (JK: 71) superannuating on 31st January, 2008. (iii) Extension of tenure of Shri N.S. Sisodia, IAS (RJ: 68) (Retd.) as Director, Institute of Defence Studies & Analysis, for a further period of three years beyond 16th August, 2008.

5773. (1-2-2008) NEW DELHI : This year's first Meeting of the Parliamentary Consultative Committee attached to Finance Ministry was held here today under the Chairmanship of the Finance Minister, Shri P. Chidambaram. He briefed the Members about the buoyancy of Indian economy and revenues and invited suggestions from the Members for the Union Budget for 2008-09. The Finance Minister said that overall macroeconomic fundamentals continue to be strong. With tax collections increasing at a healthy pace reflecting the growth potential that could be further harnessed and expenditure trends in the FY 2007-08 encouragingly pointing towards to the achievement of the fiscal targets envisaged under the FRBM mandated roadmap, further reforms in critical sectors and better implementation to ensure more efficient delivery of public services across all sections of society will see the India growth story sustained and consolidated over the Eleventh five year Plan period. Shri Chidambaram said that buoyant economic growth along with efforts to improve the tax administration system has yielded rich dividends. As a result, Central tax to GDP ratio is estimated to have increased from 8.2 per cent in 2001-02 to 11.8 per cent in BE 2007-08. This increase has provided the Central Government with additional resources which are not only being shared with State Governments but are also being utilized by the Centre for meeting expenditure in the social and infrastructure sectors and for achieving fiscal consolidation. Gross Tax Revenues are budgeted at Rs. 5,48,122 crore in 2007-08. Members presented at the meeting gave their valuable suggestions covering all sectors of economy especially the agricultural and services sectors. The Members who participated in the meeting are S/Sh. Jivabhai A. Patel, K.C. Singh Baba, Prahlad Joshi, Pusp Jain, Mohammad Salim, Tukaram G. Gadakh, P.C. Thomas, Tarit Baran Topdar, and Dr. C. Krishnan from Lok Sabha and S/

Sh. Harendra Singh Malik, Rajkumar Dhoot, A. Vijayaraghavan, S. M. Laljan Basha, Abani Roy, Bimal Jalan, B.J. Panda, Rahul Bajaj and Dinesh Trivedi from Rajya Sabha. Ministers of State for Finance, Shri S.S. Palanimanickam and Shri Pawan Kumar Bansal apart from senior officers of the Finance Ministry also attended the meeting.

5774. (1-2-2008) NEW DELHI : The world will celebrate Wetland Day tomorrow 2nd February each year is celebrated as World Wetlands Day. This year's theme is "Healthy Wetlands, Healthy People". It marks the anniversary of the adoption of the international Convention on Wetlands on 2 February 1971. Since then over a thousand wetlands have been protected by governments under the 'Ramsar' convention. Wetland is the home to a numerous of wildlife (*e.g.* Fiddler crab, mudskipper, water birds), and an important supply of natural resources (*e.g.* clean water, rice, vegetable, medicine), as well as a nature classroom. The Convention on Wetlands, usually called the Ramsar Convention after the city in Iran where it was signed, covers all aspects of wetland conservation for biodiversity and for human use. The main aim of the Ramsar Convention is the sustainable use of wetlands. As a showcase, the Convention lists Wetlands of International Importance, such as the Severn Estuary and Martin Mere. "Drawing for Wetland Conservation" Competition has been organized all over the world this year where students will present their creativity and idea on wetland conservation. People and particularly students have been encouraged to observe wetland environments, wetland plants and animals in various countries.

5775. (1-2-2008) NEW DELHI : Development of Bio-fuels as an alternative and renewable source of energy is critical in India's efforts towards self-reliance. Addressing the Second National Convention and Exhibition on Bio-diesel today Minister of State for New and Renewable Energy Shri Vilas Muttemwar said that this is corner stone of India's energy security strategy. Shri Muttemwar said 84 per cent of rural households in the country have primary source of cooking energy as fuel wood, agricultural residues and dung cakes. In such energy scenario there are major challenges in providing clean and affordable energy to all. The Minister said use of bio-ethanol and bio-diesel has positive impact on stationary applications for various rural energy systems. It has been successfully demonstrated under Village Energy Security Programme of the Ministry. The Minister also informed that a National policy on bio-fuels has been prepared and is under active consideration of the Government. The Policy outlines the strategy to achieve energy security in the country through sustainable production, conversion and application of bio-fuels. The Minister welcomed extensive research and development work to identify and promote plantation of variety of non-edible oil producing trees and shrubs in different agro-climatic regions. Shri Muttemwer informed that the Government has recently approve mandatory blending of 10 per cent of ethanol with petrol from last October in the country except in Northeastern States, some smaller States and Union Territories. The Minister stressed on need of considering availability of quality planning material, suitability of wastelands, rainfall, suitable agronomic practices for cultivation of non-edible oil seed producing plants. The stakeholders in the entire chain of bio-diesel production, conversion and utilization need to be educated and awareness needs to be created. The two-day National Convention will discuss on policy issues, feedstock, plantation and related issues.

5776. (1-2-2008) NEW DELHI : The National Rail Museum, New Delhi is celebrating its 31st Museum Day on 2nd and 3rd February 2008. During the two day celebrations, visitors can witness a fully functional miniature live steam train, the 'Indian Glory' by the renowned model maker Shri Iqbal Ahmed who finds mention in the Guinness Book of World Records. Visitors will also have an experience to discover the museum with the Indian Steam Railway Society who will conduct guided tours of the museum every hour. The programme for two day celebrations is designed in such a way that entire family can have fun filled experience. The main highlights of the celebrations include; live steam garden train, train modelling workshop, discover the world of stamps and discover the Railways through stamps in philately workshop, discover the trees of the museum in the Tree Walk conducted by Shri Pradip Krishen, the author of the famous book 'Trees of Delhi', discover the magical world of science by making toys with everyday household products, bird watching, Children's films, handicrafts, food courts etc.

5777. (1-2-2008) NEW DELHI : A delegation of the All India Federation of the Deaf called on the Vice President of India Mohd. Hamid Ansari on the first day of the Flag Week of the Deaf and pinned a flag on the self of the Vice President here today. The 49th Flag Week of the Deaf is being observed from 1st-7th February 2008 to create awareness as well apprise the people about the functions and achievements of the federation for the benefit of the hearing handicapped. Besides funds are raised through sale of flags for financing its ongoing as well as future activities. All India Federation of the Deaf, a voluntary welfare organization, established in 1955 has a track record of 52 years in the service of deaf and hearing impaired to make them self reliant and respectable citizens of the country.

5778. (1-2-2008) NEW DELHI : The Cumulative value of India's exports for the period April-December, 2007 was US $ 111049.70 million (Rs.448377.33 crore) as against US $ 91202.56 million (Rs.416175.56 crore) registering a growth of 21.76 per cent in Dollar terms and 7.74 per cent in Rupee terms during the same period last year. Exports during December, 2007 were valued at US $ 12314.97 million which was 16.04 per cent higher than the level of US $ 10612.37 million during December, 2006. In rupee terms, exports touched Rs.48569.64 crore, which was 2.54 per cent higher than the value of exports during December, 2006. India's imports during December, 2007 were valued at US $ 17680.64 million representing an increase of 18.06 per cent over the level of imports valued at US $ 14976.53 million in December, 2006. In Rupee terms, imports increased by 4.31 per cent Cumulative value of imports for the period April-December, 2007 was US $ 168871.01 million (Rs.682088.17 crore) as against US$ 134054.76 million (Rs.611521.98 crore) registering a growth of 25.97 per cent in Dollar terms and 11.54 per cent in Rupee terms during the same period last year.

5779. (2-2-2008) NEW DELHI : Shri Sis Ram Ola, Minister of Mines informed the Parliamentary Consultative Committee (PCC) here today that he was happy with the performance of National Aluminium Company Limited (NALCO) a leading example among the PSUs and symbol of excellence in public sector in general and aluminium industry in particular. The Minister was also pleased with the progress made in the execution of the company's 2nd phase expansion projects, scheduled to be completed by December, 2008. Outlining the achievements Shri Ola said that during the last three financial years, the company has made great strides in the field of production, sales and financial performance. The units of NALCO that is, bauxite mines, alumina refinery & aluminium smelter are operating near or even more than 100% rated capacity. The captive power plant is also operating at a plant load factor of nearly 80% which is much ahead of all India average of 72%. However, it was noted that the anticipated profit of the company for the year 2007-08 is expected to be at a lower level of Rs. 1620 crore as compared to Rs. 2381 crore for the year 2006-07 in view of lowering of prices of aluminium in the London Metal Exchange and the appreciation of the Rupee against the Dollar. The Minister was pleased that the company has been approved for "Navaratna" status by the Government. However, for this purpose eight Independent Directors have to be appointed on NALCO's Board, of which three such Directors have already been appointed and for the remaining five, the matter has been sent to ACC. At present, the Company has huge cash reserves as well as surplus alumina capacity. For value addition, utilizing the surplus alumina and for strengthening its market presence, the company is exploring the possibility of setting up a green field smelter and power plant elsewhere in the country or abroad depending upon availability of power. The members who attended the meeting are : S/Shri Jual Oram, K. Virupakshappa, Tushar A. Choudhary, Raghuraj Singh Shakya and Anandrao Adsul from Lok Sabha and Shri Rudra Narayan Pany from Rajya Sabha. Shri J.P. Singh. Secretary (Mines) and Senior Officers of the Ministry of Mines and NALCO were also present.

5780. (2-2-2008) NEW DELHI : As per the latest report received from the High Security Animal Disease Laboratory, Bhopal, sample collected from Canning 2 block of South 24 Parganas district of West Bengal have tested positive for Avian Influenza virus on the basis of rapid tests. The mortality of birds on 1st February 2008 was of the order of 251, all of which were reported from South 24 Parganas and Birbhum. A total mortality of 1,32,625 poultry birds has so far been reported from Birbhum, Dakshin Dinajpur, Murshidabad, Nadia, South 24 Parganas, Burdwan, Bankura, Hooghly, Malda, Coochbehar, Purulia, Howrah and North 24 Parganas districts of West Bengal. A total of 349 Rapid Response Teams were engaged as on 01.02.2008, which completed culling of 2.2 lakh birds taking the cumulative figure of culling so far to 29.43 lakh. Latest position of destruction of eggs and feed carried out till 01.02.2008 are 2,64,247 and 69,500 kg respectively. It has been decided to create a poultry depopulated zone in Assam, Bihar, Jharkhand and Orissa up to 5 kilometres from their border with West Bengal so as to prevent ingress of Avian Influenza into these States. All the concerned State Governments have been notified and advised to take further necessary action.

5781. (2-2-2008) NEW DELHI : The Minister of Information & Broadcasting and Parliamentary Affairs Shri Priya Ranjan Dasmunsi has condoled the death of veteran journalist R.K. Karanjia. In his message, Shri Dasmunsi said, "I am pained to learn that eminent veteran journalist Roussi K. Karanjia has passed away. Karanjia was a man of conviction and a fire-brand journalist. His commitment to his profession was un-flinching and deep-rooted. He introduced a unique brand of tabloid journalism in the country. In true spirit, he was free, frank and fearless-that was also the motto of his weekly ' Blitz'. Beginning his career as a war reporter, Karanjia reached the pinnacle in journalism through his investigative exposures. The huge popularity of 'Blitz' testified that he had a knack of getting to his reader's pulse. Besides his professional competence, Karanjia was a fine human being possessing qualities of heart and zest for life. In his demise, the country has lost a journalist of courage and conviction. My heart felt condolences to the bereaved family".

5782. (2-2-2008) NEW DELHI : Shri Arjun Singh, Minister of Human Resource Development has said that 'it is a clich. . to say that books are man's best friend, but sometimes it is refreshing to repeat cliches because they carry the truths of life.' Shri Arjun Singh's speech was read by Special Secretary (Higher Education) Shri K.M Acharya in his absence on the occasion of inauguration of New Delhi World Book Fair (2-10 Feb.08) at Pragati Maidan here today. In his speech, Shri Arjun Singh further said that 'as we make progress in different fields of socio-economic activities, the role of publishing industry coupled with the contribution of the writers, scientists, scholars etc., is going to assume much greater significance.' Prof. U.R. Anantha Murthy, eminent writer presided over the function. In his address he said books has romance with them and they also grow with the readers provided the reader is tolerant, curious and have a sense of patriotism. He also condemned the increasing demands of banning the books because of religious intolerance. He also appealed that we should treat all languages as equal and promote books in all languages including tribal languages. In this occasion, Andrey Y. Romanchenko, Deputy Director, Federal Agency for Press and Mass Communication complemented India for declaring Russia as the Guest of Honour. Prof. C.N.R. Rao, National Research Professor & Linus Pauling Research Professor, Jawaharlal Nehru Centre for Advanced Scientific Research, Bengalooru delivered the address as Guest of Honour. Prof. Bipin Chandra, Chairman National Book Trust moved a vote of thanks in this session. The publishing scenario in contemporary India is conceptually exciting, linguistically rich and a quantitatively diverse phenomenon. India is perhaps the only country in the world, which publishes books in more than 24 languages. There are nearly 16,000 publishers producing not less than 80,000 titles in all major Indian languages including English with an annual turnover of Rs. 100,000 million. Of these, almost forty per cent titles are published in English language alone. As a result, India ranks third in the publication of English books immediately after the USA and the UK. In recognition of its ever-expanding role in the field of publishing, India was declared the Guest of Honour Country for Frankfurt Book Fair, the largest book fair in the world, twice in 1986 and 2006. The New Delhi World Book Fair is the largest Book Fair in the Afro-Asian region. The major attraction of the Book Fair is the presentation by Russia, which is guest of honour country at the Book Fair, as the year 2008 was earlier declared the Year of Russia in India. Other outstanding features of the Fair are, the Youth Pavilion, Children's Pavilion and the Pavilion on the books on and by Mahatma Gandhi. Whereas the Children's Pavilion will showcase activities for and by children everyday, the Youth Pavilion will conduct a variety of programmes for the youth.

5783. (3-2-2008) BHUBANESHWAR: Rich tributes were paid to socialist leader and founder secretary of Orissa Unit of Communist Party Bhagabati Panigrahi here on Saturday with Left leaders calling upon cadres not to dilute the ideology the visionary leader had preached. A torch rally, which was organised by Communist Party of India (Marxist), was taken out from party's main office to Institute of Engineers' building where the memorial lecture on the occasion of the birth centenary of Late Panigrahi was staged. Describing the founder secretary of Communist Party in the State as a great socialist leader, CPI (M) general secretary Prakash Karat said Bhagabati Panigrahi believed that elimination of economic inequality would be true freedom even before independence. "I am astonished that Bhagabati Panigrahi in such a young age could able to convey the ideology to masses. He was the first person who translated communist ideology into Oriya language," Mr. Karat said.

5784. (3-2-2008) NEW DELHI : Bharatiya Janata Party is concerned about the statement of the Government of India through the Union Law Minister to the effect that the Constitution of India would be amended in order to ostensibly create parity between the three Members of the Election Commission and make the Petition seeking the removal of Shri Navin Chawla as Election Commissioner infructuous. The Bharatiya Janata Party had sought the removal of Shri Navin Chawla from the Election Commission in accordance with the provisions of Article 324(5) of the Constitution. The removal has been sought on the ground of the partisan conduct of Shri Chawla before his acquiring the membership of the Election Commission and also during his functioning as a Member of the Election Commission. It is this close proximity of Shri Chawla to the Congress Party and its political functionaries that creates an apprehension in the minds of the right thinking people that he cannot function independently and in a detached manner as a member of the Election Commission. The Petition extensively mentions the role of Shri Navin Chawla during the Emergency, the observations made by the Justice Shah Commission, his acquisitions of prime postings, grant of MPLAD funds to private trusts controlled by Shri Navin Chawla by Congress MPs and the partisan role of Shri Chawla as a Member of the Election Commission. The Election Commission should be politically detached and equidistanced. If the practice of appointing partisan persons as member of Election Commission gets established as a precedent, it will provide a temptation for future governments to pack the Election Commission with its own sympathizers. The threat is more acute because it is not an independent collegium that nominates the members of the Election Commission but the political government of the day which does so. The Union Law Minister's statement has confirmed our worst fears. Here is a Government in power which, to save Shri Navin Chawla, is willing to go to the extent of amending the Constitution. This statement is conclusive of how much value the Congress Party attaches to the continuation of Shri Navin Chawla as a Member of the Election Commission. When this statement is read in the context of the action of Prime Minister's office in not even forwarding the Petition seeking Shri Chawla's removal to the Chief Election Commissioner for his recommendations, the vested interest of the Congress Party in the continuation of Shri Navin Chawla as a member of the Election Commission gets confirmed. The Constitution deliberately provided for a Chief Election Commissioner to make recommendations whether to continue or not a member of the Election Commission. What goes on within the four-walls of the Election Commission is known only to the Chief Election Commissioner and not to the political government. If there is an allegation of bias against a member of the Election Commission of favouring the government in power, it is only appropriate that it is the Chief Election Commissioner who adjudicates the allegation of bias and not the political establishment which is the beneficiary of that bias.

5785. (3-2-2008) NEW DELHI : The Minister of Petroleum and Natural Gas, Shri Murli Deora has called upon to join in the efforts of his ministry to check/ prevent diversion of heavily subsidized domestic LPG cyclinders in a more effective manner. In this regard Shri Deora held a meeting with Maharashtra State Government officials and Senior Oil Industry officers on 2nd February, 2008 at Mumbai to review the LPG supply position including measures to arrest the diversions of highly subsidized domestic LPG cylinders in commercial and automobile use. Earlier Shri Murli Deora, met the Chief Minister of Maharashtra, Shri Vilasrao Deshmukh and discussed the problems of diversion and sought the help of the State Government to intensify the inspections of commercial establishments. He also appealed to the LPG Distributors Federation to co-operate in helping the Government in curbing the diversion of domestic LPG Cylinders in commercial applications. The Chief Minister has assured that all the help in this regard will be rendered. Shri Murli Deora urged upon all consumers and LPG distributors to refrain from diversion of LPG domestic cylinders and play the role of responsible citizen in building up a strong nation. The meeting was attended by Shri Bakshi, Principal Secretary, Civil Supplies, and Shri Jadhav, Controller of Rationing, Maharashtra along with the Senior officials of Oil Industry. Due to diversion of domestic LPG cylinders, the Government and Oil companies are forced to add to already heavy burden of subsidy. For the year 2007-08, it is estimated that on all petroleum products the subsidy burden will be approx. Rs. 80,000 crores. Hence it is imperative that this kind of diversion of domestic cylinders for non domestic use must be arrested at any cost. Action will be taken against LPG Distributors and also consumers found using domestic LPG cylinders for non-domestic applications. The offenders are punishable under Essential Commodities Act.

5786. (4-2-2008) NEW DELHI : As part of Publications Division's participation in the 18th New Delhi World Book Fair-2008, Secretary Information & Broadcasting Smt. Asha Swarup launched its Home Library Scheme here today. A book on Maulana Jalaluddin Rumi in Hindi was also released during the function by noted film maker Shri Muzaffar Ali. This book on great Sufi poet is written by Dr. Trinath Mishra. Born in 13th Century in West Asia, Rumi, along with Hafiz, is among the most illuminating stars of Persian poetry. After releasing the book the Chief Guest Shri Muzaffar Ali expressed his happiness and said that for Hindi speaking world the book on Rumi is a very important step forward by the Division. According to him, at a time when people are losing touch of their culture and philosophy the Division has successfully tried to connect them with their culture through this book. The author, a retired senior IPS officer, Dr. Trinath Mishra emphasized on the relevance of Rumi and said that Rumi is to Persian is what Tulsidas is to Hindi. While launching the Home Library Scheme, Smt. Swarup lauded Publications Division's efforts and said that the launch of the Scheme reflects the will and sincerity of the Division to reach out to book-loving Indian masses. She also hoped that the Scheme would take along the people across the country on the path of knowledge and awareness and it would be a great bonanza for book lovers. Welcoming the guests, the Additional Director General (In-Charge) in the Division Smt. Veena Jain explained that and the Scheme offers handsome discount in customer-friendly and convenient packages. She invited everybody to share the wonderful experience of going through Publication Division's books and journals-covering a variety of subjects, tastefully presented and reasonably priced. By paying a small amount of Rs. 100 annually, members of Home Library Scheme would be entitled for 20% concession on any more than 100 rupees after-rebate purchase of the Division's books. This concession will be available to members all over the country from Delhi to Thiruvananthapuram; and from Ahmedabad to Guwahati. Even this small membership amount of Rs. 100 will stand reduced to 50 rupees only for a 3-year subscription of any of its magazines.

5787. (4-2-2008) NEW DELHI : Breaking away from the traditional approach, the Indian Army together with the Indian Air Force is set to project 'manoeuvre warfare doctrine' of the Indian Armed Forces in a 'fire and manoeuvre' combat exercise, codenamed "Brazen Chariots", to be conducted at the Pokharan field firing range in western Rajasthan, on March 19. The exercise is being jointly conducted by one of the desert formations of the Indian Army in the sector, who together with the IAF will put to test an array of their latest weapon system acquisitions including the state-of-the-art missile firing tanks T-90 (Bhishma), all-weather Air Defence Gun Missile systems, Searcher Unmanned Aerial Vehicles (UAV) besides other electronic sensors and surveillance equipment. The IAF would closely support the surface forces with induction of airborne troops, provide logistical support while its frontline fighter aircraft including the Su-30 MKI, Jaguar, MiG-27, MiG-21 Bison and armed helicopters, would unleash their firepower to devastating effect. The synergy with the IAF would highlight the shape of future operations, which would be joint and seamless. A host of foreign dignitaries and Defence Attaches of friendly foreign countries will witness the exercise that is aimed at putting the mechanized formations through the paces in a simulated, deep offensive scenario in a desert terrain. The combat exercise will also include the deployment of a comprehensive communication and data linking systems incorporating Battlefield Surveillance System (BSS) and Force Multiplier Command Post (FMCP). Notwithstanding the hi-tech weaponry and war fighting support systems, essential pre-requisites to success in battle, the exercise will most certainly challenge the military leadership at various levels as their ability to synergize the application of the state-of-the-art weapon platforms towards achieving optimum results aimed at causing pre-emption, disruption and dislocation of enemy forces will be tested. Exercise Brazen Chariots has been conceptualized for exercising combat groups consisting of tanks, infantry combat vehicles and Infantry in high Mobility Vehicles, ably supported by air and complemented by weapon platforms of supporting arms and combat logistics in essential tactical applications on the battlefield.

5788. (4-2-2008) NEW DELHI : The Annual Plan for Assam for the year 2008-09 was finalized here today at a meeting between Planning Commission, Deputy Chairman Shri Montek Singh Ahluwalia and Chief Minister of Assam Shri Tarun Kumar Gogoi. The Annual Plan size has been agreed at Rs.5011 crores. This includes special plan assistance of Rs.250 crores for identified projects of the State, of this, Rs.20 crores will be earmarked for development of Majuli Island. The special plan assistance release will be conditional upon the State providing fully for its share of Centrally sponsored schemes. Deputy Chairman, Planning Commission, Mr. Ahluwalia complemented the State for improving financial health and doubling growth rate during Tenth Plan period. He said the State government should further step up efforts to accelerate development process and aim at bringing Assam at par with developed states of the country at the earliest. The State was also complemented for performance under Bharat Nirman programme. Efforts should be increased to reach targets in irrigation and drinking water sectors. The State was also advised to evolve a strategy convergence of social sector schemes so as to maximize benefits from Centrally sponsored schemes. In view of huge handloom sector potential, the State was advised to encourage cluster approach, necessary for tapping export potential. Briefing the Commission on the performance of the State the Chief Minister said Assam has achieved the objectives of eliminating the revenue deficit and reducing fiscal deficit to 3 per cent of the GSDP by 2005-06. He also informed the Commission that revenue and fiscal deficits have turned into surplus of Rs.2210.42 crores and Rs.711.35 crores respectively in 2006 and 2007. Mr. Gogoi said that the State has achieved an industrial growth rate of 8.02 per cent in the Tenth Plan and efforts are being made to encourage growth of small and cottage industry during the Eleventh Plan period. He said the survey sector has shown promising growth and Assam is likely to achieve higher growth in the sector. Mr. Gogoi asked the Commission to modify the power policy so that surplus power generated through the Mega projects in the North East Region should be first made available on priority to deficit States in the region before being evacuated to other States. He said the Government should explore the possibility of opening air links between Guwahati and Eastern Countries.

5789. (4-2-2008) NEW DELHI : The report for 3rd February, 2008, received from West Bengal shows that unusual mortality of poultry birds in the state has come down significantly. Only 14 birds were reported to have dies on the said date in Murshidabad district. This takes the cumulative mortality to 1,32,739 poultry birds, which has been reported from Birbhum, Dakshin Dinajpur, Murshidabad, Nadia, South 24 Parganas, Burdwan, Bankura, Hooghly, Malda, Coochbehar, Purulia, Howrah and North 24 Parganas districts of West Bengal. A total of 295 Rapid Response Teams were engaged on 3.02.2008, which completed culling of 1.85 lakh birds taking the cumulative figure of culling so far to 33.84 lakh.. Latest position of destruction of eggs and feed carried out till 3.02.2008 are 10,11,258 and 78,868 kg. respectively. The latest communication from HSADL, Bhopal intimates that samples of poultry birds collected from Lakhimpur Khiri and Sitapur Districts of Uttar Pradesh, which were part of the consignment transported from West Bengal have tested negative. Similarly, samples of birds received from Haryana, Uttarakhand, Tamil Nadu, Bihar and Tripura have also returned a negative result on the basis of rapid tests. The preventive culling for creating a poultry depopulated zone has already commenced in Assam. However, it is yet to start in Bihar, Jharkhand and Orissa.

5790. (4-2-2008) NEW DELHI : The Central Board of Direct Taxes have extended the due date for filing of quarterly statements of Tax Deducted at Source (TDS) and Tax Collected at Source (TCS) for the quarter ending 30th September 2007 of financial year 2007-08 to 29th February 2008. This is in view of the difficulties being faced by the tax deductors / collectors in filing statements with the correct PAN data mandatorily required to be furnished to the extent of at least 90% in the cases of salaried deductees and 70% in the cases of other deductees.

As the requirement of filing TDS / TCS certificates had been done away with, the lack of PAN of deductees was creating difficulties in giving credit for the tax deducted and collected. It was, therefore, decided that TDS returns for salaries, *i.e.* Form No.24Q with less than 90% of PAN data, and TDS returns for payments other than salaries and TCS returns, *i.e.* Form No.26Q and Form No.27EQ respectively, with less than 70% of PAN data would not be accepted for the quarter ending on 30.9.2007 and thereafter. Tax deductors and tax collectors were, therefore, advised to obtain correct PAN details of all deductees and quote the same in the TDS / TCS returns, failing which the TDS / TCS returns would not be accepted and all penal consequences under the Income Tax Act would follow. Taxpayers liable to TDS / TCS were also advised to furnish their correct PAN with their deductors, failing which they would also face penal proceedings under the Income Tax Act. It may be recalled that for and from the quarter ending 30.9.2007, in addition to government offices and companies, filing of TDS / TCS returns in electronic form has been made mandatory for (i) deductors / collectors required to get their accounts audited under section 44AB of the Income-tax Act in the immediately preceding financial year, and (ii) where the number of deductees' / collectees' records in a quarterly statement for any quarter of the immediately preceding financial year is equal to more than fifty.

5791. (4-2-2008) NEW DELHI : To mark the launch of Quasquicentennial Celebrations of Postal Life Insurance (PLI), the release of special cover and cancellation is being planned in a big way on Feb. 5, 2008 at India International Centre, New Delhi. The Secretary, Department of Posts, Shri IMG Khan will release the special cover. In its 125th year, PLI has taken significant resolutions to celebrate the mile posts. These include management of corpus within the frame work of IRDA investment regulations; up gradation of the computer system and management of data base centrally in the national data centre; and professional training to its sales force and granting license to the sales force in the pattern of IRDA regulations. Introduced on Feb. 01, 1884 for providing Life Insurance coverage to the Postal Employees, the PLI is extended to all employees of the Central Government including defence and paramilitary personnel, employees of the state Governments, public sector undertakings, autonomous bodies, universities, municipalities, nationalized banks etc. Compared to other insurance companies, PLI charges low premium from its customers and pay much higher rates of bonus. Today, number of live policies in PLI exceeds 85 lakh (including the Rural PLI). The corpus size is more than Rs. 12,500 crore. Total Sum Assured for all policies (including Rural PLI) comes to more than Rs. 31,000 crore. The fund is healthy and the current rates of bonus are Whole Life Policies-Rs. 90 for every thousand Rupees of Sum Assured; Endowment Assurance Policies-Rs. 70 for every thousand Rupees of Sum Assured; and Anticipated Endowment Policies-Rs.65 for every thousand Rupees of Sum Assured. It was primarily because of high rate of bonus, PLI has succeeded in retaining its niche market, in spite of opening up of the insurance sector and, thereby, increasing competition. PLI fund is growing at an average annual rate of 20% and RPLI fund at an average rate of more than 40% in recent years. PLI concentrates on traditional Life Insurance products and primary focus is coverage of risk and ensuring a decent return to its customers. Besides Whole Life, Endowment and Anticipated Policies, PLI offers Yugal Suraksha policies for working couples and offers add on policies for children. Starting from acceptance of proposals to settlement of claims, the operations are computerized and strict norms are followed for every aspect of customer service.

5792. (4-2-2008) NEW DELHI : The Defence Minister Shri A K Antony has called upon Defence officials to adopt a humane approach towards the requirements of Ex-servicemen so as to highlight the fact that while the country acknowledges the sacrifices being made by the jawans when they are in active service, it does not forget them after their retirement. Inaugurating the Financial Controllers' Conference here today Shri Antony said the mechanics of financial management and prudence should not be allowed to overshadow the human side of our work. 'Government attaches great importance to the welfare of ex-servicemen. The creation of an Ex-servicemen's Welfare Department in the Ministry of Defence headed by its own Secretary is an indication of the significance being attached to this area. I would like to call upon the Defence Accounts Department, which plays an important role in the management of pay and allowances and pensionary benefits, to approach the requirements of our ex-servicemen with all sensitivity and seriousness', he said. Shri Antony asked the financial managers to upgrade their procedures and techniques by drawing upon the best practises followed the world over in the fields of audit, project management, logistics and budgeting. 'The Department needs to keep abreast of the changing national and global security scenario and new developments in defence technology so that it can make meaningful contributions to our acquisition process.' The latest delegation and enhancement of financial powers is expected to result in 46 percent of the overall revenue procurement and 35 percent of capital procurement budget being spent under the delegated powers by the Services Headquarters. In this context, the Defence Minister asked the financial managers and the Services 'to sit together and work out practical solutions' so that budgetary allocations are fully utilised conforming to established procedures and the principles of financial prudence. Shri Antony said, Defence expenditure has grown considerably over the years and today it constitutes the largest single head of expenditure in our budget after interest payments. The share of capital allocations in the defence budget has increased significantly from around 25 percent in 2000-01 to over 40 percent today. The three-day conference will be deliberating upon a number of critical issues relating to defence expenditure. Others who addressed the Conference today included the Minister of State for Defence Shri M M Pallam Raju, the Defence Secretary Shri Vijay Singh, Financial Advisor (Defence Services) Smt. Neil Kamal Narang and Controller General of Defence Accounts Smt. H K Pannu.

5793. (4-2-2008) NEW DELHI : The 3rd Meeting of the Bureau of Asia Pacific Ministers Conference on Housing and Urban Development (APMCHUD) was held yesterday at Tehran, Iran. The meeting was chaired by Kumar Selja, Union Minister for Housing and Urban Poverty Alleviation and Chairperson of the Bureau of APMCHUD. India is the Chair of the Bureau represented by seven countries namely Iran, China, Jordan, Malaysia, Azerbaijan and Papua New Guinea besides India, representing various sub-regions of the Asia pacific. The meeting was hosted by H.E. Mohammed Saidi Kia, Minister for Housing and Urban Development, Islamic Republic of Iran. The meeting was participated by the representatives of the member countries of the bureau. The meeting focused on the preparations for the forthcoming second Conference of the APMCHUD scheduled to be held at Iran from 12th-14th May 2008. Addressing the Bureau, the Chairperson Kumari Selja highlighted that a strong foundation towards addressing the housing and sustainable urban development challenges has been laid with the constitution of APMCHUD. The Chairperson indicated that the setting up of the permanent executive secretariat for the Bureau is another step towards consolidating and sustaining the initiative. She further complemented the Government of Iran for the meticulous planning and preparation for the forthcoming 2nd Conference which she felt would facilitate in evolving a focused and synergic approach for addressing the daunting challenges of the sector in the region. H.E. Manoucher Kajeh Daloui, Vice Minister for Housing and Cities commended the efforts of Government of India for the specific thrust given to the initiatives of APMCHUD. He further added that the forthcoming 2nd Conference of the APMCHUD would lay a firm foundation to carry forward the initiatives and objectives enshrined in the Delhi Declaration of APMCHUD. The Iranian delegation made a detailed presentation on the status of preparation for the 2nd conference of APMCHUD scheduled at Tehran. The Chief Coordinator of the Bureau and Joint Secretary (Housing), Government of India, Mr. Sunil Kumar Singh briefed the Bureau on the initiatives made by the Executive Secretariat for establishing a mechanism for supporting the APMCHUD towards achieving its objectives. He informed that during the short period of just over a year, the Secretariat has been able to made major initial steps for institutionalizing the set up. He assured complete support of the secretariat in the organization of the 2nd Conference of the APMCHUD. The representative from UN-Habitat, Mr. Markandey Rai assured complete support of UN-Habitat to APMCHUD and the Government of Iran in organizing the conference at Tehran. The APMCHUD is a joint initiative of the countries of the Asia Pacific Region to mainstream the concerns of housing and urban development in respective countries for improving the quality of life of the citizens of the Asia pacific region and to ensure sustainable development at large.

5794. (4-2-2008) NEW DELHI : Shri Dinesh Rai, a 1974 batch IAS Officer of Uttar Pradesh cadre has taken over as the Secretary in the Ministry of Micro, Small & Medium Enterprises. Earlier, he was Vice Chairman, Delhi Development Authority. He replaced Dr. Chandrapal who retired on superannuation on 31.1.2008.

5795. (5-2-2008) NEW DELHI : The Annual Plan outlay for Uttarakhand for the year 2008-09 was finalized at a meeting, here today, between the Deputy Chairman Planning Commission, Shri Montek Singh Ahluwalia and Chief Minister of Uttaranchal Shri B C Khanduri. The Annual Plan size was agreed at Rs. 4775 crores. This includes additional Central assistance of Rs. 300 crores for infrastructure needed for Kumbh Mela and SAF Winter Games and other projects of special interest to the State. Commenting on the performance of the State, Deputy Chairman Planning Commission, Mr. Ahluwalia said that growth rate was good and even plan expenditure during the tenth plan is encouraging but per capita income remained rather low. Achievement in the agriculture sector was commendable. However, the poverty level was much higher than those at the all India level or in Himachal Pradesh in both rural and urban areas. This shows that topmost priority should be given to creating livelihood opportunities. Appreciable achievements have been reached in the tourism sector during tenth Plan period and needs to be carried forward as the State has immense potential for becoming a world class tourist centre. The State offers all types of tourism like pilgrimage, cultural, adventure, wildlife and eco-tourism. To develop high value tourism, the State should focus on developing adequate infrastructure facilities at the destinations and circuits. On industrial policy, it was pointed out that the policy seemingly was driven by subsidy. Efforts should be to have a comprehensive plan of action for identified industries. Benefits of concessions should reach far-flung areas. Briefing the Commission on the pace of development, Mr. Khanduri said that emphasis would continue on social sector. This is clearly reflected in both Eleventh Plan and Annual Plan proposal. Over 37 percent of plan outlay would be ear-marked for social services. He said efforts are on to further accelerate development of infrastructure and for this purpose four projects are being executed through external aid. These would be in roads and bridges, urban infrastructure, power and tourism development. He sought additional support from the Centre for Haridwar Maha Kumbh in 2010, South Asia Winger games and additional grant to support earthquake affected people. Mr. Khanduri said that the Centre should supplement efforts to bring at par with other developed States and in view of the state of industrialization, tax holiday period should be extended upto 2013. he also sought Central support in tackling problem of silting of dams.

5796. (5-2-2008) NEW DELHI : While releasing the special cover on the launch of Quasquicentennial celebrations, Secretary, Posts Shri I.M. G. Khan has said today, that Postal Life Insurance (PLI) is going to introduce Girl Child Insurance very soon. He further said that with a huge PLI fund, Rural Postal Life Insurance (RPLI) has come to the fore as a very exciting new interest. Its high growth rate has led the decision to invest RPLI funds in the business. Therefore an Investment Board will be set up and fund managers will be appointed by the Government to make it a real business organization than a bureaucratic one. PLI comes on its own as a business organization. Management of Corpus will be within the framework of Insurance Regulatory and Development Authority (IRDA) investment regulations.

Professional training will be given to the sales force and granting license to the sales force in the pattern of IRDA Regulations. Next step is to bring technology to make RPLI more accessible to urban people as PLI is in urban circles. Shri Khan said "technology is going to see a revolutionary change in the Postal Insurance System." There will be upgradation of computer system and management of data base centrally in the National Data Centre. All the data will be stored at the Centre to help the customers to be in touch with their day-to-day status. He also announced new Direct Agency Scheme. Having the massive network of more than 1, 55,000 Post Offices and high rate of Bonus, PLI has succeeded in retaining its place in the market despite fierce competition from private companies. PLI fund is growing at an average annual rate of 20% and Rural PLI fund at an average rate of more than 40% in recent years. PLI concentrates on traditional Life Insurance products and primary focus is coverage of risk and ensuring a decent return to its customers. Besides Whole Life, Endowment and Anticipated Policies, PLI offers Yugal Suraksha policies for working couples and offers add on policies for children. Starting from acceptance of proposals to settlement of claims, the operations are computerized and strict norms are followed for every aspect of customer service.

5797. (5-2-2008) NEW DELHI : Direct tax collections continued to record a growth of over 40 percent for the first ten months of the current fiscal. Net direct tax collections stood at Rs.2,18,538 crore, up from Rs.1,55,576 crore during the same period last fiscal, registering a growth of 40.47 percent and achieving over 81 percent of budgeted direct tax target of Rs.2,67,490 crore. Corporate Tax registered a growth of 37.54 percent at Rs.1,33,851 crore, up from Rs.97,315 crore during the previous fiscal, while Personal Income Tax (including FBT, STT and BCTT) grew by 45.45 percent at Rs.84,349 crore, up from Rs.57,990 crore. Growth in Securities Transaction Tax (STT) was 85.71 percent (Rs.6,793 crore against Rs.3,658 crore) and Fringe Benefit Tax (FBT) was 30.74 percent (Rs.5,161 crore against Rs.3,948 crore). Banking Cash Transaction Tax (BCTT) grew by 14.51 percent (Rs.460 crore against Rs.401 crore). Overall direct tax growth was highest in the Mumbai region at 64.26 percent; followed by North Western region (Chandigarh) at 48.19 percent, Pune region at 44.37 percent, Karnataka & Goa regions (Bangalore) at 43.76 percent and Andhra Pradesh region (Hyderabad) at 39.53 percent. Corporate tax growth was highest in the North-Eastern region (Guwahati) at 254.30 percent; followed by Bihar & Jharkhand regions (Patna) at 75.45 percent, Kerala region (Kochi) at 71.61 percent, eastern Uttar Pradesh (Lucknow) at 71.46 percent and Mumbai at 69.90 percent. Personal income tax growth was highest in Madhya Pradesh & Chhattisgarh regions (Bhopal) at 393.07 percent; followed by Mumbai at 54.48 percent, part of western Uttar Pradesh region (Meerut) at 52.91 percent, Andhra Pradesh region (Hyderabad) at 49.97 percent, eastern Uttar Pradesh (Lucknow) at 48.84 percent and Tamil Nadu region (Chennai) at 48.41 percent.

5798. (5-2-2008) NEW DELHI : The Government has appointed Shri Parag P. Tripathi, Senior Advocate as Additional Solicitor General of India in the Supreme Court of India with immediate effect for a period of two years. An alumni of Delhi University and Harvard Law School, Cambridge, USA, Shri Tripathi had been designated as Senior Advocate in January 2000. He has been in active practice in India since 1983 in the Supreme Court, the High Court of Delhi and other High Courts, Judicial Tribunals and Bodies, CEGAT, CLB, MRTP and Commercial Arbitrations, chambered with Mr. K.K. Venugopal, Senior Advocate (1986). His areas of specialization include Constitutional Law, Administrative Law, Commercial and Corporate Laws, including both in Court litigation and private forum litigation like arbitrations, negotiations and out of Court settlements. He has a wide range of experience in settling foreign collaborations, joint venture agreements and project finance agreements for clients. Shri Tripathi published papers in leading Law Journals and has actively participated in various seminars in India and abroad.

5799. (5-2-2008) NEW DELHI : GM crops have been developed to incorporate various traits such as insect pest resistance, herbicide tolerance, disease resistance, altered nutritional profile, enhanced storage life etc. The benefits of their use include increased crop yields, reduction in farm costs and thereby increase in farm profit as well as protection of the environment. Research is focused on a second generation of GM crops that feature increased nutritional and/or industrial traits such as easy processability. These varieties are expected to bring in more direct benefits to consumer such as correction of dietary deficiencies. The range of crops being targeted for genetic improvement include several commercially important crops such as maize, soybean, tomato, cotton, potato, mustard, rice etc. The transgenic crop show different traits like pest resistance, herbicide resistance, cold tolerance, drought tolerance, increased nutrition and plant pharmaceuticals. Its potential benefits are mainly in improved farming with cheaper food and more food. This helps in availability of more crops, better quality products, improvement in health and reduced use of chemicals and herbicides.

5800. (5-2-2008) NEW DELHI : As per the latest report received from the High Security Animal Disease Laboratory, Bhopal, samples of poultry birds collected from Bareilly and Shahjahanpur of Uttar Pradesh, which were part of the consignment transported from West Bengal, have tested negative. Mortality of 130 birds is reported on 4.2.2008 from Murshidabad, South 24 Parganas and North 24 Parganas. A total mortality of 1,32,883 poultry birds has been reported from Birbhum, Dakshin Dinajpur, Murshidabad, Nadia, South 24 Parganas, Burdwan, Bankura, Hooghly, Malda, Coochbehar, Purulia, Howrah and North 24 Parganas districts of West Bengal. This number stood at 1,32,753 till yesterday. A total of 298 Rapid Response Teams were engaged as on 04.02.2008, which completed culling of 1.34 lakh birds taking the cumulative figure of culling so far to 35.17 lakh. Latest position of destruction of eggs and feed carried out till 04.02.2008 are 14,82,323 and 79,505 kg respectively. The preventive culling of poultry birds in Assam continues. Out of the target population of 89,254 birds required to be culled in Dhubri and Kokrajhar districts of the state, 10,022 birds have since been culled. The poultry owners are also being paid compensation simultaneously with culling. Preventive culling is, however, yet to commence in Bihar, Jharkhand and Orissa

5801. (5-2-2008) NEW DELHI : Consultancy Development Centre of the Department of Scientific and Industrial Research, Ministry of Science and Technology, Government of India has launched a Study on "Status of Women Consultants in India" to assess the role of women professionals in consulting. The Study is being carried out in association with the International Management Institute (IMI), a leading business school in Delhi. The objective of the study is to map the competencies among women professionals and identify gaps, based on which a plan for competency enhancement of women professionals for consulting across sectors/disciplines and functions can be developed. Many women professionals have personal and family responsibilities that play a part in determining ability to reach their desired career paths. Finding the right opportunity to maintain an effective balance between personal and professional responsibilities is the challenge for every professional woman today. With the present IT and communication technologies, most consulting activities can be carried out from home resulting in low overheads as well as flexibility. This is an added advantage for women as it helps them in maintaining an effective balance between the professional commitments as well as the family responsibilities. Studies carried out by McKinsey, the internationally renowned consulting firm and IBM, the leading IT firm indicate that in the coming years women will be an increasing percentage of the workforce at all levels and shall play an important role as members of diverse consulting teams. The Study by CDC will include personal interviews in mini/metro cities across the country, besides desk research and questionnaire based survey. The outcome would help in evolving a Road Map including policy initiatives to be taken for development of women consultants in the country. The Study is expected to be completed in six months, leading to a series of seminars for dissemination of the findings of the Study.

5802. (5-2-2008) NEW DELHI : The Union Minister of Shipping, Road Transport and Highways, Thiru T.R. Baalu has approved a sum of Rs. 56.73 crore for Land Acquisition for construction of Kodungallur Bypass (Chandapura-Kottapuram bypass) on NH-17 from km. 401/000 to km. 404/750 in the State of Kerala. The bypass has been approved so that the existing congested and narrow stretches in the above portion passing through Kodungallur Municipality can be avoided. Bypass starts from Chandapura on North side and ends at straight approaches of existing Kottappuram bridge in the new alignment on Southern side. The existing reach is a major hurdle in the NH-17 between Edappily and Chavakkadu and by constructing the bypass, traffic management is expected to be smooth.

5803. (5-2-2008) NEW DELHI : Shri Kamal Nath, Union Minister of Commerce and Industry, has stressed upon increasing the business-to-business relations between India and Ireland at a higher levels. Supporting the promotion of bilateral trade and investment opportunities between the two countries, Shri Kamal Nath emphasized on cooperation between small and medium enterprises of both the countries. This was stated by Shri Kamal Nath when Mr. Nigel Dodds, Trade Minister of Northern Ireland, called on him here today. Both the countries expressed their keenness to cooperate on all matters of mutual interest. The bilateral trade between India and the UK during 2006-07 was US $ 9.7 billion (exports-US $ 5.5 billion and imports-US $ 4.1 billion). The major item of exports to UK include petroleum (crude & products), RMG cotton including accessories, machinery & instruments, manufactures of metals and gems & jewellery. The major item of imports from the UK include pearls, precious& semi-precious stones, machinery (except electric and electronic), gold, metalifers ores & metal scraps and transport equipments. As regards the foreign direct investment (FDI), approvals were to the tune of US $ 6.94 billion and inflows were US $ 4.06 billion. Top sectors attracting FDI from UK was fuels (power & oil refining), telecommunications, chemicals (other than fertilizers) and services sector (financial and on-financial)

5804. (5-2-2008) NEW DELHI : Mr. Marshall M. Bouton, President of the Chicago Council on Global Affairs, during his meeting with Shri Kamal Nath, Union Minister of Commerce & Industry, here today discussed the issues about increasing the bilateral trade and economic cooperation between India and USA. During the interactions, both sides agreed that there is lot of potential in both the countries and there are so many untapped areas to be concentrated, particularly in the small and medium enterprises (SMEs). USA ranks second and cumulative FDI inflows from USA is US $ 6.35 billion (9.79%) till October, 2007. Top sectors attracting FDI inflows (from January 2000 to October 2007) from USA are Computer software & Hardware (20.45%), Services Sector (financial & non-financial) (19.92%), Automobile Industry (7.50%), Consultancy Services (6.36%), and Construction Activities (4.82%). USA has been granted 1,754 technical collaborations (22.21% of the total) since, 1991. USA is India's largest trading partner. The total trade in merchandise and commodities during 2005-06 was US $ 24.9 billion achieving a growth of 20.2% over that of previous year. During the period 2006-07, India's total trade with USA was US $ 30.59 billion. Exports and imports were US $18.86 billion and US $ 11.73 billion respectively. Indian exports were US $18.86 billion while Indian imports were US $11.73 billion, giving a trade surplus of US $ 7.13 billion for India in 2006-07. Exports to USA from India constitute about 16.83% of India's total exports. The Chicago Council on Global Affairs, founded in 1922 as The Chicago Council on Foreign Relations, has been a pre-eminent forum in Chicago and the Midwest for the discussion of world affairs and U.S. foreign policy since its inception. It is a leading independent, nonpartisan organization committed to influencing the discourse on global issues through contributions to opinion and policy formation, leadership dialogue, and public learning.

5805. (5-2-2008) NEW DELHI : The Government of India has nominated the Majuli Island in Jorhat district, Upper Assam for inscription on the World Heritage List under the "Cultural Landscape" category in 2008. The Prime Minister had called a meeting in October, 2007 to discuss issues relating to Majuli with Smt. Ambika Soni, Minister (Tourism & Culture) and Prof. Saifuddin Soz, Minister (Water Resources), Government of India. These issues included the threat of erosion by the Brahmaputra river and the status of Archaeological Survey of India's preparedness to resubmit the site for consideration by UNESCO in 2008. Subsequently, a high level central team assisted by Smt. Anshu Vaish, DG, ASI visited Majuli Island in November, 2007 for an on-site review of the status on both counts. India currently has 27 World Heritage Sites, 22 of which are Cultural and 5 Natural. Red Fort was the most recent addition to the list last year. If inscribed, Majuli Island will be first world heritage site in India under the 'cultural landscape' category, which contains both cultural and natural components. Majuli is among the world's largest reverine islands. It is located in the upper reaches of the Brahmaputra river. For the past five hundred years or so, Majuli has been seen as the cradle of Assamese culture and a centre of the neo-Vaishnavite movement. It has 31 Sattras, which are institutions of culture and education, and are also the main repositories of the cultural resources of Majuli. Located in a complex delta system, Majuli is formed at the confluence of Brahmaputra and Lohit rivers. A number of other tributaries also join the rivers close to the island. The island witnesses an annual cycle of floods, erosion and siltation and has a complex and fragile eco-system, with a delicate balance of interaction between man and nature. Majuli was first nominated for World Heritage Status in 2004. The International Council of Monuments and Sites (ICOMOS), an advisory body to the UNESCO World Heritage Centre, had carried out a detailed evaluation of the Majuli Island in 2005. Based on the ICOMOS report, the World Heritage Centre sought additional information by way of the mapping of Sattras and their influence, inventory of cultural resources of the Sattras, their condition analysis, preparation of a risk preparedness strategy for the island, etc. The nomination came up for consideration before the World Heritage Committee in 2006, but was referred back for collating and providing the additional information. The Archaeological Survey of India, which acts as the nodal agency for nomination of Indian sites on the World Heritage List, has prepared a detailed document with the help of consultants and has submitted the additional information for consideration of the World Heritage Committee at its next meeting to be held at Quebec City, Canada in June 2008. Given the complexity of the site, the additional documentation has been prepared using a multi-disciplinary approach and in consultation with a number of field agencies including those under the Ministry of Water Resources and the State Government of Assam. In addition to Majuli, the Kalka-Shimla Railway has been submitted as a fresh Cultural nomination for inscription on the

World Heritage List in 2008. This nomination has also been evaluated by ICOMOS for UNESCO.

5806. (5-2-2008) NEW DELHI : Institute for Defence Studies and Analyses (IDSA), New Delhi and Institute of Strategic Studies (ISS), Islamabad have signed a bilateral institutional cooperation agreement for an initial period of five years. Shri N S Sisodia, Director General, IDSA and Dr. Shireen Mazari, Director General, ISS, signed the MoU on behalf of their respective institutes. This collaborative arrangement is considered an important Confidence Building Measures (CBM) between India and Pakistan. India had proposed establishment of bilateral ties between leading strategic think tanks from both the countries in September 2004. In fact, one of the 72 proposals listed by India then had mentioned these two institutes as the most important ones which could engage in dialogue at a non-official level and contribute to the peace process. The salient features of the MoU signed between the two institutes are: to establish direct academic and scholarly ties, exchange of ideas on issues of common concern and conduct of scholarly conferences, seminars and round-tables.

5807. (5-2-2008) NEW DELHI : Central Water Commission (CWC) under Ministry of Water Resources is monitoring storage position of 81 important reservoirs spread all over the country, of which as many as 36 reservoirs have significant hydro-power benefits with installed capacity of more than 60 MW each. The combined live storage in these 81 reservoirs at the beginning of monsoon *i.e.* 1st June, 2007 was 25 per cent of their designed capacity and stood at 50 per cent of the designed capacity as on 31st January 2008. The present storage is 93 per cent of the last year's storage and 117 per cent of last 10 years average storage during the same period. Out of these 81 reservoirs there are presently 8 reservoirs where this year's storage is 80 per cent or less than the average of previous 10 years and in the remaining 73 reservoirs the storage is more than 80 per cent of the average of previous 10 years. In order to derive the best possible benefits from the available water, Central Water Commission is keeping in touch with the Department of Agriculture and Cooperation and providing information of the weekly storage position to the Crop Weather Watch Group for evolving suitable crop strategies and also apprising the situation to various Departments and Ministries involved in Water Resources Planning. Basinwise storage position as on 31st January 2008 is as follows: The storage position in ten basins namely Ganga, Narmada, Mahi, Sabarmati, Krishna, Godavari, Tapi, Kutch, Cauvery and Neighbouring East Flowing Rivers and West Flowing rivers of South is better than average of previous 10 years. Mahanadi and Neighbouring East flowing Rivers is flowing close to normal and Indus is flowing deficient. Out of 36 reservoirs with significant hydro potential, 11 reservoirs have storage build up less than the average of last 10 years capacity.

5808. (5-2-2008) NEW DELHI : As per the latest report received from the High Security Animal Disease Laboratory, Bhopal, samples of poultry birds collected from Bareilly and Shahjahanpur of Uttar Pradesh, which were part of the consignment transported from West Bengal, have tested negative. Mortality of 130 birds is reported on 4.2.2008 from Murshidabad, South 24 Parganas and North 24 Parganas. A total mortality of 1,32,883 poultry birds has been reported from Birbhum, Dakshin Dinajpur, Murshidabad, Nadia, South 24 Parganas, Burdwan, Bankura, Hooghly, Malda, Coochbehar, Purulia, Howrah and North 24 Parganas districts of West Bengal. This number stood at 1,32,753 till yesterday. A total of 298 Rapid Response Teams were engaged as on 04.02.2008, which completed culling of 1.34 lakh birds taking the cumulative figure of culling so far to 35.17 lakh. Latest position of destruction of eggs and feed carried out till 04.02.2008 are 14,82,323 and 79,505 kg respectively. The preventive culling of poultry birds in Assam continues. Out of the target population of 89,254 birds required to be culled in Dhubri and Kokrajhar districts of the state, 10,022 birds have since been culled. The poultry owners are also being paid compensation simultaneously with culling. Preventive culling is, however, yet to commence in Bihar, Jharkhand and Orissa

5809. (5-2-2008) NEW DELHI : A dividend cheque for Rs.9.56 crore, towards the interim dividend of 35% for 2007-08, was presented to Shri Kamal Nath, Union Minister of Commerce & Industry by Dr. Arvind Pandalai, Chairman & Managing Director of State Trading Corporation of India Ltd. (STC) here last evening. During the first nine months of the current financial year (April-December 2007), STC has achieved an impressive increase of over 40% in profit over the corresponding period of the previous year. The total turnover has also crossed Rs.11000 crore mark during this period thereby surpassing the proportionate MOU target by 48%. During the period, STC's exports grew by over 60% to reach past Rs.3000 crore due to higher sales of chemicals & pharmaceuticals, gold jewellery, steel raw materials and iron ore. Total imports at Rs.7424 crore exceeded the proportionate MOU target by 36% in spite of lower wheat imports of the order of Rs.1500 crore as against about Rs.4200 crore worth of wheat imports during Apr.-Dec.'06. Imports of bullion, hydrocarbons, minerals, metals, petro-chemicals and pulses significantly grew over previous year. STC has, of late, entered into domestic tea operations. It procures tealeaves directly from small farmers in Nilgiri district in Tamil Nadu. The tealeaves are processed through leasing of a processing unit and are blended to suit to the market tastes. STC has recently launched own brand 'Tohfa' tea for sale under PDS through Gujarat State Civil Supplies Corporation. These operations by STC aim at economic upliftment of small tea growers on one hand and augmenting its own business on the other. STC is soon planning to enter into the field of bio-fuels. It has already signed an MOU with an Indian company in the field of Jatropha breeding/cultivation and identification of suitable strains of micro-algae, the production of biofuels. Under the MOU, STC shall arrange sale of all Jatropha planting material and allied products/services of the partner company. Discussions have been/are being held with a number of international companies having bio fuel refineries in the area of Jatropha plantation.

5810. (5-2-2008) NEW DELHI : Number of affected districts remains the same (14). A total population of 28.59 lakhs is under surveillance [16.08 lakhs in 0-3 Km area and 12.50 lakhs in 3-10 Km area]. In 0-3 Km area 1982 persons with fever and URI have been detected of which one had exposure to sick/infected birds. In the 3-10 Kms area a total of 1371 persons have been detected with fever & URI of which two had exposure history. These cases have been followed up.

5811. (6-2-2008) NEW DELHI : The last decade of the 20th century has seen gender emerging as basic factor for human progress. From women's problems to women's issues, finally to women's perspectives, there has been a whole reshaping of paradigms of development. Two significant factors regarding women have emerged the avenues for their participation in governance specially in the hitherto male dominated organizations and second, which is more significant, her welfare and proper representation of her perspective.

5812. (6-2-2008) JABALPUR: Mr. L.K. Advani said here that I've come here many times in the past. I very vividly remember my visit during the 1997 Swarna Jayanti Rath Yatra. Jabalpur had been rocked by a severe earthquake. I was heartened to see strong manifestation of the voluntary spirit among the people of Jabalpur and Madhya Pradesh in facing this natural calamity. Indeed, volunteers and philanthropic help had come from different parts of the country. Tragedies and crises have always united our people. Jabalpur is a cantonment city. The people of India are proud of our Armed Forces. Whenever our jawans were called upon to defend the nation, our people stood solidly behind them. We have seen this national unity most recently during the Kargil War. The Pakistani soldiers had occupied the peaks. Our Army was at the bottom of the mountains. The terrain was extremely rugged. The temperature was sub-zero. Hence, the enemy had a clear locational and visual advantage. And, yet, our brave jawans captured one peak after another and finally made the entire Pakistani Army run away. They even left their dead soldiers behind. It was our jawans who carried out the last rites as per the Islamic traditions. The Kargil War, which was fought when Shri Atal Bihari Vajpayee was the Prime Minister, was the first war in the history of independent India when we neither lost any part of our territory nor allowed any part of the territory recovered on the battleground to be bartered away in the arena of diplomacy.

5813. (6-2-2008) NEW DELHI : Shri Kamal Nath, Union Minister of Commerce and Industry, has called for improving the bilateral trade between India and Kyrgystan while observing that the present level of bilateral trade during 2006-07 is of the order of US $ 38 million (exports US $ 37 million and imports US $ 0.77 million). This he said when Mr. Ednan Karabaev, Minister of Foreign Affairs of the Kyrgyz Republic, met him here today. He further stated that the relations between the two countries are traditionally close and have over the years been reinforced by close political rapport and meaningful economic cooperation. Both sides discussed the steps for increasing the bilateral trade in the areas of food processing, textiles, agriculture, science & technology, tourism, chemical and pharmaceutical. Pointing out the difficulties faced by the Indian businessmen in obtaining the Kyrgystan visa, Shri Kamal Nath mentioned about the excellent investment climate in India and the opportunities available for the companies to take advantage of the same. Shri Kamal Nath also emphasized that "Indian skills and capacity in the IT are now globally acknowledged and we can share our expertise in this area with your country". Major commodities of export to Kyrgystan from India are RMG wool, RMG cotton including accessories, leather goods, handicrafts, machinery & instruments, cosmetics and toiletries etc., while the major commodities that India imports from Kyrgystan are raw wool, manufactures of metals, raw silk, crude minerals, Metalifers ores and metal scrap etc.

5814. (6-2-2008) NEW DELHI : Boys Sports Company, 1 Signal Training Centre (STC), Jabalpur, a joint sports venture between Army and Sports Authority of India is inviting prospective outstanding Sports Boys to appear for the Selection Rally along with their parents/guardians at Boys Sports Company, No 4 Technical Training Regiment, No. 1 STC, Mandla Road, Jabalpur Cantt on 27 February 2008 in the morning hours. Prospective Boys should have obtained 1st, 2nd or 3rd position in district level sports meet or junior national sports meet. Football players should have participated in winning teams at district level or junior national level. Prospective boys should be between 12 to 16 years of age and should have passed 6th Class at 12 years of age. Their height/weight should be respectively 155 cms, 157 cms, 162 cms, 165 cms, 170 cms / 35 Kgs, 42 Kgs 47 Kgs, 52 Kgs & 55 Kgs. Those candidates who have obtained winning positions in National/Junior National/District/School Federation/Inter Zonal Championships will be at preference. Alternatively, the candidate should display outstanding sports skills at the selection process. Candidates must pass medical examination as per army standards before selection. Selected candidates will get free boarding, lodging and education upto 10th class and will be given high class sports training to make them fit as sports soldiers, after which they will be made to go through an army recruitment selection board. Prospective boys and their parents/guardians will have to make their own arrangements for travelling, boarding and lodging at Jabalpur. Those candidates who wish to have a copy of the prospectus and admission form should send a money order of Rs 30/- only, latest by 25 Feb 2008, along with their complete address including Pin Code, to the Accounts Officer, Boys Sports Company, 4 TTR, 1 STC, Jabalpur (M.P), Pin 482 001. Those who do not wish to obtain the prospectus by money order may collect the admission form on arrival at Jabalpur and submit the completed admission form together with latest pass port size photograph and certificates of the candidate.

5815. (6-2-2008) NEW DELHI : The Minister of Foreign Affairs, Kyrgyz Republic, Mr. Ednan Karabaev today called on Minister of Tourism & Culture, Smt. Ambika

Soni. During their half-an-hour meeting here, both the leaders stressed the need to promote further cooperation in tourism and culture areas. The visiting dignitary said there is a necessity to promote tourist traffic from India to Kyrgyzstan. He said India can offer training to students from his country in tourism and hospitality sector and both the countries can sign document for strengthening bilateral cooperation in tourism sector. On the culture side, Mr. Ednan Karabaev sought India's cooperation in the field of libraries and setting up of a Centre of Hindi Studies in the premises of Diplomatic Academy in Kyrgyzstan. Showing keen interest in the proposed Library Mission in India and in the work of restoration of cultural and historical monuments, he proposed that both the countries may have a joint archaeological expedition either in India or Kyrgyzstan to promote bilateral cooperation in the field of archaeology. He said his country is keen to organize 'Days of India in Kyrgyzstan'. He expressed hope that both the countries will sign a Cultural Exchange Programme (CEP) soon. The Tourism & Culture Minister, Smt. Ambika Soni welcoming the guest said that both the countries have potential to promote tourism further bilaterally. She said exchange of writers, authors, academicians, travel writers, tour operators between the two countries will promote the understanding better between the people of the two countries. She suggested that the people of Kyrgyzstan can take advantage of beach tourism, wellness tourism and shopping festivals in India. Smt. Soni said both the Governments can exchange information on the ways of increasing tourist traffic. She said Kyrgyzstan can utilize India's expertise in the library sector particularly in building book banks.

5816. (6-2-2008) NEW DELHI : The Union Minister for Rural Development Dr. Raghuvansh Prasad Singh has advised the State administrations to ensure conducive environment for the effective implementation of centrally sponsored rural employment schemes. Presiding over the 4th meeting of Central Employment Guarantee Council here today Dr. Singh said guidelines issued for the successful implementation of National Rural Employment Guarantee Act (NREGA) should be followed in letter and spirit. The minister referred the draft CAG report and said instructions have been issued to the states for initiating corrective measures. Referring to the reported incident of attack on social activists conducting social audit of National Rural Employment Guarantee Programme (NREGP) in a State Dr. Singh said such incidents are unfortunate and deserve condemnation. Instead the social audit should be promoted and fostered as it helps check the corrupt practices, if any, Dr. Singh added. He said nobody can be permitted to prevent the momentum of NREGP and every action should be oriented to serve the interest of our rural masses who are already deprived of a lot of opportunities. Among other things the meeting discussed at length were the provision of protection to social audit teams, the status of operational guidelines of NREGA, access to NREGA related documents, crucial role of public vigilance processes, "definition" of household under the Act and remove any inconsistency between the act and guidelines in this regard, raising the financial allocation for administrative expenses under NREGA from 4 percent to 6 percent of the total NREGA costs. The members also put froth demand for the preparation of a Supplement to the Operational Guidelines, all issued related with job cards, transparency of muster rolls, pro-active disclosure of information, work applications, permissible works, works on private lands, worksite management and facilities, work management, Schedule of rates, bank payments and grievance redressal, Review of all existing job cards and preparation of a list of minimum requirements for NREGA job cards as well as of a model job card, preparation of model social audit rules and grievance redressal rules to be made available to State Governments and preparation of improved awareness generation material including a series of primers addressed to Gram Panchayat functionaries, NREGA workers, programme officers and other key participants. The members also strongly adocated for the inclusion of Panchayati Raj Ministry in the entire process. Dr. Singh assured the members for all possible help and said states have been told that the new opportunities and the impetus created in the areas of rural development should not be frittered away and the tempo needs to be maintained. He said that the need for proper monitoring and evaluation for success of any programme needs no elaboration. Earlier the Rural Development Secretary Dr. Rita Sharma briefed the modalities and detailed the action taken on the recommendations made in the previous meeting of the council. Besides Senior Officers from different States the members of the council attending the meeting included Sh. Ramachandra Khuntia, Sh. Ashk Ali, Smt. Batcha Jhansi Laxmi, Smt. Rajani Rana Pratap Singh, Sh. B.D. Sharma,I.A.S.(Retd.), Smt. Aruna Roy, Sh. Mahendra Bodh, Sh. Devi Dayal, I.A.S. (Retd.), Smt. Subhashini Ali, Sh. A. Vardarajan, Smt. Annie. Raja and Sh. Robert Minz..

5817. (6-2-2008) NEW DELHI : The Law Commission of India submitted its 204th Report on the Hindu Succession Act, 1956 to the Government. The Chairman of the Commission, Dr. Justice AR. Lakshmanan, former Supreme Court Judge presented the said Report to the Union Law Minister Dr. Hans Raj Bhardwaj on 5th February, 2008 in his office. By the 2005 Amendment Act, four (4) categories of heirs which were hitherto placed in Class II were elevated to Class I heirs namely (i) Daughter's son's son, (ii) Daughter's daughter's daughter; (iii) Daughter's son's daughter; and (iv) Son's daughter's daughter. While adding these categories to Class I, the corresponding entries in class II were not deleted. There was thus overlapping between class I and class II. In respect of these categories, the Commission has recommended that these four (4) categories should be deleted from class II heirs. The Commission has also suggested that the daughter's son's son and son's daughter's son should also be added in Class I. The Commission further noted that whereas mother of Hindu coparcenary has been included in Class I heirs but father finds mention in Class II heirs category. The Commission has suggested that father should be placed alongwith mother in Class I and both together should take one share. The Commission has also suggested revision of Class I heirs as Class I heirs list in the Schedule present, in the opinion of the Commission, quite a complex and cumbersome reading that is not amenable to easy understanding. The terms of reference with which the Commission had been set up, inter alia, enjoins upon it to revise the Central Act of general Importance so as to simplify them and to remove anomalies, ambiguities and inequities in law. Accordingly, the Commission has examined the Class I heirs list and recommended its revision in a simplified form that Class I heirs list consists of son, daughter, widow mother and father as per recommendations made herein and incase any son or daughter pre-deceased the intestate the Hindu Coparcenary dying intestate, their respective share will go to their children respectively and so on upto three generations upto great grand children. Instead of mentioning each of these descendents, it will be better to have a general provision in the matter with a view to avoid mentioning of each individual relation. Accordingly, the Commission has recommended revision of Class I heirs so as to say firstly, son, daughter, widow mother and father and secondly where any son or daughter dies before the intestate's death, then children of such son or daughter, as the case may be, and widow of pre-deceased son, if any and this will go on in succession among the heirs of the descending branches. It may be recalled that the Hindu Succession Act, 1956 was amended in 2005 by the Hindu Succession (Amendment) Act, 2005 in order to give effect to the recommendations made by the Commission in its earlier (174th) Report in respect of property rights of women under the Hindu Law of Succession. The underlying idea was to remove the discrimination as contained under section 6 of the Hindu Succession Act, 1956 by giving equal rights to daughters in the Hindu Mitakshara coparcenary property as the sons have. Accordingly, Section 6 was amended to provide that the daughter of a coparcenary will, by birth, become the coparcenary heir in her own right in the same manner as the son and will have the same rights and liabilities in the coparcenary property as she would have had if she had been a son. The Schedule of the Act too was amended accordingly to provide right of succession to the descendents through a daughter of a coparcenary dying intestate. Four additions were thus made to Class I heirs. However, while doing so, certain legislative inadvertences had crept in the law. Taking note of these discrepancies, the Commission suo-motu took up a further study of the Hindu Law of Succession.

5818. (6-2-2008) NEW DELHI : Shri Murli Deora, Minister for Petroleum & Natural Gas has said that with sustained efforts, the programme for gas hydrate coring/drilling in Indian Offshore has been successfully executed. "I am informed that we have discovered one of the best gas hydrate reservoirs in K G Area. This is a very exciting development", he added. He was speaking while inaugurating the three-day International Conference on "Gas Hydrates" at Noida, near Delhi, today. Shri Murli Deora also pointed out that production from gas hydrates is a long term goal for many developed countries but it is expected that the production of gas from gas hydrates may be realized sooner due to accelerated efforts by a few countries like India, USA and Japan. Shri Deora re-iterated Government's commitment to the development of gas hydrates, an important natural resource. With the dedicated efforts of national oil companies and the government, India has become the third country in the world to undertake such an ambitious programme on gas hydrates in offshore areas. Acknowledging the technological challenges to be overcome before gas hydrates are brought into commercial use, he expressed hope that solutions will be available in the near future with the kind of efforts being made in this area by the scientific community. "The present programme of gas hydrate coring/drilling and scientific investigations in Indian offshore is an important milestone in this direction. National oil companies such as ONGC, GAIL and OIL are taking a lead role for the exploratory efforts on gas hydrates", the Minister said. Petroleum Secretary Shri M.S. Srinivasan explained the tremendous potential gas hydrates as fuel source. He said that gas hydrates potential, if exploited fully, could make available much more fuels than the presently known conventional fuels. Shri Deora also released the results of the first advanced gas hydrate exploration programme conducted in the offshore of India through the Indian National Gas Hydrate Program (NGHP) Expedition 01. This is the most comprehensive gas hydrate field venture to date. Scientists conducted ocean drilling, coring, logging, and analytical activities to assess the geologic occurrence, regional context, and characteristics of gas hydrate deposits along India's oceans. An international team led by the U.S. Geological Survey (USGS) and the Directorate General of Hydrocarbons (under the Government of India's Ministry of Petroleum and Natural Gas) conducted the expedition. Eminent geoscientists, technologists and professionals are attending the Conference on Gas Hydrates organized by DGH from upstream oil industry from India & abroad.

5819. (6-2-2008) NEW DELHI : The Government has appointed Shri M. Chandrasekharan, senior advocate as Additional Solicitor General of India in the Supreme Court of India with immediate effect for a period of two years. Mr. Chandrasekharan has been in legal practice in India since 1962. He was appointed as Sr. Counsel for Central Government in the Delhi High Court/Supreme Court in 1985.

5820. (6-2-2008) NEW DELHI : As part of its activities in the ongoing 18th New Delhi World Book Fair, Publications Division brought out its book Lok Mein Jal here in a function today. Released by renowned author and scholar Prof. Pushpesh Pant, the book is written by celebrated author Dr. Shyamsundar Dubey. Exploring the sources, usage and availability of water, the book also points out the scarcity and need for its conservation and protection in today's world. In a flowing style, the book takes one along on a tour to folklore, history, culture, literature, language, mythology, traditions and all spheres of life related to water. The book revolves around the fact that there could be no life without water. This well researched book written in a simple language is expected to interest the common man and scholar alike. The Director and Chief Editor of 'Yojana' welcomed the guests at the function.

5821. (6-2-2008) NEW DELHI : National Cooperative Development Corporation (NCDC) has shown record performance on all major parameters in 2006-07. The

Corporation has achieved highest ever disbursals of Rs. 4010 crore and record sanctions of Rs. 6253 crore. While the sanctions recorded an impressive increase of 97%, the disbursements were higher by 74% over the previous fiscal. The recovery of NCDC's dues was the highest at 99.7% and its net NPAs reduced to 0.17% of the loans outstanding. While appreciating NCDC for its 'spectacular' performance, Agriculture Minister Shri Sharad Pawar today asked this apex financial institution in the cooperative sector to re-orient its decision making process to respond to fast emerging challenges. Addressing the General Council of NCDC here today, Shri Sharad Pawar emphasized that large investments would be required to achieve 4% annual growth of the farm sector in the XI Plan*. Though the annual growth rate has shown a rising trend in the last two years, reversing the deceleration experienced during the previous Plans would need further mobilizing resources, creating infrastructure, facilitating easy availability of inputs, organizing research and technology development, institutional support services and putting in place contingency measures to safeguard crops from natural calamities. The cooperative sector would have to play an important role in this endeavour, the Minister said. NCDC has chalked out an ambitious programme of Rs. 19640 core for the XI Plan. The Minister also informed that 'with a view to providing one time relief to all debt-ridden farmers across the country, the Central Government is seriously deliberating on a package for such farmers.'

5822. (6-2-2008) NEW DELHI : In exercise of the powers conferred by clause (1) of Article 217 of the Constitution of India, the President is pleased to appoint (i) Shri Justice Vipin Sanghi and (ii) Smt. Justice Aruna Suresh, Additional Judges of the Delhi High Court, to be Judges of the Delhi High Court, in that order of seniority, with effect from the dates they assume charge of their respective offices.

5823. (6-2-2008) NEW DELHI : Annual Plan of West Bengal for the year 2008-09 was approved today at a meeting between the Deputy Chairman, Planning Commission, Mr. Montek Singh Ahluwalia, and the Chief Minister of West Bengal, Mr. Buddhadeb Bhattacharya. The Annual Plan size was agreed at Rs 11602.38 crores. This includes additional Central Assistance of Rs. 150 crores for projects of special importance to the State. Deputy Chairman, Planning Commission, Mr. Montek Singh Ahluwalia complemented the State for improvements in the fiscal health of the State. He said both growth rate and inclusiveness of development programmes are showing healthy trend. He said State Domestic Product Growth rate was registered at 8.1 per cent in 2005-06 and per capita income was also comparable to all India figures. Mr. Ahluwalia pointed out that the State was well set to reach Eleventh Plan target of 9 per cent growth rate. He said the Commission was keen on ensuring optimum utilization of funds being allocated to the State for Centrally sponsored schemes. For this purpose, he invited suggestions to make these schemes genuinely flexible. He said the State Government should firm up strategy to implement Rastriya Krishi Vikas Yojana (RKVY) as Centre's assistance under this programme was likely to go up substantially next year. Attention was also drawn to the need for improved States' support in implementing national horticulture mission and skill development mission. Proper market mechanisms need to be put in place to reduce wastage in perishable goods. States should come forward in supplementing Central government's effort in skill development. In his comments on the performance of the State, Shri Buddhadeb Bhattacharya said that the State Government was pursuing employment oriented growth strategy. Emphasis would continue on focused attention to agriculture, small & micro enterprises (SMEs) and development of physical and social infrastructure. He said Kisan Credit Card facility has to be extended to every agriculture households. Central support to vocational training and minority welfare programmes should be increased. Banks should ensure that loans are made available to self-help groups. He said the State government was keen to improve quality of life in Sundarban region and requested Planning Commission to work out a separate master plan for the region. Support of Commission was also sought for encouraging cluster concept for small & micro enterprises. He said investment climate was improving in the State. Thrust areas for next financial year would include inclusive growth, bridging the divide, human development focused programme, sustainable agriculture growth, infrastructure build up for industrialization, intensifying industrial promotion and skill development. Human development focused programme will include enhancing livelihood opportunities, empowerment of education and improving health care facilities. Inclusive growth will have special focus on ST/SC, OBC and Minorities as well as gender and children plan at State and district level.

5824. (6-2-2008) NEW DELHI : At the instance of the Ministry of Micro, Small & Medium Enterprises, the Reserve Bank of India has set up a Working Group on Rehabilitation of sick Small and Medium Enterprises under the chairmanship of CMD, Punjab National Bank. This was stated by Shri Mahabir Prasad, Union Minister for Micro, Small & Medium Enterprises while addressing the Members of the Parliamentary Consultative Committee attached to his Ministry here today. He informed that this Group so far held meetings with various stakeholders including commercial banks/financial institutions, MSME Associations, State Governments, MSME entrepreneurs, etc. Further, in association with the MSME Association, the Group is in the process of collecting information from sick MSMEs to gain useful insight at the grassroots level. The report is being finalised. The agenda for today's meeting was "Sickness in the micro and small enterprises (MSE) sector". Shri Prasad said, as per analysis by the Reserve Bank of India recently on the position up to March 2007, the number of sick micro and small enterprises was 1.14 lakh in the country, which shows that in comparison to the year 2006 there has been a decrease in the number of sick units in the year 2007. The banks assume an important role in overcoming the problem of sickness in micro and small enterprises. Shri Prasad informed that the Reserve Bank of India took significant steps recently related to sickness. These mainly include: (i) issuing guidelines to all the public sector banks on One-Time Settlement (OTS) Scheme for small and medium enterprise accounts, (ii) issuing detailed guidelines regarding debt restructuring mechanism for all eligible small and medium enterprises, (iii) implementing a simplified one-time settlement scheme for small borrowers whose principal amount is upto Rs.25,000/- so that borrowers become eligible for fresh loans, etc. The Minister also informed that the Reserve Bank of India had also at its Regional Offices constituted Empowered Committees to review the progress in rehabilitation of sick small and medium units, which would prove to be useful in overcoming the problem of sickness. Cautioning the banks, the Minister said, "it has been noticed that more often than not the benefit of loan goes to rich entrepreneurs. This trend has to be reversed. Some of the Members were of the view that apart from agriculture, micro and small enterprises generate employment in the rural areas. Hence, the sickness of these sectors should be addressed effectively.

5825. (6-2-2008) NEW DELHI : The Central Government has released Rs. 929 crore to the States to plan and implement projects under the Rashtriya Krishi Vikas Yojana (RKVY). Considering the encouraging response from States, the initial budget provision of Rs. 900 crore was increased to Rs. 1000 crore. More funds will be made available to ensure that the implementation of the scheme is smooth. Informing this to the parliamentary Consultative Committee of the Ministry of Agriculture here today, Shri Sharad Pawar expressed the hope that this scheme would provide an incentive to States to invest more in agriculture. Explaining the need for greater public investment in the agriculture sector, Shri Pawar said that the annual growth of agriculture had slowed down to about 2% during the IX and X Five Year Plans. The growth rate did pick up during the last two years of the X Plan, but public investment needs to be stepped up to achieve growth rate of 4% in the XI Plan. Shri Pawar said that the new scheme encourages States to increase the share of expenditure on agriculture and allied sectors in their State Plans. States are required to prepare District Agriculture Plans and a State Agriculture Plan based on the local agro-climatic conditions. The scheme has wide scope and States can plan a range of agricultural activities including animal husbandry and fisheries under RKVY. States have been given a great deal of flexibility in planning and execution. Projects are sanctioned and their implementation monitored by a State Level Sanctioning Committee chaired by the Chief Secretary of the State. So far 15 States have held State Level Committee meeting to clear projects worth nearly Rs. 930 crore. Stressing that proper implementation and monitoring of the scheme was necessary for its success, Shri Pawar informed that the National Institute of Rural Development, Hyderabad would assist in monitoring and evaluation of the implementation of RKVY. The members who attended the meeting include S/Shri A. Sai Prathap, Jai Parkash, K. Francis George, M. Appadurai, K. Dhanaraju, Alok Kumar Mehata, Kailash Eaitha, and Ranen Earman (Lok Sabha) Thennala G. Balakrishna Pillai, C. Ramachndraiah, Pyarelal Khandelwal and Prof. M.S. Swaminathan (Rajya Sabha).

5826. (6-2-2008) NEW DELHI : The Ministry of Women and Child Development is organizing a workshop to sensitize senior officials of various Central Ministries towards gender responsive budgeting. The residential workshop being orgnaised on 7th-8th February at Kuchesar, District Bulandshehar will be attended by the officials of 35 Ministries. The objective is to sensitize senior officials to the needs and realities of women at the grass roots. The Government has already set up gender budgeting cells in 35 Ministries to ensure a gender perspective at various stages like programme & policy formulation, review of extant policies and guidelines, reprioritization and allocation of resources. The two-day will make workshop assessment of needs of target groups and impact of the gender budgeting so far. Case studies and feedback on the initiative and future plan of action will be deliberated upon. The Ministry has taken number of initiatives to use gender budgeting as a tool for empowerment of women. The Ministry has adopted 'budgeting for gender equity' as a Mission Statement. A strategic framework of activities to implement this mission has been framed and disseminated across all departments of the Central Government. The Ministry of finance has also mandated all Ministries to establish Gender Budgeting cells and has issued a Gender charter for the same.

5827. (6-2-2008) NEW DELHI : The Union Home Minister, Shri Shivraj Patil has expressed the hope that the people of Mumbai would not allow the peace and harmony of their city to be disturbed. In a statement issued here today, he said that the Maharashtra Government has been asked to provide protection to those who may require it. The following is the text of his statement. "Mumbai is the financial and industrial capital of India, built by people of Maharashtra and the citizens of India, coming from all parts of the country. It represents the glory and the strength of united India. People from Maharashtra and all parts of the country are living here and have enjoyed prosperity and faced adversity together. Mumbai has always been a symbol of unity which in no case should be disturbed or allowed to be disturbed and damaged. The State Government has been asked to see that no individual or group of persons is intimidated, attacked or their properties are targeted and damaged. The State Government has been asked to take necessary action against the miscreants indulging in such activities without delay and to provide protection to those who may need it or may be vulnerable. We hope, the people would not allow the peace and harmony to be disturbed. Mumbai all through its history has drawn people from far and near and its people are well known for their broad-mindedness and hospitality. They should see that this reputation of the city of the State is not allowed to be tarnished in any way."

5828. (7-2-2008) NEW DELHI : The Election Commission of India held meeting of the State Chief Electoral Officers (CEOs) today to review the status of revision of electoral rolls with 1st January, 2008 as the qualifying date and deciding a time frame for publication of photo electoral rolls for all the States/.UTs. During the meeting, the Commission apprised the CEO's an analytical framework for testing the veracity of the Electoral Rolls depending on certain broad parameters like elector-population ratio, gender ratio etc. and prescribed specific format for such analysis. The CEOs have been directed to complete such analysis and submission of reports by 29th February. In addition, the Commission also decided to put in place a verification mechanism by appointing Roll Observers in each State/UT to ensure integrity of the Rolls. While reviewing the implementation of Photo Electoral Rolls, the Commission has fixed the timeframe for implementation of Photo Electoral Rolls in all the States giving the calendar for various stages. A timeframe for final publication of photo electoral rolls was set at 31st August, 2008 for all States/UTs. The final publication of the Electoral Rolls with qualifying date as 1/1/2008 has been done in 20 States. The remaining few States, including Gujarat and Himachal Pradesh, that have just had General Elections, are in a process of finalising the revision formalities. It is expected that by the end of the first fortnight of March, 2008, the revision process would be complete in the entire country. During deliberations, the Commission laid emphasis on polling station rationalisation to be looked from the viewpoint of voter convenience and laid down fresh guidelines for creation of new polling stations and decongestion of existing polling stations. During the meeting, the preparatory activities for conversion of existing constituencies into the proposed delimited constituencies and the state of preparedness in this regard was also discussed. The CEOs were briefed about the procedure to be followed and the precautions to be taken for accurate mapping and conversion of the existing constituencies. The CEOs have been directed to undertake one case study and incorporate the lessons emerging from that before universalising the process of delimitation in the whole State/UT. The Commission has fixed 29th February, 2008 as the last date for the completion of the pilot process for all States/UTs. The Commission also reviewed the progress made in a pilot project undertaken by the CEO, Karnataka for comprehensive computerised management of Electoral Rolls. The software developed for the purpose was reviewed and it was decided that this would be adopted for the entire country in due course after incorporating changes warranted during the pilot.

5829. (7-2-2008) NEW DELHI : The Union Minister for Health & Family Welfare, Dr. Anbumani Ramadoss, today, dedicated to the Nation the first state of the art In Vitro Fertilization (IVF) Research Centre established at All India Institute of Medical Sciences (AIIMS). This facility will help those couples who are not able to have a child on their own and need some assistance to be able to conceive. Speaking on the occasion, the Minister said that this centre has been created with a mission to not only provide cost effective services to the majority, but also to foster an environment that promotes research and training. The following is the text of the Health Minister's speech: The Department of Obstetrics & Gynecology, AIIMS, has added yet another milestone in the history by adding this much needed ART centre in the Institute under the leadership of Professor Suneeta Mittal, Chief ART Centre and Head, Deptt. of Obstetrics & Gynecology, AIIMS, and I compliment her for taking this initiative in the interest of women's health in the country. All India Institute of Medical Sciences, as an institution par excellence has pioneered in health care services and research and has always kept pace with the best of medical centres in the West. Enormous scientific advancements have occurred in the past century in the field of Reproductive Medicine. Department of Obstetrics & Gynecology, AIIMS, has always excelled in providing quality health care to the women of this country. Infertility causes breech in the continuity of once genetic pedigree and thus results in substantial socio-medical problem. In 2004, it was estimated that over 186 million women worldwide experience problems in conceiving. This figure is substantially high over previous estimates, suggesting a global increase in prevalence of infertility. In India the problem affects nearly 6-8% of couples in the reproductive age group. Considering the current population statistics of India this would extrapolate to a humongous burden to the society. Until the last decade the problem of infertility received little attention, as the main focus of health services has been on efforts to slow down population growth. Defining reproductive health as a state of complete physical, mental and social well being and not merely the absence of disease or infirmity in all matters relating to the reproductive system and its function. Infertility is deeply distressing with psychological trauma and pain, a disease worthy of investigation and treatment. In a society as ours where child bearing defines a woman's identity and motherhood of great social significance, infertility leaves unhealed scars traumatizing the couple socially and emotionally. Out of a population of 1000 million Indians, an estimated 25% (250 million individuals) are conservatively estimated to be attempting parenthood at any given time; by extrapolating the WHO estimate, approximately 13 to 19 million couples are likely to be infertile in the country at any given time. Prevention and appropriate treatment of infertility has been included in the ICPD (International Conference on Population and Development) Programme of Action; it follows that alleviation of infertility should be included as a component of the primary health care system.

5830. (7-2-2008) NEW DELHI : Income Tax Department had recently carried out a search operation against a group of Gurgaon engaged in development of real estate and running a private airline. On the basis of evidence collected during that search, surveys were subsequently conducted by the Department at 11 different locations in Delhi, Mumbai and Gurgaon on two leading groups of builders having close business connections and transactions with the group searched earlier. On the basis of evidence collected during these surveys, the two groups of builders admitted to unaccounted income of Rs.63 crore and Rs.31 crore, respectively. During the course of survey at another builder's premises huge amount of cash was found. As a result, search was also conducted at the residence of its directors and cash amounting to Rs.2 crore was seized. This builder also admitted unaccounted income of Rs.10 crore.

5831. (7-2-2008) NEW DELHI : Krishak Bharati Cooperative Limited (KRIBHCO) today presented a dividend cheque of Rs.53.54 crore to the government of India. The Chairman of KRIBHCO Shri Chandra Pal Singh handed over the cheque to the Minister for Steel, Chemicals and Fertilisers Shri Ram Vilas Paswan here. The company has announced 20 per cent dividend for the year 2006-07. It produced 34.75 lakh tonnes of urea last year. Minister of State for Chemicals and Fertilisers Shri B.K.Handique, Secretary, Department of Fertilisers Dr. J.S. Sarma and other senior officials were present.

5832. (7-2-2008) NEW DELHI : The Steel Authority of India Limited (SAIL) today presented a dividend cheque of Rs. 670.49 crore as the interim dividend to the Government of India. The cheque was handed over to the Minister for Steel, Chemicals & Fertilisers Shri Ram Vilas Paswan by SAIL Chairman, Shri S.K. Roongta. SAIL had announced interim dividend of 19 per cent last month. The Public Sector steel giant has earned a net profit of Rs. 5160 crore during the first nine months of this year.

5833. (7-2-2008) NEW DELHI : Union Power Minister, Shri Sushilkumar Shinde today said that power projects to the tune of 60,214 MW already under construction while in the 11th Plan during the period April, 2007 to January, 2008 a total of 7263 MW has already been added. Interacting with the Media at a Press Meet in New Delhi the Minister said that 56,722MW capacity addition has taken place during the last three Plans. The Capacity Addition during the 8th Plan was 16,423 MW and in the 9th Plan it was 19,119MW while in the 10th Plan it was 21,180 MW. On the power scenario in the country, the Minister said that the current installed capacity is over 1,40,300 MW comprising of 90,645 MW Thermal (64.7%),34,681 MW Hydro (24.7%), 4120 MW Nuclear (2.9%) 10,855 MW Renewable (7.7%). He said that for the 11th Plan 78,577 MW has been proposed for capacity addition. In addition 14,000 MW is expected through Renewables and another 12,000 MW from captive route. Shri Shinde said that orders for machinery of projects to the tune of 10,950 MW will be placed by the end of March 2008. The total generation of electricity in the country during the current year (April to December 2007) was 526 billion units, as compared to about 493 billion units during the corresponding period last year, an increase of 6.6%. The Plant Load Factor (PLF) of thermal power stations in the country during April to December 2007 was 77.2% compared to 75.3% during the previous year. The PLF of central sector generating stations during the current year increased from 82.3 % last year to 85.4% this year.

5834. (7-2-2008) NEW DELHI : 315 projects with a Culturable Command Area (CCA) of 28.68 million hectare have been included under the Centrally Sponsored Command Area Development and Water Management (CADWM) Programme. After deletion of 164 projects, clubbing of 23 projects into 8 projects and inclusion of some new projects, the Programme is presently being implemented in 136 projects. Construction of field channels (which is the main activity under the Programme) has been completed in about 18.7 million hectare till end of X Plan.

From the inception of the Programme till December 2007, an amount of Rs. 3435 crore (including Rs. 217 crore during 2007) has been released to the State Governments as Central Assistance under the Programme. The Centrally Sponsored Command Area Development (CAD) Programme was started in the year 1974 on the recommendations of the National Irrigation Commission (1972) and a Committee of Ministers (1973) with the objective to bridge the gap between irrigation potential created and that utilized through micro level infrastructure development and efficient farm water management to enhance agricultural production and productivity and to improve socio-economic conditions of the farmers. With effect from 1st April 2004, the Programme was restructured and renamed as "CADWM" Programme.

5835. (7-2-2008) NEW DELHI : Shri Kamal Nath, Union Minister of Commerce and Industry, during his call on the Finland Prime Minister, Mr. Matti Vanhanen, here today, informed that India is a vibrant economy and huge opportunities are available for doing business with India. India has a large skilled human resource base, which can be combined with Finland's technology and investment to create a win-win situation for both sides, he added. Shri Kamal Nath stated that initiative for cooperation in renewable energy sectors needs to be encouraged. The Commerce Minister also reiterated that India looks forward to early conclusion of comprehensive trade and investment negotiations with European Union (EU), as these agreements provide building blocks for successful economic relationship. "India recognises the importance of small & medium enterprises (SMEs) to exploit the potential of the growing Indian markets and participate in projects related to infrastructural development in particular", the Minister added. A large high-level delegation representing both official and business, were present at the interactions. Shri Kamal Nath emphasised that both the governments need to encourage businesses to explore new areas and sectors, to widen and deepen the trade basket. "Trade between India and Finland is concentrated in a few products, such as readymade garments, machinery and electronic goods", he said. During the interactions with Finland Prime Minister, Shri Kamal Nath underlined the areas of bilateral cooperation in the areas such as, energy including renewable & clean development mechanism, forestry & forest industries, information technology, civil aviation, environment, science & technology, air services, ports & shipping, culture, tourism and financial cooperation. As regards the multilateral trade, Shri Kamal Nath stated that India remains committed to a rule-based multilateral trading system and informed about the current state of play in the Doha Round. India has been engaging constructively and actively with other fellow member countries of the World Trade Organisation (WTO) towards achieving an early conclusion of the round. Bilateral trade between India and Finland during the year 2006-07 was to the tune of US $ 804 million as against US $ 782 million in 2005-06. The main exports to Finland were drugs, pharmaceuticals & fine chemicals, RMG cotton including accessories, manufactures of metals, coffee, machinery and instruments etc. while the main imports from Finland were electronic goods, machinery except electrical & electronics, computer software, paper board & manufactures, transport equipments etc. In the comparative list of countries for FDI approvals, Finland ranks 42nd and actual FDI inflows during the year 1991 to June 2007 was US $ 54.2 million. Sectors attracting Finnish investments are: fuels (power & oil refinery), telecommunications, electrical equipments (including computer software & electronics); services sector (financial and non-financial services) and paper & pulp (including paper). More than 70 Finnish companies have made investments in India including, Nokia Telecommunications OY (Communications); Wartsila Diesel Oy (electrical equipment); Kone Oy (lifts) and Oy Airam Electric AB.

5836. (7-2-2008) NEW DELHI : The Parliamentary Committee have invited memoranda containing suggestions/views/comments from the interested organisations/institutions/individuals on the cleanliness and sanitation in Indian Railways with a view to improve systems for maintenance of sanitation and related infrastructure in the Railways. The Committee on Public Accounts headed by Prof. Vijay Kumar Malhotra, M.P. has taken up the subject "Cleanliness and Sanitation on Indian Railways" as a subject of study for detailed examination and submitting a report to Parliament. The subject is primarily based on Chapter II of the Report of the Comptroller and Auditor General (C&AG) of India for the year ended March 2006, No. 6 of 2007 (Performance Audit), Union Government (Railways) related to "Cleanliness and Sanitation on Indian Railways". The contents of the C&AG Report are available on the website: www.cag.nic.in. Those desirous of submitting memoranda to the Committee may send their written memoranda, either in English or Hindi on the above subject to Shri Brahm Dutt, Director, Lok Sabha Secretariat, Room No. 403, Parliament House Annexe, New Delhi-110001 (Tel. NO. 23034403 and Fax 23010756) or can e-mail at E-mails: compac@sansad.nic.in or bdutt@sansad.nic.in within fifteen days of publication of this advertisement. The memorandum submitted to the Committee would form part of the records of the Committee and would be treated as confidential and would enjoy privileges of the Committee. Those who are willing to appear before the Committee, besides submitting memoranda are requested to indicate so. However, the Committee's decision in this regard shall be final.

5837. (7-2-2008) NEW DELHI : Shri Mahabir Prasad, Minister of Micro, Small and Medium Enterprises launched Rajiv Gandhi Udyami Mitra Yojana here today. The scheme aims to provide handholding assistance to first generation entrepreneurs through lead agencies or Udyami Mitra, who shall provide guidance to the potential entrepreneurs and help them in completion of various tasks and formalities necessary for the establishment of the enterprise. Launching the scheme, the Minister said that the Ministry was running many schemes for development of Micro, Small & Medium Enterprises, under which entrepreneurship and skill development training programmes were organised and technical assistance, marketing assistance and financial assistance were being provided. He said, our further endeavour should be that new enterprises established under these schemes run successfully and play meaningful role in economic development and prosperity of the country. The Minister said, "the youth population of our country was maximum in the world today. If we can give employment to this young labour force of ours, none can stop India from becoming a superpower in the world. For this purpose we need to train the youth thereby converting them into entrepreneurs." He further stated, "we can generate employment opportunities in every part of the country as well as achieve inclusive growth, taking along all sections of the society only through micro and small enterprises. This is our main aim in the 11th Five Year Plan." Under the newly launched Rajiv Gandh Udyami Mitra Yojana, the selected lead agencies *i.e.* Udyami Mitras would provide guidance and assistance to the potential entrepreneurs registered with them, in preparation of project report, arranging finance, selection of technology, marketing tie-ups with buyers, installation of plant and machinery as well as obtaining various approvals, clearances and NOCs etc. Udyami Mitras are expected to be the friend, philosopher and guide of the new entrepreneurs, assisting them in the establishment and successful running of the enterprise. For providing this handholding assistance to the new entrepreneurs, the Udyami Mitras shall be paid handholding charges under the scheme, including nominal contribution of the concerned entrepreneur. However, the beneficiaries belonging to SC/ST/physically handicapped/women and beneficiaries from North Eastern Region will not be required to pay any contribution for the establishment of service enterprises of micro manufacturing enterprise. The scheme is expected to fill a critical void between the entrepreneurship development training and the actual establishment of enterprises, as even after undergoing the EDP training, the entrepreneurs face difficulties in availing full benefits under various schemes and complying with various formalities. Rajiv Gandhi Udyami Mitra Yojana is expected to provide an integrated and end-to-end support for creation of new micro and small enterprises. The launch of the scheme was followed by a National Workshop on the modalities of the scheme which was attended by representatives of various State Governments, industry associations and other organizations involved in the training as well as promotion and development of industries.

5838. (7-2-2008) NEW DELHI : Prof. Saifuddin Soz, the Union Minister for Water Resources has described the death of veteran journalist and well-known political and social activist Shri P.N. Jalali as a great loss to the people of Jammu and Kashmir. Prof. Soz said that late Shri Jalali had a rich and an eventful past spanning over 50 years which saw him playing an active role in diverse fields of life in Kashmir. He recognized Jalali Sahib as a proud and dedicated Kashmiri who got involved deeply in freedom movement and the uplift of backward sections of society. The Minister said that Shri Jalali wielded a powerful pen as a veteran journalist and always used it for promoting the cause of Jammu and Kashmir people. Paying tributes to late Shri Jalali, he said that Kashmir would be poorer by the loss of this great son. Prof. Soz visited the residence of the deceased and conveyed condolences to his son Shri Rahul Jalali who happens to be President of the Press Club of India.

5839. (7-2-2008) NEW DELHI : Shri Kamal Nath, Union Minister of Commerce and Industry, while sharing his views on the Doha Round stated that the negotiations are poised at a critical stage at the moment. While they hold the promise for a conclusion by the end of this year, unless sagacity and statesmanship is on view from the countries, which have benefited chiefly from globalization so far, the negotiations can also move sharply away from convergence. Shri Nath stated that after the resumption of talks exactly a year ago in February 2007, considerable progress has been achieved in the negotiations on Agriculture. However, certain key issues like the cuts in overall trade distorting domestic support, product specific limits in the Amber and Blue Boxes, Green Box disciplines, sensitive products and tariff rate quotas, special safeguard, special products, special safeguard mechanism, tariff simplification, tariff capping, tariff escalation, tropical products and preference erosion etc. are yet to be resolved. The trade distorting measures resorted to by the developed countries have an impact on global agricultural prices, affecting the livelihoods of millions of farmers in the developing world. In order to live up to the avowed agenda of a Development Round, the Doha Round has to deliver on a significant and effective reduction in the agriculture subsidies being given by the developed countries. Firm commitments in this regard are yet to be come from these countries. Therefore, while the progress made in the past one year has been appreciable, considerable work still remains to be done. The Minister expressed the hope that the revised text on Agriculture, which is scheduled to be brought out any day now, will reflect truly the actual progress made and the convergence achieved. However, Shri Kamal Nath felt that the NAMA Draft Modalities text was unbalanced and reflected the views and ambition of only one set of developed countries, while almost completely disregarding the views of more than a hundred developing countries. In order for the Doha Round to reach a successful conclusion, the Minister stated, it is imperative that the views of the membership are reflected faithfully in any document that is brought out and the document helps in actually moving forward the negotiations rather than acting as a divisive and precipitating factor among countries. Shri Nath stated that it is his earnest expectation that the revised text on NAMA, also scheduled to come out immediately, will not belie the expectations of a vast majority of the WTO membership, specially the developing countries, including India. The third major pillar of the negotiations, *viz.* Services, has only shown halting progress during the past year, according to the Commerce Minister. He mentioned in this context that the ambition level in Services has been clearly delineated in the Hong Kong Ministerial and any attempt to reopen this issue in order to pitch an overweening ambition in only a limited part of the Services arena, without showing a comparable level of ambition in the other parts of the arena. For India, Services are an important sector in the Doha negotiations and market access in Modes 1 and 4 with disciplines in Domestic Regulations are a must have and not negotiable. Shri Nath acknowledged that there are other areas of the negotiations which are also significant in their own right, *e.g.* Trade Facilitation, amendment to TRIPS etc.. However, he made a special mention of the Rules negotiations. In his opinion, the Draft Modalities on Rules reflect the views of one country mainly in the Anti-dumping sphere, to the detriment of the vast majority of the membership. On Fisheries Subsidies, Shri Kamal Nath said that the absurd disciplines sought to be imposed on developing countries within even their own territorial waters, ostensibly to prevent over fishing and building up of excess capacity, is unacceptable because it threatens the livelihoods of millions of small, artisanal fisherfolk. Shri Kamal Nath said that in order to move the negotiating process forward, a revised text on Fisheries Subsidies, addressing the livelihood concerns, was essential. On the process to be adopted to reach convergence in the talks, Shri Nath mentioned that it was important to lend a sense of urgency to the proceedings. The Minister stated that it is content and not artificial timelines that are important. Thus the urgency had to be calibrated against the backdrop of realism and had to match the aspirations of the developing world in terms of an outcome that truly lived up to the promise of a Development oriented Round. Towards this end, it was important to make comparable progress in not only Agriculture but NAMA, Services and Rules as well. Only when the membership is satisfied that there is sufficient convergence across at least Agriculture, NAMA, Services and Rules, with perhaps just a few issues remaining to be resolved, could there be a horizontal process involving the highest decision making body of the WTO, *viz.* a Ministerial meeting.

5840. (7-2-2008) NEW DELHI : The IOR extends from 20 degree East longitude to 147 degree East longitude and covers 73.6 million sq Kilometres. This region is the third largest water body on this planet and constitutes 20% of the world's oceanic area. The importance of this region and its impact on the global maritime scenario can be understood from these statistics. As a part of its contribution towards consolidating the growing recognition of the importance of the Indian Ocean Region (IOR), the Indian Navy has taken the initiative and proposed setting-up of an inclusive and consultative regional forum, to be known as the Indian Ocean Naval Symposium (IONS). Thirty-three countries (including India) have been identified as littoral nation states of the IOR. Navies and maritime security organizations (in respect of countries who do not have any formal navy) of these nation states shall form part of this Naval Symposium. The Symposium is also being widely attended by various think-tanks of the Ministry of Defence and the Ministry of External Affairs. This maiden Symposium aims to increase maritime cooperation among participating navies/ maritime agencies by providing a forum for discussion of maritime issues, both global and regional, and in the process generate a flow of information and opinion between naval professionals leading to common understanding and possible agreements on the way ahead.

5841. (7-2-2008) NEW DELHI : In its short life, Internet has become an agent of revolutionary change and is one of the fastest tools to promote and defend freedom and to facilitate democratic access to information and knowledge. It has emerged as today's greatest instruments of progress and has gradually become a part of the vital infrastructure of global social, economic, cultural and political life. The Internet's effect on our lives is pervasive. Over the past decade, the use of e-mail, the web and blogs have become part of the daily routine of more than a billion Internet users. Today the Internet access touch points have outgrown the traditional PC based Internet browsers (Internet Explorer, Firefox) to desktop applications, mobile phones and satellite navigational devices in vehicles and living rooms. More and more people are buying movie tickets, air tickets, travel pacakages, railway tickets, paying bills online. Online gaming is projected to increase by 141% by 2011 in the Asia Pacific Region and mobile gaming to increase by 119% by a leading gaming industry. Very soon we will see the dawn of the video age when video will be used for buying, communicating, learning and socializing. Online chat and blogs is reducing the gap between private and public life of the present generation. Cyber cafes have taken over pubs and bars for socializing in spite of the opposing forces of regional borders, copyright, censorship, network blocking, etc.

5842. (7-2-2008) NEW DELHI : GM crops using recombinant DNA techniques have advantages over the conventional crops. However as more and more GM crops are being released for field-testing and commercialization, concerns have been expressed regarding the risks arising from their use due to potential risks to both human health and environment. These apprehensions arise because GM technology crosses the species barrier as compared to classical selection techniques, thereby permitting the gene transfer among microorganisms, plants and animals. There is no evidence that any unique hazards exist in the development of GM crops, because of novel combinations of genes. It is not true that all GM crops are toxic or are likely to proliferate in the environment. However, specific crops may be harmful by virtue of novel combinations of traits they possess. This means that the concerns associated with use of GMOs can differ greatly depending on the particular gene-organism combination and therefore a case-by-case approach is required for assessment of safety concerns. Potential risks from the use of GM crops broadly fall under two categories, risks to human and animal health as well as risks to environment.

5843. (7-2-2008) NEW DELHI : The Indira Gandhi Rashtriya Uran Akademi (IGRUA) today signed a management contract with CAE of Canada. A Joint Venture Agreement was also signed by the Airports Authority of India and the CAE to develop the Rajiv Gandhi National Flying Training Institute (RGNFTI). This was done in the presence of Shri Ashok Chawla, Secretary, Civil Aviation. For IGRUA, the management contract is for ten years initially. The first 12 months of the fiscal year 2008-09 will be a ramp up period wherein new facilities and aircraft will be added. The number of pilots being trained in the Akademi will increase from the present 40 to 100 by March 2009. Besides increase in the number the quality of training of pilots will also be upgraded. CAE will manage IGRUA's existing flight school activities, including maintenance of aircraft, flying operations, air traffic control, runway maintenance, NAV aids, fire fighting facilities, medical facilities, security, staff and student facilities, as well as transportation. Indira Gandhi Rashtriya Uran Akademi opened in 1986 and is the government's national flying school located at the Fursatganj Airport in Rae Bareli, Uttar Pradesh. The Rajiv Gandhi National Flying Training Institute will have the capacity to train 100 pilots initially, which will be increased to 200 pilots. The foundation stone for this Institute will be laid by the Prime Minister, Shri Manmohan Singh on 9th February 2008 in Gondia, Maharashtra. The RGNFTI will be a joint venture between CAE and AAI. The Institute will include a state-of-the-art facility equipped with classrooms, a hostel, a library, a workshop, a cafeteria, a guesthouse and a club. The school will operate new aircraft, and will use CAE's courseware and innovative training methodologies. The total investment for RGNFTI is approximately US$25 million. This step is expected to help augment the availability of pilots and to address the shortage of pilots being faced in India due to the high growth in the civil aviation sector. In the next few years there will be approximately 500 more aircraft being inducted by the various airlines in the country and therefore, thousands of pilots will be required. Thus there will be race against time to produce human resources to man the cabins of the aircraft, which will soon by flying the Indian skies.

5844. (7-2-2008) NEW DELHI : The Cabinet Committee on Economic Affairs today gave its approval for one-time interim grant of Rs.200 crore as Non-Plan funds to the Fertilizers and Chemicals Travancore Ltd. to enable it to sustain its operations till 31 March 2008. This would help FACT to recover the losses due to inadequate compensation for input costs and fertilizer products.

5845. (7-2-2008) NEW DELHI : The Congress party has said here that there is a limit to the hypocrisy and double facedness of the BJP. Day in and day out, they talk of terrorism to deliberately generate insecurity and mislead the people. They use the court judgment in the hijacking case as an excuse to attack the Congress and UPA on terrorism? What is their record during the BJP led NDA Government where the then Home Minister was also the Deputy Prime Minister? The Nation wants to know what transpired between the Deputy Prime Minister and the Foreign Minister on the one hand and the Taliban diplomats, the Afghanistan officials and the hijackers on the other, between December 24 and December 31, 1999? Instead of misleading people at Jabalpur, Shri Advani should tell the Nation what led to the sudden capitulation on December 31, 1999 at Kandahar after 7 days? Why did the self appointed "Loh Purush" became the "Soft" Home Minister, sending the Indian Foreign Minister to escort terrorists to Kandahar? Why was Mr. Advani's government unable to control, prevent or abort Akshardham, Raghunath Mandir, Indian

Parliament, Red Fort and innumerable similar instances? What happened to his "Sankalp"? Why did the BJP release Masood Azhar, Omar Sheikh and Zargar? Why could they not prevent or avert operatives of the Lashkar-e-Toiba who attacked Red Fort in January 2001? Why did they ignore this and invite Musharaff later in 2001 for the Agra Summit? Did they not ask Musharaff about Pakistan's role in the hijack and with the Taliban and the hijackers? And was not the BJP and NDA an utter failure in diplomacy at Agra? And shortly after that, the same Azhar and his Jaish-e-Mohammed attacked Parliament? This was the same person whom Mr. Advani's government had released at Kandahar. When the NDA and the BJP lecture us on terrorism, they remind us of the person who decides to go on a pilgrimage after committing a thousand sins. " Sau Choohon Ko Mar Kar Billi Haj Karne Nikli Hai" We do not believe in playing politics on the subject nor at finger-pointing, nor at creating a climate of insecurity and fear. The BJP believes in all three. The facts speak for themselves and expose the hypocrisy of no less than a former Home Minister. Published figures show an improvement of 70%-repeat 70%-as far as terrorism in J&K is concerned. As far as Naxalism is concerned, the most affected was Andhra Pradesh. That has been a decline of 70%-repeat 70%. 80% of all Naxalite activity is found in 3 states – Chhatishgarh, Orrisa and Jharkhand. The first two are NDA states and third was so, till a couple of years ago. Mr. Advani needs to set his own house in order, do some soul searching, stop being irresponsible and first berate and condemn his own, or his allies' Chief Ministers. What is the use of creating a climate of fear and insecurity by saying that 1/3rd of the country is in the grip of terrorism and Naxalism? Even if 1 village in a district is Naxalite affected, one cannot call the whole district Naxal affected. Actually, out of 14,000 police station across the country, only 300 are Naxalite affected *i.e.* less than 2%. The BJP and Mr. Advani have always thrived on hypocrisy and preached without practice. That is their true culture. But that is also grossly irresponsible. The people of India have seen through such double-faced manoeuvres. What is amazing is that Peter Bleach accused and convicted of sedition—the most serious and national offence known to law—was released and sent abroad by Shri Advani, then home minister and deputy prime minister and by the NDA. No pardon, no remission, no proceeding. Even more amazing, Afzal Guru was arrested by the NDA government and released before the Parliament attack. Who is now shedding crocodile tears? To a question that in a recent speech the Congress President said Naxalism is the strongest threat in the country today, Shri Singhvi said, it is no doubt a threat where it exists. I am not condoning it.

5846. (7-2-2008) NEW DELHI : The Cabinet Committee on Economic Affairs today gave its approval for electrification of 809 route kilometres of Barauni-Katihar-Guwahati section of East Central and Northeast Frontier Railways at a cost of Rs.505.68 crore. Electrification of Barauni-Katihar-Guwahati will facilitate running long distance freight and passenger trains including Rajdhani and Garib Rath Express towards North East end-to-end on electric traction. Electrification will contribute to the flexibility by way of continuity of traction and economic operation. Electrification will also cater to the anticipated increase in passenger and freight traffic by the year 2012 and will also offset requirement of imported crude and diesel, in addition to environmental benefits that accrue. The project is likely to be completed by 2011-12 *i.e.* in four year's time.

5847. (7-2-2008) NEW DELHI : The Cabinet Committee on Economic Affairs today gave its approval for the transfer of administrative control of M/s. Bharat Wagon & Engineering Company Ltd. (BWEL), Patna a subsidiary of Bharat Bhari Udyog Nigam Limited (BBUNL) to the Ministry of Railways.

5848. (7-2-2008) NEW DELHI : The Cabinet Committee on Economic Affairs today gave its approval for Continuation of the Central Sector Scheme of Rajiv Gandhi National Fellowship (RGNF) w.e.f. 2007-08 for ST Students for pursuing higher studies such as M.Phil and Ph.D courses and effecting changes in the rates of fellowship as and when required, to keep them at par with the UGC fellowship rates. The Scheme would be continued in the XIth Plan period and thereafter. The scheme covers all universities/institutions recognized by the University Grants Commission under section 2(f) of the UGC Act. Fellowships will be available only for undertaking regular M.Phil/Ph.D. courses. The maximum duration of the fellowship will be 5 years. The total number of fellowships every year will be 667. An outlay of Rs.26 crore will be spent during the year 2007-08 and during the XI Five Year Plan the expenditure is projected at Rs.175.985 crore. 12079 number of ST students during the XI Five Year Plan.

5849. (7-2-2008) NEW DELHI : The Union Cabinet today gave its approval to the scheme for implementation of National projects by providing financial assistance to ongoing spilled over projects of 10th Plan and new projects taken up in 11th Plan under Accelerated Irrigation Benefits programmes (AIBP) with a total outlay of Rs.43700 crores. Cabinet also gave its approval to the proposal for implementation of National Projects with central assistance of 90% of the cost of the project as grant falling in the following selection criteria: i) International projects where usage of water in India is required by a treaty or where planning and early completion of the project is necessary in the interest of the country. ii) Inter-State projects which are dragging on due to non-resolution of inter-State issues relating to sharing of costs, rehabilitation, aspects of power production etc., including river interlinking projects. iii) Intra-State projects with additional potential of more than 2,00,000 ha. and with no dispute regarding sharing of water and where hydrology is established. This will help to complete ongoing /irrigation projects under AIBP to augment irrigation facilities in the country. This will also help in a big way to achieve targeted irrigation potential under Bharat Nirman. This will help in utilizing share of water in rivers governed by the international Treaties apart from creation of additional irrigation potential in the country.

5850. (7-2-2008) NEW DELHI : The Union Cabinet today gave its approval for enhancement of governing powers of the Board of Directors of Nuclear power

Corporation of India Limited (NPCIL) to incur capital expenditure, investment towards establishing financial joint ventures and wholly owned subsidiaries in India or abroad, and for delegation of powers to Secretary, Deptt. of Atomic Energy (DAE) to approve the tours abroad of Chairman and Managing Director (CMD), NPCIL. The enhanced delegation would facilitate NPCIL to incur capital expenditure upto Rs. 500 crore without government approval, within the overall ceiling of 15% of the net worth of the company in one project with overall ceiling on all projects put together restricted to 30% of the net work of the company with a view to reduce gestation period and also to invest its surplus funds in establishing financial joint ventures & subsidiaries.

5851. (7-2-2008) NEW DELHI : The Union Cabinet today gave its approval for signing of a Memorandum of Understanding between India and South Africa on agricultural cooperation between India and South Africa. MoU will promote further bilateral cooperation through joint activities and exchanges in the areas of agriculture including animals, fisheries, poultry, agricultural extension, land and water management and its conservation; promotion of agricultural trade and investment, agricultural biodiversity management and conservation etc. through exchange of scientific delegations and experts between the two countries. MoU will be valid for a period of five (5) years.

5852. (7-2-2008) NEW DELHI : The Union Cabinet today gave its approval for signing of an Agreement between India and Zambia for the Avoidance of Double Taxation and the Prevention of Fiscal Evasion with respect to taxes on income. The Agreement will stimulate the flow of investment, technology and services from India to Zambia and vice versa. It will provide tax stability to the residents of India and Zambia and facilitate mutual economic cooperation.

5853. (7-2-2008) NEW DELHI : The Prime Minister, Dr. Manmohan Singh, has said that Government of India will adopt a responsible and forward looking stance aimed at promoting sustainable development. Delivering his inaugural address at the Delhi Sustainable Development Summit here today, the Prime Minister said that the impact of climate change falls differently on people and the poor are the worst hit. "We need technology innovations for reduction of energy use by industry and other user sectors," he added. He further said "we need massive action for afforestation, drought proofing, flood protection and the need to protect our coastal areas and glaciers that feed our river systems." Dr. Singh emphasized the need to ensure an acceptable standard of living for all our people following sustainable path for that development. Climate justice must, therefore, inform all efforts at international collaboration in act of human solidarity, he added.

5854. (8-2-2008) NEW DELHI : The Union Minister for Rural Development Dr. Raghuvansh Prasad Singh has emphasized the need to develop synergy between the State Government, the Central Government and banks for skill development and entrepreneurship development programmes to generate self-employment opportunities. Addressing the 11th meeting of the Central Level Coordination Committee (CLCC) of Swarnajayanti Rozgar Yojana (SGSY) held here today the minister reiterated that the objective of SGSY is to bring the rural BPL families above the poverty line by ensuring appreciable increases in in come on a sustainable basis. Dr. Singh said under the National Skill Development Mission the Planning Comission has also proposed to set up one Rural Development and Self Employment Training Institute (RUDSETI) in each district of the country by his ministry. The CLCC was convened to discuss means to remove the bottlenecks /deficiencies in the implementation process of providing physical as well as financial assistance to Self-Help Groups and Sawrozgaries under the SGSY. The minister recalled of the survey made by the Bankers Institute of Rural Development (BIRD),Lucknow in the states of Andhra Pradesh, Bihar, Chhattisgarh, Kerala, Orissa, Tamil Nadu and Uttarpradesh and said there is a need for physical and financial inclusion of SC and ST families for inclusive growth and development. Expressing concern over the discretionary power of Banks for charging interest rates, High/variable interest rates on loans under SGSY scheme and poor performing bank branches under this scheme Dr. Singh said these issues need to be discussed and sorted out to facilitate smooth implementation of the scheme which has the objective of economic amelioration of the rural poor. Under the SGSY at the National Level the percentage of utilization of total available funds during the current year 2007-08 (upto 21-08-2008) is 53.84%. The Credit mobilization target of Rs. 3743.55 crore has been fixed under SGSY for the current financial year, though only Rs. 1359.49 crores (55.87%) of the credit targets have been achieved by the banks till 31.12.2007. Again during the current year 2007-08 a total of 4,36,518 applications were submitted to banks under SGSY. However, loans have been sanctioned on 2,44,338 applicationes and loan has been disbursed in respect of 2,08,712 loan applications. There were 1,78,681 applications were pending with banks as on 31.12.2007. Due to this the proportion of SHGs which have taken up economic activity via-a-vis formation of SHG fored remained at 20.43% only. It is evident that a memorandum of understanding (MoU) for extending financial assistance to RUDSETI was signed on 21st December, 2005 between the Institute and Ministry of Rural Development for developing their campus and infrastructure for the existing five centres at Bhopal, Bhubaneshwar, Jaipua, Agra and Ananthapur at an estimated cost of Rs.487.50 lakhs and @ Rs.97.50 lakhs per centre. The Project cost will be shared between the Ministry of Rural Development and RUDSETI in the ratio of 75:25. The Ministry would provide financial assistance in three instalments of 30%, 40% and 30%. The duration of project will be three years. The Institute will impart training to at least 1.22 lakh rural youths from BPL house holds over a period of five years. So far, Ministry of Rural Development has releasedits share for twa instalments to RUDSETI for the Jaipur, Agra and Ananthapur centres and one instalment to Bhubaneshwar and Bhopal centres.

5855. (8-2-2008) NEW DELHI : A three-day seminar on noted Urdu Poet and political activist Makhdoom Mohiuddin was inaugurated today. In a message sent by the Human Resource Development Minister, Shri Arjun Singh described Makhdoom a genuine poet who gave topmost importance to his social concerns. His poetry still fills the people with energy and enthusiasm. "Makhdoom was truly a people's poet. His primary identity today is that of a poet. It was through his poetry that he spread his political message", remarked CPI General Secretary Shri A.B. Bardhan while inaugurating a three-day national seminar on noted progressive poet and a great political leader of Tilangana Movement of fifties, Makhdoom Mohiuddin. Inaugural session of the seminar was chaired by noted theatre personality Habib Tanvir. He spoke about different aspects of Makhdoom's life, and his role in the Tilangana movement. The three-day seminar is being organized by National Council for Promotion of Urdu Language (NCPUL) during 8-10 February at India Islamic Cultural Centre at New Delhi. Others speakers on the occasion included senior Congress leader Shri P. Shiv Shankar, Shri G. Venkataswami, Shri Sudhakar Reddy, MP from Andhra Pradesh. Describing Makhdoom a great communist leader, Shri G. Venkataswami talked about his association with Makhdoom said that throughout his life Makhdoom was concerned with the problems of common people. He led a simple life with great ideas. He demostrated immense courage in his struggle to achieve his goals. Makhdoom was a great leader of workers and a source of inspiration for the people of Andhra Pradesh. This seminar is a part of celebrations of birth centenary year of Makhdoom Mohiuddin.

5856. (8-2-2008) NEW DELHI : The Annual Plan for Jharkhand for the year 2008-09 was finalized at a meeting, here today, between the Deputy Chairman Planning Commission, Shri Montek Singh Ahluwalia and the Chief Minister of Jharkhand, Shri Madhu Koda. Plan size for the current year was agreed at Rs.8015 crores. This includes additional Central assistance of Rs.50 crores for projects of special interest to the State. Mr. Ahluwalia appreciated the efforts of the State Government for improving the pace of development. He said plan expenditure for the current year was much better than the previous years. He said efforts should be expedited to further improve pace of development with focused attention of human development. Since the economy of the State was characterized by higher incidence of poverty, unemployment and low per capita income, higher attention and allocation to social sector development was needed. He said the State Government should take benefit from the new schemes being introduced by the Central Government which are aimed at making growth more inclusive. Allocations to new initiatives like AIBP, Food Security & Rashtriya Krishi Vikas Yojana is likely to be improved and States should make advance preparations to operationalize them. In view of natural potential for horticulture & floriculture, the State Government was advised to take optimum advantage of national horticulture mission and establish marketing network. It was pointed out that development of physical infrastructure should be expedited for rapid industrialization of the State. Briefing the Commission on the performance of the State, Mr. Koda said that the State Government had embarked on overhauling the processes and systems with a view to make delivery systems more effective, transparent, responsive and cost effective. ICT tools and new delivery models including PPP were being encouraged. Villages were being empowered and processes being simplified. Efforts were on improve human development index. Higher allocations are being made to social services. Over 38 per cent of outlay is being ear-marked to social service which includes 13.24 per cent to education. He sought Planning Commission's intervention in seeking additional support from Centre for up-gradation of Highways, expedite environment clearance of irrigation projects and free power to host States where pithead thermal power projects are planned.

5857. (8-2-2008) NEW DELHI : Government of India have announced the sale (re-issue) of "6.57 percent Government Stock, 2011" under Market Stabilization Scheme for a notified amount of Rs. 4,000 crore (nominal). The Government Stock will be sold through price based auction using multiple price method. The auctions will be conducted by the Reserve Bank of India, Mumbai Office, Fort, Mumbai on February 14, 2008(Thursday). Up to 5 per cent of the amount notified for the sale of stock is reserved for allotment to eligible individuals and Institutions on non-competitive basis as per the Scheme for Non-Competitive Bidding Facility in the Auction of Government Securities. Bids in the prescribed form obtainable from the Regional Director, Reserve Bank of India, Mumbai Office (Public Debt Office), Fort, Mumbai-400 001 and RBI website www.rbi.org.in should be submitted to that Office on February 14, 2008. The NDS members should submit competitive as well as non-competitive bids in electronic format using Primary Market Operation (PMO) module of NDS. All bids should be submitted by 12.30 P.M. The result of the auctions will be announced on February 14, 2008and payment by successful bidders will be during banking hours.

5858. (8-2-2008) NEW DELHI : The BJP said here that the comments of the Congress against the NDA government in general and Shri L K Advani in particular on the issue of handing terrorism is not only amusing but also is an attempt to conveniently gloss over its own dismal record which had led to the growth, consolidation and spread of the menace of terrorism across vast tracks of the country leading to the loss of more than 70,000 lives so far. If Jammu & Kashmir simmers even today, if the north east continues to be in turmoil with anti India sentiments being kindled in many areas, if the naxalite problem has acquired menacing proportions, then the Congress will have to apportion substantial blame for the manner in which they have treated these problems indifferently and with criminal negligence at times for nearly 52 years that they have ruled the country either directly or in coalition with others. The core issue is whether one fights terror and terrorists with commitment and conviction or with convenience and an eye on the vote bank. This is the crucial benchmark that differentiates the BJP and the NDA as against the Congress and the UPA. Yes, during the NDA regime, there were terrorist attacks but the perpetrators were either killed on the spot or promptly convicted under due process of law using effective anti-terror laws like POTA. Moreover, a resurgent security force given full freedom by the political leadership of the NDA to take tough action without interference, bore the fruits. This happened in the case of the attacks on Akashardham, Raghunath Mandir in Jammu and in the attack on the Parliament. What is the record of the Congress? Afzal Guru, the mastermind of the Parliament attack case, was convicted by the trial court, and this was further affirmed in appeal by the Delhi High Court and finally given the seal of approval by the Supreme Court. Even the review petition and the curative petition by Afzal Guru has been rejected. Yet the Congress led UPA government is dithering for the last one and half years in executing the final orders, on the nebulous plea of clemency which can be decided in a single day by the government. Sometime the vote bank of the UP elections forces the postponement, and sometimes the illusory hope of a victory in Gujarat leads to its deferment.

5859. (8-2-2008) NEW DELHI : It is hereby informed that the Central Government has, with immediate effect, prohibited any export of Non-Basmati Rice under the Transitional arrangements under Para 1.5 of the Foreign Trade Policy, 2004-09 (as amended from time to time). It may be recalled that export of Non-Basmati Rice was prohibited vide Notifications No. 38 & 44 w.e.f. 10.10.2007. However, in order to honour the prior commitments of exporters, Non-Basmati Rice exports were being undertaken against valid irrevocable commercial letters of credit as provided in Para 1.5 of the Foreign Trade Policy. With the Notification No. 77 dated 7.02.2008 (available on website of the DGFT-http:// www.dgft.gov.in), export of Non-Basmati Rice against letters of credit as per Para 1.5 of the Foreign Trade Policy, 2004-09 (as amended from time to time) has been prohibited.

5860. (8-2-2008) NEW DELHI : As per data compiled by Agriculture Ministry as on today, wheat sowing is over. Wheat has been sown in 276.89 lakh ha as compared to 282.14 lakh ha last year. 21.49 lakh ha area has come under winter rice as against 21.74 lakh ha last year. Coarse cereals have been sown in 67.87 lakh ha as compared to 70.4 lakh ha by this time in 2007. Barley and maize have been grown in more area than last year's {barley 7.57 lakh ha, maize 10.35 lakh ha}. Rabi oilseeds have been sown in 89.3 lakh ha as compared to 97.01 lakh ha in the last rabi. Mustard/rapeseed coverage has reached 59.81 lakh ha (last rabi, up to this time: 66.68 lakh ha). Rabi pulses cover 133.28 lakh ha (last year: 138.99 lakh ha). Gram coverage has reached 80.27 lakh ha (vs. 83.72 lakh ha by this time last year).

5861. (8-2-2008) NEW DELHI : Finance Minister Shri P. Chidambaram has said that we should care young talents who have lost their childhood as many children move into adulthood bypassing the joy of childhood because of harsh realities of life. All efforts should be made to identify and bring forth the creativity of the socially challenged children. Stating this Shri Chidambaram said that the requirement for their food, clothing and even shelter are usually met but what is most important is to encourage the creative and natural talents which these children possess but are not expressed as they do not get a proper platform for expression.

Shri Chidambaram said that children possess original and natural talents which should be encouraged particularly in the field of Songs, Music, Dances and other similar arts. The Finance Minister appreciated the original idea and initiative by two professionals Alpana & Neeraj who with the assistance and enrolment of other professionals organized a show called "Small Wonders" to bring forth the creativity and talents of these special children at a function here last evening at the prestigious Balyogi Auditorium of the Parliament. Appreciating the role of different voluntary institutions working for the welfare and development of socially challenged children (Orphans) like Ashadeep, Shishu Sangh Open Griha/St. Michel's Hostel, Bhatia School and Bal Bhawan, the Finance Minister said that similar efforts should be made to empower the children by exploring & then developing their potential. The programme, which was based on the theme of Basant Panchmi, will be telecast on Lak Sabha TV Channel from 4 to 5 p.m. on Sunday *i.e.* 10th February, 08.

5862. (8-2-2008) NEW DELHI : Historian and scholar in Jamia Millia Islamia University, Dr. Rizwan Qaiser released two books on the First War of Independence today in the ongoing 18th New Delhi World Book Fair. Brought out by Publications Division, Ministry of Information and Broadcasting, these books '1857-The Uprising' and Delhi in 1857 are part of the Division's prestigious series of books to commemorate the 150 years of 1857 uprising. Author Gautam Gupta introduced his book '1857-The Uprising'. This book presents an analysis of the events that shaped the final outcome of this eventful struggle and changed the destiny of India. This well-researched book is different from most of the available writings on this subject, which are by British authors presenting British point of view, while this book narrates the activities of the heroes of the revolt on the Indian side. The other book 'Delhi in 1857' written by Dr. Prabha Chopra with Delhi in focus, gives an account of how the historical city of Delhi was turned into battlefield overnight. Delhi was ruined several times and every time it rose like a phoenix out of the ashes with renewed glory. The British atrocities were worst. But ultimately it revived to become the capital city of free India. The Additional Director General (in-charge) of Publications Division welcomed the guests in the function.

5863. (8-2-2008) MALAPPURAM: This is my school! Chirped 55yrs old Fathima showing a small tiled roofed hall. "When do I get my books for 7th standard?" she asks. This is the attitude of most of the much enthused 1508 new literates of Nilambur Grama Panchayat in Malappuram District of Kerala. All thanks to Jyothirgamaya, a total primary education programme implemented by the Gram Panchayat with the help of State Literacy Mission in Nilambur Gram Panchayat. Thanks to which, January 8, 2008 went down in the history of the country and mainly the Panchayat when Shri R L Bhatia, Governor of Kerala declared it as the "first Gram Panchayat in the country to achieve total primary education". The success of the programme completely rests on the people's participation who contributed in money as well as man power beyond political, religious and social differences, informed Shri Aryadan Shaukat, the Panchayat President, who is today all smiles on the success of this programme. Out of the total expenditure of Rs. 21 lakh, Rs 3.1 lakh was the only contribution from the government, the rest by the people. The whole concept of the project triggered off when after coming to power in 2005, the present Panchayat Committee realized more than anything else that the people of the Panchayat should be given the light of knowledge. The Committee approached the State Literacy Mission and presented the issue. A survey in January 2006 showed, that 1050 people between the age group of (15-50 years) were illiterate or semi-illiterate. Out of them about 90% were women. In coordination with the State Literacy Mission, the "Jyothirgamaya", the dream project of the panchayat, was formulated. As many as 300 teachers or facilitators as they are called, contributed their services through 142 study centres. Facilitators were given training in teaching. The major problem faced by the facilitators was teaching the beneficiary who had no touch with learning or writing and most of them were daily workers. An Academic Committee was constituted to prepare study materials incorporating functional teaching and then to design the syllabi of the Literacy Mission. The learners were provided with textbooks equivalent to those for the fourth standard. As the classes progressed, it was found that many of them had poor eyesight. The Panchayat promptly acted to solve this problem. The Panchayat in coordination with private eye hospital organized a free eye camp were 800 people were given spectacles free of charge. The first phase of the programme began in March 2006 that concluded with the annual examination conducted by the State Literacy Mission in December, 2006. The external assessment was done by two teams of evaluators, one headed by C. Nazeema of the Centre for Adult and Continuing Education and Extension, University of Calicut and the other led by K. Sivadasan Pillai of the Literacy Mission. The reports of both the teams were approved by the National Literacy Mission. The course was made interesting by conducting cultural competitions, excursion tours and providing vocational training to students who participated with great enthusiasm. Follow-up activities were conducted by introducing 55 mobile libraries in the area with stock of over 3,000 books. Each student and facilitator has an experience to narrate about the programme. For Sainatha, the project is a dream come true. Today she has a set of poems penned by her and published in the State Literacy Mission's magazine. For 64 year old Pathummakutty of Cheruvathu kunnu 3rd ward, the programme will help to fulfil her life's wish to go for Haj. The Certificate provided by the Government of Kerala is an authentic document for proving the date of birth, name, spouse's name, address etc. With its help Pathummakutty can apply for Passport! For Shakila a facilitator, married when she was in 8th standard left by her husband with a son. The class gave her a new lease of life, a new meaning. She feels elated to teach students of her mother's age! No doubt, "Jyothirgamaya", as it means, has led many from darkness to light and made priceless contribution to the social, cultural and educational sectors of the region.

5864. (8-2-2008) NEW DELHI : A major rescue operation was carried out today in Jammu and Kashmir, which saved the life of 45 people including women and children. The operation was carried out in Gulabgarh village near Kajigund of south Srinagar, when an avalanche hit the village at 7in the morning. After getting the information, the army's Avalanche Rescue Team rushed to the spot by 8.10 am and started the operation. Negotiating with heavy snowfall, the team succeeded in rescuing the buried personal in four and half hours. Three of the rescued people were very critical and instant first aid was provided to them but one of them succumbed. The rescue team was led by two officers comprising 26 other ranks of 49 Rashtriya Rifles, a section of 2 Rashtriya Rifle.

5865. (8-2-2008) NEW DELHI : Hindustan Latex (HLL), a mini ratna enterprise under the Ministry of Health and Family Welfare of the Government of India has set up HINDLABS-the Diagnostic Centre-a partnership venture with the CGHS (Central Government Health Scheme). This Centre located at the CGHS Dispensary in Sector-12 at R. K. Puram in New Delhi will start functioning from tomorrow and provide quality diagnostic services to the CGHS beneficiaries at CGHS rates. The same services will also be provided to patients outside the CGHS too at affordable rates.

5866. (8-2-2008) NEW DELHI : The Spanish Minister of Environment, Ms. Cristina Narbona, and the Ambassador of Spain in India, Mr. lon de la Riva, called on the Union Minister of Water Resources Prof. Saifuddin Soz here today. The Spanish Minister of Environment is currently in New Delhi to participate in Delhi Sustainable Development Summit 2008. The two Ministers discussed matters of mutual interest with regard to water resources, environmental issues, the need for cleaner atmosphere etc. The Spanish Minister earnestly requested Prof. Soz to ensure India's participation in the Expo Zaragoza, 2008 (Spain) being held from June 14 to Sep 13, 2008. Prof. Soz assured that he had already taken up the matter with the concerned authorities for India's participation. The Spanish authorities would be hosting an International Exposition devoted to Water and Sustainable Development wherein countries of all the world's climate regions will be participating. The future of water and its sustainable development, it will be recalled, is one of the 21st century's most important challenges.

5867. (8-2-2008) NEW DELHI : Nathpa Jhakri Hydro Power Station has become the first single hydro power station of the country to surpass 6000 Million Units of electricity generation on 7.2.2008; 53 days ahead of the close of the Financial Year. This highest generation has been achieved besides all odds which the plant faced like adverse hydrology, flash floods and high-silt contents. Besides benefiting the beneficiaries and country as a whole, this would bring higher revenues to equity partner Govt. of Himachal Pradesh with 12% free power and 22% power on account of their energy share. The power generation of Nathpa Jhakri Hydro Power Station during the last financial year was 5941 million units and during the current year already surpassed 6000 MU with 53 days of the current financial year yet to go, this was stated by Shri R.P. Singh, Director (Electrical) of public sector Satluj Jal Vidyut Nigam Ltd. which had implemented this project. As a result of such performance, the Company has been able to pay dividend to the shareholders *i.e.* Govt. of India and Govt. of Himachal Pradesh from the very first year of its commercial operation itself. Shri R.P. Singh informed that the generation during the current period has also surpassed the MoU targets entered into with the Ministry of Power. Shri Singh hopes that the power station will be able to meet the MoU targets of 6400 million units for the year 2007-08. Shri Singh also stated that the Company had established spectacular achievements during the financial year 2006-07 and recorded net profits of Rs.732.71 crore as well as paid dividends of Rs. 235 crore to the equity partners for its performance during the financial year 2006-07. Since 2003 the power station has been energizing the northern states namely Delhi, Haryana, Punjab, Rajasthan, Uttar Pradesh, Uttarakhand, J&K, Chandigarh and the home state Himachal Pradesh with valuable power.

5868. (8-2-2008) NEW DELHI : The Internet Corporation for Assigned Names and Numbers (ICANN), the body charged with overseeing Internets addressing system is holding its 31st International Public Meeting in New Delhi beginning next Monday. This is the first meeting of the ICANN in India and it assumes significance as India is fast emerging as a country and a region at the forefront of the waves of changes to the Internet. ICANN is a multi-stakeholder body. The Government Advisory Committee (GAC) is one of the components of ICANN. GAC advises ICANN on various Public Policy issues relating to Internet. The Government of India is a member of the GAC. Furthermore, the Secretariat of the GAC is presently housed in the Department of Information Technology, Government of India for a five year period from 2006 to 2010. The meeting of ICANN is scheduled to discuss the mid-term review of ICANN's Joint Project Agreement (JPA) with the US Government and its goal of continued transition of its role to the private sector. It may be recalled that ICANN was created through a Memorandum of Understanding (MoU) between the US Department of Commerce and ICANN, a public private partnership, to transition management of the Domain Names System (DNS) from the U.S. government to the global community. The last JPA was signed between the U.S. Department of Commerce and ICANN in October, 2006, a pact for three years extending the U.S. Department of Commerce over sight of the body while leaving the possibility open of the Group becoming independent as early as April this year. Another issue which is likely to figure prominently in the New Delhi meeting is a workshop on Internationalized Domain Names (IDNs) in the Indian languages and scripts. IDNs is one of the critical factors for democratization and universalisation of the Internet. Already 13 languages test names have been introduced by ICANN which include Devnagari and Tamil scripts. With 22 official languages, India is pushing for more language names at the top level so that internet becomes accessible and available to those sections which do not understand English. India believes that multi-lingual internet will increase local interests in internet contents and increase the possibilities for all language groups to share and access information in their own language.

5869. (8-2-2008) NEW DELHI : The total approximate earnings of Indian Railways on originating basis during 1st April 2007-31st January 2008 were Rs. 57282.51 crore compared to Rs. 50765.01 crore during the same period last year, registering an increase of 12.84 per cent. The total goods earnings have gone up from Rs. 34415.58 crore during 1st April 2006-31st January 2007 to Rs. 38747.90 crore during 1st April 2007-31st January 2008, showing an increase of 12.59 per cent. The total passenger revenue earnings during first ten months of the financial year 2007-08 were Rs. 16134.95 crore compared to Rs. 14126.97 crore during the same period last year, registering an increase of 14.21 per cent. The revenue earnings from other coaching and sundry amounted to Rs. 2399.66 crore during April 2007-January 2008 compared to Rs. 2222.46 crore during the same period last year, showing an increase of 7.97 per cent. The total approximate number of passengers booked during April 2007-January 2008 were 5559.87 million compared to 5267.44 million during the same period last year, showing an increase of 5.55 per cent. In the suburban and non-suburban sectors, the number of passengers booked during April 2007-January 2008 were 3074.10 million and 2485.77 million compared to 2923.69 million and 2143.89 million during the same period last year, an increase of 5.14 per cent and 6.06 per cent respectively.

5870. (8-2-2008) NEW DELHI : Congress spokesman Smt. Jayanthi Natrajan said the nation has been shocked by the uncovering of this major racket in kidney transplantation and unsuspecting victims—over 500 known victims of this shameful network— in which the arrest of one or two of the main accused has just happened. This has exposed a very ugly face of our society and shocked the conscience of the nation because it represents what is possibly the most revolting and obscene form of exploitation of poverty. Racketeering in human organs is a fowl and reprehensible crime and those who have sunk so low as to engage themselves in it should be given the most exemplary punishment. Although the Human Organs Transplantation Act was passed in 1994, I am not aware—subject to correction—of any convictions that have actually happened under the Act and it is well-known that in some parts of the country, this has become a very shameful, flourishing trade which exploits the ignorance and helplessness and poverty of the poorest of the poor. Under the 1994 Act, the state and the Central government appoint appropriate authorities who are supposed to review the procedure of donation of kidneys or any other human organs but apart from monitoring the registration of hospitals which conduct these transplants, in actual point of fact, the Act has not been successful in addressing this extremely serious problem. It is also a fact that the appropriate authority does not have the manpower to implement this Act and when police actually arrest one or two accused, under this Act, they book them under Sections of the Indian Penal Code and not under the relevant Act. Finally, under the present Human Organs Transplantation Act, the quantum of punishment is laughable and pitiful. It is basically between 2 to 5 years for the main tenure of imprisonment and ten thousand rupees fine. This is by no means a deterrent for a crime that shocks the human conscience and therefore the Indian National

Congress would like to request the government to take a fresh look at the Act. The Hon'ble Health Minister has already mentioned that this would be done but we would like to urge that any society, leave alone a political party, that has a modicum of concern for the citizens of the country, the common man, should insure that this exploitation is stopped in its tracks. This requires a fresh look at the law, redrafting a law with greater teeth and insuring that the implementation of the law is absolutely rigid as well as dynamic. We would also like to call upon the various governments and the CBI to insure that not just the present culprits but the entire network of all those involved in this should be brought to justice and punished in the most exemplary fashion. To a question whether on the Sethusamudram project issue is your government now junking this project as it seems it is gearing up to go for archaeological study of the project, Smt. Jayanthi said, the stand of the Indian National Congress is well-known and while the Sethusamudram project is a long-standing demand of the people of Tamil Nadu and the present Sethusamudram project and alignment were initiated, cleared and taken forward by the NDA government. Since some sections of the people have raised various objections and since the matter is currently sub-judice, all sensitivities will be considered and the matter taken forward thereafter. To a question that the top leadership has spoken of Cabinet reshuffle for some time now is the government doing something about it, Smt. Jayanthi said, it is the prerogative of the prime minister.

5871. (8-2-2008) NEW DELHI : Retail prices of farm commodities monitored by the Department of Consumer Affairs have generally remained steady or shown mixed trend over the week ending February 1, 2008. During the week ending February 1, 2008 prices of wheat remained steady at most of the monitoring centres. Prices increased only at Bhopal, and declined at Ahmedabad. Prices of sugar remained steady at all the monitoring centres and decreased at Shillong. Prices of gram dal increased at Kolkata and Shillong and declined at Bhopal. Prices of tur dal remained steady at almost all the monitoring centres. Prices increased at Ahmedabad and declined at Delhi, Bhopal and Kolkata. Out of 14.02 lakh tonne pulses contracted for import, 10.7 lakh tonne have arrived in the country by 5.2.08. In Delhi, prices of atta, gram, rice, wheat, tea, potato and onion held steady for one week. Prices of sugar, groundnut, milk and salt held steady for one month. Prices of mustard oil and vanaspati, however, rose by Re 1 per kilo respectively. Prices of tur dal decreased from Rs. 42 to Rs. 41 per kg.

5872. (8-2-2008) NEW DELHI : The Appointments Committee of the Cabinet has approved the appointment of Shri A.P.V.N.Sarma, IAS(AP:74), presently in the cadre as Secretary, Department of Shipping, Ministry of Shipping, Road Transport and Highways in the vacancy of Shri A.K.Mohapatra, IAS(HP:71).

5873. (8-2-2008) NEW DELHI : The Internet Corporation for Assigned Names and Numbers (ICANN), the body charged with overseeing Internets addressing system is holding its 31st International Public Meeting in New Delhi beginning next Monday. This is the first meeting of the ICANN in India and it assumes significance as India is fast emerging as a country and a region at the forefront of the waves of changes to the Internet. ICANN is a multi-stakeholder body. The Government Advisory Committee (GAC) is one of the components of ICANN. GAC advises ICANN on various Public Policy issues relating to Internet. The Government of India is a member of the GAC. Furthermore, the Secretariat of the GAC is presently housed in the Department of Information Technology, Government of India for a five year period from 2006 to 2010. The meeting of ICANN is scheduled to discuss the mid-term review of ICANN's Joint Project Agreement (JPA) with the US Government and its goal of continued transition of its role to the private sector. It may be recalled that ICANN was created through a Memorandum of Understanding (MoU) between the US Department of Commerce and ICANN, a public private partnership, to transition management of the Domain Names System (DNS) from the U.S. government to the global community. The last JPA was signed between the U.S. Department of Commerce and ICANN in October, 2006, a pact for three years extending the U.S. Department of Commerce over sight of the body while leaving the possibility open of the Group becoming independent as early as April this year. Another issue which is likely to figure prominently in the New Delhi meeting is a workshop on Internationalized Domain Names (IDNs) in the Indian languages and scripts. IDNs is one of the critical factors for democratization and universalisation of the Internet. Already 13 languages test names have been introduced by ICANN which include Devnagari and Tamil scripts. With 22 official languages, India is pushing for more language names at the top level so that internet becomes accessible and available to those sections which do not understand English. India believes that multi-lingual internet will increase local interests in internet contents and increase the possibilities for all language groups to share and access information in their own language.

5874. (9-2-2008) NEW DELHI : Union Minister for Science and Technology and Earth Sciences Mr. Kapil Sibal has held discussions with Senator Kim Carr, Australian Minister for Innovation, Industry, Science and Research at Melbourne. Both Ministers agreed to step up scientific cooperation between the two countries. Mr. Sibal is visiting Australia as Guest of the Australian Government from February 7 to 12, 2008 and his visit is being coordinated by the Australian Department of Prime Minister and Cabinet. He is also the first Indian Minister to visit Australia after the new Government led by the Leader of the Australian Labor Party, Mr. Kevin Rudd MP, was sworn in on 3rd of December 2007. Taking note of the ongoing 21 projects under the India-Australia Strategic Research Fund, the two Ministers agreed to further strengthen bilateral scientific cooperation focussing on industrial research and development and high technology areas such as nano-composites, bio-energy, health and agricultural bio-technology, climate change and renewable energy particularly using photo-voltaic technology. They also agreed to set-up a Joint Working Group (JWG) to create a roadmap for strengthening bilateral S&T cooperation in the next six months. During the visit, Mr. Sibal met with Senator Ms. Penny Wong, Minister for Climate Change and Water, and Mr.

Robert McClelland, MP, Attorney General. He also met the Victorian Governor, Professor David de Kretser,AC: Victorian Minister for Environment, Climate Change and Innovation, Mr. Gavin Jennings, MLC: and NSW Minister for Science and Medical Research, Ms. Verity Firth, MP. Mr. Sibal also visited three of the Austria's group of eight Universities (University of New South Wales, University of Sydney and the University of Melbourne), amongst the leading universities of the world, as well as some of the Premier R&D institutions *e.g.* Wolter and Eliza Hall Institute of Medical Research, centenary Institute of Cancer and Cell Biology and Bio21 Institute. Mr. Sibal also addressed the Australia-India business council at Sydney, and invited the Australian Industry to jointly work with their Indian counterparts for accessing global market for the production of world class products at affordable prices using complimentary strengths available in two countries.

5875. (9-2-2008) NEW DELHI : The Vice President of India Mohd. Hamid Ansari inaugurated a Seminar on "Contours of Ageing in India-Seeking Peace and Security" organized by The Guild of Service with the cooperation of the Ministry of Social Justice & Empowerment here today. In his address, the Vice President said that we should not forget our old traditional values and the elderly people should be given due respect and should be treated as assets. The Vice President called upon the people to re-examine the status of elderly people in our country and to develop ways to provide them greater safety and security. He appreciated the efforts of the Guild in support of elderly people. The Guild of Service is a voluntary organization working with a mandate of serving and strengthening the marginalized persons in India. Smt V. Mohini Giri, Chairperson of Guild of Service and many dignitaries were present on the occasion.

5876. (9-2-2008) NEW DELHI : The Minister of Petroleum and Natural Gas, Shri Murli Deora, has condoled the sudden demise of Baba Amte in whose passing away the country has lost a true Gandhian entirely dedicated to the uplift of the downtrodden and the disadvantaged section of our society. In his message Shri Deora described Baba Amte as a great human being, a social reformer and the one who adopted noble path to get justice for the downtrodden. Shri Deora further said, "This has been a big personal loss to me as I was a beneficiary of Baba Amte's guidance and support as and when needed." Shri Deora said that his work for improving the lot of those afflicted with leprosy speaks volume about his sheer determination and conviction, which would always inspire people to attempt overcoming insurmountable difficulties. The Minister added, " I would ever cherish my association and frequent meetings with Baba Amte to support his crusade for well being of humanity."

5877. (9-2-2008) NEW DELHI : The Prime Minister, Dr. Manmohan Singh, has said that the UPA government has launched an ambitious programme to make elementary education available to all. He said that he has dubbed the 11th Five Year Plan as "National Education Plan", because of the stress that has been laid on public investment in education. He said that the country needs a system that will prepare every one of our children for the challenges of the future, and not make them prisoners of the past.He was speaking at Mahindra United World College of India at Pune today.

5878. (9-2-2008) NEW DELHI : The Vice President of India Mohd. Hamid Ansari has deeply condoled the death of eminent public personality Shri Baba Amte. In his condolence message, the Vice President said that Shri Baba Amte served the people, especially the poor and downtrodden, and earned their love and adulation. In his passing away, we have lost a great Indian. Following is the text of Vice President's condolence message : "I am deeply grieved to learn about the sad demise of Shri Baba Amte, an eminent public personality. His death is a great loss to the country. Shri Baba Amte served the people, especially the poor and the downtrodden, and earned their love and adulation. In his passing away, we have lost a great Indian."

5879. (9-2-2008) NEW DELHI : The Prime Minister Dr. Manmohan Singh has expressed his condolences on the passing away of the famous Gandhinian leader, Baba Amte. The Prime Minister said in his condolence message: "It is with a deep sense of grief and loss that I heard about the demise of Baba Amte. A true Gandhian who worked hard to uphold Gandhian values in their true spirit, Baba Amte became a legend in his own lifetime. The work he did for the upliftment of leprosy affected people at Anandvan alone puts him in a unique class of great national figures who lived for the betterment of their fellow human beings. His life long struggle to unite people across the length and breadth of the country on national and Gandhian lines and to eliminate all forms of discrimination and bias truly make him a saint of our times. The footprints of Baba Amte will be permanently embedded in the sands of time and will be a guiding beacon for all those working for the common good. In this hour of sorrow, my heart reaches out to all those associated with Baba Amte and his millions of admirers across the nation. I pay homage to a truly great son of India and pray that his departed soul rests in peace."

5880. (10-2-2008) NEW DELHI : To mark the 97th anniversary of the Corps of Signals, the "Information Warriors" of the Indian Army, presented a colourful daring display of martial arts (Taekwondo, Kalaripayattu), and motorcycle stunts and their latest communication equipment, here today. Corps of Signals is responsible for planning, establishing and managing entire Information and Communication Technology (ICT) set up for the Indian Army. The ICT infrastructure apart from catering for the communication requirements for conventional operations also provides communication support to our forces involved in Counter Insurgency operations, United Nation Missions and for emergency communications during natural calamities. Under the able guidance of Lieutenant General S P Sree Kumar, Signal Officer-in-Chief, Corps of Signals has taken active measures for stabilizing, fine tuning and consolidating the architecture and performance of various communication networks fielded in the recent past. The process of consolidation is aimed at effectively providing secure, reliable, real time communications, round the clock by creating a pan Indian consolidated Army network of networks, which ensured that the aim of transforming Indian Army into a Network Centric Force in near future is fulfilled. Successful implementations of Project Mercury Connect, an OFC project in rugged North Eastern Sector and Project Mobile Cellular Communication System (MCCS) for extending mobile services to our soldiers in Counter Insurgency Operations in Northern Sector are a few major steps taken by the Corps in achieving the aim. The Corps of Signals with its responsibility to provide Cyber Security for the Indian Army has ensured Information assurance to the field formations with its trained personnel and resources to thwart any cyber threats. Electronic Warfare and Signal Intelligence units are force multipliers and valuable assets for all future wars. The Corps has also enhanced the technology savvy image of our Army internationally by establishing Computer Training Laboratories in friendly foreign countries. Signals have always been at the forefront of sports and adventure activities. Sportsmen of the Corps have achieved distinction in Hockey, Wrestling, and Athletics at various national and international level competitions. Motorcycle display team of the Corps famously known as "Dare Devils" hold the distinction of having their feat mentioned in Guinness Book of World records. In the recently concluded 4th Military World Games conducted at Hyderabad and Mumbai the responsibility of Communication, Information Technology and Accreditation was entrusted to Corps of Signals and was executed to perfection.

5881. (11-2-2008) NEW DELHI : The Fifth All India IAF Civilians Inter Command Football Tournament was flagged off today by Air Officer-in-Charge Personnel, Air Marshal VR Iyer, AVSM, at 412 Air Force Station Football ground New Delhi. The proceedings started with a grand March Past by all the participating teams in their Command Colours with Air Marshal Iyer taking the salute. The inaugural match was played between Western Air Command and Southern Air Command with WAC defeating SAC by 5-Nil. The Indian Air Force has moved ahead by forming Air Force Civilian Sports Board approved and budgeted by the Government. In order to enhance the morale of the civilian workforce and further integrate them with their service counterparts, the Board is holding All India Inter Command Tournaments in other fields of All India Cultural Programme by the Civilian employees, other sports championships in Carom, Table Tennis, Volleyball & Chess. The finals will be held on 22 Feb 08 with the Chief of the Air Staff, Air Chief Marshal FH Major, as the Chief Guest.

5882. (11-2-2008) NEW DELHI : The Defence Minister Shri A K Antony will visit Gas Turbine Research Establishment (GTRE), Electronics and Radar Development Establishment (LRDE), Aeronautical Development Agency (ADA) and Aeronautical Development Establishment (ADE) during his day long visit to Bangalore tomorrow. At the ADA, Shri Antony will hold discussions with senior officials and is expected to take a look at the System Design and Evaluation Facility, Weapons Rig and an exhibition. The ADA is the nodal agency for the design and development of Light Combat Aircraft-Tejas for Air Force and Navy with Hindustan Aeronautical Limited as principal partner. Eight limited series production aircrafts are being manufactured by ADA. During his visit of the Aircraft Research and Development Centre, the minister will be taken to the Iron Bird and the Hanger of the Light Combat Aircraft-'Tejas'. This will be followed by his witnessing a Flight Demonstration of the Tejas at the National Flight Test Centre. At ADE, scientists will brief the minister on products and exhibits on display there as well as simulation activities at the centre. Established in 1959, the thrust areas of ADE are Unmanned Aerial Vehicles, flight simulation, combat aircraft systems and air weapons. The major projects executed by ADE are Lakshya, Nishant UAV, LCA Simulator and Sudarshan Laser Guided Gun. A visit to the Kaveri Engine Assembly Bay and Test House at GTRE and display of Radars at LRDE, as well as an exhibition on the activities of ADE have also been lined up for the Defence Minister. LRDE is one of the premier R&D establishments set up under the DRDO to address the Services needs in the field of Radar, communication systems and related technologies. The laboratory has on its hand two major active phased array radar projects,-a radar for an airborne platform dedicated for early warning, surveillance and control (AEW&C) and a 'Medium Power Radar' for the Indian Air Force with 300 km range.

5883. (11-2-2008) NEW DELHI : The North Eastern region comprises of the states of Arunachal Pradesh, Assam, Manipur, Meghalaya, Mizoram, Nagaland, Sikkim and Tripura. While Sikkim is a little away perched on top of the narrow Siliguri corridor in West Bengal, Assam is surrounded by the other six states-all of them sharing borders with Assam. Assam is dominated by plains and the mighty Brahmaputra while the other states are predominantly hilly. The region is characterized by high biodiversity, heavy precipitation, annual floods along the Brahmaputra and high seismicity. The geographical setup and the terrain of the region ensures poor accessibility and renders communication difficult in the region. The North East region has also an extraordinary diverse ethno-geographic diversity. There are many tribes in the region with their own rich languages, social practices and traditions. However, because of the complex problems of historical neglect, rapid social and political changes, the region could not develop to its full potential. Political evolution, reorganization of state boundaries, insurgency, low resource base inhospitable terrain, remoteness from the mainland and late introduction to Planning process for some of the states have, among other factors, contributed to the region remaining under developed especially in terms of infrastructure, communication, health care facilities and human resources. Keeping this in mind, the Central Government has earmarked 10% of its Plan funds consistently since 1998-99 in order to enable the North East to catch up with the rest of the country, especially with regard to its infrastructure deficiencies.

5884. (11-2-2008) NEW DELHI : 13 States namely Andhra Pradesh, Assam, Bihar, Chattisgarh, Goa, Gujarat, Karnataka, Kerala, Madhya Pradesh, Maharashtra, Orissa, Rajasthan and Tamil Nadu have enacted the Participatory Irrigation Management (PIM) till December 2007. So far 54330 Water Users Associations (WUAs) covering an area of 12.32 million hectare have been formed in various states. The Ministry of Water Resources has been emphasizing Participatory Approach for Management of Water Resources by involving not only the various Government agencies but also the users and other stakeholders in an effective and decisive manner in various aspects of planning, designing, development and management of water resources. The Ministry has circulated a draft bill on PIM with a view to ensure an appropriate legal and organizational framework for beneficiary participation in the management of irrigation water.

5885. (11-2-2008) NEW DELHI : ICANN, The 31st International Public Meeting of ICANN (Internet corporation for Assigned Names and Numbers) got underway in New Delhi this morning with a call to make IPv4 amd IPv6 interoperable since the pool of IPv4 addresses may get exhausted in the next 3 to 4 years. In his welcome address to the 900 delegates gathered for the ICANN meeting, Secretary, Information Technology Mr. Jainder Singh said that IPv6 will not only expand the address space but also enable internet connectivity between a large number of devices. He said India will continue to work closely with ICANN on this issue. The Secretary said there was a need for ensuring participation of all linguistic groups inside the space. The Internet is a key factor in developing a more inclusive information society which stresses diversity, he said. Setting the tone for the week long meeting, the Chairman of the Board of ICANN, Mr. Peter Dengate Thrush said that the introduction of Internationalized Domain Names IDNs), is an obvious path for further expansion of internet in the country. He said that such a system would allow delivery of internet naming system that allows virtually any language to be recognized in a script that people can recognize. ICANN is in the process of deliberating whether scripts other than ASCII can be used for IDNs at the top levels. Other topics to be debated in the ICANN Board meeting and the Public meeting are new gTLDS so that business opportunities on the net expands. The CEO of ICANN Mr. Paul Twomey welcomed the business outsourcing IT service industries in India that have been booming. He said one of the main reasons behind this boom was single global internet that can seamlessly serve the customers both in India and off-shore. He said as opposed to physical trade where there are tariff and non tariff barriers, delivery of services in the online environment is globally seamless. Mr. Twomey also mentioned about the Joint Project Agreement with US Department of Commerce which was coming up for review this year and will try to take ICANN into the transition phase where it will be responsible for more of its own activities. The ICANN itself is an interesting public/private experiment and the world is watching how it performs. Principles such as inclusiveness, transparency, openness, and for the technical coordination of the internet. Introduction of IDNs and DNS security issues are of great importance to ICANN and areas where the world will look for positive influence of ICANN. The New Delhi meeting is the first of the three public ICANN meetings in 2008. These meetings are crucial because ICANN's policies are created through a bottom-up, transparent process involving internet Community.

5886. (11-2-2008) NEW DELHI : On 23 Feb 2008, when the Honourable Raksha Mantri Shri AK Antony formally inducts the Hawk 132 Advanced Jet Trainer (AJT) into service, an important milestone in the history of the IAF will be reached. This event will mark the fulfilment of a long-standing requirement of the IAF for an AJT that will effectively bridge the gap between the slow jet trainer such as the Kiran and the advanced fighter aircraft currently in IAF's inventory. The need for an AJT was first articulated by the IAF in 1982 and ever since has remained high on IAF's agenda for procurement. The IAF felt that there existed a quantum difference in the skill and judgement levels required of a yong fighter pilot as he transited to state of the art fighters such as the Su-30 MKI, Mirage 2000 and MiG-29. The Hawk 132 would adequately serve as lead in trainer for these advanced aircraft. The Hawk 132 is a variant of the highly successful BAE Systems Hawk It incorporates an open architecture mission computer, glass cockpit and a state of the art avionics suite including a new generation Inertial Navigation System with GPS (INGPS). It is also equipped with several Indian made components such as the communication sets, dentification Friend or Foe (IFF) system and the radio altimeter. In addition to being an advanced jet trainer, Hawk 132 is fully combat capable and can carry air to air missile and air to ground armament. It could also be used as a lightweight fighter. The contract for supply of the Hawk AJT was signed between the IAF and BAE Systems in 2004. The deal envisaged a supply of 66 aircraft, 24 built in the UK and 42 license produced by HAL at Bangalore. IAF pilots and technicians were trained at BAE Systems facilities at Warton and Brough in UK. The initial four Hawk aircraft were flown from Warton to Bidar by a combined team of BAE Systems' and IAF pilots. Bidar airfield, located in the North West of Karnataka, approx 150 Km from Hyderabad, was chosen as the main operating base for the Hawk. This base has been a training establishment for budding fighter pilots of the IAF since 1963. To ensure the smooth induction of the Hawk, the Air Warriors under the command of Air Commodore Ramesh Rai have worked tirelessly to put the required infrastructure in place. They were, at all stages, assisted by the local civil authorities and population. The work services included extension of the two runways, improvement in landing facilities and creation of servicing facilities for the technology intensive Hawk aircraft. The first two aircraft arrived at Bidar on 12 Nov 2007 and were welcomed to Indian skies by Air Marshal GS Chaudhry, Air Officer Commanding-in-Chief, Training Command, IAF, Bangalore. Since then, IAF pilots and technicians have been hard at work coming up to operational status on this combat capable aircraft. The formal induction of the Hawk 132 on 23 Feb 2008 by the Honourable Raksh Mantri Shri AK Antony marks the operationalisation of the aircraft. It will be an important milestone in training of future fighter pilots.

5887. (11-2-2008) NEW DELHI : The Ministry of Women & Child Development has proposed public-private partnership for strengthening the Integrated Child Development Scheme (ICDS). The partnership may include resource mobilistion for construction of anganwadi centres, creating facilities such as child friendly toilets, kitchen, drinking water, pre-school education kits and regular health check-ups at ICDS health centres. Addressing a national workshop on Public-Private partnership in ICDS, the Minister of Women & Child Development Smt. Renuka Chowdhury said that the ICDS, the largest programme in the world for intervention to correct malnutrition caters about 60.63 million young children through about 9 lakh anganwadis. But still there were some gaps which could be filled through the participation of other stakeholders of the society especially private industry. She said that investment in the children would provide better human resource to the industry and better citizen to the country. Smt. Renuka Chodhury said ever since the IC DS was initiated, it was envisaged a purely Governmental programme. However, with the gradual passage of time through field experience, it was felt that the programme could yield much better results if participation of private sector is also elicited in its implementation. As of now, the Government has only collaborated with few voluntary organizations and Panchayati Raj Institutions across the country which has paid rich dividends. Taking all these developments into consideration, the Government is of the view that ICDS could be developed as people's programme with the partnership of private sectors which would be mutually beneficial to all concerned, she added. Listing the areas for public private partnership the Minister said that the private sector could help the Government to reach remotest areas to create awareness about health & nutrition, provide training to enhance the capacities of ICDS functionaries, making anganwadis more child friendly, upgrading infrastructure and monitoring the implementation of various ICDS schemes. The meeting was organized by the Ministry of Women & Child Development to explore possible avenues for PPP in ICDS. Besides, representatives of Public Sector Banks, Corporate Houses, NGO and international agencies the States where partnership has already been initiated were also present in the workshop.

5888. (11-2-2008) NEW DELHI : The National Mineral Development Corporation (NMDC) produced 20.1 million tonnes of iron-ore during April-December 2007 recording a growth of 12.5 per cent over the production during the same period last year. It also surpassed the target set in the Memorandum of Understanding by 6 per cent. NMDC sold 19.86 million tonnes of iron ore during the first nine months of FY 08 as against 17.49 million tonnes during the same period in FY 07. During the period the company earned net profit of Rs. 2234.01 crore compared to Rs. 1609.20 crore during the previous year. Making a presentation at the performance review meeting chaired by the Minister for Steel, Chemicals and Fertilisers Shri Ram Vilas Paswan, NMDC Chairman Shri Rana Som said transport bottlenecks and threats from Maoists has led to shortfall in despatch of iron ore. He said, the company will set up an Investigation and Exploration Centre at

Raipur. The Centre will assist State governments in mineral exploration activities free. Shri Som said, recruitment for the Centre has already started. Complimenting NMDC for getting 'Navratna' status and continued excellent performance, the Minister said, it should complete all its expansion projects in a time bound manner. Shri Paswan also assured NMDC that he will take up the issue of availability of railway rakes with the concerned Ministry. The Minister asked the company to expedite the complementation of its activities under the Corporate Social Responsibility.

5889. (11-2-2008) NEW DELHI : Forest Secretaries and officials of Forest Departments from all over the country are meeting tomorrow to discuss issues relating forest areas, management of protected areas, man-animal conflicts and other forest and wildlife related issues. This two-day Conference has been organized by the Ministry of Environment and Forests. Forest Secretaries, Principal Chief Conservators of Forests and Chief Wildlife Wardens from all the States and Union Territories will participate in the Conference. They will discuss issues relating to increasing forests and tree cover in the country. To achieve the target of National Forest Policy 1988 to increase the forest cover of the country, radical reforms and concerted actions will be discussed. The Conference will deliberate on a unique proposal to develop plantation banks to facilitate the compensatory afforestation through Green Credit Scheme. Besides this, implementation of scheduled tribes and other traditional forest dwellers (Recognition of Forest Rights) Act 2006, Tiger Conservation, Man-Animal Conflicts, better facilities for front-line staff, recommendations of National Forests Commission and Forest Protection including wildlife conservation will be discussed. The main thrust of the Conference will be on progress of the implementation of the management plans of Protected Areas and man-animal conflicts. The management plans are important tools for scientific management of protected areas. If they are based on sound scientific and ecological data, they help in augmenting water resources of respective region. The National Wildlife Action Plan (2002-2016) has also emphasized this. The Man-Animal conflicts spread over the country in a variety of forms, including monkey menace of the urban centres, crop raiding by ungulates and wild pigs, depredation by elephants and cattle and human lifting by tigers and leopards. These are results of degradation of habitats, depletion of the natural prey base, changing crop patterns and others. The Conference will disucss on various aspects and management interventions to mitigate these conflicts. Representatives from Ministry of Tribal Affairs, Ministry of Health and Family Welfare (AYUSH), Ministry of Panchayati Raj, Ministry of Agriculture, Ministry of Rural Development and Planning Commission will attend the Conference. The officials of the Ministry of Environment and Forests and its Institutions such as Wildlife Institute of India, Forest Survey of India, Indira Gandhi National Forest Academy, Indian Plywood Research and Training Institute (IPRTI), Indian Council Forestry Research & Education, Indian Institute of Forest Management will also participate in this two-day Conference.

5890. (11-2-2008) NEW DELHI : Number of affected districts remains the same (14). A total population of 27.79 lakhs is under surveillance [12.77 lakhs in 0-3 Km area and 15.02 lakhs in 3-10 Km area]. In 0-3 Km area 1083 persons with fever and URI have been detected of which four had exposure to sick/infected birds. In the 3-10 Kms area a total of 1186 persons have been detected with fever & URI of which two had exposure history. These cases have been followed up.

5891. (11-2-2008) NEW DELHI : Number of affected districts (14 districts) remains the same. In these districts, 48 blocks and five municipalities are involved. A total population of 22.92 lakhs is under surveillance [9.69 lakhs in 0-3 Km area and 13.22 lakhs in 3-10 Km area]. In 0-3 Km area 704 persons with fever and URI have been detected of which 4 had exposure to sick/infected birds. In the 3-10 Kms area a total of 835 persons have been detected with fever & URI of which two had exposure history. These cases have been followed up. In the hospitals, 714 patients with Fever and URI have reported of three of them are admitted.

5892. (11-2-2008) NEW DELHI : Number of affected districts remains the same (14). A total population of 27.79 lakhs is under surveillance [12.77 lakhs in 0-3 Km area and 15.02 lakhs in 3-10 Km area]. In 0-3 Km area 1083 persons with fever and URI have been detected of which four had exposure to sick/infected birds. In the 3-10 Kms area a total of 1186 persons have been detected with fever & URI of which two had exposure history. These cases have been followed up. No suspected human cases of Avian Influenza have been detected in any of the affected Districts.

5893. (11-2-2008) NEW DELHI : Shri Shantanu Consul today took over as Secretary (Border Management) in the Ministry of Home Affairs. He replaces Shri U.N.Panjiar who has been appointed Secretary, Union Ministry of Water Resources. Shri Shantanu Consul is a 1974 batch IAS officer and belongs to the Karnataka cadre. Before taking over as Secretary (Border Management), he was the Administrator of the Universal Services Obligation Fund, Department of Telecommunications. Apart from serving in various positions in his cadre, he has also had the experience of working in the Department of Civil Aviation and the Union Ministry of Chemicals & Fertilizers.

5894. (12-2-2008) NEW DELHI : Telecom and IT companies will be showcasing their products and services for the first time in the DEFEXPO 2008, Shri Pradeep Kumar, Secretary, Defence Production, said here today. Addressing a press conference ahead of the four-day Exposition, Shri Kumar said 273 companies from over 30 countries would display weapon systems for army and navy. The United States with 46 exhibitors is the largest participant while 43 exhibitors will represent France. Major participants include Russia and UK, besides Israel, South Africa, Germany, Italy, Czech Republic, Poland, Ukraine, Sweden and South Korea. The Defence Minister Shri A K Antony will inaugurate the 5th DefExpo-

2008 at Pragati Maidan on Saturday, February 16th. Organised by the Department of Defence Production, the exhibition will continue till February 19th. The Confederation of Indian Industry (CII) is its event manager. Reflecting the increased role of private sector in defence industry, the Defence Production Secretary said over 200 Indian private sector companies besides defence undertakings would participate in the exhibition. Dedicated to global land and naval systems business activity-from suppliers to manufacturers, technology providers to services-the DefExpo also offers an opportunity to the international defence industry to promote and showcase their products and services. As many as 90 products would be launched by domestic and foreign companies during the DefExpo, Shri Pradeep Kumar said. Shri Kumar said the DefExpo would project the emergence of India as an attractive market as well as an investment destination for joint ventures in defence industry. The exhibition has generated attention globally and has carved a niche amongst major defence exhibitions around the world, he added. The DefExpo was conceptualised in 1998 with an objective to promote defence exports from India and exhibit the capabilities of Indian defence R&D and production. The first exhibition was held in 1999 and subsequently in 2002, 2004 and 2006. While a modest 197 exhibitors participated in the first DefExpo, the biennial event will feature 475 companies in its 5th edition this year. Delegations from 47 countries including Afghanistan would attend the deliberations.

5895. (12-2-2008) NEW DELHI : Following is the text of the opening remarks made by the Prime Minister, Dr. Manmohan Singh, at the joint press interaction with Russian Prime Minister, Mr. Victor Zubkov, here today. "I am very pleased to welcome Prime Minister Zubkov and his distinguished delegation to India. Prime Minister Zubkov's visit to India comes within three months of my own visit to Russia in November, 2007. Such high level exchanges between India and Russia reflect the time tested nature of the close and special ties that exist between our two countries. Prime Minister Zubkov and I have had an extremely productive and comprehensive discussion on all aspects of our relationship. I conveyed to the Prime Minister the importance we attach to his participation in the meeting of the Indo-Russia Forum on Trade and Investment and the "Year of Russia" in India. Later today, I will be accompanying the Prime Minister to formally inaugurate the "Year of Russia" in India. In our discussions, we agreed to re-double our efforts to tap the full potential of our two economies. We agreed on the need to diversify our trade basket, and expand cooperation in sectors such as minerals, diamonds, transport and infrastructure, investment and services, and high technology. For this we will operationalise the Joint Task Force to implement recommendations to increase bilateral trade to US$ 10 billion by 2010 and consider a Comprehensive Economic Cooperation Agreement. We agreed that there was vast potential for mutually beneficial cooperation in the area of hydrocarbons. I expressed my hope that ongoing discussions between our oil and gas companies would result in finalization of joint projects in India, Russia and third countries. We expressed our satisfaction at the status of our ongoing collaboration in the fields of science and technology, space and civil nuclear cooperation. We have finalised negotiations in regard to reaching an agreement on cooperation in the construction of additional nuclear power plants in India. We reaffirmed our commitment to build upon our defence relations which is an important pillar of our Strategic Partnership. Our talks today have reaffirmed our joint commitment to further strengthen Indo-Russian relations for the mutual benefit and prosperity of our two peoples, and for our region and the world. Thank you"

5896. (12-2-2008) NEW DELHI : Union Minister for rural Development, Dr. Raghuvansh Prasad Singh has emphasized on the correct presentation of figures related with the implementation of the Swarnajayanti Gram Swarozgar Yojana (SGSY). The Minister was presiding over a meeting to review the guidelines of SGSY pertaining to the special project currently under implementation here today. Dr. Singh retaliated that in view of the National Sample Survey Organization (NSSO) reports and the demand to enhance the coverage of the scheme from different states it will be apt to reconsider some of the guidelines for corrections so that more and more persons belonging to the BPL families are benefitted. The SGSY targets and their speedy implementation in the states of Bihar and Jharkhand also came up in the discussion and it was observed that keeping in view the 2001 Census data and the new data made available by NSSO need a through check up and yearly targets should be set up accordingly. As per the datas of the 8.29 crore population of Bihar there were 7.43 crore persons residing in the rural areas. This accounted to nearly 1.48 crore rural households. The BPL families constituted nearly 67 lakh at the time of carving out of the State of Jharkahand.

5897. (12-2-2008) NEW DELHI : The Union Home Minister, Shri Shivraj Patil reviewed here today the Naxal situation in Jharkhand and Chhattisgarh. Senior officers of the two States briefed him about the situation and the steps taken by the State Governments to deal with it. They also apprised him of the utilization of the funds, provided by the Central Government. The Home Minister accepted the request of the Jharkhand Government to provide additional five companies of Para Military Forces for the required period. The Chhattisgarh Government's request for additional Para Military Forces will also be considered by the Ministry. Shri Patil, however, asked the two State Governments to make use of the Para Military Forces for operational purposes and not for normal law and order or static guard duties. The Centre has already provided 13 battalions of Para Military Forces to Chattisgarh and 5 to Jharkhand. Expressing concern over the slow pace of filling up of vacancies in the two states, the Home Minister said that the process required to be speeded up. This will not only help strengthen security, but also provide employment to local people. He asked the two State Governments to strengthen their intelligence wings and also ensure optimal and timely utilization of the funds granted under various central schemes. The Home Minister expressed satisfaction at some successful anti-Naxalite operations carried out recently, and emphasized the need to follow a pro-active strategy in both the States. The review meeting on Jharkhand was attended, among others, by the DGP of the State and the meeting on Chhattisgarh, among others, by the Chief Secretary and DGP of the State. Both the meetings were attended, among others, by the Union Home Secretary, Shri Madhukar Gupta, DG, CRPF, Shri S.I.S. Ahmed and senior officers of the Home Ministry.

5898. (12-2-2008) NEW DELHI : BJP challenges Congress to spell out the action plan on how they are going to combat terrorism without POTA like stringent anti-terror law. The latest arrest of six Lashkar-e-Tayyeba (LeT) from Uttar Pradesh is a case in point. These fidayeen have confessed to their role in attack on CRPF camp in Rampur and attack on Indian Institute of Sciences (IISc) in Bangalore along with their planning to attack BSE and Church Gate Station in Mumbai. Three of them are from Pakistan. But all these confessions are not admissible in court of law under present laws. Unless police comes out with direct evidences such cases can't be conclusive and most likely these terrorists will be on bail instead of being in jail. The inadequate provisions of our present day laws can't effectively deal with such a terrorist module in absence of a stringent anti-terror law. Law does not make confession admissible and the terrorist can't be put under detention for longer duration. Law can't effectively act against over ground supporters of such a module either. POTA enables the custodial confessions admissible as evidence in court of law. Such terrorist can be detained for 180 days without presenting them in the courts. Investigating agency can withhold identity of witnesses. POTA was effective as far as action against over ground supporters of such a module, without whose sympathy and support the modules can't operate. POTA had a provision whereby presumption of guilt was made against accused. Without a POTA like act the agencies stand on loosing ground, as direct evidence in such cases is difficult to surface. India is the only country with high killings at the hands of terrorists without any anti-terror law. Indian Government must raise issue of cross border terrorism with Pakistan, as many LET fidayeens from Pakistan are involved in recent terrorist attacks. The joint mechanism has miserably failed to tackle such problems. Congress led UPA can't fight terrorism with proper legal, political, diplomatic response as its mindset is bogged down with political overtone of vote bank politics. Scrapping of POTA, relief package to dependents of terrorists and Prime Minister's infamous "Lost Sleep" over pains of suspected terrorists is the manifestation of such a mindset. The CMP of UPA does not mention any priority to fight terrorism. Government's decision to offer relief package to dependents of terrorist amounts to the government rewarding the terrorists for killing our brave soldiers and innocent citizens. No country in the world supports tacitly those families, whose members have fought against the integrity of the country.

5899. (12-2-2008) NEW DELHI : The Ministry of Rural Development has released Rs. 24,14,88,000/- (Twenty four crore fourteen lakh eighty eight thousand) only towards Central share for the implementation of Swarna Jayanti Gram

Swarozgar Yojana (SGSY) to the States of Bihar, Madhya Pradesh and Uttar Pradesh during the current financial year (2007-08). Of the sanctioned amount the District Rural Development Agencies (DRDA) of Jamui, Munger, Patna, Saharsa and Sheikhpura in Bihar will get Rs, 9,98,01,000/- (Nine crore ninety eight lakh one thousand) as 1st instalment from the Central Allocation of Rs. 19.66 crores. The amount of 1st instalment for these districts consist of Rs. 2.12 crore, 1.32 crore, 3.33 crore,2.46 crore and 72.19 lakh respectively. In the case of Madhya Pradesh the grant is for Rs. 5,27,31,000/- (Five crore twenty seven lakh thirty one thousand) only. From it the DRDAs of Balaghat, Rewa, Shivpuri and Vidisha are to receive the 2nd instalment of grant of. 2.49 crore, 1.46 crore, 58 lakhs and 73 lakhs respectively. The DRDAs of Uttar Pradesh will receive Rs.8,89,56,000/- (Eight crore eightynine lakh fifty six thousand) only as second instalment of SGSY. This include Banda (Rs.1.24 crore), Hardoi (Rs.4.79 crore) and Kanpur Dehat (Rs.2.86 crore). The release of funds is subject to audit by Internal Audit of the Ministry of Rural Development and the amount should be utilized on the programmes as per approved guidelines of SGSY. The funding pattern will be 75:25 by the Centre and State.

5900. (12-2-2008) NEW DELHI : All tax deductors / collectors are required to file the TDS/TCS returns in Form No.24Q (for salaries), Form No.26Q (for payments other than salaries) or Form No.27EQ (for TCS). These forms require details of all tax deductions with name and permanent account number (PAN) of parties from whom tax was deducted. It had earlier been decided that Form No.24Q with less than 90% of PAN data and Form No.26Q & Form No.27EQ with less than 70% of PAN data will not be accepted for the quarter ending on 30.09.2007 and thereafter. The said decision has since been reviewed. It has now been decided to enhance the threshold limit for PAN quoting without which TDS/ TCS returns will not be accepted. The limit has been enhanced to 95% from 90% n case of Form 24Q and to 85% from 70% in case of Forms 26Q and 27EQ. The enhanced limits will be applicable for and from the quarter ending 31.03.2008. These threshold limits will also apply to all those TDS/TCS returns, which are filed for any of the earlier quarters on or after 01/04/2008. Tax deductors and tax collectors are, therefore, advised to obtain correct PAN of all deductees and quote the same in their TDS / TCS returns. Deductees are also advised to furnish their correct PAN with their deductors, failing which they will not only have difficulty in getting credit of TDS/TCS in their income tax assessments but will also face penal proceedings under the Income Tax Act.

5901. (12-2-2008) NEW DELHI : Total country level population of tiger is 1411 with a 17.43 per cent coefficient of variation. The lower limit is 1165 and the upper limit is 1657. Making a presentation about Tiger census in a press conference today Dr. Rajesh Gopal, Member Secretary, Tiger Project explained that the assessment shows that though the tiger has suffered due to direct poaching, loss of quality habitat, and loss of its prey, but there is still hope. The government has declared more eight new tiger reserves to strengthen the population of tigers. He said an area of around 31111 sq.km. of tiger habitat has been notified/identified by tiger states as per provisions of the wildlife (Protection Act). New and additional methods have been used in Tiger Census. Giving the details the Minister said The Project Tiger Directorate (now the National Tiger Conservation Authority) of the Ministry of Environment and Forests initiated refinement of the ongoing process of tiger estimation using pugmarks (footprints) in 2002. This was a collaborative initiative with the Wildlife Institute of India and 17 Tiger States. Based on a pilot study done in the Satpura Landscape of Madhya Pradesh, the methodology was mainstreamed as a country-level process, which was endorsed by the Tiger Task Force. The new process has been conceived, financially supported and implemented by the Ministry of Environment and Forests (now the National Tiger Conservation Authority), with internal and external peer review during field data collection. Dr. Rajesh Gopal informed that results pertaining to four major tiger States (Madhya Pradesh, Maharashtra, Chhattisgarh and Rajasthan) were finalized / released in May 2007. This report evaluates the current status of tigers, co-predators and their prey in India. The Member Secretary informed that the status of tiger, its co-predators, prey and its habitat has not significantly / adversely changed in the Tiger Reserves and Protected Areas. However, there is a decline in the same in outside areas. The spatial occupancy of tigers and other animals have been done for all the 17 tiger States, and mapped in the GIS domain.

5902. (12-2-2008) NEW DELHI : The Indian Ocean Naval Symposium, saw its first delegation arrive at New Delhi today to participate in the inaugural "IONS Seminar 2008" being conducted jointly by the Indian Navy and the National Maritime Foundation. The Saudi Arabian delegation, headed by His Highness Vice Admiral Prince Fahd bin Abdullah Al Saud, Commander of the Royal Saudi Naval Forces, arrived here at Indira Gandhi International Airport in the morning today. His Highness, the Commander of the Royal Saudi Naval Forces, was received by Rear Admiral BR Rao, Chief Hydrographer of the Indian Navy, who was the personal representative of the Chief of the Naval Staff, Admiral Sureesh Mehta. The 12 member Saudi delegation is one of the largest. Coming in from the opposite flank of the Indian Ocean was the Singapore delegation, which also arrived in the capital today. The delegation, headed by Rear Admiral CHEW Men Leong, Chief of the Navy, Republic of Singapore Navy, was received by Rear Admiral HCS Bisht, ACCP. The Singaporean Naval Chief was accompanied by his staff officer and the Head, Naval Intelligence of the Republic of Singapore Navy. Delegations from Eritrea, Brazil, Seychelles, Kuwait, Qatar, Mauritius, Malagasy, Myanmar, Oman, Sri Lanka, the UAE, Kenya, Djibouti, Egypt, Mozambique, South Africa, Sudan, Tanzania, Malaysia, Maldives, Indonesia, Australia, Thailand and France, will all arrive tomorrow. Each delegation would be received and welcomed at the airport by a Flag Officer, representing the Chief of Naval Staff of the Indian Navy. The IONS initiative is ready to be launched.

5903. (12-2-2008) NEW DELHI : Following is the text of the speech by her Excellency the President of India, Shrimati Pratibha Devisingh Patil, at the presentation of "Lakshmipat Singhania-IIM, Lucknow National Leadership Awards 2007" in New Delhi today: It is a great pleasure to participate in the Lakshmipat Singhania-IIM, Lucknow National Leadership Awards. I congratulate the award winners Shri Sunil Bharti Mittal, Dr. Anil Kakodkar and Smt. Aruna Dalmia for the leadership qualities that they have shown in their respective fields for which they richly deserve the awards. I would also like to congratulate Shri R. Subramanian, Dr. Atish Dabholkar and Shri Dipendra Manocha who have been conferred the Young Leader Awards. I wish them luck and am confident that they would continue to achieve success in their work. I have noted that Lakshmipat Singhania-IIM Lucknow National Leadership Awards have been given in three fields-business; Science and Technology, community services and social upliftment. All three are important aspects of the corporate world-all are interconnected and represent a holistic approach. While, undoubtedly, carrying out business is the basic function of industry, there is a constant need to use better methods of production and innovative technologies to improve productivity. In fact, the world is now technology driven which makes research and development a critical input for growth. Industry should extend support to scientific and research institutions to retain the cutting edge. Similarly, the entire purpose of a business should not be to just make profits but also to give back to society, in whose well-being they must invest. They have a social duty to perform and those who do so deserve recognition so that others are motivated. Indian industry is growing fast and is making rapid strides. Manufacturing, Communications, Business Process Outsourcing, knowledge based industries especially information technology, biotechnology and pharmaceuticals have demonstrated their strength and sustainability. Indian industry is also expanding globally and has production units and service centres in many parts of the world. Businesspersons have the responsibility to ensure that their products and services are of a quality that satisfies consumers both in the domestic and the international markets. The "Made in India" brand should be associated world over with quality, efficiency and assured services. This would result in a higher growth rate for industry and a better image for India. As industry grows, it needs to reflect on its responsibilities. Questions regarding good corporate governance and corporate responsibility have assumed centre-stage position. Corporate governance is about working ethically and finding a balance between economic and social goals. It includes the ability to function profitably while obeying laws, rules and regulations. A set of principles voluntarily agreed to by the business world and corporate houses in India could be developed into a self-imposed code of conduct. I have often spoken about corruption as a menace in our country that needs to be uprooted.

5904. (12-2-2008) NEW DELHI : A state of the art Energy Conservation Technology Centre for display of energy efficient products and technologies was inaugurated by Shri S. Sundareshan, Addl. Secretary, Ministry of Petroleum &

Natural Gas at Sanrakshan Bhawan, New Delhi today. The centre set up by Petroleum Conservation Research Association (PCRA) provides a common platform to the manufacturers of such items that have the potential to contribute significantly towards savings of energy. Across the country, such products are being developed not only through research and development works in established laboratories and workshops but also through innovations and entrepreneurship at individual levels with little or no support. The CTS has been set up to fill up the gap of effective information dissemination on energy efficient products and technologies to general public. Apart from products, the CTC is also intended to be a nodal point for exposition of energy efficient technologies, both nascent and in different stages of development. Some of the energy efficient items on display are industrial equipment like motors & lighting, products of mass consumption such as kerosene lamps & stoves that have been developed after painstaking research, energy labeled white consumer goods like air conditioners and refrigerators, innovative building components that save energy. The centre also showcases technological advances in bio diesel, wind energy, fuel efficiency in transport sector. The centre is designed to be a stimulant for young scientists in schools and colleges who can contribute to the development of energy efficient products by their ideas, experiments and researches. By setting up the CTC, which is a first of its kind centre, PCRA has taken pro-active step to lend voices to and create visibility for innovations in energy efficient products and technologies and also build up capacity through mass participation.

5905. (12-2-2008) NEW DELHI : As part of the initiative and efforts of the Ministry of Tourism, Govt. of India, to create a large platform for showcasing its rich cultural heritage and tourism products, the Ministry of Tourism, in conjunction with various State Governments/Union Territories will be organizing "Shopping Festivals for promotion of Handicrafts and Rural Tourism" in six regions of the Country every year. The regions are East, West, South, North, Central and the North-East. The first in line in the "Shopping Festival for Promotion of Handicrafts and Rural Tourism" is the " Toshali National Crafts Mela" to be held in BHUBANESHWAR, Orissa, in the Eastern Region from February 15-27, 2008. The event is being organised by the Department of Tourism, Govt. of Orissa with the assistance of Ministry of Tourism Govt. of India. Union Minister for Tourism & Culture, Smt. Ambika Soni will inaugurate the event on February, 16, 2008 and the event will continue till February, 27, 2008. Over 150 craft persons will be participating at the event showcasing the finest Handicrafts & Handlooms of India. Eighteen Rural Tourism projects of the Ministry of Tourism, Govt. of India supported by UNDP will exhibit the specialized crafts and handlooms of these areas, enabling visitors to interact with the skilled artisans from Raghurajpur & Pipli (Orissa), Sualkuchi (Assam) Nepura (Bihar), Hodka (Gujrat), Chitrakote & Nagarnar (Chhatisgarh), Pranpur-Chowgn (M.P), Samod (Rajasthan), Ballavpur Danga, Mukutmonipur (West Bengal). These highly skilled artisans will display an amazing variety of unique products from different parts of the country. Visitors will also be able to see the craftsmen at work, producing beautiful pieces of art. Amidst the village ambience, a variety of cultural programmes during the day will provide a glimpse of the colours and traditional art forms of rural India. Cultural programmes every evenings will be held to include classical and folk performances like Odissi dance, Kathak, Bharat Natyam, Gazals and folk performances by renowned artists. The choice of multi-cuisine food stalls serving popular and traditional delicacies will be a treat for the entire family.

5906. (12-2-2008) NEW DELHI : Addressing the press persons here today, Shri Kamal Nath, Minister of Commerce and Industry, welcomed the Revised Draft Modalities texts on Agriculture and NAMA, which had been brought out in Geneva on 8 February. He commended the Chairs of the two negotiating groups for their efforts in seeking convergence and for putting together the complicated texts. Shri Nath clarified that a final view on the two texts would be possible only after holding consultations with other Ministries, domestic stakeholders, and India's partner countries in Geneva. This could take some more time. However, the Minister shared his preliminary assessment of the two texts. The Minister stated that the Agriculture text distils the progress made in negotiations between September 2007 and January 2008. While convergence has been achieved in some areas, the Chair has also put out brand new text in some other unresolved areas and these would require detailed deliberations *e.g.* Special Products (SPs), Special Safeguard Mechanism (SSM), Special Safeguards, Tropical Products, Tariff Simplification etc. There are also some other issues on which large divergences still exist, *e.g.* OTDS, market access in Sensitive Products, Tariff Capping etc. The Minister said: "Significant and effective reduction of trade distorting subsidies of the developed countries is an issue on which there can be no compromise because they impact adversely upon the livelihood of millions of our poor farmers". He added that: "Indian agriculture cannot be expected to carry the burden and most definitely not in a Development Round". The Minister expressed satisfaction at the fact that the original G-20 proposal of a minimum 54% cut in agricultural tariffs for developed countries and a maximum tariff cut of 36% for developing countries was back on the table. "India had always espoused the concept of two thirds proportionality between developed and developing countries in tariff reductions" he added. Striking a note of caution, Shri Kamal Nath stated that a lot of work still remains to be done on Special Products (SPs). India has already indicated that one of its "must-haves" on SPs was a significant number of tariff lines which did not have to take any tariff cuts. Also, logic demands that the cuts for other SPs had to be more favourable than for Sensitive Products. The Minister was firm that "The livelihood of Indian farmers and the food security of the nation is of paramount importance and must be protected at all costs". On the Special Safeguard Mechanism, the Minister opined that some of the proposals in the text were likely to render the SSM unworkable and detract from its utility. The SSM was a defensive instrument to safeguard livelihood issues: "How can a weak instrument provide the required protection?" he asked. Volume and price triggers have to be sensitive and independent of each other. This has to be recognized. India has always maintained that a simple, easy-to-use SSM was in the best interests of all. Shri Nath noted that though the Revised NAMA text continues with the earlier proposals on Swiss coefficients, it reflects that there are other points of view held by many countries. However, the Minister expressed surprise at the removal of the numbers on the para 8 flexibilities for developing countries, which have been on the table since the Framework of July 2004. He stated that these numbers were the very least that the developing countries, including India, needed in order to protect their infant industries, small-scale industries, and vulnerable sectors. "We need greater flexibilities" he added. The Chair should not have withdrawn the numbers from the text and left room for ambiguity to creep in. The Minister expressed the hope that the Chair of the Rules Negotiating Group would take a cue from the NAMA Chair and now come out with a Revised text, which truly reflects the views of the membership rather than representing just the views of one country, as in the case of the anti-dumping proposals. The Minister stated that the text on fisheries subsidies has to be radically revised in order to take into account the actual conditions in which small, artisanal fisheries in the developing world have to operate. "This is an issue that critically impinges upon the livelihood of millions of poor fisherfolk in India and other countries. It cannot be left unaddressed" he added. Sounding an optimistic note, the Minister stated that the revised texts can form the basis for constructive engagement and negotiation in the coming weeks. However, a lot of hard work still lies ahead. For instance, there are around 170 square brackets in the Agriculture text alone, which have to be reduced through intensive negotiations to a small and manageable number. "There are admittedly a number of areas where there are strong differences of opinion. Convergence in these areas will have to be incrementally achieved in these areas" the Minister said. It is vitally important to bear in mind the overarching Development mandate of the Round. If India's developed country trading partners recognize this, it would hasten the process of removing the square brackets and reaching convergence. India is committed to concluding the Doha Round quickly. "Now is the time for progress in other areas of interest to the WTO membership, *viz.* Rules and Services. There must be simultaneous progress on all fronts if we are to clinch a deal by end 2008" he concluded.

5907. (12-2-2008) NEW DELHI : The total import of sensitive items for the period April-December 07 has been Rs.20589 crores as compared to Rs.18532 crore during the corresponding period of last year thereby showing an increase of 11.1%. The gross import of all commodity during same period of current year was Rs.682088 crore as compared to Rs.611522 crore during the same period of last year. Thus import of sensitive items constitute 3.0% of the gross imports during last year as well as current year. Imports of spices, marble & Granite and milk & milk products have shown a decline at broad group level during the period. Imports of items *viz.* edible oil, fruits & vegetables (including nuts), food grains, cotton & silk, automobiles, products of SSI, rubber, Alcoholic beverages and Tea

& Coffee have shown increase during the period under reference. In the edible oil segment, the import has increased from Rs.7929 crore last year to Rs.8433 crore for the corresponding period of this year. The import of both crude oil as well as refined oil have gone up by 5.6% and 13.1% respectively. The increase in edible oil import is mainly due to significant growth in import of Crude palm oil and its fractions, which has gone up by 11%. Imports of sensitive items from Indonesia, Canada, China P RP, United States of America, Russia, Brazil, Sri Lanka DSR, Germany, Thailand, Japan, Guinea Bissau, Ukraine etc. have gone up while those from Argentina, Myanmar, Malaysia, Cote D' Ivoire, Australia etc. have shown a decrease.

5908. (12-2-2008) NEW DELHI : Sustainability of Forest Eco System is an essential component of the environment conservation and any degradation of forests will have an adverse impact on various life support systems. Inaugurating a two-day Conference of Forest Secretaries, Principal Chief Conservators of Forest and Chief Wildlife Wardens today, Thiru S. Regupathy, Minister of State for Environment and Forest said that the support systems like water resources, agriculture, bio-diversity, environment, climate change and human health will be affected. Shri Regupathy said inadequate public awareness about multiple function of forests, undervaluation of the contribution of forests to gross domestic products, technological weakness etc. are the issues unique to forestry sector. Explaining the principal aim of the National Forest Policy the Minister said that it is to provide environment stability and ecological balance including atmospheric equilibrium. This policy gives priority to the sustenance and livelihood needs of the forest dependent communities, particularly tribals. Shri Regutpathy informed that at present more than 22 million hectare forests have been assigned to communities under joint forest management in the country. Regarding Forest and Tree cover Shri Regupathy said we have set a target of 30 per cent by 2012. It is most crucial to achieve this target as besides other requirements it will help to solve the problem of global warming. The National Forest Commission has suggested 360 recommendations to achieve mandate of National Forest Policy. The Ministry is in general agreement with the recommendations except few. The Ministry has set apart around 4.8 per cent of the geographical area for inclusive conservation of its biodiversity in the form of protected areas. Currently there are 659 protected areas in the country. He urged States to submit requirements for tiger results, tiger conservation, constitution committees and creation conservation fund. Earlier, Secretary Miss Meena Gupta said forests can act as source as well as sink of Carbon dioxide. She said the forestation and forest degradation contributes nearly 20 per cent of the total green house gases emissions at global level. This is an area of concern for entire global community. The Bali Action Plan has addressed this issue and put forests on the centre stage. In our country the forests and tree cover is more or less stabilize at around 24 per cent of total land marks. However, the decline in good quality forests cover should be our area of concern. The Scheduled Tribes and Other Traditional Forests Dwellers (Recognition of Forests

Rights) Act, 2006 recognizes and vests the forest rights and occupation in forest land in forest tribes and other traditional forest dwellers. The Forest Department will have to check number of pro-active actions to ensure effective implementation of this Act in true spirit. She cautioned to protect forests against unlawful claims of occupation. Regarding the allocation of forests and wildlife sector she said the next Plan period that double allocation *i.e.* Rs.5039 crores. The Conference will deliberate on a unique proposal to develop plantation banks to facilitate the compensatory afforestation through Green Credit Scheme. Besides this, implementation of scheduled tribes and other traditional forest dwellers (Recognition of Forest Rights) Act 2006, Tiger Conservation, Man-Animal Conflicts, better facilities for front-line staff, recommendations of National Forests Commission and Forest Protection including wildlife conservation will be discussed.

5909. (12-2-2008) NEW DELHI : India and Netherlands signed a Memorandum Of Understanding (MoU) here today in the various areas concerning shipping and port sectors. The MoU was signed by the Minister of Shipping, Road Transport and Highways Thiru T.R. Baalu on behalf of India and Mr. Camiel Eurlings, Minister of Transport, Public Works and Water Management on behalf of Netherlands. The MoU envisages cooperation in the fields of Port planning and development; Maritime transport and logistics; Shipbuilding; Research and development; safety and security and stimulation of cargo flows between the two countries. The MoU will help in boosting ties between the two countries in the area of maritime sector. Speaking on the occasion, Thiru Baalu said that India and the Netherlands have in recent times come very close through trade and technical cooperation as is clear from the fact that the total two-way trade between India and Netherlands has reached a total of € 2.77 billion in 2006 from € 1 billion in 1997. However, Indian share in overall Dutch trade continues to be small, he added and said that it needs to be enhanced. Thiru Baalu informed the Dutch delegation about the National Maritime Development programme under which an investment of about 1000 billion rupees is envisaged. He said that India is also in the process of setting up of two international size shipyards one each at the eastern and western coast. The Minister said that India and Netherlands can cooperate in all these areas. Apart from this, dredging is another area in which the Netherlands can share their expertise, he said. Similarly Inland Water Transport which is in a nascent stage in India with lot of potential, can be another area of cooperation. India plans to setup an International Maritime University at Chennai with campuses at Mumbai, Kolkata, Visakhapatnam and expertise of Netherlands in this area would be welcome, Thiru Baalu added. On this occasion, the Netherlands side announced twelve scholarships for Indian Martime officers and engineers. It was also decided that a study would be conducted for supply chain management for carriage of goods form Indian hinterland to Netherlands Ports.

5910. (12-2-2008) NEW DELHI : Dr. Ashwani Kumar, Minister of State for Industry, has stated that technology and innovation are identified as two major focus areas for knowledge management and added that while technology provides the hardware and software aspects for managing knowledge, the brainware or the mindware phenomenon are promoted by the innovative capabilities of human resources. He was speaking at the International Conference on "Technology & Innovation for Knowledge Management" here today, which was organised by the National Productivity Council (NPC). Dr. Kumar emphasised that these two factors supplement and complement each other and provide complete solutions to many problems encountered by the knowledge managers. Shri Ajai Shankar, Secretary, Department of Industrial Policy & Promotion and other senior officials from the NPC spoke on the occasion. Speaking on the occasion, Dr. Kumar said: "In the 21st century, the paradigms of the global economies are changing, as increasingly the creation of wealth is dependent on 'knowledge assets' as compared to the 'material assets' of the previous years. India is fortunately blessed with both natural material wealth as well as knowledge assets in its people. In order to face global competition and simultaneously evolve to reach our targets of becoming a developed country by 2020, it would be essential to harness our assets to attain maximum productivity levels". Dr. Kumar commended the initiatives of NPC and Asian Productivity Organisation (APO) in making efforts to bring together various stakeholders of the Asian countries, to discuss the global practices in knowledge management with resource speakers and experts from both the West and East of the World. "In order to make substantial gains out of the intellectual wealth which is natural embodiment of our people, the government is also consciously promoting 'knowledge' based development in all forms of economic activities. The government has constituted the "Knowledge Commission" to identify priority areas of action to promote knowledge based wealth creation and the commission has already provided many action plans for development and implementation. India's economy is now much more integrated with "Knowledge Economy" and has been benefited from this integration in many ways. The outstanding success of IT and IT-enabled services (ITES) has demonstrated what Indian skills and enterprise can do-given the right environment. Similar strength is now evident in sectors such as pharmaceuticals, bio-technology, space research, health services, financial services etc. These gains in competitiveness are now spreading to other sectors also. National Productivity Council, the apex institution spearheading the productivity movement in the country, would be completing 50 years of its existence this month, has been offering consultancy, training, research & awareness creation activities to spread the message of productivity in all sectors of the Indian economy. With the development of services and manufacturing sector as a crucial factor towards gaining leadership in the knowledge economy, NPC has been developing services in the area of knowledge management

5911. (12-2-2008) NEW DELHI : Indian Railways have carried 643.73 million tonnes of revenue earning freight traffic during the first ten months (*i.e.* April 2007-January 2008) of the current financial year 2007-08. The freight carried shows an increase of 50.06 million tonnes over the freight traffic of 593.67 million tonnes actually carried during the corresponding period last year, reflecting an increase of 8.43 per cent. During the month of January 2008, the revenue earning freight traffic carried by Indian Railways was 72.38 million tonnes. There is an increase of 6.64 million tonnes over the freight traffic of 65.74 million tonnes actually carried by the Indian Railways during the same period last year, reflecting an increase of 10.10 per cent.

5912. (12-2-2008) NEW DELHI : There has been exponential growth in the Indian Civil Aviation Sector in the recent past. The domestic passenger traffic grew from 32.67 million in 2006 to 43.29 million in 2007 registering a growth of 32.15%. This is very significant considering. There was a very high growth of 46% last year. There are 13 schedule airlines in operations and about 65 non-schedule operators. The number of aircraft has increased from about 300 in 2003-04 to about 600 now. Additionally helicopter operations have increased in the recent years for election and executing flying. As a result, the air traffic in India has increased many times. With this phenomenal growth, aviation safety has also assumed greater importance and is needed to be addressed with more care to ensure safe journey and secured movement. The operators have to adopt all the prescribed safety norms, even if the cost is high. The safety comes first. It cannot be compromised. Safety should not be evaluated in terms of static or operating cost. The exponential growth of Civil Aviation has created high demand of trained manpower. There is shortage of skilled manpower to operate these aircraft. Many airlines have employed foreign pilots and engineers to meet the shortage. Foreign pilots flying Indian aircraft are issued authorizations subject to English proficiency check and knowledge of Indian Civil Aircrafts Rules and regulations as a safety measure. 1000 foreign pilots have been issued authorization by DGCA. However it has to be ensured that Airlines implement phasing out of foreign pilots as per their programme. There is no doubt that India Pilots who are more familiar with out airports and skies will give passengers more confidence to fly. DGCA had carried out a number of safety audits. It has carried out audits in which the operator adherence to safety standards set up by DGCA in the form of Rules, CAR etc. are checked. A number of measures have been taken to ensure safety of aircraft operations which include implementation of recommendations emanating from Investigation of Aircraft Accidents and Hazardous Incidents, dissemination of Safety Information, safety audit of operator, periodic spot checks, prevention of bird strike incidents etc. Action against defaulters has also been taken wherever necessary. To deal with the menace of bird strikes, various preventive measures like proper disposal of garbage, prevention of water-logging, scaring and shooting of birds, modification of take off and approach procedures etc. have been put in place. Also Aircraft Act has been amended suitably to make disposal of garbage in open within 10 kms. of the airport a cognizable offence. DGCA has issued Civil Aviation Requirements (CAR) for mandatory installation of safety equipment such as Airborne Collision Avoidance System (ACAS) on aircraft, Mode 'S' transponder, Digital Flight Data Recorder (DFDR), Cockpit Voice Recorder (CVR), enhanced

Ground Proximity Warning System (GPWS). The above steps are to enhance safety of aircraft operations in flight by providing means to avoid air miss and ATC related incidents. To cope with the ever-increasing air traffic in the Indian airspace, perspective plans for improved air space management have also been introduced which include introduction of flexi use of airspace. The indigenous development of Space Based Augmentation System (SBAS)-GAGAN, jointly by Indian Space Research Organisation (ISRO) and Airports Authority of India (AAI), is also on traxk for implementation. However, no initiative is fully complete unless results are there to see. And for the Indian skies due to effective measures taken by the Government, the past seven years have been totally accident-free years. No fatal accident has occurred to any of the scheduled airlines. The tremendous growth in a short span of time has put pressure on the available resources and infrastructure of the DGCA. DGCA has to keep pace with the new challenges. There is a need for re-engineering of our Safety Regulator. The government is aware of this and steps are being taken in this direction. Presently DGCA is performing dual role of regulator and investigator. The time has come, when there should be an independent investigative authority. This will definitely make operators and regulator more responsible, and will be in line with the best international practices. The India Skies are safe. But this does not mean that there should be complacency. There are new challenges ahead. Both Operators and Regulator shall endeavour together to make the sky safer. Placing importance on safety in aviation would go a long way in sustaining the growth and development of air transport services.

5913. (13-2-2008) NEW DELHI : In exercise of the powers conferred by clause (1) of article 217 of the Constitution of India, the President is pleased to appoint (i) Shri Justice Shrishen Ratanlal Dongaonkar, and (ii) Shri Justice Vikas Ramchandra Kingaonkar, Additional Judges of the Bombay High Court, to be Judges of the Bombay High Court, in that order of seniority, with effect from the dates they assume charge of their respective offices.

5914. (13-2-2008) NEW DELHI : Eight envoys presented their credentials to the President of India, Smt. Pratibha Devisingh Patil at a ceremony at Rashtrapati Bhavan in New Delhi today. The Envoys who presented their credentials were:- His Excellency Mr. Savenaca Kaunisela, the High Commissioner of Fiji, His Excellency Mr. Rupert Holborow, the High Commissioner of New Zealand, Her Excellency Ms. Nimisha Madhvani, the High Commissioner of Uganda, His Excellency Mr. Oscar Alfonso Silva, the Ambassador of Chile, His Excellency Dato Tan Seng Sung, the High Commissioner of Malaysia, His Excellency, Mr. Brian Bowler, the High Commissioner of Malawi, His Excellency, Mr. Stavros Lykidis, the Ambassador of Greece and His Excellency Mr. Dick Esparon, the High Commissioner of Seychelles. The President during her interaction with the Head of Missions stated that India is committed to promoting peace and prosperity in the world and to have friendly relations with all countries. She wished the

Ambassadors/High Commissioners success during their tenure in India. The credential presentation ceremony was attended by the senior members of the diplomatic missions, senior officials of the Ministry of External Affairs and of the Rashtrapati Bhavan.

5915. (13-2-2008) NEW DELHI : The Annual Plan for Himachal Pradesh for the year 2008-09 was finalized at a meeting, here, today between the Deputy Chairman Planning Commission, Shri Montek Singh Ahluwalia and the Chief Minister of Himachal Pradesh, Shri Prem Kumar. Plan size for the current year was agreed at Rs. 2400 crores. This includes additional Central assistance of Rs.450 crores for projects of importance to the State. Deputy Chairman, Planning Commission, Mr. Montek Singh Ahluwalia complemented the State Government for implementing the development programmes in totality despite a very difficult fiscal situation. He said despite difficult climatic condition, the State has succeeded in maintaining healthy growth performance and good human development index. Performance in social sector specially Sarva Shiksha Abhiyan and Mid-day Meal was appreciated. It was pointed out that State has achieved 100 per cent rural electrification target. The State was advised to modal district planning in a way that optimum benefit can be taken from the Central scheme. In view of vast potential for the growth of horticulture, floriculture and herbs, the State should help in setting up marketing network. Focused attention should also be given to promotion of handicraft. The Chief Minister said that the major objectives of the 11th Plan of Himachal Pradesh would include the provision of essential public services, increasing farm incomes, developing better infrastructure, nurturing human capital, protecting the environment and improving governance. The focus would remain on reduction of poverty, enhancing equity among various sections of the society and a balanced regional development. The Chief Minister suggested that Centre should allow States' to introduce a nominal generation tax on power produced. He also wanted compensation for not exploiting forest wealth in national interest. Setting up of AIIMS level institutions, National Institute of Fashion Technology, IIM and Institute of Information Technology was also demanded.

5916. (13-2-2008) NEW DELHI : Incidents of piracy on the high seas have declined considerably since India ratified a regional agreement one-and-a-half years ago. This was pointed out in talks between Brigadier General (NS) Tay Lim Heng, Chairman of the Regional Cooperation Agreement on Combating Piracy and Armed Robbery against ships in Asia (ReCAAP), and Vice Admiral RF Contractor, Director General, Indian Coast Guard (DGICG) and Vice Chairman of ReCAAP, here yesterday. Brig. General Tay Heng is leading a four member ReCAAP delegation on a visit to India to discuss steps to enhance cooperation and force building. India acceded to the ReCAAP on June 6, 2006. The agreement aims at enhancing cooperation amongst its 16 member countries, including the ASEAN, China, Japan, South Korea, Bangladesh and Sri Lanka. It enables the maritime forces to seize ships or aircraft involved in piracy and armed robbery besides information sharing, capacity building and cooperation for extradition and mutual legal assistance. In the ASEAN only Malaysia and Indonesia have not ratified the treaty. The ReCAAP achieved a distinction when it concluded an agreement with the International Maritime Organisation in December last year. During his stay in New Delhi, Brig. General Tay Heng also held discussions with Shri PK Rastogi, Special Secretary, Ministry of Defence. The four-member ReCAAP delegation will visit the Maritime Rescue Coordination Centre (MRCC), which is also the Piracy Reporting Centre in India, and participate in a table top exercise on piracy control during their visit to Mumbai over the next two days. The Coast Guard is India's nodal agency for the ReCAAP. The role of the Indian Coast Guard shot into fame when it tackled the 1999 piracy incident of MV Alondra Rainbow.

5917. (13-2-2008) NEW DELHI : In a spectacular display of musicianship, the 90 piece Indian Naval Symphonic Orchestra thrilled the audience of Delhi at a scintillating treat of Music at the Siri Fort Auditorium on the 13 Feb 08. Her Excellency Smt Pratibha Devisingh Patil, the Hon President of India graced the musical fare. The history of the Naval Orchestra dates back to 1945 when the orchestra was formed from the naval central band under the aegis of then Lt Cdr S E Hills, MVE, RNVR. From its small beginning, this band has grown into the orchestra which was on stage. The presentation of music commenced with a fanfare which was one of the best ever written by Radley tilted Twentieth Centurey Fox and arranged for Military band by BN Anthony, Leading Musician. The opening piece, a quick march, by Tieke presented to showcase the quality of martial music, was followed by the first movement of Mozart's 40th symphony. The contrast between the items showcased the wide versatility of the naval musicians by shifting from pure marital music to western classical. The bravura and skill of percussionists of the Navy was highlighted in a Xylophone duet titled titbits composed by Captain SA Anchees. This was the debut performance of this piece in Delhi. Cornet solo played by Sivi Thomas, Petty Officer Musician, performing Sir Arthur Sullivan's Lost chord was received with applause. For the very first time the Naval Orchestra attempted the bagpipe played by Somenath Dey Leading Musician, in their presentation of Highland Cathedral composed by Ulrich and Michael and arranged for the orchestra by Captain SA Anchees. That the naval musicians are extremely versatile came to the fore in their presentation of fusion music based on raga Humsadhwani. The theme, Vatapi Ganapathi was arranged by Manoj Sebastian, Petty Officer Musician for bamboo flute played by Pratapan Leading Musician. On the saxophone played in Jazz style I D Rao, Leading Musician. The percussion in this piece included the jazz set, timpany, tabla, mrudangam and for the first time idikkya. This arrangement by Manoj Sebastian, who is also training to become a musician officer, was conducted by him. The orchestra then took us to Western India, covering the folk lure of Gujarat with Pankhida, Maharastra with Nagoba dolaila Laagla and Dagaila Laagli Kada, and finally brought us to Goa with some famous rythemic Mandos. This selection, which was making its debut was conducted by Lt Cdr Vijay D Cruz. A song originally vocalised by Martin McBride title With a Broken Wing written by James, Sam and Phil was presented by a young and talented singer Natasha Anchees. Silver threads among the Gold, Somewhere over the Rainbow and Feelings arranged by Lt Cdr Sateesh Champion, another debut performance took us through memory lane. This selection was conducted by the arranger himself. This selection was followed by another set of evergreen melodies in Hindi with titles such as Aayega, Ajeeb daastan, and Hawa mein Udta Jaaye arranged as a selection by Lt Cdr D Cruz made the audiences reminiscent of the days gone by. A surprise item to welcome our guests from foreign land, Naval Chiefs visiting our country for the IONS-2008 titled It's a small world, after all... brought out the message of peace, love and harmony and delineation of borders. This song brought out the true meaning of the presentation by the Indian Naval Symphonic Orchestra. It was arranged and conducted by Lt Cdr Champion. The finale, an integration of the three services titled Desh Rakhsak compiled by the Central Naval Band and arranged by KPN Nath Master Chief Petty Officer Musician covering the song Jai Bharti, composed by M Dias, the Air Force song composed by Mrs. Zora Shaw and Kadam Kadam Badhaye Jaa the Army song composed by Captain Ram Singh INA with visuals from the three services in action ended with ever arousing and soul inspiring patriotic song Saare Jahaan Se Achha by Iqbal brought down the curtains to the annual concert by the Indian Naval Symphonic Orchestra at Delhi.

5918. (13-2-2008) NEW DELHI : The President of India, Smt. Pratibha Devisingh Patil will undertake her first visit to Bihar since she assumed office. The President shall be in the state from February 15th to 16th. During her two-day visit, Smt. Patil will address and attend the 1st Inter University Cultural Festival hosted by Magadh University at Bodh Gaya on February 15th. The President will also launch the, "Mukhyamantri Kanya Vivah Yojna" and inaugurate and address the International Conference on Hyperthermia. Both events will be in Patna. During the tour, the President shall also visit places of historical importance at Nalanda, Bodh Gaya and Vaishali, as well as Gurudwara Patna Sahib in Patna.

5919. (13-2-2008) NEW DELHI : The Mughal Gardens and other Rashtrapati Bhavan Gardens will be opened for public viewing this year for the general public from February 16th to March 28th. The Gardens will be open from 10 AM to 5 PM on all days except on Mondays on account of maintenance. Further the Gardens shall also remain closed on March 21st and 22nd. Entry into the Gardens will be only upto 4 PM. Entry and exit to the Gardens shall be from Gate No. 35 of President's Estate, which is located near North Avenue at the extreme end of Church Road about 300 meters West of Cathedral Church. Entry for physically challenged persons using Wheelchairs will be through the Rashtrapati Bhavan Reception. Such persons can arrive at Rashtrapati Bhavan through Hukmi Mai Marg or Rajpath along with their escorts. Visitors are requested not to bring any water bottles, briefcases, handbags/ladies purses, cameras, radios/transistors, cell phones, umbrellas, arms/ammunitions and eatables. Such articles, if any, will not be allowed to be carried into the Mughal Gardens and other Gardens and will have to be deposited at the entry point at the owner's risk.

5920. (13-2-2008) NEW DELHI : Consultancy Development Centre (CDC), an autonomous institution of Department of Scientific and Industrial Research, Ministry of Science and Technology has carried out a study for export potential of Engineering and Management Consultancy Services for Ministry of Commerce and Industry. The basic objectives of the study were to explore the potential of export of Engineering and Management Consultancy services from India as well as to build database of Consultants, Consultancy organizations and Associations to strengthen the strategic alliances with local consulting partners. The report has discussed at length a whole spectrum of issues ranging from priority sector, consulting market size, perception about Indian consultants, competitiveness of Indian consultants viz-a-viz international consulting firms, gaps. An action plan has also been given for action by various stakeholders *viz.* consultants, industry associations, consulting nodal organization, government etc. The findings have revealed that Vietnam is a booming economy growing at rate of about 8% GDP and offers a lot of consulting opportunities in infrastructure sector *viz.* construction, urban development, water management, energy, telecommunication besides offering short to long term consulting opportunities in sectors such as education, IT and IT enabled services, environment, transport, manufacturing etc. The study also reveals that there is an immediate match between the consulting skill sets available with Indian consultants and opportunities available in the Vietnam in these sectors. Moreover the consulting industry in Vietnam is not very well developed, thereby a large gap exists between local consulting capabilities and demand which can be leveraged by Indian Consultants by virtue of their strong consulting capabilities and cost competitiveness. The study is expected to benefit various stakeholders, consulting firms, individual consultants, experts, government and academia through collaboration with local consultants and opportunities for competing for assignments in Vietnam. This would enhance India's knowledge presence in Vietnam besides enhancing business opportunities to all the stakeholders.

5921. (13-2-2008) NEW DELHI : The Government is taking urgent steps to hold elections very soon in cantonments across the country. Announcing this at the meeting of the Parliamentary Consultative Committee attached to his ministry, here today, the Defence Minister Shri A K Antony said the democratisation process of the cantonments have been finally achieved with the Cantonments Act, 2006 which came into force on December 18, 2006. The Act was amended after a gap of 82 years. There are 62 cantonments all over the country spanning over 1.9 lakh acres including civil area of nearly 30,000 acres. Civil area is an area within the cantonment specifically notified as a measure of democratisation under Section 46 of the Cantonments Act, 2006. The new Act establishes parity between the elected and non-elected members. The non-elected members were more than the elected members as per the Cantonments Act of 1924. Shri Antony said the

Cantonment Electoral Rules, 2007 have already been notified under which the division of cantonments into wards and reservation of seats for SCs and STs have been notified in all the cantonments. The reservation of wards for women has been notified in respect of 61 cantonment boards. Historically, the first cantonment was established in Barrackpore in 1765 and the second at Danapore in the same year. Taking part in the discussion, the Minister of State for Defence Shri M M Pallam Raju said, over the years due to better land management, cantonments have become good real estate. He said the efforts of the government are not only directed to fully safeguard this valuable asset of the nation, but also to make optimal use of land. 'We have initiated computerisation of land records of cantonments to achieve this purpose', he said. Members of Parliament who took part in the discussion called for effective measures to prevent encroachment on defence land. However, many of them were of the view that civic amenities and other welfare measures taken by the State Governments should also be implemented for the civilian population living in the cantonment areas. Some members brought to the notice of the Defence Minister that the provision of octroi still continues in 7 cantonments which is causing hardship to the civilian population. Shri Antony assured the members that the issue will be taken up after the elections by which time alternative source of income for these cantonments may be worked out. The Members of Parliament, who attended today's meeting included Shri Naveen Jindal, Shri MA Kharabela Swain, Smt Jayaben B Thakkar, Shri Samik Lahiri,, Shri Sanjay Dhotre, Shri Shankhlal Majhi, Shri Braja Kishore Tripathy, Shri Madhu Goud Yaskhi from Lok Sabha and Shri Syed Azees Pasha, Shri Dharam Pal Sabharwal from Rajya Sabha.

5922. (13-2-2008) NEW DELHI : The Secretary, Ministry of Civil Aviation, Shri Ashok Chawla today inaugurated the public interface facility in the office of Directorate General of Civil Aviation (DGCA) today. This facility is expected to address the problems of public on various queries relating to DGCA regarding aviation matters ranging from status of application by airlines to queries from trainee pilots. The facility has been totally computerized to help in tracking of files, receiving application and fees for RTI and addressing queries/clarifications from the different departments of DGCA. The Facility Centre will be attended by officials from the different units of the DGCA which have interactive business relating to different aviation related matters with the public.

5923. (13-2-2008) NEW DELHI : The Union Home Minister, Shri Shivraj Patil will be on a day-long visit of Chhattisgarh tomorrow. He will discuss the Naxal situation in the State with the Chief Minister, Dr. Raman Singh and senior officers of the State Government. He will also hold a meeting with the Governor of Chhattisgarh, Shri E.S.L. Narsimhan. The Union Home Minister will be accompanied by the DG, CRPF, Shri S.I.S. Ahmed, Special Secretary (Internal Security) in the Ministry of Home Affairs, Shri M.L. Kumawat and other senior officers of the Ministry.

5924. (13-2-2008) BHUBANESHWAR: The Nationalist Congress Party (NCP) will organise a Paribartan Samabesh in BHUBANESHWAR on February 19. National president of the party Sharad Pawar will address the rally that was likely to be attended by a large number of people coming from all the 30 districts in the State. At a press conference here, senior NCP leader Bijoy Mohapatra said that the rally would highlight the need for unseating the Naveen Patnaik Government as it had 'failed' in almost every field. Mr. Mohapatra informed that the party had already held meeting all the districts to prepare people for attending the rally. "The response has been very positive as people in every part of the State had realised that the present government had failed to deliver the goods," Mr. Mohapatra said. The rally was not being organised to show the party's strength but to spread the message about the need for a change in the government, he said.

5925. (13-2-2008) NEW DELHI : Shri Siddharth Sinha of the Film and Television Institute of India (FTII) has won the Silver Bear in the Brelinale Shorts Section of the Berlin Film Festival. Shri Sinha won the Award for his film 'Udedh Bun', a story of Ashu who is leaving his boyhood behind and growing up to be a man. He needs to reinvent himself. The Silver Award has been given for the film's modern narration and a sharp focus that relies on a harmony between images and sound rather than words.

5926. (13-2-2008) BANGLORE : Shri L.K. Advani said here at a function that Shri B.S. Yediyurappa, former chief minister of Karnataka, Shri Ananth Kumar, MP and general secretary of the BJP, Shri G.M. Siddeshwara, MP and chairman of Srishyla Education Trust, teachers and students of GM Institute of Technology, ladies and gentlemen, It gives me great pleasure to be with all of you at this wonderful educational institution. The college building that I have been asked to inaugurate is truly a great work of aesthetics. An elegant building and a beautiful campus are as essential for good education as well-qualified teachers. It is, therefore, rightly said that we shape our buildings, and thereafter they shape us. Nowhere is it as true as it is in the case of buildings of educational institutions. But I would hasten to add that we need better architectural and aesthetic sensitivity in everything we build-indeed, in nation-building as a whole. We should build better and more beautiful cities and towns for today's young Indians and for the future generations to live in. We are not paying enough attention to this aspect. As in the case of so many other aspects of nation-building, this also is linked to the theme of good governance. At the outset, I would like to pay homage to the late G. Mallikarjunappa, the founder of this institution and a widely respected political leader from Davanagere. He was my party's valued colleague in Parliament. I would also like to express my deep appreciation of all those institution-builders in the field of education in Karnataka. Your state has truly made tremendous strides in professional education, most of this progress being due to non-governmental initiatives. I must especially pay tribute to all those religious establishments in Karnataka that have established a large network of educational institutions of high standards-medical and engineering colleges, management institutes, vocational training centres, colleges in traditional streams and, of course, primary and secondary schools. Other states should emulate Karnataka in this regard.

5927. (13-2-2008) NEW DELHI : As per the provision of DPCO, 1995 National Pharmaceutical Pricing Authority (NPPA) has to revise and fix the norms for Conversion Cost (CC), Packing Charges (PC), Process Loss (PL) and Packing Material (PM) for the year' 2008. These norms for CC, PC, PL & PM are to be worked out based on actual cost data/information received from various manufacturers & formulators. Two detailed questionnaire in printed form have already been sent to pharma units and Industry Associations. Soft copies of both the questionnaire are available on the official website of NPPA *i.e.* www.nppaindia.nic.in. The Pharma manufacturing units & companies have been requested to furnish the information/data to NPPA in a soft copy on Compact Diskette (CD) along with duly signed hard copy as also the copy of the Annual Report of the company for the last two years *i.e.* 2005-06 & 2006-07. The last date of submission of the aforesaid data and information was 31st January, 2008. However, NPPA has received representations from some Pharma companies to extend the deadline for submission of data. In view of request of the Pharma companies, it has been decided to extend the deadline for submission of data till 28.02.2008. Pharma manufacturing units and companies are requested to please furnish the required information and data by that date, *i.e.* before the 28th February 2008 to enable NPPA to complete the exercise and revise and fix the norms at the earliest.

5928. (13-2-2008) NEW DELHI : There are no further reports from the HSADL, Bhopal of any sample testing positive from any part of the country, including West Bengal. No unusual mortality was reported in West Bengal on 12th February, 2008. The culling operations have been completed in the state of West Bengal. A total of 196 Rapid Response Teams (RRTs) were engaged (78 for surveillance / mopping and 118 for disinfection and sanitization), which completed culling of 19,014 birds in the mopping exercise, taking the figure of cumulative culling to 38.15 lakh. The latest figures of eggs and feed destroyed till 12.02.2008 are 14,89,978 and 80,033 kg respectively. As reported earlier also, the first round mopping operation has already been completed in both the districts of Assam *i.e.* Dhubri and Kokrajhar. The second round of mopping up operation is continuing. In Bihar, 28% of the culling task has been completed with 1,32,314 birds already culled. The culling has been completed in the notified areas of the Purnia district.

5929. (13-2-2008) NEW DELHI : The meeting of the Consultative Committee of the Members of Parliament attached to the Ministry of Civil Aviation was held here today. All Members applauded the growth in the sector and congratulated the Minister and the Ministry officials for facilitating this growth. Welcoming the Members of the Committee to the first meeting this year, the Chairman and the Minister for Civil Aviation Shri Praful Patel, briefly summed up the major activities that had taken place in 2007. He informed the Committee that during the year 2007, domestic airline passenger traffic had grown from 326.28 lakhs to 432.89 lakh-a growth of 32.51% vis-a-vis 2006. And considering the fact that the base is also growing, the Minister said that on a higher base the sector is registering a considerable growth. He also informed the Members about the new category of airline services, the Scheduled Air Transport(Regional) Services-which has been introduced to promote regional connectivity especially to the Tier-II and Tier-III cities. Four airlines have been given NOC in this category-M/s. Star Aviation for Southern Region, Jagson Airlines for Northern Region, M/s. MDLR Airlines Pvt. Ltd., for Northern Region and M/s. Zav Airways for North-East/Eastern Region. The Minister also informed that the merger process of Air India and Indian Airlines is underway and several working groups and an Integration Team have been formulated to move the merger process forward. A III-Tier Grievance Redressal Machinery and an Inter-Ministerial Grievance Redressal Committee have been put into place to address employee grievances. The fleet augmentation by NACIL was also underway. Of the 111 state-of-the-art aircraft that is to be added to its fleet, three Boeing 777-200LR, three Boeing 777-300ER, ten Boeing 737-800, six A319 and five A321 aircraft have already been received. The remaining will be received by 2011. He also informed that Air India has been invited to become the Member of Star Alliance-one of the biggest alliance of airlines in the world. Air India will become the full-fledged member of the Alliance formally by 2009, by when the IT Integration and other issues will be completed. Specialized teams at Air India, Star Alliance and its member carriers are now working on the integration process. Shri Patel spoke about the in-principle approval given by the Government to the setting up of Greenfield airports in Kannur (Kerala), Navi Mumbai and about the international airport at Jewar, Greater Noida that was under the consideration of a Group of Ministers as per the direction of the Union Cabinet. The Minister also spoke about the change in FDI caps in a number of sectors in civil aviation. He said that this change would boost civil aviation in the country. The Minister informed about the Ministry of Civil Aviation consistent efforts to talk to the State Governments on various issues of civil aviation. These talks have started yielding results-yesterday the Andhra Pradesh State Government announced the reduction in the sales tax on ATF from 33% to 4%. The Members raised a number of issues-issues of safety and security, pilot training, on-time performances and losses of Air India, status of merger of Air India and Indian Airlines, the new airports, connectivity across the country, rules for permitting airline to fly abroad etc. Members of Parliament who were present at the meeting were: S/Shri Madhu Goud Yashki, Sachin Pilot, Ratilal K. Verma, Ashok Argal, Ramswaroop Koli, Tarit Baran Topdar, A. Krishnaswamy, Anandrao Adsul, Santosh Bagrodia, Dr. M.S. Gill, Tarlochan Singh, Dinesh Trivedi, Dr. Farooq Abdullah and Vijay Darda.

5930. (13-2-2008) NEW DELHI : Teheran has shown keenness to have presence of Indian media persons in Iran. This was conveyed by the Iranian Vice Minister and Foreign Ministry Spokesperson, Mr. Seyed Mohammad Ali Hosseini when he called on the Minister of Information & Broadcasting and Parliamentary Affairs, Shri P. R. Dasmunsi today. In his response Shri Dasmunsi said that the Ministry will discuss the issue and would make speedy effort to fill this gap. Giving a broad view of the media scene in India, Shri Dasmunsi said that freedom of the media is guaranteed by our Constitution and is one of the pillars of our democracy. For print media, an autonomous body Press Council of India is the authority to address any complaints whereas Cable and Television Network Act is in place to address issues related to the electronic media. The Government never gives any dictation or direction to the media. The Minister said that India being a free press country, media reports generating from India may not necessarily be taken as Government's viewpoint. The visiting dignitary said that the mutual deliberations between the two countries will further strengthen our relationship of traditional friendship. He said, Iran has five news agencies, which are ready to have extended cooperation with India. Our proposal is to establish friendship society between India and Iran and arranging interaction between the media from the two sides, he said. He appreciated the views expressed by the Minister which he felt can pave the way for a broad cooperation in the media sector. He informed that an arrangement is in place with PTI in this regard and can be further extended. Mr. Abdul Reza Bondi, Iranian News Agency (IRNA), Chief of Bureau, in his remarks said that they didn't have a single difficulty throughout IRNA's 30 year long presence in India. He, however, felt that more interaction with Iranian media could project the Indian viewpoint up to the Iranian public in a better way. Pr. Director General (M&C), Smt. Deepak Sandhu in her remarks referred to the excellent participation of the Iranian films and film makers at International Film Festival of India every year. She said that further efforts would be made to facilitate Iranian media interaction at the Government level.

5931. (13-2-2008) NEW DELHI : Deputy Prime Minister & Minister of Culture, Republic of Tatarstan (a region in Russia), Ms. Zilya Valeeva today called on Minister of Tourism and Culture Smt. Ambika Soni. During their 45 minutes meeting here, both the leaders discussed the matters related to Culture and tourism sectors. Welcoming the guest, Smt. Ambika Soni recalled the traditionally warm relations with the people of all the regions of Russia and stressed the need for increased cultural exchanges between India and Russian regions. She said like Tatarstan India is also a multi-cultural country with Constitution of India allowing freedom to all religions. She said India has signed a Cultural Exchange Programme (CEP) with Russia in 2007 and exchange of cultural delegations with Tatarstan would be taken up within the scope of the CEP. Smt. Soni exchanged views about the status of women, libraries and museums and cinema in India with the visiting dignitary. She also stressed the need to increase people to people contact between India and Russia through promotion of tourism. Ms. Zilya Valeeva describing India as a unique country with a rich heritage said her region is interested in exchange of cultural delegations, information on museums and libraries with India. She also said that every year, a week of Indian films is being organized in

Tatarstan. She said she is looking forward to have Indian film artists in Tatarstan to promote further understanding about Hindi cinema. She said places such as Qutab Minar can attract lot of tourists from her region. The visiting dignitary showed keen interest in Ajanta and Ellora cave paintings and enquired if exhibition of these paintings can travel to Tatarstan.

5932. (13-2-2008) NEW DELHI : Shri Kamal Nath, Union Minister of Commerce and Industry, co-chaired the Second Session of the India-Russia Forum on Trade and Investment in New Delhi (February 12-13, 2008) along with Mrs. Elvira. S. Nabiullina, Minister of Economic Development & Trade of the Russian Federation. Mrs. Nabiullina participated along with a high profile Russian delegation, including government officials and businessmen. The Indian delegation included representatives from the Ministry of Commerce & Industry and Ministry of External Affairs and businessmen and representatives from the Confederation of Indian Industry (CII), Federation of Indian Chambers of Commerce & Industry (FICCI) and Associated Chambers of Commerce & Industry (ASSOCHAM). Speaking on the occasion, Shri Kamal Nath mentioned about the positive investment climate in India as also the huge investment opportunities in infrastructure, metallurgy, real estate, pharmaceuticals and other sectors. He emphasized that the level of economic engagement between the two countries, in terms of trade and investment relations, should increase. A Protocol was signed by Shri Kamal Nath and Mrs. Nabiullina, underlying to resolve to cooperate in several spheres of mutual interest as mentioned above. It was decided by both the sides that enhancement of the bilateral investment and trade cooperation is one of the important steps to advance qualitatively trade and economic relations and to widen strategic partnership and cooperation between India and Russia. Both sides also agreed on early commercialisation of new and innovative technologies as one of the prospective spheres of cooperation. The next meeting of the Forum would be held in 2009 or earlier in Russia on a mutually agreed date India's export to Russia was US $ 1.10 billion in 2006-07 while its import was US$ 2.99 billion. India has received FDI of US$ 94.0 million from Russia so far. Some of the sectors attracting FDI from Russia are chemicals, telecommunications, trading and consultancy services. Indian approved investment in Russia, on the other hand, amounts to US $ 2839.6 million up to March, 2007. The opening session of the Forum was convened on 12th February 2008 wherein, besides the two Ministers co-chairing the event, Russian Prime Minister Mr. Victor A. Zubkov also attended the session. Shri Ajay Shankar, Secretary, Department of Industrial Policy & Promotion, Shri G.K. Pillai, Secretary, Department of Commerce, along with representatives of CII and FICCI also addressed the delegates. The presentations and speakers of the Russian side included among others Mr. V. Fadeyev, Chairman of the Board of Directors of Business Council of Cooperation with India, Mr. German Gref, President, Chairman of the Board of Directors, JSC Sberbank of Russia and Mr. Aleksand Kogoin, Minister for Industry and Trade of the Tatarstan Republic. Shri Nath and Mrs. Nabiullina discussed the steps required for realizing the outcome of the meet. On the second day of the Forum held on 13th February 2008, four parallel sessions were held on sectors of mutual interest such as mines and minerals, energy & power, transport & infrastructure including inland waterways, ports, railways construction, civil aviation & automobiles, pharmaceuticals, biotechnology, IT, chemicals, Telecom and High Technology. A session on business environment, financial services and commodities, co-chaired by Shri G.K. Pillai from the Indian side, also took place on 12th February 2008. The India-Russia Forum on Trade & Investment was set up on 16th March 2006 through the signing of a Joint Communique between the Ministry of Commerce & Industry of India and the Ministry of Economic Development & Trade of the Russian Federation. It was felt that there is a need to strive for stable development of Indo-Russian trade, economic and investment cooperation.

5933. (13-2-2008) NEW DELHI : 4.45 million dug wells of beneficiary farmers are to be taken up for recharging Ground Water. The concerned State Governments are being asked to take all necessary steps for implementation before the monsoon of 2008. The Government approved the scheme of "Artificial Recharge of Ground Water through Dugwells in Hard Rock Areas" in seven States namely Andhra Pradesh, Maharashtra, Gujarat, Karnataka, Rajasthan, Tamil Nadu and Madhya Pradesh in November 2007. The scheme has been approved for a total cost of Rs. 1798.71 crore with net cost of subsidy to Government in terms of civil works being Rs. 1499.27 crore. The scheme provides 100 per cent subsidy to marginal and small farmers and 50 per cent subsidy to other farmers.

5934. (13-2-2008) NEW DELHI : Number of affected districts (14 districts) remains the same. In these districts, 48 blocks and five municipalities are involved. A total population of 10.82 lakhs is under surveillance [5.47 lakhs in 0-3 Km area and 5.34 lakhs in 3-10 Km area]. In 0-3 Km area 337 persons with fever and URI have been detected. No one had exposure to sick/infected birds. In the 3-10 Kms area a total of 297 persons have been detected with fever & URI. No one had exposure history. In the hospitals, 413 patients with Fever and URI have reported and two of them are admitted.

5935. (13-2-2008) NEW DELHI : A cheque of Rs. 1992.50 crore was presented by Shri T. Sankaralingam, CMD, NTPC to the Union Minister of Power, Shri Sushilkumar Shinde, as the share of Government of India towards interim dividend for the FY 2007-08. The total interim dividend works out to Rs. 2226.28 crores, @ 27% on the paid-up capital of the company. This is the highest ever interim dividend declared by the Company. Shri Anil Razdan, Secretary (Power) and other senior officials from Ministry of Power and NTPC were present on the occasion. This is the 15th consecutive year that NTPC has paid dividend. NTPC, which is globally comparable thermal generation company in terms of size and performance, has the vision to be a world class integrated power major, with increasing global presence. NTPC presently has an installed capacity of 28644 MW (including 1794

MW JVs). It is diversifying into Hydro power, coal mining, power distribution, power trading, power equipment manufacturing, EPC etc.

5936. (14-2-2008) NEW DELHI : Major steel producers agreed for a partial roll back on the price rise carried out by them in February 2008, by Rs.1000/- per tonne for TMT and rounds and Rs.500/- per tonne for other steel products, to be effective immediately. This was done in response to appeal made by the Union Minister of Steel, Shri Ram Vilas Paswan. The steel producers also agreed to the appeal of Shri Paswan to maintain their price line. The Minister conveyed the concern of his Government regarding the impact of sudden price hike in steel commodities carried out by the steel producers in the last two months period. He stated that the price hike, apart from hitting the common man due to its cascading effect on inflation, would also affect many of the downstream consumer industries such as small and medium manufacturers and construction sectors. The steel industry also expressed its concern over the rising input costs due to steep hike in the prices of iron ore, coking coal, metcoke, ferro alloys and cost of transportation. Concerned with the recent price hike in steel commodities, Shri Paswan, convened a meeting with the CEO's of major steel producers here today. The meeting was attended by SAIL, RINL, Tata Steel, Essar Steel, JSW Steel, Jindal Steel & Power and Ispat Industries Limited. A preliminary discussion with these major steel producers had already taken place in a meeting under the Chairmanship of Steel Secretary, to discuss the issues concerning steel price. Shri Paswan thanked the Indian steel industry for responding to the request of the Government in the interest of the nation. He also assured the Indian steel industry regarding the commitment of the Government in initiating suitable policy directives as well as facilitating the growth of the steel sector as a whole so as to augment the supply side in order to bridge the demand-supply gap and maintain a stable price line.

5937. (14-2-2008) NEW DELHI : The PSU Oil Marketing Companies (IOCL, HPCL and BPCL) have been moderating the impact of high oil prices, which have touched record highs and are currently at approximately $90 per barrel. This has resulted in OMCs incurring under-recoveries amounting to more than Rs. 71,000 crores. To protect the common man from the inflationary impact of high international oil prices, Government has been following the principle of 'equitable burden sharing' wherein the burden of high oil prices is equitably shared amongst the three stake holders namely the Government, PSU oil companies and consumers, with the Government and the PSU oil companies taking the major portion of the burden. Previously, Government had reduced the retail prices of petrol and diesel by Rs. 4/litre and Rs.2/litre in two consecutive reductions of Rs. 2/litre and Re 1/litre respectively in November 2006 and February 2007. In line with the principle of equitable burden sharing, Government has decided a partial restoration in retail prices where in an increase of Rs.2/litre for petrol and Re.1/litre for diesel may be made in the retail selling prices (at Delhi) with effect from 15.2.2008. Increases in other locations will be made in line with net increase at Delhi and applicable taxes and duties. Keeping its commitment to the common man, no increase has been made in the prices of PDS kerosene and domestic LPG. In addition, Government will issue the required quantum of oil bonds to ensure good financial health of PSU oil marketing companies. Government is committed to protecting the interests of the common man as well as the ensuring financial health of the PSU oil marketing companies which is essential for energy security of the country.

5938. (14-2-2008) NEW DELHI : Head of the Federal Agency for Tourism of the Russian Federation Mr. V. Strzhalkovskiy today called on Minister of Tourism and Culture, Smt. Ambika Soni. During their 40 minutes meeting here, both the leaders agreed that India and Russia have unlimited potential in tourism sector and there is a need to increase tourist traffic from India to Russia and vice versa. The Tourism and Culture Minister, Smt. Ambika Soni said that her Ministry has chalked out a plan to have Road Shows in Russia and other countries in the adjoining area by August-September 2008 to promote India as a tourist destination. She said her Ministry will also make tourism related films with specific target area of Russia and translate brochures, tourism related literature and CDs etc. in Russian language to attract tourists from Russia. She said for better understanding of India, her Ministry will invite travel writers, media persons and tour operators from Russia to India for short duration stay so that once they go back to Russia, they should write about India, its rich heritage and places of tourist interest. She also exchanged views on visa procedures, hotel accommodation and Budget hotels. She said her Ministry is expecting some concessions in the forthcoming Union Budget of India to give a boost to Budget hotels in the country. Smt. Soni elaborated to the visiting dignitary about the long-term visa of 5 years with multiple entries and the visa on arrival scheme which is being worked out. She thanked the Russian leader for his country's support to India during the election of UNWTO Executive Council where India was elected as Chairman. The Russian leader recalling the traditional friendship between the two countries said India and Russia have huge tourist potential and exchange of travel writers and tour operators will increase the tourist traffic between the two countries. Exchanging views on visa procedure for tourists, he said Russia is making all efforts to make it tourist friendly. He said India has great potential in tourism sector as it has many interesting places such as Goa, Agra, Rajasthan, Backwaters of Kerala and Jammu & Kashmir. He wanted better air connectivity for the Russian tourists in India particularly in Mumbai-Goa sector. He invited India to take part in Tourism Exhibitions in Russia as such participation will contribute significantly in promotion of tourism between the two countries.

5939. (14-2-2008) NEW DELHI : The Union Minister for Rural Development, Dr. Raghuvansh Prasad Singh has called for the need to establish Self-employment Training institutes in each district for training the poor in income generating activities. The emergent need was for skill development of the uneducated members of the BPL families, he said. He gave an example of rural development and self-training institutes in Karnataka, which could be replicated by other States and banks. Dr. Singh reiterated the need for adequate marketing support for rural products. He urged the Banks to initiate steps to open bank branches in blocks where there are no banks and also urged them for a uniform rate of interest to be charged under the Swarnjayanti Gram Swarozgar Yojana (SGSY). He expressed concern about the large number of loan applications pending, the low percentage of the credit mobilized and large number of banks that have achieved less than 25% credit target. He added that Banks have a very important role in the SGSY Scheme as they are responsible for sanction of loan applications under SGSY, credit mobilization and disbursal. The Minister was addressing the 11th Meeting of the Central Level Coordination Committee (CLCC) under SGSY, which was held in New Delhi recently. The Minister presided over the meeting, which was attended by the senior officers of the Ministry of Rural Development, State Rural Development Secretaries, representatives of various Ministries, RBI, NABARD, Commercial Banks and NGOs. CLCC is an apex level institution that act as an interface between those involved in administration of rural development programmes, especially, SGSY, which is a credit based programme and the credit is routed through the banks. In her opening remarks, Dr. Rita Sharma, Secretary, Ministry of Rural Development emphasized on the need for holding regular meetings of SGSY Committees at block, district and State level for better performance and monitoring of the programme. The CLCC is a forum to discuss the ways and means to make a frontal attack on rural poverty, she said. SGSY is flagship programme of the Ministry of Rural Development that helps BPL families to generate income and develop skills for self employment. The total number of SHGs (Self Help Groups) formed under the scheme is 27.32 lakh. The financially assisted SHGs are 5.57 lakh.

5940. (14-2-2008) NEW DELHI : There are no further reports from the HSADL, Bhopal of any sample testing positive from any part of the country, including West Bengal. Certain press reports appearing on 13th February, 2008 mentioned unusual mortality of birds in a farm in Jalpalguri district of West Bengal. Enquiries made with the State Government of West Bengal revealed that 800 poultry birds in a broiler farm died during the period 9th to 12th February 2008, which was found to be on account of starvation, suffocation, unhygienic conditions and improper temperature management. On 13th February, only 31 birds died at the said farm. No mortality has been noticed at the neighbouring farms. The State has been asked to immediately forward sample to the HSADL, Bhopal. No further mortality in any other district of West Bengal was reported on 13th February, 2008. A total of 285 Rapid Response Teams (RRTs) were engaged (147 for surveillance / mopping and 138 for disinfection and sanitization), which completed culling of 33,114 birds with cumulative culling to 38.48 lakh. The culling being done now is part of the mopping up exercise. The latest figures of eggs and feed destroyed till 13.02.2008 are 14,89,486 and 80,033 kg respectively. As part of the preventive culling in Assam two rounds of mopping up operation have been completed in both the districts. Cleaning and disinfection of poultry premises have also been completed simultaneously. Thus the poultry depopulation operation in the identified zone in Assam has practically been completed. In Bihar, 34% of the culling has been completed.

5941. (14-2-2008) NEW DELHI : Television can play an important role in socio-economic development of the people. Doordarshan being the sole public service television broadcaster has been playing a leading role in the socio-economic development of the country since its beginning in 1959. At present when over 300 TV channels are beaming programmes from within and outside the country and are competing for attracting more and viewers, the responsibility of Doordarshan in providing healthy media support to socio-economic development of the country has gained more importance. Presently Doordarshan has 30 channels and a DTH service. These channels include: Five national channels (DD1 National, DD News, DD Sports, DD Bharati, DD Urdu), 11 regional language satellite channels (DD Bangla, DD Oriya, DD Saptagiri, DD Podhigai, DD Chandana, DD Malayalam, DD Sahyadri, DD Gujarati, DD Punjabi, DD Kashir, DD North-East), 1111 regional service state network (Rajasthan, Uttar Pradesh, Madhya Pradesh, Bihar, Jharkhand, Chhattisgarh, Haryana, Himachal Pradesh, Uttrakhand, Mizoram, Tripura), one international channel (DD India), DD Rajya Sabha, DD Gyandarshan and a DTH service (DD Direct Plus). Two of these channels *viz.* DD1 National and DD News are in both terrestrial and satellite modes. Besides this, there are regional networks and regional language satellite channels which have terrestrial support. The rest three channels namely DD Sports, DD Bharati and DD India are satellite channels telecasting in satellite mode only. Present terrestrial coverage of Doordarshan is 79.1 per cent area and 91.4 per cent population of the country. In the bouquet of Doordarshan DTH service (DD Direct Plus) there are 36 TV channels and 20 Radio channels and it is a free to air service. From the very beginning Doordarshan has earmarked a sizable chunk of its time for telecasting various programmes to provide media support to socio-economic development activities of the country. Agriculture programme, programmes for rural development, women, children, family welfare, adult education, youth, civic sense and public awareness, science & technology, special programmes during natural calamities like flood, earth quake, epidemics etc. are some of important programmes for socio-economic development of the country. DD News channel provides news and current affairs programmes on the development taking place in different parts of the country and in various fields. In order to manage these development programmes more efficiently Doordarshan has created two separate wings namely Development Communication Division, and Narrowcasting. Development Communication Division concentrates on health and sanitation and other development issues; while Narrowcasting deals with agriculture and allied subjects.

5942. (14-2-2008) NEW DELHI : At its 31st Public meeting currently underway in New Delhi, the Internet Corporation for Assigned Names and Numbers (ICANN) is exploring the possibility of introducing top level domain names in the local language and local scripts. At present while India has introduced domain names at the secondary level in the local language, the top-level domain names are still in the American ASCII code. In a special session on Internationalized Domain names (IDNs), the ICANN experts currently meeting in New Delhi held detailed discussions on the possibility. The Indian experts in charge of language development in the Ministry of IT as well as Programme Head of CDAC, Mr. Mahesh Kulkarni shared India's experience in developing a primer on how the 22 Indian languages can be categorized and what scripts and script families are. Development of language tables, policy issues for Indic scripts also figured in the discussions. Senior experts from ICANN debated on the complexities involved in non-English languages. Alternate spellings pose a problem. In conclusion, Indian experts explained that only homographs are being considered and CDAC has achieved Unicode character set finalization for inclusion in IDN. The public meeting on ICANN, which began on 11th February, draws to a close on 15th February. Speaking on the meeting, ICANN's Board Chairman, Mr. Peter Dengate Thrush said "India and Asia are at the heart of the Internet's future-a future that ICANN is working on. Internet penetration in India is at just over five percent and growing fast-considering that one per cent is 11 million people coming online. ICANN's work on Internationalized Domain Names and new top-level domains has the potential to reach out to rest of India and begin remaking the Internet as people connect in their own languages and scripts." ICANN's IDN programme is making about close to 100,000 characters from the languages of the world available at the top level-the part after the dot—so users can benefit from a domain name in fully localized language or script," said Tina Dam, ICANN's IDN Program Director. "India has 22 official languages and has done a great deal of foundation work on how languages and scripts-or the collection of characters used in a language-can be categorized and used. There are a lot of lessons for the world coming out of the work being done in India." "As ICANN moves forward to making the scripts and languages of the world available in all levels of domain names, the work being done in India, and the lessons learnt, will make an immeasurable contribution to the people of the world being able to get their name in their language for their Internet," Dam said.

5943. (14-2-2008) NEW DELHI : In exercise of the powers conferred by clause (1) of Article 224 of the Constitution of India, the President is pleased to appoint (i) Shri Ravi Vijaykumar Malimath, and (ii) Smt. Bangalore Venkataramiah Nagarathna to be Additional Judges of the Karnataka High Court, in that order of seniority, for a period of two years, with effect from the dates they assume charge of their respective offices.

5944. (14-2-2008) NEW DELHI : The Export Credit Guarantee Corporation of India Limited (ECGC) has paid an interim dividend of Rs.80 crore to the government. The dividend cheque was handed over to Shri G.K. Pillai, Commerce Secretary by Shri A.V. Muralidharan, Chairman-cum-Managing Director of ECGC here on 11th February, 2008. The Board of Directors of ECGC approved the payment of interim dividend in their meeting held on 8th February, 2008, in view of overall excellent performance upto the end of 3rd quarter.

5945. (14-2-2008) NEW DELHI : With a view to have detailed discussions in matters relating to the air services between the two countries, India and Bangladesh delegations held bilateral air services consultations on 11-13 February, 2008 in New Delhi. The Indian delegation was led by Shri Ashok Chawla, Secretary (Civil Aviation). After detailed discussions both sides reached an agreement and an MOU was signed between the two sides. Both sides have agreed to further liberalize the existing SAARC offer and all existing caps for the operations of Bangladesh carriers to/from different points in India have been removed. Now, the designated airlines of each side are entitled to operate 61 services per week in each direction to/from any points in each other's territory specified in the Route Schedule with any type of aircraft, without any restriction or capping. Also, in order to facilitate tourism, the designation airlines of both sides can operate any number of services to/from 18 tourist gateways in India *viz.* Patna, Lucknow, Guwahati, Gaya, Varanasi, Bhubaneshwar, Khajuraho, Aurangabad, Goa, Jaipur, Port Blair, Kochi, Trivandrum, Kozikode, Amritsar, Visakhapatnam, Ahmedabad and Tiruchirapalli. The Bangladesh side agreed to grant Sylhet in Bangladesh as an additional point of call for the Indian designated carriers. In order to enhance the air services operations and to make the operations more commercially viable, the provision of cooperative marketing arrangement has been agreed. Another important outcome of these discussions is reflected in the form an agreement on cargo operations where the designated airlines of each side are entitled to operate 7 all-cargo services per week between each other's territory with any type of aircraft.

5946. (14-2-2008) NEW DELHI : The Appointments Committee of the Cabinet has approved the appointment of Shri Ashok Kumar, IAS (AGMU: 74) presently in the cadre, as Vice Chairman, Delhi Development Authority in the rank and pay of Additional Secretary.

5947. (14-2-2008) NEW DELHI : Retail prices of farm commodities monitored by the Department of Consumer Affairs have generally remained steady or shown mixed trend over the week ending February 8, 2008. During the week ending February 8, 2008 prices of wheat remained steady at all the monitoring centres. Prices of sugar remained steady at all the monitoring centres. Prices of gram dal increased at Jaipur and declined at Chennai. In all other centres, prices of gram remained unchanged. Prices of tur dal remained steady in most centres. Prices increased at Delhi and declined at Kolkata and Chennai. Out of 14.02 lakh tonne pulses contracted for import, 10.7 lakh tonne have arrived in the country by 5.2.08. In Delhi, prices of wheat, rice, atta, groundnut oil, sugar, vanaspati, mustard oil, and onion held steady for one week. Prices of tea (loose), gram, milk, potato and salt held steady for one month. Prices of tur dal increased from Rs. 41 to Rs. 42 per kg.

5948. (14-2-2008) NEW DELHI : In a presentation made by the Ministry of Human Resource Development to the Consultative Committee of Parliament, the key objectives of expansion of secondary education in the country were outlined to be availability and access to every child within 5 kms. for secondary schools and within 7-10 kms. for higher secondary schools, and improvement of quality. The Consultative Committee meeting was chaired by Human Resource Development Minister Shri Arjun Singh who expressed the hope that perceptible change may be noticed on these attainable targets in the 3rd year of the Plan. He also said that vocationalization of secondary education will also be taken up on a massive scale. It was also mentioned in the meeting that universalisation of access to secondary education will be ensured by the end of the 11th Plan. It will include strengthening of existing schools to achieve prescribed norms; expansion of capacity of existing schools; upgradation of higher primary schools to secondary level; expansion of facilities for open distance learning and stepping up allocation to secondary education from 0.9% of GDP to 1.5% of GDP. Expansion of secondary education will also involve upgradation of physical infrastructure (class rooms, playgrounds, library, science lab, computer lab, toilet, drinking water, electricity, telephone etc.), recruitment and training of teachers and extensive use of ICT. This will also include incentives to girls and weaker sections including SCs/STs/ Minorities, curriculum revision, examination reforms and monitoring & supervision. The members of the Consultative Committee offered several suggestions. The main suggestions being special efforts to reduce dropout specially for girls, creation of social and parental awareness, accessible and affordable education; emphasis on moral and value education & yoga; in service training for teaching staff; hostel facilities for girls to reduce the drop out; development of the Public Private Partnership, improvement of infrastructure in existing schools, and systemic reforms in the educational system. The members were apprised that as a follow up of Prime Minister's Independence Day announcement, 6000 new high quality schools will be opened at the rate of one school per block. Out of these, 2500 schools will be in Public Private Partnership (PPP) model. Another component of the expansion of secondary education is a proposal for establishment of one girls' hostel of capacity 100 in each Educationally Backward Block (EBB). The members were also informed that one lakh Merit-cum-Means scholarships of Rs. 6000 per annum would be awarded each year from class IX to class XII. The meeting was attended by the Minister of State for Human Resource Development Smt. D. Purandeswari and Members of Parliament: Shri Babulal Marandi, Shri D. Raja, Shri Harisinh Chavda, Shri Haribhau Jawale, Smt. Kanimozhi, Dr. K. Kasturirangan, Prof. P. J. Kurien, Shri Ramesh Dube, Shri Raashid Alvi,Dr. Vallabhbhai Kathiria & Shri Vijay Krishna.

5949. (14-2-2008) NEW DELHI : The Union Cabinet today approved a proposal for signing of the Agreement between India and South Africa on the abolition of visa requirement for the holders of diplomatic and official / service passports and its implementation. This decision will facilitate visa-free travel for diplomatic and official passport holders while entering, transiting through the existing from the territory of the other country and issue of residence visa valid for duration of the assignment to the members of diplomatic / consular Mission.

5950. (14-2-2008) NEW DELHI : The Union Cabinet today gave its approval for proposing to the Economic and Social Commission for Asia and the Pacific of the United Nations (UNESCAP) for following amendments to the route of AH-2, and AH-48 defined in the List of Asian highway Routes of the Inter-Governmental Agreement on the Asian Highway Network, for consideration by the Working Group on the Asian Highway :-(i) Including "Phulbari" between Banglabandha and Siliguri and defining the route of AH-2 at this location as "… Banglabandha-Phulbari-Siliguri-Kakarbhitta…", (ii) Providing link to Bhutan by extending route or AH-48 from "Thimphu-Phuentsholing-Jaigaon-Hasimara-Jalpaigui-Phulbari" in place of "Phuentsholing-Border of India", as indicated now, and consequently connect with AH-2 at Phulbari in India. By extending the AH-48 from Thimphu-Phuentsholing (Bhutan) to Jaigaon, Border Point in India, and giving connectivity to AH-2 in India will provide connectivity of Asian Highway Route from Bhutan to India, as well as to both Bangladesh and Nepal. This will help in increase in trade and tourism amongst these countries.

5951. (14-2-2008) NEW DELHI : The Union Cabinet today approved a proposal for introduction of a Bill in the Parliament for amending the Maternity Benefit Act, 1961. The existing ceiling of Rs. 250/- as Maternity Bonus under Maternity Benefit Act, 1961 is inadequate in the present economic scenario. Hence, there is an urgent need to increase the amount to Rs. 1000/- so that it could be a source of financial support to working women as far as maternity benefits are concerned. This decision will empower the Central Government to revise the medical bonus after every three years payable under the Maternity Benefit Act, 1961, subject to the maximum limit not being more than an amount of Rs. 20000/- (Rupees Twenty Thousand) by issuing notification.

5952. (14-2-2008) NEW DELHI : The Mughal Gardens of Rashtrapati Bhavan including the Musical Garden, the Spiritual Garden, the Herbal Garden, the Biodiversity Park and the Nakshatra Gardens, are being opened for viewing by the general public from February 16th. The Gardens will be open to the general public on all days from 16th February to 24th March from 1000 hrs. to 1700 hrs. except on Mondays being maintenance days. Entry into the Gardens will close at 1600 hrs. The gardens shall also remain closed on March 21st and 22nd. The Mughal Gardens, contiguous to the main building of Rashtrapati Bhavan cover an area of 15 acres. They were designed by Sir Edwin Lutyens inspired by the beautiful gardens of Jammu and Kashmir, the gardens around the Taj Mahal and Persian and Indian miniature paintings. The Mughal Gardens comprise three parts: the first is the Rectangular Garden adjacent to the main Rashtrapati Bhavan building, which is divided into four quarters, each with terraced gardens on either side. The Central Lawn is the venue of numerous receptions and 'At Homes' hosted by The President. The Rectangular Garden has several beds of Tulips. This garden will be the centre of attraction this year having 8 different varieties of Tulips. Tulips do not last long. Single colour Tulips are in full bloom now. One can enjoy their beauty upto 22nd February and Hybrid multicolour Tulips from Kashmir will be in full bloom approximately from 22nd to 2nd March 2008. The second is the Long Garden, leading on to the third part, which is the Circular Garden. The Long Garden has several beds of roses with a dwarf-trimmed hedge, giving the effect of 'coloured knots on a vast carpet'. This year 7 different varieties of roses have been added. The Circular Garden, also known as the 'Pearl Garden' or the 'Butterfly Garden', presents a feast of colours, with each tier overflowing with annual flowers and separated from the next, by a patch of greens having a centrally located fountain. This year the flowering is delayed on account of adverse weather conditions. The Garden derives its evergreen character from trees like Moulsiri, Putranjiva, Saru, Juniper, China Orange, Roses and varieties of Climbers etc. The Garden has 135 varieties of roses this year like Sentimental, Memorial Day, Garden Party, Aishwarya, Welwyn Garden, Glory, Taj Mahal, Pasadena, Pusa Arjun etc. and Ink Spot, Black Baccara, Oklahoma, which is nearest to being black. In blues it has Rhapsodie in Blue, Fragrant Plum, Lady X as well as the Green Rose. Various annuals are grown in beds and formal borders according to their heights and colours to produce harmonious effect and provide longer period for the bed to be full of blooms. Winter flowers like Calendula, Antirrhinum, Alyssum, Dimorphotheca, Eschscholzia, Larkspur, Gazania, Gerbera, Godetia, Lineria, Mesembryanthemum, Brachycome, Metucharia, Verbena, Viola, Pansy, Stock etc. grow well in flowerbeds. Dahlias, Carnations and Sweet Pea stand out because of their range of colours. Naturalizing effect is created by bulbous flowering plants like Crocus Narcissus, Hyacinth, Daffodils, Gladiolus, Lilies, Tulips and Iris. 55 Types of annuals are in bloom now. Sweet Pea an annual that covers the walls with flowers and is more beautiful than other annuals is eye catching. The Long Garden or the 'Purdah' Garden, so called because of its shape is enclosed by high walls and lies to the West of the main garden. It has 16 square attractive rose beds hemmed in low hedges. Along the walls are lined the resplendent China Orange whose ornamental fruits outnumber the leaves.

5953. (14-2-2008) NEW DELHI : The Prime Minister Dr. Manmohan Singh inaugurated the Indian Ocean Naval Symposium Seminar in New Delhi today. Speaking on the occasion, Prime Minister said that there is a need for a greater cooperation between the navies of the littoral states of the Indian Ocean for preventing transnational crimes and maintaining the biological diversity of the seabed in the region. Following is the text of Prime Minister's speech: "It is a matter of great privilege for me to be present in your midst with you on the occasion of the launch of the Indian Ocean Naval Symposium. This is a unique gathering of Chiefs of Navies and Heads of Maritime Security Organizations representing the littoral states of the Indian Ocean. I extend very warm welcome to each one of our guests from various parts of the world. Spanning 28 million square kilometres, the Indian Ocean is host to a third of the world's population. The littoral states of the Indian Ocean account for 25% of the global landmass and 40% of the world's energy sources. They have a rich heritage and share close socio-cultural ties. Above all, they are linked by a history of sea faring. A significant share of international trade passes through the sea-lanes of the region. Regrettably the Indian Ocean also accounts for 70% of the world's natural disasters. These are all reasons why we must pool our knowledge and resources and act for the common good of all our people. Your presence here today is a testimony to your belief in the need for cooperative action. Indian Ocean littoral States have witnessed rapid economic growth in recent years. These high levels of growth are translating into increased intra-regional trade and global trade, a significant portion of which is sea borne. The sea-lanes of the region have thus emerged as one of the most important lines of communication in the world. Container handling at the ports of Colombo, Mumbai, Chittagong, Bangkok and Malaysia's Port Klang are registering double-digit growth rates. A growing percentage of the world's large merchant ships and bulk carrier ships fly an Asian flag. This expansion in trade and economic growth dictates the need to ensure the safety and security of the sea-lanes. Recent years have seen a rise in crimes such as terrorism, smuggling, including of narcotics, arms and weapons, piracy, and robbery. These activities not only pose a threat to our growing naval commerce but also affect innocent fishermen and tourists. In addition there is the abominable practice of trafficking in human beings. The perpetrators of these crimes are well-organized and well-funded transnational crime syndicates who take full advantage of the vastness of the oceans. The need for cooperation among the Navies of the region in preventing such international crimes is therefore of paramount importance. The monsoons play a vital role in the lives of the peoples of the Indian Ocean littoral states. They have also been pivotal in determining the sea routes that would transport precious cargo, be it spices from western India or rubber from the plantations of Malaysia. Recent years have witnessed a marked rise in incidents of natural disasters. We look upon our Navies to protect our citizens from natural disasters and mitigate the effects on our coastal zones from phenomena like cyclones and tsunamis. Our coastal ecosystems sustain livelihoods and they are host to a diverse species of marine life. We must have robust capabilities to deal with environmental emergencies. Our coastal ecosystems sustain livelihoods and they are host to a diverse species of marine life. The United Nations Convention on the Law of Sea sets out the legal framework within which all activities in the oceans and the seas must be carried out.

5954. (14-2-2008) NEW DELHI : The Prime Minister, Dr. Manmohan Singh said the " Recent years have seen a rise in the crimes such as terrorism, smuggling, including of narcotics, arms and weapons, piracy and robbery. These activities not only pose a threat to our growing naval commerce but also affect innocent fishermen and tourists. In addition there is the abominable practice of trafficking in human beings". The prime minister was speaking at the Inaugural of the IONS 2008. He said, " India remains committed to an Indian Ocean region that is stable and peaceful. We would like to cooperate with all like minded countries so as to ensure the freedom of the seas for all nations and to deepen trade and economic linkages between the Indian Ocean rim countries" Speaking on the occasion, the Defence Minister said, "The maritime domain is demanding and deserving of continuous study, discussion and debate. The fact that the littoral states of the Indian Ocean Region too, realize this and understand its implications is clearly evident from your presence here at the launch of the Indian Ocean Naval Symposium". Shri AK Antony added that " We are all here to....'dream the Indian Ocean Dream'... We have come together to share and explore the contours of a grand vision of a coalesced, prosperous and progressive Indian Ocean. This is a vision that is neither diminished nor daunted by our diversity." The Chief of the Naval Staff Admiral Sureesh Mehta, said "IONS should be seen as a construct in our region that focuses on issues related to, or, which can be influenced through the maritime environment. In doing so, it would perhaps help in creating conditions for regional cooperative efforts to spill over to other fields as well." The Admiral said "The threat from malevolent non-state actors presents a clear and present danger to not just one or some but to all of us. The response from us must, therefore, be from not just one or some, but from all of us."

5955. (15-2-2008) NEW DELHI : On completion of the term of Shri M.Damodaran, the Central Government has appointed Shri C.B. Bhave, presently Chairman & Managing Director, National Securities Depository Limited as Chairman of the Securities & Exchange Board of India. In view of a few proceedings initiated or under consideration by SEBI in respect of NSDL, Mr. Bhave has requested to be recused from these proceedings and to put in place a mechanism to oversee the conduct of these proceedings. Having considered this request, the Central Government has advised the SEBI Board that in order to ensure objectivity in the handling/conduct of these pending proceedings, these matters be handled by a team of non-Whole Time Members of SEBI who were not party to the initiation or processing of such proceedings. Neither Shri Bhave who was heading NSDL nor the nominee of the Ministry of Finance on the SEBI Board will be involved in this special arrangement. These proceedings will be overseen by a three member team comprised of part time members of the Board. The team will associate an eminent legal expert for professional advice.

5956. (15-2-2008) NEW DELHI : A section of media has reported quoting Petroleum Secretary Shri M.S.Srinivasan as having said that Government will issue Oil Bonds with SLR status to Oil Marketing Companies (OMCs). In this regard, Petroleum Secretary has clarified that no such statement attributed to him has been made. He further clarified that the matter regarding all issues relating to Oil Bonds to be released to OMCs are under consideration of the Government.

5957. (15-2-2008) NEW DELHI : The Ordnance Factories have started offering warranty on their products including small ammunition, bombs, rockets and weapon systems, Disclosing this at a news conference on the eve of the 5th DefExpo, 2008 here today, the Ordnance Factories Board (OFB) Chairman Shri Sudipta Ghosh said all the 40 ordnance factories spread across the country have recently earned the ISO-9002 certificate. Refuting concerns about the quality of OFB products, Shri Ghosh assured that the malfunctions, if any, are attended to by experts or the product is replaced to the customers' satisfaction. In another milestone in the OFB's history of over 200 years, the OFB Chairman will hand over the first batch of an upgraded Pinaka rockets, developed in collaboration with the DRDO, to the Indian Army on February 27. The Vice Chief of Army Staff Lt. Gen. Milan Naidu will receive the rockets at a ceremony at Ordnance Factory, Chanda in Maharashtra. The OFB will supply 300 Pinaka rockets to the Army this year and 1,000 next year. The Ordnance Factory, Trichy, only yesterday handed over at a ceremony the first consignment of 10 Anti-Material Rifles to the BSF. Revealing plans for the future, Shri Ghosh said the Ordnance Factories are open to the idea of joint ventures as foreign vendors scout for partners to fulfil the offset clause in defence purchases above 300 crore rupees stipulating for ploughing back 30 percent of the contract money into the country. The 40 Ordnance Factories, participating in a big way in the DefExpo, the Naval and Land-based weapon systems exposition, will showcase their products alongside major foreign companies in a bid to grab a slice of the emerging markets, he added. Shri Ghosh said the OFB has raised its R&D budget over the years to upgrade an array of guns, rockets, launchers, tanks and APCs. Towards this end, about 20 engineers are undergoing training abroad, he said. Keeping itself abreast of the changing patterns in modern warfare, Shri Ghosh said the OFB is upgrading existing land systems to adapt to a net-centric environment. Several new products are being developed either inhouse or in collaboration with the DRDO and foreign partners. OFB is also developing new ammunition with longer range for the artillery in various calibres. The new or upgraded weapons and systems which have already been evaluated, include the 155 mm ERFB BB Ammunition, 130 mm Cargo Ammunition, Kavach Launcher Mark-2, Mine Protected Vehicles, 5.56 mm Excalibur Rifle, Anti-Material Rifle, 100-120 kg Air Bomb, CRN-91 Naval Gun, T 90 tanks, AK 630 Naval Gun, 84 mm Rocket Launcher Mark-3, Pinaka Rocket, Armoured Ambulance, Armoured Engineering Reconnaissance Vehicle, NBC (Nuclear-Biological-Chemical) Recce Vehicle and Combat Free fall Parachute.

5958. (15-2-2008) NEW DELHI : The Annual Plan for Sikkim for the year 2008-09 was finalized here today at a meeting between Deputy Chairman, Planning Commission Shri Montek Singh Ahluwalia and Chief Minister of Sikkim, Shri Pawan Chamling. The Plan outlay was agreed at Rs.852 crores. This includes additional Central assistance of Rs.77 crores for projects of special importance to the State. In his remarks, Mr. Ahluwalia complemented the State for alround performance and said that the human development indicators of the State were better than majority of States. The State was doing well in areas of health, education and other priority programmes. Emphasis should continue on social and physical infrastructure. Efforts to promote public private partnership in the development process were appreciated. Performance during Xth plan was satisfactory. State had almost achieved the growth targets set for the tenth plan. The State was advised to maintain progress achieved in agriculture with concerted efforts aimed at increasing area under agriculture without compromising in efforts aimed at improving growth in horticulture and floriculture. Cluster approach in promoting horticulture and floriculture was recommended. Thrust areas should include tourism, horticulture/floriculture and human resource development. These will not only generate revenue but also generate employment opportunities. In his comments on the development strategy for Eleventh Plan, the Chief Minister Mr. Chamling said the State would have continued emphasis on social sector and over 40 per cent of funds would be ear-marked for the sector. With in the sector education will get highest priority with 17% allocation. He said the State Government was keen on skill development specially in the area of tourism where trained manpower was needed. He said efforts would continue to further improve fiscal health. He said elections to rural local bodies have been completed and this would help further accelerate pace of development. He said in addition to promotion of tourism, horticulture and floriculture and citizen friendly services, setting up of low volume, high value and eco-friendly industries would encouraged. Policy initiatives have helped in creating investment friendly environment and more than Rs.1000 crores of investment have been committed. He sought adequate financial assistance from the Central Government for settingup of centre of excellence projects and establishment of Central University in Sikkim.

5959. (15-2-2008) NEW DELHI : The Government has appointed Shri C.B. Bhave as the new Chairman of Securities and Exchange Board of India (SEBI) for a period of three years from the date he assumes office upon the completion of term by Shri M. Damodaran. Shri C.B. Bhave is presently the Chairman and Managing Director of National Securities Depository Limited (NSDL).

5960. (15-2-2008) NEW DELHI : In exercise of the powers conferred by clause (1) of Article 217 of the Constitution of India, the President is pleased to appoint (i) Shri Justice Prafulla Chandra Pant, (ii) Shri Justice Brahma Singh Verma and (iii) Shri Justice Dharam Veer, Additional Judges of the Uttarakhand High Court, to be Judges of the Uttarakhand High Court, in that order of seniority, with effect from the dates they assume charge of their respective offices.

5961. (15-2-2008) NEW DELHI : The GB Pant Institute of Himalayan Environment & Development (GBPIHED) has taken significant strides in identifying problems. Releasing a document "GBPIHED-Over the Years (Stakeholder driven research and development)" of the institute, Shri Namo Narayan Meena, Minister of State for Environment & Forests said that the institute has developed region specific approaches. It has efficiently disseminated the information to various needed stakeholders. The Minister said that the institute had addressed diverse problems related to ecology. Shri Meena said the document not only presents the outcome of major research and development activities carried out over the years, but also gives an account of stakeholder's responses towards this outcome. The document aims at meeting the expectation of various stakeholders, including the policy makers. The institute was established in 1988 as an autonomous institute of the Ministry of Environment & Forests. It has area of operation covering 5, 91,000 sq.km. It covers nearly 15 million people spread over 12 states of India, *i.e.* Jammu & Kashmir, Himachal Pradesh, Uttrakhand, Sikkim, Arunachal Pradesh, Nagaland, Manipur, Mizorum, Tripura, Meghalaya, Assam and West Bengal hills. The institute's thematic area includes watershed process and management, biodiversity conservation, environmental assessment and management, socio-economic development, biotechnological applications and knowledge products as well as capacity building The recently concluded findings of Glaciers Study Unit have given a new inside in rate of retreat of Himalayan Glaciers. This unit generated time series authentic datasets on rate of recession of Himalayan Glaciers. The institute has addressed diverse problems pertaining to different issue of Himalayan Environment & development, livelihood options, land restoration and awareness and outreach on different issues. To achieve problem solving approaches and to make them acceptable the institute has also established demonstration of best practices. This compilation will be useful to scientist's academia ions, stakeholders and policymakers. Besides this it will help in improving their synergy with the institute for promoting ecological and economic development of the Indian Himalayan Region.

5962. (15-2-2008) NEW DELHI : The first Seminar conducted under the aegis of the Indian Ocean Naval Symposium (IONS) came to an end at New Delhi today. It was attended by heads of navies of 27 nations of the Indian Ocean Region (IOR). The Symposium founded a cooperative and inclusive forum of IOR countries and would also provide a platform for the conduct of training exchanges, seminars, table-top exercises, workshops etc. Whilst the seminar on 'Contemporary Trans-national Challenges-International Maritime Connectivities' was underway at Vigyan Bhavan, the Chiefs of Navies / heads of respective maritime organisations met at a Conclave of Chiefs to deliberate upon the charter of the IONS. The Conclave of Chiefs will continue its discussions during the second session scheduled at Goa on 16 and 17 February 2008. The Chiefs will also visit the naval base, INS Hansa. Earlier, the Vice President of India, Mohd Hamid Ansari addressed the Conclave of Chiefs impressing upon common concerns and the need for collective response including security issues in the IOR.

5963. (15-2-2008) NEW DELHI : In a first of its kind initiative, the Indira Gandhi National Open University (IGNOU) in collaboration with the Agricultural and Processed Food Products Export Development Authority (APEDA) of the Ministry of Commerce & Industry, has developed a 6-month duration course on Certificate in Organic Farming. Shri Jairam Ramesh, Minister of State for Commerce, launched this newly developed educational programme on Organic Farming here today. IGNOU Vice Chancellor, Prof. V.N. Rajasekharan Pillai; APEDA Director, Shri S. Dave; and Prof. B.S. Hansra, Director of IGNOU's School of Agriculture were present at the launch ceremony. Shri Ramesh stated that the study programme is expected to address vast manpower requirement for trained personnel in organic farming sector in India and added that after taking this course, successful candidates can find employment avenues as Organic Farming professionals, advisors, entrepreneurs, quality certifiers, marketing and export trade facilitators. He further said that organic farming in India is set to get a major boost in the country due to the rising income levels and health consciousness among large section of people, as the programme has been designed with the help of experts from different organizations / universities across the country. The IGNOU-APEDA Organic Farming programme will be the first such full-fledged educational and training programme being offered in the country. The programme would be made available to students, progressive farmers and certifying personnel seeking enrolment to the course from the coming academic year. As it would be imparted in IGNOU's Open and Distance Learning (ODL) mode, persons with Secondary School qualification (10+2) in any part of the country could enroll in it. IGNOU's School of Agriculture which developed the training programme in organic farming has the main objective of promoting sustainable agriculture by broad-basing and upgrading the knowledge level of the Indian farming community. The delivery of IGNOU's organic farming programme to the students and farmers would be backed up by student practical classes and counselling being arranged through different Programme Study Centres (PCS) of IGNOU. These programme study centres are established in State Agricultural Universities, Krishi Vigyan Kendra, NGOs, ICAR institutions etc. Currently, India is having 1.7 million hectares of area under certified organic farming. The organic market in the country is valued at Rs.100 crore with an annual growth rate steadily going up from 35% to 50% by 2010. India is fast becoming a major base for production and supply of organically produced agricultural products to the world market. The global market for organic farm produce is expected to touch US$ 100 billion by 2010. Realizing the potential for export of organic products, Ministry of Commerce has set up National Programme for Organic Production (NPOP) in April 2000. A National Steering Committee (NSC) was set up by the Ministry of Commerce under NPOP. Maintaining strict quality control standards, India's National Programme for Organic Production (NPOP), ensures the export of only those products which qualify the National Standards for Organic production. APEDA has been designated as the secretariat for NSC under NPOP and it performs the lead role for promotion of export of organically grown agro-products. APEDA is also responsible for accreditation of Certification Bodies in the country.

5964. (15-2-2008) NEW DELHI : The Indian Air Force and Pawan Hans Helicopter Ltd (PHHL) signed a Memorandum of Understanding (MoU) today at Air

Headquarters (Vayu Bhawan) enabling IAF to share its expertise in operations with Pawan Hans. Under the agreed terms and conditions, helicopter pilots nearing the end of their flying career in IAF for induction into Pawan Hans. The MoU was signed by Air Vice Marshal LK Malhotra, Assistant Chief of Air Staff (Personnel Officers) on behalf of IAF and Shri GP Srivastava, GM (P&HRD) for Pawan Hans. This would ensure Pawan Hans, India's leading helicopter service provider, benefits from the extensive operation experience of IAF pilots. At the same time, it will offer a second career option to IAF helicopter pilots would be able to utilize their flying skills even after their career in IAF. The accrued training and expertise of IAF pilots nearing the end of their terms of service would therefore be effectively harnessed in furtherance of the national cause. Present during the signing of MoU, Air Chief Marshal Fali Major said "The signing of this MoU is indicative of IAF's commitment to growth of aviation in the country, be it civil or military. The MoU will not only promote mutual benefits to both the organization but will prove to be a milestone for Indian Aviation as such". AVM LK Malhotra, who signed the MoU on behalf of IAF said during the ceremony "the MoU will enable IAF pilots to get opportunity for growth and a longer, fruitful second career upto 65 years of age. Similary Pawan Hans would also be benefited by augmenting their strength of qualified pilots. The inclusive HR policies of IAF would yield positive results for over all growth of aviation in the country". Shri RK Tyagi, CMD of Pawan Hans Ltd mentioned that Pawan Hans Helicopter Ltd is looking forward for a massive fleet expansion as well as to enter new areas of operation such as inter and intra city transportation besides setting up a state of art maintenance centre and also new helicopters at Delhi, Mumbai and other viable areas. It is understood that PHHL is poising for acquiring new helicopters during next financial year for which requirement of more qualified pilots is paramount.

5965. (15-2-2008) NEW DELHI : Internet Corporation for Assigned Names and Numbers (ICANN) concludes its meeting in New Delhi today. The meeting was attended by 726 participants cutting across 76 countries with a large Indian presence of 294 persons. In the week-long meeting, the issues relating to domain names in the local languages, local scripts and issues with wide range to variants, spellings were discussed. Domain Names Security (DNS) issues also figured prominently. ICANN has already successfully concluded tests in local non-English languages including Devnagari and Tamil languages. The meeting in New Delhi enabled the participants to share the experiences with experts from C-DAC, Department of Information Technology (DoIT) and the National Internet Exchange of India (NiXi), on variants and spellings and how expert organizations are overcoming the security issues arising out of spelling variations. There is need to proliferate IPv6 in the country as more and more devices are connected to the Net. In fact, India has been emphasizing the need of IPv4 and IPv6. The Internet exchange of India (NiXi) which is the main registry of.in Domain Name held discussions with ICANN on issues relating to issues relating to India. The highlight of the ICANN meeting was the signing of Memorandum of Understanding between

ICANN and the Internet User Groups who participated in the Asia Pacific Regional At-Large Organisation (APRALO) on its first general meeting in New Delhi as part of ICANN's 31st International Public Meeting. They discussed issues that will affect Internet users through out the region and the world. The Internet user groups who are part of APRALO are incredibly diverse, and include users from India, Japan, China, Australia, New Zealand, Hong Kong, and the United Arab Emirates.

5966. (15-2-2008) NEW DELHI : National Commission for Protection of Child Rights (NCPCR) has organized national Round Table Consultations on Juvenile Justice and Child Rights to review the implementation and to explore Legislative reforms in the area. Following visits to a number of States recently the NCPCR has felt that Juvenile Justice system requires intensive review of implementation mechanism and Legislative reform. The Commission has initiated a national review process identifying priority areas for targeted implementation support as well as recommending effective strategies for undertaking reform and comprehensive JJ Act implementation. As a part of the consultation process the commission is holding a series of Round tables with States to ensure comprehensive input and judges of High Courts and child right activists and representatives of various departments to establish national consensus on priority commitments for implementation and reforms for protection of child rights and welfare.

5967. (15-2-2008) NEW DELHI : Following is the text of the address of Vice President of India Mohd. Hamid Ansari to the assembled Chiefs/Heads of Navy of the entire Indian Ocean at the "IONS Seminar 2008" here today : "Once upon a time the commander-in-chief of a rising land power, unfamiliar with seafaring and uneasy about it, asked one of his field commanders to describe the sea and seafarers to him. The officer dutifully reported: 'Verily I have seen a great creature [that is, the sea] ridden by a small one [that is, man]. When it is calm it renders the heart with anxiety, and if it is agitated it leads the mind into confusion. On it certainty shrinks and doubt increases. Those who are on it are like a worm on a twig; if it bends he is drowned, and if he is saved he is astounded'. In another region of the world, in the island of Bali, the traditional belief considered the sea to be full of demons; hence to be approached with care if not avoided. In both cases, perhaps, the immenseness of the body of water and the mysteries in its depths acted as a deterrent. These examples can be multiplied. History is witness to great land powers failing to comprehend the relevance of the sea as an instrument of statecraft. The historian Paul Kennedy attributes the rise of European powers, sixteenth century onwards, to 'technological change and military competitiveness'; he may have added, with equal justice, that seafaring was an equally relevant ingredient of promoting trade, competing with rivals, and eventually overcoming them. The fact nevertheless remains that for a good percentage of humankind, the sea is not in the same category of familiarity as the land. This may be no more than an accident of natural history and the manner in which humans assumed a centrality on this planet. On the other hand, certain facts relating to this planet of ours may suggest correctives to such a slanted approach. Earth is a planet of oceans. They constitute 71 percent of its total area. In a very real sense, they sustain life on earth. Cheap transportation is possible through them. They are in increasing measure a source of food, energy and minerals.The Indian Ocean is the third largest ocean in terms of area but unquestionably the first in terms of its impact on human civilisation. The reason for this is obvious; some of the oldest civilisations took shape and blossomed in lands around the Indian Ocean or the seas adjacent to it. They interacted with each other principally through trade. For this reason alone, a gathering of people from Indian Ocean lands would provide a useful collection of perspectives. Today's conference, I believe, goes beyond an exercise in history and ethnology. Its timing and purpose are sharply focused on the world of today and tomorrow. A look at recent history provides the perspective. The Portuguese discovery of the sea route to India was of such critical importance that the King of Portugal thought it fit to reflect it in his formal titles. Its wording is to be noted: 'Lord of Conquest, Navigation and Commerce, of Ethiopia, Arabia, India and Persia'. Their hegemony lasted for two centuries, to be replaced by the British who followed the pattern and the new jewel in the Crown justified the additional title of Empress of India. The end of the British era saw the enhancement of the role of the United States. Alongside, the Cold War witnessed super-power rivalry extended itself in the Indian Ocean littoral. In each of these, the external impulse remained the dominant one. The littoral states themselves had little or no input into it. Whatever be the past, the imperative today is of a qualitatively different situation in the Indian Ocean littoral. The external impulses have in good measure given way to internal dynamics of individual societies. This, however, is not easily comprehended and older patterns of thinking persist. A few years back a scholar in Honolulu delved in futurology pertaining to the Indian Ocean: 'We do not yet understand the political geography of the 21st century. However, no region is likely to feature as prominently in that geography as the Indian Ocean due to its combination of oil, Islam and the likely rise-and probable mutual rivalry of both India and China. Indian Ocean regionalism, or regional integration, remains quite retarded when perceived through an economic lens. Sadly, however, it is the converse conclusion that seems warranted when the region is perceived through the prism of geopolitics and nuclear weapons'.

5968. (16-2-2008) NEW DELHI : National Commission for Protection of Child Rights (NCPCR) has expressed concern over the plight of juveniles in the country and has stressed the need to make the Government, police and Judiciary more sensitive about the protection and welfare of children. Addressing the inaugural session of the first National consultations with representatives of judiciary, police and State Governments, Dr. Shanta Sinha, Chairperson of the commission said that over 5000 cases against juveniles have been pending in the courts with many of them languishing for over 12 years. But this is not the only challenge that children in need of juveniles justice face. There is also variance in the standards meted out by various authorities. Dr. Sinha said that recently, the Commission visited a number of States to review implementation of government policies on children and found that there was almost no provision for or linkage to remedial bridge school education for children with limited or disrupted education. "Our imperative must be to ensure that all children coming into juvenile justice system are sent back to school and their families. In fact, I believe that the extension of the right to education through appropriate remedial mainstreaming is one of the most important factors which can fight criminalisation and institutionalization of these children," said Shanta Sinha. Over the past few months the NCPCR has established independent expert committees focused on Children's Homes and the Juvenile Justice Boards to identify the gaps in the delivery of justice and implementation of Juvenile Justice Act, and the tendency towards either treating them as criminals or putting them into Homes and forgetting about them. The studies have shown that the length of the time spent in institution is too long most of the time and rate of restoration to the families is not satisfactory. Rehabilitation of children with proper education and their protection from abuse require greater attention, the chairperson of NCPCR revealed. Briefing about the objective of consultation, Ms. Dipa Dixit member NCPCR said that the national studies have also revealed that more than 50 per cent of children's homes do not provide any counselling services across the country. In addition, more than 80 per cent caretakers do not have any proper training to handle children. Physical punishment is dominant method to discipline the children at these children homes. Another member of NCPCR, Mrs.Sandhya Bajaj stressed the need to sensitize to the judiciary, police and government machinery to protect the children. She said that plight of the children in the children homes is a matter of concern and corrective steps are urgently needed.

5969. (16-2-2008) NEW DELHI : The Defence Minister Shri AK Antony has categorically ruled out allowing middlemen or commission agents in defence deals. Addressing a press conference shortly after inaugurating the fifth edition of DefExpo India-2008 here today, Shri Antony said the government's stand on the issue is very clear-"No question of middlemen in defence deals." He, however, discounted apprehensions about timely procurement of weapon systems and platforms for the forces saying that the government would be able to spend budget allocations on capital expenditure head and would be asking for more resources in the next budget. The Defence Minister, however, ruled out any compromise on transparency. "Of course, we cancelled two-three contracts. Do you want us to compromise on transparency? Even at a later stage when we find something is wrong somewhere, we are not concerned about the status of the company; we will cancel it. So we have gone for fresh RFP," he said. Shri Antony replied to a wide range of questions. He said that the Defence Procurement Procedure 2008 will be ready by April and it is being fine-tuned with a great deal of diligence after taking into account the suggestions received from various stakeholders including the services and the industry. Giving a detailed reply on the status of the Light Combat Aircraft being jointly developed by the DRDO and HAL, Shri Antony said major breakthroughs in the project have been achieved in recent times and he is confident that "it will be in the sky within a few years." He said the Indian Air Force, which was not willing to accept even one of this aircraft earlier, has now decided to receive two squadrons, indicating their confidence in the aircraft. The Defence Minister admitted that there are still problems with the high-powered Kaveri engine and negotiations are on for a suitable partnership. As a result, development of a fully operational Kaveri engine may take some more time but "we will not abandon the project," he declared. Earlier inaugurating DefExpo India-2008 on a balmy morning at Pragati Maidan, Shri Antony said that the DPP-2008, which is going to be announced by April, will address concerns and opinions of various stakeholders relating to issues like banking of offset credits, Transfer of Technology (ToT), licensing requirement for software industry and so on. Shri Antony stressed the need for far greater synergy between the private players and the government. The Def Expo India exhibition was conceptualised in the year 1998 by the Department of Defence Production, Ministry of Defence, Government of India in partnership with the Confederation of Indian Industry with an objective to promote defence exports from India and at the same time exhibit the capabilities of Indian Defence R&D and production. The Def Expo India exhibition which began in 1999 with 197 exhibitors has grown to one of the most internationally recognised defence exhibitions in the world, with a total of 475 exhibitors, of which foreign exhibitors are 273 and Indian exhibitors are 202. Dedicated to global land and naval systems business activity-from suppliers to manufacturers, technology providers to services-it allows the international defence industry to promote and showcase their products and services to an international ness audience. First time in Defexpo India '08 both Telecom and IT companies will be showcasing their products and services. 47 Official Delegations would be visiting Defexpo India 2008 including 6 Ministerial delegations from Afghanistan, Belarus, Ghana, Mozambique, Namibia and Nigeria. The 4th Indian Defence Industry Summit on Indian Defence Industry Policy & Procurement Processes will be held on 16th February, 2008. A major highlight of DEFEXPO India 2008 this year is the inclusion of 16 seminars coinciding with DEFEXPO INDIA 2008, to enable exhibitors to make technology / product specific presentations to target audience from Indian Defence establishments, R&D Institutions, visiting official delegations, Defence Public Sector Undertakings, Ordnance Factories and Indian Industry. Additionally, a new feature this year is that CII will be organising a Def Expo India-Golf Tournament on Sunday, 17 February 2008 at the Army Golf Course New Delhi. International participation in Defexpo India '08 is from over 30 countries, displaying an array of technology and new products.

5970. (17-2-2008) NEW DELHI : The President of India said here that I am very happy to participate at the "National Conclave of North Eastern States for Access to Justice to Women of the Region" to discuss impediments of access to justice and the convergence of schemes pertaining to social justice in the region. I am privileged to be in the midst of participants from the North Eastern States at this Conclave. I had advised the organizers to hold the conference in the North Eastern region, but due to certain constraints, it could not be held there. I hope in near future it will be held in one of the North Eastern States. The North-East is a very special part of India. It is a land of exquisite natural landscapes with snow mountains, rivers and dense forests; with a large variety of flora and fauna; and with rich natural resources. Its brave and strong people belonging to its different tribes with their vibrant culture flowing out of the diversity of languages, customs, traditions, dance and music have enriched our country. These patriotic and hardworking people are proud Indians with a great sense of national integrity. The region is a land of beauty and is also a land of great potential. The challenge is to realize the potential of the region and bring development there in an atmosphere of peace. As we are holding this meeting on Access to Justice to Women of the Region, I am also pleased to note that the 5th North-East Trade Expo is also being held in New Delhi under the auspices of the Ministry for the Development of the North-Eastern Region. I understand that at the Expo products from the region are on display and there is an opportunity to taste the special cuisines as well as watch the different cultural performances from the region. The North East Crafts and Culture Festival is another event currently underway in New Delhi. I would encourage the frequent holdings of events from the North-Eastern States in the National Capital and in other parts of India as they promote better understanding and appreciation of each other's cultures and traditions. Bringing the North Eastern region closer and developing the region, both are an essential part of our national endeavour. Geographical features have, for too long, acted as a constraint to the overall development of the region. The states of the North-East are required to be made more accessible for the easy flow of not only commerce and trade but also of ideas and new technological developments. Infrastructure development of road, rail, air and tele-communications would help in realizing the potential of the region and will provide better connectivity with rest of India, making people-to-people contacts easier. Dr. Mohini Giri has raised some points in her speech. I will look into them. The Constitution of India has assured to all its citizens, political social and economic justice. We have been working for this objective for the last six decades. Success has been achieved in many areas, work is in progress in others and in some areas challenges remain. We have demonstrated to the world that a developing country of over a billion people can live harmoniously and move forward within the framework of a secular democracy. This has been possible due to the effort of each and every citizen of India. Like all people of India, those from the North Eastern region, are also looking for progress and prosperity.

5971. (18-2-2008) NEW DELHI : The Prime Minister, Dr. Manmohan Singh has expressed his condolences on the passing away of Shri Harishchandra Singh, father of Samajwadi Party Leader Shri Amar Singh. In his condolence message the Prime Minister said: "I am deeply grieved to learn of the sad demise of Shri

Harishchandra Singh, father of Samajwadi Party Leader Shri Amar Singh. The tragedy of losing an elderly person of the family is difficult to bear. The sense of loss is very overpowering for the kith and kin and all those who were close to him sharing his vision and values. In this hour of grief I stand by Shri Amar Singh and other members of the bereaved family. Shri Harishchandra Singh is no longer with them in physical form and his passing away has caused a deep void. I deeply mourn his unfortunate passing away and convey my heartfelt condolences to all those who suffered this bereavement. May his soul rest in peace."

5972. (18-2-2008) NEW DELHI : The BJP said here that we are grateful to the Election Commission for giving us time, at such a short notice. Despite being the largest single party in the recently dissolved Karnataka Assembly the BJP has been deprived of the opportunity to serve the people of Karnataka. The party strongly advocates the termination of the President's Rule and the installation of a democratically elected government at an early date. We therefore urge upon the Commission to announce the Poll schedule at an early date and the completion of the Polls before end May. At the same time, the Party is keen to have the Elections conducted on the basis of the recommendations of Delimitation Commission, already gazetted, for Karnataka. BJP has always been urging the early implementation of the recommendations of the Delimitation Commission. There is an apprehension that the Commission may not be able to conduct the polls before end May, once the Presidential notification of the date is issued for making the Delimitation orders operational. We feel that it is not necessary, statutorily or otherwise, for the Commission to wait for the notification for initiating the preparatory work for giving effect to the recommendation of the Delimitation Commission on ground. In Karnataka by and large all assembly constituencies are sited within the same district. It is therefore possible to empower the Deputy Commissioners to restructure the polling booths and allocate the electoral rolls for the ACs falling within his jurisdiction. All the ground work can thus be compressed within a short time frame and the framework kept ready for completing the polls before end May 2008. The BJP is totally opposed to the extension of President's rule in Karnataka, based on specious procedural grounds of the Commission not being in a position to complete the procedural work. We earnestly hope the Commission will rise to the occasion and find administrative solutions for resolving this problem. The Party assures the Commission for all help and assistance that may be required in making this possible.

5973. (18-2-2008) NEW DELHI : Government of India have announced the issue of '7.95 per cent Fertilizer Companies' Government of India Special Bonds, 2026' for Rs.3,610 crore (nominal), The second and final tranche of the Special Bonds are being issued at par to 23 Fertilizer Companies as compensation towards fertilizer subsidy during the current financial year on February 18, 2008 (Monday). The investment in the Special Bonds by the banks will not be reckoned as an eligible investment in Government securities by banks and insurance companies for their statutory requirements. However, such investment by the insurance companies will be eligible to be reckoned as investment under "other Approved Securities" category as defined under Insurance Regulatory and Development Authority (Investment) Regulations, 2000. Further, the investment by the Provident Funds, Gratuity Funds, Superannuation Funds, etc. in the Special Bonds will be treated as an eligible investment under the administrative order of the Ministry of Finance. The Special Bonds will be transferable and eligible for market ready forward transactions (Repo). The bonds, however, will not be an eligible underlying security for ready forward transactions (Repo/Reverse Repo) with the Reserve Bank of India.

5974. (18-2-2008) NEW DELHI : Following is the text of the keynote address delivered by the Defence Minister Shri AK Antony to the National Seminar on "Defence Cooperation as a tool for enhancing National Interest," here today: The most visible manifestation of a strategic relationship between two countries is cooperation in the sphere of defence. Strong political and economic ties between two countries can be further enhanced through closer defence cooperation, provided the potential challenges are identified and addressed and there is clarity on its terminal benefits. Most countries build defence relationships that promote specific national security interests, develop friendly military capabilities for building mutual confidence and trust as also to imbibe 'best practices' for various aspects of defence functioning. Defence cooperation also leads to optimizing action in the field of UN peacekeeping as well as disaster management. Globalization has affected defence as much as any other activity and there is a need to continually find avenues for exchanging points of view with armed forces of other countries, as well as learning from successful innovations being implemented elsewhere. Defence cooperation may be defined as any arrangement between two or more nations where their Armed Forces work together to achieve mutual aims and objectives. This can include exchanges and liaison visits, individual and joint training, joint military exercises, common doctrine and equipment procurement. The objectives of defence cooperation between countries are to promote intra and extra regional peace and stability through dialogue and cooperation in the field of defence and security, to promote mutual understanding on defence and security challenges as well as to enhance transparency and openness and to imbibe 'best practices' in various military fields by observing specific aspects of functioning of the militaries of more advanced countries. Defence cooperation offers a range of benefits. It helps build trust and confidence, as also facilitates cooperation at political and economic level between nations. Expertise available with various militaries can be shared for development of mutual concepts and operational doctrine. Advanced countries have access to superior technology in weaponry and systems. Such technologies can be available to the Armed Forces of developing countries through means of Defence cooperation. Cooperation can be most successful when forces have inter-operable systems and weapons which facilitate functional cooperation when undertaking peacekeeping or disaster management operation together. The efforts of various countries can be optimized in new innovations in rapidly changing operational environment through joint development and production of military equipment. Through Defence cooperation mechanism, countries make mutual arrangements for Promotion of Regional security and economic interests in the maritime zone through protection of Sea Lines of Communication. India has very wide ranging international defence and military cooperation. It has been used as an effective tool of foreign policy and forms one of the main forms of engagement with many countries such as Russia, Singapore, UK, USA, France, Indonesia, Israel, Japan, Mauritius, Myanmar, Maldives, Nepal, Sri Lanka, Bangladesh, South Africa, Tajikistan, Oman and Bhutan. The range of international military cooperation arrangements includes formal defence agreements which could be bilateral or multilateral; bilateral forums for meetings are at the strategic, military and technological levels. Military to military activities include high level visits, attendance at courses at military training institutions, professional defence and military expert exchanges, joint exercises, courses, defence equipment and technology-transfer, military assistance programmes, sports and adventure activity and cooperation in UN Peace Keeping Operations. Obviously, the levels of military cooperation with each and every country cannot be at the same level. These would be dependent on our national interests and our foreign policy goals and priorities. An analysis of the levels of existing cooperation indicates that there is scope for us to further enhance international defence and military cooperation with many countries, particularly those located within India's strategic periphery. India's approach to international defence cooperation has been reasonably effective and is in sync with the national foreign policy. India can claim many successes in this; however, much more can be done to create conditions of peace, stability and security in the region for economic and social development of the country and its people.

5975. (18-2-2008) NEW DELHI : The Plan outlay for the Union Territory of Pondicherry for the year 2008-09 was finalized, here today, at a meeting between the Deputy Chairman Planning Commission, Shri Montek Singh Ahluwalia and the Chief Minister of Pondicherry, Shri N. Rangaswamy. Plan size for the current year was agreed at Rs.1750 crores. Deputy Chairman, Planning Commission, Mr. Montek Singh Ahluwalia complemented the Union Territory for growth in the manufacturing and service sectors. However the GSDP growth rate is less than the national average. Focus should be on improving utilization of resources. The State was complemented for efforts aimed at promoting tourism and involving private sector. Human development indices are better than the national average. Performance in health & education sector is satisfactory. The Commission offered non-lending technical assistance for procuring Master Plan on tourism development. The State was advised to rationalize subsidy and encourage rainwater harvesting. Attention was also drawn to coastal erosion. Mr. Rangaswamy said that the Eleventh Plan will focus on social sector development with allocations stepped up for up-gradation of rural roads, better drinking water supply, slum up-gradation, primary & secondary education, primary health care services and public distribution system. He said infrastructure facilities were being improved to attract investment for industrial development, tourism and IT related industries. Natural resource based integrated farming system model with crop diversification and livestock integration would be promoted.

5976. (18-2-2008) NEW DELHI : In the margins of his visit to Tokyo, where he addressed a high level business summit, Dr. Ashwani Kumar, Minister of State for Industry, called upon former Prime Minister Mr. Shinzo Abe and conveyed to him the greetings of Government and people of India. Dr. Kumar who was the accompanying minister to Prime Minister Abe during the latter's visit to India in August 2007, assured former Prime Minister Abe that India seeks a comprehensive economic and strategic Partnership with Japan, and that India and Japan are on same side in meeting global challenges. Former Prime Minister Abe assured Dr. Kumar that he was committed to making the relationship between India and Japan a special one and that it was his considered view that the new global order in the making warrants a close partnership between India and Japan. Mr. Abe sought India's cooperation in Environment protection and said that he understood India's need to explore alternate sources of clean energy to fuel its economic growth. He informed Dr. Kumar that Japan was looking forward to Prime Minister Manmohan Singh's visit later this year and assured Dr. Kumar that he would personally continue to support all efforts to deepen Indo-Japan relationship. Dr. Kumar also met with Minister Akira Amari the minister for Economy Trade and Industry and discussed the progress in the implementation of dedicated freight corridor and DMIC. Dr. Kumar informed Mr. Amari that India welcomes Japanese investments and Technology in a manner that may be mutually beneficial. He urged Mr. Amari to assist in Japan becoming a large investor in the Indian manufacturing and Food Processing sectors. Dr. Kumar informed Mr. Amari that India was committed to an early conclusion of EPA and for forging a Comprehensive Economic Partnership Agreement with Japan. Mr. Amari assured Dr. Ashwani Kumar of Japanese Govt desire to increase Japanese FDI in India consequent upon liberalization of the FDI norms. He expressed the hope that EPA would be concluded soon so as to give a fillip to the relationship. Dr. Kumar also met Mr. Yushimi Watanabe, Minister for Financial Services and Administrative Reforms and discussed a wide range of issues between India and Japan.

5977. (18-2-2008) NEW DELHI : Congress spokesman Shri Abhishek Singhvi said the president of the BJP Shri Rajnath Singh has proudly announced that he has no regrets over Kandahar. It should not surprise you or us. The basic thought-process, the basic approach of the BJP has never left any scope for improvement and there is no hope for change as far as their mansikta is concerned. Regret, of course, is not a word in their Dictionary. They have no regret about Kandahar, about writing an unprecedented and unheard and an unthinkable chapter in History. They have no regret for creating history of a kind where the Indian Central government sent a senior minister to escort with great care, concern and compassion three of the most dangerous terrorists to Kandahar. They have no regret for the provision of this special escort service which no terrorist, in his wildest and most expectant dreams, could expect or hope for. The BJP has no regrets not only for Kandahar but also not for Kargil. They have no regrets of the fact that throwing dust in the eyes of the NDA government, hundreds of square miles of Indian territory were captured by Pakistan but for the extraordinary bravery and the supreme sacrifice of our brave soldiers we would have had a most insulting end to an act which was not done on Indian territory by Pakistan from 1971 to 1998. The BJP has no regrets over Babri Masjid, over the Lucknow saree scandal and is not disturbed when raj dharma is upset or disturbed in Gujarat and they have no regrets over Tehelka or Judev. The BJP has no regrets for its new-found love, for their new mascot and icon Jinnah. Far from having regrets for their love for Jinnah they have rewarded the supporter of Jinnah with the post of prime minister-in-waiting. If there is any regret which the BJP has, it is for the stoppage in their mad lust for power, in their ambitions, a stoppage put by the fact that the UPA to the regret of the BJP has the common man with it. If only the BJP understood that if they did have regret for their blunders, they would not have been thrown out by the junta in 2004 in the way in which they have been thrown out. To a question that have you sent a reply to the Election Commissioner to their notice on Sonia Gandhi, Shri Singhvi said, we have received the notice a couple of days ago and we have three weeks for the reply. We will give a strong and befitting reply in which we will show that the notice taken as given deserves to be rejected at the threshold, discloses no actionable claim and that it is in the realm of the completely false, frivolous and vexatious complaint. To a question that some sections of the media are blaming Smt. Ambika Soni for escorting Smt. Sonia Gandhi to Belgium, Shri Singhvi said, I have already said that the facts which are clear, available, even taking the complaint as given, do not make a case for notice and there is no question of allocating blame any where. I have said we will give a befitting reply. Smt. Sonia Gandhi has not sought, has not been granted any membership of any association. She has not paid any subscription, she has no pecuniary benefit, she holds no office of profit and to receive a civil decoration and to call it a foreign allegiance or adherence is way of the mark. All this will be elaborated with materials, in our reply which will be sent, within time in due course. To a question that the BJP wants elections in Karnataka and are accusing the Congress Party of using every possible excuse to stop the election, Shri Singhvi said, there is absolutely no warrant for us to react to speculative rumours and reports.

5978. (18-2-2008) NEW DELHI : Addressing a JIBCC, FICCI sponsored Business summit attended by over 200 Japanese companies in Tokyo, Dr. Ashwani Kumar, Minister of State for Industry, called for the need to expand the level of India-Japan economic engagement. Speaking to the Japanese investors, he stated that the present share of Japan in India's global trade was a mere 2.3% in 2006-07. He reminded the Japanese Business leaders, of India's plans to spend 7-8% of

GDP into development of Indian infrastructure which in monetary terms would be of the level of 450 billion USD out of which 150 billion would have to come from the private sectors including foreign investors. Dr. Kumar invited Japanese investment in the development of Indian Power Sector, Civil Aviation, Logistics, Biotechnology, Nano-technology and also in the Agro Processing and Clean technology. Speaking with reference to the DMIC and Delhi Mumbai Freight Corridor, Dr. Kumar said that these two projects are the most ambitious projects ever undertaken by India and that Japan being a partner in the project is a step forward in forging a meaningful Special Economic Partnership between India and Japan. The project involves a capital outlay of USD 90 billion and is expected to generate 3 million additional jobs. Japanese companies, he said are likely to invest USD 5 billion in the DMIC over the next three years.

5979. (18-2-2008) NEW DELHI : Power for All by 2012 is the goal set by the Ministry of Power. This entails provision of adequate reliable power, at affordable cost with access to all citizens. Electricity is a concurrent subject. The primary responsibility of structuring its availability and distribution is of the States. The Government has been facilitating this process through coordinated planning, regional electricity boards, inter-state transmission links and a few central generating stations. With the establishment of major central generating companies like National Thermal Power Corporation (NTPC), National Hydroelectric Power Corporation Ltd. (NHPC), North Eastern Electric Power Corporation (NEEPCO) and the Central Transmission Utility, Powergrid, as well as with the decline in the financial and operational health of State Electricity Boards or other utilities, the role of the Government has got enlarged. Seeing the state of household electrification, particularly in rural areas, the Rajiv Gandhi Grameen Vidyuteekaran Yojana (RGGVY) was launched in 2005. This has been preceded by major intervention schemes like Accelerated Generation and Supply Programme (AG&SP) to boost state sector generation and Accelerated Power Development and Reform Programme (APDRP) to address the severe malady of high Sub Transmission, Distribution and Commercial losses. Along with restructuring the opaque monolithic electricity boards, an independent tariff setting regime under the regulatory commissions has been put in place. There is need for a growing and urgent realization that the power sector is not merely a welfare activity. It is an industrial and commercial venture which must not only be self supporting but also provide for improvements and expansion, besides being an activity which is deemed to be a profitable venture for private investment.

5980. (18-2-2008) NEW DELHI : There are no further reports from the HSADL, Bhopal of any sample testing positive from any part of the country, including West Bengal. No unusual mortality was reported in West Bengal on 17th February, 2008. The latest report from West Bengal reveals that a total of 143 Rapid Response Teams were engaged (9 for surveillance / mopping and 134 for disinfection and sanitization). The cumulative culling of poultry birds stands at 39.05 lakhs.

The cumulative figures of eggs and feed destroyed till 17.02.2008 are 14,90,785 and 80,033 kg respectively. In Assam, the poultry depopulation operation in the identified zone has been completed on 13.02.2008. The progress of preventive culling in Bihar and Jharkhand is continuing. Out of three districts in Bihar, culling has been completed in Purnia and Kishanganj districts. In the third district of Katihar, it is likely to be completed by 20th February, 2008. The preventive culling in Jharkhand involves two districts *viz.* Jamtara and Pakur. The culling was started in the state on 15.02.2008 and has since been completed in Jamtara district. It is expected to commence in Pakur district today.

5981. (18-2-2008) NEW DELHI : The first Indian Ocean Rim Association for Regional Cooperation (IOR-ARC) Film Festival will be hosted in New Delhi from 22nd February, 2008. India had offered to host this Festival at the 7th Council of Ministers Meeting of IOR-ARC held in March 2007. IOR-ARC is a regional cooperation initiative established in Mauritius in March 1997 with the aim of promoting economic and technical cooperation, including expansion of trade and investment and comprises 18 members: Australia, India, Kenya, Mauritius, Oman, Singapore, South Africa, Indonesia, Madagascar, Malaysia, Mozambique, Sri Lanka, Tanzania, Yemen, Bangladesh, Iran, Thailand and United Arab Emirates. There are five Dialogue Partners of IOR-ARC, namely, France, Japan, UK, Egypt and China. (Seychelles withdrew from IOR-ARC in 2003). The IOR-ARC Film Festival is being held at Siri Fort Auditorium in New Delhi from 22 February to 1 March 2008 in partnership with the Directorate of Film Festivals, Ministry of Information and Broadcasting, Government of India. The Minister of State for External Affairs Shri Anand Sharma will inaugurate the Festival on 22 February, 2008 at 1830 hrs. at Siri Fort Auditorium. Ten films are being screened at the Festival from IOR-ARC member countries, *viz.* Australia, Bangladesh, Iran, Mauritius, Sri Lanka, Thailand, Kenya, South Africa, Tanzania and India. The Australian film "Yolngu Boy" has been selected to be screened at the inauguration. The Directors of the films from Australia, Mauritius and Bangladesh are expected to be present at the time of inauguration of the Film Festival and the directors of the films from Kenya and Tanzania on the concluding day on the 1st of March 2008.

5982. (18-2-2008) NEW DELHI : The Chief Minister of Uttar Pradesh, Kum. Mayawati called on Prime Minister, Dr. Manmohan Singh to discuss issues pertaining to development of the State. The Prime Minister assured the Chief Minister of Uttar Pradesh that the Central Government will take all necessary steps to promote the development of the State and the welfare of the people of Uttar Pradesh. The Prime Minister referred to the special group he had constituted for preparing a road map for the rapid economic development of UP under the Chairmanship of Shri B.K. Chaturvedi, Member, Planning Commission. He assured the Chief Minister that a special plan for development of Bundelkhand region will be prepared with the help of the Planning Commission. The Prime Minister also drew attention to financial allocation made to the State under various Central Government programmes, including Bharat Nirman, National Rural Employment Guarantee Scheme, National Rural Health Mission, Sarva Shiksha Abhiyan, Jawaharlal Nehru National Urban Renewable Mission and Roads, Railways and Power Development Projects. He hoped these programmes will be properly implemented by the State Government. The total resources available to the State under 11th Plan will be Rs.2,80,000 crore amounting to 3.5 times the resources made available in the 10th Five Year Plan. Central assistance alone will be over Rs.80,000 crore during the Plan period. The Prime Minister also assured the Chief Minister that the State's energy and connectivity needs will be met. He said that a Group of Ministers is presently considering the proposal for setting up an International Airport in Gautambudh Nagar district.

5983. (18-2-2008) NEW DELHI : Addressing the Parliamentary Consultative Committee Meeting of the Ministry of Commerce & industry, here on Friday (15th February) evening on "Industrial Infrastructure Development", Shri Kamal Nath, Union Minister of Commerce and Industry, has said that "it will be our endeavour to fine tune our strategies and develop a more holistic and integrated approach towards the development of infrastructure for Industry. He indicated that the government has taken several initiatives to provide a fillip to the development of industrial infrastructure. Some of these initiatives, particularly the Industrial Infrastructure Upgradation Scheme (IIUS), can be seen as successful interventions. Members who participated in the meeting were: S/Shri Sambasiva Rao; Ram Singh Kaswan; P. Karunakaran; Sudhangshu Seal; Rajeev Shukla; Sharad Joshi; Shantaram Naik, M. Rajasekara Murthi and Naresh Gujral. Dr. Ashwani Kumar, Minister of State for Industry, Shri Ajay Shankar, Secretary, Department of Industrial Policy and Promotion; and Shri G.K. Pillai, Commerce Secretary also attended the meeting. While welcoming the Members Shri Kamal Nath explained that the primary responsibility for development of infrastructure vests with the State Government and State Industrial Development Corporations provide basic infrastructure to industrial units by setting up industrial estates in self-contained geographical areas. Most State Governments have set up industrial estates and the experience so far has been mixed. The Central Government also supplements the efforts of the State Government through various schemes for the development of industrial infrastructure. The Minister underlined that the IIUS launched recently, focused on infrastructure upgradation of existing industrial clusters. 25 projects are currently under implementation and 5 of these projects are nearing completion. "We expect this scheme to continue in the 11th Plan with suitable modifications based on the outcome of the ongoing critical evaluation", he said. As regards the Industrial Park Scheme, the Minister stated that Income Tax exemption is available to infrastructure developers for any ten consecutive years out of fifteen years beginning from the year in which the eligible projects commence operation. The response to this scheme has been good and it is estimated that close to Rs.14000 crore have been invested towards the creation of infrastructure for industry.

Explaining the recent initiatives, Shri Kamal Nath said: "We have also initiated a novel approach for infrastructure development along the proposed Delhi-Mumbai Rail Freight Corridor through creation of high impact/market driven nodes such as Integrated Investment Regions (IRs) and Industrial Areas (IAs). These nodes/ regions are proposed to be self-sustained industrial townships with world-class infrastructure, road and rail connectivity for freight movement to and from ports and logistics hubs, served by domestic/international air connectivity, reliable power, quality social infrastructure so as to provide a globally competitive environment for setting up businesses". Shri Joshi, Rajasekara Murthy, Sudhangshu Seal and Ram Singh Kaswan stressed the need for further investments in the industrial infrastructure for a balanced growth of industry in all areas and particularly the backward areas. Shri Naresh Gujral desired that the focus should be given to skill development for enabling youth to get the jobs. Shri Rajeev Shukla and Shri Shantaram Naik drew the attention towards real estate valuation in setting up of industrial estates and requested for exploring the possibilities for development of industrial infrastructure on wastelands. Shri Sambasiva Rao thanked the Minister for approving the Spice Park at Guntur (Andhra Pradesh). Shri Kamal Nath noted all the points while seeking further guidance from the Members for development of industrial infrastructure.

5984. (19-2-2008) NEW DELHI : The Union Minister for Rural Development, Dr. Raghuvansh Prasad Singh informed the Members of the Consultative Committee that various flagship programmes of the Ministry are doing well and asked members for their active participation to achieve further success. He was addressing the members of the Consultative Committee attached to his Ministry in New Delhi, yesterday. The Minister asked the Members to study any shortcomings in the implementation of programmes, like National Rural Employment Guarantee Programme (NREGP), Pradhan Mantri Gram Sadak Yojana (PMGSY), Total Sanitation Campaign (TSC) and Swarnjayanti Gram Swarozgar Yojana (SGSY) and bring it to the notice of the Ministry. He appreciated the work done under various programmes and informed the members that the Ministry of Rural Development in coordination with the Government is very close to achieving the targets. He also informed the members that NREGP, which is a demand-based programme is doing very well in most of the States. However, there are certain problems in its implementation at some places, as also pointed out by the Draft CAG report & various Social Audit Groups and the Ministry is taking all possible steps to remove these problems. The Ministry is in touch with the respective State Governments and monitoring the situation very closely. The Members raised various points about category of work to be offered under NREGA, minimum wages to be paid, the enhancement of minimum wages at certain places where it is very low, increase in the cost of construction of latrines in rural households and definition of BPL families. Some Members also raised the issue of diversion of funds under NREGP to various other programmes of the State Governments, in some States. The Minister assured that the matter will be looked into and action will be taken accordingly. The Ministry of Rural Development presented a Power Point Presentation to the Members about the achievements during 2007-08 under various programmes and also suggestions for improvement.

5985. (19-2-2008) NEW DELHI : The First meeting of the 'Committee on State Agrarian Relations and the Unfinished Task in land Reforms' took place under the Chairmanship of Dr. Raghuvansh Prasad Singh, Union Minister for Rural Development in New Delhi today. The terms of reference of the Committee were finalized in consultation with the Members of the Committee. Welcoming the Members the Minister said that the Government gives greater emphasis on the effective implementation of the various components and schemes of Land Reforms so that the benefits reach the gross root level. The Government has urged the Chief Ministers of the States for having a thorough review of implementation of Land Reform programmes and schemes as land reform related issues essentially fall in the domain of the State Governments. However, in order to give comprehensive recommendations on the matter the Centre has constituted the Committee, which met under the chairmanship of the Minister today. The Minister said that wasteland at the disposal of the Government should be distributed to the eligible rural poor and the Central Government will make every effort in helping States to achieve the targets. In some States the Bhudan movement has met with considerable success. Tenancy Reform and Prevention of alienation and restoration of alienated tribal lands in another important area of the programme. The Members raised various uses like ensuring the responsibility and accountability, transfer of land by market forces, ecological factors, market oriented solutions, implementation of Act in tribal areas, the role of Panchayati Raj in implementation of Land Reform Policy. The Minister asked the officials to incorporate all the suggestions of the Members in the terms of reference. Five sub-groups were formed by the Committee to work in detail on various aspects of the Land Reforms Policy, which will help in achieving the Agrarian reform, and to complete the Land Reform programme. Some of the Members who attended the meeting were S/Shri T. Haque, V.K. Pipersenia, R.D. Munda, K.P. Saxena, P.K. Jha, Subhash Lomte, A.K. Singh and Ms. Nilima Khaitan and other members of the Committee. Secretary (LR), Ms. Rita Sinha coordinated the meeting.

5986. (19-2-2008) NEW DELHI : The Annual Plan of Punjab for the year 2008-09 has been approved in a meeting between the Deputy Chairman, Planning Commission, Shri Montek Singh Ahluwalia and the Chief Minister of Punjab Sardar Prakash Singh Badal, here today. The Annual Plan size was agreed at Rs.6210 crores. This includes additional Central assistance of Rs.200 crores for projects of special interest to the State. Deputy Chairman, Planning Commission, Mr. Ahluwalia complemented the State for the initiatives taken to ensure inclusive growth and efforts to encourage private sector participation in development. He said initiatives aimed at rejuvenating agriculture, skill development and manufacturing sector are steps in the right direction. The State Government was asked to take lead in agro-marketing and amend APMC. Emphasis should be on skill up-gradation through public private partnership, crop diversification, genetic up-gradation of major crops and power sector reforms. It was pointed out that policy of free power needs to be reviewed as it was leading to over exploitation of ground water. The State's efforts to improve growth rate and catch up with the national trend was appreciated. In his comments on development programme, Shri Badal appreciated the initiatives of the Central Government like skill development mission and setting up of international airport at Chandigarh. On development policy of the State, he said it would focus on removing intra-regional imbalances, generation of productive employment, improving quality of life by providing better health care facilities, sanitation, safe drinking water, education and greater access to food. He said focus would be on improving performance on social indicators to match its economic progress. Concerns of the development of women & children will be addressed with greater emphasis and more attention would be given to economic and social advancement of under privileged and disadvantaged groups. He said to improve employability of Punjab youth a new department of employment generation has been created and focused attention is being given to improving delivery of public services in the health education sectors. High priority will be given to energy sector and social services. Shri Badal requested for enhancement of Grant under Indira Awas Yojana to Rs.50000 each from present level of Rs.15,000/-. He also requested for setting up of an IIT & IIM in the State. Extension of freight corridor to Wagah was also suggested.

5987. (19-2-2008) NEW DELHI : Union Minister of Power, Shri Sushil Kumar Shinde today called upon the States and Union Territories to jointly address the various issues and problems facing the power sector. Addressing the Conference of the Chief Secretaries of all States and Union Territories in New Delhi he said that the Government is fully committed to achieving the target of quality power for all, at an affordable rate by the end of 11th Plan. However, the States also have to play a major role in achieving this goal. He said that the set target of capacity addition of 78,577 MW for the 11th Plan period can be possible only if there is rigorous monitoring of various milestones in the implementation of each and every project. The Central Government is monitoring the capacity addition programme very closely. However, success cannot be assured unless the State Governments also participate in the process actively. Observing that over the last four decades, the Central share in the generation has been constantly increasing while that of the States has been decreasing the Minister made it clear that States should actively pursue their capacity addition programmes and not depend only on the Central Sector or Private Sector projects. Shri Shinde also pointed out that thought it was unanimously decided that placement of orders for power projects proposed to be commissioned during 11th Plan had to be completed by December 2007, the orders for projects aggregating to 11,125 MW in the State sector are yet to be placed. He told the representatives of the States to ensure that all the orders are placed latest by 31st March 2008. To reduce the AT&C losses to less than 15%, the Minister suggested better governance and administrative practices, restructuring of utilities to make them more focused, deployment of better manpower and use of better technology. Emphasizing the need for concerted efforts to ensure that every village is electrified by 2009 and every household has electricity connection by 2012 Shri Shinde advised the States to pay closer attention to their capacity addition programme. For the 11th Plan, he said, the allocation for the Rajiv Gandhi Grameen Vidyutikaran Yojana has been enhanced to Rs. 28,000 crores. The Minister informed that the scheme has been extended to cover habitations with population of 100 and above and now it is also stipulated that prior to release of any subsidy under RGGVY, the State Government has to guarantee a minimum daily supply of 6-8 hours of electricity in the RGGVY network. He said that the States have to be very pro-active in the implementation of RGGVY. They need to actively pre-empt bottlenecks in supply of materials. On open access in transmission and distribution Shri Shinde observed that while Central transmission utility has fully operationalised open access in transmission the same cannot be said about the States. He urged the States to prepare a clear programme for the expansion and strengthening of their transmission and distribution systems with definite timelines and monitor their implementation closely. Earlier, Secretary, Ministry of Power, Shri Anil Razdan welcomed the delegates. Secretary, Ministry of New & Renewable Energy, Shri V. Subramanian and several heads of CPSUs under the Power Ministry were also present on the occasion. The day long Conference was convened by the Ministry of Power to discuss several issues related to power sector under various themes such as accelerated capacity addition, reduction of AT&C losses, rural electrification, implementation of open access in transmission and distribution, strengthening intra-state transmission and distribution under the state sector and grid interactive solar PV power generation, etc.

5988. (19-2-2008) NEW DELHI : BEML Limited, a Defence PSU has declared an interim dividend of 55% for the current financial year. Announcing this in New Delhi today, the CMD Shri VRS Natarajan said that this is a new record by the company. He said during the last financial year, BEML has paid 40% interim dividend. Shri Natarajan said, BEML Limited has an MoU target of 2756 crores for FY 07-08. Referring to the latest products developed by the company and displayed in the DefExpo-08, Shri Natarajan said these include Command Post Vehicle, TATRA Driving Simulator, Armoured Recovery vehicle built in collaboration with M/s. Bumar, Poland, Crash Fire Tender built in collaboration with M/s. Tatra UK, and Weapon Loading System (BHIMA). He said the company is displaying for the first time aircraft towing tractor with ground power unit and Pontoon End shore section and road laying section built indigenously with 100% indigenous R&D efforts. BEML has emerged as a major base for manufacture and supply of various land and ground support equipments and critical aggregates in the country. With BEML planning to increase its contribution to defence sector. The company has been making strenuous efforts diversifying the portfolio of products in Defence. BEML also provides effective logistics support to the armed forces in terms of training of service men and stocking of spare parts across the country. Referring to the new technology tie ups, he informed that BEML has signed Memorandum of Association with General Dynamics, Canada for four wheeled Armoured Patrol Vehicle (Duro APV MK III). This vehicle is Small Arms and mine protected. This MoU will be for producing & Marketing for Indian and global market. He also said that BEML has signed MoA with M/s. WFEL, UK to offer 46 mtrs Dry Support Bridges to Indian Army. Shri Natarajan said that BEML has extended the MoU with M/s. TATRA SIPOX,UK for Technology transfer, production and marketing of 20 tons to 25 tons capacity Tippers to Indian Metal, Mining & Coal Market. This range of vehicle have great demand in Mining sector and M/s. TATRA has also agreed to offer the complete ToT for BS II Engines for 4x 4, 6x6 and 8x 8 BEML TATRA Defence Trucks for India with global outsourcing for overseas market.

5989. (19-2-2008) NEW DELHI : The Minister of State for Defence Shri MM Pallam Raju visited the DefExpo India-2008 here today. He showed keen interest in the exhibits and praised the efforts of Defence PSUs like BEML, BEL, BDL, Mazagon Docks Ltd, Garden Reach Shipbuilders and Engineers (GRSE) and others. Shri Pallam Raju appreciated the indigenization efforts of the DRDO and the 39 Ordnance Factories which are participating in a big way at the DefExpo. He commended the Defence Exhibition Organisation for drawing a good response from major defence manufacturers worldwide for India's biennial exposition on land and naval weapons and systems. With foreign manufacturers now keen to share the hitherto highly guarded and hi-tech weaponry, Shri Pallam Raju hoped the Indian DPSUs and the private sector would take advantage of the Offsets in the Defence Procurement Procedure, which would be liberalised further, and form joint ventures to indigenously produce defence hardware. The DefExpo was conceptualised in the year 1998 by the Department of Defence Production in partnership with the Confederation of Indian Industry (CII) with an objective to promote defence exports from India and at the same time exhibit the capabilities of Indian Defence R&D and production. The Def Expo India exhibition which began in 1999 with 197 exhibitors has grown to one of the most internationally recognised defence exhibitions in the world, with a total of 475 exhibitors, of which foreign exhibitors are 273 and Indian exhibitors are 202. Dedicated to global land and naval systems business activity-from suppliers to manufacturers, technology providers to services-it allows the international defence industry to promote and showcase their products and services. For the first time in the 5th Defexpo India'08, Telecom and IT companies also showcased their products and services which find wide application in today's network centric warfare. Over 30 countries participated in the DefExpo this year, including the US, Russia, Israel, UK, France, Germany, Italy, Poland, Russia, South Africa, Sweden and Ukraine. 47 official delegations, including 6 ministerial delegations from Afghanistan, Belarus, Ghana, Mozambique, Namibia and Nigeria, visited the four-day DefExpo, which came to a close today.

5990. (19-2-2008) NEW DELHI : Shri Subodh Kant Sahai, Minister for Food Processing Industries said Institute of Crop Processing Technology will help the farmers to get better profit for their products. He laid foundation stone for the Institute of Crop Processing Technology at Thanjavur in Tamil Nadu. Shri Sahai further said this Institute is step towards Intensive focused and comprehensive Research and Development initiatives for the food processing sector specializing in post harvest processing technologies, processes and products in food grains. The Central Government allotted fifty crore for the Institute for the construction of additional building, procurement of equipments and creation of new post for scientist, he added. On this occasion Union Minister for Shipping and Road Transport, Shri T. R. Balu said the Institute will be a boon to the Paddy sector in Tamil Nadu. This Institute will have provision for primary processing, storage handling and product development. A technology dissemination centre and food analysis lab will be an added attraction to the Institute. Shri Balu further said that it will serve as a centre for research education and training in the area of post harvest, processing of crops of wet land, flood, cyclone and storm prone areas. The major objectives of the Institute are reduction of post harvest losses in paddy, millets, pulses and oilseeds and establish processing divisions for these crops. On this occasion Union Minister of State for Finance, Shri S. S. Palanimanickam and Minister for Commercial Tax of State Shri S. N. M. Ubayadulla were present.

5991. (19-2-2008) NEW DELHI : Government has issued Notification No. 3/2008-ST, dated 19.02.2008, extending the scheme to refund service tax paid by exporters on taxable services, which are not in the nature of "input services" but could be linked to export of goods, to following three more taxable services: (i) Services provided by the Goods Transport Agency in relation to transportation of export goods from the place of removal to the actual place of export *i.e.* inland container depot / port / airport. (Section 65[105][zzp]), (ii) Services provided in relation to transportation of export goods in containers by rail from the place of removal to the actual place of export *i.e.* inland container depot / port / airport. (Section 65[105][zzzp]) (iii) Courier Services provided to an exporter in relation to transportation of documents, goods or articles relating to export, to a destination outside India. (Section 65[105][f] of the Finance Act, 1994)

5992. (19-2-2008) NEW DELHI : A total eclipse of the Moon will occur in the early morning of Thursday, the 21st February 2008 (2 Phalguna 1929 Saka Era) from 0713 Hrs to 1039 Hrs IST. The eclipse is visible in the region covering Arctic, western parts of Asia, most of Arabia, Africa except Madagascar, Europs and the Americas. The beginning of the umbral phase will be visible from the Indian Ocean, Crozet Island, Mauritius, Maldives, extreme north Western tip of Indian and western parts of Russia. The ending will be visible from the Pacific ocean, western parts of Alaska and extreme north eastern parts of Russia.

5993. (19-2-2008) NEW DELHI : The Railways have generated Rs. 38292.04 crore of revenue earnings from freight traffic during the first ten months (*i.e.* April

2007-January 2008) of the current financial year 2007-08 as compared to Rs. 34087.14 crore during the corresponding period last year, registering an increase of 12.34 per cent. Railways carried 643.70 million tonnes of freight traffic during April 2007-January 2008 as compared to 593.67 million tonnes carried during the corresponding period last year, reflecting an increase of 8.43 per cent. The Net Tonne Kilo Metres (NTKM) went up from 389211 million during the months of April 2006-January 2007 to 415432 million during April 2007-January 2008, with an increase of 6.74 per cent. The earnings from freight traffic during the month of January 2008 was Rs. 4534.15 crore, compared to Rs. 3844.30 crore during the corresponding period last year showing an increase of 17.94 per cent. Railways carried 72.35 million tonnes of freight traffic during the month of January 2008 as compared to 65.74 million tonnes of freight traffic during the corresponding period last year, registering an increase of 10.05 per cent. The Net Tonne Kilo Metres (NTKM) went up from 42950 million during the month of January 2007 to 47829 million during January 2008, showing an increase of 11.36 per cent. Of the total earnings during the month of January 2008, Rs. 1681.31 crore came from transportation of 30.65 million tonnes of coal, followed by Rs. 745.28 crore from 12.26 million tonnes of iron ore, Rs. 377.56 crore from 3.99 million tonnes of foodgrains, Rs. 375.47 crore from 7.24 million tonnes of cement, Rs. 249.41 crore from 2.39 million tonnes of iron & finished steel, Rs. 254.94 crore from 3.06 million tonnes of petroleum oil and lubricant (POL), Rs. 214.35 crore from 3.24 million tonnes of fertilizers, Rs. 182.17 crore from 2.45 million tones of container service, Rs. 74.70 crore from 1.07 million tonnes of raw material for steel plants except iron ore and Rs. 378.96 crore from 6.00 million tonnes of other goods.

5994. (19-2-2008) NEW DELHI : The scheme of "Flood Management Programme" under state sector has been approved with an estimated cost of Rs. 8000 crore during 11th plan period (2007-12). Under the scheme, State Governments will be provided necessary assistance for taking up works for river management, flood control, anti-erosion, drainage development, flood proofing works and restoration of damaged flood management works in the critical reaches in the whole country. The scheme will also cover the remaining works recommended by Task Force on Flood Management/Erosion Control 2004 in Ganga Basin and Brahmaputa Basin. Under the scheme, the proposals received from the State Governments having all mandatory clearances will be considered for central assistance by a committee headed by Secretary (Finance) on the following approved funding pattern : For Special category-90 per cent central and 10 per cent State; for Non-special category-75 per cent central and 25 per cent State; and for Restoration of damaged works(all states)-90 per cent central and 10 per cent state.

5995. (19-2-2008) NEW DELHI : The Ministry of Tribal Affairs has stressed the need for implementation of Forest Rights Act in time bound manner and urged the States to complete the preliminary work for identification of beneficiaries by the mid of March, 2008. In two day meeting of State Secretaries of Tribal Development concluded here today the Secretary of the Ministry of Tribal affairs, Shri G.B. Mukherji said that the Centre gives very high priority for the implementation of Scheduled Tribes and Other Traditional Forest Dwellers (Recognition of Forest Rights) Act, 2006 and urged the States to draw action plan and set up effective monitoring mechanism at various levels for continuous review of the implementation of the Act. Chairing the meeting, Shri G.B. Mukherji reviewed the progress of the implementation of the Act so far and explained various points related with its implementation. The meeting was also addressed by Secretary, Ministry of Panchayati Raj and senior officials of the Ministry of Environment and Forests. Making presentations of the preparatory actions already taken towards the implementation of the Forest Rights Act, most of the States ensured that exercise of convening Gram Sabha meetings would be initiated from 28th February, 2008 and will be completed by mid of the next month. The actionable points for the States and the roles of the Ministries of Environment & Forests and Panchayati Raj as envisaged in the Act were also explained in the meeting. The representative of the Ministry of Environment & Forest pointed out that the Forest Rights Act was also recently discussed in a meeting of the State Forest Secretaries/PCCFs/CWLWs organized by that Ministry last week. He explained the role of the Ministry of Environment & Forests in implementation of the Act and highlighted certain issues from the forestry angle. Secretary (Panchayati Raj) stated that the provisions of the Forest Rights Act and the rules framed thereunder were in complete harmony with the PESA Act and the Act needed to be implemented in its letter and spirit.

5996. (20-2-2008) NEW DELHI : The Prime Minister, Dr. Manmohan Singh, has condoled the passing away of Prof. Amaresh Bagchi. The PM in his condolence message described Prof. Bagchi as one of our most distinguished and influential fiscal policy experts. The text of the PM's condolence message is as follows: "I learnt with profound sadness the news of the passing away of Prof. Amaresh Bagchi. I had the privilege of knowing him for a long time in various capacities. Prof. Bagchi was one of our most distinguished and influential fiscal policy analysts and experts. He has left a lasting imprint both in the field of academic research in fiscal policy as well as on public policy formulation. It is no exaggeration to state that Amaresh has been associated with almost every major fiscal policy reform of the past thirty years. As Member of the Finance Commission, he contributed to major policy initiatives in the field of Centre-State Finances. In his passing away, the country loses the experience and knowledge of one of our most distinguished fiscal policy experts. Prof. Amaresh Bagchi was a true nationalist and a patriot deeply committed to the welfare of our people. I wish to convey my heartfelt condolences to Smt. Ratna Bagchi and to his children and other members of his family and his many students, colleagues and friends."

5997. (20-2-2008) NEW DELHI : The Vice President of India Mohd. Hamid Ansari called upon the people to change their attitude towards female child and reiterated that the age long problem of female foeticide should be rooted out completely from our society as it is a curse. Inaugurating a function "Kanyabhrun Hatya Ke Khilaf Sarvdharm Maha Abhiyan Samaroh" organized by National Integration Committee here today, he said that mere framing rules will not serve the purpose and the people at large will have to be motivated against it. It is not only inhuman but badly affecting our society also. He expressed his happiness that now the society has been awakened to root out this problem. He congratulated the organizers of the function to start this noble cause as a movement The Vice President received a copy of the book entitled "The Unborn Curse" by Acharaya Shri Lokesh on the occasion. The founder of Ahimsa Vishwa Bharti Acharya Shri Lokesh in his address cautioned that if the problem of female foeticide is not solved in time it may have more dangerous consequences than Aids or Cancer. The root cause of this social evil will have to be found. Shahi Imam of Fatehpuri Masjid, Dr. Mufti Mohd. Mukarram and the Chief Editor of Rajasthan Patrika Shri Gulab Kothari also addressed. A number of dignitaries were present on the occasion.

5998. (20-2-2008) NEW DELHI : The All-India Consumer Price Index Number for Agricultural Labourers (Base: 1986-87=100) for January, 2008 remained stationary at 413 (Four hundred and thirteen) points while it increased by 1 point to stand at 414 (Four hundred and fourteen) points for Rural Labourers. The rise/ fall in index varied from State to State. In the case of Agricultural Labourers, 9 States reflected an increase in index ranging between 1 and 5 points; in 10 States the declining trend in index ranged between 1 and 9 points while in 1 State *i.e.* Haryana, the index remained constant. Haryana with 441 points topped the index table whereas Manipur was at the bottom with the index level of 366 points. In the case of Rural Labourers, in 9 States, index reflected an increase ranging between 1 and 4 points; in 9 States the declining trend in index ranged between 1 and 9 points whereas in 2 States the index remained constant. Haryana and Punjab were at the top of the index table with 439 points each whereas Manipur was at the bottom with 367 points. The Consumer Price Index Number of Kerala for Agricultural Labourers registered the highest increase of 5 points whereas in the case of Rural Labourers Kerala, Manipur and Rajasthan experienced the highest increase of 4 points each mainly due to increase in the prices of rice, wheat atta, fish fresh/dry, milk, mustard oil, gingelly oil, pan leaf, firewood and cinema ticket. On the other hand, the indices in respect of Tripura registered the highest fall of 9 points each for Agricultural Labourers and Rural Labourers mainly due to decrease in the prices of rice, mustard oil, poultry, fish fresh, onion and vegetables & fruits. Point to point rate of inflation based on the CPI-AL decreased from 5.90% during December, 2007 to 5.63% in January, 2008 whereas it increased from 5.63% during December, 2007 to 5.88% in January, 2008 for Rural Labourers.

5999. (20-2-2008) NEW DELHI : There are no further reports from the HSADL, Bhopal of any sample testing positive from any part of the country, including West

Bengal. No unusual mortality was reported in West Bengal on 19th February, 2008. The latest report brings out that a total of 173 Rapid Response Teams (RRTs) were engaged (19 for surveillance / mopping and 154 for disinfection and sanitization). The cumulative culling of poultry birds is 39.05 lakhs. The cumulative total of eggs and feed destroyed till 19.02.2008 are 14,90,785 and 80,033 kg respectively. There is also no change in the amount of compensation of Rs. 8.40 crores (approx.) paid to the affected families; which was reported yesterday. In Assam, the poultry depopulation operation in the identified zone has been completed on 13.02.2008. Out of three districts in Bihar, culling has been completed in Purnia and Kishanganj districts. There are five blocks in Katihar district involved in the preventive culling. The exercise has been completed in four of the five blocks. The task is also expected to be completed in the remaining block today. In Jharkhand, culling has been completed in Jamtara district, as already reported. The exercise is currently in progress in Pakur district, which is also expected to be completed by 21.02.2008. No culling has yet been taken up in Orissa. The Reserve Bank of India has issued guidelines to the banks on 19th February 2008 for implementation of relief measures for poultry industry. These include, one year's moratorium on repayment of outstanding loans, conversion of working capital loans into term loans and reschedulement of term loans, etc.

6000. (20-2-2008) NEW DELHI : Direct tax collections continued to record a growth of over 40 percent for the 1st April 2007 to 15th February 2008 in the current fiscal. Net direct tax collections stood at Rs.2,28,745 crore, up from Rs.1,61,776 crore during the same period last fiscal, registering a growth of 41.40 percent and achieving over 85 percent of budgeted direct tax target of Rs.2,67,490 crore. Corporate Tax registered a growth of 38.78 percent at Rs.1,38,073 crore, up from Rs.99,488 crore during the previous fiscal, while Personal Income Tax (including FBT, STT and BCTT) grew by 45.64 percent at Rs.90,356 crore, up from Rs.62,040 crore. Growth in Securities Transaction Tax (STT) was 84.64 percent (Rs.7,878 crore against Rs.4,267 crore) and Fringe Benefit Tax (FBT) was 29.75 percent (Rs.5,216 crore against Rs.4,020 crore). Banking Cash Transaction Tax (BCTT) grew by 16.81 percent (Rs.478 crore against Rs.409 crore). Mumbai region has recorded the highest overall growth at Rs.83,363 crore compared to Rs.50,227 crore in the same period last fiscal (*i.e.* 65.97 percent) and its contribution to the direct tax collections in the country so far is 36.86 percent. Among type of taxes, self-assessment tax (paid voluntarily before filing of tax return) recorded a growth of 62.9 percent while tax deducted / collected at source recorded a growth of 51.9 percent, indicating improved tax administration and better tax compliance levels.

6001. (20-2-2008) NEW DELHI : The BJP is committed for providing 33% reservation for women in Parliament and the state assemblies. The BJP is the only party in the country to provide 33% reservation for women within the organisation and has recently in the National Council Meeting amended its Constitution for implementing this change. Further to the National Council meeting, the BJP Mahila Morcha is organizing a huge women national rally on 21st February at the Ramlila Maidan in New Delhi with the objective to pressurize the UPA government to table the Women's Reservation bill in Parliament. This rally is being attended by about 1 lakh women workers of the party from each and every corner of the country. Women participants from Uttar Pradesh, Rajasthan, Maharashtra, Bihar, Haryana, Punjab, Chandigarh, Delhi, Madhya Pradesh, Gujarat, Jharkhand, Karnatak, Tamil Nadu, Kerala, Andhra Pradesh, Goa, Mumbai, Orissa including North-Eastern states have either already reached or will be reaching the capital in thousands to participate in this historic rally for their rights. In addition to these states, women from Laskshyadweep, Daman Dio, Dadra, Nagar Haweli and Andaman Nicobar Islands are also participating in this great congregation of women. Many of them have already reached Delhi. All the major arrangements for the rally have been completed. The delegates coming by road will be welcomed at the borders of Delhi and thereafter will be guided to their respective accommodations. The stay arrangements have been made at the Ramlila Maidan and also at the residences of party workers of the Delhi State BJP. Food arrangements for all delegates have also been made at the residences of party workers. All the members of the BJP National Executive have also been invited to participate in the rally. The Senior National Leaders of the party, who would be addressing this rally include Sh. L.K. Advani, Leader of Opposition Lok Sabha, Sh. Rajnath Singh, All India President of the BJP, Smt. Sushma Swaraj, Ms. Vasundhara Raje, CM of Rajasthan, Smt. Sumitra Mahajan, & the National Incharge, BJP Mahila Morcha, Dr. Najma Heptullah, Smt. Mridula Sinha and Smt. Jaywanti Ben Mehta, Smt. Maya Singh, Smt. Surma Padhey, Smt. Kanta Nalawade, Ex-National Presidents of BJP Mahila Morcha among others. Women and development are synonyms to each other. No nation can boast of comprehensive development without the upliftment of the women. History provides ample examples that whenever and wherever women have been ignored, that society and that country has not been able to keep pace with the development in the world. Therefore, the BJP believes that now when the party has resolved to ensure that this 50% segment of our population now will be involved in the decision making process, nothing can stop women from coming forward. The party also condemns the manner in which women are being ignored and sidelined because of the bad governance of UPA and Congress government. The BJP will is committed that the women of this country should regain their lost glory and dignity, which the other political parties have consistently been holding back. The BJP is of the firm belief that the all round upliftment of women is a must for a prosperous and developed nation.

6002. (20-2-2008) NEW DELHI : In a significant development towards setting up a world-class petroleum technology institute in India, Smt Sonia Gandhi, Member of Parliament and UPA Chairperson laid the foundation stone of Rajiv Gandhi Institute of Petroleum Technology (RGIPT) at Jais, near Raebareli in Uttar Pradesh on 20th February 2008. The Ministry of Petroleum and Natural Gas piloted the enactment of the Rajiv Gandhi Institute of Petroleum Technology (RGIPT) Act 2007 with a view to incorporate RGIPT as an 'Institute of National Importance' under an Act of Parliament having a governance structure as well as legal empowerment to grant degrees in a manner similar to that enjoyed by the IITs. Special function held for the purpose was presided over by Shri Rahul Gandhi, Member of Parliament. Shri Murli Deora, Minister of Petroleum and Natural Gas and Shri Dinsha Patel, Minister of State for Petroleum and Natural Gas were also present with senior officers of the Ministry and oil PSUs. The Rajiv Gandhi Institute of Petroleum Technology (RGIPT) is envisaged to serve as the fountainhead for nurturing world class technical human resources capable of serving as the leaders and innovators of tomorrow in the field of Petroleum Technology. The total estimated capital cost of the project is Rs.435 crore which would be met partially through budgetary support of Rs. 285 crore and Rs.150 crore from Oil Industry Development Board. The total estimated recurring expenditure of Rs. 260.58 crore would be met from the accrual of interest on Endowment Fund of Rs. 250 crore to be created with the contribution of Oil Public Sector Undertakings (PSUs), student fees, donations and other earnings of the Institute through Research & Development, consultancies, students' placement fees, etc. The Institute is envisaged to be self sufficient and self-reliant by the year 2015-16. It may be noted that the year 1999 witnessed the advent of the New Exploration Licensing Policy which has been progressively made more and more attractive. This policy has evoked great enthusiasm among foreign companies as well as Indian private and public sector companies for acquiring exploration acreages in India. As on date, only 30% of the sedimentary basins in India has been explored. It is planned to increase the exploration coverage to an extent of 100% by the year 2015. In this context, apart from technology, availability of adequate number of qualified personnel would be a prime requirement in the coming years. In a recent study conducted by consultant PriceWaterhouseCoopers for Petrofed, the gap between the availability and requirement of trained manpower in India is projected to be about 36,000 by the year 2019 and the existing institutes may not be adequate to meet the increasing requirement of technical manpower in the petroleum sector. The proposed Rajiv Gandhi Institute of Petroleum Technology is expected to meet this shortfall to a significant extent. The Institute will commence its academic operations by admitting students from the academic year 2008-09. To start with, there will be two undergraduate courses namely B. Tech. in Petroleum Production & Reservoir and B. Tech. in Petroleum Refining and one MBA course on Petroleum Management. The Institute will become fully operational in 2015-16and would have 7 B. Tech, 6 Integrated Masters Degrees, 8 M.Tech/MBA and 12 PGD and Ph.D programmes. It is proposed that RGIPT would have a high degree of autonomy in terms of its academic, administrative and financial functioning.

6003. (20-2-2008) NEW DELHI : The Project for Repair, Renovation and Restoration (RRR) of Water bodies is being expanded throughout the country with external assistance. The World Bank Loan agreement has been signed with Tamil Nadu for Rs. 2182 crore to restore 5763 water bodies having a Culturable Command Area (CCA) of 4 lakh hectare, Andhra Pradesh for Rs. 835 crore for restoration of 3000 water bodies with a CCA of 2.5 lakh hectare and Karnataka Government for Rs. 259 crore. The projects in respect of Orissa and West Bengal are under appraisal. The 'National Project for RRR of Water Bodies directly linked to Agriculture' was sanctioned in January 2005 with an estimated cost of Rs. 300 crore. The Scheme was approved for 26 district projects in 15 states, namely, Andhra Pradesh, Bihar, Chhattisgarh, Jharkhand, Karnataka, Madhya Pradesh, Orissa, Rajasthan, Tamil Nadu, West Bengal, Himachal Pradesh, Jammu and Kashmir, Gujarat, Kerala and Maharashtra at an estimated cost of Rs. 299.92 crore and Central Share of Rs. 179.73 crore has been released to the states so far. These projects cover 1098 water bodies with total original CCA of 1.72 lakh hectares. After RRR works, an additional irrigation potential of 0.78 lakh hectare is likely to be generated. The physical works for restoration have been completed in 736 water bodies in 11 states so far.

6004. (20-2-2008) NEW DELHI : Smt. Jayanthi said the Budget session of Parliament will begin on Feb 25 and we would like to make sincere appeal to all the Opposition parties to cooperate in running the business of Parliament, in legislative business and to discuss various important pieces of legislation and important issues of the day concerning the ordinary citizens of the land in a spirit of mutual cooperation so that important issues can be brought to light can be highlighted and discussed in a constructive manner. Ever since the UPA government has been elected there has been a systematic attempt by some sections of the Opposition to subvert the functioning of both houses of Parliament. During every Parliament session the running of the House is brought to a standstill, issues are not discussed in a constructive manner. During this important Budget session we would like to call upon all parties to cooperate and conduct the business of the House in a constructive manner. As you are all aware, there was a meeting in AICC where the party offered suggestions to Hon'ble Finance Minister regarding how the Budget should incorporate measures that will of be greatest benefit for common man, for farmers and most disadvantaged sections of the society. Thereafter yesterday, the Minister for Women and Child Development Renuka Choudhary, led a delegation of eminent women. And we would like to appeal to the Hon'ble Finance Minister to give special attention to the impact of the Budget on women which consists not merely of allotments in favour of women but also to consider a macroeconomic impact of all policies upon women in all sections of society.

6005. (20-2-2008) NEW DELHI : The President of India, Smt. Pratibha Devisingh Patil has greeted fellow citizens on the occasion of Guru Ravidas Jayanti, which will be celebrated tomorrow. In a message, the President has said, "On the occasion of the Birthday of Guru Ravidas, I extend my greetings and good wishes to all my countrymen. Ravidasji led a life of faith and devotion and dedicated himself to the cause of the poor irrespective of cast, creed and religion. His philosophy of service and his commitment to create a caring society is relevant even today. May his message of love, compassion and equality inspire us to serve humanity with dedication and devotion".

6006. (20-2-2008) NEW DELHI : We welcome the victory of the democratic forces in the recently concluded elections in Pakistan and the end of a decade of dictatorial darkness in that country. We hope that the democratic forces will provide Pakistan with a truly representative government with full peoples' participation. We also hope that they will be able to exercise proper democratic control over the Pakistan army which was responsible for the Kargil war and continues to unleash cross border terrorism against India. We expect the new rulers of Pakistan to work for a negotiated and peaceful settlement of all issues between India and Pakistan and to make constructive contribution to regional peace and cooperation. We, however, note with dismay the very limited role of minorities, specially the Hindu minority in these elections. We hope that the new rulers of Pakistan will take proper care of the minorities.

6007. (20-2-2008) NEW DELHI : The Prime Minister, Dr. Manmohan Singh, greeted the Nation on the auspicious occasion of Ravidas Jayanti. In his message, the Prime Minister said that Guru Ravidas embodied the spirit of humility and human dignity. Revered by Hindus and Sikhs, the compositions of Guru Ravidas have been a source of knowledge and wisdom. His life and teachings would always inspire us to create a humane and just society, where every individual is given due dignity, regardless of his or her caste, creed, religion or gender.

6008. (21-2-2008) NEW DELHI : Will the Finance Minister axe the taxes in this Budget 2008-09, is the moot question on all minds be they in the corporate sector, professionals or the 'aam admi'. The run-up to the Budget has been rife with speculation on whether it would be a populist Budget or a balanced one given the ongoing global economic scenario. The main source of revenue for any Government, taxation is one area any Finance Minister finds hard to touch. While the direct tax collection has been buoyant, the indirect tax scenario has not been so cheerful. Decelerating customs revenue growth and low excise revenue are obviously the main problems confronting the Finance Minister as he chalks up the taxation plans. He is thus expected to focus on better mobilization of earnings through direct and service taxes But then, if anything, the Finance Minister has the comfort factor of presenting the Budget in the backdrop of a booming economy. In line with a GDP growth of 9.4 per cent recorded last fiscal, the economy is expected to record a growth rate of over 9 per cent in 2007-08. The annual inflation rate, as measured by the Wholesale Price Index (WPI) is in the range of 4 per cent to 5 per cent. On the other hand, while the Indian cereal output of around 200 million tonnes projected for the current fiscal may raise comfort levels as far as food security is concerned, India cannot expect to stay isolated from global conditions, especially with a spiralling crude oil prices. The fiscal situation too has improved. The aggregate gross fiscal deficit relative to the GDP declined considerably in 2006-07 and is further expected to go down in 2007-08 to touch 2.6 per cent of GDP, about 70 basis points lower than the estimated 3.3 per cent. The revenue deficit too has improved to around 0.9 per cent of GDP, 60 basis points lower than the 1.5 per cent Budget target for 2007-08. The Government is hopeful of achieving the targetted zero revenue deficit by the end of 2008-09, the terminal year of the Fiscal Responsibility and Budget Management Act, 2003. The most significant and notable source of improvement, however, has been in the collection of central taxes, mainly the personal and corporate income taxes. Direct tax revenues are likely to cross Rs 325,000 crore, which is Rs 68,000 crore more than the Budget Estimates. Indirect tax revenues are also expected to cross the Budget Estimates by about Rs 4,000 crore. Economists peg the factors responsible for the unprecedented growth in revenue collection to include moderate tax rates, change in taxpayer behaviour, better compliance owing to easier tax laws and a technology driven Income Tax Department, which has become more taxpayer friendly. The one thing that is feared to derail this rosy picture is agriculture, with its painfully slow growth rate. Appreciating Rupee is another area of concern, with exporters taking a severe hit this year. This has had a fall-out on several sectors, including manufacturing, which contributes a major bulk of the tax revenue, as well as the IT services. The other factors that pose a potential risk to the growth outlook are infrastructure bottlenecks, high inflation rate of assets, especially housing prices in the international market, widening trade deficits and turbulent global financial market. In this backdrop, there is pressure on the Finance Minister to churn out a more benevolent Budget as far as taxes are concerned. Industry as well as economists have suggested widening the tax base and increasing the tax revenue to check tax avoidance. They have also called for rationalisation of the provisions of direct tax laws. Acknowledging that no Finance Minister would like to upset the apple cart when the going is good, the economists, however, see merit in reduction of tax rates, wherever appropriate, while maintaining the rigour of fiscal administration.

6009. (21-2-2008) NEW DELHI : Certain sections of electronic media are showing a news misquoting the Minister of State for Railways, Shri R. Velu saying that there will be no hike in the fares in the Railway Budget 2008-09. This is to clarify that while interacting with the media after the Conference on High Axle Load at Vigyan Bhawan here today, the Minister only said that the budget will be people friendly and refused to make any comment when one of the media representatives asked about the fare hike in the Budget. The Minister made no mention about fares as it is obvious that budget proposals are not made public prior to presentation of the Budget by the Hon'ble Minister of Railways in the Parliament.

6010. (21-2-2008) NEW DELHI : The first meeting of the India-Pakistan Standing Committee on Delhi-Lahore, Amritsar-Lahore and Amritsar-Nankana Sahib Bus

Services was held here today. The Indian delegation was led by Mr. Saroj Kumar Dash, Joint Secretary (Transport), Ministry of Shipping, Road Transport and Highways and the Pakistan delegation was led by Mr. Mohammad Abbas, Additional Secretary, Ministry of Communications. Both sides noted with satisfaction the continuing operations of the bus services and discussed further measures for its improvement. It has been decided to increase the frequency of Delhi-Lahore bus service from two trips per week to three trips per week from each side. It was also decided to rationalize the bus fare. In addition, the quota for the return tickets would be increased form the existing 6 (six) seats to 10 (ten) seats. The two sides agreed that enroute, the Amritsar-Nankana Sahib bus service would make a halt at Lahore to enable the passengers to disembark/embark whereas, Lahore-Amritsar bus service would continue to operate as per existing arrangement. It was decided that the concerned financial officials of the two sides would meet every year, alternately in Delhi and Lahore in July for reconciliation of accounts. The new arrangements will come into effect from 17th March 2008. The meeting was held in a friendly and cordial atmosphere.

6011. (21-2-2008) NEW DELHI : There are no further reports from the HSADL, Bhopal of any sample testing positive from any part of the country, including West Bengal. No unusual mortality was reported in West Bengal on 20th February, 2008. The latest report from West Bengal shows that a total of 123 Rapid Response Teams (RRTs) were engaged (22 for surveillance / mopping and 101 for disinfection and sanitization). No culling is being done from 17.02.2008. The cumulative culling of poultry birds is 39.05 lakhs. No egg and feed was destroyed on 20.02.2008. The cumulative figures of eggs and feed destroyed are 14,90,785 and 80,033 kg respectively. The task of creating 5 km. poultry depopulated zone in their border areas with West Bengal has been completed in Assam and Bihar. While the culling work has been completed in Jamtara district of Jharkhand, it is in progress in Pakur district of the state.

6012. (21-2-2008) NEW DELHI : Shri Vayalar Ravi, Minister for Overseas Indian Affairs inaugurated the International Seminar on "Diasporic Writing: The Dynamics of Be/Longing" at IGNOU, New Delhi today. Addressing the participants, he said that Diaspora communities today are wide spread with the advent of information and communication technology and fast modes of transport. Diaspora Communities therefore have an impact both globally and nationally. He further said that the emigrant/immigrant expatriate experience is a life changing one both for those who live and those who are left behind. These experiences have found expression in the writing of diasporian. Exile and emigrant narratives are not necessarily narratives of trauma. Therefore, the writers can cover a vast range of issues traversing geo-politics, religion, cast culture and community. Shri Ravi said that the two-day seminar would cover all the issues related to Diaspora. This is an area full of potential and could very well form the framework of a complete course on diasporic writings, he added.

6013. (21-2-2008) NEW DELHI : The Union Cabinet today gave its approval to modify the earlier decision of the Cabinet to the extent that the Government may subscribe to the Rights Issue of equity shares of SBI amounting to Rs.9995.99 crore by issue of "Special Marketable Government Securities" instead of "SLR Marketable Government Securities." The Government is likely to receive around Rs.1449 crore additionally by way of dividend and taxes from the Bank during the years 2008-09, as against an expenditure of around Rs.825 crore as interest to be paid to the Bank for the proposed Securities. However, in subsequent years, the Government is likely to receive higher amount of additional revenues (Rs.1683 crore in the year 2009-10 and Rs.2049 crore in the year 2010-11 and thereafter). The additional growth of the bank due to its increased capital base will also have multiplier effect on the overall performance of the Bank, which will gain in terms of its position in the industry, ratings-both in international as well as domestic markets, and in increased valuation of its stock, besides boost to the economy at large. On receipt of the approval of the Cabinet, the transaction will be completed within the current financial year and, thereafter a "securities redemption fund" will be created to redeem these securities on due date.

6014. (21-2-2008) NEW DELHI : The Union Cabinet today gave its approval to the following proposals: i) a maximum amount of Rs. 200 crore to be contributed by the Central Government to the Financial Inclusion Fund over a maximum period of five years; and ii) a maximum amount of Rs.200 crore to be contributed by the Central Government to the Financial Inclusion Technology Fund over a maximum period of five years. The Finance Minister, in the Union Budget speech for 2007-08 announced the Constitution of FIF and FITF with an overall corpus of Rs.500 crore each with initial funding to be contributed by the Central Government, Reserve Bank of India and the National Bank for Agriculture and Rural Development. The objectives of the FIF shall be to support "developmental and promotional activities" with a view to securing greater financial inclusion, particularly among weaker sections, low income groups and in backward regions/ hitherto unbanked areas. The objectives of FITF shall be to enhance investment in Information Communication Technology (ICT) aimed at promoting financial inclusion, stimulate the transfer of research and technology in financial inclusion, increase the technological absorption capacity of financial service providers/users and encourage an environment of innovation and cooperation among stakeholders. The constitution of these funds would ensure access to timely and adequate credit and financial services by vulnerable groups such as weaker sections and low-income groups at an affordable cost.

6015. (21-2-2008) NEW DELHI : The Union Cabinet today gave its approval to the Agreement for Avoidance of Double Taxation and Prevention of Fiscal Evasion with respect to Taxes on income and on capital between the Government of India and the Government of the Grand Duchy of Luxembourg. The Agreement will stimulate the flow of capital, technology and personnel from India to

Luxembourg and vice-versa. It will provide tax stability and reduce any obstacles in providing mutual cooperation. India has so far signed and notified such bilateral treaties for avoidance of double taxation with 71 other countries. In more than 20 DTAAs the scope of the agreement includes capital taxes.

6016. (21-2-2008) NEW DELHI : The Union Cabinet today gave its ex-post-facto approval for the Bilateral Agreement signed on 12th November 2007 at Moscow between India Russian Federation on cooperation to combat illicit trafficking in narcotics, psychotropic substances and their precursors. The Agreement will help in mutual cooperation in the regulation of narcotic drugs and psychotropic substances for medical and scientific use and in combating drug trafficking. Such bilateral agreements have already been executed with various countries such as the USA, Afghanistan, Mauritius, Russian Federation, Myanmar, Zambia, UAE, Egypt, China, Iran, Bulgaria, Romania, Italy, Tajikistan, Turkey, Lao PDR, Israel, Bangladesh and Kuwait.

6017. (21-2-2008) NEW DELHI : The Union cabinet today approved a proposal for introduction of the Bill in Parliament by making an amendment of the Supreme Court (Number of Judges) Act, 1956 for increase in the number of judges in the Supreme court to augment the strength of the Supreme Court Judges, excluding the Chief Justice of Indian, from 25 to 30. The increase in the number of judges will allow Supreme Court to function more efficiently and effectively towards attaining the ultimate goal of rendering speedy justice to the litigant public.

6018. (21-2-2008) NEW DELHI : The Union cabinet today approved a proposal for the establishment of the North Eastern Institute of Folk Medicine at Pasighat, Arunachal Pradesh at a cost of Rs. 32.88 crores as an Autonomous Institute under the Deptt. of AYUSH. This decision will facilitate systematic and comprehensive documentation, presentation and validation of the folk medicine traditions of the North-Eastern region.

6019. (21-2-2008) NEW DELHI : The Union Cabinet today gave its approval for issuing a Central Order under Section 3 of the Essential commodities Act, 1955, for extending the validity of the Central notification dated 29-08-2006, 27-02-2007 and 31-08-2007 for a further period of six months beyond 29-02-2008. This would empower the State Governments to undertake de-boarding operations and to control the prices of wheat and pulses.

6020. (21-2-2008) NEW DELHI : The Government today approved continuation of the Credit Linked Capital Subsidy Scheme (CLCSS) for Micro & Small Enterprises during 11th Plan. The Cabinet Committee on Economic Affairs (CCEA) gave its approval here today. The Ministry of Micro, Small & Medium Enterprises has been operating for technology upgradation of Small Scale Industries under which 15% capital subsidy on the Institutional Finance was provided in specified sub-sectors/products for induction of well established and improved technologies approved under the scheme. The validity of this scheme was upto 31.03.2007 *i.e.* the end of X Five Year Plan. During initial period of five years, very few units could take advantage of the scheme, therefore, the scheme was modified and made more attractive by increasing the rate of subsidy from 12% to 15% and raising the ceiling of loan from Rs.40 lakh to Rs. 1.00 crore in September, 2005. The period of validity which was expiring on 30 September, 2005 was also extended upto 31.03.2007. Consequently, the Scheme became popular among Micro and Small Enterprises with about 2400 units availing financial assistance (term loan) of Rs.727 crore (approx.) from the financial institutions and utilising a subsidy of Rs.80 crore (approx.) under the Scheme in a period of one-and-a-half years of its operation. In addition, about 2400 more units have already obtained financial assistance of about Rs.833 crore and are awaiting subsidy clearance of about Rs.115 crore. At the request of many prominent Associations of Micro and Small Enterprises, the Ministry of Micro and Small Enterprises took initiative to extend the period of validity of CLCSS during XI Plan period for the benefit of Micro and Small Enterprises. With the extension of the CLCSS during XI Five Year Plan period, the Micro and Small Enterprises will be able to modernise their plants & machineries and upgrade their manufacturing technologies and will be able not only to survive in the most competitive environment of the present era of liberalisation and globalisation but will also be able to make remarkable progress and provide employment to many people and contribute to the national economy.

6021. (21-2-2008) NEW DELHI : The Union Minister of Shipping, Road Transport and Highways, Thiru T.R. Baalu has approved a total sum of Rs. 532.89 lakh for road improvement works and reconstruction of minor bridges at National Highway-208 in the state of Tamil Nadu. An amount of Rs. 270.77 lakh has been approved for strengthening of a stretch between Pudupatti and Thirumangalam Road of NH-208. This is an important National Highway of inter-state connectivity and passes through many important towns as Tenkasi, Rajapalayam and Srivilliputtur. It also connects two important tourism centres of Coutrallam and Madurai. The riding surface of the road was badly damaged during the last monsoon season and therefore, it has become absolutely necessary to repair this stretch. An amount of Rs 262.12 lakh has been approved for reconstruction of five minor bridges in NH-208. All these five minor bridges, located between Sethur and Rajapalayam have developed cracks and are in damaged condition. Taking into consideration the deteriorated condition of these bridges, the reconstruction as per the National Highway standards, has been approved by Thiru T.R. Baalu.

6022. (21-2-2008) NEW DELHI : The total approximate earnings of Indian Railways on originating basis during the period 1st February-10th February 2008 were Rs. 2156.16 crore compared to Rs. 1736.15 crore during the same period last year, registering an increase of 24.19 per cent. The total goods earnings have gone up from Rs. 1194.47 crore during 1st February-10th February 2007 to Rs. 1465.47 crore during 1st February-10th February 2008, showing an increase of

22.69 per cent. The total passenger revenue earnings during the period 1st to 10th February 2008 were Rs. 624.16 crore compared to Rs. 474.98 crore during the same period last year, reflecting an increase of 31.41 per cent. The revenue earnings from other coaching amounted to Rs. 47.92 crore during this period compared to Rs. 47.18 crore during the same period last year, showing an increase of 1.57 per cent. The total approximate number of passengers booked during the period 1st to 10th February 2008 were 180.40 million compared to 182.66 million during the same period last year, showing a decrease of 1.24 per cent. In the suburban and non-suburban sectors, the number of passengers booked during 1-10 February 2008 were 102.06 million and 78.34 million compared to 105.49 million and 77.17 million during the same period last year, registering a decrease of 3.25 per cent and an increase of 1.52 per cent respectively.

6023. (21-2-2008) NEW DELHI : The Cabinet Committee on Economic Affairs today gave its approval for providing immediate relief to the exporters by way of providing interest subvention to mitigate hardships on account of unanticipated and steep rupee appreciation. The measure will ensure mitigation of the effect of rupee appreciation across the export sectors and will make them internationally competitive and will also enable them to achieve export targets.

6024. (21-2-2008) NEW DELHI : The Cabinet Committee on Economic Affairs today gave its approval for Continuation of the Credit Linked Capital Subsidy Scheme (CLCSS) for Micro and Small Enterprises during XI Plan also. The continuation of the CLCSS during XI Plan will encourage micro and small enterprises to undertake modernisation through technology upgradation to remain competitive.

6025. (21-2-2008) NEW DELHI : Shri Koshy Koshy will be the new Director General of the Bureau of Police Research & Development (BPR&D). Shri Koshy Koshy, a 1973 batch Haryana cadre IPS officer, is currently holding the post of Director General, National Disaster Response Force & Civil Defence (NDRF&CD). He will continue to hold the post of Director General, NDRF&CD as additional charge.

6026. (22-2-2008) NEW DELHI : The first-ever Film Festival of Indian Ocean Rim Association for Regional Cooperation (IOR-ARC) countries got underway here today. The Festival is jointly organized by the Directorate of Film Festivals, Ministry of I&B and the Ministry of External Affairs. Minister of State for External Affairs, Shri Anand Sharma formally inaugurated the Festival by lighting the ceremonial lamp. In his remarks, Shri Sharma said that IOR-ARC is an important association for cooperation in various fields among the member countries. Initiatives like the Film Festival offer understanding of the cultural perspective of member countries through the medium of cinema. Secretary, I&B, Smt. Asha Swaroop in her remarks said that it is a matter of great pride for India to be hosting this Festival. Such a Festival would pave the way for more cultural exchanges between the member countries in future. It is indeed a rare opportunity to see films from these countries as they are often not released commercially in India. Current Chairman of IOR-ARC, Mr. Syed Mehdin Nabizadeh, the Ambassador of the Islamic Republic of the Iran and the Director of the opening film 'Yolngu Boy' were also present on the occasion. The Festival will be on till March 1, 2008 at the Siri Fort Auditorium. In all 10 films will be screened at the Film festival from IOR-ARC member countries, *viz.* Australia, Bangladesh, Iran, Mauritius, Sri Lanka, Thailand, Kenya, South Africa, Tanzania and India.

6027. (22-2-2008) NEW DELHI : Prime Minister Dr. Manmohan Singh chaired a meeting here today to review Tiger conservation status in the country and the functioning of the National Tiger Conservation Authority. While expressing concern about the decline in Tiger population, Prime Minister noted that recent estimates of Tiger population, arrived at on the basis of a new methodology, cannot be compared with earlier estimates. Stating that the Government of India is fully committed to Tiger conservation, the Prime Minister said the Central Government will further enhance financial and organizational support for efforts in this direction. Prime Minister directed that the Centre should fund modernization of Tiger Reserves management, including recruitment of staff from local population and providing them adequate equipment. He sought a State-specific strategy for such central assistance. Government has recently approved an enhanced relocation package of up to Rs. 10 lakhs per family for families living in Tiger Reserves. Schemes for rehabilitation of traditional hunters; for supporting new Tiger Reserves; for supporting eco-tourism benefitting local communities; for deployment of anti-poaching staff; and, for improving service conditions of forest officers have also been taken up. Noting that some States have a better record of Tiger conservation than others, the meeting stressed the importance of concerned State Governments paying focused attention. Chief Ministers have been asked to take personal charge of Tiger conservation and forest management. The Prime Minister will convene a Conference of Chief Ministers of States with Tiger Reserves to put in place a coordinated response to the challenge of Tiger conservation. The meeting was attended by the Minister of State for Forests, Shri Regupathy, Deputy Chairman, Planning Commission, senior officials of the Prime Minister's Office and ministry of environment and forests, and Director, National Tiger Conservation Authority.

6028. (22-2-2008) NEW DELHI : On the recommendation of the Minister of Tourism and Culture, the President has appointed Shri Ashok Vajpeyi as pro-tem Chairman of the Lalit Kala Akademi with immediate effect. He will continue to hold the office till a regular chairman is appointed. Shri Vajpeyi is an eminent Hindi Poet and critic. He is a widely respected person and has held various important positions. He has served as Vice-Chancellor, Mahatma Gandhi International Hindu University, Chairman, Bharat Bhavan Trust, Trustee, Indira Gandhi National Centre of the Arts, Member, Indian Council of Cultural Relations, and Executive Board Member of Sangeet Natak Akademi. A leading Poet, Essay

Writer, Shri Vajpeyi has a number of publications to his credit. He has also won Dayavati Modi Kavi Shekhar Samman, 1994 and Sahitya Akademi Award, 1994.

6029. (22-2-2008) NEW DELHI : The outstanding balance of 12.15 per cent Government Stock, 2008 is repayable at par on March 25, 2008 and no interest will accrue thereon from the said date. In the event of a holiday being declared on March 25, 2008 by any State Government under the Negotiable Instruments Act, 1881, the Loan will be repaid by the paying offices in that State on the previous working day. To facilitate repayment of the Loan on the due date, holders may tender the securities, duly discharged, at the Public Debt Offices, Treasuries/ Sub-Treasuries and branches of State Bank of India and its Associate Banks (at which they are enfaced / registered for payment of interest) 20 days in advance of the due date for repayment.

6030. (22-2-2008) NEW DELHI : 6.5% Savings Bonds, 2003 (Non-Taxable) issued in terms of Government of India, Ministry of Finance, Department of Economic Affairs Notification No. F. 4(9)-W&M/2003 dated March 13, 2003 will start maturing for repayment with effect from March 24, 2008. The holders may note that "no interest would be payable on the Bonds after maturity". As per sub regulations 24 (2) and 24 (3) of Government Securities Regulations, 2007, payment of maturity proceeds to the registered holder of a Government security, held in the form of Bond Ledger Account (BLA) and Stock Certificate (SC), shall be made by a pay order incorporating the relevant particulars of his bank account or by credit to the account of the holder in any bank having facility of receipt of funds through electronic means. To facilitate repayment of the above bonds on the due dates, holders of BLAs / SCs may furnish the relevant particulars of their bank account to the issuing offices well in advance so that the automatic redemption of BLAs / SCs can be made on due date without requiring to give any discharge upon the security / Annexure 1A. Holders may, therefore, submit the relevant particulars of their bank account for automatic redemption of the maturity value on the due date. However, in the absence of relevant particulars of bank account / mandate for receipt of funds through electronic means, repayment will be made on receipt of discharge upon the security (in case of SC) and on Annexure-1 A (in case of BLA).

6031. (22-2-2008) NEW DELHI : In exercise of the powers conferred by clause (1) of Article 217 of the Constitution of India, the President is pleased to appoint (i) Shri Justice Syed Ali Naqvi, and (ii) Shri Justice Subhash Chandra Vyas, Additional Judges of the Madhya Pradesh High Court, to be Judges of the Madhya Pradesh High Court, in that order of seniority, with effect from the dates they assume charge of their respective offices.

6032. (22-2-2008) NEW DELHI : The President of India Smt. Pratibha Devisingh Patil will confer the prestigious Sangeet Natak Akademi Fellowship and Akademi Awards for 2007 at a special ceremony on 26 February 2008 in New Delhi. The

Akademi Fellowship (Akademi Ratna) and Akademi Awards (Akademi Puraskar) are recognized as the highest national honour conferred on practicing artists, gurus and scholars and have come to stay as the most coveted honour which the artistes aspire to. Past recipients of Akademi Fellowship and Awards include eminent personalities such as Alauddin Khan, Hafiz Ali Khan, Ariyakudi Ramanuja Iyenga, Omkar Nath Thakur, T. Balasaraswati, Rukmini Devi Arundale, Kelucharan Mohapatra, Sachin Deb Burman, Satyajit Ray, Sombhu Mitra, P.L. Deshpande, C.C. Mehta, Mohan Rakesh, B.V. Karanth to name a few. The Fellowships and Awards are decided by Akademi's General Council, the apex body consisting of eminent artistes, scholars and representatives of different States and Union Territories of the country. This year the most coveted honour of Akademi Fellowship (Akademi Ratna) will be conferred on eminent scholar and Professor of aesthetics, Dr. S.K. Saxena. He will receive a purse money of Rs. one lakh, besides a citation, an angavastram and a tamrapatra. 33 eminent persons will be conferred the Akademi Awards for the year 2007 carrying purse money of Rs. 50,000/-, citation, angavastram and tamrapatra. The Sangeet Natak Akademi was established by the Government of India on 31 May 1952 as the National Academy of Music, Dance and Drama. It was created as the apex body in the country for the task of preservation and promotion of the performing arts of India. One of the important activities of the Akademi has been to give recognition and honours to artistes for setting standards in performing arts and restoring the art and artists to their rightful place in independent India.

6033. (22-2-2008) NEW DELHI : While Congress President Smt. Sonia Gandhi was giving lips sympathy to the farmers in Raibareli, 11 more farmers committed suicide in last 72 hours in Vidarbha region. 3 farmers from Amaravati and Washim district and 2 from Yawatmal and 1 each from Bhandara, Nagpur and Wardha are the unfortunate farmers, who were failed by the hollow promises of Central and State Congress government. Farmers suicide continue unabated and figure since January 1, 2008 has crossed over 140 in 50 days. Congress is shedding crocodile tears on the condition of farmers without any concrete action plan. It is the Congress economics, which has deprived Indian farmers, of their dues and have never got remunerative prices. The agrarian crisis won't be over till remunerative prices and irrigation facility is made available to the Indian farmers. The BJP demands immediate acceptance of recommendations of Commission for Agriculture Costs and Prices (CACP) about MSP for various crops. The Commission for Agriculture Costs and Prices (CACP) has recommended MSP of Rs. 1,000 for wheat and paddy and has recommended substantial increase in MSP for all crops across the board. CACP has recommended Rs. 2,000 for Arhar and Rs. 2,520 for Moong Dal. It has also recommended Rs. 2,100 for Groundnut, Rs. 1,350 for Soyabean and Rs. 2,215 for Sunflower. Cotton growers have been recommended a price tag of Rs. 2,500-3,000 for different verities. Though these are not fully in tune with the recommendations of Swaminathan Commission, which has suggested MSP with a formula of 50% addition on the cost of production. Unless, farmer get remunerative prices the plight of farmers will never improve. CACP recommendations are the first step to ensure remunerative prices. The recent National Sample Survey Organisation (NSSO) has found out that 43 million farmers (48% of 90 million farmers) were indebted. This is the result of not assuring remunerative prices to the farmers. If the prices had been assured, the farmers would have definitely repaid their outstanding loans. BJP demands immediate announcement of agriculture loan remission policy and write off loans upto Rs. 50,000 as one time measure. Loan waiver should be treated as overdue payment to farmers being adjusted in their loan accounts. Heavy public investment in accelerated irrigation projects, changes in Land Acquisition Act 1894, more institutional credit, farm income guarantee insurance scheme and ensuring more productivity with technology transfer is needed to revive the agriculture in the country.

6034. (22-2-2008) NEW DELHI : A seven-Member Vietnamese delegation led by Mr. Nguyen Thanh Xuan, Vice Chairman called on the National Commission for Minorities. Welcoming the delegation, the Chairperson of the Commission, Shri Mohamed Shafi Qureshi drew attention to India's secular ethos and unity strengthened by the common thread of peaceful co-existence and communal harmony despite being a multi-cultural, multi-religious, multi-lingual and multi-racial society. Mr. Nguyen Thanh Xuan gave an account of the religious policy in Vietnam and highlighted the similarities between the two countries on equality of rights and secularism. He also mentioned about the institutional mechanism of Religious Committees to cater to the religious needs of the people. The two delegations had wide ranging discussions. The Commission's role in guarding the rights and interests of religious minorities and to facilitate their socio-economic development were shared. The grievance redressal mechanism in place and its efficacy in securing justice and the rights of the minorities in the country also formed part of the discussions. Strengthening of human bonds and relations between India and Vietnam despite wide disparities in languages, culture and religion through such interactions were emphasized by both countries. Both the sides underlined the need to strengthen ties between India and Vietnam.

6035. (22-2-2008) NEW DELHI : The technology 'Method for diagnosis of tuberculosis by smear microscopy, culture and polymerase chain reaction using processed clinical samples and kit thereof' developed by All India Institute of Medical Sciences (AIIMS), New Delhi, was transferred by Biotech Consortium India Limited (BCIL) to Arbro Pharmaceuticals Ltd., a Delhi based pharmaceutical and diagnostics company. The licence agreement was executed by Dr. Purnima Sharma, Executive Director & CEO, BCIL and Shri Vijay Kumar Arora, Managing Director, Arbro Pharmaceuticals Ltd. The technology developed by Dr. Jaya Sivaswami Tyagi, Professor, Department of Biotechnology, at AIIMS with support from the Department of Biotechnology, Government of India, enables TB detection (pulmonary and extra-pulmonary infection) with high sensitivity and specificity.

M/s. Arbro Pharmaceuticals Limited is leading manufacturer and exporter of pharmaceutical and diagnostic products. The company has state-of-the-art facilities that have been certified and internationally accredited for Good Manufacturing Practices (GMP). Arbro Pharmaceuticals Limited has been awarded the status of Star Export House. Its Analytical Division is a well equipped lab which has been rated amongst the top five labs of India and has been accredited by number of national agencies. It has been the vision of Mr. Vijay Kumar Arora, MD of Arbro to bring the highest level of healthcare within the reach of the common man. In the area of diagnostics Arbro manufactures kits for detection of diseases like tuberculosis, Hepatitis and food and water borne pathogens. Till now these products have mainly been imported at exorbitant costs keeping them out of the reach of masses. Biotech Consortium India Limited (BCIL) that has facilitated this technology transfer, is a company promoted by Department of Biotechnology (DBT), Government of India and set up by all India financial institutions including IDBI, ICICI, IFCI, etc. BCIL has been engaged in facilitating accelerated commercialization of biotechnology based products for more than a decade by establishing linkages among the various stake holders which includes industry, R&D institutions, Government, financial institutions and international agencies. Also, the company provides access to technologies, creating awareness about business opportunities, regulatory and biosafety requirements, drafting feasibility and detailed project reports and manpower training and placement. The diagnostic technology, designated as USP technology, comprises of a robust sample processing procedure and provides a single platform for performing conventional and nucleic acid-based tests for the laboratory diagnosis of pulmonary and extrapulmonary tuberculosis using any type of clinical specimen. USP smear microscopy can reproducibly detect positive specimens containing as low as 300-400 bacilli/ml, which is nearly 30 times more sensitive than the direct method of smear microscopy (detection limit of ~10,000 bacilli/ml). The USP smear test promises to be a rapid and inexpensive technique for the rapid diagnosis of paucibacillary disease, especially in sputum. According to Dr. Atul Thatai (VP, Biotechnology, Arbro Pharmaceuticals) this technology has the potential to replace the 66 million conventional TB smears which are carried out each year in our country because of its sensitivity and ease of use. The devR gene of M. tuberculosis was identified in Dr. Jaya S. Tyagi's laboratory at AIIMS and used to develop PCR assays. The PCR test is based on amplification of a short segment of the devR gene. The sensitivity of PCR is >90 % in both sputum and CSF samples and 45-85 % in extra pulmonary samples including pleural fluid, pleural tissue and lymph node biopsy specimens. The specificity has ranged between 66-100% in various studies carried out on pulmonary and extra pulmonary samples. The performance of PCR is significantly better than the conventional tests and PCR promises to be a very valuable tool for rapidly diagnosing extra pulmonary tuberculosis.

6036. (22-2-2008) NEW DELHI : Demand for new and more effective antibiotics continues to grow particularly as bacterial resistance to existing antibiotics spreads.

The market for antibiotic drugs is huge. In 2005, worldwide sales of oral antibiotics totaled USD 25 Billion including US sales of $8.5 billion ($7.0 billion for adults and $1.5 billion for children). Apart from being huge, the market is also growing at a significant rate, with adult and pediatric prescriptions growing in 2005 at 8.5% and 10.8% respectively. Department of Biotechnology has recently initiated a network project called "Screening for Bio-molecules from microbial diversity collected from different ecological niches". The project involves nine institutes, with NPIL Research & Development Limited (NRDL) as an industrial partner. The total cost of the project is Rs.24.86 crores with DBT contribution of Rs.17.98 Crores. Rs. 6.88 Crores is being contributed by NRDL.

6037. (22-2-2008) NEW DELHI : Congress spokesman Shri Manish Tewari said this is my maiden press briefing and I have to begin with a rather intiguing story of Patan, a small town in Gujarat, which has been witness to a very horrific incident whereby a young trainee teacher was gang-raped for over six months by six of her teachers. This girl belongs to a poor Dalit family and the incident came to light around the 4th of February when she mustered courage to bring these facts to light and filed an FIR. Though the accused have been arrested, the story has implications that this was a systematic process of abuse which had been going on in the institution for over a decade. The National Commission for Women, the National Commission for SC/STs, my colleague in the AICC Shri Sudhakar Reddy all of them visited this institute in Patan and spoke to the parents and the fact that emerged is that there is a concerted effort by the state government to hush up the incident. The reason is not far to discern. The MLA of Patan, the Revenue Minister of Gujarat Smt. Anandi Behn Patel, who is supposedly the lady Friday of Gujarat Chief Minister, is extremely close to two of the accused who have been arrested in the matter. The National Commission for Women and the National Commission for SC/STs have demanded a CBI inquiry into the incident. The Indian National Congress reiterates the demand and would like to call upon the Gujarat government that it would be in the interest of justice if the investigation of this case is handed over to the CBI at the earliest. It is unfortunate that a party which has been tom-toming about women's empowerment, their chief minister in Gujarat did not even have the courtesy of meeting a delegation of young girl students from this institute when they called upon him, so much of the commitment which the BJP as a party has to women's empowerment. Three states in the North-East namely Meghalaya, Nagaland and Tripura would be holding elections to their respective State Assemblies over the next fortnight. This is strategically an important and a diverse region of India that is usually not in the focus of the National Media. Given the fact that both the UPA Chairperson and Prime Minister have visited these states and would be doing so again over the next fortnight; it would be an appropriate occasion to focus on some of the salient initiatives taken by the UPA Government over the last 3 years and 8 months on improving the lives of people in this region. Broadly speaking the UPA Governments policy towards the North-East can be summed up as establishing peace for development. There can be no development without peace and vis-a-versa no peace without development. It would be noteworthy to point out that Mizoram in the North-East has the distinction of being perhaps the only state in India where insurgency was brought to an end through a negotiated political settlement. It was in 1986 that Late Prime Minister Sh. Rajiv Gandhi oversaw the signing of a historic accord between the Government of India and the Mizo National Front (MNF). Significantly even after 22 years of the accord not only is the peace holding but the erstwhile insurgents have been fully integrated in to the National Mainstream. Incidentally it was the INC which restored peace in the North West – Punjab through an astute combination of firmness in dealing with terror and reinvigorating democratic institutions. Over the past 3 ½ years the NSCN(I/M), NSCN(K) in Nagaland, National Liberation Front of Tripura NLFT (NB) and NLFT (KMK) in Tripura and the Achick National Volunteers Council (ANVC) in Garo-hills, Meghalaya have entered into agreements with the UPA Government to suspend insurgency operations. This has brought relative succor to the lives of ordinary people. An agreement has been signed between Bru National Liberation Front of Mizoram (BNLF) and the Government of Mizoram for the return of BRU / Reang Tribe from Tripura to Mizoram leading to a large number of people being rehabilitated in the process. Development projects worth Rs.225 crore have been sanctioned for the area and assistance of Rs.100 crore annually is being released since the year 2004-05 to the Council. The UPA Government has implemented various schemes for surrender and rehabilitation of militants in the North-East. 20% of vacancies of constables in the Border Guarding Forces (BGF) would be filled up from areas affected by the militancy in the North-East in order to create employment opportunities and wean youth away from the path of violence. The Security Related Expenditure reimbursement facility has also been extended to Meghalaya, Nagaland and Tripura. Operation Sadbhavana Programme which is being implemented in J&K to counter alienation among the local population in the context of counter insurgency operations has been extended to the North-East. A Special Accelerated Road Development Programme to the North-East (SARDP-NE) is being implemented. It envisages improvement of about 7,639 km of National Highways and state roads. 34 District Headquarters unconnected so far would be connected to the National Highways under the aegis of this Programme. The total cost on this would be 12,123 crores. New railway lines are being laid in the Kumarghat-Agartala and Jiribam-Tupul (Imphal Road) sectors respectively. The Lumding-Silchar lines are being converted from meter-gauge to broad gauge.

6038. (22-2-2008) NEW DELHI : The twenty-first century is witnessing a gradual increase in life expectancy. The cause of morbidity and mortality world over is shifting from communicable diseases a few decades ago to non-communicable diseases. The leading causes of mortality among aged people comprise respiratory problems, heart diseases, cancer and stroke. Significant causes of morbidity among this group is chronic inflammatory and degenerative conditions such as Arthritis, Diabetes Osteoporosis, Alzheimer's disease, depression, psychiatric disorders, Parkinson's disease and age related urinary problems. The biggest challenge with geriatric problem is that in most of the cases the condition cannot be attributed to a single cause or in certain conditions of neuro-psychiatric disorders like, Senile dementia, Alzheimer's depression, the structural cause is unknown. In such cases the conventional medical therapy fails to come out with effective management plan and hence is severely compromised. Another challenge with conventional medical therapy is that it does not have health-promoting agents. Ayurveda on the other hand has interventions like chayavanaprasha, triphala that enhance physiological processes that influence metabolic and immunological status. Such interventions are significant in the context of geriatric care.

6039. (22-2-2008) NEW DELHI : Under the Scheme of Assistance to Disabled persons for purchase/fitting of aids/appliances (ADIP Scheme), the aids and appliances are distributed to persons all over the country as per eligibility. This scheme covers disabilities where aids and assistive devices can be used. Number of beneficiaries who have received help apparatus under the said scheme and the amount spent on them during the last three years is at annexure. During the current financial year i.e 2007-08, no grant has been released to any of the National Institutes/NGOs.

6040. (22-2-2008) NEW DELHI : Dr. Ambedkar Foundation is providing financial assistance under the Dr. Ambedkar Medical Aid scheme to the Scheduled Caste Patients, whose annual income is less than 50,000/- and who are suffering from major ailments that need surgery, such as Heart, Kidney, Liver, Cancer, Brain etc. or any other life threatening diseases. Fifty percent of the total cost of the treatment will be reimbursed to the hospital concerned directly with maximum ceiling limited to Rs.75,000 in each case, out of which Rs.25,000 will be reimbursed before surgery and the remaining about after the surgery and the remaining amount after the survey. The Scheme is presently implemented in 10 States through 10 hospitals identified under the scheme. It has been proposed to include K.S. Bowring Hospital, Bangalore, Kidwai Institute of Oncology, Bangalore, Kastuba Hospital, Meanipal and Civil Hospital, Oorgaon.

6041. (22-2-2008) NEW DELHI : Keeping in view the wide gap between the literacy levels of SC girls and boys, a proposal has been formulated by the Ministry of Social Justice & Empowerment to raise the existing 50 percent central assistance to 100 percent to the State Governments for construction of hostels for Scheduled Caste girls, so as to encourage their enrolment and arrest the drop out rate. However, in the case of construction of hostels for SC boys, the existing level of 50 per cent central assistance will remain unchanged. The Government is implementing various schemes for SC boys and girls, which include: (i) Upgradation of Merit of SC students; (ii) Free Coaching including call centre training for BPO industry; (iii) Post-Matric Scholarship Scheme; (iv) Rajiv Gandhi National Fellowship; (v) National Overseas Scholarship Scheme; and (vi) NGO schemes for running schools and training centres.

6042. (22-2-2008) NEW DELHI : Under the Overseas Citizenship of India (OCI) Scheme of the Ministry of Overseas Indian Affairs, eligible Overseas Indians are issued an OCI Registration Booklet and a life-long multiple entry, multi-purpose visa sticker. OCIs are also granted parity with Non-Resident Indians (NRIs) in the economic, financial and educational fields; Government is also considering to extend parity to OCIs with NRIs in all fields except those specified under Section 7(B) (1) of the Citizenship Act, 1955; (ii) Scholarship Programme for Diaspora Children (APDC) launched in 2006 provides admission-cum-scholarships to children of overseas Indians in technical and higher educational institutions in India; and (iii) a policy framework for setting up a NRI-PIO University at a suitable place in the country, ensuring flexibility in the choice of disciplines and courses offered, has been approved by the Government. The Schemes will meet the aspiration of the overseas Indian and also fulfil commitment made at the highest level to overseas Indians. Engagement with Indian Diaspora is mutually beneficial.

6043. (23-2-2008) NEW DELHI : The Vice President of India, Shri Mohd. Hamid Ansari inaugurated a seminar on "India and the Gulf" organized by the Association of Indian Diplomats here today. Following is the text of inaugural address". "I am delighted to be here today, amidst friends, and to talk about a subject that, by accident rather than design, became a life long pursuit. Confusion about nomenclature is avoidable. The correct name of this body of water is the Persian Gulf (PG). This is recognised by the United Nations, the US Department of State, and by historical maps of the region. This confusion about name is reflected in practical usage; at times we are exclusive and make 'the Gulf' synonymous with the GCC, and at others we include all the littoral states in the term. The Persian Gulf, and its littoral states, has been described as India's 'proximate neighbourhood'. Our task then is to locate India in relation to the PG states. This necessitates identifying the perception, in self, of the other: to determine (a) how we see these states and (b) how do PG states perceive India? Both are necessary to bring about a convergence of interests and the establishment of mutually beneficial relationships.

6044. (24-2-2008) NEW DELHI : The Defence Minister, Shri AK Antony, visited the forward Areas of the desert sector today. He was accompanied by the Chief of the Army Staff, General Deepak Kapoor, Lieutenant General Noble Thamburaj, GOC-in-C, Southern Command and Lieutenant General SN Handa, GOC of the Desert Corps. During his visit, the Raksha Mantri visited the border area in Tanot Sector and was briefed by Lieutenant General SN Handa on operational and border management aspects. Thereafter, he witnessed a demonstration of the 'Battle of Laungewala' fought in 1971, during which the Pakistani onslaught with armour and infantry was stopped dead in its tracks by a company of 23 PUNJAB and the Indian Air Force. The grit and determination exhibited by the Indian Army during the Battle of Laungewala is a shining example of valour and sacrifice of our soldiers in the face of the enemy. In addition to his interaction with Senior Commanders and officers of the Desert Corps, he addressed a large gathering of troops of the Desert Corps. In his address, Mr. Antony commended the troops for their high state of operational readiness to meet any eventuality and called upon all ranks to continue their good work. Mr. Antony exhorted the troops of the Desert Corps to emulate the valiant acts of bravery displayed by those defending Laungwala Post and called upon them to persevere in their efforts in defending the territorial integrity of the nation. Shri AK Antony joined the troops for a barakhana and had an informal interaction with them.

6045. (25-2-2008) NEW DELHI : Annual Plan size for Haryana for the year 2008-09 was finalized here today at a meeting between the Deputy Chairman, Planning Commission, Shri Montek Singh Ahluwalia and Chief Minister Shri Bhupinder Singh Hooda. The Plan outlay for 2008-09 was agreed at Rs.6650 crores. This includes onetime additional Central assistance of Rs.100 crores provided for specific projects of special interest to the State. In his comments on the performance of the State, Mr. Ahluwalia said that the State has been achieving excellent growth rate and overall performance of the State is much above expectations. During tenth plan period, it achieved growth of 9 per cent against the target of 7.9 per cent. Accordingly, the Planning Commission has fixed ambitious target of 11 per cent for the Eleventh plan. He said per capita income of the State is much above national average. Appreciating the efforts being made in improving human development index, attention was drawn to the need to bridge the gaps. Mr. Ahluwalia said the policy initiatives clubbed with the efforts to improve infrastructure has helped in creating investment friendly environment. Central Government's initiatives of providing freight corridor link and National Highway connectivity to the State would further improve its status as favorite investment destination. The State was also advised to improve private sector participation in development of new townships, reduce transmission &distribution losses and encourage social forestry. On fiscal performance the State government was complemented for bringing down fiscal deficit within FRBM targets and transforming it to revenue surplus State. Expenditure realization during Tenth Plan period was expected to be more than 100 per cent with anticipated expenditure for the Plan reported at Rs.12675.70 crores against approved outlay of Rs.12000 crores. Briefing the Commission on the development strategy, the Chief Minister pointed out that besides additional resource mobilization measures, efforts are on to further improve social sector performance and number of initiatives have been taken to benefit those who have not fully realized fruits of development. He said luxury tax was being levied on premium hotel & banquet halls and stamp duty rates for registration of sale of properties have been rationalized. To improve quality of education compulsory computer education is being introduced in secondary schools and Edusat Network has been extended in all schools in the State. Special package for institutional deliveries has been introduced to reduce IMR/MMR in SC women. Health institutions are being modernized and up-graded to meet Indian public health standards. He said sprinkle irrigation was being popularized to ensure optimum utilization of scarce water and sought subsidy enhancement to promote this effort. Ground water recharge through tube wells in depleting water zones and restoration of old water bodies was being taken on priorities. Industrial promotion Act has been enacted to provide single window time-bound clearance and new labour policy has been put in place to facilitate private investment. Investments of Rs.28000 crores have already been made while another Rs.60000 crores are in the pipeline. He said tax incentives for industries in Aravali, Mewat and Shivalik regions of the State should be at par with hill States.

6046. (25-2-2008) NEW DELHI : The Minister for Civil Aviation, Shri Praful Patel alongwith the senior officers of the Ministry of Civil Aviation and the Airports Authority of India (AAI) held a meeting with the representatives of AAI Employees Union here today. A number of issues including the closure of Bangalore & Hyderabad Airports raised by the Union representatives were discussed. It has been decided that the Ministry will look into these matters in detail and another round of discussion will be held with the Union representatives in the near future. Meanwhile, the Union representatives have agreed to defer their strike which was to begin tomorrow.

6047. (25-2-2008) NEW DELHI : Minister of State for Law and Justice K. Venkatapathy has said that all concerned agencies should take special care to ensure speedy justice for women. Delivering his address at the "National Conclave of North Eastern States on Access to Justice to Women of the Region" Shri Venkatapathy said, in this context, the role of law as an instrument of justice dispensation for the aggrieved assumes significance. The Minister said, the Constitution of India has assured to each citizen political social and economic justice. However, assurance of political justice is of no substance if the citizens are perpetually denied of their social or economic rights. Social Justice would be a hollow proposition, if it were not accompanied by just distribution of economic resources with equitable access to the opportunities to people. He said, legislatures at the national and State level have contributed by creating a plethora of laws in the realm of social welfare. Statutory declarations alone do create rights but they have to be followed up by the executive who is duty-bound to enforce those rights and make them meaningful. In order to dispense justice to people, we will need to have harmonious relationship between the Executive, Judiciary and the Legislature and Convergence of the multi sectoral schemes created for citizens' welfare. Since independence, India has taken successful strides in almost all walks of life. Yet the promises of equality, liberty and justice to everyone remain mostly a dream for the masses. The Minister said, it is a matter of great satisfaction that the concept of legal aid and advice has now been evolved and recognized as a statutorily guaranteed right to "legal service". Shri Venkatapathy said, judicial pronouncements have only reinforced the view of evolving the right to free legal aid services as an essential element of "reasonable, fair and just procedure" vis-a-vis the poor and needy. Steps need to be taken to spread awareness of the legal provisions and institutions, which can render necessary help to in securing these rights. Laws must be simplified so that ordinary persons understand them better. The objectives of the National Legal Literacy Mission must be taken forward with great speed. It is important to ensure that the people have the ability to approach a legal institution and claim the enforcement of a right. An institution must make procedures as simple as possible for persons to gain access to it. The institution must ensure that the remedy it is able to offer in fact reaches those who need it most.

6048. (25-2-2008) NEW DELHI : Lt Gen PC Bhardwaj, presently GOC 14 Corps has been promoted as Army Commander and posted as GOC-in-C Northern Command. He replaces Lt Gen HS Panag who has been posted as GOC-in-C Central Command. Lt Gen HS Panag replaces Lt Gen OP Nandrajog who retires on 29 February 2008. Lt Gen VK Singh, presently GOC 2 Corps has been promoted as Army Commander and posted as GOC-in-C Eastern Command. He replaces Lt Gen KS Jamwal who also retires on 29 February 2008. All the Army Commanders will assume their new assignments from 01 March 2008. As for other appointments on promotion, Maj Gen JP Singh, presently the Deputy Commandant of Armoured School and Centre is to be the GOC of 2 Corps, while Maj Gen VK Ahluwalia, presently the Additional Director General of Military Training is to be the GOC of 14 Corps.

6049. (25-2-2008) NEW DELHI : The Board of Approval of the Special Economic Zones (SEZs) met on 25th February, 2008 to consider proposals for setting up of Special Economic Zones and also approve other miscellaneous requests pertaining to SEZs. Addressing the Board of Approval members, the Chairman informed that so far formal approvals have been granted for setting up of 439 SEZs out of which 201 have been notified as on date. He informed that over Rs.67347 crore have been invested in these notified SEZs during this short span of time. Direct employment of the order of 97478 persons has been generated in the new generation SEZs, which is in addition to the employment provided by the 7 Central Government established SEZs which is over 1.83 lakh persons. In this meeting, 14 proposals for setting up SEZs, including 3 proposals for conversion of in-principle approvals to formal approvals. The Board recommended grant of 10 Formal approvals.

6050. (25-2-2008) NEW DELHI : Thirty-one new RM radio channels were commissioned during January, 2008. With this, the total number of operational FM channels in India has gone up to 187. The Government also received a sum of Rs. 9,94,21,745/- as licence fee from the private FM radio broadcasters during the period. The newly commissioned FM radio channels are, 'Oolala' by Positive Radio for Agartala and Shillong; 'S.FM' by Kal Radio for Pondicherry, Rajahmundry, Trishur, Trichi, Varanasi and Vijaywada; 'BIG FM' by Adlabs Films for Jodhpur, Mangalore, Pondicherry and Rourkela; 'My FM' by Synergy Media for Jodhpur and Raipur, 'Best FM 95' by Asianet Communications for Kannur and Trishur; 'Mango FM' by Malayala Manorama for Kannur; 'Club FM' by Mathrabhumi for Kannur; 'Tomoto FM' by Pudhari Publications for Kolhapur; 'Hello FM' by Malar Publications for Pondicherry and Trichy; 'Radio Dhamaal' by B.A.G. Infotainment for Ranchi; 'Mantra FM' by Shri Puran Multimedia for Ranchi; 'Radio Mirchi' by ENIL for Raipur and Thiruvananthapuram' 'Radio City' by MBPL for Sangli; Kushal Global for Ajmer; Muthoot Finance for Chennai; PCM Cemments for Siliguri and Syntech for Siliguri.

6051. (25-2-2008) NEW DELHI : Inaugurating the National Yoga Week-2008 organized by the Morarji Desai National Institute of Yoga (MDNIY), the Union Minister for Health & Family Welfare, Dr. Anbumani Ramadoss said the treatments in the modern medical hospitals are becoming expensive affairs for general public and so Yoga is gradually making a new niche in the healthcare sector. It is a traditional system of Indian medicine and has the vast potential of prevention and therapeutic dimensions. Smt. Anita Das, Secretary, AYUSH, Dr. R.K. Srivastava, DGHS and other senior officials from the Ministry of Health were present at the function organized in technical collaboration with DGHS and WHO The following is the summary of the Health Minister's speech: Yoga is a holistic system of health care and has a legacy of in-depth prospective of spiritual, social and medicinal values, especially in the era of Liberalization, Privatization and Globalization (LPG), where every one wants peace, harmony and satisfaction from the untidy and hyperactive social milieu. With the advancement of modernization, busy and hectic schedule of the social life, the significance of Yoga have greatly increased and gradually becoming a blissful way of life. In spite of being a discipline of spiritual advancement in the ancient days, Yoga has fittingly unleashed its horizon all over the world, particularly in the western hemisphere like USA, Canada, England, Germany, France and many other nations of the world. At the same time, it is conveying profound thought and getting worldwide popularity for its physical, physiological and psychological healing responses. However, this is not the end; the community of Scientists, Yoga researchers, Educationists, and Therapists has started churning the very possible use and zest of Yoga in every field and walk of life. This enthusiasm will facilitate a new paradigm of Yoga for overall development of human beings. A large number of researches and studies are going on in various medical institutions and research centres both at the national and international level on Yoga so that the importance of this unique form of treatment can be visualized at a larger level. Yoga has the capability of developing self-realization with in-depth potential of spiritual and ethical values. In the age of urbanizations and globalization, the various components of Yoga are gaining momentum and becoming popular field of medicine to treat the several health problems and malaises of the present day. Even in a number of places, it is given preferences to the modern medicine because of larger faith and beliefs of the people. It is also playing a pivotal role in the management of diseases that is generally declared incurable by the physicians. Yoga converts distress to de-stress and disease to ease. Yoga practices help in alleviating distress and thus producing therapeutic benefits. It has also the potential to strengthen the inner vigor. It is a proven system of techniques used to create health of mind and body by well-controlled experiments. It has become imperative to gain maximum from our ancestral medical practices like Yoga so that maximum advantage can be harnessed where modern medical sciences have limited to offer. The Morarji Desai National Institute of Yoga is engaged in multifarious and multidimensional activities and programmes related to Yoga. The Institute is putting its best efforts to bring the system of Yoga in the mainstream of health care delivery system. The Institute has also taken a new initiative of starting Yoga Therapy and Research Centres in Government and Tertiary Hospitals of Modern medicine. Its contribution in Yoga demonstration and participation in AROGYA melas organized by the Ministry is much more appreciated by all. It has initiated to publish a quarterly journal-YOGA VIJNANA. I hope these unique moves will gather momentum to the propagation of Yoga and create more avenues for the public to use Yoga for their health problems. I appreciate the sincere efforts of the MDNIY for the promotion and propagation of Yoga by keeping the traditional values intact. The National Yoga Week is a Mass Awareness Programme for Health, Happiness and Harmony through Yoga. It is a good initiative from the Institute where eminent Yoga experts, professionals and experts of allied sciences will share their enriched knowledge for stimulating and inspiring holistic approach for the betterment of the society. A need was being felt for a forum where active and dynamic researchers of this area can meet periodically to report new experiments and theoretical developments to examine hypothesis, explain physical phenomenon, and discuss common problems faced by people working in this domain. I hope the deliberations in this National Yoga Week would lead us to explore possible collaborations at multilateral fronts for systematic development of Yoga in all its aspects at the regional and global levels. On the same wavelength, the various Yoga Institutions and Departments in different parts of the country should take an initiative to organize National Yoga Week event simultaneously on the said theme/events at least for a day or two to preserve the very purpose and sanctity of this event so as to make it a truly national event in the days to come.

6052. (25-2-2008) NEW DELHI : The Union Public Service Commission (UPSC) today declared the result of Combined Defence Services (CDS) Examination (I)-2007. 254 candidates (225* + 29^) have finally qualified on the basis of the results of the CDS Examination (I)-2007 conducted by the UPSC and interviews held by the Services Selection Board of the Ministry of Defence for admission to the (i) *Officers' Training Academy, Chennai for 87th Short Service Commission Course (for men); and (ii) ^1st Short Service Commission (Women Non-Technical) Course, commencing in April, 2008. The list of 87th Short Service Commission Course (for men) also includes the names of the candidates who were recommended earlier on the basis of the result of the same examination for admission to the Indian Military Academy-Dehradun/Naval Academy-Goa Course and Air Force Station-Begumpet, Hyderabad Course (s). The number of vacancies as intimated by the Government, for (i) 87th Short Service Commission Course (for men) is 175; and for (ii) 1st Short Service Commission (Women Non-Technical) Course is 11. The result of Medical Examination of candidates has not been taken into account in preparing the merit list. The candidature of all the candidates is Provisional. UPSC have a Facilitation Counter near Examination Hall Building in its Campus.

6053. (25-2-2008) NEW DELHI : Dr. Mohamed ElBaradei, Director General, International Atomic Energy Agency (IAEA) has established a "Commission of Eminent Persons" for making recommendations to the Board of Governors, regarding longer term priorities and funding of IAEA. He has invited Dr. R. Chidambaram, Principal Scientific Adviser to the Govt. of India (PSA to GOI) to be a member of this Commission. The first meeting of the Commission is being held at Vienna, Headquarters of the IAEA from 24-26 February, 2008. Dr. Chidambaram is now in Vienna attending the first meeting of the Commission.

6054. (25-2-2008) NEW DELHI : As a token of goodwill and friendship, Inidan army presented two stallions and four mares to Bangladesh army. The reins of the horses were handed over by Gen Deepak Kapoor, Chief of Army Staff to his Bangladesh counterpart, General Moeen U Ahmed here today. The presentation ceremony followed a guard of honour to the visiting dignitary and his laying a wreath at Amar Jawan Jyoti, India Gate. Lt Gen Sudhir Sharma, Quartermaster General and Lt Gen N Mohanty, Director General Remount Veterinary Services were also present at the handing over ceremony alongwith other dignitaries. These stallions and mares will form a strong breeding germ-plasm for production of quality horses for Bangladesh Army and promote multifarious equestrian activities in that country. The two stallions and the four broodmares have been bred and produced at Equine Breeding Studs of remount Veterinary Corps, Indian Army at Hisar & Babugarh. These horses will be transported to Indo-Bangladesh border under arrangement of Indian Army by road. The horses will finally be handed over to Bangladesh Army at Haridaspur-Banipole on Indo Bangladesh border. General Moeen U Ahmed is also scheduled to visit Indian Military Academy at Dehradun and other Army institutions during his six day visit to India.

6055. (25-2-2008) NEW DELHI : The 4-day biannual International Microbicides 2008 Conference was inaugurated yesterday (24.2.2008) by the Union Minister for Health & Family Welfare, Dr. Anbumani Ramadoss. Congratulating the Indian Council for Media Research (ICMR) for organizing this important international event, the Minister particularly emphasized the need for an active participation and collaboration amongst all stakeholders in achieving the goal of developing a safe, effective, and accessible microbicide for a woman more than a man to deal with behavioral change. It is for the first time that this meeting is being held in the Asian region in which over 1100 delegates comprising researchers, public health workers, communities and advocacy organizations have gathered together from across the Globe to discuss and deliberate current research and development of an effective microbicide. Microbicides refers to a range of different products that share one common characteristic: the ability to prevent the sexual transmission of HIV and other sexually transmitted infections when applied topically. A variety of microbicides are being researched which could be delivered in many forms: gels, creams, suppositories, films, sponge or ring. Microbicides are currently under research & development. The biannual International Microbicides Conference has become one of the most important international scientific and networking conferences in the fight against HIV/AIDS. Maintaining global commitment to this effort requires continued pressure from the scientists and advocates who are working on microbicides, and this conference allows this critical research field to be continuously profiled and developed. The conference provides updates on recent Microbicides research, creates a forum for the discussion of new developments in Microbicides research and to present opportunities for knowledge sharing between Microbicides researchers, public health workers, advocates, communities and civil society organizations. Despite the knowledge of successful HIV prevention strategy, HIV continues to spread at an alarming rate especially among women in developing countries. Specifically, there are about 2.5 million cases of HIV in India. The prevalence rate of HIV amongst 15-49 years age group is 0.9 % and a mere 0.1 % increase in the HIV prevalence would result in addition of 0.5 millions new cases. The use of current HIV controlled methods such as abstinence, monogamy and condoms-males / females are not always feasible. Therefore, there is an urgent need to have other HIV prevention technologies which are women initiated. The 4-day meet (24th-27th February, 2008) with an international scientific advisory committee with eminent medical scientist Dr. N.K. Ganguly, formerly Director-General, ICMR as the Chair and national organizing committee with Shri. Naresh Dayal, Secretary, Ministry of Health & Family Welfare as Chair, will be discussing at length various issues in four simultaneous tracks-basic science, clinical, social science and community & advocacy under eminent Chairpersons. Specifically, there will be nine plenary sessions, and presentations of 553 Original researches [oral, poster, book] as also cross track sessions, round table discussion sessions including poster sessions and exhibitions.

6056. (25-2-2008) NEW DELHI : Congress spokesman Shri Abhishek Singhvi said delegations of farmers, associations of farmers met the Hon'ble Prime Minister and the Congress President. The Congress Party strongly stands by the legitimate and just demands of diverse sections of the farming community, the agricultural community. The Congress Party has always played a pioneering and historic role in the development of the entire agricultural sector. After 2004, the budgets by the Congress-led UPA have provided unique initiatives, tailored and focused on the agricultural sector. If you will recollect, the agricultural rural credit, more schemes started since 2004 under the successive budgets than for years and years before. If you will remember the irrigation schemes and allocations, more initiatives started from 2004 than for years and decades before. If you will hearken back to the largest ever agricultural support programme regarding Vidarbha, announced by the Prime Minister some time ago, there have been many more initiatives but we feel sure that the government will respond positively to the many just and legitimate concerns of the farmer, in particular to the legitimate and just concern regarding waiver or significant softening of the loan burden. We also want to remind you that the initiatives of the Congress-led UPA government have led to a continuous and sustained decrease in the unfortunate incidents of suicides in certain vulnerable areas. This is not to say that it is in the hands of the government to altogether prevent it but very strongly targeted ameliorative measures have, in the recent past, significantly dealt with in a positive manner the scourge of suicides facing our farming community. It is the Congress Party, if you go back longer into history, ushered in the Green Revolution. It is the Congress Party which has always believed that if democracy is of the people, by the people, for the people then it is first and foremost of the farmers, by the farmers for the farmers. We also believe that this is not a mere focus on one sector because the impact and the effect of this is cross-sectoral. When we feel proud of our 8%, 9% hopefully 10% growth, we cannot sustain it without stepping up the agricultural sector growth rate. And it is with that comprehensive approach that the Congress Party hopes and trusts that the economic initiatives in the next few days will address the legitimate concerns of this vulnerable community. To a question that the BJP had asked the Lok Sabha Speaker regarding the suspension of question hour, Shri Singhvi said, let me be clear, any and every discussion is welcome. It has to be as per rules, it has to be a genuine discussion and there is no problem if you want to have discussion. Parliament is the grand inquest of the nation but on the pretext of discussion, on the supposed excuse of discussion please do not disrupt the normal functioning of the House. I am not here to comment on the notice given as it is to be decided by the presiding officers and nobody is supposed to interfere but if you have question hour or zero hour, zero hour takes a short while. You have to see the record of proceedings of the last two sessions and the opposition has not lived up to its promise. But if what you have said is correct, we welcome a discussion but it can be easily done without disrupting any parliamentary procedures. To a question that your Party's leaders in Bihar have said that though it is your Party in Maharashtra and at the Centre why then the exodus of Biharis and Upites from Maharashtra, Shri Singhvi said, it is not proper to evaluate and give judgement on certain incidents. The concerned state and the Centre as also the Congress Party have condemned the exodus. We have, as per law, taken appropriate steps. The situation is now under control and cases have been filed against those involved. To a question that the Left parties have once again raised the issue of the nuke deal, what is your take on this, Shri Singhvi said, there is no change in any body's stand. As far as the desirability of the deal is concerned we must emphatically state that we stand for the deal and equally we agree to disagree. No amount of statements is going to change either our stand or the position we agree to disagree.

6057. (25-2-2008) NEW DELHI : The President of India, Smt. Pratibha Devisingh Patil witnessed a ballet programme titled, "Smruti Sankalp Yatra" which included a cultural and musical presentation on the social evil of female infanticide and the environmental issue of global warming at Rashtrapati Bhavan today. The programme was presented by the Yuvak Biradari (Bharat) of Mumbai and supported by the Sangeet Natak Academy. The programme highlighted the evil of female infanticide through a ballet called "Ajanmika", which combined folk and classical dance forms. The show also highlighted the pressing problem of global warming and also included a cultural presentation depicting India's freedom struggle from 1857 to 1947 through song and dance with ballet in various languages of the country. Some 200 school children and about 40 professional theatre artistes performed in the show. The following schools were also associated with the show:- the Nalanda Nrutya Kala Mahavidyalaya, Mumbai, the Fulma Dance Academy, Vadodara, the R.D. Public School, New Delhi, the Prelude School, Agra and the Sumermal Jain School, New Delhi. The Yuvak Biradari (Bharat) was formed in 1974 aimed at being an engine for social development and youth welfare. The organisation concentrates on the social, educational and cultural advancement of society.

6058. (25-2-2008) NEW DELHI : The Prime Minister, Dr. Manmohan Singh addressed the thanksgiving rally of Punjab farmers in Delhi today. The farmers expressed gratitude to the government for waiving off the loans of Punjab farmers and also submitted a charter of demands to the Prime Minister. Speaking at the occasion, Dr. Singh said: "You have come here in such large numbers. I understand the agony of the people of Punjab especially farmers. Even last year our government had waved off the loans of the Punjab government. The budget is expected in another two three days and it would be inappropriate for me to discuss these issues in detail. But I would like to assure you that under the leadership of Smt Sonia Gandhi, our government would pay attention to the demands listed in the Memorandum that has been submitted. Smt Sonia Gandhi ji, Congress Party and the UPA government desire that Punjab should progress and prosper. With these words, I thank you all once again for coming here. Akali Dal is taking out rallys, organizing public gatherings to convey that UPA government is not protecting the Punjab farmers. This is absolutely wrong and by coming here in such large numbers, you have proved it. The rights and interests of the people of Punjab are safe in the hands of the UPA government"

6059. (26-2-2008) NEW DELHI : The Annual Plan for Arunachal Pradesh for the year 2008-09 was finalized here today at a meeting between Deputy Chairman, Planning Commission Shri Montek Singh Ahluwalia and Chief Minister of Arunachal Pradesh, Shri Dorjee Khandu. The Plan outlay has been finalized at Rs. 2065 crores. Deputy Chairman, Planning Commission, Mr. Ahluwalia in his comments on pace of development pointed out that the State needs to explore all options for generating more resources. He said focused attention should be given to the development of horticulture, floriculture, tourism and power generation. He said the State needs to have a medium term policy to exploit available hydro potential as it will substantially add to State resources. It was pointed out that inadequate transport infrastructure was a major constraint in the development efforts. Efforts to involve private sector in providing health services and education was appreciated. The State should take advantage of Central programmes in improving horticulture and skill development. Vast natural resources, particularly enormous hydro power potential, oil and natural gas and tourism offer a strong advantage to transform this strategically located State into one of the richest State in the country. It should also work on rich heritage of traditional handlooms & handicrafts. The Chief Minister, Mr. Khandu said that efforts were being made to improve resources and given transparent administration to the people. He said a number of new initiatives are being planned but resource constraint is a major bottleneck. He sought Planning Commission's help in changing the guidelines for Centrally Sponsored Schemes so as to enable to the State to execute them.

6060. (26-2-2008) NEW DELHI : The following is the text of the address of the Vice President of India, Shri Mohd. Hamid Ansari at the 'Golden Jubilee Foundation Day Function of Maulana Azad Medical College' (MAMC), here today: "It is my pleasure to be here today at the Golden Jubilee Foundation Day function of the Maulana Azad Medical College (MAMC). Since its inception in 1958, it has evolved as a premier institution in medical education in the country. It is also an institution with a unique history. Built in a previous jail complex, its role in the pre-independence era is associated with several historical events. Thousand of freedom fighters were jailed here and many freedom fighters hanged at the gallows at this jail complex. As Pt. Govind Ballabh Pant noted while laying the foundation stone of the College in 1959, "a symbol of our people's suffering was to become a place which would now help to relieve it". It is also very appropriate that the college is named after Maulana Abul Kalam Azad, a great scholar, visionary political leader and the country's first Education Minister who over saw the establishment of our national education system and institutions of higher education. Maulana Azad's message of nurturing our multiple identities within the framework of a strong, united and secular India has acquired new relevance in the India of today. The young medical students of the college today, and their predecessors, have been fortunate to be trained in such an institution. I come to this institution of excellence also to talk about the crisis in medical education in our country. To quote the National Knowledge Commission, "health related education and training has become more urban oriented, doctor-centric and technology-driven;....it is directionless, unregulated and non-standardised;... the quality, quantity and distribution of the health oriented human resources being produced leaves much to be desired".

6061. (26-2-2008) NEW DELHI : The National Institute of Ocean Technology (NIOT), Chennai, an autonomous institute under Ministry of Earth Sciences (MoES) has designed and developed a Remotely Operated unmanned Submersible which is 2.53 m long, 1.80 m wide with height of 1.70 m. This can carry a payload of 150 kg. The complete hardware and software for the instrumentation and control system was developed by Indian Scientists. An integrated navigation system comprising Hydro Acoustic Navigation System (HANS), Inertial Navigation System and Doppler Velocity Log has also been developed. This would benefit researchers in carrying out various research works like sampling, seabed, photography, inspection of underwater vehicles, pipelines, etc. This information was given by Union Minister for Science & Technology and Earth Sciences, Shri Kapil Sibal, in the Lok Sabha today.

6062. (26-2-2008) NEW DELHI : A new medical college, Army College of Medical Sciences (ACMS), Delhi Cantt is to commence its first MBBS course in the next academic sesion. ACMS, affiliated with Guru Gobind Singh Indraprasth University, Delhi has been established under the aegis of Army Welfare Education Society (AWES). This college is for wards of Army personnel, including Short Service officers who have served the Army for ten years. Children of officers from Army Medical and Dental Corps presently serving in the Airforce or Navy but have served the Army for 10 years and are members of Army Officers Benevolent Fund will also be eligible to apply. Similarly wards of Military Nursing Services and Army Postal Service who have served in the Army for ten years are also eligible. Admissions to 100 seats will be based on a common entrance test to be conducted by Guru Gobind Indraprasth University. Eligible Candidates short listed on the basis of CET marks will be called for counselling at ACMS in Jul. 2008. After completing the course, the candidates will have to join the Army as short service officers in Army's Medical Corps. The Army already has dental and engineering colleges at Secunderabad and Pune respectively.

6063. (26-2-2008) NEW DELHI : Congress spokesman Smt Jayanthi Natrajan said that the Indian National Congress congratulates the Railway Minister for having presented a people-friendly, growth-oriented, extremely productive Railway Budget. The Railway Minister has continued the trend of success which he has already set in the last few years and in this Budget as well, oriented the Budget to serve the needs of the central focus of the UPA government which is the aam admi. Passenger fares have been reduced, special concessions have been given to senior citizens and to students as also to patients travelling for treatment for HIV and AIDS. There are also very welcome provisions of making travel easier by introducing parking facilities, reducing queues and overall better management. More importantly, the Hon'ble Railway Minister has attempted successfully to spread the benefit of new innovations and facilities for the rail-travelling Budget all over the country. This is a very positive, productive, people-friendly Budget and we welcome it. To a question that Shri Karat and Shri Yechuri attended the rallies by your adversaries and even met them saying not much has been done for the farmers, Smt Jayanthi said, one of the primary focus of the UPA government is farmers and issues relating to welfare of the people in the agriculture sector. So it is absolutely incorrect to say that the UPA government has failed to deliver or concentrate upon issues relating to farmers. Insofar as certain leaders who are supporting us from outside are attending any rally being conducted by other parties, it has no connection whatsoever to the support that they are extending to the UPA government. This is a very strong alliance which will continue. To a question on the Sethusumandram project as to what is the Congress Party's stand since in the Cabinet committee on political affair there was a war of words as the government wanted the affidavits withdrawn and is now considering dismissing the PILs, Smt Jayanthi said, the Congress Party's stand is very clear. I am not aware of any war of words in the Cabinet. The Sethusamundaram project is a long-standing demand of the people of Tamil Nadu. The matter is now in the Supreme Court and we will await the decision on the subject but as far as the alignment and progress is concerned, all these will be governed by the directions of the Supreme Court. As far as the Party is concerned it would like to take all aspects of public opinion into consideration and ensure that the aspirations of the people of Tamil Nadu are fulfilled on the one hand and public opinion is not hurt on the other hand. To a question that Darul Uloom in UP's Deoband district passed a declaration condemning terrorism and blamed the UPA government that it could not protect innocent Muslims. What is your reaction, Smt. Jayanthisaid, first, we welcome any declaration and believe all the people of India should join in fighting terrorism with all the strength at our command and the government, the political system and every citizen will stand as one to uproot terrorism form our soil and from anywhere else. Hence determination to fight terrorism is welcome. The UPA government and its allies will never allow harassment of innocent citizens of the country of any religion.

6064. (26-2-2008) NEW DELHI : Based on the information furnished by University Grants Commission (UGC), there are 415 Universities/Institutions in the country as on 31.12.2007 and 6680 Colleges under Section 2(f) and 12(B) of UGC Act, 1956. The State-wise details is Annexed. There are 1820 teaching posts and 5067 non-teaching posts lying vacant in Central Universities as on 31.3.2007 and 627 teaching posts lying vacant in 74 State Universities as on 1.5.2007. The UGC has been directing all the Central Universities to fill up the vacant posts in Universities. The UGC has issued a circular dated 23.3.2006 to all Universities of State Governments to fill up the vacant posts on regular basis as per norms of Commission since continuation of appointment of faculty in contract, part time and guest faculty on long terms basis effects the quality of education. The Central Government has already increased the age of superannuation from 62 years to 65 years in respect of teachers of Centrally Funded Technical and Higher Educational Institutions which come under the purview of Ministry of Human Resource Development, in view of acute shortage of experienced teachers. The State Governments were also requested that they too may take a similar view in view of the prevailing circumstances.

6065. (26-2-2008) NEW DELHI : The President Smt. Pratibha Devisingh Patil presented the prestigious Sangeet Natak Akademi Fellowship and Akademi Awards for 2007 at a special ceremony here today. Presenting the Awards the President said, Indian art and music must look at the social role that they can play. Dance and drama are a powerful medium and can be used to effectively convey social messages particularly to fight social evils like female foeticide, female infanticide, dowry and addiction to drugs and alcohol. They can also educate the population on various issues such as health, literacy and the values of truth, tolerance and harmony. She called upon the social organizations to promote music and art as a means of bringing about awareness, harmony and peace in society. Expressing concern that some of our traditional folk arts were fast disappearing for want of patronage, she said we must look at how the "patrons of arts" in our society-whether corporate houses, musical societies, local artist groups-can be encouraged to support the classical and the traditional arts. The President called upon all the people of the country to participate in the learning, understanding and preservation of our diverse and rich culture. Earlier, congratulating the award winners the Minister for Culture and Tourism Smt. Ambika Soni said the Government was acting as a facilitator for promoting art, culture and the diversity and plurality of our country. She said 'Incredible India' did not relate to tourism alone, its all about our rich art, culture and heritage. Smt. Soni said recently Indian artistes performed abroad to celebrate 60 years of our independence. It showcased the traditional Indian art in the world arena. This year the most coveted honour of Akademi Fellowship (Akademi Ratna) was conferred on eminent scholar and Professor of aesthetics, Dr. S.K. Saxena. The award contains a purse money of Rs. one lakh, besides a citation, an angavastram and a tamrapatra. 33 eminent persons were conferred the Akademi Awards for the year 2007 carrying a purse money of Rs. 50,000/-, citation, angavastram and tamrapatra.

6066. (26-2-2008) NEW DELHI : With a view to provide assistance to State Government, a scheme for "Flood Management Programme" with an estimated cost of Rs. 8000 crore has been approved under State sector of Central Plan. A Central Sector scheme for "River Management Activities and Works related to Border Areas" under Central Plan has also been envisaged in XI Plan under which various activities for Ministry of Water Resources and its organizations are undertaken. Guidelines for providing central assistance to States under the scheme for Flood Management Programme have been issued to all Sates in December 2007. This information was given by the Minister of State for Water Resources, Shri Jai Prakash Narayan Yadav in response to a question by Smt. Supriya Sule in the Rajya Sabha today.

6067. (26-2-2008) NEW DELHI : There is no proposal to bring any river under Central ambit by identifying it as National River. Government has already enacted Inter-State Water Dispute Act in 1956 for adjudication of water disputes and amended the same in 2002 for time bound adjudication of the disputes and the "Act is now called Inter State River Water Dispute Act, 1956. This information was given by the Minister of State for Water Resources, Shri Jai Prakash Narayan

Yadav in response to a question by Shri Mahmood A. Madani, Smt. Supriya Sule, Shri Gireesh Kumar Sanghi, Shri Jesudasu Seelam and Shri Santosh Bagrodia in the Rajya Sabha today.

6068. (26-2-2008) NEW DELHI : The releases under AIBP are regulated by the State Wise ceilings of grant for Accelerated Irrigation Benefits Programme (AIBP) fixed by the Planning Commission. For the year 2007-08, initial ceiling proposed by the Planning Commission for Rajasthan was of Rs. 125 crore which was subsequently revised to Rs. 250 crore. The Ministry of Finance released Rs. 100.26 crore as AIBP grant for the State of Rajasthan on 9h April 2007 for the AIBP proposals fo the State for the year 2006-07. Since the grant was released during the year 2007-08, the same is adjustable against the grant ceiling for the year 2007-08. However, as stated above, the Planning Commission has subsequently raised the grant ceiling under AIBP for the Rajasthan to Rs. 250 crore resulting in available balance amount of ceiling of Rs. 149.74 crore for release during 2007-08. This information was given by the Minister of State for Water Resources, Shri Jai Prakash Narayan Yadav in response to a question by Shri Lalit Kishore Chaturvedi in the Rajya Sabha today.

6069. (26-2-2008) NEW DELHI : The Government has proposed to set up 93 AIR transmitters and 41 Doordarshan transmitters in the country during 2007-2008 and 2008-2009. in addition, 100 Low Power Transmitters (LPTs) will also be set up in the North Eastern States. The total estimated cost in respect of All India Radio is 182 crores. The same in respect of Doordarshan is 198.37 crores. The criteria followed by the Government for establishment of Radio and TV transmitters include factors such as extent of resultant coverage to urban and rural population; provision of coverage to tribal, hilly, remote and border areas; terrain conditions etc., and it has no linkage to the number of cities. This information was given by Minister of Information & Broadcasting and Parliamentary Affairs, Shri P. R. Dasmunsi in written reply to a question in Lok Sabha today.

6070. (26-2-2008) NEW DELHI : The Swedish Parliamentary delegation led by Mr. Per Westerberg, Speaker of the Riksdag today called on Minister of Information & broadcasting and Parliamentary Affairs, Shri P. R. Dasmunsi. Shri Dasmunsi apprised the visiting dignitaries of the functioning of the Parliamentary system in India. He also gave them an overview of the committee system in Indian Parliament as well as the role of the Speaker. The two sides discussed the areas of mutual cooperation between the two countries and shared policy perspective on issues that have global import. The visiting dignitaries appreciated the faster pace of economic growth of Indian economy.

6071. (26-2-2008) NEW DELHI : State and Union Territories-wise Gross Enrolment Ratio for Primary (classes I-V), Middle (classes VI-VIII) and Secondary/ Senior Secondary (classes IX-XII) and Dropout Rates for classes I-V, I-VIII and I-X for the period from 2002-03 to 2004-05 are given at Annexure I, II & III.

Annual class-wise enrolment figures are not collected for urban and rural areas separately. Drop out rate for standard XII is not calculated. A multi-pronged approach has been adopted under Sarva Shiksha Abhiyan (SSA) for reducing dropout rates. One set of interventions are towards strengthening of schools and improving the quality of education through improvement in school infrastructure, recruitment of additional teachers, annual school grants, regular training of teachers, regular academic support to teachers etc. In addition, several interventions under SSA also aim at community support, flexible schooling for children who are drop-outs, older children or children in difficult circumstances, and special provisions to promote education of girls, children from disadvantaged sections of society or children with special needs. Central Government is committed to make secondary education of good quality available, accessible and affordable to all young persons. At present, Central intervention in secondary education is through various centrally sponsored schemes like, Information and Communication Technology (ICT) in schools, Integrated Education for Disabled Children and strengthening of Boarding and Hostel facilities for Students of Secondary and Higher Secondary Schools.

6072. (26-2-2008) NEW DELHI : To assess progress of States and Union Territories towards universalization of elementary education, an Educational Development Index (EDI), has been developed by National University of Educational Planning and Administration (NUEPA). The EDI is based on four broad parameters of access, infrastructure, teacher related indicators and elementary education outcomes. State-wise ranking on a composite index for primary and upper primary level of education for the year 2006-07 data, is at Annexure. EDI details are taken into regard in approving Annual Work Plan & Budgets of States/ districts, in order to address, inter-alia, gaps in infrastructure, equity issues and quality outcomes, by the Government of India. This information was given by the Minister of State for Human Resource Development Shri M.A. A. Fatmi in a written reply in Lok Sabha today.

6073. (26-2-2008) NEW DELHI : The University Grants Commission (UGC) has constituted a Committee to prepare draft Regulations for admission and fee structure in self financing Universities and Colleges. In the XI Plan document, the Planning Commission has, inter-alia, suggested that since most university students come from top 10 per cent of the population by income levels, they would be able to pay fees amounting to 20 per cent of the operating cost of general higher education. The fee levels should, therefore, be increased gradually in existing institutions but the new norms could be implemented in new institutions from the start. This information was given by the Minister of State for Human Resource Development Smt. D. Purandeswari in a written reply in Lok Sabha today.

6074. (26-2-2008) NEW DELHI : The US Secretary of Defence, Dr. Robert Gates arrived in New Delhi this afternoon on a two day visit to India. Dr. Gates is making his first visit to India since assuming office on 18th December, 2006. Secretary Gates' visit takes place in the last of the eight year Bush Presidency that witnessed unprecedented acceleration in India-US engagement and qualitative transformation in the relationship, in particular in Defence. India and US have a strong framework of defence cooperation established by the 2005 Defence Framework Agreement and a comprehensive institutional framework of exchanges. Secretary Gates' visit will give a further impetus to the ongoing defence cooperation between our two countries. During his stay, Secretary Gates will be meeting the External Affairs Minister Shri Pranab Mukherjee, the Defence Minister Shri AK Antony, the National Security Advisor Shri MK Narayanan and the leader of the Opposition Shri L K Advani. His visit to India reaffirms the importance of the Indo-US relations and the strong political support in the US for our strategic partnership. India also reiterates its interest in looking forward to broad-based defence ties with the USA.

6075. (26-2-2008) NEW DELHI : Following is the text of the address by Her Excellency the President of India, Shrimati Pratibha Devisingh Patil, at the presentation of the fellowship and awards of the Sangeet Natak Akademi for the year 2007 in New Delhi today: I am glad to be present here at the award ceremony of the Sangeet Natak Akademi. I would like to congratulate Dr. Sushil Kumar Saxena for being elected a Fellow of the Akademi. I would also like to convey my congratulations to all the 33 artists who have been conferred the Sangeet Natak Akademi Awards for the year 2007 in recognition of the excellence they have achieved in their respective fields of performing arts. Since its inception in 1952 the Sangeet Natak Akademi, as the apex body of the performing arts, has contributed to the preservation and conservation of our cultural heritage. It sponsors festivals, seminars and conferences on performing arts; encourages exchange of ideas and enrichment of techniques between different regions with respect to performing arts; helps to revive and preserve folk music, folk drama and folk dance and also promotes the development of children's theatre and research in the field of Indian music, dance, and drama. Its annual awards are the highest national recognition of the contribution made by artistes to various fields of performing arts. We must encourage the Sangeet Natak Akademi to continue its work in the field of art and culture. India occupies an important place on the cultural map of the world. We can be justly proud of our rich and varied culture. We are one of the oldest and continuous civilizations of the world. This has been possible because of our inherent strengths and resilience as well as our ability to incorporate change and cope with new ideas without losing our basic character and values. Resultantly, today, we have inherited a valuable range of art, literature, monuments, customs and traditions that enrich our lives. Each one of us must honour the cultural legacy left to us by our forefathers and contribute to its preservation for our future generation. Under the Constitution, it is the duty of each and every citizen of India to value and preserve the rich heritage of our composite culture. I call on the people of the country to participate in the learning, understanding and preservation of our diverse and rich culture. Performing arts, both classical and folk, are basic to our identity. Whether it is the sound of the Sitar, the Sarod, the Veena, or

Nadhaswaram and other musical instruments or it is the dance forms of Kathak, Kathakali, Bharatanatyam, Kuchipudi, Mohiniattam, Odissi or other folk dances, all these have the capacity to arouse the feeling of "being an Indian" in each one of us. The world over in the minds of people all these are associated with India. One of the aims of Sangeet Natak Akademi should be to encourage the best talent from all parts of the country and also to reach the performing arts to a large a number of people as far as possible. We have to spread dance, music and drama to the masses. This is one of the participatory ways for the preservation of our culture. This approach in our policy for the cultural development of the country could result in people becoming patrons of the performing arts and stakeholders in the efforts for the preservation of our rich civilizational history of more than 5,000 years. Some of our traditional folk arts are fast disappearing for want of patronage. We must look at how the "patrons of arts" in our society-whether corporate houses, musical societies, local artist groups-can be encouraged to support the classical and the traditional arts. We are living in times of considerable change and in a globalised world, in which there is a constant interaction and flow of ideas. In such a scenario, it becomes imperative for the Akademi to ensure that its various schemes and programmes, address themselves adequately to the traditional arts in the changing environment. It should look at using the different media of the new world like the Internet and multimedia systems, in addition to innovatively using the electronic media for promoting performing arts. Our special efforts should be to reach out to the new generation and to inculcate in them an appreciation for our culture. Our artists and musicians should attract them to learning music and dance. The Sangeet Natak Akademi should encourage budding young artists through Youth Talent awards and through grant of sponsorships and scholarships, in cases where the young artists do not have adequate financial resources. Attaining excellence in the performing arts is the result of very hard work. Music, dance and drama all require considerable amount of discipline and riyaz. The greatest of our musicians spend long hours practicing. I call on the youth to show commitment and dedication for learning and excelling in the fields of music, dance and theatre. Indian art and music must also look at the social role that they can play. Dance and drama are a powerful medium and can be used to effectively convey social messages particularly to fight social evils like female foeticide, female infanticide, child marriages, dowry and addiction to drugs and alcohol. They can also educate the population on various issues such as health, literacy and the values of truth, tolerance and harmony. I would call on social organizations and corporate houses to promote music and art as a means for bringing about awareness, harmony and peace in society.

6076. (26-2-2008) NEW DELHI : The national level campaign for the coming kharif season took off today with the Centre exhorting States to make the best use of newly launched schemes, NFSM and RKVY, and to integrate animal husbandry activities in their agricultural plans. Inaugurating the two-day National Conference on Agriculture for Kharif Campaign, Agriculture Secretary, Dr. P.K.

Mishra informed that States had been very prompt in operatinalising the National Food Security Mission (NFSM) and Rastrihya Krishi Vikas Yojana (RKVY) launched a few months back. Though the impact of these schemes would be known only after their implementation for a number of crop seasons, the intermediate parameters are already showing improvement, he said. For example, distribution of quality seed of wheat has shown remarkable increase in Bihar and Rajasthan and that of pulses in Chhattishgarh. So far, Rs. 360 crore have been released for NFSM and Rs. 986 crore for RKVY. Shri Mishra asked the States to make full use of the flexibility provided to them in formulation and implementation of schemes under RKVY. Agriculture Secretary also underlined the importance of extension and marketing in rejuvenating the farm sector. While extension helps in reaching the latest know-how and technology to the farmer, a proper marketing infrastructure helps farmers to get remunerative prices for their produce, he explained. He also informed that as provided in the budget, over 300 ATMAs have been set up this year to give fillip to farm extension. This nationwide network of extension agencies must be initiated by States to disseminate relevant information and advice to farmers, he said. Secretary, Animal Husbandry, Dairying and Fisheries, Dr. Pradeep Kumar, requested the States to increase the share of animal husbandry activities in State and District level agricultural plans. He expressed concern at low importance being given by States to animal husbandry. He said that as against over 30% contribution of livestock related activities to the agriculture sector and their tremendous potential for increasing farm income, only 10% of the RKVY funds are presently being used for livestock-related schemes. Secretary, DARE and DG (ICAR), Dr. Mangala Rai, emphasized on the need to popularize quality seed to farmers. For this, he suggested distribution of seeds of improved varieties in villages for demonstration affect, and need to provide training to farmers to produce hybrid seed. Principal Adviser, Dr. S.M. Jharwal and CEO, National Rainfed Area Authority, Dr. J.S. Sarma also addressed the conference. Besides State Agriculture Secretaries and Agriculture Production Commissioners, Vice Chancellor of state universities, heads of research institutions under ICAR and officials from various departments of central government are participating in the two-day conference.

6077. (26-2-2008) NEW DELHI : During the 10th Plan a composite Centrally Sponsored Scheme of "Quality Improvement in Schools" was introduced by converging the following 5 earlier schemes of the Department as its components:- (i) Improvement of Science Education in Schools (ii) Environmental Orientation to School Education (iii) National Population Education Project (iv) Introduction of Yoga in Schools; and (v) International Science Olympiads Expenditure Reforms Commission had recommended discontinuation of the scheme of Yoga and Environment Education on the ground that the allocations under these schemes were too low to make country-wide impact. After considering the matter, the Committee of Secretaries was of the view that Environment Education and Yoga are important components of quality education and should continue in an expanded form. The scheme of Quality Improvement in Schools was formulated in this background. The component "Improvement of Science Education in Schools" has been transferred to the State Governments/Union Territory Administrations as a State Sector Scheme w.e.f. 1.4.2006 since with limited allocation available, it was not possible to make an impact and since it was felt that the States would be in a better position to articulate their priorities through the State Sector Plan. This information was given by the Minister of State for Human Resource Development Shri M.A.A. Fami in a written reply in Lok Sabha today.

6078. (26-2-2008) NEW DELHI : The National Council of Educational Research and Training (NCERT) has made efforts to revamp the curriculum of school education, including primary education, in order to encourage creative thinking among children. This exercise carried out under the National Curriculum Framework (NCF), 2005 has made a significant shift in school education towards a constructivist paradigm for teaching and learning. Suitable modifications have been made in development of textbooks, classroom transaction and learners' assessment. Based on the recommendations of NCF-2005 and Focus Group papers on different subjects, new syllabi have been developed. Subsequently the new textual material for classes I to V have been developed. These textbooks are child-friendly and provide space for creative thinking. The content of the textbooks is child centred which provide her/him space to explore and construct knowledge. It encourages children to move away from rote learning to creative learning. The NCF-2005 views assessment at all levels, as a meaningful and comprehensive process pertaining to the quality and extent of a child's learning, construction of knowledge and her/his interest attitudes towards leaning, which may be manifested in various activities. The new vision of the curriculum articulated in NCF-2005 has profound implications for creative thinking on the above concerns related to assessment/evaluation of children. Keeping this in view, NCERT has developed a Source Book for assessment at the primary level and it is being 'trialled' out in 10 selected States across the country. This information was given by the Minister of State for Human Resource Development Shri M.A.A. Fami in a written reply in Lok Sabha today.

6079. (26-2-2008) NEW DELHI : According to the National University of Education Planning and Administration's (NUPEA) District Information System for Education (DISE), elementary education the percentage enrolment of Muslim children in the 6-14 years age group compared to the communities' share in the population, shows a national coverage of 9.39% at primary and 7.62% at upper primary level for the year 2006-07. In the case of UP it is 9.24% and 7.18%, in Bihar 8.95% and 6.60%, in West Bengal 27.9% and 19.63%, while in Kerala it is 10.13% and 9.59%, respectively. Data collected on muslim children Under DISE system for elementary education, was done for the first time in September 2006. The data sets stabilize in a few years. While Sachar Committee has not made any estimate of enrolment in proportion to population, based on the data of National Sample Survey organization (NSSO), the committee has estimated that in Kerala, Karnataka, Delhi, Maharashtra and some other states the enrolment rates among Muslims are higher than state average. On the other hand, in states like UP, Bihar, Jharkhand and Uttrakhand enrolment rates are estimated by the committee to be lower than the state average. Under the Sarva Siksha Abhiyan, focused targeting of funds in 88 districts with substantial muslim population is being done. Furthermore, under the Kasturba Gandhi Balika Vidhyalaya's 270 residential schools have been sanctioned in educationally backward blocks with substantial muslim population.

6080. (26-2-2008) NEW DELHI : The World Bank in its 2007 in its 2007 study 'Unleashing India's Innovation: Towards Sustainable & Inclusive Growth" has referred to the said findings of the study conducted by Mckinsey (a consulting firm). For improvement of quality, the University Grants Commission identifies the Universities and Colleges with potential for excellence and gives a maximum financial assistance to Universities of Rs. 30 crores for a period of five years and Rs. 35 lakhs to Rs. 1 crore to colleges. It is also implementing a Special Assistance Programme (SAP) wherein assistance of Rs. 40-100 lakhs is given to eligible Department of Universities having potential for quality teaching and research in various disciplines. The UGC also approves vocational courses in several universities. For improving the quality of technical education the Government is implementing the Technical Education Quality Improvement Programme (TEQIP) in country. The All India Council for Technical Education (AICTE) has also an All India Board of Studies in Information Technology, which advises the Council on, inter-alia, the model curricula for IT courses and their upgradation. Besides, a programme of Finishing School for unemployed engineering graduates, so as to prepare them for the IT/ITeS Industries, has been taken up since 2007-08. This information was given by the Minister of State for Human Resource Development Smt. D. Purandeswari in a written reply in Lok Sabha today.

6081. (26-2-2008) NEW DELHI : Plant based oils are indispensable in the human food as also in several industrial uses. Vegetable oils in India were traditionally used for illuminating lamps even before the arrival of kerosene. These oils and their by-products are increasingly being used in modern industries for various purposes like cosmetics, varnishes, paints, lubricants, resins, adhesives, dyes & inks, explosives, cell phones, pesticides, pharmaceuticals, bio-diesels etc. More than 100 species of plants occurring in wild or cultivated in India have been identified to bear seeds possessing fixed oils in commercially extractable proportions. Certain essential plant oils, widely used as fragrances and flavours in the perfume and food industries, have long been reputed to repel insects. Recent investigations in several countries confirm that some plant essential oils not only repel insects, but have contact and fumigants insecticidal actions against specific pests, and aimed at the development of reduced-risk pesticides based on plant essential oils, toxic and sublethal effects of some essential oil terpenes and phenols have been investigated using the tobacco cutworm (Spodoptera litura) and the green peach aphid (Myzus persicae) as model pest species. They have medicinal properties as well. The antimicrobial properties of 21 plant essential oils and two essences were investigated against five important food-borne pathogens, Camphylobacter Jejuni, Selamonella enteritidis, Escherichia coil, Staphylococcus aureus and Listeria monocytogenes. The oils of bay, cinnamon, clove and thyme were the most inhibitor, each having a bacteristatic concentration of 0.75% or less against all five pathogens. In general, Gram-positive bacteria were more sensitive to inhibition by plant essential oils than the Gram-negative bacteria. Campylobacter jejuni was most resistant of the bacteria investigated to plant essential oils, with only the oils of bay and thyme having a bactericidal concentration of less than 1%. At 35'C, L. monocytogenes was extremely senstiv to the oil of nutmug. A concentration of less than 0.01% was bacteriostatic and 0.05% was bacteriocidal, but when the temperature was reduced to 4'C, the bacteriostatic concentration was increased to 0.5% and the bacteriocidal concentration to grater than 1%. These days, people have a notion that low-fat, high carbohydrate diets are essential for health has grown into an obsession. It is driven largely by an effort to reduce heart dieses and, more recently, certain types of cancer. We know that saturated fatty acids are more closely associated with risk factors for heart disease than are unsaturated fatty acids. Many people believe that plant-based diets are healthy because they are low in fat. However, plant-based diets are not necessarily low-fat. In true plant-based diets, unsaturated fatty acids predominate. Plant-based diets include foods that contain fats, such as nuts and such as nuts and seeds and oils from grains and seeds. The fats in these foods are not associated with increased risk for heart disease. In addition, for people with insulin resistance, higher-fat diets products against the heart disease risk factors of low HDL-cholesterol concentration, hypertriglyceridemia, hypergly-cemia, and hyperinsulinemia. Here are few plants with their qualities and usages in various fields.

6082. (26-2-2008) NEW DELHI : Constraint of resources will not be allowed to stand in the way of the aim of achieving 4% growth in agriculture and necessary funds will be provided to States for all their agricultural schemes. This was stated by Agriculture Minister, Shri Sharad Pawar here today. He was addressing the National Conference on Agriculture for Kharif Campaign. The target for agricultural growth in the Plan has been fixed at 4% per annum. To achieve this target, action on several areas will be required-bringing technology to farmers, improving efficiency of investments, increasing systems support and rationalizing subsidies, diversifying and at the same time protecting food security concerns and fostering inclusiveness through a group approach by which the poor will get better access to land, credit and skills, Shri Pawar said. Shri Pawar applauded the farming community and the State Governments for achieving record production of rice, maize, soyabean, sugarcane and cotton in 2007-08. He informed that as per the second advance estimates, the production of foodgrains in 2007-08 is estimated at a record level of 219.32 million tonnes which is higher than the 217.28 million tonnes for 2006-07. The production of rice is estimated at 94.08 million tonnes compared to 93.35 million tonnes during the previous year. The production of coarse cereals is estimated at 36.09 million tonnes which is higher than the 33.92 million tonnes produced in the previous year. Cotton production at 233.81 lakh bales during 2007-08 is a record. The Minister asked State Governments to work out a Plan of Action for implementation of the National Policy for Farmers, keeping in view the grassroot level requirements. He also exhorted States to intensively monitor NFSM and RKVY. On ways to maximize Kharif output, the Minister said that States should popularize hybrid rice technology through demonstrations and availability of quality seeds. For cotton, increasing availability of treated quality seeds with emphasis on de-linted seeds is required. Efficient use of irrigation water through drip and sprinklers should be encouraged. In horticulture, emphasis should be on superior quality planting material. Earlier, the Minister launched e-pest surveillance device, a hand-held gadget for capturing data on pests and sending it to centralized database. He also released a book, Glimpses of Indian Agriculture, edited by Dr. S.M. Jharwal and Shri R.S. Deshpande.

6083. (26-2-2008) NEW DELHI : An investment of Rs.75,000 crore will be made over the next seven years to augment line capacity on identified routes to create the required capacity for carrying an additional 310 million tonnes. This was announced by the Minister of Railways, Shri Lalu Prasad, while presenting the Railway Budget 2008-09 in the Lok Sabha today. The Minister said that a blue print on the route-wise detailed study has been prepared and accordingly, route-wise works would be undertaken in a phased manner. This would include 124 works of doubling, third and fourth lines, bye-passes, flyovers, crossing stations, intermediate block stations, automatic signaling works and yard re-modelling. Shri Lalu Prasad said that the above works include construction of the Eastern and Western Corridors and informed that 104 throughput enhancement works, already in progress, would be completed over the next two years.

6084. (26-2-2008) NEW DELHI : The Minister of Railways, Shri Lalu Prasad has announced reduction in passenger fares of various classes while introducing the Railway Budget for 2008-09 in the Lok Sabha today. There will be a reduction of one rupee in the second-class fares of up to rupees fifty for non-suburban mail/express and ordinary passenger trains. The second-class fares of all mail/express and ordinary trains will be reduced by 5% for the tickets costing more than fifty rupees per passenger to benefit long distance passengers. The Railway Minister also announced a reduction in the fares for newly designed Sleeper Class coaches by 2%. Fare reduction by 2% for the newly designed AC 3 tier and AC Chair Car coaches has also been announced. This reduction will be only half for popular trains and during the peak period. To make the fares for higher classes more competitive, the Railway Minister announced reduction of fares for AC-I class by 7% and AC-2 tier by 4%. This reduction would only be half for popular trains and during the peak period. With this reduction, the process of rationalization of AC class fares has now been completed.

6085. (26-2-2008) NEW DELHI : Presenting the Rail Budget in the Lok Sabha today, the Railway Minister, Shri Lalu Prasad said to sustain magical turnaround in Railway's performance a 'Vision 2025' document would be finalized within six months. The document will set forth targets for the coming 17 years for operational performance and upgradation of services. It will also have a detailed action plan for achieving the stipulated targets and necessary investment plans thereof. Reiterating the commitment for passengers' amenities Shri Lalu Prasad said the proposed document would also contain details of customer-centric modern passenger services and various freight schemes to sharpen the competitive edge of the railways. Route wise planning would be done to reduce traffic bottlenecks, expand the network and modernize the railways. Passenger services will be governed by two words-'comfort and convenience'. A multi-departmental innovation promotion group will also be set up in the Railway Board. All Railway employees and citizens will be able to send their innovative suggestions to this group. Shri Lalu Prasad expressed the hope that proposed initiatives would inspire the Railway management and its employees for new experiments and would lay a solid foundation for resurgent Railways.

6086. (26-2-2008) NEW DELHI : Presenting the Railway Budget for 2008-09 in the Lok Sabha today, the Minister of Railways, Shri Lalu Prasad proposed to increase contribution to the Staff Benefit Fund of Railway employees from Rs. 35/- to Rs. 350/- per employee for the year 2008-09. Appreciating contribution of 14 lakh railway employees in financial turnaround of the Railways, Shri Lalu Prasad said 13 new works would be taken up at a cost of Rs. 101 crore for improving health services for the employees. Northern Railways' Central Hospital building at Delhi will be made centrally air-conditioned. The works of upgradation of two divisional hospitals to Central Hospitals at Jaipur and Hubli on Western and South Western Railway respectively, a new divisional hospital at Ranchi and construction of an OPD block at Integral Coach Factory (ICF) would be taken up.

6087. (26-2-2008) NEW DELHI : With the objective of increasing the carrying capacity, from 2008-09 onwards, manufacture of 20.3 tons axle load BCN and BOXN wagons will be stopped and only 22.9 tons axle load stainless steel wagons will be manufactured. The newly designed stainless steel BCN wagon has a lower tare weight. Due to the shorter length of these wagons, instead of 40 wagons, the BCN wagon train will now accommodate 58 wagons, like BOXN wagon trains. Thus, the payload of the BCN trains will increase by 78% from 2300 tons to 4100 tons. Similarly, the payload of open wagon trains will increase by 22% to 4100 tons. To realize the full potential of the newly designed high capacity wagons, in 2008-09, 5000 open wagons will be upgraded to stainless steel body, thereby reducing their tare weight by about two tons. In order to develop the wagon leasing market, a new wagon leasing policy has been prepared under which, rail customers and container operators will be able to take wagons on lease. For getting registered under the scheme, wagon leasing companies should have minimum net worth of Rs. 250 crore and will have a deposit Rs. 5 crore as registration fee. Registration will be valid for 20 years and will be renewable for another 10 years on rendering satisfactory services. Leasing companies have been give full rights to choose or change their lessees. These companies will lease out special purpose wagons, high capacity wagons and container wagons. The construction work of Eastern freight corridor from Ludhiana to Dankuni situated near Kolkata and Western corridor from Delhi to JNPT will commence in 2008-09. Detailed feasibility study for North-South, East-West, East-South and South-South dedicated Freight Corridors are being carried out and action will be taken to expedite sanction for construction of these corridors.

6088. (26-2-2008) NEW DELHI : Presenting the Railway Budget for 2008-09 in the Lok Sabha today, the Minister of Railways, Shri Lalu Prasad announced availability of rail ticket, monthly season ticket and platform ticket on smart card in Mumbai Suburban Service. This service would be launched by the end of next month. The Central Railways has already started trial run for this purpose through public-private partnership. The Railway Minister informed that the multi purpose card has been named 'Go Mumbai Card' and sale of bus tickets of BEST on this card has already started. These cards will be available at stations, bus depots of BEST and various other locations in the city. He clarified that there would be no extra burden on passenger for buying tickets through the smart card. However, only a marginal fee would be payable on buying and recharging of the card. Shri Lalu Prasad expressed the hope that the initiative would end long queues at ticket counters for daily train passengers in Mumbai suburban.

6089. (26-2-2008) NEW DELHI : A new railway coach factory is to be set up in Kerala. The Kerala Government has made available 1000 acres of land for the factory. The decision follows steady increase in the demand for metro coaches. Announcing the decision to this effect, Railway Minister Shri Lalu Prasad said last year the Ministry had decided to set up a new coach factory at Rae Bareilly. Coach supply orders have been received from Malaysia, Philippines, Vietnam, Sri Lanka, Bangladesh, Tanzania, Mayanmar, Angola, Senegal and Male during last few years. He also announced that a new wagon reconstruction unit at a cost of Rs. 40 crore would be set up at Garkha in Chapra district for reconstruction of old wagons. This follows growing need for wagon maintenance and reconstruction. He also proposed modernization of Lilluah Workshop in West Bengal, Perambur Loco Workshop and Ajmer Loco Workshop at a cost of about Rs. 200 crore. Jamalpur Workshop would also be modernized at a cost of Rs. 82 crore to enable its development like a production unit.

6090. (26-2-2008) NEW DELHI : In view of the long pending demand of licenced porters, the Minister for Railways, Shri Lalu Prasad in his Budget speech announced that the Railways have decided on a one time basis to appoint them as gangmen and to other Group D posts after due screening. Porters working on stations belong to Scheduled Castes and Tribes, other backward castes, minorities and other weaker sections of society. They have been carrying the luggage of passengers for years. There are thousands of vacant posts of gangmen. A large number of additional vacancies will arise due to promotion of gangmen as gatemen for manning of unmanned level crossings gates.

6091. (26-2-2008) NEW DELHI : Presenting the Railway Budget for 2008-09 in the Lok Sabha today, the Minister of Railways, Shri Lalu Prasad said that his Ministry has issued directions for setting up minority cells in all Zonal Railway offices and in the Railway Board for promoting minorities' welfare and ensuring their adequate representation in railway services. It has been made mandatory to have one member from the minority community in all the recruitment boards and committees. It has also been decided to issue recruitment notices in Urdu newspapers, published in the States having Urdu as the second official language. Instructions have also been issued to permit Urdu also as a medium of examination for Group 'D' posts in such states. Shri Lalu Prasad informed the House that a special campaign had been launched to clear the backlog vacancies of Scheduled Castes and Scheduled Tribes and nearly 99 per cent identified vacancies had been filled up so far. He said that recruitment from SC, ST and Other Backward Classes in Group 'D' had in fact exceeded their respective earmarked quota in 2007-08.

6092. (26-2-2008) NEW DELHI : The Railway Minister, Shri Lalu Prasad today announced completion of the process of rationalization of freight structure, initiated four years back. He said, barring a few light commodities, the difference between the highest and the lowest rates is not more than two times. With the rationalization of freight structures, freight rates for petrol and diesel would be further reduced by about 5%. The freight rates for these commodities will thus be brought down by 17% in three years' time. He announced reduction by 14% in the freight rates for fly ash. The policy of discount under empty flow direction freight discount scheme has been further liberalized. The rate of discount has been increased from 30 to 40 per cent. Shri Lalu Prasad also announced that the Indian Railways will give 6% discount for traffic originating from other States for the North Eastern States barring a few commodities. As part of the Central Government's commitment to all round development of the North Eastern States, last year, he announced a discount of 6% in freight rates for traffic originating from the region for other States. It has been decided that commodities not covered in goods tariff will be charged at a composite rate and not at the highest class rate as being charged at present. The move is expected to increase freight basket of various commodities and attract piecemeal traffic. As a special incentive for the Merry-Go-Round System, the Railway Minister announced that a lump sum rate of about Rs. 25 per ton would be charged for loading of rakes of BOXN for a distance of 30 kms.

6093. (26-2-2008) NEW DELHI : Presenting the Rail Budget today in Parliament, the Railway Minister, Shri Lalu Prasad announced introduction of 10 Garib Rath trains to provide better comfort at lower fare. He also proposed introduction of

53 new trains and extension of 16 trains. Besides this, frequency of 11 trains will be increased. In view of tercentenary function of Shri Guru Granth Sahib Gurta Gaddi at Nanded, the Railway Minister proposed special trains from Anandpur Sahib and Patna Sahib to Nanded during the celebrations. A special train between Pune and Delhi during Commonwealth Youth Games in Pune in October is also proposed.

6094. (26-2-2008) NEW DELHI : Presenting the Railway Budget, the Minister of Railways, Shri Lalu Prasad announced that Anti Collision Device would be introduced in Southern, South Central and South Western Railway in the next two years. This follows encouraging results from the North East Frontier Railways where a Pilot Project is already in place. A multi-pronged scheme has been prepared to reduce human failure. It envisages provision of automatic safety devices. The Railway Minister said, sustained efforts have led to significant improvement in safety and consequential fall in accidents. From 234 in 2005-06, the number has come down to 195 in 2006-07. Train accidents per million train kilometres have come down to 0.23 in 2006-07 as compared to 0.28 in 2005-06. The work of replacing 16538 kms of overage track and overage signals at 2359 stations and rehabilitation of 2251 bridges utilizing Special Railway Safety Fund would be completed by the end of this year. Railways are also taking due precaution to make adequate provision under Depreciation Reserve Fund (DRF) for timely replacement of overage assets. The provision in DRF has been increased to Rs. 7000 crore in 2008-09 from Rs. 5450 in 2007-08.

6095. (26-2-2008) NEW DELHI : The Minister of Railways, Shri Lalu Prasad today announced several new initiatives to make the travel experience pleasant, comfortable and secure. Presenting the Railway Budget for 2008-09 in the Lok Sabha, he said that a multi-pronged strategy using information technology has been prepared to permanently terminate long queues at railway ticket reservation counters within two years. The Railways are exploring the option of issuing tickets through mobile phones besides increasing number of UTS counters to 15000 and Automatic Ticket Vending Machine counters to 6000 to facilitate availability of ticket in neighbourhood. The Railway Minister also announced extension of e-ticketing to wait-listed passengers and of Jansadharan Ticket Booking Seva to all Zonal Railways. These steps would provide employment to thousands of unemployed youth besides ensuring easy availability of railway tickets. Shri Lalu Prasad said that now all overnight mail and express trains will have on-line coach indication display boards to give information about running of the trains and likely time of arrival of approaching stations continuously. This facility would be very helpful to the passengers deboarding trains at night. The public address system which is presently available only in Rajdhani and Shatabdi trains will be made available to other select mail and express trains. Information boards displaying on line information about train arrival-departure and platform berthing will be installed at parking lots and entrance gates besides platforms of 100 'A' and 'B' category stations. On-line reservation availability information boards will also be installed at reservation offices of all 'A' and 'B' category stations. The Railway Minister said that to make the travelling more comfortable it has been decided that all Rajdhani trains will have LHB design coaches by March 2010 and remaining Shatabdi trains by March 2011. LHB coaches with stainless steel ICF bogies, which are more comfortable and have 10-16 per cent more carrying capacity will also be provided in mail and express trains besides Rajdhani and Shatabdi trains. To make the journey more comfortable, the Railway Ministry has decided to upgrade all low and medium level platforms by increasing their height. Lifts and escalators will also be installed at 50 major stations. Beside this, every platform of all 'D' category stations will be provided shelters to give relief from heat, cold and rain. All 'B' & 'D' category stations which have high level platforms will be provided with foot over bridges to check inconvenience to passengers. Platforms of 30 stations will be extended during the current year for running longer passenger trains, multi-level car parking lots and modernized car parking facilities will be created at 30 major stations. Stressing on cleanliness in the Railway network, Shri Lalu Prasad said that the Railway had started a pilot project for onboard cleaning by professional agencies on some Rajdhani and Shatabdi trains which had resulted in satisfactory results. Therefore, it has been decided that onboard cleaning will be introduced on all Rajdhani, Shatabdi and Superfast mail and express trains, using modern machines. All 36000 coaches would be provided clean toilets by the end of the 11th Plan at a cost of Rs. 4000 crore to put a permanent end to the problem of discharge from the train toilets. Besides this, all LHB coaches will have ergonomically designed modular toilets with attractive interiors for better hygiene and cleanliness.

6096. (26-2-2008) NEW DELHI : The Minister of Railways, Shri Lalu Prasad today announced biggest ever annual plan for the Railways. He said, the Ministry of Railways proposes to invest Rs. 37,500 crore, which is 21% more than the previous year. The plan size includes a total budgetary support of Rs. 7874 crore including Rs. 774 crore to be provided from the Central Road Fund. The annual plan will have Internal and External Budgetary Resources (IEBR) funding of 79%. Under this plan, priority has been given to enhancement of rail capacity, modernization of the railway, throughput enhancement on High Density Network routes, traffic facility works and expansion and development of the network. Construction of flyovers, bypasses, Intermediate Block System (IBS), upgradation of goods shed etc., traffic facilities works will be completed on priority. The outlay for doubling works has been increased to Rs. 2,500 crore, traffic facility works to Rs. 984 crore and an outlay of Rs. 1535 crore has been proposed for projects under implementation by Rail Vikas Nigam Limited (RVNL). Provision of Rs. 1730 crore for new lines, Rs. 2489 crore for gauge conversion, Rs. 626 crore for electrification and Rs. 650 crore for Metropolitan Transport Projects has been made. On safety related plan heads, provision has been made for Rs. 3600 crore for track renewals, Rs. 1520 crore for signal and telecommunication works, Rs.

700 crore for Road Over Bridges and Road Under Bridges and Rs. 600 crore for manning of unmanned level crossings. The Railway Minister also sought additional funds to the tune of Rs. 1712 crore from Ministry of Finance for national projects of Udhampur-Srinagar-Baramulla, Jiribam-Imphal Road, Dimapur-Kohima, Azra-Byrnihat and Kumarghat-Agartala new line, Bogibeel Rail-cum-Road Bridge and Lumding-Silchar-Jiribam, Rangia-Murkongselek gauge conversion. During the year 2300 km broad gauge lines are likely to be completed. The target for construction of broad gauge lines in 2008-09 is 3500 km. The construction of new line between Kakapore and Badgam in the Kashmir valley has already been completed and the remaining portion in the valley will be completed in 2008-09. Expressing gratitude to the Hon'ble Prime Minister for deciding the funding of National Projects in the North Eastern region, through 25% funds from Railways Gross Budgetary Support and balance 75% as an additionality, he proposed to create a non-lapsable Northeast Rail Development Fund to expedite track construction process in this region.

6097. (26-2-2008) NEW DELHI : Reaffirming Indian Railways commitment to the security of passengers, the Railway Minister, Shri Lalu Prasad today announced drawing up of an Integrated Security Plan to strengthen railway security through installation of Close Circuit TVs at important stations and metal detectors, baggage screening systems and explosive detection and disposal systems for screening passengers and their luggage at vulnerable stations. Railway Protection Force (RPF) will be equipped with all modern equipment and adequate funds will be provided for this. Shri Prasad said, 5700 vacant posts of constables and 993 vacant posts of sub-Inspectors in RPF will be filled up by May this year. 5% of vacant posts of constables and 10% in Sub-Inspectors have been reserved for women. The Government has also created 973 additional posts for which recruitment would be done next year.

6098. (26-2-2008) NEW DELHI : Several new concessions have been announced for rail travel. These include extension of the scheme of free monthly season tickets for students, concession for senior lady citizens, concession for Ashok Chakra Awardees and for AIDS affected persons. Extended concessions for students include free monthly season tickets for girl students up to graduation and for boy students up to 12th standard. At present, free monthly season tickets for second class travel between school and home are provided to girl students up to 12th standard and boy students up to 10th standard. The Union Railway Minister, Shri Lalu Prasad also announced that passenger fare concession for lady senior citizens will be increased to 50% from 30% at present for all classes of travel. Ashok Chakra awardees will now be provided facility to travel in Rajdhani and Shatabadi trains on card passes. For AIDS patients, a concession of 50% has been announced in second class passenger fares for travel to nominated ART centres for treatment. Rajiv Gandhi Foundation and Indian Railways will collaborate in running a Mother-Child Health Express of seven coaches on a pilot bases for providing medical facilities to the mother and the child. This train will be run by railways at concessional fares and would have facilities like delivery operation room and child health centre.

6099. (27-2-2008) NEW DELHI : In a major welfare measure, the Border Roads Organisation (BRO) has proposed to insure its large casual workforce. Presiding over a Border Roads Development Board (BRDB) here today, the Minister of State for Defence Shri MM Pallam Raju said the measure would benefit over 70,000 labourers laying roads in difficult and terrorist infested border areas. He said a special package to provide Life Insurance cover to the casual labourers is being considered by the government. Lt. General AK Nanda, Director-General, Border Roads, said the casual labourers are presently provided free shelter, rations from BRO units and free clothing besides wages. The BRDB, meeting for the second time in the current financial year to review and plan various projects, approved the BRO's proposal to outsource certain work to civilian construction agencies wherever feasible. This would enable the BRO to add capacity and undertake more road, bridge and tunneling work. The BRO presently constructs about 1,100 kms of roads and lays bridges over three kilometres long worth over 2,600 crore rupees every year. It plans to more than double the target for the next financial year, 2008-09, with road construction of about 2,500 kms and five kms length of bridges worth over 4,000 crore rupees. The DGBR, Lt. Gen. Nanda informed the meeting that strategic projects including roads along the China border, Prime Minister's reconstruction package for Jammu and Kashmir and Special Road Development Programme for the North-East would be completed within the stipulated timeframe. The BRO has drawn up a five-year perspective plan for the purpose. Shri Pallam Raju assured priority to the BRO's airlifting needs of equipments and other resources in remote and high altitude areas. More than 1,500 tons of material has been airlifted this year and about 4,000 tons airlift is planned next year. Among those who attended the BRDB meeting were the army and air force vice chiefs and senior officials of the ministries of Road Transport and Highways, Environment and Forest, External Affairs and Home Affairs besides the Planning Commission.

6100. (27-2-2008) NEW DELHI : A farmers' delegation led by BKU leader Shri MS Tikait met Agriculture Minister, Shri Sharad Pawar here today. The delegation submitted a memorandum of demands to the Minister. Shri Pawar apprised the farmers about the steps taken by the government in the recent past for improving their earnings and to remove their hardships. The farmers appreciated the initiatives taken by the government, especially the remarkable rise in MSP of major crops in the last three years. They held discussions with the Minister on wide-ranging issues including the need to provide loans at low interest and to reduce the unit area for crop insurance purposes. The Minister expressed the government's commitment to protect their interests in WTO negotiations. Agriculture Minister assured the delegation that he would personally look into the suggestions made by them in the memorandum, and invited them for a more detailed discussion next week.

6101. (27-2-2008) NEW DELHI : The National Conference on Agriculture for Kharif Campaign 2007-08 concluded here today. The deliberations among Central government departments, State governments and scientists resulted in a number of crop-specific and issue-specific recommendations for the coming kharif season. States have been advised to submit their Action Plans for kharif in the first week of March. They must take all necessary steps in time for maximising kharif production including ensuring input supply, energising the extension network and promoting best agronomic practices. Earlier, presentations were made by division heads on WTO issues, national policy for farmers, RKVY and NFSM, plant protection and extension system and discussed with the states. In their presentations, individual states presented the position relating to rabi assessment and kharif prospects, initiatives taken for implementing NFSM and RKVY, steps taken to encourage private investment and market reforms, and status relating to availability of quality seed and fertilizers.

6102. (27-2-2008) NEW DELHI : The nation will observe National Science Day on 28 February 2008 with "Understanding Planet Earth" as the theme. Most research laboratories will organize "open-day" inviting members of the public to visit their facilities and interact with researchers. Universities are organizing lectures by eminent scientists on the theme. The Outreach Campaign for Understanding Planet Earth was launched by the Prime Minister, Dr. Manmohan Singh, on January 03, 2008 at Andhra University, Vishakhapattnam. Community awareness programmes have been initiated on issues of climate change, natural hazards, coasts and oceans, urbanization and health of the planet. The national function for Science Day will have the eminent agriculture scientist Dr. M.S. Swaminathan, sharing his views on the theme. The national awards for science and technology communication for outstanding work done in the past 5 years by institutions and individuals will also be presented. These include science and technology communication, science communication through books and magazines, science popularization among children, science and technology communication in print medium and science and technology communication through electronic medium. These awards were instituted in 1987 by the government with a view to encouraging and recognizing the efforts in the area of science and technology communication and were first announced on National Science Day in 1988. No award is being given for the category of science translation in Indian languages this year. A Science Exhibition would also be organized on this occasion at Technology Bhavan, New Delhi. A number of science communication software materials have been developed for different target audiences including teachers and students on various aspects of Planet Earth in connection with International Year of Planet Earth 2008.

6103. (27-2-2008) NEW DELHI : Sewage treatment plants have been set up in different identified towns as one of the core pollution abatement schemes under the Ganga Action Plan (GAP) and Yamuna Action Plan (YAP). These plants are meant for treating the intercepted and diverted sewage to the desired standards before it is disposed into the receiving body. Rs 727.65 crore has been sanctioned to set up these STPs in the states implementing GAP and YAP. Under the Centrally Sponsored Schemes of National River Conservation Plan (NPCP), the Government of India has sanctioned various pollution abatement schemes namely, Interception and Diversion of sewage, low cost sanitation works, electric/improved wood crematoria, river front development works besides setting up of STPs. The NRCP presently covers pollution abatement works in 164 towns along polluted stretches of 35 riverbeds.spread over 20 states.

6104. (27-2-2008) NEW DELHI : All the Chief ministers have been asked to adequately protect critical wildlife habitats while implementing the Scheduled Tribes and Other Traditional Forest Dwellers (Recognition of Forest Rights) Act,2006,expeditiously in keeping with the rules provided under it. Under the Section 4 of the Act, they have been requested to provide protection to critical wildlife habitats also. The Scheduled Tribes and Other Traditional Forest Dwellers (Recognition of Forest Rights) Act,2006 has been enacted to recognize and vest the forest rights and occupation in forest land in forest dwelling Scheduled Tribes and Other traditional forest dwellers who have been residing in such forests for generation but whose rights could not be recorded.

6105. (27-2-2008) NEW DELHI : Movement of troops by the Army is carried out as a routine based on operational requirements such as commitments for internal security duties, management of Field/Peace profiles of units and other administrative considerations. The present politico security situation in Pakistan does have an impact on the levels of infiltration in J&K. Although no deluge of terrorists from across is expected, some form of uncalibrated and uncontrolled infiltration can be expected to ease out pressure from within Pakistan. Indian Army is suitably deployed along the borders and maintains requisite level of operational preparedness to ensure the sanctity and integrity of our borders. This information was given by the Defence Minister Shri A K Antony in a written reply to Smt. Supriya Sule in Rajya Sabha today.

6106. (27-2-2008) NEW DELHI : The Integrated Guided Missile Development Programme (IGMDP), launched in 1983 headed by Dr. APJ Abdul Kalam, in DRDO is not being abandoned. The following missiles and technology demonstration systems have been developed under Integrated Guided Missile Development Programme (IGMDP)-Agni, a technology demonstration project for re-entry technology; Prithvi, surface-to-air missile with 150, 250 & 350 Km range for Army, Air Force and Navy; Akash, surface-to-air missile with a range of 25Km and multi-target handling system; Nag, third generation "fire & forget" and "top attack" anti-tank missile; Development of Trishul missile system has been completed as technology demonstration.

6107. (27-2-2008) NEW DELHI : Government have acquired the Landing Platform Dock (LPD) USS Trenton and UH-3H Helicopters from the US Government. These were commissioned into the Indian Navy in June 2007 as INS Jalashwa. Government have also signed Letters of Offer and Acceptance for the procurement of weapons and equipment required by the Special Forces of the Indian Army and for six C-130J-30 aircraft for the Indian Air Force. The C-130J-30 aircraft are the latest variant of the C-130 aircraft and are different from the aircraft being operated by Pakistan. This information was given by the Defence Minister Shri AK Antony in a written reply to Shri Amar Singh in Rajya Sabha today.

6108. (27-2-2008) NEW DELHI : Congress spokesman Shri Manish Tewari said both Houses of Parliament had to be adjourned, ostensibly on the farmer's issue. The UPA government has been extremely sensitive to the plight of farmers ever since this government assumed office in May 2004. In fact, over the past few days, both the President of the Indian National Congress and the Prime Minister have been meeting series of delegations of farmers and farmers' associations from across north India who have been sensitizing them to what is going on the agricultural sector. I would like to appeal to the opposition that in a parliamentary democracy there is no substitute to debate and discussion. They must allow the House to function so that whatever concerns they may have are all discussed threadbare and certain solutions could be found. It is unfortunate that the BJP which is the principal Opposition party has been in the forefront of shedding crocodile tears on the plight of farmers. Yesterday the President of the BJP, addressed a rally organized by its ally, the Siromani Akali Dal (SAD) in New Delhi and supported certain specific demands raised by them. But in the BJP ruled states, especially Rajasthan, Madhya Pradesh and Chatishgarh their governments have anti-farmer attitude. Here is an example of a case study of what happened in Rajasthan recently where crops worth over Rs.1,000 crores were destroyed in over 22 districts in Rajasthan because of frost as a result of a long spell of cold. This damage to the mustard, wheat and gram crops have affected 05 lakh families in the state and over 10 lakh hectares of land. The Rajasthan government without even getting a proper survey conducted through the respective District Authorities has announced a package of Rs. 126 crores which is barely 1/10th of the cumulative damage suffered by the farmers. The Rajasthan government is very cleverly trying to hide behind the fact that the norms of the Calamity Relief Fund (CRF) scheme do not allow it to utilize moneys from this fund to provide relief to the farmers. They ostensibly claim that they have written to the Union Government to relax these norms. This is nothing else except a crude political manoeuvre to pass the buck on the Central Government. The Calamity Relief Fund (CRF) scheme operative from the financial year 2005-06 to 2009-10 clearly mandates that whatever is the unspent balance in the fund at the end of 5 years would automatically become a part of the Plan Expenditure of the state at the end of the year 2010 if the scheme is discontinued. Thus there is nothing which stops the state government from providing relief to the farmers out of its own resources if it so desires, because eventually unspent CRF fund would flow to their coffers. It would be noteworthy to mention in the past 4 years the UPA Government has provided Rs.1171.46 cores to the Rajasthan government under the CRF Scheme. In addition to this, Rs.216.79 crores was provided in 2004-05 and Rs.100 crores in 2006-07 under the National Calamity Contingency Fund (NCCF) also. This is in addition to the funds which have been provided to Rajasthan. The anti-farmer attitude of the BJP is further evidenced by the fact that in the past 4 ½ years many incidents of police firing on farmers has taken place which has resulted in the death of over 35 farmers and thousands more had been implicated in false cases which imposes a heavy legal burden on them. It would be appropriate to point out that the Rajasthan BJP government in its election manifesto in November 2004 had promised that it would establish 'Kisan Kalyan Kosh' with a corpus of Rs.250 crores and in its budget for the financial year 2005-06 announced that it would establish 'Kisan Kalyan Kosh' with a corpus of Rs. 175 crores. Not only is there glaring inconsistency between the two pronouncements within one year of each other but incidentally both these commitments remain unimplemented even as the term of the BJP government in Rajasthan draws to a close. The Rajasthan government has further compounded the misery of the farmers of the state by increasing the agriculture tariff on electricity by Re.1.00 per unit, while the electricity supply has come down from 8 hours to 4 hours per day. To a question that whether in the CRF norms is frost covered and why is the Central government not considering it? Shri Tewari said, the CRF norms do not specifically cover for frost. So if a particular calamity is not covered under the CRF norms then the way around it is that if the state government is interested, it can actually provide relief from its own sources and the funds which flow into the CRF, 75% of which is Central contribution, if they are unutilized, they ultimately get added back to the planned expenditure of the state when the scheme is discontinued or comes to an end. Therefore, trying to crudely pass on the buck to the Central government by saying that the norms do not permit it, a much better way would have been if the Rajasthan government would have taken a pro-active position and said yes, we recognize it. The Central government is considering it because in addition to frost there are representations which have come from other states to include various other calamities which the agricultural sector is inflicted by in the CRF norms. To a question that is your government trying to pass the buck to the Supreme Court and junking the Sethusamudaram project, Shri Tewari said, the money for the feasibility study of this project was provided by the NDA government in 2000-2001. There was a provision of 4.8 crores which was made by the then NDA government and the feasibility was carried out.

6109. (27-2-2008) NEW DELHI : There is neither lack of funds nor shortage of scientists in DRDO to conduct research on strategic projects. Time overrun of various projects is mainly due to-Technical complexities; Technological embargo/ sanctions and various control regimes; Non-availability of infrastructure within the country; Extended and long lasting user trials; Revision of systems specifications during development phase. There is no shortage of scientists at any level.

6110. (27-2-2008) NEW DELHI : The total population of tiger is 1411; the lower limit is 1165 and the upper limit is 1657. The methodology involved was double sampling. All forested habitats in 17 tiger states have been surveyed for tigers, prey presence and human pressure to determine tiger occupancy and generation of indices. Remotely sensed data and variables were modeled on the GIS domain along with tiger occupancy/indices. Tiger densities were estimated in representative areas based on the indices using camera traps in a statistical framework. These densities were than correlated withabove indices and extrapolated for contiguous, similar landscapes.

6111. (27-2-2008) NEW DELHI : The Ministry of Environment and Forests while granting environmental clearance to Nhava Sheva Port (now Jawaharlal Nehru Port) stipulated that the level of traffic at Mumbai Port should gradually be reduced. The other condition stipulated was that Port's land which is not required for operational purpose should be made available for greening and recreation. In 2006-07 Mumbai Port handled 52.36 Million Tonnes. About 62% of the above is liquid cargo transported through pipe lines, 12% is moved through water ways, 6% by rail and 14% by road. 58% of the cargo moving on the road is meant for city consumption and 42% goes out of city. Traffic destined to and from city uses 3 arterial roads connecting NH-4. The usage of Port's Land in the city is governed by the city development plan finalized under Maharashtra Regional and Town Planning Act 1966. This plan is valid upto 2012-13 and has earmarked land for greenery and recreation. Traffic at Indian Ports have shown upward trend and infrastructure needs to be consistently enhanced for supporting the Economic Growth. Development of ports is an ongoing process. As a part of this process the proposals for development/ expansion of Mumbai Port are considered and appropriate decisions taken after necessary clearances, keeping in view the demands of Maritime Trade.

6112. (27-2-2008) NEW DELHI : There is no proposal for levying of any Cess on the cargo handled in the country. This was stated by the Minister of Shipping, Road Transport and Highways, Thiru T.R. Baalu in a written reply in the Lok Sabha today.

6113. (27-2-2008) NEW DELHI : The Minister for Petroleum and Natural Gas Shri Murli Deora has directed Oil Marketing Companies (OMCs), IOC, BPCL, HPCL to urgently take remedial steps regarding complaints of hardships faced by domestic LPG consumers in West Bengal. Shri Deora assured the ex-Member of Parliament (Rajya Sabha) Shri Batin Sengupta, who met the Minister in Delhi, that Government is already seized of the issue regarding LPG supply backlog in some parts and has taken initiatives to enhance availability as well as check diversion of domestic LPG for unintended use. The Minister informed that additional imports have been tied up by the oil companies besides operating LPG bottling plants during extra hours and holidays. Shri Sengupta had complained about delay in LPG supply to the consumers in West Bengal.

6114. (27-2-2008) NEW DELHI : Twenty two mills will be modernized by National Textiles Corporation (NTC) itself by inducting new machineries, rationalization of manpower, capital restructuring etc. Out of forty mills, remaining 18 mills will be modernized through Joint Venture route. Private partners to run 5 of these mills have been finalized. This was stated by the Minister of State for Textiles, Shri E.V.K.S. Elangovan, in the Rajya Sabha today, in a written reply to a question by Shri Amir Alam Khan. Giving further details of the Modified Rehabilitation Scheme, 2006 approved by BIFR and Group of Ministers (GOM), the Minister informed the House that out of the total 52 mills, 12 mills have been identified for further closure where there was no production activity and most of the employees opted for benefits of Modified Voluntary Retirement Scheme (MVRS). Out of these, 2 mills have been closed, raising the number of closed mills from 65 to 67. National Textiles Corporation (NTC) was incorporated in 1968 with the main objective of managing the affairs of 16 sick textile mills taken over by the Government. NTC took over more sick textile mills under 3 Nationalization Acts. (1974, 1986 & 1995), raising its number upto 119 mills in 1995. As per the Rehabilitation Scheme, 2002, the Board for Industrial and Financial Reconstruction (BIFR) approved revival of 53 viable mills and closure of 66 unviable mills. 65 unviable mills were closed under the Act. 2 Mills (one viable and one unviable) located in the Union Territory of Pondicherry have been transferred to the Government of Pondicherry. With this, NTC was left with 117 sick mills, *i.e.* 52 viable mills and 65 closed mills.

6115. (27-2-2008) NEW DELHI : During the Sixth Pravasi Bharatiya Divas, 2008 held at New Delhi on 7th to 9th January, 2008, a Plenary Session on 'Diaspora Philanthropy: Empowerment of Rural Woman' was organized to discuss the modes of participation and the kind of Institutional support that the overseas Indians would require to channelise their philanthropic propensities for rural development and empowerment of women in India. A proposal to establish a 'not-for-profit' Foundation to channelise diasporic capital into India is under examination. This proposed Foundation will serve as a credible institutional mechanism to assist the Overseas Indians to contribute to the social causes including rural development and empowerment of rural women. This information was given by the Minister of Overseas Indian Affairs, Shri Vayalar Ravi in a written reply in Lok Sabha today.

6116. (27-2-2008) NEW DELHI : The Ministry of Overseas Indian Affairs proposes to set up Overseas Indian Centres in the Indian Missions and posts at Dubai, Kuala Lumpur and Washington to cater to the interests of the Indian diaspora. The objectives of the centres are to provide legal, medical and financial services to the Indian diaspora. While the Dubai centre will look after the entire Gulf region, the centre at Kuala Lumpur will cater to the diaspora in Malaysia, Singapore and Brunei. The Washington centre will perform similar functions for USA and Canada. Workers are exploited both in India by recruiting agents and overseas by the foreign employers and their agents. Legal services are required both to make them aware of their rights and obligations and advise them in cases of disputes with employers. Health services, including psychiatric counselling, are needed, particularly for the women emigrant workers. Most Overseas Indian Workers also need financial advice on transfer of funds, savings and investments. There is also a need to access the knowledge sector to help India tap the large pool of experience and expertise of the local diaspora. NRI women who are victims of fraudulent marriages require legal and other forms of assistance. To make the Indian centres functional, six posts in CGI, Dubai and HCI, Kuala Lumpur and five posts in EOI, Washington have been created which include one post each of Director, Assistant and PA and three (two in Washington) posts of Professionals with legal, medical and financial expertise. The selection for the posts of Director Community Welfare (Development) at these stations is in process in consultation with DoPT. The remaining posts are proposed to be filled locally. This information was given by the Minister of Overseas Indian Affairs, Shri Vayalar Ravi in a written reply in Lok Sabha today.

6117. (27-2-2008) NEW DELHI : Two regional offices under the Registrar of Newspapers for India (RNI) in line with the existing regional offices at Mumbai, Kolkatta and Chennai are proposed at Guwahati and Bhopal. It is envisaged that the regional offices at Guwahati and Bhopal would be operational in 2007-08 and 2008-09 respectively. These offices would coordinate between Headquarter of Registrar of Newspapers for India (RNI) and publishers of the region on the matter relating to registration, title etc. To cater to the needs of Maharashtra State, a Regional Office of RNI is already functioning at Mumbai. This information was given by Minister of Information & Broadcasting and Parliamentary Affairs, Shri P. R. Dasmunsi in written reply to a question in Rajya Sabha today.

6118. (27-2-2008) NEW DELHI : The Eleventh Plan document mentions that the Plan will aim for inclusive growth by introducing National Urban Health Mission (NUHM), which along with National Rural Health Mission (NRHM) will form the Sarva Swasthya Abhiyan. The NRHM has already been approved for the period 2007-2012 and is under implementation. It provides for accessible, affordable, equitable, accountable and quality health care to the people especially those living in rural areas. NRHM ensures to provide concurrent service guarantee in respect of skilled attendants at all births, full coverage of childhood diseases/ health conditions, maternal diseases/health conditions, blindness due to refractive errors and low vision, leprosy, tuberculosis, vector borne diseases, inpatient treatment of childhood diseases, inpatient treatment of maternal diseases, life style diseases, hypertension, providing secondary care services at district hospitals, meeting unmet needs and spacing and permanent family planning services, for RTI/STI and counselling for HIV/AIDS services for adolescents. A NUHM is also proposed for the urban poor with focus on those living in urban slums. The allocation for Eleventh Five Year Plan under NRHM is Rs. 89478 crore and for NUHM is Rs. 4495 crore and the proposed outlay for the annual plan of 2008-09 is Rs. 11930 crore for NRHM and Rs. 50 crore for NUHM. However, the year-wise and State wise allocation in respect of these two programmes cannot be given as explained below. The Five Year Plan Scheme-wise outlay is an indicative one. The State-wise and Scheme-wise allocation is made during the year based on the Annual Plan outlay communicated by the Planning Commission which is normally less than the Annual Plan proposals projected by the Departments. Moreover, the Scheme-wise Annual Plan proposals are made based on the priorities assigned to each Scheme depending upon the State specific importance assigned to it. NRHM seeks to achieve its objective through the process of communitisation through untied funds and involvement of Panchayats etc. improved management, capacity through skill augmentation and infusion of managerial skills, flexible financing, monitoring progress against standards through Indian Public Health Standards, innovation in human resource management, partnership with non-government providers, etc. This information was given by the Minister for Health & Family Welfare, Dr. Anbumani Ramadoss in a reply to a question in the Lok Sabha.

6119. (27-2-2008) NEW DELHI : In order to examine the possibility of ensuring availability of doctors in rural areas by introducing compulsory one year rural posting of medical student before grant of permanent registration, a Committee was constituted under the Chairmanship of Dr. R. Sambasiva Rao, Additional Director General of Health Services. The Terms of reference of the Committee was to elicit the opinion of various sections of the society on the issue of making rural posting for MBBS student compulsory. The Committee has submitted its report and the same is under examination. This information was given by the Minister of State for Health & Family Welfare, Smt. Panabaaka Lakshmi in a written reply to a question in the Lok Sabha.

6120. (27-2-2008) NEW DELHI : The National Rural Health Mission [NRHM] has been launched with the objective of providing accessible, affordable, accountable, effective and reliable primary health care facility especially, to the poor and vulnerable section of the population. It further aims to provide overarching umbrella to the existing programmes of Health & FW including RCH II across the country including Orissa State. The National programmes include Malaria, Blindness, Iodine deficiency, Filaria, Kala Azar, Tuberculosis, Leprosy and Integrated Disease Surveillance. The preventive and curative health care is provided through a three-tier network of Sub Centres, Primary Health Centres and Community Health Centres. Orissa is one of the High Focus States under NRHM so as more resources could be allocated for the health programmes. During the Financial Year 2007-08 an amount of Rs. 10373 Lakhs has been released under RCH Flexi pool and Rs. 9028 Lakhs has been released under Mission Flexi pool upto December 2007 out of which the State has utilized an amount of Rs. 6286.27 lakhs and Rs. 1087.435 lakhs (including the spill over from the previous year) respectively. The implementation of NRHM in the State is reviewed from time to time. This information was given by the Minister of State for Health & Family Welfare, Smt. Panabaaka Lakshmi in a written reply to a question in the Lok Sabha.

6121. (27-2-2008) NEW DELHI : The launch of Chandrayan-I slated for April, 2008 has been shifted to June-July, 2008 to ensure thorough and appropriate testing of various subsystems and the spacecraft to ensure the mission performance. The payloads are being received from various agencies and the satellite integration is progressing as planned. This information was given by the Minister of State in the Prime Minister's Office, Shri Prithviraj Chavan, in the Lok Sabha today.

6122. (27-2-2008) NEW DELHI : Nurses are the largest work force of health care delivery system cycle. Nursing personnel are also frontline health care providers in the community. Their role and significance has grown immensely with introduction of primary health care services and health for all strategies. In order to meet the shortage of nurses in the country it is proposed to start a new scheme of Development of Nursing Services (Human Resource). The proposal in the scheme envisages establishment of Centres of Excellence in 24 States, strengthening of State Nursing Councils and Nursing Cells in 17 States, opening of 145 ANM and 137 GNM Schools, establishment of 6 Colleges of Nursing and 4 Regional Institutes of Nursing. Proposed locations for opening of more nursing colleges under the scheme can be seen at Annexure. This information was given by the Minister of State for Health & Family Welfare, Smt. Panabaaka Lakshmi in a written reply to a question in the Lok Sabha.

6123. (27-2-2008) NEW DELHI : The National Family Health Survey-3 (NFHS-3) was conducted in 29 States during the year 2005-06, collected information on various health indicators including Mortality, Marriage & Fertility, Family Planning, Maternal and Child Health, Immunization of children, child feeding practices, Nutritional status of children and adults, prevalence of anemia among children and adults, obesity among men & women, Knowledge, attitude and behaviour with regard to HIV/AIDS and its prevalence and treatment seeking behaviour for TB & malaria. In order to promote maternal and child health care, the Government implemented the Reproductive and Child Health programme, Phase-I (RCH-I) for a period of five years from 1997-98 to 2002-03. Based on the experience of the programme as exhibited through regular monitoring and evaluation, the second phase of the RCH programme was launched from 2005 to 2010. Subsequently, the programme has been integrated under the National Rural Health Mission (NRHM), launched in April, 2005. The National Rural Health Mission seeks to provide accessible, affordable and quality health care to the rural population, especially to the poor and the vulnerable sections of the population. It also seeks to reduce Maternal Mortality Ratio, Infant Mortality Rate and the Total Fertility level within the seven year period of the Mission, ending in 2012. The Mission seeks to provide accountable, effective, reliable and quality primary health care through creation of a cadre of Accredited Social Health Activities (ASHA), strengthening of Public Health Delivery System at all levels, improved hospital care measured through Indian Public Health Standards (IPHS), provision of untied funds to all the facilities to enable local action, decentralization of programme to district level to improve intra and inter-sectoral convergence and effective utilization of resources. Flexibility has been given to the States to devise need based Programme Implementation Plan (PIP). The outcomes are being monitored through regular performance reporting and periodic surveys like NFHS. This information was given by the Minister of State for Health & Family Welfare, Smt. Panabaaka Lakshmi in a written reply to a question in the Lok Sabha.

6124. (27-2-2008) NEW DELHI : National Medicinal Plants Board has been implementing Contractual Farming Scheme under which financial assistance @ 30% of the project cost subject to a maximum of Rs. 9.00 lakhs, is provided to farmers / growers for cultivation of identified medicinal plants. The Scheme is implemented through State Medicinal Plant Boards. The Board had identified list of 32 medicinal plants for cultivation and development on priority can be seen at Annexure-I. However, as per Operational Guidelines, projects for cultivation of other commercially important plants can also be considered for which assured market exists. The Board has since revised list of prioritized plants for cultivation and development under its schemes can be seen at Annexure-II. This information was given by the Minister of State for Health & Family Welfare, Smt. Panabaaka Lakshmi in a written reply to a question in the Lok Sabha.

6125. (27-2-2008) NEW DELHI : Jammu & Kashmir and Andhra Pradesh are the only two States who have not adopted the Transplantation of Human Organs Act, 1994, as they have their own laws similar to this act. The Hon'ble High Court of Delhi in CWP No. 813/2004 vide its order dated 6.9.2004 had set up a Committee to examine the provisions of Transplantation of Human Organs Act, 1994 and the Transplantation of Human Organs Rules, 1995. The report was submitted on 25.5.2005. A National Consultation was held on 18.5.2007 and the report was submitted in the second fortnight of August, 2007. The recommended changes required amendments in the Transplantation of Human Organs Act, 1994 and the Rules framed there under. These changes are intended to facilitate genuine cases, increase transparency in transplantation procedures and to provide deterrent penalties for violation of the law. In so far as the Act is concerned, the following amendments have been proposed: i) To empower Union Territories, specially Government of NCT of Delhi to have their own appropriate authority instead of DGHS and /or Additional DG (Hospitals). ii) To make the punishments under the Act harsh and cognizable for the illegal transplantation activities to deter the offenders from committing this crime. iii) To provide for registration of the centres for removal of organs from the cadavers and brain stem dead patients for harvesting of organs instead of registration of centres for transplantations only. iv) To allow swap operations between the related donor and recipients who do not match themselves but match with other similar donors / recipients. Sale / purchase of human organs is already prohibited under Transplantation of Human Organs Act, 1994. Appropriate authorities established under this Act are responsible and empowered to check the illegal activities of human organs trafficking. This information was given by the Minister for Health & Family Welfare, Dr. Anbumani Ramadoss in a reply to a question in the Lok Sabha.

6126. (27-2-2008) NEW DELHI : The State-wise and year-wise details of reported number of HIV positive AIDS cases and deaths in different States of the country during the last three years as per information received from State AIDS Control Societies can be seen at Annexure 'A' & 'B' respectively. In order to make people aware about HIV/AIDS and promote safe behaviours, National AIDS Control Organisation and State AIDS Control Societies conduct regular IEC campaigns through mass media and inter-personal communication channels. NACO's programmes "Jeewan Hai Anmol" and "Lets Talk AIDS" was aired on 174 AIR stations in 24 languages. The special episodes of "Kalyani" health magazine on Doordarshan is telecast. Special awareness programme through Song & Drama Division and Directorate of Field Publicity have been organized in the areas where regular mass media presence is low. Besides this, the sensitization of members from Gram Sabhas, Panchayati Raj Institutions, Aanganwadi workers, Self Help Groups and media is also undertaken on a regular basis. A Red Ribbon Express was launched on 1st December, 2007 to spread awareness messages in 50,000 villages over a period of one year. Phase III of the National AIDS Control Programme has been formulated to control the spread of HIV by up scaling targeted interventions among the high risk groups, behaviour change communication for improved awareness, expanding, counselling and testing services, blood safety support and treatment of HIV infected persons including the treatment of opportunistic infections, provision of anti-retroviral drugs and mainstreaming of HIV intervention strategies. This information was given by the Minister of State for Health & Family Welfare, Smt. Panabaaka Lakshmi in a written reply to a question in the Lok Sabha.

6127. (27-2-2008) NEW DELHI : The programme grant agreement has been signed between the Government of India and the Global Fund to Fight AIDS Tuberculosis and Malaria (GFATM) on 20-12-07 for the phase-II of Round IV which will end in August, 2010 under this project, antiretroviral treatment is being provided to HIV/AIDS infected persons in 6 high prevalence states and NCT Delhi. Under this agreement financial grant of US $ 122,668,637 will be received from GFATM to establish 78 new ART centres, including 10 centres in the corporate sector. Approximately 84.7 lakh persons will be screened and 1.8 lakh PLHAs will be provided treatment at the ART centres. Facilities for CD4 testing will be made available at 188 ART centres in a phased manner. Medical, nursing, counselors, lab technicians and other health personnel working in the ART centres will be trained. The terms and conditions of the said agreement are: (i) Funding is consistent with the funding policies that may be set by the Global Fund Board; (ii) No Grant fund shall be used to finance any customs duties, tariffs, import taxes, or other similar levies and taxes associated with the import, manufacture, or sale of products or commodities, or the procurement of services for the programme; (iii) The Auditor shall be the Comptroller and Auditor General of the Government of India; (iv) The Global Fund shall consult the Country Coordinating Mechanism prior to selecting a new entity to serve as LFA. (v) The Global Fund and the Principal Recipient commit to use their best efforts to resolve any issues related to procurement under the programme in a collaborative fashion; (vi) The National AIDS Control Organisation (NACO) of the Ministry of Health and Family Welfare will be the implementing agency for the purposes of this Agreement. GFATM Round IV covers 6 high prevalent States (Tamil Nadu, Maharashtra, Karnataka, Andhra Pradesh, Manipur and Nagaland) and NCT Delhi. Under Phase I (September 2005-September, 2007) of GFATM Round IV, 105 ART centres have been established. The total PLHAs covered under ART in these centres were 79,390 as against target of 59,007 and 215,698 episodes of opportunistic infections were treated against the target of 2,37,559 during Phase I. A total of 51 health care facilities with laboratory capacity to conduct CD4 counts have been established. 1129 services providers including doctors, counselors, lab technicians, data entry operators have been trained in counselling, technical and attitudinal areas. 4,068,929 persons were counselled and tested for HIV in high prevalence States and NCT Delhi during phase I of GFATM Round IV. Three operational research studies have also been undertaken. This information was given by the Minister of State for Health & Family Welfare, Smt. Panabaaka Lakshmi in a written reply to a question in the Lok Sabha.

6128. (27-2-2008) NEW DELHI : There is no substantial enhancement of heavy mineral deposit in the coastal stretches of Tamil Nadu and Pondichery. However, Tsunami has resulted in enhancement of nearly 0.46 million tones of llmenite and 0.03 million tones of Rutile in the known deposits of Chavara, Kerala. Government has allocated Rs. 99.50 crore for setting up a 500 tons per year titanium sponge plant at Kerala Minerals and Metals Limited, Kollam based on the technology developed at Defence Metallurgical Research Laboratory. The beach sand mineral sector has been liberalized and private sector is also encouraged to set up titanium extraction plants. This information was given by the Minister of State in the Prime Minister's Office, Shri Prithviraj Chavan, in the Lok Sabha today.

6129. (27-2-2008) NEW DELHI : There are a total of 7274 Sub Centres [SCs], 1073 Primary Health Centres [PHCs] and 273 Community Health Centres [CHCs] functioning as on March, 2007 in the State of Gujarat. Under the National Rural Health Mission [NRHM] Programme Implementation Plan [PIP] 2007-08, proposals have been received for opening of new SCs, PHCs and CHCs from Government of Gujarat. An amount of Rs. 800 lakhs have been approved for construction of 200 new SCs @ Rs. Four Lakhs per SC, Rs. 658 Lakhs has been approved for construction of new PHC and an amount of Rs. 510 Lakhs has been approved for construction of five new CHCs. This information was given by the Minister of State for Health & Family Welfare, Smt. Panabaaka Lakshmi in a written reply to a question in the Lok Sabha.

6130. (27-2-2008) NEW DELHI : ISRO is planning to launch a satellite called Aditya to study the sun. Aditya will carry an instrument intended to study the outmost region of the sun called corona. It will also study the coronal mass ejection and the crucial physical parameters of space weather, such as, the coronal magnetic field structures and evolution of the coronal magnetic field. The mission is intended to enhance the scientific knowledge of the sun's radiation and the continuous monitoring of the sun's atmosphere. This data will also help to design the satellites to withstand adverse effects of solar environment. This information was given by the Minister of State in the Prime Minister's Office, Shri Prithviraj Chavan, in the Lok Sabha today.

6131. (27-2-2008) NEW DELHI : The 3-day (25-27 February 2008) International Conference on "Moving towards gender sensitisation of trade policy" organised by the United Nations Conference on Trade and Development (UNCTAD) concluded here today. The Conference was inaugurated by Mrs. Meira Kumar, Minister for Social Justice and Empowerment on 25th February. Dr. Supachai Panitchpakdi, Secretary-General of UNCTAD and Shri G.K. Pillai, Commerce Secretary, also participated in the Conference and spoke on the occasion. The conference provided a forum for Indian and international trade and gender experts to discuss and raise awareness on trade performance and gender linkages in India and globally and propose actions and directions towards enhanced and more effective gender sensitisation of trade policy with particular reference to India and generally to developing countries. While inaugurating the Conference, Mrs. Meira Kumar said that equitable distribution of gains from trade among the genders is a development objective which needs to be addressed through trade policies and trade agreements. Dr. Supachai Panitchpakdi highlighted a number of findings that have emerged from a new empirical study by the UNCTAD/DFID/India Project in collaboration with UNDP, on the impact of trade and globalization on gender in India, he stated that women are significant stakeholders in the process of trade, growth and development. This must be recognized and harnessed by Government to make globalization more inclusive with pro-poor impact. Women's groups must be consulted to a greater extent and in a systematic and structured manner, in the formulation of trade policies or negotiating positions, so as to integrate the gender dimension, he suggested. Broadly, the Conference deliberations suggest a strong and direct relationship between trade performance, gender empowerment and development, explicit and specific attention to gender issues in policy and operational actions, as well as in attitudes, are key conditions for maximizing the gains for gender empowerment through trade and minimizing the costs that can arise. This is important because overall the situation in India and in many developing countries presently is that there is progress towards gender empowerment through trade. Moreover, a gender-sensitive approach to trade must involve a vision of trade as an integral component of wider development efforts to eradicate poverty and promote inclusive, people-centred development.

6132. (27-2-2008) NEW DELHI : Although violence and militancy has continued in some parts of the country, the overall situation remains largely under control. In fact, there has been a significant improvement in so far as the situation in Jammu & Kashmir is concerned, and even in the North Eastern Region, the situation has improved considerably in some States such as Tripura and Meghalaya, while coordinated measures are being taken to check and control the activities of militant groups in the other affected States in the region *viz.*, Assam, Manipur and Nagaland. In the naxal affected areas also the overall level of extremist violence has, more or less, remained at a similar level in the last few years and, has in fact, shown improvement in a number of areas, but for a few major incidents in some States like Chhattisgarh, Jharkhand, etc. The State Governments have been urged to take focused and coordinated measures to deal with the situation, and all possible help and assistance is being provided by the Government of India to them in this regard. As far as terrorism in the hinterland is concerned, although some incidents have occurred in different States, close coordination is being maintained between the Central and State agencies, including regular sharing of information and intelligence. As a result, a large number of terrorist modules have been busted and possible major terrorist incidents averted. Institutional arrangements have also been put in place so that sharing and analysis of information can be done on a continuing basis in a systematic and coordinated manner. The State Governments have also been urged to strengthen the State police forces, by filling up vacancies and improving the police-population ratio, as also to take special measures to strengthen their intelligence set up. Assistance for these purposes is also been given under the Police Modernisation Scheme, under which the States have also asked to prepare sub-plans for strengthening the intelligence related arrangements for which the assistance of Central agencies is also being provided. All this is in addition to deployment of Central forces to assist the civil authorities in the States, liberal sanctions for raising of India Reserve (IR) battalions and assistance for general and specialized training for the State security forces. This information was given by Shri Sriprakash Jaiswal, Minister of State in the Ministry of Home Affairs in reply to a question in Rajya Sabha today.

6133. (27-2-2008) NEW DELHI : The Government proposes to issue Multi-purpose National Identity (smart) Card (MNIC) to the citizens in the country. The project envisages providing unique National Identity Number (NIN) to each person in the National Population Register. However, keeping in view the complexities involved both in the processes and technology, a pilot project has been under implementation on an experimental basis covering a population of 30.95 lakhs in the selected areas in 12 States and 1 Union Territory. Under the pilot project, identity (smart) cards are being issued to the citizens of age 18 years and above. The production and distribution of identity cards to be completed by March this year has been undertaken through Central Public Sector Undertakings. It is proposed to decide on the implementation of the scheme in the entire country in the light of the experiences gained and lessons learnt from the pilot project. This information was given by Shri Manikrao H. Gavit, Minister of State in the Ministry of Home Affairs in reply to a question in Rajya Sabha today.

6134. (27-2-2008) NEW DELHI : Dr. Raghuvansh Prasad Singh, the Union Minister of Rural Development informed that there is no proposal at present under consideration of the Government for increasing the number of working days under National Rural Employment Guarantee Scheme from 100 to 150. In reply to a question in Rajya Sabha today, Dr. Singh further informed that the aim of National Rural Employment Guarantee Act is to provide for the enhancement of livelihood security of the rural households by providing at least 100 days of guaranteed wage employment in every financial year to every household whose adult members volunteer to do unskilled manual work. NREGA is demand based. Under the Act, employment is provided to a wage seeker for the number of days of employment demanded subject to an over all ceiling of 100 days per household in a financial year.

6135. (27-2-2008) NEW DELHI : The Kaladan Multi-Modal Transit Transport Facility envisages connectivity between Indian ports on the eastern seaboard and Sittwe Port in Myanmar thereby providing an alternate route for transport of goods to North-East India through Myanmar. The approximate cost of the project is expected to be Rs. 545 Crores. The time-frame for the project is 5 years from the date of actual commencement of the project, which will be after the Agreement and the Protocols are signed by the two Governments. The above information was given by the External Affairs Minister, Shri Pranab Mukherjee in written reply to a question in Lok Sabha today.

6136. (27-2-2008) NEW DELHI : Prime Minister Dr. Manmohan Singh visited China from 13 to 15 January 2008. PM held official talks with Premier Wen Jiabao and had separate meetings with Chinese President Hu Jintao and Chairman of the Standing Committee of the National People's Congress of China, Wu Bangguo. PM and Premier Wen Jiabao signed a joint document on 'A Shared Vision for the 21st Century' of the Republic of India and the People's Republic of China'. They also witnessed signing of ten other documents covering cooperation in various fields, namely: for Cooperation between the Planning Commission and National Development and Reform Commission of China; on Cooperation between the two Ministries of Railways; MoU between Ministry of Housing and Urban Poverty Alleviation of India and Ministry of Construction, PRC; for Cooperation in Land Resource Management, Land Administration and Rehabilitation; MoU on Joint Medical Mission to commemorate the Indian Medical Mission to China between Indian Council for Cultural Relations (ICCR) and the Chinese People's Association for Friendship with Foreign Countries (CPAFFC); MoU for cooperation between ICCR and CPAFFC; on Cooperation in the area of Geo-sciences; on Cooperation in traditional medicine; MoU on mutual cooperation between NABARD and Agricultural Development Bank of China; and Protocol of Phytosanitary Requirements for the Export of Tobacco Leaves from India to China. Both sides agreed that India-China relations are of regional and global significance. They recognised their 'significant historical responsibility to ensure comprehensive, balanced and sustainable economic and social development of the two countries and to promote peace and development in Asia and the world as a whole'. India-China relations are not targeted at any country, nor will it affect their friendship with other countries. Both sides agreed to intensify further high-level exchanges between the leaders of the two countries. Both sides agreed that the Foreign Ministers of India and China will exchange visits in 2008. They also agreed to continue deepening the mutual understanding and trust between the armed forces and welcomed the successful conclusion of the first joint military training exercise and agreed to hold a second exercise in India in 2008. It was decided to increase the bilateral trade target from 40 billion US dollars by 2010 to 60 billion US dollars. The two Prime Ministers mandated their Ministers of Commerce to examine the Feasibility Study on the benefits of a Regional Trading Arrangement and make recommendations at an early date. It was also decided to establish a high-level Business Leaders Forum to advise the two Prime Ministers on the future of economic ties. PM conveyed India's appreciation for China's assistance in providing flood season data for some trans-border rivers. Both leaders agreed to expand cooperation in this area through the Expert Level Mechanism. In pursuance of the India-China Science & Technology Partnership agreed during the visit of Chinese President to India in November 2006, both sides have now identified earthquake engineering, disaster management, climate change, biotechnology and nano sciences as areas for further cooperation in the priority area of science and technology. The two Prime Ministers welcomed the progress made by the Special Representatives in seeking a framework for settlement of the boundary question that is fair, reasonable, mutually acceptable, and based on the agreement on Guiding Principles and Political Parameters signed in April 2005. While the SRs continue their efforts, both sides reiterated their mutual commitment to maintaining peace and tranquillity in the border areas. PM's visit has led to a broadening of our functional cooperation in bilateral areas and to the deepening of mutual understanding between our two countries. The above information was given by the Minister of External Affairs, Shri Pranab Mukherjee in response to a question in Lok Sabha today.

6137. (27-2-2008) NEW DELHI : A meeting on the subject was chaired by External Affairs Minister on October 31, 2007. At the meeting, the importance of internal transportation connectivity in all modes for the development of North Eastern region was highlighted. The meeting was also informed of the efforts being made by the Government, to increase international connectivity. To this end, discussions are being held with concerned neighbouring countries, both in the bilateral and multilateral framework to enhance economic, commercial and trade links with these countries. The Ministry of Development of North Eastern Region, being responsible for the overall development of North Eastern States, including the building up of the physical infrastructure, will be providing state-wise details on the specific steps being taken by them in due course. The above information was given by the External Affairs Minister, Shri Pranab Mukherjee in written reply to a question in Lok Sabha today.

6138. (27-2-2008) NEW DELHI : External Affairs Minister, Shri Pranab Mukherjee informed the Lok Sabha today in written reply to a question that 460 Indian fishermen were taken into custody by the Pakistan Maritime Security Agency (PMSA) in 2005, 365 in 2006, 124 in 2007 and 22 in 2008. 251 boats were similarly taken into custody between 2003 and 2005, 58 in 2006, 29 in 2007 and 4 in 2008. As per information available, 372 Indian fishermen and 342 boats continue to be in the custody of the Pakistan authorities. The fishermen and boats are mostly from Gujarat and the Union Territory of Diu and Daman. Since 2005, 1579 fishermen have been released by Pakistan including those taken into custody before 2005. Government have been taking up the issue of the release of fishermen and their boats regularly with the Government of Pakistan including at the highest level. A Judicial Committee comprising judges from India and Pakistan has been formed to expedite the release of prisoners in either country.

6139. (27-2-2008) NEW DELHI : China disputes the international boundary between India and China. Since 1993, the two Governments have agreed to maintain peace and tranquillity along the line of actual control in the India-China border areas, without prejudice to their respective positions on the alignment of the line of actual control as well as on the boundary question. In the meantime, pending a final settlement, both sides have agreed to clarify the LAC and to take up perceived violations through established mechanisms including the Joint Working Group, the Expert Group, border personnel meetings, flag meetings and diplomatic channels. The above information was given by the Minister of External Affairs, Shri Pranab Mukherjee in response to a question in Lok Sabha today.

6140. (27-2-2008) NEW DELHI : Rs. 62 crores is provided for assistance to National Sports Federations for various activities, including training of athletes. For the Commonwealth Games, a separate scheme has been worked out titled "Preparation of Indian Teams for Commonwealth Games 2010". After extensive discussions with National Sports Federations, a programme for providing training, foreign exposure, scientific backup, equipment etc. of high standard has been drawn up for the elite athletes who will represent India in the Commonwealth Games, 2010. Current estimates indicate an expenditure of Rs 802.00 crore for this training over the period 2007-08 to 2010-11, out of which expenditure on foreign exposure would be substantial so that the elite athletes could get the best in terms of training and foreign competitions. This information was given by Shri Mani Shankar Aiyar, Minister of Panchayati Raj, Youth Affairs & Sports and DoNER in the Lok Sabha today in a written reply to a question by Shri Sarvey Sathyanarayana.

6141. (27-2-2008) NEW DELHI : The allotment of National Games to States is done by the Indian Olympic Association (IOA). IOA have informed Government that only Uttar Pradesh bid for the 35th National Games. As the 35th National Games have already been allotted to Uttar Pradesh, it is not possible now to allot the 35th National Games to any other State. This information was given by Shri Mani Shankar Aiyar, Minister of Panchayati Raj, Youth Affairs & Sports and DoNER in the Lok Sabha today in a written reply to a question by Shri P.C. Thomas.

6142. (27-2-2008) NEW DELHI : The Union Minister of Shipping, Road Transport and Highways, Thiru T.R. Baalu has approved a sum of Rs. 1492.49 lakh for road improvement work at National Highway-47B in the state of Tamil Nadu. The Minister has given the approval for strengthening of a stretch for a length of 22 km from Nagercoil-Parvathipuram Junction to Kavalkinaru via Aralvai Mozhi in NH-47B. This is an important National Highway connecting NH-7 and NH-47. The riding surface of the road was badly damaged during the last monsoon season and lot of potholes and patches developed on the existing carriageway. Therefore, it has become absolutely necessary to repair this stretch.

6143. (28-2-2008) NEW DELHI : Union Minister for Science and Technology and Earth sciences Shri Kapil Sibal has said that Food security, Health and Environment are the challenges the world is facing in the 21st century and called upon the scientists to think out of the box to find solutions to sustain life. Addressing a gathering of eminent scientists on the occasion of National Science Day celebrations in New Delhi today, he said, solution lies in Science and Technology, particularly in integration of biology with chemistry. The theme this year is "Understanding Planet Earth" Shri Sibal observed that Global warming is relocating the habitat in the world as the process of civilization is changing the order of nature. Culture of science, therefore, he said, has to be to work with nature and not against it. Citing the example of coal as a natural resource he said that nature does value addition to itself but human beings want to destroy what has taken nature millions of years. Paying tribute to great scientists like C.V. Raman whose achievements are remembered by celebrating National Science Day, the Minister said the world would not have been what it is without their passion for Science. He said that science is about discovering the unknown, about future and hope and unless it is understood so, there will be neither future nor hope. The Minister also gave away the National Awards for Science Communication. Earlier, the noted scientist Prof. M S Swaminathan who graced the occasion as the Guest of Honour called for an "Evergreen Revolution" in his Science Day lecture. Dr. T. Ramasami, Secretary, Department of Science and Technology also spoke on the occasion.

6144. (28-2-2008) NEW DELHI : Fluctuation in the population of wildlife is a natural phenomenon. The status of population of wild animals on a yearly basis is not collated at Government of India level. There are no reports to indicate a continuous sharp decline in the population of endangered species in general. However, habitat degradation and other disturbances can have adverse effect on the natural population of wildlife. The All India Estimation of Tiger, co-predators and its prey was carried out recently in the tiger range states of the country using a modified and integrated methodology as recommended by the Tiger Task Force. The details are at Annexure I. However, in view of the modified new methodology adopted in the process, which is a benchmark in itself, it cannot be compared with the previous estimation of wild animals. Similarly, the all India enumeration of wild population of elephants in the country was carried out in 2007, except the North Eastern States. The details are at Annexure II. The Government has taken number of steps to protect wildlife and prevent poaching. They are enactment of the Wildlife (Protection) Act, 1972 to deal with the issues of wildlife crime. Stringent penalties are imposed on the offenders for the contravention of the provisions of the Act. A network of National Parks and Wildlife Sanctuaries has been set up across the country, Wildlife Crime Control Bureau, with a network a five Regional and three Sub Regional Offices, has been set up to control wildlife crime, providing financial support under the Centrally Sponsored Scheme-Development of National Parks and Sanctuaries, Project Tiger and Project Elephant, to State/UT Governments for the conservation and development of wildlife and its habitats etc. India is a signatory to the Convention on International Trade in Endangered Species of Wild Fauna and Flora (CITES) that regulates international trade in wildlife and its derivatives as well as India has bilateral arrangements with China and Nepal on combating wildlife crime.

6145. (28-2-2008) NEW DELHI : A draft notification on Regulatory Regime of Wetlands in the country has been proposed to be brought out under the provisions of the Environment Protection Act 1986. Since the notification is still in the draft form, modalities of maintenance and upkeep will be worked out after its finalization. Recognizing the value of Wetlands and taking cognizance of the fact that there does not yet exist a formal system of Wetland Regulation, the National Environment Policy (NEP), 2006, as approved by the Cabinet in May 2006 sought to set up a legally enforceable regulatory mechanism for identified valuable Wetlands to prevent their degradation and enhance their conservation. A series of meetings were held by the Multi Disciplinary Expert Group constituted for this purpose. The Expert Group prepared its recommendations on the Categories of Wetlands for Regulation, Process and Procedure for Identification, Composition of Regulatory Authority, Functions of the Authority, and Activities to be Regulated. A draft notification is proposed to be brought out under the provisions of the Environment Protection Act, 1986. At present, 103 wetlands have been identified under National Wetland Conservation Programme, out of which four wetlands, *viz.*, Chilika, Kanjia, Kunaria and Daha wetlands are located in Orissa.

6146. (28-2-2008) NEW DELHI : Breeding of Gharials in captivity has been successfully standardized and as and when required, captive bred Gharials are released in wild also. As per the last census conducted in 2007, the estimated number of Gharials in various Sanctuaries has been about 1645. Around 105 Gharials have been reported dead during the period between 8.12.2007 and 21.2.2008. No particular reason could be attributed to this mortality of Gharials. However, possibility of nephro-toxin entering via the food-chain could not be ruled out. The Government has taken important steps to check the Gharial mortality are as follows: (i) The Ministry of Environment & Forests has constituted a Crisis Management Group to coordinate the efforts to control Ghariyal mortality. (ii) Expertise of international experts has been obtained for the investigation purpose. Tissues/Blood samples have been sent for laboratory investigations. (iii) Immediate financial assistance to the tune of Rs. 12. 08 lakhs has been provided to the State of Madhya Pradesh, Rajasthan and Uttar Pradesh for mitigation of Gharial mortality apart from grant of Rs. 27.295 lakhs for the National Chambal Gharial Sanctuary, for the year 2007-08. (iv) All efforts have been made by the State Governments to stop illegal sand mining thus avoiding any damage to the habitat of Gharials. Further, inter-state collaboration amongst the States of Madhya Pradesh, Rajasthan and Uttar Pradesh are taken up for conservation & management of Gharials and their habitats.

6147. (28-2-2008) NEW DELHI : The principal outcome of Bali Conference which was held at Bali as the thirteenth Conference of Parties (COP-13) to the United Nations Framework Convention on Climate Change (UNFCCC) and the third Meeting of Parties (MOP-3) to Kyoto Protocol was to launch a comprehensive process called Bali Action Plan (BAP) that would enable the full, effective and sustained implementation of the UNFCCC through long-term cooperative action, now, up to and beyond 2012. It is expected that an agreed outcome would be reached and a decision adopted regarding BAP, at the fifteenth Conference of Parties (COP-15) to be held in December 2009. The Conference of Parties serving as Meeting of Parties at Bali also took crucial decisions in respect of the Kyoto Protocol, the Adhoc Working Group on further commitments of developed countries (beyond 2012) finally established a deadline of 2009 for the completion of its work and forwarding to COP-15 for a decision, its recommendations on quantified emissions limitation and reduction commitments of Annex I Parties (developed countries). Several other significant decisions which are beneficial to developing countries were also reached at Bali. These include operationalization of the Adaptation Fund to provide assistance to developing countries to adapt to climate change; agreement on guidance for the further implementation and improvement of the Clean Development Mechanism; policy approaches and positive incentives on issues relating to reducing emissions from deforestation and forest degradation in developing countries and the role of conservation, sustainable management of forests and enhancement of forest carbon stocks in developing countries; "transfer of technologies", including licenses to support the access to and transfer of low carbon technologies, and know how. It is expected that the decisions taken at Bali would enhance the implementation of the UNFCCC and as a responsible country, India will engage constructively in these negotiations.

6148. (28-2-2008) NEW DELHI : We can never forget the love and affection you have showered on us during our visits to Nagaland. We deeply cherish our interactions with the elected representatives of Nagaland and also with various Naga leaders during the six-year rule of the National Democratic Alliance at the Centre. We fully understand that the overwhelming desire among Naga people is for a permanent peace with honour, dignity and respect for Naga history and culture. It is this understanding which guided all the sincere and sustained efforts of the NDA government to ensure speedy and meaningful progress of the peace process. A lot of progress was, indeed, achieved for which we heartily thank the people of Nagaland and their leaders. Nagaland is going to the polls to elect a new Assembly on 5 March 2008. Much depends on the strengthening of the democratic process in your state, since it is inextricably linked to our commonly cherished goals of peace and development. The Bharatiya Janata Party has fielded candidates in the Assembly elections. The BJP is tried and tested. Our party's commitment to ensuring a better future for Nagaland has been proven. Peace is a precondition for development. Without development, there can be no employment. The BJP's goal, both in Nagaland and in the rest of India, is to remove poverty, social disparities and regional imbalances, and enhance the quality of life of all citizens, irrespective of their religious, ethnic or linguistic affiliations. The BJP assures you that our candidates, when elected, will do their utmost to further these objectives. We appeal to you to elect BJP candidates in large numbers. Once again, our best wishes to all of you.

6149. (28-2-2008) NEW DELHI : The Supreme Court of India advised Government not to release more funds for Ganga clean up (GAP) without the State showing utilization certificates for earlier grants. In its orders dated 5th December, 2007, the Hon'ble Supreme Court, among other points, has observed that if further funds are allocated by the Union of India, the Planning Commission may verify whether those funds are duly utilized for the States effectively. The subject order has been provided by the Ministry to the Planning Commission for necessary compliance. The States implementing the Ganga Action Plan have also been directed in the order by the Hon'ble Court to file proper affidavits with details of utilization certificates for the funds received under the Plan. Control of pollution in rivers is a continuous process. Fund releases under the Plan are made to Implementing Agencies of the States in the form of recurring grants commensurate with the status of the projects on receipt and scrutiny of Utilisation Certificates from time to time in respect of the earlier releases and the details of their deployment in the approved schemes for pollution abatement. Unspent balances if any, are duly taken into account while effecting subsequent releases for the sanctioned works. The releases are made taking into account the overall requirement of funds assessed on the basis of the progress achieved in the pollution abatement works and the amounts utilized as per the Utilization Certificates.

6150. (28-2-2008) NEW DELHI : The State Environmental Impact Assessment Authority (SEIAA) of Uttar Pradesh has accorded environmental clearance to Ganga Expressway Project in August, 2007. They received representations for the project in which issues such as intensification of sedimentation of Ganga river, impact on bio-diversity, reduction in the flow have been raised. The Project proponents have been asked by the Secretariat of SEIAA, UP to carry out comprehensive environmental impact assessment and make necessary changes incorporating the environmental issues.

6151. (28-2-2008) NEW DELHI : The Board of Governors (BOG) NYKS has emphasized that in two years a lot of strengthening of Nehru Yuva Kendra Sangathans has been done and several streamlining measures have been taken. This includes structuring of programmes with emphasis on youth clubs becoming part of its activities. In the last 2 years NYKS functioning has also increased and major initiatives are under way to improve the performance of NYKS. One such initiative includes a detailed study by IIM Ahmedabad on NYKS and its programmes. IIM Ahemdabad has finished this in depth study and will submit its report in mid March 2008. The Board of Governors further discussed the expansion of NYKS to all districts of the country which is necessary for the development of youth. The BOG requested the Minister of Youth Affairs and Sports Mr. Mani Shankar Aiyar to put forth this request for extension to the Government of India. The Minister assured them that their request would be sent to the Finance Ministry for consideration. The meeting of the BOG was held on 26th February 2008.

6152. (28-2-2008) NEW DELHI : Ministry of Social Justice and Empowerment is implementing a plan scheme namely 'An Integrated Programme for Older Persons' under which financial assistance upto 90 per cent of the project cost is provided to NGOs for establishing and maintaining Old Age Homes, Day Care Centres, Mobile Medicare Units and to provide non-institutional services to older persons. In addition, the government is also offering various other facilities/ benefits like old age pension, higher threshold limit of exemption under Income Tax, higher rates of interest on saving schemes of senior citizens; exclusive Health Insurance Schemes through Public Sector Insurance Companies for senior citizens; travel concessions, etc. Further, the Government has recently enacted the maintenance and Welfare of Parents and Senior Citizens Act, 2007 for providing need-based maintenance and better healthcare facilities to the senior citizens, setting up of old age homes in every district of the country and for institutionalization of the mechanism for protection of life and property of the senior citizens. This information was given by the Minister of State for Social Justice and Empowerment, Smt. Subbulakshmi Jagadeesan in a written reply to a question in Lok Sabha today.

6153. (28-2-2008) NEW DELHI : According to the Census 2001, there are 2.19 crore persons with disabilities in India who constitute 2.13 per cent of the total population. The mentally retarded persons are 22.64 lakhs and constitute approximately 0.23 per cent of the total population in the country. The total population of mentally challenged persons as per census 2001 is 22,63,821. The physical, social and psychological empowerment of persons with disabilities is promoted through Deendayal Disable rehabilitation Scheme (DDRS) and Assistance to Disabled Persons for Purchase/Fitting of aids/Appliances (ADIP) Scheme. The seven National Institutes also take up programmes for empowerment of persons with disabilities through their outreach progrmmes. Government has been promoting the self-employment of persons with disabilities by providing vocational training and loan on concessional rates through National Handicapped Finance and Development Corporation (NHFDC). This information was given by the Minister of State for Social Justice and Empowerment, Smt. Subbulakshmi Jagadeesan in a written reply to a question in Lok Sabha today.

6154. (28-2-2008) NEW DELHI : Congress spokesman Dr. Shakeel Ahmed said it is unfortunate that today also no business could be transacted in Parliament and the Hon'ble Speaker also expressed regret that the opposition parties have formed a habit of disrupting the House repeatedly and want to become martyrs as a saying in Urdu goes, "apply blood and pretend to die as martyrs". The Finance Minister has said that our prime focus is towards the agricultural sector and education. And the opposition when it got the hint about this fact, did not let any business to be transacted. They give the impression that they are the well wishers of both the sectors and this not good in a democracy. The peoples' representatives who have been sent to Parliament to debate and discuss matters pertaining to their problems are wasting the precious time of Parliament in disruption and obstruction. To a question regarding Ramsethu issue. Dr. Ahmed said, the details of the affidavit filed by the government has not been announced and if the matter is sub-judice I therefore cannot comment on it. To a question that there has been a deliberate attempt to leak the Budget, Dr. Ahmed said that it is altogether wrong to say that the Budget has been leaked. It is easy to blame others and the opposition is deliberately playing blame game. These charges are not true and we totally dismiss it. To a question that Congress MLA in Tamil Nadu made some objectionable remarks about Dr. B. R. Ambedkar, Dr. Ahmed said that Shri Arun Kumar has not said anything about Dr. Ambedkar which might hurt the feelings of a section of the society. But if it has hurt the sentiments of any section of the society he has unconditionally apologized. To a question about Shri Rahul Gandhi meeting with the Prime Minister, Dr. Ahmed said that our spokesperson Shri Abhishek Singhvi is bringing the information about the same. Shri Abhishek Singhvi who joined in said that the delegation led by Shri Rahul Gandhi met with the PM for complimenting him for the implementation of the National Rural Employment Guarantee Act (NREGA). The delegation felt that it was their duty to give voice to the poor of this country by drawing the attention of the PM to the scope for improving the implementation of NREGA. A Press release on the meeting of Shri Rahul Gandhi and the delegation of young MPs who met Prime Minister is also being distributed.

6155. (28-2-2008) NEW DELHI : The Government has constituted a Commission consisting of a Chairperson, a Member and a Member Secretary to consider the proposal for reservation for the economically Backward Classes not covered by the existing reservation policy. The terms of references of the Commission are: (i) to elicit the views of State Governments/UTs and other Commissions on the subject; (ii) to suggest criteria for identification of economically backward classes; (iii) to recommend the welfare measures and quantum of reservation in education and Government Employment in consultation with the National Commission for Religious and Linguistic Minorities; (iv) to suggest the necessary constitutional, legal and administrative modalities as required for the implementation of their recommendations. This information was given by the Minister of State for Social Justice and Empowerment, Smt. Subbulakshmi Jagadeesan in a written reply to a question in Lok Sabha today.

6156. (28-2-2008) NEW DELHI : The Minister of Petroleum and Natural Gas Shri Murli Deora informed the Lok Sabha in a written reply today that Public Sector Oil Marketing Companies (OMCs) have reported that at present, there is no overall shortage of LPG in the country and LPG supplies to distributors are being made by the OMCs through indigenous production and imports in accordance with the genuine demand of customers registered with the LPG distributors. He also said that OMCs have further reported that they have supplied 8450 TMT (Thousand Metric Tonnes) of domestic LPG in the country during the period-April, 2007-January, 2008 as against 8030 TMT during the corresponding period of last year, showing a growth of 5.2%. However, OMCs had reported backlog in LPG supplies in certain States in the country due to reduction in supply of bulk LPG by Reliance Industries Limited (RIL) & Essar Oil Limited in January 2008, delay in movement of bulk LPG by rail from Jamnagar to the Northern Region, increased demand in the States due to severe cold which resulted in panic booking by the customers, strikes by contract labour, agitational activities, delays in berthing of vessels at Haldia Port due to reduced draft, bandhs etc. The Minister told the House that Government has advised OMCs to liquidate the backlog in the States by operating the bottling plants on holidays and during extended hours. Increased bottling is also being done during the working days for early clearance of backlog. Shri Deora also said that at present the indigenous production of LPG is inadequate to meet domestic requirements. The shortfall in availability is met through imports.

6157. (28-2-2008) NEW DELHI : The Minister for Petroleum and Natural Gas Shri Murli Deora informed the Lok Sabha in a written reply today that India has been pursuing the import of natural gas from Iran through the Iran-Pakistan-India (IPI) transnational gas pipeline. Shri Deora told the House that important issues concerning the implementation of the Project are under discussion amongst the participating countries. He also said that as per current indications, pipeline within Iran upto Iran-Pakistan border will be laid and operated by an agency to be nominated by Iran. Iran wants to sell gas at Iran-Pakistan Border. So all responsibility for safety and security of the pipeline within Iran will vest with Iran. Safety and security of pipeline and gas within Pakistan will be provided by the Pakistan Government for which a transit fee would be levied. Discussions regarding the security package by the Pakistan Government and the transit fee are continuing. Suitable provisions will be included in the contract with the Pakistan side for safety & security of the pipeline. It has been agreed that the pipeline proposed to be laid in Iran, Pakistan and India will be constructed as per the international standards, incorporating all safety features. It is envisaged to provide round-the-clock communication and supervisory control system all along the pipeline. Shri Deora emphasized that such multilateral projects involve protracted discussions, as all the aspects have to be carefully examined and deliberated upon to the satisfaction of the participating countries to protect each country's interests and avoid any problems in the future in the successful operation of the project. He added, "No official communication has been received regarding China joining IPI gas pipeline Project."

6158. (28-2-2008) NEW DELHI : The Minister for Steel, Chemicals and Fertilisers Shri Ram Vilas Paswan today launched the Online Complaint Submission and Redressal System of the National Pharmaceutical Pricing Authority of India (NPPA) here today. He also handed over the ISO 9001-2000 Certificate to the Chairman, NPPA; and also released a compendium containing prices of scheduled bulk drugs and scheduled formulation packs. The Online Complaint Submission and Redressal System has been developed by NPPA in association with NIC for speedy redressal of complaints and for effective and efficient monitoring of complaints relating to availability and prices of medicines. Action on any complaint received through the system will be initiated within 30 days. Any individual or organization can lodge the complaint through internet and if the complainant is not able to upload documents like Cash Memo or copy of the Strip/Label, he/she can forward the same by post so that it reaches NPPA within 15 days of filling of the complaint. Speaking on the occasion the Minister complemented NPPA for its efforts to bring in transparency. He said the National Pharma Policy now under the consideration of the Group of Ministers will be cleared very soon. Shri Paswan said, while the efforts of the Government is to support the pharmaceutical industry for its growth, the Government remains committed to ensure availability of medicines at affordable prices. He said only 28 per cent of the sector is under price control and appealed to the industry to keep the interest of common man in mind before fixing prices. Shri Paswan also released the first ever directory of Pharmaceutical units of the country and also announced the launching of a census of Pharmaceutical units. The census will provide inputs for policy making. The Chairman of NPPA Shri Ashok Kumar, senior official of the Ministry of Chemicals and Fertilisers, Consumer Affairs, Industry and Consumer representatives were present on the occasion.

6159. (28-2-2008) NEW DELHI : "Unorganised Manufacturing Sector in India-Input, Output and Value Added "-Report No. 526 based on the survey of unorganised manufacturing enterprises carried out by National Sample Survey Organisation (NSSO) of the Ministry of Statistics and Programme Implementation, Government of India, as part of 62nd round survey of NSS, has been released. The fieldwork of the survey was carried out during July 2005-June 2006. This report is the third and the last in a series of three reports brought out based on the survey on unorganised manufacturing enterprises. The first report contained information on various operational characteristics of enterprises like location of enterprise, nature of operation, maintenance of accounts etc. in detail. The second report presented detailed information on employment, assets and borrowings of these enterprises. The present report provides input, output and value added of unorganised manufacturing enterprises at all India level for different industry groups and at the level of States / UTs for all the industry groups taken together. The term 'unorganised manufacturing enterprises ' under the coverage of 62nd round referred to all manufacturing enterprises, which were not covered by Annual Survey of Industries (ASI). All government and public sector undertakings were also outside the coverage. All States / Union Territories were covered by the survey except some interior areas of Nagaland, Andaman and Nicobar Islands and Leh and Kargil districts of Jammu & Kashmir. A dual frame approach was followed in the survey with a view to improving the reliability of the overall estimates by separating out apparently large units into one frame (list frame) and covering the remaining units within the coverage through the area frame. A sample of 82897 enterprises were actually surveyed out of which 2,260 enterprises belonged to list frame and the remaining were spread over 9,923 sample villages/urban blocks in the area frame.

6160. (28-2-2008) NEW DELHI : The Government in October, 2005 has approved the expansion plan of Vishakhapatnam Steel Plant (VSP) at an estimated cost of Rs. 8692 crores (base June 2005 prices) for increasing its liquid steel capacity from 3 million tonnes to 6.3 million tonnes per annum by the 2009. While considering the proposal for expansion, an assessment has been made in respect of the international market, export trends and internal consumption vis-a-vis the projected rate of return on the investment. Assessment of returns on the investment for Expansion Phase-I has already been made in the Project Report. The entire capital cost of the expansion plan will be met by the VSP from internal resources and extra budgetary resources at an incremental debt equity ratio of 1:1. Giving this information in a written reply in the Lok Sabha today the Minister of State for Steel Dr. Akhilesh Das said Vishakhapatnam is not dependent on continued demand only from China.

6161. (28-2-2008) NEW DELHI : In order to maintain its predominance in the Indian steel sector and to face global competition, the Steel Authority of India Limited (SAIL) has drawn up an expansion plan covering its five integrated steel plants and special steel plants. SAIL proposes to increase production of hot metal from present level of 14.6 million tonnes per annum (2006-07) to 26.2 million tonnes per annum by the year 2010-11 at a present indicative cost of Rs. 54,000 crores. The financing of investment would be met by SAIL primarily from its internal resources and balance from market borrowings, if required. Besides capacity enhancement, the growth plan adequately addresses the need of SAIL Plants towards eliminating technological obsolescence, energy saving, enriching product mix, pollution control, developing mines & collieries to meet higher requirement of key inputs, introduce customer centric processes and have matching infrastructure facilities in the Plant to support higher production volumes. This information was given by the Minister of State for Steel Dr. Akhilesh Das in a written reply in the Lok Sabha today.

6162. (28-2-2008) NEW DELHI : The Government proposed to change the present policy for leasing of Lignite/Coal blocks. This information was given by the Minister for Coal, Dr. Dasari Narayana Rao in the Parliament. In order to make the policy for leasing of Lignite and Coal blocks more transparent and objective in the context of increasing number of applications and declining number of coal and lignite blocks, the Government is contemplating to introduce a system of auctioning through competitive bidding for allocation of such blocks by making necessary amendments in the Mines and Minerals (Development and Regulation) Act, 1957. The Government proposed to transfer the entire resource raised through competitive bidding to the concerned state government where the coal block is located. Under the existing provisions of the Act, prior approval of the Central Government is necessary before State Governments can grant mining lease in respect of Coal/Lignite and other minerals included in the First Schedule of the Act.

6163. (28-2-2008) NEW DELHI : There is a large community of persons of Indian origin in Malaysia who are citizens of that country and are well integrated in the Malaysian society. The population of Malaysian citizens of Indian origin stands at about 1.9 million, which accounts for about 8% of the total population of Malaysia. Indians are the third largest ethnic group in Malaysia, after Malays and Chinese. Malaysia officially celebrates customs, traditions and religions of its multi-racial population. The people of Indian origin are active in various walks of the Malaysian society, economy and polity, including in the government, and their rights as Malaysian citizens are also derived from the Malaysian constitution. Members of Indian community have, however, also articulated their concerns and grievances regarding their standing in the country. Recently, a rally was organised by the Hindu Rights Action Force (HINDRAF) in Kuala Lumpur on 25 November 2007 with the stated purpose of handing over a petition to the British High

Commission in Kuala Lumpur seeking the support of Queen Elizabeth II for a class action suit filed in the UK for the exploitation of Indians who were brought to Malaysia as indentured labour. During this rally as well as subsequently, difficulties and concerns pertaining to economic and social conditions and religious rights of the Indian community in Malaysia have been highlighted. It may be recalled that in a suo motu statement made in Parliament on 30 November 2007, the Minister of External Affairs referred to concerns expressed by Hon'ble Members of Parliament regarding the alleged harassment of participants of the rally organised by the HINDRAF in Kuala Lumpur on 25 November 2007 and subsequent related matters. The Minister of External Affairs stated that Government remain deeply solicitous for the welfare of people of Indian origin living abroad and noted that there is a large community of people of Indian origin in Malaysia who are citizens of that country. He added that we have friendly relations with Malaysia and we are in touch with the Malaysian authorities in the related matter. During our interactions with Malaysian authorities, concerns expressed in India, including in the Parliament, regarding developments pertaining to the Indian community in Malaysia have been suitably conveyed. The above information was given by the Minister of External Affairs, Shri Pranab Mukherjee in response to a question in Rajya Sabha today.

6164. (28-2-2008) NEW DELHI : External Affairs Minister, Shri Pranab Mukherjee informed the Rajya Sabha today in written reply to a question that Government are aware that there have been delays in obtaining of Pakistan visa for pilgrims visiting religious shrines including Nankana Sahib. A proposal to increase both the number of shrines and pilgrims under the Bilateral Protocol on Pilgrimages has been pursued with the Government of Pakistan for over three years. A new visa agreement is also being discussed with Pakistan which should, when finalised, help in easing travel between the two countries including for those intending to visit religious shrines in Pakistan such as Nankana Sahib.

6165. (28-2-2008) NEW DELHI : China illegally claims approximately 90,000 square kilometres of Indian territory including Tawang in the State of Arunachal Pradesh. According to a report in 'The Statesman' dated 1 November 2007, the former Chinese Ambassador to India, Mr. Zhou Gang reportedly said, "As the Chinese people would never accept 'McMahon Line', India must make substantial adjustment in the Eastern sector." The fact that Arunachal Pradesh is an integral part of India has been conveyed by Government to the Chinese side. Indian territory under the occupation by China in Jammu & Kashmir is approximately 38,000 sq. kms. In addition, under the so-called "China-Pakistan Boundary Agreement" of 1963, Pakistan illegally ceded 5,180 sq. kms. of Indian territory in Pakistan Occupied Kashmir to China. China illegally claims approximately 90,000 sq. kms. of Indian territory in Arunachal Pradesh and about 2000 sq. kms. in the Middle Sector of the India-China boundary. The Special Representatives of India and China are presently seeking a framework for settlement of the boundary question that is fair, reasonable, mutually acceptable and based on the agreement on Guiding Principles and Political Parameters signed in April 2005. The above information was given by the Minister of External Affairs, Shri Pranab Mukherjee in response to a question in Rajya Sabha today.

6166. (28-2-2008) NEW DELHI : Following is the text of the statement made to the media by Finance Minister, Shri P. Chidambaram after placing Economic Survey in the Parliament House, here today:-The economy has decisively moved to a higher growth trajectory during the five years to 2007-08. In terms of GDP, the growth rate has averaged 8.7 per cent per annum during these five years. This indicates stability and sustainability. The growth is reflected in a near doubling of the pace at which the average income of our people is growing. If the rate of growth of per capita GDPmp continues at the five year average of 7.2 per cent per year, average income would now double in a decade instead of a generation or more, earlier. The acceleration in improvement of the condition of the common man is also reflected in a near doubling of the rate of growth of per capita private consumption to 5.1 per cent per annum (from 2.6 per cent in the previous 11 years). With better targeting of government services and an increase in their quality we can ensure that the overall welfare of the common man in terms of both private consumption and supply of public goods continues to increase rapidly. The higher economic growth trajectory and the projected growth of 8.7 per cent in 2007-08 is based on a quantum jump in savings and investment rates. The rate of investment (GCF) was 35.9 per cent of GDP in 2006-07 and is projected to increase in 2007-08. This is an unprecedented level of investment and shows the firm foundations on which the growth acceleration has been built. The saving rate has similarly scaled new highs reaching 34.8 per cent of GDP in 2006-07. Given this solid foundation of domestic investment and saving, we are confident of meeting the Eleventh Plan (2007-08 to 2011-12) target of 9 per cent average growth. We will be able to mobilise the resources for meeting the growth target of 9 per cent, as set for the Eleventh Five Year Plan. Macro-economic fundamentals continue to inspire confidence and the investment climate is full of optimism. This is reflected, for instance, in the significant surge in capital inflows into the economy in the recent period, even when the global economy is showing distinct signs of slowing down. Buoyant growth of Government revenues has made it possible to maintain fiscal consolidation as mandated under the FRBMA. At the same time, we have the means to bridge and address the chronic gaps and weaknesses in our physical and social infrastructure. Inflation, which had risen during the second half of 2006-07, has been brought under control. The year on year rate of inflation declined to less than 4% in August 2007 and had remained below 4 per cent for 23 consecutive weeks since then. The price inflation in primary articles has similarly been brought down to 3.8 per cent in January 2008. Given the high level of food, oil and other commodity prices in international markets, the risks to inflation remain. Thus keeping inflation under control in an uncertain global environment will be one of the major challenges in 2008-09. There are, also downside risks to growth arising from the slowdown and possible recession in the global economy. There are several challenges to inclusive growth, namely agriculture, infrastructure, education and skill development. The last few years have seen a resurgence of the manufacturing sector and a continued broad based growth of the services sector. The agriculture sector/ dependent as it is on the monsoon, continued to fluctuate, though the five year period ending 2007-08 had the second lowest year to year variation since the five years ending 1956-57. We need to accelerate the pace of growth in agriculture on a sustained basis. Despite efforts to accelerate the pace of Infrastructure development, the demand for infrastructure services has grown even faster than the supply. It is imperative to augment and upgrade infrastructure both physical and social. This requires mobilisation of unprecedented amount of capital with macroeconomic stability, which can only happen if both the public and private sectors have the incentive and motivation to perform at their best. We have to harness our demographic potential and promote inclusive growth by providing the basic education and skills needed in the job market. I am optimistic about growth and containment of inflation in the coming year. It will be my priority to continue to provide a conducive investment climate and manage the macro economy to facilitate non-inflationary growth. We have to ensure that the benefits of this growth percolate to the most marginal and vulnerable segments of the society. If you wish me to sum up in one phrase the outlook for 2008-09, I would say "optimism, but with caution as the watchword." There are a number of things going in favour of India. We need to capitalize on these opportunities while at the same time responding to the evolving situation in the global economy in a manner that our growth story is not affected."

6167. (28-2-2008) NEW DELHI : External Affairs Minister, Shri Pranab Mukherjee informed the Rajya Sabha today in written reply to a question that the Government are aware of the offensive use of images of Mahatma Gandhi, Tricolour and Jawaharlal Nehru on undergarments by a US based online supplier. The Embassy of India in Washington wrote to the President of the company immediately to express outrage, requesting that this practice be discontinued. The matter has been followed up actively. Further, the US Government has also been apprised of this offensive practice of the said US company.

6168. (28-2-2008) NEW DELHI : The Government of Australia introduced new citizenship test w.e.f. October 1, 2007. The test does not adversely affect persons of Indian origin applying for Australian citizenship. The Australian Citizenship Amendment (Citizenship Testing) Act, 2007 amended the Australian Citizenship Act to require applicants for Australian citizenship to have successfully completed a test before applying for Australian citizenship. The citizenship test is to ensure that the applicant possesses a basic knowledge of the English language, has an adequate knowledge of Australia and of the responsibilities and privileges of Australian citizenship. All the questions in the test are drawn from information in a booklet entitled "Becoming an Australian Citizen". The booklet is available to applicants free of charge. For applicants with a low level of English literacy, officials at the testing centre provide assistance by reading the questions and possible answers. To be eligible for this assistance the applicant must have completed at least 400 hours of English language tuition under the "Adult Migrants English Programme". The above information was given by the Minister of External Affairs, Shri Pranab Mukherjee in response to a question in Rajya Sabha today.

6169. (28-2-2008) NEW DELHI : There is no proposal of two-laning of all single-lane NHs across the country on BOT basis, which are not covered under approved phases of NHDP. However, NHDP-Phase-IV, involving upgradation of NHs to two-lane standards with paved shoulders primarily on BOT basis, is yet to be approved by the Government. The Eleventh Five Year Plan (2007-12) endorsed by the National Development Council (NDC) during its meeting held on 19.12.2007 recommended that the targets for stretches other than NHDP have to be prioritised according to their importance to the national economy so that the available resources are not spread thinly among competing projects. The major targets for non-NHDP components include: i. Accelerated efforts to bring NHs network to a minimum of two-lane standard within the next ten years and four-laning small segments of non-NHDP stretches. ii. Removing existing deficiencies, like inadequate capacity, insufficient pavement thickness, etc. in the road network by strengthening the National Highway network/improving riding quality. The condition of the National Highways (NHs) is monitored on regular basis. Further, the development and maintenance of NHs is a continuous process to keep them in traffic worthy conditions and are taken up as per the availability of funds, traffic intensity and inter-se priority. This information was given by the Minister of State for Shipping, Road Transport and Highways, Shri K.H. Muniyappa in a written reply in the Rajya Sabha today.

6170. (28-2-2008) NEW DELHI : As per the extant policy guidelines of the Ministry of Shipping Road Transport & Highways, speed breakers are not permitted on National Highways being obstruction to free flow of traffic and safety hazard. However, Ministry's policy circular recommends provision of properly designed rumble strips at places like approaches to sharp curves or level crossings, congested or accident prone sections etc. where control of speed on National Highways is unavoidable. There are 12 numbers of speed breakers on NH-11 from Jaipur to Agra and 8 numbers of speed breakers on NH-12 from Jaipur to Kota. As per the Ministry's extant policy, concerned executive agencies have been instructed to take urgent necessary action in co-ordination with the local authorities for removing of speed breakers existing on National Highways and replace the same with properly designed rumble strips, only at unavoidable locations. This information was given by the Minister of State for Shipping, Road Transport and Highways, Shri K.H. Muniyappa in a written reply in the Rajya Sabha today.

6171. (28-2-2008) NEW DELHI : The Minister of State for Housing & Urban Poverty Alleviation, Kumari Selja informed the Rajya Sabha today, in a written reply to a question by Shri Jesudasu Seelam & Shri Gireesh Kumar Sanghi that the National Housing Bank which is a Subsidiary of Reserve Bank of India had prepared a Concept Note for construction of Low Cost houses under a programme titled "Aam Aadmi Aawaas." Accordingly, a provision of Rs.30 crores has been made in the budget Grant of this Ministry for the year 2007-08 for an Interest Subsidy Scheme for Housing the urban Poor. The Scheme seeks to improve affordability and accessibility of institutional finance to poorer sections with preference to Scheduled Castes, Scheduled Tribes and Minorities in accordance with Government's Policy. The details are being worked out.

6172. (28-2-2008) NEW DELHI : The road construction on National Highway No. 8 between Delhi and Gurgaon has been completed. The total project cost was estimated as Rs. 555 crore. The work was awarded on Build, Operate and Transfer (BOT) basis at a negative grant of Rs.61.06 crore. The entire construction cost of the project has been borne by the Concessionaire. The Change of Scope works amounting to Rs.155.25 crore (including share of Haryana Government) was approved as per the requirement of Haryana and Delhi Governments and keeping in view requirement of traffic due to rapid development in Gurgaon in the last 4 to 5 years. This was borne by the National Highways Authority of India. The total cost of construction is approx. Rs. 710 crore. This information was given by the Minister of State for Shipping, Road Transport and Highways, Shri K.H. Muniyappa in a written reply in the Rajya Sabha today.

6173. (28-2-2008) NEW DELHI : Meetings at high levels including the Group of Ministers, Lt. Governor, GNCTD, Cabinet Secretariat etc. are regularly held to assess preparations for the Commonwealth Games. Action Taken Reports on decisions taken in such meetings are reviewed during the course of the next meeting to ensure that required actions have been taken by the agencies concerned. Most recently, the Prime Minister's Office took stock of the progress made and advised all concerned to expedite matters. Government are conscious of the need to ensure proper planning and timely preparation for the Commonwealth Games, 2010 and to this end a number of institutional arrangements have been made. These include a Core Group of Ministers (GoM) under the co-Chairmanship of the Minister for Human Resource Development and the Home Minister for coordinating the various works related to the conduct of the Games; an Apex Committee headed by the Minister for Youth Affairs and Sports to oversee preparations; an Organizing Committee (OC) headed by the President, Indian Olympic Association for the Conduct of the Games; and a Committee of Secretaries headed by Cabinet Secretary which is responsible for monitoring the implementation of the decisions of the GoM and taking decisions on other related matters. In addition to these arrangements at the Central level, there is a sub-committee under the Chief Minister of Delhi to take decisions in respect of all matters pertaining to infrastructure and other preparations for the Games within the jurisdiction of the Government of NCT of Delhi. The Lt. Governor Delhi has been entrusted with the overall responsibility for matters coming under DDA and with specific reference to security, law and order. An Empowered Committee has been set up under the chairmanship of Chief Secretary, GNCTD, with representatives from all the agencies/authorities concerned to facilitate speedy clearances in respect of Games-related projects. Another Committee has been set up under Secretary, Ministry of Urban Development to facilitate clearances pertaining to the Delhi Urban Arts Commission (DUAC). Keeping in view the need for developing adequate tourist accommodation in readiness for the large expected influx of visitors for the Commonwealth Games, an inter-Ministerial Task Force has been set up under the Ministry of Tourism (MoT) for monitoring and coordinating further action in this regard by all the agencies concerned. A Committee for expediting Central Government clearances in respect of hotels coming up in Uttar Pradesh has also been set up under the Chairmanship of Secretary, Ministry of Youth Affairs and Sports. Locations for the various competitions/training venues and the International Broadcasting Centre (IBC)/Main Press Centre (MPC) have been agreed among the stakeholders. All stakeholders have indicated specific time-lines with reference to key milestones, *viz.*, finalization of detailed designs and estimates, commencement of the tendering process, award of the work, commencement of the work, completion of the work; and handing over to OC. The work on all the major sports venue infrastructure projects has commenced and the venues will be handed over to the OC by the end of 2009. Ministry of Youth Affairs & Sports has also set up a web based monitoring system to monitor and review the projects related to the Commonwealth Games To improve the performance of the Indian contingent in the Commonwealth Games, 2010, extensive discussions have been held with all stakeholders and a programme for providing training, foreign exposure, scientific backup, equipment etc. at an estimated cost of Rs.802.00 crore has been drawn up for the elite sportspersons who will represent India in the Commonwealth Games, 2010. Government have approved project proposals of the Sports Authority of India for an amount of Rs.1000 crore (± 10%) for the upgradation/creation of sports venue infrastructure; upgradation of the tennis venue by the All India Tennis Association at a cost of Rs.30 crore (± 15%); and an expenditure budget for the Organizing Committee on a revenue neutral basis of Rs.767 crore (± 15%) for the 'Conduct of the Games'. The Expenditure Finance Committee have considered the proposal of the Delhi Development Authority (DDA) for about Rs.765.00 crore for the International Zone etc. in the Games Village (the Residential part of which is being developed in the Public Private Partnership Mode) and sports infrastructure at the Village/other venues belonging to DDA.

6174. (28-2-2008) NEW DELHI : India will be hosting the AFC Challenge Cup from 30 July to 10 August 2008 and not in 2011. All India Football Federation (AIFF) have selected players from all over the country and intensive training is being given to them to create a "formidable" team for the event. Apart from the training, the All India Football Federation has also planned to give them international exposure through friendly matches and combined training with foreign teams. As per the regulations of the All India Football Federation, the clubs have to release the players as and when the players are to attend national coaching camps. AIFF have informed us that the training academies to be set up by the All India Football Federation at Gurgaon and Goa will be moddled on the best football academies in Europe and Japan with necessary technical staff. This information was given by Shri Mani Shankar Aiyar, Minister of Panchayati Raj, Youth Affairs & Sports and DoNER in the Rajya Sabha today in a written reply to a question by Shrimati Syeda Anwara Taimur and Shri Vijya J. Darda.

6175. (28-2-2008) NEW DELHI : The Government has decided to revive Nepa Ltd. through Joint Venture partner by disinvestment of Government of India Equity, preferably to the extent of 74% or 100%. Nepa Limited (Disinvestment of Ownership) Bill 2007 was introduced in Lok Sabha for getting Parliamentary approval of disinvestment of Nepa Ltd. The Bill has been referred to Department related Parliamentary Standing Committee on Industry on 17.12.2007. The Bill provides that every officer or other employee of the Nepa Ltd., except the Chairman and Directors, serving in its employment immediately before the disinvestment of the Nepa Ltd., shall continue in office or service after such disinvestment, on the same terms and conditions as if the disinvestment of the Nepa Ltd., had not been made and shall continue to do so until the expiry of the period of one year from the date of such disinvestment. Where an officer or other employee of the Nepa Ltd. opts not to continue in the employment or service of the Nepa Ltd., such officer or other employee shall be deemed to have resigned. This information was given by the Minister of State for Heavy Industries and Public Enterprises, Smt. Kanti Singh in a written reply to a question in Lok Sabha today.

6176. (28-2-2008) NEW DELHI : Economic Survey 2007-08 says, FDI inflows into India accelerated in 2006-07 due to reforms in policies, better infrastructure and a more vibrant financial sector. On a gross basis, FDI inflows into India after rising to a level of US $ 6.2 billion in 2001-02 has risen to US $ 23.0 billion in 2006-07. The trend continued in the current Financial Year with gross FDI inflows at US $ 11.2 billion in the first six months. FDI inflows continued to be preponderantly of the equity variety, broad-based and spread across a range of economic activities like financial services, manufacturing, banking services, information technology services and construction. FDI grew by 179.5 per cent on a net basis during 2006-07 while the growth was 150.2 per cent on gross basis. Even as FDI into India grew substantially, a simultaneous pick up in outward investment moderated the over all net inflows. Outward investment by India shot up from levels less than US $ 2.4 billion in the period 2003-04 to 2004-05 to reach US $ 14.4 billion in 2006-07. Thus, over all net FDI in 2006-07 was at US $ 8.5 billion. The trend continued in the current year also with FDI inflows in the period April-September 2007 being moderated by outward investment of US $ 7.3 billion to yield net flows of US $ 3.9 billion. The proportion of payments to receipts under FDI into India was 0.7 per cent and 0.4 per cent in 2005-06 and 2006-07 respectively. This indicates the lasting and stable nature of FDI flows in India.

6177. (28-2-2008) NEW DELHI : The Economic Survey 2007-08 says that about 70 per cent of the export target for the present year was achieved during April-December 2007, reaching a level of US $111 billion. The major drivers of export growth were petroleum products, engineering goods and gems and jewellery. The growth of engineering exports has been sustained by machinery and equipment, transport equipment and manufacturers of metals. There was a revival of the gems and jewellery sector with export growth 20.4 per cent for April-September 2007, after a deceleration in 2006-2007. India's merchandise exports and imports (in US $, on customs basis) grew by 22.6 per cent and 24.5 per cent respectively in 2006-07, recording the lowest gap between growth rate after 2002-03. Petroleum products (59.3%) and engineering goods (38.1%) were the fastest growing exports. The perceptible increase in share of petroleum products in total export reflected India's enhanced refining capacity and higher POL prices. The rising share of engineering goods reflected improved competitiveness. The imports grew by 25.9 per cent during April-December 2007 due to non-POL imports growth of 31.9 per cent, implying strong industrial demand by the manufacturing sector and for export activity. The trade with top 12 trading partners increased by over 11.2 per cent since 2001-02 to 53.8 per cent of total in 2006-07. The share of the United States, the largest trading partner declined by 2.5 per cent to 9.8 per cent in 2006-07 while China became the second largest partner in 2006-07 with its share increasing by 5.2 percentage points over the decade. China's trade share during April-October 2007 is even higher than that of the United States by Rs.600 crore. India's export of services grew by 32.1 per cent to US $ 76.2 billion in 2006-07. Software services, business services, financial services and communication services were the main drivers of growth. Commercial Services exports were almost 60 per cent of merchandise exports in 2006-07. India has continued to favour multilateral trading arrangements, which are both transparent and fair to the developing economies.

6178. (28-2-2008) NEW DELHI : The Economic Survey 2007-08 has said that the prospects for growth of tourism in India are bright. The overall development of tourism infrastructure coupled with other efforts by the Government to promote tourism such as appropriately positioning India on the global tourism map through the "Incredible India" campaign, according greater focus to newly emerging markets such as China, Latin America and CIS countries, and participating in trade fairs and exhibitions will facilitate tourism growth. The rate of growth of tourism sector in India has been way above the world average in the last few years. 2006-07 is the fourth consecutive year of high growth in foreign tourist arrivals and foreign exchange earnings from tourism. 2006-07 saw arrival of approximately 46.33 lakhs foreign tourists in India, thereby registering a growth of 13 per cent over the previous year. As per advance estimates, foreign exchange earned during

2006-07 due to tourism was $ 9696 million-a growth of 23.5 per cent over the previous year.

6179. (28-2-2008) NEW DELHI : The production of non-food crops, particularly sugarcane, cotton and jute (including mesta) exceeded both the targets and the levels achieved in the previous year. In the current year, as per the second advance estimates of crops' production, a shortfall is expected in rabi crops. The Economic Survey 2007-08 presented in Parliament today by the Finance Minister, Shri P. Chidambaram has stated that the overall foodgrains production in 2007-08 is expected to fall short of the target by 2.2 million tonnes though it is expected to be 10.1 million tonnes higher compared to the second estimates for 2006-07. Production of sugarcane is estimated to exceed the target, though it will be lower than the previous year. A shortfall of 2.8 million tonnes (10%) is expected in the production of oilseeds compared to the target though it is still expected to be higher by 2.9 million tonnes compared to the final estimates of 2006-07. The overall production of foodgrains was estimated at 217.3 million tonnes in 2006-07, an increase of 4.2% over 2005-06. The Survey, however, pointed out that compared to the target set for 2006-07, it was lower by 2.7 million tonnes. The increase in production in 2006-07 was largely because of higher production of wheat by 6.5 million tonnes (9.3%) and of pulses by 0.8 million tonnes (6%). There was a decline in production of oilseeds (3.7 million tonnes or 13%) compared to the production in 2005-06. The actual production of foodgrains on an average was 93% of the target. Production of sugarcane and cotton, however, overachieved their respective targets in 2005-06 and 2006-07.

6180. (28-2-2008) NEW DELHI : The fiscal deficit of the Centre as a proportion of GDP came down from 5.9% in 2002-03 to 3.4% in 2006-07. The deficit is estimated to further decline to 3.3% in 2007-08 (BE). This was stated in the Economic Survey 2007-08 presented in Parliament today by the Finance Minister, Shri P. Chidambaram. The revenue deficit also declined from 4.4% in 2002-03 to 1.9% in 2006-07 and is estimated to further decline to 1.5% in 2007-08 (BE). The revenue deficit as a percentage of fiscal deficit has declined from 79.7% in 2003-04 to 56.3% in 2006-07 and it is further estimated to improve to 47.4% in 2007-08 (BE) implying a progressively better utilization of borrowed resources towards asset creation.

6181. (28-2-2008) NEW DELHI : The Economic Survey 2007-08 says that the 9.2 per cent growth achieved during April to November 2007 by the industrial sector, when seen against the backdrop of the robust growth during the preceding four years suggests that the buoyancy in this sector has continued, though with a degree of moderation. The first eight months of the current fiscal witnessed a moderate slowdown in the growth of the industrial sector which has mainly been on account of the manufacturing sector. The mining and quarrying sector grew at a faster pace, while the growth in electricity remained unchanged from April-November 2006. The Survey highlights the two important changes that have occurred in the growth pattern of the use-based industrial categories during April-November 2007 compared to the corresponding period of 2006. First, capital goods have grown at an accelerated pace over a high base attained in the previous years which augurs well for the required industrial capacity addition. Second, the consumer durables basket that forms part of the index of industrial production showed negative growth during the period. Interestingly, the Survey has pointed out that while one segment of automobiles-commercial vehicles, jeeps and passenger cars-catalyzed manufacturing growth, the slump in the production of motor cycles dampened it. Items like insulated cables/wires, telecom cables, etc., wood products, sugar computer systems and their peripherals, and scientific equipment drove growth with their outstanding production performance. Major dampeners of manufacturing growth were telephone instruments, cine film, X-rays, photo-roll films other than motor cycles and scooters.

6182. (28-2-2008) NEW DELHI : Robust economic growth and improved performance of the manufacturing and services sectors have helped the government keep tax revenues buoyant during the last five years, says Economic survey-2007-08. Average annual growth of revenue receipts of the Central Government between 2003-04 and 2007-08 (BE) was 16.2%. Improved growth of tax revenue at 20.7% during the same period generated an overall high growth of revenue receipt. Gross tax revenue of the government recorded an average annual growth of 20.5%, higher than the 13.8% rate of growth of GDP (at market prices) during this period. The Survey further states that the gross tax GDP ratio, which had stagnated at 8-10% for more than a decade, increased to 11.4% in 2006-07 and is expected to improve further to 11.8% in 2007-08 (BE). The Economic Survey, however, points out that the Revenue Expenditure in 2006-07 (actual) grew by 17% and was higher than the budgeted expenditure by 5.4%. Capital expenditure on the other hand recorded a moderate growth of 3.6% and was lower than the budgeted expenditure by 9.3%.

6183. (28-2-2008) NEW DELHI : Substantial irrigation potential has been created in the country through major, medium and minor irrigation schemes. The total irrigation potential in the country has increased from 81.1 million ha in 1991-92 to 102.8 million ha in 2006-07. pThis was stated in the Economic Survey 2007-08 presented in Parliament today by the Finance Minister Shri P. Chidambaram. Irrigation is one of the six components for the development of rural infrastructure under the Bharat Nirman. During 2005-06 and 2006-07, 1.68 million ha and 1.94 million ha of irrigation potential, respectively, is reported to have been created.

6184. (28-2-2008) NEW DELHI : The Economic Survey 2007-08 says, the number of participants in the insurance sector has gone up to 37 from six insurers in the year 2000 in the life, non-life and re-insurance segments. This includes specialized insurers, *viz.*, Export Credit Guarantee Corporation; Agricultural Insurance Company and two stand along health insurance companies. Of the 17 life insurance companies, as many as 15 are in joint venture with foreign partners.

In the Life Insurance Industry, the first year premium underwritten during the period under report was Rs.44,696 crore as against Rs.44,073 crore in the corresponding period of the previous year. The total premium underwritten by the industry has grown from Rs.34,898 crore in 2000-01 to Rs. 1,56,041 crore in 2006-07. During the current year, the non-life insurers underwrote premium of Rs. 18,509 crore during April to November 2007 as against Rs. 16,560 crore in the corresponding period of the previous year. Post-de-tariffing, while the growth in premium has slowed down on account of reduction in rates, the number of policies underwritten has shown an increase. The Economic Survey says the IRDA has carried forward the process of detariffing of the general insurance sector, creation of the motor pool effective April 1, 2007 during 2007-08. Several policy initiatives were taken in the insurance sector during 2007. These include, de-tariffing of the general insurance industry, obligations towards the rural and social sectors and micro insurance. With a view to synergizing the efforts of all State Governments which are promoting the poverty alleviation programmes, the IRDA has requested the State Governments to publicize the concept of micro-insurance through their various agencies. As per data available (as on February 1, 2008) approximately 2.85 lakh employees were covered under the NPS. An amount of approximately Rs.1,177 crore, including the Government contribution and interest component has been credited into the pension account. Nineteen State Governments have also notified similar schemes for their new recruits. The Pension Fund Regulatory Act Development Authority (PFRDA) has appointed three sponsors for pension funds for managing the corpus under the New Pension System for the Government employees after due consideration. The entire architecture of the NPS is expected to be operationalized by May 31, 2008. The Economic Survey says that the growing importance of insurance and pension funds would provide impetus and broaden the horizon of the Government securities market.

6185. (28-2-2008) NEW DELHI : The Economic Survey 2007-08 has said that the real challenge before the country lies in strengthening the foundations of sustained industrial growth. One of the biggest challenges to sustaining and stepping up industrial growth lies in removing the infrastructural impediments in road-both rural and urban-rail, air and sea transport and power. The Survey has pointed out that growth in infrastructure not only alleviates the supply side constraints in industrial production, but also stimulates additional domestic demand required for industrial growth. Another issue in industrial growth is the swiftness and efficacy with which the skill deficit felt in many areas of manufacturing is bridged. This will facilitate research and development and technological innovations, which are urgently called for in important industries like chemicals, automotives and pharmaceuticals. The Economic Survey has also said that there is an imperative need to facilitate the growth of labour intensive industries, especially by reviewing labour laws and labour market regulations. This is particularly important in reversing the current not-so-encouraging manufacturing employment trends. Besides, the growth in many industries is constrained by the acute scarcity/depleting reserves of important raw materials like coal, iron ore, natural gas and forest resources. The Survey feels that sectorally differentiated initiatives may be required for skill upgradation, supply augmentation of inputs and promotion of research and development.

6186. (28-2-2008) NEW DELHI : Bank Credit has grown by 1.5 per cent upto January 4, 2008 during the current Financial Year due to policy interventions, says the Economic Survey 2007-08. Concomitantly, the non-food credit by scheduled commercial banks (SCBs) as on the date under referene was well below the indicative target of 24-25 per cent growth for 2007-06. The credit deposit ratio was 71.8 per cent compared to 74 per cent on the corresponding date in 2007. As per the Economic Survey 2007-08, the credit to the priority sectors on the last reporting Friday of November, 2007 increased by 20.5 per cent over the corresponding month of the previous year. The flow of credit to agriculture sector was Rs.1,37,760 crore (during this period of 8 months) which is about 61 per cent of the target for the year. In the micro finance sector, bank loan of Rs.20,114 crore was availed of by 30.51 lakh Self Help Groups with the average bank loan availed of per SHG being Rs. 65,924. The outreach of the SHG-bank linkage programme has enabled an estimated 427 lakh poor households to gain access to micro finance. The Current Financial Year witnessed a spurt in Statutory Liquidity Ratio (SLR) investments of the commercial banks due to continued higher aggregate deposit mobilization coupled with lower offtake of credit. On a year to year basis as on January 4, 2008, the increase in SLR investments was Rs. 1,89,349 crore. The investment-deposit ratio as on this date was 32 per cent, the same as the last year figure. Under the Rural Infrastructure Development Fund of NABARD, the amount sanctioned and disbursed to the State Governments as on January 11,2008 was Rs.69.883 crore and Rs.41.360 crore respectively. During 2007-08 (up to January 11, 2008), the amount sanctioned and disbursed was Rs.8,592 crore and Rs.3800 crore respectively, says the Economic Survey 2007-08. Efforts to widen and intensify the credit delivery mechanism have continued. To ensure steady flow of credit to various segments of SSI, new instructions were given in April and July 2007. The banks have been encouraged to make available "no-frills" bank counts with "nil" or very low minimum balances making such accounts accessible to public at large. Convenor banks have been advised to initiate action for identifying at least one district in their State/Union Territory for 100 per cent financial inclusion.

6187. (28-2-2008) NEW DELHI : The Indian Capital Market attained further depth and width during 2007, says the Economic Survey 2007-08. BSE sensex scaled a high of 20,000 mark at the close of calendar year 2007 and NSE Index rose to close about 6100 mark. Both the indices more than tripled between 2003-07. The total amount of the capital raised through different instruments in the Primary Market was 31.5 per cent higher in 2007 compared to 2006. Component wise, private placement at Rs. 1,11,838 crore (upto November 2007) accounted for the major share during 2007. The total equity issues mobilized Rs. 58, 722 crore, of which Rs.33,912 crore was accounted for by the Initial Public offerings (IPOs). During 2007, the total number of IPOs issued was 100 as compared to 75 in the previous year. Similarly, the net flow of savings into mutual funds increased by over 30 per cent in 2007 to Rs.138,270 crore. Of this 1,20,766 crore was in Private Sector, 8,259 in the public sector and Rs.9245 crore in UTI funds. In the secondary market, the activity expanded further during 2007-08 with BSE and NSE indices scaling new peaks. On a point to point basis, sensex and Nifty indices rose by 47.1 and 54.8 per cent respectively during 2007. Amongst NSE indices, both Nifty and Nifty Junior delivered record annual equity returns of 54.8 per cent and 75.7 per cent respectively during the calendar year. BSE Sensex yielded a compounded return of 36.5 per cent between 2003 and 2007. Sensex has given an annual return of over 40 per cent during the last three years. The market capitalization in India nearly doubled in 2007. The BSE 500 capitalized to Rs. 64,70,881 crore, BSE Sensex capitalized to Rs.28,61,341, Nifty to Rs. 35,22,527 crore and Nifty Junior to Rs.3,33,693 crore from Rs. 33,36,509 crore, Rs. 17,58,65 crore, Rs. 19,75,603 crore and Rs.3,33,693 crore respectively in 2006. The price to earnings (P/E) ratio was higher at around 27 by end December, 2007 as compared to 21 in the previous year. The valuation of Indian stocks as reflected in P/E multiples of around 27 times end December 2007 was the highest amongst the select emerging market economies such as South Korea (15.04), Thailand (19.92), Malaysia (16.07), Indonesia (18.43) and Taiwan (20.14). In India, Market capitalization (BSE 500) at US$ 1,638 billion was 150 per cent of GDP, which compares well with the other economies such as China (137.3) Japan (104.4), South Koria (116.2) and USA (128.8). In the derivative market the NSE and BSE turnover added upto Rs.1,21,60,701 crore during 2007 showing a quantum growth over the previous years. As per the Economic Survey, Policy and Regulatory changes for the capital markets introduced during the year include, amendments to Disclosure and Investor Protection Guidelines; appointment of a sub-committee on Disclosures and Accounting for integrating initial and continuous disclosures of companies; stipulation that Permanent Account No. would be the sole identification number for all participants in the security markets; successful completion of demutualization process by 16 stock exchanges; SEBI permitting short selling by Institutional investors and waiver of entry load by mutual funds for investors making applications for investment in mutual fund schemes directly.

6188. (28-2-2008) NEW DELHI : The Economic Survey of 2007-08 states that if India can get the skill development act right, the country will be harnessing a "demographic dividend". In India the "demographic dividend" which manifests in the proportion of working age group of 15-64 years will be increasing steadily from 62.9 per cent in 2006 to 68.4 per cent in 2026. For actual tapping of the "demographic dividend", it is necessary not only to ensure proper health care but also a major emphasis on skill development and encouragement of labour intensive industries. The projected decline in the dependency ratio (ratio of dependents to the working age population) from 0.8 in 1991 to 0.73 in 2001 is expected to further decline sharply to 0.59 by 2011. This decline sharply contrasts with the demographic trend in the industrialized countries and also in China, where the dependency ratio is rising. Low dependency ratio gives India a comparative cost advantage and a progressively lower dependency ratio will result in improving competitiveness. The Survey says that a thrust is required on creating a pool of skilled persons in appropriate numbers with adequate skills in line with the requirements of the ultimate users such as the industry, trade and service sectors. Such an effort is necessary to support the employment expansion envisaged as a result of inclusive growth including in particular, the shift of surplus labour from agriculture. However, the Survey cautions that if skills are not adequately created India could well be facing a "demographic nightmare."

6189. (28-2-2008) NEW DELHI : The stock position of foodgrains in the country as on January 1, 2008 was 19.2 million tonnes comprising 11.5 million tonnes of rice and 7.7 million tonnes of wheat. This along with projected arrivals of wheat imports would be adequate for meeting the requirement under TPDS and welfare schemes during the current financial year. This information was given in the Economic Survey-2007-08 presented in Parliament today by the Finance Minister, Shri P. Chidambaram.

6190. (28-2-2008) NEW DELHI : Recognizing the importance of development of adequate infrastructure for sustaining the growth momentum and to ensure inclusiveness of the growth process, the Government will continue to play a lead role in infrastructure development during the Eleventh Plan. The Economic Survey 2007-08 tabled in Parliament today, states that accompanying the recent moderation in industrial growth, the growth performance of some segments of the infrastructure such as power generation and movement of railway freight and also the production of universal intermediates like steel, cement and petroleum have shown a subdued performance during April-December 2007-08 as compared to the corresponding period last year. In the power sector, though the plan capacity addition is unlikely to be achieved, the growth in capacity in the current year is distinctly higher than in the previous years. The movement of cargo handled by major ports and air cargo has showed improved performance as compared to the corresponding period last year. The highly competitive telecom sector has maintained its phenomenal growth, the Survey adds. With the rapid growth of economy in the recent years, the importance and urgency of removing infrastructure constraints have increased. The Government has made an effort to facilitate the entry of private enterprise into this sector through changes in the legal framework. The Survey mentions that the role of private sector participation has also been facilitated by technological change that allows unbundling of infrastructure so that the public and the private sectors can take up the components according to their capacities. The Survey states that the recent moderation in the growth in the industrial sector has raised concerns in some quarters about sustainability of high growth of the sector. To deal with the situation emerging from the slow down of some export oriented sectors of relatively low import intensity including textiles, handicrafts, leather etc. the Survey states that the Government took certain measures to tide over the situation in short run. It emphasises that, over the medium term, there is little choice but to improve productivity even if there are issues pertaining to the exchange rate of currencies of competing countries. During the Eleventh Five Year Plan, the power sector is expected to grow at 9.5 per cent per annum. The Survey mentions that a capacity addition of 78,577 MW has been proposed for the plan period to fulfil the objective of the National Electricity Policy 2005. A number of projects envisaged for the Eleventh Plan have made steady progress and most of these are in a position to be commissioned well within the Plan period. It is expected that the total capacity addition during the current financial year would be 10,821.8 MW with thermal, hydro and nuclear accounting for 8,015 MW, 2,587 MW and 220 MW respectively. The Survey also mentioned that for development of coal based Ultra Mega Power Projects (UMPPs) each with a capacity of 4,000 MW or above, project specific shell companies have been set up as wholly owned subsidiaries of the Power Finance Corporation Limited to facilitate tie up of inputs and clearances. The bidding process in respect of Sasan, Mundra and Krishnapatnam UMPPs have been completed. For the development of hydro power potential, the Survey also states that a task force has been constituted under the Chairmanship of Minister of Power. The task force shall examine and resolve issues relating to hydro power development. To achieve the goal of electrifying all unelectrified villages and hamlets and providing access to the electricity to all households as envisaged under the Rajiv Gandhi Grameen Vidhyutikaran Yojana (RGGYY), the Government has approved its continuation during the Eleventh Five Year Plan period. With an initial outlay of Rs. 28,000 crore, about 1.15 lakh unelectrified villages and 2.34 crore rural BPL households have been envisaged to be covered in Phase-1 of the scheme.

6191. (28-2-2008) NEW DELHI : The Economic Survey 2007-08 presented by the Finance Minister, Shri P. Chidambaram in Parliament today says that with the Indian Economy moving to a higher growth path, the new challenge is to not only maintain growth but also raise it further to double digit levels. To meet the demand for infrastructure services, there is a heightened urgency to augment and upgrade infrastructure both physical as well as social and in particular power, roads and ports. This requires mobilization of unprecedented amounts of capital with macroeconomic stability, which can only happen if both the public and private sectors have the incentive and the motivation to perform at their best. According to the Economic Survey, the public sector requires the effective addressing of the persistent institutional weaknesses and implementation constrains at different levels of government in the country.

6192. (28-2-2008) NEW DELHI : The Economic Survey 2007-08 presented by the Finance Minister, Shri P. Chidambaram in Parliament today says that the economy has moved decisively to a higher growth phase. With growth in GDP at market prices exceeding 8 per cent in every year since 2003-04 the projected economic growth of 8.7 per cent for 2007-08 is fully in line with this trend. There was acceleration in domestic investment and saving rates to drive growth and provide the resources for meeting the 9 per cent (average) growth target of the Eleventh Five Year Plan. Macroeconomic fundamentals continue to inspire confidence and the investment climate is full of optimism. Buoyant growth of government revenues made it possible to maintain fiscal consolidation. Inflation flared up in the last half of 2006-07 and was successfully contained during the current year, despite a global hardening of commodity prices and an upsurge in capital inflows. Expressing concern over slowdown in the consumer goods segment of industry and infrastructure constraints, the Economic Survey calls for additional reforms to raise growth to double digit. Growth in 2006-07 initially estimated at 9.2 per cent in February 2007 was revised upwards to 9.4 per cent in May 2007 and further to 9.6 per cent on January 31, 2008, suggesting that upward adjustments in the 2007-08 projections are possible. GDP at current market prices is projected at Rs. 46,93,602 crore in 2007-08. Thus, in the current fiscal year, the size of the Indian economy at market exchange rate will cross US$ 1 trillion. The growth in the services sector continued to be broad based with "transport and communication" being the fastest growing with an average of 15.3 per cent per annum during the 10th Five Year Plan followed by "construction". The contribution of the construction sector increased to 10.8 per cent while that of telecom to 11.4 per cent. There was 13.9 per cent growth in the financial services comprising banking, insurance and business services in 2006-07.

6193. (29-2-2008) NEW DELHI : The Union Minister for Steel, Chemicals & Fertilizers hailed the Union Budget as progressive and pro-aam admi. Shri Ram Vilas Paswan commended the Union Finance Minister for having reduced the Excise Duty on drugs from 16% to 8% and said that this would be a major step in bringing down the prices of medicines. As per the stated position of the UPA in the NCMP to make available drugs to the common man at affordable prices, Shri Paswan said that his Ministry had been demanding a cut in the Excise structure. This reduction is expected to reduce the retail prices of drugs by at least 5% and he hoped that the industry would pass on the entire benefit to the consumer. The move to also reduce Customs Duty, on certain life saving drugs and bulk drugs used for its manufacture, from 10% to 5% would lead to reduction in the prices of drugs for the treatment of Hepatits B, Diabetics, Thyroid, Cancer, Asthma as also certain vaccines. The reduction of customs duty on steel melting scrap would help in making available rods and rounds, used by the common man in construction activity, was an issue close to my heart, Shri Paswan said. The Minister had also assured the secondary steel manufacturers in the Steel Consumer's Council meeting held in 2007 that he would take up the issue with the Finance Ministry and expressed happiness that the same has been reflected in the Union Budget 2008-09. The reduction of CST to 2% from the existing 3%, would further aid in making steel available at reduced rates to the consumers, Shri Paswan said. Reduction of customs duty on project import of capital goods would boost steel investments in a large way, he said. This would help the existing steel majors who have embarked on a major expansion cum modernization programme as also new investors in this sector.

6194. (29-2-2008) NEW DELHI : Indian Civil Accounts Organisation Day will be observed tomorrow *i.e.* on 1st March, 2008. It was on this day in 1976 that the Departmentalisation of Union Accounts Act came into force. This momentous legislation led to the creation of Indian Civil Accounts Service which mans the Departmentalised accounting of the Civil Ministries in Government of India. The move ensured decentralisation of Government accounting, better transparency, more user friendly system and smooth functioning in this core activity of the Government. On this occasion, Shri V.N.Kaila. Controller General of Accounts (CGA) will deliver a key note address at the Institute of Government Account and Finance (INGAF), New Delhi. He will also release training calendar and brochure of INGAF. Over the past three decades, Institution of CGA has taken several new initiatives in making the government accounting system more effective and modern in line with the changing needs and technological revolution. Some of the initiatives taken include core accounting solution, computerisation of accounting, disbursal and treasury functions of civil Ministries, monitoring and accounting of all Central and Centrally sponsored schemes etc. Chief Controller of Accounts, (CCAs) Controller of Accounts (CAs) and Pay and Accounts Officers (PAOs) etc. all are part of the significant system of Government Accounting.

6195. (29-2-2008) NEW DELHI : The Minister of Petroleum and Natural Gas Shri Murli Deora has welcomed the people-friendly proposals made in the general Budget 2008-09, which was presented in the Lok Sabha today. Describing the Budget as another milestone achieved by the UPA Government towards ensuring the welfare of the common man, Shri Deora specifically welcomed the tax rationalization by the Finance Minister in excise duties on unbranded petrol and diesel. Referring to the conversion of the advalorem part of the excise duty to specific duty on these products, the Minister said that this is a major step forward towards rationalizing tax structure of petroleum products. He also said that reduction of import duty on project imports from 7.5% to 5% would give a boost to fresh investment in the oil and gas sector, along with other industrial sectors. Hailing the Budget as a land mark one, he said that the critical agriculture sector had been given due importance in ensuring that India continues on the high growth path. He also pointed out that the UPA Government's approach on inclusive development found ample reflection in the quantum jump in fund allocations to the social sector schemes, especially for vulnerable and backward sections of the society. Shri Deora congratulated Finance Minister on announcing several measures for the welfare of farmers and added that ordinary tax payers have also benefited significantly.

6196. (29-2-2008) NEW DELHI : All India Consumer Price Index Number for Industrial Workers (CPI-IW) on base 2001=100 for the month of January 2008 remained stationary at 134 (one hundred and thirty four). During January 2008, the index recorded an increase of 3 points each in Bhilai, Bangalore, Pondicherry, Warrangal, Salem and Srinagar centres, 2 points in 10 centre and 1 point in 17 centres. The index decreased by 5 points in Tripura centre, 3 points in 4 centres, 2 points in 5 centres and 1 point in 15 centres while in the remaining 20 centres the index remained stationary. The increase in indices of most of the centres during January, 2008 is mainly because of increase in House Rent Index, while in additon that of 3 points in Bhilai centre is due to Rice, in Bangalore centre due to Dairy Milk, in Pondicherry centre due to Fish Fresh, Vegetable and Fruit items and Bus fare, in Warangal centre due to Rice and Goat Meat, in Salem centre due to Rice, Arhar Dal, Groundnut Oil, Goat Meat and Vegetable items, in Srinagar centre due to Rice, Wheat Atta and Mustard Oil. The decrease of indices in most of the centres is due to decrease in the prices of Vegetable items and that of 5 points in Tripura centre is also due to Rice, Wheat Atta, Onion and Chillies Dry.

6197. (29-2-2008) NEW DELHI : Following is the Text of the valedictory address delivered by the Minister of State for Defence Shri M M Pallam Raju at the presentation of the inaugural M Phil degree in 'Defence & Strategic Studies' by the Madras University to members of the 46th National Defence College (NDC) course : It gives me great pleasure to deliver the valedictory address on the occasion of the award of the inaugural M Phil degree in 'Defence & Strategic Studies' by the Madras University to members of the 46th NDC course. Pandit Jawaharlal Nehru while inaugurating this great institution in April 1960 said and I quote "Defence itself is not an isolated subject. It is intimately connected with the economic aspects, industrial aspects, and many other aspects in the country. India today has become positively and actively defence conscious, more than at any time since independence. Our desire is to continue to live peacefully and cooperatively with all our neighbours. Nevertheless, no defence apparatus can exist in a purely idealistic way. It has to be very realistic and remain prepared for any emergency. The National Defence College has become a positive necessity to meet defence problems as they are likely to be in the future." These immortal words ring true even today. With the continued changes in the dynamics of the society, both internally and externally, the role of the armed forces has expanded far beyond traditional military matters. The traditional role of armed forces is to defend the territorial integrity and sovereignty of their nations. The non-traditional roles, however, vary from country to country, depending on the unique circumstances that they find themselves in. The changing defence and security environment in recent years has resulted in an expansion of such roles. It is clear that future conflicts in the complex defence and security environment will require a more integrated multi-state and multi-agency approach. Preparing military officers, police officers and civilian bureaucrats to deal with the complex security environment of the future will necessarily have to be addressed in a holistic and comprehensive manner. Military officers and defence officials at all levels will be faced with very important strategic decisions, and they will need to possess a depth of understanding not previously demanded of them. The present security environment demands that you senior officers engage in critical thinking and analysis. It also demands that you should be capable of working with a variety of other organizations in complex and demanding circumstances. Therefore, nations need senior military officers and bureaucrats who can both be experts on war fighting and provide well-informed and enlightened advice on security and defence to political leadership. This societal demand on the intellect and professionalism of top military and bureaucratic leadership has added a new dimension to the profession of arms. With non-defence officials being part of the security arena, a more complex level of integration is necessary to face the challenges. This specifically relates to challenges in the academic field with special reference to the various aspects of Defence and Strategic Studies. It is here that I would like to compliment the leadership of the National Defence College and the University of Madras for anticipating this need and adapting the present curriculum to meet this urgent requirement. There is a clear requirement for officers to understand government policies that emanate from political objectives and translate them into well defined objectives on the ground. Inclusion of civil bureaucrats in the National Defence College curriculum has done enormous good in meeting the civil service's knowledge of national security issues and inculcating in them the strategic culture. I am sure the M Phil programme, would go a long way in broadening the perspectives of the selected senior officers and equip them suitably to meet their nations' challenges. Another feature that I consider relevant and important is that I see this M Phil programme to be a bridge between the different educational needs and philosophies of universities such as the Madras University and institutions delivering professional strategic based education such as the National Defence College. Developing the NDC into becoming a full fledged Research Centre will also lead to the professional development of both such hallowed institutions. Without tie ups such as this, military institutions risk falling by the wayside and will eventually isolate themselves from mainstream education. To this end the conceptualisation and subsequent establishment of the National Defence University will ensure that no such isolation will take place. In fact, on the contrary, the National Defence College, thanks in no small measure to this affiliation with the University of Madras is ideally positioned to be the flagship of the National Defence University. I am aware that your curriculum embraces subjects like the politico-social study of India, its economy, science and technology, international affairs, India's strategic and immediate neighbourhood and the like. Strategic education warrants interaction amongst civil-military bureaucrats, academicians and experts for deeper understanding of the cross-cutting interplay at the national, regional and international levels with their attendant ramifications.

6198. (29-2-2008) NEW DELHI : The Chief Minister of Jammu and Kashmir Shri Gulam Nabi Azad called on the Union Minister of Shipping, Road Transport and Highways, Thiru T.R. Baalu here today to discuss the development and maintenance of road network in the State. The Chief Minister raised some specific issues concerning road development in J&K : Second instalment of Central Road Fund (CRF) funds due to the state to be released by the Ministry of Shipping, Road Transport and Highways; Release of funds for Bhaderwah-Chamba road from the Inter State Connectivity (ISC) fund; Release of outstanding amount under CRF from previous years; start of four laning of National Highway No.1 A from Srinagar side; and Street lighting of Jammu bypass Thiru Baalu informed that second instalment amounting to Rs. 16.95 crore has already been released and further release shall be made on submission of utilization certificate by the state Government. On the issue of Bhaderwah-Chamba road, it was informed that estimate is in advanced stage of sanction and funds shall be released soon after the sanction of the estimate. As far as the other issues raised by the Chief Minister, the Minister promised to have them examined at the earliest possible.

6199. (29-2-2008) NEW DELHI : It was expected that the Govt. will try to give a populist budget keeping an eye on the coming general elections. But the Govt. has failed in this endeavour. The Govt. has waived of the banking loans of small farmers, but there is no plan to give relief to large number of farmers, who are trapped in the clutches of money lenders. The growth rate in agriculture is again a dismal 2.6%. No reduction in the interest rates of agriculture loan despite the persistent demand of bringing it to 4%. No Scheme or provision for ensuring a fixed income for farmers and a total eye wash to the recommendations of Farmer's Commission are clearly indicating that the future will remain as problematic for farmers as it is today. The Govt. has tried to give a tip to the farmers but has given nothing to empower them. Now its clear that Roti Kapda Aur Makan will consistently become scarce for a common man in a coming time. Though I myself demanded to raise the Income Tax limit to 1.5 lakh in the presidential address of our National Council. But since the 6th Pay Commission will become effective from this year so the increase in the IT limit shall have practically no meaning. This Budget has set up an unprecedented and ignominious record of communal budgeting in the history of India. Which remind us the Communal Award of British time. Today the entire economy is on the low, the interest rates are high, the inflation is high, the agriculture growth is miserably low. All this indicates that under the four year rule of UPA our economy has become diseased. But Govt. is only trying to cure the symptoms not the disease. So, I am quite skeptical about the real solution of problems in coming times.

6200. (29-2-2008) NEW DELHI : Lieutenant General SPS Dhillon, Deputy Chief of Army Staff (Information System and Training) addressed the Indian Army Contingent earmarked to represent the country in United Nations Mission in Sudan (UNMIS). The Indian Army Contingent comprises of 2 NAGA, 5/1 Gorkha Rifles and other units. 2 NAGA was raised on 11 Feb 1985 and is the second battalion of the youngest regiment of the Indian Army. 2 NAGA is the proud recipient of the Chief of Army Staf Unit Citation 'twice' and has been bestowed with Battle Honour' Maskoh' and Theatre Honour ' Kargil' for their splendid performance during Operation Vijay. The unit has won one Maha Vir Chakra, two Vir Chakra, one Yudh Seva Medal, two Sena Medals, two Vishisht Seva Medals and other awards. 5/1 Gorkha Rifles was re-raised on 01 Jan 1965. During Bangladesh Operation in 1971, the battalion has been honoured with Battle Honour 'Darsana' and Theatre Honour 'East Pakistan'. In addition the unit has been awarded the Chief of Army Staff's Unit Citation. The unit has been awarded three Maha Vir Chakra and two Vir Chakra. Both the battalions will be supported by Force Signal Unit, 619 Transport company and level II hospital of the Indian Army. The Deputy Chief of Army Staff (IS&T) mentioned the outstanding track record of the battalions. He apprised the troops of the excellent work done by Indian Contingents in various UN Peace Keeping Operations in the past and exhorted all to carry out their assigned tasks with self dedication, devotion and humanitarian approach.

6201. (29-2-2008) NEW DELHI : Chitranjan Locomotive Works (CLW) produced 154 electric locomotives against the target of 154 electric locomotives and Diesel Locomotive Works (DLW) produced 190 diesel locomotives against the target of 181 diesel locomotives during first ten months of the fiscal 2007-08 (April 2007-January 2008). Rail Coach Factory (RCF) produced 1194 coaches against the target of 1178 coaches where as Integral Coach Factory (ICF) produced 1006 coaches against the target of 1021 coaches during the same period. Rail Wheel Factory (RWF) produced 116677 wheels and 39979 axles against the target of 106504 wheels and 40031 axles during April 2007-January 2008. During the month of January 2008, CLW, DLW, ICF, RCF and RWF have produced 20 electric locomotives, 20 diesel locomotive, 100 coaches, 141 coaches, 15170 wheels and 6030 axles respectively against the target of 22 electric locomotives, 18 diesel locomotive, 115 coaches, 134 coaches, 11301 wheels and 5982 axels. The punctuality percentage of mail/express trains was 88.7 per cent in Broad Gauge and 99.5 per cent in Metre Gauge during the month of January 2008 compared to 87.9 per cent and 99.5 per cent respectively during the same period last year. Railways have realized an amount of Rs. 21 crore approximately during the month of January 2008 through ticket checking.

6202. (29-2-2008) NEW DELHI : The total approximate earnings of Indian Railways on originating basis during the period 10th January-20th January 2008 were Rs. 2211.38 crore compared to Rs. 1816.30 crore during the same period last year, registering an increase of 21.75 per cent. The total goods earnings have gone up from Rs. 1271.76 crore during 11th January-20th January 2007 to Rs. 1524.67 crore during 11th January-20th January 2008, showing an increase of 19.89 per cent. The total passenger revenue earnings during the period 11th to 20th January 2008 were Rs. 618.38 crore compared to Rs. 480.34 crore during the same period last year, reflecting an increase of 11.63 per cent. The revenue earnings from other coaching amounted to Rs. 49.26 crore during this period compared to Rs. 44.68 crore during the same period last year, showing an increase of 10.25 per cent. The total approximate number of passengers booked during the period 11th to 20th January 2008 were 190.96 million compared to 180.54 million during the same period last year, showing an increase of 5.77 per cent. In the suburban and non-suburban sectors, the number of passengers booked during 11-20 January 2008 were 108.21 million and 82.75 million compared to 104.56 million and 75.98 million during the same period last year, registering an increase of 3.49 per cent and an increase of 8.91 per cent respectively.

6203. (29-2-2008) NEW DELHI : The Finance Minister, Shri P. Chidambaram has announced two major interventions for the vulnerable sections of our society in the General Budget 2008-09. Every worker in the unorganized sector of the country falling under the BPL category will be provided a health cover of Rs. 30,000 under Rashtriya Swasthya Bima Yojana. He announced that most of the States have agreed to join the Yojana and it will be launched in Delhi and in the States of Haryana and Rajasthan on April 1, 2008. The Government proposed to provide Rs. 205 crore as the Centre's share of the premia in 2008-09. The other major initiative is for the elderly. The Finance Minister said, a National Programme for the Elderly with a Plan outlay of Rs. 400 crore will be started in 2008-09. Besides, during the Eleventh Plan period, two National Institutes of Ageing, eight regional centres and a department for geriatric medical care in one medical college/tertiary level hospital in each State will also be established.

6204. (29-2-2008) NEW DELHI : NTPC Limited and Uttar Pradesh Rajya Vidyut Utpadan Nigam Limited (UPRVUNL) have signed a Joint Venture Agreement (JVA) for implementation of 1320 MW (2X 660 MW) coal based thermal power plant at Meja, Distt. Allahabad, UP. The project shall be implemented by (50:50) JVC of NTPC and UPRVUNL on Build, Own and Operate (BOO) basis. The Agreement was signed in the presence of Shri Ranveer Upadhyay, Energy Minister, UP, by Shri T. Sankaralingam, CMD, NTPC and Shri G.B. Patanayak, CMD, UPPCL for and on behalf of UPRVUNL. Shri R.S. Sharma, Director (Commercial), NTPC, Shri Alok Tandon, MD, UPRVUNL and Shri I.B. Pandey, Regional Executive Director (North), NTPC and other senior officials were present on the occasion.

6205. (29-2-2008) NEW DELHI : NTPC Limited has signed a loan agreement for Euro 68.56 million with the Nordic Investment Bank (NIB), a multilateral financial institution owned by the Nordic and Baltic countries, to part finance the capital expenditure of its projects. The loan has a maturity of 12 years including availability period of 3 years. The loan carries a floating rate of interest linked to EURIBOR and is without sovereign guarantee. This is the first loan that NTPC has tied up with NIB. The loan agreement was signed in Helsinki, Finland by Shri A.K.Kundu, Executive Director (Finance) on behalf of the Company. NTPC is the largest power producer in the country with generating capacity of 28664MW, contributing about 28% of India's power generation.

6206. (29-2-2008) NEW DELHI : The total allocation for the education sector (including NER) has been increased by 20% from Rs. 28,674 crore in 2007-08 to Rs. 34,400 crore in 2008-09. Of this, Sarva Shiksha Abhiyan (SSA) will be provided Rs. 13,100 crore; the Mid-day Meal Scheme will be provided Rs. 8000 crore; and secondary education will be provided Rs. 4,554 crore. The Finance Minister, Shri P. Chidambaram while presenting the General Budget 2008-09 in Lok Sabha today, pointed out that the focus of SSA would shift from access and infrastructure at the primary level to enhancing retention; improving quality of learning; and ensuring access to upper primary classes. The Finance Minister said that a Model School programme, with the aim of establishing 6,000 high quality model schools, would be started in 2008-09. An amount of Rs. 650 crore has been proposed for the new scheme.

6207. (29-2-2008) NEW DELHI : The Finance Minister, Shri P.Chidambaram in the General Budget 2008-09 has proposed reduction in the custom duty on crude and unrefined sulphur from 5 per cent to 2 per cent, in order to support domestic fertilizer production. The duty exemption on naphtha for use in the manufacture of polymers has been withdrawn and normal rate of 5 per cent customs duty has been imposed. This is to remove the distortions which arise due to its export from refineries and import by manufacturers of polymers. However, naphtha imported for the production of fertilizers will continue to the exempt from import duty. The duty on bactofuges has been reduced from 7.5 per cent to nil. This will benefit the dairy industry by increasing the shelf life of milk. In order to reduce the cost of manufacture of cattle and poultry feeds, the Budget proposes reduction in the duty on vitamin premixes and mineral mixtures from 30 per cent to 20 per cent and on phosphoric acid from 7.5 p.c. to 5 p.c..

6208. (29-2-2008) NEW DELHI : The anti AIDS drug 'Atazanavir' as well as bulk drugs for its manufactures have been totally exempted from excise duty in the General Budget 2008-09 proposals. Excise duty on water purification devices, veneers and flush door, sterile dressing pads, specifying package material and breakfast cereals has been reduced from 16 to 8 per cent.. The duty on filter as well as non-filter cigarettes has been enhanced. To encourage cold chain facility, refrigeration equipment above 2 tonne refrigeration (TR) utilizing power of 50 KW and above on end use basis has been totally exempted from excise duty.

6209. (29-2-2008) NEW DELHI : No change has been effected in the peak rate of customs duty in the General Budget 2008-09. Customs duty has been reduced for certain industries with a view to provide a fillip or to remove anomalies. Customs duty on project imports has been reduced from 7.5 per cent to 5 per cent. However, a special CVD of 4 per cent would be imposed on some specified projects in the power sector. The duty on steel melting scrap and aluminium scrap reduced to nil from 5 per cent. Specified parts of Set Top Boxes and specified raw materials for using IT/Electronic industry have been fully exempt from customs duty. The duty on convergence products has been lowered to 5 per cent from 10 per cent. Customs duty on certain specified life saving drugs has been brought down from 10 per cent to 5 per cent. Bulk drugs used for manufacture of such drugs have been totally exempted from customs duty or countervailing duty. In order to conserve chrome ore and make it available for value added manufacture in India, export duty on this item has been raised to Rs.3000 per MT from Rs.2000 per MT.

6210. (29-2-2008) NEW DELHI : Four additional service sectors have been brought under the Service Tax Act in the General Budget 2008-09. They are, Asset Management Service provided under ULIP, to bring it on par with those under Mutual Funds; services provided by stock/commodities exchanges and clearing houses; customized software, to bring it on par with packaged software and other IT services; and right to use goods, in cases where VAT is not payable. It has been clarified that the money changers, persons running games of chance and tour operators using contract carriage vehicles are liable to service tax. Threshold limit of exemption for small service providers is proposed to be increased from Rs.8 lakhs p.a to Rs..10 lakhs per annum. The measure is expected to benefit 65,000 small service providers.

6211. (29-2-2008) NEW DELHI : In the Budget Estimates 2008-09, the total expenditure is estimated at Rs.750,884 crores. Of this, the Plan Expenditure is placed at Rs.243,386 crore. As a proportion of total expenditure, it will be 32.4 per cent. Non-Plan Expenditure is estimated at Rs. 507,498 crore. The revenue deficit for the current year will be 1.4 per cent (against a BE of 1.5 per cent) and the fiscal deficit will be 3.1 per cent(against a BE of 3.3 per cent). The revenue receipt of the Central Government for 2008-09 are projected at Rs.602,935 crore and the revenue expenditure at Rs.658,119 crore. Consequently, the revenue deficit is estimated at Rs.55,184 crore, which amount to 1.0 per cent of GDP. The fiscal deficit is estimated at Rs.133,287 crore which is 2.5 per cent of GDP. The Budget estimates say, the target for fiscal deficit under the FRBM Act will be easily achieved. In the case of revenue deficit, the target of annual reduction of 0.5 per cent will be met. However, because of the conscious shift in expenditure in favour of health, education and the social sector, one more year may be need to eliminate the revenue deficit.

6212. (29-2-2008) NEW DELHI : The General Budget 2008-09 has proposed to add the business of production of seeds and manufacture of agricultural implements to the list of exempt category on in-house scientific research. They will be allowed a weighted deduction of 150 per cent on any expenditure on in-house research as available hitherto to companies engaged in certain businesses. In order to promote outsourcing of research, a weighted deduction of 125 % has been allowed on any payment made to companies engaged in R & D. Income rising from saplings or seedlings grown in a nursery has been exempted from tax on the lines of agricultural income.

6213. (29-2-2008) NEW DELHI : The Finance Minister has at the end of his speech quoted the immortal words of Saint Tiruvalluvar that generous grants, compassion, righteous rule and succor to the downtrodden are the hallmarks of good governance. I am surprised that the Finance Minister has been reminded of these immortal words only in the last year of his office. This government came into power on the slogan of the aam admi. But, it is the aam admi, especially the aam aurat who has suffered the most during the last four years as a result of back-breaking price-rise and insecurity of life and limb. The farmers have suffered no end as a result of agrarian distress and thousands of them have been compelled to commit suicide during the last four years. All these years, the government has merely looked on. Now, in the last year of their office, they are reminding us of the elements of good governance. I have no doubt that people will easily see through this charade. The highlight of the budget, namely, the waiver of farm loans has come too late. It is also insufficient. A large number of farmers in our country have taken loans from private money-lenders. Arrangements should have been made to provide relief to them also. The rate of interest on farm loans should also have been reduced to 4%. The farmer should also have been covered under an assured income insurance scheme. Farm loans are supposed to be remitted by 30th June this year, but the Finance Minister has said nothing about the administrative arrangements needed for such an exercise. I am also surprised at the heavy communal overtones of the budget. It is a throw back to the Liaqat Ali days, the consequences of which are well-known. So far, the record of this government has been one of being long on promise and short on delivery. This year may not be any different.

6214. (29-2-2008) NEW DELHI : In the General Budget 2008-09, a five year tax holiday has been announced for setting up Hospitals anywhere in India, specially in tier-2 and tier-3 towns in order to serve the rural interland. Certain specified urban agglomerations will not be covered. This window will be open for the period April 1,2008 to March 31, 2013, during which the hospital must commence operations. For the purpose a new sub-section 11 C in Section 80-IB will be inserted. Similarly, a five year holiday from income tax has been announced for two, three and four star hotels established in specified districts which have UNESCO-declared 'World Heritage Sites'. The hotel should be constructed and start functioning during April 1,2008 to March 31, 2013. The measure has been taken in view of significant rise in tourist arrivals, specially for cultural tourism.

6215. (29-2-2008) NEW DELHI : In the General Budget 2008-09, Banking Cash Transaction Tax (BCTT) has been withdrawn w.e.f. April 1, 2009. The step is in view of the fact that the information gathered by means of BCTT is also available to the Income Tax Department through other instruments introduced in the last few years. Relief has been provided in the Fringe Benefit Tax (FBT) for certain class of tax payers. Crèche facilities, sponsorship of an employee-sportsperson, organizing sports events for employees and guests will be excluded from the purview of FBT.

6216. (29-2-2008) NEW DELHI : The General Budget 2008-09 has provided relief in the Dividend Distribution Tax (DDT). A parent company is now allowed to set off the dividend received from its subsidiary company against dividend distributed by the parent company, provided that the dividend received has suffered DDT and the parent company is not a subsidiary of another company. Changes have been effected in the Securities Transaction Tax (STT). STT will now be treated like any other deductible expenditure against business income. Further the levy of STT in the case of options will be only on the option premium where the option is not exercised, and the liability will be on the seller. In case where the option is exercised, the levy will be on the settlement price and the liability will be on the buyer. However, there will be no change in the present rates. Commodities Transaction Tax (CTT) has been introduced in this year's Budget on the same lines as STT on options and futures.

6217. (29-2-2008) NEW DELHI : While presenting the Budget proposals for the year 2008-09 in the Lok Sabha today, the Finance Minister Shri P Chidambaram said that in anticipation of the Unorganized Sector Workers' Social Security Bill, 2007 being made into law, the Government has introduced three schemes viz Aam Admi Bima Yojana, Rashtriya Swasthya Bima Yojana and Indira Gandhi National Old Age Pension Scheme with an objective to provide social security to workers in the unorganized sector in a phased manner. The Finance Minister proposed to place an additional sum of Rs. 1000 crore with Life Insurance Corporation (LIC) in the year 2008-09 to cover another one crore poor households under the Aam Admi Bima Yojana in the second year. Expressing the happiness, Shri Chidambaram announced that in the first year of Yojana, LIC will cover one crore landless households by 30th September, this year. He further announced that Rashtriya Swasthya Bima Yojana will be implemented with effect from 1st April, 2008. Regarding the Indira Gandhi National Old Age Pension Scheme, which was in large with effect from November 19, 2007 to include all persons over 65 years falling under Below Poverty Line (BPL) category, the Finance Minister proposed to allocate Rs. 3,443 crore in 2008-09 as against Rs. 2,392 crore in 2007-08 because of expansion of coverage from 87 lakh to 157 lakh beneficiary under the scheme.

6218. (29-2-2008) NEW DELHI : Keeping in view the higher cost of construction of houses, the Finance Minister, Shri P Chidambaram has proposed to enhance the subsidy per unit in respect of the new houses sanctioned after 1st April 2008 from Rs. 25,000/- to Rs. 35,000/- in plain areas and Rs.27,500/- to Rs. 38,500/ - in hilly / difficult areas for the construction of new houses for the poor through the Indira Awas Yojana (IAY) as a part of Bharat Nirman Programme. While presenting the Budget proposals for the year 2008-09 in the Lok Sabha today, the Finance Minister informed the House that the subsidy for upgradation of houses will be increased from Rs. 12,500/- per unit to Rs. 15,000/-. He further added that a beneficiary will still need own funds to complete the house. Accordingly the Public sector banks will be advised to include IAY houses under the differential rate of interest scheme and lend upto Rs. 20,000/- per unit at an interest rate of 4 percent. He further informed that the housing for the poor is one of six elements of Bharat Nirman and is implemented through IAY. Against a target of 60 lakh houses, 41.13 houses have been constructed upto December 2007 and cumulative number will be 51.77 lakh houses by the end of March, this year.

6219. (29-2-2008) NEW DELHI : The Backward Regions Grant Fund was given Rs. 5,800 crore in the current year. While presenting the Budget proposals for the year 2008-09 in the Lok Sabha today, the Finance Minister, Shri P Chidambaram has proposed to keep the allocation for the Backward Regions Grant Fund for the next year at the same level. He added that nearly 45% of the amount is likely to be allocated to the States of Bihar, Orissa and Uttar Pradesh.

6220. (29-2-2008) NEW DELHI : With a view to project India's music, literature, dance, art, cuisine and especially films around the world, the Finance Minister, Shri P Chidambaram has proposed to provide Rs. 75 crore to the Indian Council of Cultural Relations to design and implement a programme to achieve this objective. While presenting the Budget proposals for the year 2008-09 in the Lok Sabha today, he said, "this is the 'soft power' of India and must be projected in a sophisticated and subtle manner.

6221. (29-2-2008) NEW DELHI : For the fourth year in succession, the Finance Minister, Shri P Chidambaram has proposed to make a special grant of Rs. 100 crore each to three institutions of excellence. While presenting the Budget proposals for the year 2008-09 in the Lok Sabha today, he informed that awards for the year 2008 go to Mahatma Phule Krishi Vidyapeeth, Rahuri, Maharashtra; University of Mysore, Mysore; and Delhi University, Delhi.

6222. (29-2-2008) NEW DELHI : The Finance Minister, Shri P Chidambaram has informed that the 6th Central Pay Commission will submit its report by 31st March, 2008. While presenting the Budget proposals for the year 2008-09 in the Lok Sabha today, he expressed the confidence that the report will meet the legitimate expectations of Government employees.

6223. (29-2-2008) NEW DELHI : The Finance Minister, Shri P Chidambaram has provided Rs 624 crore for the Commonwealth Games. While presenting the Budget proposals for the year 2008-09 in the Lok Sabha today, he said that the Games are only 947 days away and urged the authorities concerned to adhere to the strict time lines and quality standards.

6224. (29-2-2008) NEW DELHI : The Finance Minister, Shri P Chidambaram has proposed to increase the allocation for defence by 10 percent from Rs. 96,000 crores to Rs. 105,600 crore. While presenting the Budget proposals for the year 2008-09 in the Lok Sabha today, he assured that any further amount needed for defence forces, especially for capital expenditure will be provided.

6225. (29-2-2008) NEW DELHI : The Finance Minister, Shri P Chidambaram has announced setting up of one fully-fitted mobile soil testing laboratory each to 250 districts of the country before March 2009. While presenting the Union Budget 2008-09 in the Lok Sabha today, the Finance Minister said a one time allotment of Rs. 75 crore will be given to the Ministry of Agriculture to provide the mobile soil testing laboratories. In addition to this, 500 soil testing laboratories will be set up in the public private sectors during the 11th Plan with Government's assistance of 13 lakh per laboratory. Special thrust is being given to the revival of crops such as coconut, cashew and peeper under the National Horticulture Mission (NHM). An outlay of Rs. 1,100 crores has been allocated for the same. NHM now covers 340 districts in 18 states and 2 Union Territories. An area of 2,76,000 hectares has been brought under horticulture crops and an area of 56,000 hectares of old plantations has been rejuvenated.

6226. (29-2-2008) NEW DELHI : In anticipation of upgrading 300 more Industrial Training Institutes (ITIs) in 2008-09, the Finance Minister, Shri P Chidambaram has proposed to provide Rs.750 crores in the Union Budget. While presenting the Budget proposals in the Lok Sabha today, he said that the upgradation of ITIs is proceeding apace. Under the World Bank assisted scheme, 238 ITIs are undergoing upgradation. Under the public private partnership scheme, 309 ITIs in 29 States have been identified with corresponding industry partners and agreements have been signed in 244 cases, he informed.

6227. (29-2-2008) NEW DELHI : To continue the buoyancy in tax revenues, the Finance Minister, Shri P Chidambaram has announced reduction in excise duty on agriculture related items while presenting the Union Budget 2008-09 in the Lok Sabha today. In order to reduce the cost of manufacture of cattle and poultry feeds, duty on vitamin premixes and mineral mixtures has been reduced from 30% to 20%. Duty on Phosphoric acid has been reduced from 7.5 to 5 percent. The duty on bactofuges is reduced from 7.5percent to Nil. This will increase the shelf life of milk and benefit the dairy industry. In order to support domestic fertilizer production, the minister reduced the customs duty on crude and unrefined sulphur from 5% to 2%.